S0-CRE-390

OCÉANO ATLÁNTICO

○La Habana

CUBA

Santiago ●

San Juan

REPÚBLICA DOMINICANA ○

HAITÍ ●Ponce

Santo Domingo **PUERTO RICO**

JAMAICA

MAR CARIBE

AS

lpa

NICARAGUA

○

Lago de Nicaragua

○ Caracas

Río Orinoco

VENEZUELA

COSTA RICA

Canal de Panamá ○

○ San José Panamá

PANAMÁ

Río Magdalena

○Bogotá

COLOMBIA

BRASIL

¿Qué tal?

AN INTRODUCTORY COURSE · SECOND EDITION

An abridged version of *Puntos de partida*

Thalia Dorwick

Martha Alford Marks

Marty Knorre, *University of Cincinnati*

Bill VanPatten, *University of Illinois, Urbana–Champaign*

Theodore V. Higgs, *San Diego State University*

Text of photo essays by
María José Ruiz Morcillo, *University of California, Berkeley*

Random House *New York*
This book was developed for Random House by Eirik Børve, Inc.

Second Edition

9 8 7 6

Library of Congress Cataloging-in-Publication Data
Dorwick, Thalia, 1944–
    ¿Qué tal?

    "An abridged version of Puntos de partida."
    English and Spanish.
    Includes index.
    1. Spanish language—Text-books for foreign speakers—English. I. Martha Alford Marks.
II. Marty Knorre. III. Title.
PC4129.E5D66 1987   468.2′421   86-29707
ISBN 0-394-35314-5
Manufactured in the United States of America.

Text design: Adapted from Dare Porter/Graphic Design, San Francisco
Cover Design: Janet Wood
Production: Stacey Sawyer, Montara, California
Art: Axelle Fortier
Typesetting: Interactive Composition

The rooster on the cover was adapted by Dare Porter from a design of a rooster, a good luck symbol, on an earthenware ceiling tile from Paterna, made at Valencia about A.D. 1500.

Dr. Thalia Dorwick is the coordinator of the project (text and supplementary materials) and the author of most of the grammar explanations and most of the exercises and minidialogues; she also served as project editor. Dr. Martha Alford Marks is the coordinator of the text and the author of many grammar explanation sections, exercises, minidialogues, and **Vocabulario: Preparación** sections, as well as all of the **Situaciones** role-play activities; she is also the coauthor of the *Instructor's Manual*. Dr. Marty Knorre (University of Cincinnati) is the author of many of the activities and exercises and all of the *Study Hints*; she is also coauthor of the *Instructor's Manual*. Dr. Bill VanPatten (University of Illinois, Urbana-Champaign) is the author of many of the **Vocabulario: Preparación** sections and other activities and the author of all of the **Antes de leer** sections and the comprehension and writing activities that follow the cultural readings. Dr. Theodore V. Higgs (San Diego State University) is the author of the cultural readings and of some of the culturally based review exercises. María José Ruiz Morcillo (University of California, Berkeley) prepared the photo essays **(Imágenes del mundo hispánico).**

Cartoons on pp. 96, 310, 380—© Antonio Mingote; pp. 248, 299, 305, 386—© Quino; p. 164—reprinted with special permission of King Features Syndicate, Inc.; p. 283—© *Blanco y negro*; p. 384—© *Semana*; advertisement on p. 312 © Shell International Petroleum Company Limited.

CONTENTS

Katharine A. Lambert/Kay Reese & Associates

PREFACE

During the last several years, *¿Qué tal?* has successfully met the needs of many instructors who are eager to implement a truly communicative approach in their classrooms but who also seek a brief, manageable text. *¿Qué tal?* has proved that a concise text can teach functional material very effectively by concentrating on essential vocabulary and grammar and on teaching for communication through pair and group activities.

The goals of the second edition of this lively first-year program, based on the highly successful *Puntos de partida*, are identical to those of the first: *to help students develop proficiency in the four skills and cultural awareness considered essential to truly communicative language learning.*

¿Qué tal? *and the Proficiency-Oriented Classroom**

The conceptualization of the first and second editions of *¿Qué tal?* coincides with many aspects of the proficiency movement.

- an insistence on the acquisition of vocabulary during the early stages of language learning (the **Pasos preliminares**) and then in each chapter throughout the book;

- an emphasis on personalized and creative use of language to perform various functions or achieve various goals; careful attention to skills development rather than only on grammatical knowledge;

- a cyclical organization in which vocabulary, grammar, and language functions are consistently reviewed and re-entered;

- an integrated cultural component that embeds practice in a wide variety of culturally significant contexts;

- content that aims to raise student awareness of the interaction of language, culture, and society.

Within each chapter, text materials are sequenced to facilitate and maximize progress in communication skills: from vocabulary acquisition activities, to grammar practice in structured, contextualized situations, to divergent activities that stimulate student creativity. The overall text organization progresses from a focus on for-

mulaic expressions, to vocabulary and structures relevant to the "here and now" (desciptions, student life, family life, and so on), to survival situations (ordering a meal, travel-related activities, and so on), to topics of broader conceptual interest (the individual and society, current events, and so forth). Some material is introduced functionally in small "chunks" before the entire paradigm is presented. Major grammar topics such as the subjunctive and the past tenses are introduced, then reentered later in the text; most grammar topics and language functions are continually reviewed and reentered throughout the text and its ancillaries.

Organization of the Second Edition

The chapter organization of *¿Qué tal?* has not been radically altered in this edition, although there are minor changes and fewer chapters overall. The text begins with four mini-lessons, the **Pasos preliminares,** which introduce students to the sounds of Spanish and to the text and which provide students with a preliminary vocabulary that they can use immediately for communication. Twenty-eight chapters follow, most organized in this manner.

- **Vocabulario: Preparación** This section presents and practices the thematic vocabulary that students will need for self-expression and to cope with the situations and activities they will encounter in the chapter.

- **Pronunciación** This section, a feature of the first thirteen chapters, focuses on individual sounds that are particularly difficult for native speakers of English. It continues the presentation of the sounds of Spanish begun in the **Pasos preliminares.**

- **Minidiálogos y estructura** This section presents one to three grammar points, most introduced by a minidialogue, cartoon, or brief reading and followed by a series of contextualized exercises and activities that progress from controlled to open-ended. Practice materials, carefully ordered to lead students from guided to free responses, include paraphrase, interview, partner, role playing, and creative language use in a cultural and often humorous context.

- **Repaso** New to the second edition, these sections combine and review grammar and vocabulary presented

*See also *Using ¿Qué tal? in the Proficiency-Oriented Classroom,* by Martha Alford Marks, available as part of the Instructor's Package of Optional Materials, from Random House.

in the chapter, as well as important grammar from previous chapters. Material such as **ser** versus **estar**, the preterite and the imperfect, and so on, is thus continually recycled. In Chapters 23–27, these sections (called **Repaso general**) are expanded to include functional vocabulary and conversational strategies (**A propósito...**   ) with follow-up activities and role-play activities (**Situaciones**).

• **Un paso más**   In even-numbered chapters, these sections consist of a cultural reading (**Lectura cultural**) with prereading exercises (**Antes de leer**, new to the second edition) and post-reading comprehension and writing activities. In odd-numbered chapters, the sections consist of brief photo essays (**Imágenes del mundo hispánico**, new to the second edition) on appealing aspects of the current Spanish-speaking world as well as on its history and civilization.

• **Vocabulario**   This chapter vocabulary list includes all important words and expressions considered to be active.

The last two chapters of the text present no new grammar points, but focus instead on review/recombination activities and on vocabulary and expressions useful for travel or living abroad.

Additional features of importance include:

• **¿Recuerda Ud.?**   Brief review sections that provide a link between previously studied grammar points and new material that builds on them. Answers to the brief review exercises are included in the Instructor's Manual.

• **Un poco de todo**   Review sections that follow every fourth chapter. They include some convergent grammar practice as well as functional vocabulary and conversational strategies (**A propósito...**) with follow-up activities, role-play activities (**Situaciones**), and cultural and humorous activities. (Beginning in Chapter 23, they are replaced by the in-chapter **Repaso general** sections.)

• *Study Hints*   Sections that give students specific advice on how to acquire language skills: how to learn vocabulary, how to use a bilingual dictionary, and so on. *Hints* are placed at logical points throughout the text.

Major Changes in the Second Edition

Language: Skills Development and Content

• In response to comments by many adopters of the text, the **Pasos preliminares** have been shortened to four.

• The total number of chapters has been reduced from thirty to twenty-eight.

• The conceptual "fit" between the vocabulary and grammar of many chapters and their cultural themes or situations has been refined so that grammar, vocabulary, and culture work together as interactive units.

• Grammatical detail has been trimmed in certain areas. Some points have been omitted, others minimized by being treated as lexical items in the **Vocabulario: Preparación** sections.

•   When possible, grammar topics are presented in terms of what students can do with the language: talking about the past, expressing desires and requests, and so on. Some material (**me gustaría...** , for example) is introduced when the cultural theme or situation demands it, although the entire paradigm (the conditional) is not presented until later on in the text.

• The number of new grammar points has been reduced to one in later chapters of the book and review/re-entry activities are increased.

• All exercises have been contextualized. Many paraphrase, interview, partner, role-playing, and problem-solving exercises have been added to all parts of the chapters. The odd-chapter activities sections from the first edition have been replaced by photo essays, but the activities themselves have been integrated into the exercise sequences.

•   Review and re-entry has been expanded, especially in the new **Repaso (general)** sections, which regularly review major topics such as **ser** and **estar**, preterite and imperfect, and so on. The content of the **Un poco de todo** review sections, which now occur every four chapters, has been totally reworked with an emphasis on activities that present functional material and stimulate creative language use.

• Some minidialogues have been rewritten to stress realistic situations, and the exercises that follow them are now more functional, helping students to use new structures actively.

• Functional minidialogues, two in most chapters and new to the second edition, present brief models of interaction in realistic language situations.

• A new reading-strategies section (**Antes de leer**) precedes the cultural readings in the first fourteen chapters (and continues in the *Instructor's Manual* through the end of the text).

Culture: An Integral Part of Language Learning

• Most cultural readings have been totally rewritten to accurately reflect the realities of the contemporary Spanish-speaking world, as well as to focus student attention on areas of cultural similarity and contrast.

• The black-and-white photo essays, **Imágenes del mundo hispánico** (new to the second edition), invite students to explore topics and geographical areas of interest in the Spanish-speaking world and to learn about its civilization and culture.

• The new color photo insert vividly presents the wide variety of people, places, and activities of the Hispanic world, as well as its artistic heritage.

• Some cultural themes have been abbreviated and others elaborated to enrich and expand the cultural content. Themes added or treated in greater detail include holidays and festivals, technology and computers, sports and other leisure-time activities, environmental questions, and the individual's place in society.

Supplementary Materials for the Second Edition

The *Workbook*, by Alice Arana (Fullerton College) and Oswaldo Arana (California State University, Fullerton), continues the format of the first edition, providing additional practice with vocabulary and structures through a variety of controlled and open-ended exercises, review sections, and guided writing and composition activities. Review/re-entry exercises have been added to each chapter in the second edition.

• The *Laboratory Manual* and *Tape Program*, by María Sabló Yates, have been substantially rewritten. All exercises have been contextualized, and greater emphasis is placed on listening comprehension and on interesting comprehension activities. In particular, more effective use is made of dialogue materials, and each chapter now contains a number of interview and dialogue activities in which students interact with the speakers.

• The *Instructor's Manual* contains section-by-section teaching suggestions, many supplementary exercises for developing listening and speaking skills, and abundant variations and follow-ups on student text material. It also offers an extensive introduction to teaching techniques, general guidelines for instructors, suggestions for lesson planning and for writing semester-quarter schedules, sample tests (one per chapter), and quizzes.

• An optional instructor's package, linked to the communicative and cultural themes of each chapter, is available to each instructor. It includes transparency masters, communicative games and activities, additional realia pieces, and a pamphlet detailing the proficiency orientation of the text. In addition, a set of color slides, with descriptive commentary, is available.

• A *Computerized Language Program*, with sets of both conventional and interactive (game format) exercises, is available for use in conjunction with *¿Qué tal?*

• A video-tape program consisting of twenty three-part segments linked to the cultural themes and situations of the text is also available. The program includes a pamphlet containing the complete scripts and suggested pre- and post-viewing activities.

Acknowledgments

Special thanks go to the following instructors, who participated in an in-depth review of parts of the second edition. The appearance of their names does not necessarily constitute endorsement of the text.

Shirley J. Bialek, Monterey Peninsula College; Mary A. Boutiette, Northland Community College; Aristeo Brito, Pima College; Susan Brushaber, University of Wisconsin at Madison; Marvin D'Lugo, Clair University; Margaret Florio, College of DuPage; Jill H. Geletko, Community College of Allegheny County; Donald B. Gibbs, Creighton University; George Greenia, College of William and Mary; William H. Heflin, Jr., University of Tennessee at Knoxville; Ernest E. Norden, Baylor University; María E. Pérez, Iona College; Gerald W. Peterson, University of Nevada at Reno; Ronald P. Redman, Cypress Junior College; Claire Rogers, Arapahoe Community College; Shirley A. Rogers, University of Texas at Austin; Ann Stewart, Auburn University; Alain Swietlicki, University of Wisconsin at Madison; Ana B. Waisman, Olympic College.

Also gratefully acknowledged are the contributions of the following individuals: Dr. William H. Heflin, Jr. (University of Tennessee) and Professor Fabián Álvarez Samaniego (University of California, Davis) for their suggestions and guidance during the planning stages of the first edition; Dr. Shaw Gynan (Western Washington University) for a detailed review of all aspects of the first edition. Thanks also are due to the following professional friends who made helpful suggestions and comments in conversations with the authors: Drs. Donald Gibbs and Maryjane Dunn-Wood (Creighton University); Professor Deanne Flouton (Naussau Community College); Professor Maryo Walters (Coastline Community College).

Many other individuals deserve our thanks and appreciation for their help and support. Among them are the people who, in addition to the coauthors, read the manuscript to ensure its linguistic and cultural authenticity and pedagogical accuracy: Alice Arana (United States), Oswaldo Arana (Peru), Laura Chastain (El Salvador), María José Ruiz Morcillo (Spain), María Sabló Yates (Panama). Aristóbolo Pardo (Colombia), Paul Figure (Chile), Begoña Zubiri (Spain), and Feliz Menchacatorre (Spain) read manuscript in earlier drafts.

Pasos preliminares

Katherine A. Lambert/Kay Reese and Associates

Universidad de Chile, Santiago, Chile

¿Qué tal? means *Hi, how are you doing?* in Spanish. This textbook, called *¿Qué tal?*, will provide you with a way to begin to learn the Spanish language and to become more familiar with the many people here and abroad who use it.

Language is the means by which humans communicate with one another. To learn a new language is to acquire another way of exchanging information and of sharing your thoughts and opinions with others. *¿Qué tal?* will help you use Spanish to communicate in various ways—to understand Spanish when others speak it, to speak it yourself, and to read and write it—and function in many kinds of real-life situations. This text will also help you to communicate in Spanish in nonverbal ways—via gestures and through an awareness of cultural differences.

Learning about a new culture is an inseparable part of learning a language. "Culture" can mean many things: everything from great writers and painters to what time people usually eat lunch. Throughout *¿Qué tal?* you will have the opportunity to find out about the daily lives of Spanish-speaking people and the kinds of things that are important to them. Knowing about all these things will be important to you when you visit a Spanish-speaking country, and it may also be useful to you here. If you look around, you will see that Spanish is not really a foreign language but rather a widely used language in the United States today.

The **Pasos preliminares** (*First Steps*) are a four-part section that will introduce you to the Spanish language and to the format of *¿Qué tal?*

PASO UNO

Saludos° y expresiones de cortesía

Greetings

1.

ANA: Hola, José.
JOSÉ: ¿Qué tal, Ana? (¿Cómo estás?)
ANA: Así así. ¿Y tú?
JOSÉ: ¡Muy bien! Hasta mañana, ¿eh?
ANA: Adiós.

---

1. ANA: *Hi, José.* JOSÉ: *How are you doing, Ana? (How are you?)* ANA: *So-so. And you?* JOSÉ: *Fine! (Very well!) See you tomorrow, OK?* ANA: *'Bye.*

2.

SEÑOR ALONSO: Buenas tardes, señorita López.

SEÑORITA LÓPEZ: Muy buenas, señor Alonso. ¿Cómo está?

SEÑOR ALONSO: Bien, gracias. ¿Y usted?

SEÑORITA LÓPEZ: Muy bien, gracias. Adiós.

SEÑOR ALONSO: Hasta luego.

¿Qué tal?, ¿Cómo estás?, and **¿Y tú?** are expressions used in informal situations with people you know well, on a first-name basis.

¿Cómo está? and **¿Y usted?** are used to address someone with whom you have a formal relationship.

3.

MARÍA: Buenos días, profesora.

PROFESORA: Buenos días. ¿Cómo se llama usted?

MARÍA: (Me llamo) María Sánchez.

PROFESORA: Mucho gusto.

MARÍA: Igualmente. (Encantada.)

¿Cómo se llama usted? is used in formal situations. **¿Cómo te llamas?** is used in informal situations—for example, with other students. The phrases **mucho gusto** and **igualmente** are used by both men and women when meeting for the first time. In response to **mucho gusto,** a woman can also say **encantada;** a man can say **encantado.**

Otros saludos y expresiones de cortesía	
buenos días	good morning (*used until the midday meal*)
buenas tardes	good afternoon (*used until the evening meal*)
buenas noches	good evening, good night (*used after the evening meal*)
señor (Sr.)	Mr., sir
señora (Sra.)	Mrs., ma'am
señorita (Srta.)	Miss

Note that there is no standard Spanish equivalent for *Ms.* Use **Sra.** or **Srta.,** as appropriate.

2. MR. ALONSO: *Good afternoon, Miss López.*   MISS LÓPEZ: *'Afternoon, Mr. Alonso. How are you?*   MR. ALONSO: *Fine, thanks. And you?*   MISS LÓPEZ: *Very well, thanks. Good-bye.*   MR. ALONSO: *See you later.*   **3.** MARÍA: *Good morning, Professor.*   PROFESORA: *Good morning. What's your name?*   MARÍA: *(My name is) María Sánchez.*   PROFESORA: *Pleased to meet you.*   MARÍA: *Likewise. (Delighted.)*

Práctica

A. Practice Dialogues 1 through 3 several times with another student, using your own names.

B. How many different ways can you respond to the following greetings and phrases?

1. Buenas tardes.   2. Adiós.   3. ¿Qué tal?   4. Hola.
5. ¿Cómo está?   6. Buenas noches.   7. Buenos días.
8. Hasta mañana.   9. ¿Cómo se llama usted?   10. Mucho gusto.

C. **Situaciones.** If the following persons met or passed each other at the times given, what might they say to each other? Role-play the situations with another student.

1. Mr. Santana and Miss Pérez, at 5:00 P.M.
2. Mrs. Ortega and Pablo, at 10:00 A.M.
3. Miss Hernández and Olivia, at 11:00 P.M.
4. you and a classmate, just before your Spanish class

CH. **Entrevista** (*Interview*). Turn to the person sitting next to you and do the following.

• Greet him or her appropriately.
• Find out his or her name.
• Ask how he or she is.
• Conclude the exchange.

Now have a similar conversation with your instructor, using the appropriate formal forms.

El alfabeto español

There are thirty letters in the Spanish *alphabet* (**el alfabeto**)—four more than in the English alphabet. The **ch, ll,** and **rr** are considered single letters even though they are two-letter groups; the **ñ** is the fourth extra letter. The letters **k** and **w** appear only in words borrowed from other languages.

Listen carefully as your instructor pronounces the proper names and the place listed with the letters of the alphabet.

Letters	Names of Letters	Examples		
a	a	Antonio	Ana	la Argentina
b	be	Benito	Blanca	Bolivia
c	ce	Carlos	Cecilia	Cáceres
ch	che	Pancho	Concha	Chile
d	de	Domingo	Dolores	Durango
e	e	Eduardo	Elena	el Ecuador
f	efe	Felipe	Francisca	la Florida
g	ge	Gerardo	Gloria	Guatemala
h	hache	Héctor	Hortensia	Honduras
i	i	Ignacio	Inés	Ibiza
j	jota	José	Juana	Jalisco
k	ka	(Karl)	(Kati)	(Kansas)
l	ele	Luis	Lola	Lima
ll	elle	Guillermo	Guillermina	Sevilla
m	eme	Manuel	María	México
n	ene	Nicolás	Nati	Nicaragua
ñ	eñe	Íñigo	Begoña	España
o	o	Octavio	Olivia	Oviedo
p	pe	Pablo	Pilar	Panamá
q	cu	Enrique	Raquel	Quito
r	ere	Álvaro	Clara	el Perú
rr	erre or ere doble	Rafael	Rosa	Monterrey
s	ese	Salvador	Sara	San Juan
t	te	Tomás	Teresa	Toledo
u	u	Agustín	Lucía	el Uruguay
v	ve or uve	Víctor	Victoria	Venezuela
w	doble ve, ve doble, or uve doble	Oswaldo	(Wilma)	(Washington)
x	equis	Xavier	Ximena	Extremadura
y	i griega	Pelayo	Yolanda	el Paraguay
z	zeta	Gonzalo	Esperanza	Zaragoza

Práctica

A. The letters on the following page represent the Spanish sounds that are the most different from their English counterparts. You will practice the pronunciation of these letters in upcoming sections of *¿Qué tal?* For the moment, pay particular attention to their pronunciation when you see them. Can you match the Spanish spelling with its equivalent pronunciation?

Spelling	Pronunciation
1. ch	**a.** like the *g* in English *garden*
2. g before **e** or **i;** also **j**	**b.** similar to *dd* of *caddy* or *tt* of *kitty* when pronounced very quickly
3. h	
4. g before **a, o,** or **u**	
5. ll	**c.** like *ch* in English *cheese*
6. ñ	**ch.** like Spanish **b**
7. r	**d.** similar to a "strong" English *h*
8. r at the beginning of a word or **rr** in the middle of a word	**e.** like *y* in English *yes* or like the *li* sound in *million*
9. v	**f.** a trilled sound, several Spanish **r**'s in a row
	g. similar to the *ny* sound in *canyon*
	h. never pronounced

B. Spell your own name in Spanish, and listen as your classmates spell their names. Try to remember as many of their names as you can.

C. Identify as many of your classmates as you can, using the phrase **Te llamas** _____ (*Your name is* _____). Then spell the name in Spanish.

MODELO   Te llamas María: **M** (eme) **A** (a) **R** (ere) **Í** (i acentuada) **A** (a).

CH. Spell these U.S. place names in Spanish. All of them are of Hispanic origin: Toledo, Los Angeles, Texas, Montana, Colorado, El Paso, Florida, Las Vegas, Amarillo, San Francisco. Pronounce the names in Spanish before you begin to spell them.

Los cognados

Many Spanish and English words are similar or identical in form and meaning. These related words are called *cognates* (**los cognados**). Spanish and English share so many cognates because a number of words in both languages are derived from the same Latin root words, and also because Spanish and English are "language neighbors," especially in the southwestern United States. Each language has borrowed words from the other and adapted them to its own sound system. Thus, the English word *leader* has become Spanish **líder,** and Spanish **el lagarto** (*the lizard*) has become English *alligator*. The existence of so many cognates will make learning some Spanish vocabulary words easier for you and increase the number of words that you can recognize immediately.

Many cognates are used in the **Pasos preliminares.** Don't try to memorize all of them—just get used to the sound of them in Spanish.

Here are some Spanish adjectives (words used to describe people, places, and things) that are cognates of English words. Practice pronouncing them, imitating your instructor. These adjectives can be used to describe either a man or a woman.

cruel	independiente	pesimista
eficiente	inteligente	realista
egoísta	interesante	rebelde
elegante	liberal	responsable
emocional	materialista	sentimental
idealista	optimista	terrible
importante	paciente	valiente

The following adjectives change form. Use the **-o** ending when describing a man, the **-a** ending when describing a woman.

extrovertido/a	introvertido/a	serio/a
generoso/a	religioso/a	sincero/a
impulsivo/a	romántico/a	tímido/a

DIRECTORIO			
PLANTAS FLOORS ETAGES			
4ª	SALA DE PROMOCIONES ESPECIALES CAMPING	SALON DE PROMOTIONS SPECIALES CAMPING	PROMOTIONAL ROOM CAMPING
3ª	Tienda joven Deportes Oportunidades Cafetería	Teenage shop Sports Opportunities Snack bar	Boutique Sports Opportunités Snack bar
2ª	Muebles Ropa de hogar Tejidos Alfombras	Furniture Home clothes Tissues Carpets	Meubles Lingerie Tissus Tapis
1ª	Señoras Caballeros Niños	Women fashion Men fashion Children	Mode femmes Mode hommes Enfants
Baja Ground floor Rez-de-Chaussee	Zapatería Bolsos Perfumería Juguetes Ag. de viajes	Shoes Hand bags Perfumes Toys Travel agency	Souliers Sacs Parfums Jouets Agence Voyages
Sótano Underground Sous-sol 1	Hogar Radio - T V Supermercado	Home Radio - T V Supermarket	Maison Radio - T V Supermarché
Sótano Underground Sous-sol 2-3	Aparcamientos	Parking	Parking

Rogers/Monkmeyer Press Photo Service

¿Cuántos (How many) cognados hay (are there) en el directorio de este almacén (this department store) de Madrid (España)?

Práctica

A. Describe Don Juan, the famous lover, in simple Spanish sentences that begin with **Don Juan es** (*is*)... or **Don Juan no es** (*is not*)... .

B. Think of a well-known person—real or imaginary—and describe him or her. Try to describe as many qualities of the person as you can. For example:

- **El presidente es/no es...**
- **Jane Fonda es/no es...**

¿Cómo es usted?

You can use these forms of the verb **ser** (*to be*) to describe yourself and others.

(yo) **soy**	*I am*
(tú) **eres**	*you* (familiar) *are*
(usted) **es**	*you* (formal) *are*
(él, ella) **es**	*he/she is*

Práctica

A. **¿Cómo es usted?** (*What kind of person are you?*) Describe yourself, using adjectives from **Los cognados: Yo soy... Yo no soy...**.

B. **Entrevista.** Use the following adjectives, or any others you know, to find out what a classmate is like. Follow the model.

MODELO —¿Eres generoso? (¿Eres generosa?)
—Sí, soy generoso/a. (No, no soy generoso/a.)

Adjectivos

sincero/a eficiente emocional inteligente impulsivo/a liberal

Now find out what kind of person your instructor is, using the same adjectives. Use the appropriate formal forms.

Spanish as a World Language

Although no one knows exactly how many languages are spoken
around the world, linguists estimate that there are between 3,000 and
6,000. Spanish, with 266 million native speakers, is among the top five
languages. It is the language spoken in Spain, in all of South America
(except Brazil and the Guyanas), in most of Central America, in Mexico,
in Cuba, in Puerto Rico, and in the Dominican Republic—in
approximately twenty countries in all.

   Like all languages spoken by large numbers of people, modern
Spanish varies from region to region. The Spanish of Madrid is different
from that spoken in Mexico City or Buenos Aires, just as the English of
London differs from that of Chicago or Dallas. Although these
differences are most noticeable in pronunciation ("accent"), they are also
found in vocabulary and special expressions used in different
geographical areas. In Great Britain one hears the word *lift*, but the
same apparatus is called an *elevator* in the United States. What is called

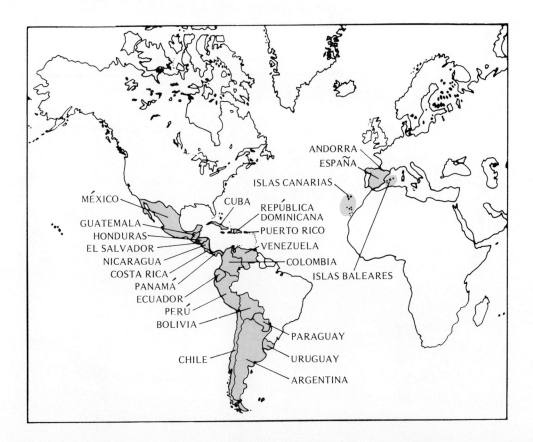

an **autobús** (*bus*) in Spain may be called a **guagua** in the Caribbean. While such differences are noticeable, they result only rarely in misunderstandings among native speakers, since the majority of structures and vocabulary are common to the many varieties of each language.

PASO DOS

Más expresiones de cortesía

gracias	thanks, thank you
muchas gracias	thank you very much
de nada	you're welcome
por favor	please (*also used to get someone's attention*)
perdón	pardon me, excuse me (*to ask forgiveness or to get someone's attention*)
con permiso	pardon me, excuse me (*to request permission to pass by or through a group of people*)

Práctica

A. Are these people saying **por favor, con permiso,** or **perdón**?

1.

2.

3.

4.

5.

6.

B. **Situaciones.** Role-play situations similar to those shown in **Práctica A** with a classmate, who should respond with an appropriate Spanish phrase.

Pronunciación

You have probably already noted that there is a very close relationship between the way Spanish is written and the way it is pronounced. This makes it relatively easy to learn the basics of Spanish spelling and pronunciation.

Many Spanish sounds, however, do not have an exact equivalent in English, so you should not trust English to be your guide to Spanish pronunciation. Even words that are spelled the same in both languages are usually pronounced quite differently. It is important to become so familiar with Spanish sounds that you can pronounce them automatically, right from the beginning of your study of the language.

Las vocales (Vowels): A, E, I, O, U

Unlike English vowels, which can have many different pronunciations or may be silent, Spanish vowels are always pronounced, and they are almost always pronounced in the same way. Spanish vowels are always short and tense. They are never drawn out with a *u* or *i* glide as in English: **lo** ≠ *low*; **de** ≠ *day*.

■ **¡OJO!** *The English* uh *sound or schwa (which is how all unstressed vowels are pronounced:* canal, waited, atom*) does not exist in Spanish.*

a: pronounced like the *a* in *father*, but short and tense
e: pronounced like the *e* in *they*, but without the *i* glide
i: pronounced like the *i* in *machine*, but short and tense*
o: pronounced like the *o* in *home*, but without the *u* glide
u: pronounced like the *u* in *rule*, but short and tense

Práctica

A. Pronounce the following Spanish syllables, being careful to pronounce each vowel with a short, tense sound.

---

*The word **y** (*and*) is also pronounced like the letter **i.**

1. ma fa la ta pa   4. mo fo lo to po   7. su mi te so la
2. me fe le te pe   5. mu fu lu tu pu   8. se tu no ya li
3. mi fi li ti pi   6. mi fe la tu do

B. Pronounce the following words, paying special attention to the vowel sounds.

1. hasta   tal   nada   mañana   natural   normal
fascinante
2. me   qué   Pérez   usted   rebelde   excelente
elegante
3. así   señorita   así así   permiso   diligente   imposible
tímido
4. yo   con   cómo   noches   profesor   señor
generoso
5. uno   usted   tú   mucho   Perú   Lupe   Úrsula

Más cognados

Although some English and Spanish cognates are spelled identically (*idea, general, gas, animal, motor*), most will differ slightly in spelling: *position*/**posición**, *secret*/**secreto**, *student*/**estudiante**, *rose*/**rosa**, *lottery*/**lotería**, *opportunity*/**oportunidad**, *exam*/**examen**.

The following exercises will give you more practice in recognizing and pronouncing cognates. Remember: don't try to learn all of these words. Just get used to the way they sound.

Hay (*There are*) muchos cognados en este letrero (*this sign*) en una clínica de Miami (Estados Unidos). ¿Cuántos (*How many*) reconoce usted?

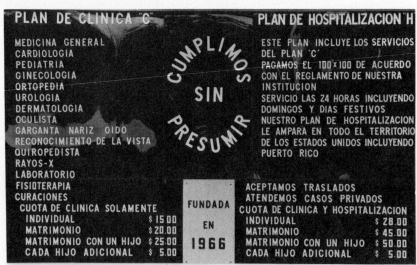

PLAN DE CLINICA "C"

MEDICINA GENERAL
CARDIOLOGIA
PEDIATRIA
GINECOLOGIA
ORTOPEDIA
UROLOGIA
DERMATOLOGIA
OCULISTA
GARGANTA NARIZ OIDO
RECONOCIMIENTO DE LA VISTA
QUIROPEDISTA
RAYOS-X
LABORATORIO
FISIOTERAPIA
CURACIONES
CUOTA DE CLINICA SOLAMENTE
INDIVIDUAL $ 15.00
MATRIMONIO $ 20.00
MATRIMONIO CON UN HIJO $ 25.00
CADA HIJO ADICIONAL $ 5.00

CUMPLIMOS SIN PRESUMIR

FUNDADA EN 1966

PLAN DE HOSPITALIZACION "H"

ESTE PLAN INCLUYE LOS SERVICIOS
DEL PLAN "C"
PAGAMOS EL 100×100 DE ACUERDO
CON EL REGLAMENTO DE NUESTRA
INSTITUCION
SERVICIO LAS 24 HORAS INCLUYENDO
DOMINGOS Y DIAS FESTIVOS
NUESTRO PLAN DE HOSPITALIZACION
LE AMPARA EN TODO EL TERRITORIO
DE LOS ESTADOS UNIDOS INCLUYENDO
PUERTO RICO

ACEPTAMOS TRASLADOS
ATENDEMOS CASOS PRIVADOS
CUOTA DE CLINICA Y HOSPITALIZACION
INDIVIDUAL $ 28.00
MATRIMONIO $ 45.00
MATRIMONIO CON UN HIJO $ 50.00
CADA HIJO ADICIONAL $ 5.00

Alan Carey/The Image Works

Práctica

A. Pronounce each of the following cognates and give its English equivalent.

NACIONES: la Unión Soviética, el Japón, Italia, Francia, España, el Brasil, China, el Canadá

PERSONAS: líder, profesor, actriz, pintor, político, estudiante

LUGARES (*places*): restaurante, café, museo, garaje, banco, hotel, oficina, océano, parque

CONCEPTOS: libertad, dignidad, declaración, contaminación

COSAS (*things*): teléfono, fotografía, sofá, televisión, radio, bomba, novela, diccionario, dólar, lámpara, yate

ANIMALES: león, cebra, chimpancé, tigre, hipopótamo

COMIDAS Y BEBIDAS (*food and drink*): hamburguesa, cóctel, patata, café, limón, banana

DEPORTES (*sports*): béisbol, tenis, vólibol, fútbol americano

INSTRUMENTOS MUSICALES: guitarra, piano, clarinete, trompeta, violín

B. **¿Qué es esto?** (*What is this?*) Pronounce these cognates and identify the category to which they belong, using the following sentences.

Es **un** lugar (concepto, animal, deporte, instrumento musical).*
Es **una** nación (persona, cosa, comida, bebida).*

MODELO　béisbol → Es un deporte.

1. calculadora
2. burro
3. sándwich
4. golf
5. México
6. actor
7. clase
8. limonada
9. elefante
10. refrigerador
11. universidad
12. fama
13. terrorista
14. Cuba
15. turista
16. rancho
17. serpiente
18. chocolate
19. básquetbol
20. acordeón
21. democracia

C. **¿Qué es esto?** With another student, practice identifying words, using the categories given in **Práctica B,** above.

MODELO　—¿Qué (*What*) es un hospital? →
　　　　　—Es un lugar.

---

*The English equivalent of these sentences is *It is a place* (*concept . . .*); *It is a nation* (*person . . .*). Note that Spanish has two different ways to express *a* (*an*): **un** and **una.** All nouns are either masculine (*m.*) or feminine (*f.*) in Spanish. **Un** is used with masculine nouns, **una** with feminine nouns. You will learn more about this aspect of Spanish in Grammar Section 1. Don't try to learn the gender of nouns now, and note that you do not have to know the gender of nouns to do the exercise.

1. un saxofón	**4.** un doctor	**7.** una enchilada
2. un autobús	**5.** Bolivia	**8.** una jirafa
3. una estación	**6.** una Coca-Cola	

CH. Situaciones. Can you identify these figures of the Spanish-speaking world? With another student, ask and answer questions according to the model. Use the names, categories, and countries given below as a guide.

MODELO   PRIMER (*First*) ESTUDIANTE: ¿Cómo se llama usted?
SEGUNDO (*Second*) ESTUDIANTE: (Me llamo) Juan Carlos.
PRIMER ESTUDIANTE: Y ¿quién (*who*) es usted?
SEGUNDO ESTUDIANTE: Soy rey (*king*).* Soy de (*from*) España.

Personas	Categorías	Naciones
Diego Rivera	actor (actriz)	México
Fernando Valenzuela	militar	España
Geraldo Rivera	cantante (*singer*)	los Estados
Fidel Castro	muralista	Unidos
Rita Moreno	jugador (*player*)	Puerto Rico
Ricardo Montalbán	de béisbol	Cuba
Lee Treviño	jugador de golf	
Julio Iglesias	reportero	
Severiano Ballesteros		

Gustos° y preferencias   *Likes*

—¿Te gusta el béisbol?
—Sí, me gusta, pero (*but*) me gusta más (*more*) el vólibol.

To indicate that you like someting in Spanish, say **Me gusta** _____. To indicate that you don't like something, use **No me gusta** _____. Use the question **¿Te gusta** _____**?** to ask a classmate if he or she likes

---

*Note that the indefinite article (**un, una**) is not used before unmodified nouns of profession.

something. Use **¿Le gusta _____?** to ask your instructor the same question.

In the following exercises, you will use the word **el** to mean *the* with masculine nouns and **la** with feminine nouns. Don't try to memorize which nouns are masculine and which are feminine. Just get used to the idea of using the words **el** and **la** before nouns.

Práctica

A. Indicate whether you like the following things.

MODELOS ¿la clase de español? → (No) Me gusta la clase de español.
¿estudiar? → (No) Me gusta estudiar.

1. ¿la música moderna? ¿la música clásica?
2. ¿el océano? ¿el parque?
3. ¿la universidad? ¿la residencia (*dorm*)? ¿la cafetería?
4. ¿la actriz Joan Collins? ¿el actor Emilio Estévez? ¿el presidente de los Estados Unidos?
5. ¿estudiar español? ¿esquiar (*to ski*)? ¿jugar (*to play*) al tenis? ¿jugar al fútbol? ¿jugar al golf? ¿jugar a la lotería?
6. ¿beber (*to drink*) vino? ¿beber café? ¿beber té? ¿beber Coca-Cola? ¿beber chocolate?

B. Entrevista. Ask another student if he or she likes the following things.

MODELO ¿nadar (*to swim*)? →
—¿Te gusta nadar?
—Sí, me gusta nadar. (No, no me gusta nadar.) (Sí, me gusta, pero me gusta más jugar al tenis.)

1. ¿comer (*to eat*) tacos? ¿comer hamburguesas? ¿comer en la cafetería? ¿comer en un restaurante elegante?
2. ¿hablar (*to speak*) español? ¿hablar otras lenguas? ¿hablar por teléfono? ¿hablar ante (*in front of*) muchas personas?
3. ¿tocar (*to play*) la guitarra? ¿tocar el piano? ¿tocar el violín?
4. ¿ir a (*to go to*) clase? ¿ir al cine (*movies*)? ¿ir al bar? ¿ir al parque? ¿ir al museo?

Now use the preceding cues to interview your instructor about his or her likes and dislikes.

Hispanics in the United States

The importance of the Spanish language is not limited to other
countries. The Spanish language and people of Hispanic descent have
been an integral part of United States life for centuries, and Hispanics
are currently the fastest-growing cultural group in the country. The map
below shows the number of Hispanics living in the United States in
1980.

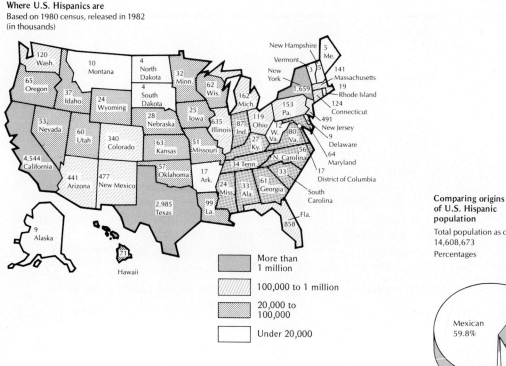

Where U.S. Hispanics are
Based on 1980 census, released in 1982
(in thousands)

	More than 1 million
	100,000 to 1 million
	20,000 to 100,000
	Under 20,000

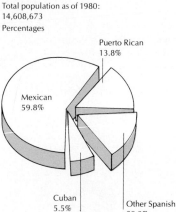

Comparing origins of U.S. Hispanic population
Total population as of 1980:
14,608,673
Percentages

Mexican 59.8%
Puerto Rican 13.8%
Cuban 5.5%
Other Spanish 20.9%

   People of Hispanic origin were among the first colonizers of what is
now the United States, and descendants of those early settlers live in all
parts of this country today. Large groups of more recent arrivals can be
found in many large cities, especially New York and Miami.

Hispanics in the United States come from many different ethnic and social backgrounds. Their rich cultural heritage has helped to shape many aspects of life in this country, and they are now found in virtually every walk of life. Some, like Luis Tiant, David Concepción, Carlos Aguilar, Lee Treviño, and Nancy López, became sports celebrities. Others, like Anthony Quinn, Vicki Carr, Rita Hayworth, Martin Sheen, Ricardo Montalbán, José Feliciano, and Rita Moreno, are well-known entertainers. In the field of politics, people such as Henry Cisneros and César Chávez have achieved national recognition. Many others, whose names are not as familiar, regularly make important contributions in the fields of education, law, business, social work, science, and so on. Clearly our second language, Spanish will be increasingly important in the future as a language for communication and commerce both in this country and abroad.

Laimute E. Druskis/Taurus Photos

Hay muchos estudiantes de origen hispano en los Estados Unidos. Aquí (*Here*) unos estudiantes conversan en el «campus» del Bronx Community College.

PASO TRES

¿Qué día es hoy?°

¿Qué... What day is today?

Los días de la semana

lunes	Monday	**jueves**	Thursday	**domingo**	Sunday
martes	Tuesday	**viernes**	Friday		
miércoles	Wednesday	**sábado**	Saturday		

el lunes, el martes...	on Monday, on Tuesday . . .
los lunes, los martes...	on Mondays, on Tuesdays . . .
los sábados, los domingos...	on Saturdays, on Sundays . . .
hoy	today
mañana	tomorrow
pasado mañana	the day after tomorrow
el fin de semana	(on) the weekend
los fines de semana	(on) the weekends
Hoy es viernes.	Today is Friday.
Mañana es sábado.	Tomorrow is Saturday.
Pasado mañana es domingo.	The day after tomorrow is Sunday.

Práctica

A. ¿Qué día es hoy? ¿Qué día es mañana? ¿Qué día es pasado mañana?

B. Si (*If*) hoy es miércoles, ¿qué día es mañana? ¿Qué día es pasado mañana? ¿Y si hoy es domingo? ¿lunes? ¿viernes?

C. ¿Qué días de la semana hay (*are there*) clases? ¿Qué días de la semana no hay clases?

CH. Choose items from each column to indicate what you like to do—or don't like to do—on different days of the week.

MODELO   Los lunes me gusta estudiar.

los lunes		estudiar
los miércoles	(no) me gusta	dormir hasta muy tarde (*to sleep very late*)
los sábados		comer (*to eat*) en un restaurante
los fines de semana		comer en la cafetería
		comer en casa (*at home*)
		jugar al tenis (al golf, al vólibol, al _____)
		ir al cine (*to go to the movies*)
		ir al bar (al parque, al museo, _____)
		mirar (*to watch*) la televisión

Pronunciación: Diphthongs and Linking

Two successive weak vowels (**i, u**) or a combination of a strong vowel (**a, e,** or **o**) and a weak vowel (**i** or **u**) are pronounced as a single syllable, forming a *diphthong* (**un diptongo**).

When words are combined to form phrases, clauses, and sentences, they are linked together in pronunciation. In spoken Spanish, it is usually impossible to hear the word boundaries—that is, where one word ends and another begins.

Práctica

A. Más práctica con las vocales

1. Ana	nada	patata	calabaza
2. trece (13)	elefante	clase	general
3. Pili	jirafa	practicar	presidente
4. los	dólar	novela	político
5. gusto	lugar	Cuba	universidad

B. Practique las siguientes palabras. (*Practice the following words.*)

1. historia	secretaria	gracias	ciencias
2. bien	viernes	siete (7)	diez (10)
3. secretario	Julio	adiós	diccionario
4. Guatemala	Eduardo	el Ecuador	Managua
5. buenos	nueve (9)	luego	Venezuela

C. Practice saying each phrase as if it were one long word pronounced without a pause.

1. Buenas tardes.	**5.** Puerto Rico y el Canadá
2. ¿Cómo está usted?	**6.** sábado y domingo
3. Tomás y Pilar	**7.** Colorado y Nuevo México
4. el tigre y el chimpancé	**8.** un jugador de fútbol

Los números 0–30

Canción infantil
Dos y dos son cuatro,
cuatro y dos son seis,
seis y dos son ocho,
y ocho dieciséis.

A children's song Two and two are four, four and two are six, six and two are eight, and eight (makes) sixteen.

0	cero				
1	uno	11	once	21	veintiuno
2	dos	12	doce	22	ventidós
3	tres	13	trece	23	veintitrés
4	cuatro	14	catorce	24	veinticuatro
5	cinco	15	quince	25	veinticinco
6	seis	16	dieciséis*	26	veintiséis
7	siete	17	diecisiete	27	veintisiete
8	ocho	18	dieciocho	28	veintiocho
9	nueve	19	diecinueve	29	veintinueve
10	diez	20	veinte	30	treinta

The number *one* has several forms in Spanish. **Uno** is the form used in counting. **Un** is used before masculine singular nouns, **una** before feminine singular nouns: **un señor, una señora.** Note, also, that the number **veintiuno** becomes **veintiún** before masculine nouns and **veintiuna** before feminine nouns: **veintiún señores, veintiuna señoras.**

Use the word **hay** to express both *there is* and *there are* in Spanish. **No hay** means *there is not* and *there are not.* **¿Hay... ?** asks *Is there?* or *Are there?*

Hay treinta estudiantes en la clase.	*There are thirty students in the class.*
No hay un tigre en la clase.	*There isn't a tiger in the class.*
¿Cuántos hay?	*How many are there?*

Práctica

A. Practique los números.

1. 4 señoras	**6.** 1 clase (*f.*)	**11.** 28 bebidas
2. 12 noches	**7.** 21 ideas (*f.*)	**12.** 5 guitarras
3. 1 café (*m.*)	**8.** 11 tardes	**13.** 1 león (*m.*)
4. 21 cafés (*m.*)	**9.** 15 estudiantes	**14.** 30 señores
5. 14 días	**10.** 13 teléfonos	**15.** 20 oficinas

B. Problemas de matemáticas: + (y)   − (menos)   = (son).

MODELO $2 + 2 = ?$ → Dos y dos son cuatro.
$4 - 2 = ?$ → Cuatro menos dos son dos.

1. $2 + 4 = ?$	**4.** $3 + 18 = ?$	**7.** $1 + 13 = ?$	**10.** $13 - 8 = ?$
2. $8 + 17 = ?$	**5.** $9 + 6 = ?$	**8.** $15 - 2 = ?$	**11.** $14 + 12 = ?$
3. $11 + 1 = ?$	**6.** $5 + 4 = ?$	**9.** $9 - 0 = ?$	**12.** $23 - 13 = ?$

*The numbers 16 to 19 and 21 to 29 can be written as one word (**dieciséis... veintiuno**) or as three (**diez y seis... veinte y uno**).

C. Preguntas (*Questions*)

1. ¿Cuántos días hay en una semana? ¿Hay tres? (No, no hay...) ¿catorce? ¿nueve? ¿Cuántos días hay en un fin de semana?
2. Hoy en la clase, ¿hay un elefante? ¿una jirafa? ¿Cuántos estudiantes hay en la clase hoy? ¿Hay tres profesores o un profesor (una profesora)?
3. Hay muchos edificios (*many buildings*) en una universidad. En la universidad de usted, ¿hay cafetería? ¿teatro? ¿cine? ¿laboratorio de lenguas? ¿bar? ¿clínica? ¿hospital? ¿museo? ¿muchos (*many*) estudiantes? ¿muchos profesores?

CH. **¿Cuánto es?** (*How much does it cost?*) You have asked a clerk the prices of three different models or brands of something you want to buy. In each case you want to buy the least expensive model. What is the price of the item you finally select?

1. tres pesos, trece pesos, treinta pesos
2. dieciocho dólares, veintiocho dólares, ocho dólares
3. veintidós pesos, doce pesos, quince pesos
4. dieciséis pesetas, catorce pesetas, diecisiete pesetas
5. veintiún dólares, veintisiete dólares, veintinueve dólares
6. once pesetas, veintiuna pesetas, veintisiete pesetas

Now make up five similar sets of prices, and present them orally to your classmates, who will select the lowest price.

¿Qué hora es?° (Parte 1)

¿Qué... What time is it?

Es la una.

Son las dos.

Son las cinco.

Son las cinco y diez.

Son las dos $\begin{cases} \text{y media.} \\ \text{y treinta.} \end{cases}$

Es la una $\begin{cases} \text{y cuarto.} \\ \text{y quince.} \end{cases}$

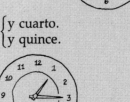

Son las ocho y veinticinco.

In telling time, one says **Es la una,** but **Son las dos** (**las tres, las cuatro,** and so on). Note that from the hour to the half-hour, Spanish, like English, expresses time by adding minutes or a portion of an hour to the hour.

Otras expresiones útiles	
de la mañana	A.M., in the morning
de la tarde (noche)	P.M., in the afternoon (evening)

Práctica

A. ¿Qué hora es?

1. 1:00	**4.** 7:30	**7.** 3:15	**10.** 2:10
2. 6:00	**5.** 1:30	**8.** 4:15	**11.** 5:25
3. 11:00	**6.** 10:30	**9.** 9:15	**12.** 12:18

B. ¿Qué hora es? ¿de la mañana, de la tarde o de la noche?

1. 3:20 P.M.	**3.** 9:10 A.M.	**5.** 4:15 A.M.
2. 5:07 P.M.	**4.** 11:14 P.M.	**6.** 10:04 P.M.

C. La excursión es a (*at*) _____ .

1. 2:19 P.M.	**4.** 7:30 A.M. on Monday
2. 8:15 A.M.	**5.** 10:15 A.M. on Saturday
3. 9:00 P.M.	**6.** 3:15 P.M. on Wednesday

CH. Situaciones. How would the following people greet each other if they met at the indicated time? Role-play each situation with another student.

1. el profesor Martínez y Gloria, a las diez de la mañana
2. la Sra. López y la Srta. Luna, a las cuatro y media de la tarde
3. usted y su (*your*) profesor(a) de español, en la clase de español
4. Jorge y María, a las once de la noche

HOY

PRIMERA CADENA

11,30 Dinastía. Episodio 122. Alexis se entera de que el rey Galen continúa vivo, aunque los revolucionarios de Moldavia exigen por su rescate diez millones de dólares.

12,25 Avance telediario.

12,30 Teletexto.

13,30 Programación regional.

15,00 Telediario 1.

15,35 El halcón callejero. «Alas incendiarias». Wiel Gassner, un importante hombre de negocios, recibe un tercer ataque en otro de sus edificios, que queda destruido por el fuego.

El mundo hispánico (Parte 1)

Antes de leer

In the following brief reading, note that the word **está** means *is located;* **está** and other forms of the verb **estar** (*to be*) are used to tell where things are. You will learn more about the uses of **estar** in Grammar Section 12.

The reading also contains a series of questions with interrogative words. You are already familiar with **¿cómo?, ¿qué?,** and **¿cuántos?** (and should be able to guess the meaning of **¿cuántas?** easily). The meaning of other interrogatives may not be immediately obvious to you, but the sentences in which the words appear may offer some clues to meaning. You probably do not know the meaning of **¿dónde?** and **¿cuál?,** but you should be able to guess their meaning in the following sentences.

Cuba está en el Mar Caribe. <u>¿Dónde</u> está la República Dominicana?
Managua es la capital de Nicaragua. <u>¿Cuál</u> es la capital de México?

Use the statements in the reading as models and the geographical and population information in the maps to answer the questions.

¿En cuántas naciones de la América Central se habla español? Hay setenta y un (*71*) millones de habitantes en México. ¿Cuántos habitantes hay en Guatemala? ¿en El Salvador? ¿en las demás (*other*) naciones de la América Central? ¿Cuál es la capital de México? ¿de Costa Rica?

Cuba está en el Mar Caribe. ¿Dónde está la República Dominicana? ¿Qué parte de los Estados Unidos está también (*also*) en el Mar Caribe? ¿Dónde está el Canal de Panamá?

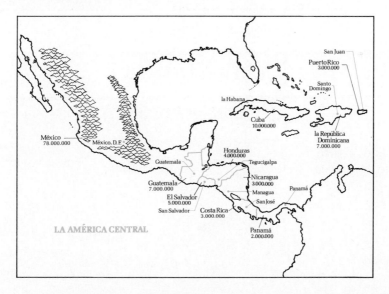

LA AMÉRICA CENTRAL

¿En cuántas naciones de Sudamérica se habla español? ¿Se habla español o portugués en el Brasil? ¿Cuántos millones de habitantes hay en Venezuela? ¿en Chile? ¿en las demás naciones? ¿Cuál es la capital de cada (*each*) nación?

España está en la Península Ibérica. ¿Qué otra (*other*) nación está también en esa (*that*) península? ¿Cuántos millones de habitantes hay en España? No se habla español en Portugal. ¿Qué lengua se habla allí (*there*)? ¿Cuál es la capital de España? ¿Está en el centro de la península?

PASO CUATRO

¿Qué hora es? (Parte 2)

Son las dos { menos cuarto.
{ menos quince.   Son las ocho menos diez.   Son las once menos veinte.

From the half-hour to the hour, Spanish expresses time by subtracting minutes or a portion of an hour from the next hour.

Otras expresiones útiles	
Es la una menos cuarto **en punto.**	It's exactly 12:45. (It's 12:45 on the dot.)
¿A qué hora?	At what time?
A las once de la noche.	At 11:00 P.M.

Práctica

A. ¿Qué hora es? ¿de la mañana, de la tarde o de la noche?

1. 2:45 P.M.
2. 8:45 A.M.
3. 5:45 A.M.
4. 7:50 P.M.
5. 4:35 P.M.
6. 6:31 A.M.
7. 10:55 P.M.
8. 11:40 A.M.

B. Situaciones. You are a travel agent. Your clients want to know when (**¿cuándo?**) they're going to arrive at their destinations. With another student, role-play this situation according to the model.

MODELO   a Guanajuato / 9:00 A.M. →
—¿Cuándo llegamos (*do we arrive*) a Guanajuato?
—A las nueve de la mañana.

1. a Sevilla / 11:00 A.M. exactly
2. a Buenos Aires / 11:54 P.M. on the dot
3. a Los Ángeles / 1:15 P.M. exactly
4. a Miami / 8:31 P.M. on Wednesday
5. a Málaga / 5:35 A.M. on Sunday
6. a Cali / 2:30 A.M. on Tuesday

C. Entrevista. Ask a classmate what time the following events or activities take place. He or she will answer according to the cue or will provide the necessary information.

MODELO   la clase de español (10:00 A.M.) →
—¿A qué hora es la clase de español?
—Es a las diez de la mañana… ¡en punto!

1. la clase de francés (1:45 P.M.)
2. la sesión de laboratorio (3:10 P.M.)
3. la excursión (8:50 A.M.)
4. el concierto (7:30 P.M.)
5. _____ (programa de televisión)

Now ask what time your partner likes to perform these activities. He or she should provide the necessary information.

MODELO   estudiar español →
           —¿A qué hora te gusta estudiar español?
           —A las ocho de la noche.

1. comer (*to eat*)   3. jugar (*to play*) al vólibol
2. mirar (*to watch*) la televisión   4. ir (*to go*) a la cafetería

CH. ¿Qué hora es? Complete each statement, telling what time it probably is if the activity is taking place. Give a day of the week when possible.

MODELO   _____ ; estudio (*I'm studying*) en la cafetería. →
           Es lunes. Son las doce; estudio en la cafetería.

1. _____ ; el profesor (la profesora) llega (*arrives*) a la clase de español.
2. _____ ; yo llego a la clase de español.
3. _____ ; hablo (*I'm speaking*) español en clase.
4. _____ ; estudio español.
5. _____ ; tomo (*I'm drinking*) café.
6. _____ ; miro (*I'm watching*) *Miami Vice*.
7. _____ ; el profesor (la profesora) prepara un examen.
8. _____ ; hay una fiesta en mi casa (*at my house*).

Las palabras interrogativas: Un resumen

You have already used a number of interrogative words and phrases to get information. (You will learn more in subsequent chapters of *¿Qué tal?*) Note the accent over the vowel you emphasize when you say the word and the use of the inverted question mark.

¿cómo?	¿Cómo estás? ¿Cómo es don Juan? ¿Cómo te llamas?
¿cuál?*	¿Cuál es la capital de Colombia?
¿cuándo?	¿Cuándo es la fiesta?
¿cuánto?	¿Cuánto es?
¿cuántos?, ¿cuántas?	¿Cuántos días hay en una semana? ¿Cuántas naciones hay en Sudamérica?
¿dónde?	¿Dónde está España?
¿qué?*	¿Qué es un hospital? ¿Qué es esto? ¿Qué hora es?

*Use **¿qué?** to mean *what?* when you are asking for a definition or an explanation. Use **¿cuál?** to mean *what?* in all other circumstances. See also Summary of Interrogative Words (**Capítulo 7**).

¿a qué hora?   ¿A qué hora es la clase?
¿quién?   ¿Quién es usted?

Note that in Spanish the voice falls at the end of questions that begin with interrogative words.

¿Qué es un tren?   ¿Cómo estás?

Práctica

A. What interrogative words do you associate with the following information?

1. A las ocho de la noche.
2. En la universidad.
3. Soy médico.
4. Muy bien, gracias.
5. ¡Es muy arrogante!
6. Hay cinco millones (de habitantes).
7. Dos pesos.
8. (La capital) Es Caracas.
9. Es un instrumento musical.
10. Mañana, a las cinco.
11. Son las once.
12. Soy Roberto González.

B. Now ask the questions that would result in the answers given in **Práctica A.**

C. Situaciones. What question is being asked by each of the following persons?

MODELO   El hombre pregunta (*The man is asking*): ¿_____?
          La mujer (*woman*) pregunta: ¿_____?

1. ¿la película (*movie*)?

2. ¿el libro?

3. ¿el regalo (*gift*)?

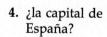

4. ¿la capital de España?

5. ¿el libro?

6. ¿el fantasma?

CH. Use interrogatives to form as many questions as you can about each of the preceding pictures.

MODELO   Dibujo (*drawing*) 1: ¿Dónde está el cine?
                              ¿Quién es el hombre?

El mundo hispánico (Parte 2)

Antes de leer

You will recognize the meaning of a number of cognates in the following reading about the geography of the Hispanic world. In addition, you should be able to guess the meaning of the underlined words from the context (the words that surround them); they are the names of geographical features. You have learned to recognize the meaning of the word **¿qué?** in questions; in this reading, **que** (with no accent mark) means *that* or *which*.

La geografía del mundo hispánico es impresionante y muy variada. En algunas° regiones hay de todo.° Por ejemplo, en la Argentina hay pampas extensas en el sur° y la cordillera de los Andes en el oeste. En partes de Venezuela, Colombia y el Ecuador, hay regiones tropicales de densa selva, y en el Brasil está el famoso río Amazonas. En el centro de México y también en El Salvador, Nicaragua y Colombia, hay volcanes activos que producen erupciones catastróficas. El Perú y Bolivia comparten° el enorme lago Titicaca, situado en una meseta entre los dos países.°

Cuba, Puerto Rico y la República Dominicana son tres islas situadas en el Mar Caribe. Las bellas playas° del Mar Caribe y de la península de Yucatán son populares entre° los turistas de todo el mundo.

España, que comparte la Península Ibérica con Portugal, también tiene° una geografía variada. En el norte están los Pirineos, la cordillera que separa a España del° resto de Europa. Madrid, la capital del país, está situada en la meseta central, y en las costas del sur y del este hay playas tan bonitas como las de° Latinoamérica y el Caribe.

Es importante mencionar también que el mundo hispánico tiene una variedad de ciudades.° En la Argentina está la gran° ciudad de Buenos Aires. Muchos consideran a Buenos Aires «el París» o «el Nueva York» de Sudamérica. En Venezuela está Caracas, y en el Perú está Lima, la capital, y Cuzco, una ciudad antigua de origen indio.

En fin,° el mundo hispánico es diverso respecto a la geografía. ¿Y Norteamérica?

some / *de... a bit of everything*
south

share
naciones

beaches
among

has

from the

tan... as pretty as those of

cities / *great*

En... In short

George Gerster/Rapho/Photo Researchers, Inc.

Extremadura, España

Peter Menzel

Los Andes, el Perú

Dieter Grabitzky/Monkmeyer Press Photo Service

La Cascada de Iguazú, entre (*between*)
el Brasil y la Argentina

George Holton/Photo Researchers, Inc.

El río Amazonas, cerca de (*close to*) Iquitos (el Brasil)

Comprensión

Demonstrate your understanding of the words underlined in the reading and other words from the reading by giving an example of a similar geographical feature found in the United States or close to it. Then give an example from the Spanish-speaking world.

MODELO   un río → *the Mississippi*, el río Amazonas

1. un lago	**4.** una isla	**7.** un mar
2. una cordillera	**5.** una playa	**8.** un volcán
3. un río	**6.** una costa	**9.** una península

Frases comunes en la clase

Here are some phrases that you will hear and use frequently during class. Don't try to memorize all of them. You will learn to recognize them with practice.

Los estudiantes
Practice saying these sentences aloud. Then try to give the Spanish as you look at the English equivalents.

Tengo una pregunta (que hacer).	*I have a question (to ask).*
¿Cómo se dice *page* en español?	*How do you say "page" in Spanish?*
Otra vez, por favor. No entiendo.	*(Say that) Again, please. I don't understand.*
No sé (la respuesta).	*I don't know (the answer).*
Cómo no.	*Of course.*

Los profesores
After you read these Spanish sentences, cover the English equivalents and say what each expression means.

¿Hay preguntas?	*Are there any questions?*
Escuche.	*Listen.*
Repita.	*Repeat.*
Lea (en voz alta).	*Read (aloud).*
Escriba (la oración).	*Write (the sentence).*
Conteste en español, por favor.	*Answer in Spanish, please.*
Abra el libro en la página _____ .	*Open your book to page _____ .*
Pregúntele a otro estudiante _____ .	*Ask another student _____ .*

Práctica

Your instructor will say the following commands and questions. Respond with an appropriate action or rejoinder.

1. Abra el libro en la página 20.
2. ¿Hay preguntas?
3. Repita la oración: Soy estudiante.
4. Escriba: Hola. ¿Qué tal?
5. Escuche.
6. Lea una oración.
7. Conteste en español: ¿Cómo está usted hoy?
8. Pregúntele a otro estudiante: ¿Cómo te llamas?

VOCABULARIO: PASOS PRELIMINARES

Although you have used many words in the **Pasos preliminares** of *¿Qué tal?*, the following words and phrases are the ones considered to be active vocabulary. Be sure you know all of them before beginning **Capítulo 1.**

SALUDOS Y EXPRESIONES DE CORTESÍA

Buenos días. Buenas tardes. Buenas noches.
Hola. ¿Qué tal? ¿Cómo está(s)?
Así así. (Muy) Bien.
¿Y tú? ¿Y usted?
Adiós. Hasta mañana. Hasta luego.
¿Cómo te llamas? ¿Cómo se llama usted? Me llamo _____ .
señor (Sr.), señora (Sra.), señorita (Srta.)
(Muchas) Gracias. De nada.
Por favor. Perdón. Con permiso.
Mucho gusto. Igualmente. Encantado/a.

¿CÓMO ES USTED?

soy, eres, es

GUSTOS Y PREFERENCIAS

¿Te gusta _____ ? ¿Le gusta _____ ? Sí, me gusta _____ . No, no me gusta _____ .

¿QUÉ DÍA ES HOY?

(el/los) lunes, martes, miércoles, jueves, viernes, sábado(s), domingo(s)
hoy, mañana, pasado mañana, el fin de semana/los fines de semana

LOS NÚMEROS 0–30

cero, uno, dos, tres, cuatro, cinco, seis, siete, ocho, nueve, diez, once, doce, trece, catorce, quince, dieciséis, diecisiete, dieciocho, diecinueve, veinte, treinta

¿QUÉ HORA ES?

es la..., son las..., y/menos cuarto, y media, en punto, de la mañana (tarde, noche), ¿a qué hora?, a la(s)...

PALABRAS Y FRASES INTERROGATIVAS

¿cómo?, ¿cuál?, ¿cuándo?, ¿cuánto? ¿cuántos? ¿cuántas?, ¿dónde?, ¿qué?, ¿quién?
¿qué es esto?

PALABRAS ADICIONALES

sí yes
no no
y and
o or
también too, also
de of; from
en in; at
a to; at (*with time*)

está is (*located*)
hay there is/are
no hay there is not/are not
¿hay? is/are there?

Introduction to *¿Qué tal?*

¿Qué tal? is divided into twenty-eight brief chapters. Each chapter has its own theme—university life here and abroad, travel, foods, and so on. Important vocabulary and expressions related to these situations are included in **Vocabulario: Preparación. Pronunciación** (in the first thirteen chapters) will introduce you to more aspects of the Spanish sound system.

The section called **Minidiálogos y estructura** contains brief dialogues, drawings, or readings that introduce new structures. The explanations are followed by exercises and activities that will help you function in realistic situations in Spanish and express yourself creatively by answering questions, describing pictures and cartoons, completing sentences, and so on. Throughout the **Minidiálogos y estructura** section, the word **¡OJO!** (*Watch out!*) will call your attention to areas where you should be especially careful when using Spanish. The exercises called **Repaso** will help you review material learned in each chapter as well as previous material. Another kind of review section that is scattered throughout the **Minidiálogos y estructura** sections is called **¿Recuerda Ud.?** (*Do you remember?*). These brief sections will help you review structures you have already studied before you learn new structures based on these points.

The final section in each chapter, **Un paso más** (*One more step*), contains photo essays **(Imágenes del mundo hispánico)** and cultural readings **(Lectura cultural)** in alternating chapters. The sections called **Antes de leer,** two of which you have already seen in **Pasos 3** and **4,** offer strategies that will make reading Spanish easier for you. In the **Vocabulario** you will find a complete list of all new (active) words for the chapter.

Every four chapters, in the sections called **Un poco de todo** (*A little bit of everything*), you will find exercises, activities, and role-plays that will help you review what you have learned up to that point. The words and phrases presented in the **A propósito...** (*By the way . . .*) boxes will help you handle situations you might encounter in a Spanish-speaking country or area of the United States, as well as hints on how to communicate more successfully with others in Spanish.

Una invitación al mundo hispánico

One aspect of understanding another people's culture is understanding what they do all the time without thinking about it. Many times a familiar action—a particular gesture, for example—has a different meaning in another culture. Sometimes you see people doing things that just seem "wrong" to you. You will find shops closed when your culture tells you they "should" be open, and open when they "should" be closed.

In learning about another culture, you also learn more about your own. A culture is a structure that provides for basic human needs: personal safety, making and maintaining friendships, dealing with strangers, and so on. Each culture meets these needs in its own way. Your job as a visitor to another culture is to learn to observe this structure without immediately judging it, to compare by using the terms "same/different" and not "right/wrong." As you do this, your understanding and appreciation of yourself and of other people will continually grow, and you will be increasingly able to participate actively in many new and exciting experiences. Many of the photographs and dialogues in *¿Qué tal?*—especially the **Lecturas culturales** at the end of even-numbered chapters—will help you develop your understanding of culture.

People often use the word *culture* to refer to another aspect of human activities: the history of a people or country as well as their contributions to the fields of art, architecture, literature, music, science, and so on. Knowledge of culture is vital for a complete understanding of a national group and helps us to place our individual heritage, whatever it may be, in the context of world history and civilization. You will learn about culture in the photo essays, **Imágenes del mundo hispánico,** that come at the end of each odd-numbered chapter.

El pasado monumental: Cabeza (*Head*) olmeca (Museo Antropológico, México)

David Kupferschmid

Omikron/Photo Researchers, Inc.

Un pionero de las nuevas tendencias: Pablo Picasso, «Guernica» (1937, Museo del Prado, Madrid, España)

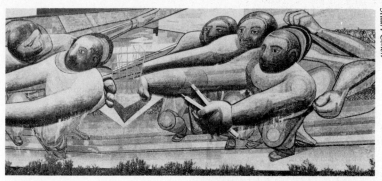

Stuart Cohen

Las universidades: Una forma de mirar (*looking*) al futuro (UNAM, México)

Peter Menzel

La tradición culta: Manuscrito medieval en latín y español (Biblioteca [*Library*] del Monasterio de El Escorial, España)

Ciudades (*Cities*) grandes y multicolores: Caracas, capital de Venezuela

Peter Menzel

Allan Cash/Rapho/Photo Researchers, Inc.

Una constante: la mexcla (*mixture*) de tradiciones. Ayer (*Yesterday*) mezquita; hoy, Catedral católica de Sevilla (España)

Bienvenidos
al mundo hispánico

Chichén Itzá,
México
(© Peter Menzel)

Barcelona, España (© Stuart Cohen)

Córdoba, España (© Peter Menzel)

Playa del Carmen, México (© Peter Menzel)

Bogotá, Colombia (© Georg Gerster/Photo Researchers)

Las personas

Madrid, España (© Mangino/The Image Works)

Ponce, Puerto Rico (© Porterfield/Chickering/Photo Researchers)

Juárez, México (© Buddy Mays)

Madrid, España (© Peter Menzel)

La Argentina (© Stuart Cohen)

Santo Domingo, República Dominicana (© Peter Menzel)

Guatemala (© George Holton/Photo Researchers)

Arte mural en Oakland, California (© Peter Menzel)

Las actividades

Monterrey, México (© Mangino/The Image Works)

Puerto Vallarta, México (© Karen Rantzman)

La Paz, Bolivia (© Will McIntyre/Photo Researchers)

Madrid, España (© Ronny Jaques/Photo Researchers)

Málaga, España (© Susan McCartney/Photo Researchers)

San Sebastián, España (© Stuart Cohen)

Ciudad de México, México (© Peter Menzel)

Sevilla, España (© Peter Menzel)

El Ecuador (© Karen Rantzman)

La pintura

España

Francisco de Goya: *Fusilamientos del Tres de Mayo*
(Prado, Madrid, España/Art Resource)

Pablo Picasso: *Tres músicos* (Collection, The Museum of Modern Art,
New York. Mrs. Simon Guggenheim Fund)

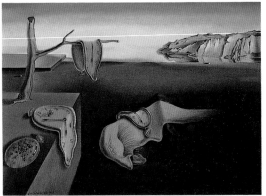

Salvador Dalí: *La persistencia de la memoria*
(Collection, The Museum of Modern Art, New York)

Rufino Tamayo: *Olga* (Museum of Modern Art of Latin America/OAS)

David Alfaro Siqueiros: *Eco de un grito*
(Collection, The Museum of Modern Art, New York.
Gift of Edward M. M. Warburg)

José Clemente Orozco:
La trinchera (Museum of Modern Art
of Latin America/OAS)

Wilfredo Lam: *La jungla* (Collection, The Museum of Modern Art,
New York. Inter-American Fund)

Carlos Mérida: *El joven rey*
(Museum of Modern Art of Latin America)

Fernando Botero:
La familia presidencial (Collection,
The Museum of Modern Art, New York.
Gift of Warren D. Benedek)

CAPÍTULO 1

En la universidad

VOCABULARIO: PREPARACIÓN

LA UNIVERSIDAD / THE UNIVERSITY

la biblioteca the library
la clase the class

el edificio the building
la librería the bookstore

la oficina the office
la residencia the dormitory

LAS COSAS / THINGS

el escritorio the desk

la pizarra the chalkboard

la silla the chair

LAS PERSONAS / PEOPLE

el consejero the (male)
adviser
la consejera the (female)
adviser
el estudiante the (male)
student

la estudiante the (female)
student
el profesor the (male)
professor

la profesora the (female)
professor
el secretario the (male)
secretary
la secretaria the (female)
secretary

En el campus

—Por favor, ¿dónde está el departamento de Historia?
—Está en el edificio Bolívar.
—Muchas gracias.
—De nada.

David Kupferschmid

Universidad de Costa Rica

A. ¿Dónde están? (*Where are they?*) Indique el edificio o lugar (*place*). Luego (*Then*) identifique las cosas y las personas usando las letras.

1. Están en _____. →

   __c__ la profesora   _____ el bolígrafo
   _____ la estudiante   _____ la mesa
   _____ el papel   _____ la silla
   _____ el lápiz   _____ la pizarra

← 2. Están en _____.

   _____ el libro   _____ la mesa
   _____ el diccionario   _____ el estudiante
   _____ el cuaderno   _____ la silla
   _____ el bolígrafo

3. Están en _____. →

   _____ la estudiante   _____ el bolígrafo
   _____ el lápiz   _____ el dinero
   _____ el cuaderno

← 4. Están en _____.

   _____ la secretaria   _____ el escritorio
   _____ la consejera   _____ el diccionario
   _____ el profesor

B. Identificaciones. ¿Es hombre o mujer (*man or woman*)?

MODELO   ¿La consejera? → Es mujer.

1. ¿El profesor?   3. ¿El secretario?
2. ¿La estudiante?   4. ¿El estudiante?

Study Hint: Learning New Vocabulary

Vocabulary is one of the most important tools for successful communication in a foreign language. What does it mean to "know vocabulary"? And what is the best way to learn vocabulary?

1. Memorization is only part of the learning process. Using new vocabulary to communicate requires practicing that vocabulary in context. What do you associate with this word? When might you want to use it? Create a context—a place, a situation, a person or group of people—for the vocabulary that you want to learn, or use a context from the text. The more associations you make with the word, the easier it will be to remember. Practice useful words and phrases over and over—thinking about their meaning—until you can produce them automatically. You may find it useful to "talk to yourself," actually saying aloud the words you want to learn.

2. Carefully study the words in vocabulary lists and drawings. If a word is a cognate or shares a root with an English word, be especially aware of differences in spelling and pronunciation. For example, note that

clase is spelled with only one **s**; that **estudiante** begins with **es-**, not **s-**; and that **diccionario** has a **-cc-** combination, not a **-ct-**. Keep in mind that an "almost but not quite perfect" spelling may lead to a miscommunication: **el libro** (*the book*) versus **la libra** (*the pound*); **la mesa** (*the table*) versus **el mes** (*the month*); **el consejero** (*male adviser*) versus **la consejera** (*female adviser*). You also need to remember which words require **el** and which require **la** to express *the*, as well as which words require a written accent—**el lápiz, el bolígrafo,** for example—and where the accent occurs.

3. After studying the list or drawing, give the English equivalent of each Spanish word.

4. When you are able to give the English without hesitation and without error, reverse the procedure; cover the Spanish and give the Spanish equivalent of each English word. Write out the Spanish words (using **el** or **la** where appropriate) once or several times and say them aloud.

5. Vocabulary lists and flash cards can be useful as a review or as a self-test.

Los números 31–100

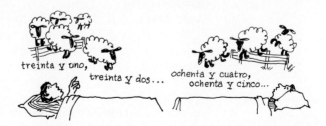

treinta y uno, treinta y dos...

ochenta y cuatro, ochenta y cinco...

En la residencia

Continúe la secuencia: treinta y uno, treinta y dos...
ochenta y cuatro, ochenta y cinco...

31	treinta y uno*	40	cuarenta
32	treinta y dos	50	cincuenta
33	treinta y tres	60	sesenta
34	treinta y cuatro	70	setenta
35	treinta y cinco	80	ochenta
36	treinta y seis	90	noventa
37	treinta y siete	100	cien
38	treinta y ocho		
39	treinta y nueve		

Beginning with 31, Spanish numbers are *not* written in a combined form; **treinta y uno,*** **cuarenta y dos**, **sesenta y tres**, and so on, must be three separate words. **Cien** is used before nouns and in counting.

cien sillas	*a (one) hundred chairs*
noventa y ocho, noventa y nueve, **cien**	*ninety-eight, ninety-nine, one hundred*

A. Más (*More*) problemas de matemáticas

1. 30 + 50 = ?	**4.** 77 + 23 = ?	**7.** 84 − 34 = ?
2. 45 + 45 = ?	**5.** 100 − 40 = ?	**8.** 78 − 36 = ?
3. 32 + 58 = ?	**6.** 99 − 39 = ?	**9.** 88 − 28 = ?

B. Telephone numbers in many countries are written and said slightly differently than in the United States. Using the model, give the following phone numbers.

MODELO   9-72-64-87 → nueve–setenta y dos–sesenta y cuatro–ochenta y siete

LA GUÍA TELEFÓNICA

Fierro Aguilar[†]	Amalia	Avenida Juárez 86	7-65-03-91
Fierro Navarro	Teresa	Calle Misterios 45	5-86-58-16
Fierro Reyes	Gilberto	Avenida Miraflores 3	5-61-12-78
Figueroa López	Alberto	Calle Zaragoza 33	5-32-97-77
Figueroa Pérez	Julio	Avenida Iglesias 15	5-74-55-34
Gómez Pérez	Ana María	Calle Madero 7	7-94-43-88

---

*Remember that when **uno** is part of a compound number (**treinta y uno, cuarenta y uno,** and so on), it becomes **un** before a masculine noun and **una** before a feminine noun.

cincuenta y **una** mesas	*fifty-one tables*	setenta y **un** libros	*seventy-one books*

---

†Note the two last names characteristic of people of Hispanic origin. You will learn about these last names in the **Lectura cultural, Capítulo 4.**

Gómez Valencia   Javier   Avenida Córdoba 22   3-99-45-52
Guzmán Ávila   José Luis   Avenida Montevideo 4   6-57-29-40
Guzmán Martínez Josefina   Avenida Independencia 25 2-77-22-70

Now give your phone number according to the model.

MODELO   —¿Cuál es tu teléfono?
          —Es el siete–veinticuatro–ochenta y tres–sesenta y uno.
            (724-8361)

C. **Situaciones.** It is inventory time at the local bookstore. The
    following items are left over from last season's merchandise. Read
    the list to your supervisor, who will write it down. Hint: Most
    words that end in **-a** are feminine.

50	radios	49	lápices
100	cuadernos	91	calculadoras
71	enciclopedias	64	lámparas
30	diccionarios	87	calendarios
25	bolígrafos	100	novelas

PRONUNCIACIÓN: Stress and Written Accent Marks

In the words **habl*a*r**, **pap*á***, **bol*í*grafo**, and **ofic*i*na**, the italicized vowel is
stressed (given more emphasis than the others). In Spanish, *stress* **(la
acentuación)** can be predicted based on the written form of the word.

1. If a word ends in a *vowel*, **n**, or **s**, stress normally falls on the
    next-to-the-last syllable.

    me-sa   **si**-lla   **cla**-se   di-**ne**-ro   ne-ce-**si**-tan
    prac-**ti**-can   **li**-bros   e-di-**fi**-cios

2. If a word ends in any other consonant, stress normally falls on the
    last syllable.

    us-**ted**   es-pa-**ñol**   pa-**pel**   doc-**tor**   ac-**triz**   ha-**blar**

3. Any exception to these two rules will have a *written accent mark* **(un
    acento ortográfico)** on the stressed vowel.

    a-**sí**   **nú**-me-ro   na-**ción**   te-**lé**-fo-no   **lá**-piz   **dó**-lar
    bo-**lí**-gra-fo

4. When one-syllable words have accents, it is to distinguish them
    from other words that sound like them. For example: **tú** (*you*)/**tu**
    (*your*); **él** (*he*)/**el** (*the*); **sí** (*yes*)/**si** (*if*).

5. Interrogative and exclamatory words have a written accent on the stressed vowel. For example: **¿quién?** (*who?*); **¿dónde?** (*where?*); **¡cómo no!** (*of course!*).

Práctica

A. Practique las siguientes palabras.

1. cosa   cliente   biblioteca   consejero   mañana   lunes
   silla   hombre   semanas   pizarra   cuaderno
   diccionarios
2. desear   hablar   mujer   papel   español   universidad
   general   sentimental   gustar   profesor
3. práctico   Ramón   miércoles   adiós   lápiz   perdón
   francés   bolígrafo   librería   sábado   Gómez   José

B. Indicate the stressed vowel of each word in the following list. Give the rule that determines the stress of each word.

1. dependiente	5. profesor	9. plástico
2. libertad	6. romántico	10. menos
3. martes	7. Guillermo	11. lugar
4. número	8. edificio	12. escritorio

MINIDIÁLOGOS Y ESTRUCTURA

En *la clase: El* **primer** *día*

PROFESORA: ... y para mañana, es necesario traer *los libros* de texto, *papel, un cuaderno y un diccionario.*

ANA: Perdón, *profesora*, pero... ¿ya hay *libros* para esta *clase* en *la librería?*

PROFESORA: Creo que sí.

ANA: ¿Y *diccionarios?*

PROFESORA: ¿No hay en *la librería?*

PEDRO: Sí, hay... pero *el problema* es *el precio.*

Complete las oraciones en una forma lógica.

1. *Para mañana es necesario traer* _____ .
2. *En la librería hay* _____ .
3. *El problema con* (with) *los libros de texto es* _____ .

In class: The first day.   INSTRUCTOR: *. . . and for tomorrow, it's necessary to bring the textbooks, paper, a notebook, and a dictionary.*   ANA: *Pardon me, ma'am (professor), but . . . are there books for this class in the bookstore already?*   INSTRUCTOR: *I think so.*   ANA: *And (what about) dictionaries?*   INSTRUCTOR: *Aren't there any in the bookstore?*   PEDRO: *Yes, there are . . . but the problem is the price.*

1 ¿Masculino o femenino?
Singular Nouns: Gender and Articles*

A *noun* (**un sustantivo**) is a word that names a person, place, thing, or idea. In Spanish, all nouns have either masculine or feminine *gender* (**el género**). This is a purely grammatical feature of nouns; it does not mean that Spanish speakers perceive things or ideas as having male or female attributes.

	Masculine Nouns		Feminine Nouns	
Definite Articles	**el** hombre **el** libro	*the man* *the book*	**la** mujer **la** mesa	*the woman* *the table*
Indefinite Articles	**un** hombre **un** libro	*a (one) man* *a (one) book*	**una** mujer **una** mesa	*a (one) woman* *a (one) table*

A. Nouns that refer to male beings and most nouns that end in **-o** are *masculine* (**masculino**) in gender: **hombre** (*man*), **libro** (*book*).

Nouns that refer to female beings and most nouns that end in **-a**, **-ción**, **-tad**, and **-dad** are *feminine* (**femenino**): **mujer** (*woman*), **mesa** (*table*), **nación** (*nation*), **libertad** (*liberty*), **universidad** (*university*).

   ▪ **¡OJO!** *A common exception is the word* **día,** *which ends in* **-a** *but is masculine in gender:* **el día.** *Many words ending in* **-ma** *are also masculine:* **el problema, el programa, el drama,** *and so on.*

Nouns that have other endings and that do not refer to either males or females may be masculine or feminine. Their gender must be memorized: **el lápiz, la clase, la tarde, la noche,** and so on.

B. In English, *the* is the *definite article* (**el artículo definido**). In Spanish, the definite article for masculine singular nouns is **el;** for feminine singular nouns it is **la.**

C. In English, the singular *indefinite article* (**el artículo indefinido**) is *a* or *an.* In Spanish, the indefinite article, like the definite article, must agree with the gender of the noun: **un** for masculine nouns, **una** for feminine nouns. **Un** and **una** can also mean *one* as well as *a* or *an.* Context determines the meaning.

[Práctica A–B]†

---

*The grammar sections of *¿Qué tal?* are numbered consecutively throughout the book. If you need to review a particular grammar point, the index will refer you to its page number.

---

†This reference is a regular feature of the grammar sections of *¿Qué tal?* It means that you are now prepared to do Exercises **A** and **B** in the **Práctica** section.

CH. Some nouns that refer to persons indicate gender according to the
following patterns:
If the masculine ends in **-o**, the feminine ends in **-a**:

> **el** amig**o**   *the (male) friend*   **la** amig**a**   *the (female) friend*
> **el** niñ**o**   *the little boy*   **la** niñ**a**   *the little girl*

If the masculine ends in a consonant, the feminine has a final **-a**:

> **un** profesor   *a (male) professor* → **una** profesor**a**   *a (female) professor*

Many other nouns that refer to people have a single form. Gender is
indicated by the article: **el estudiante, la estudiante; el cliente** (*the
male client*), **la cliente** (*the female client*). A few nouns that end in **-e**
have a feminine form that ends in **-a: el dependiente** (*the male clerk*),
la dependienta (*the female clerk*).

D. Since the gender of all nouns must be memorized, it is best to learn
the definite article along with the noun; that is, learn **el lápiz** rather
than just **lápiz.** The definite article will be given with nouns in
vocabulary lists in this book.

[Práctica C–E]*

Práctica

A. Cambie (*Change*): artículo definido → artículo indefinido
artículo indefinido → artículo definido

1. el diccionario	**5.** el bolígrafo	**8.** un cliente
2. la librería	**6.** una silla	**9.** un estudiante
3. el profesor	**7.** una residencia	**10.** una oficina
4. la residencia		

B. Dé (*Give*) el artículo definido.

1. escritorio	**4.** pizarra	**7.** mujer
2. biblioteca	**5.** hombre	**8.** nación
3. bolígrafo	**6.** universidad	**9.** secretario

Dé el artículo indefinido.

10. día	**13.** lápiz	**16.** papel
11. mañana	**14.** clase	**17.** condición
12. problema	**15.** noche	**18.** programa

C. **Escenas de la universidad.** Haga oraciones según el modelo.
(*Form sentences following the model.*)

---

*The notation [Práctica C–E] means that you are now prepared to do the rest of the exercises in the **Práctica** section.

MODELO   estudiante / librería →
Hay un estudiante en la librería.

1. consejero / oficina
2. profesora / clase
3. lápiz / mesa
4. cuaderno / escritorio
5. cliente (*f.*) / librería
6. bolígrafo / silla
7. palabra (*word*) / pizarra
8. oficina / biblioteca

CH. **Definiciones.** Defina en español según el modelo.

MODELO   biblioteca / edificio → La biblioteca es un edificio.

1. consejero / persona
2. universidad / lugar
3. residencia / edificio
4. dependienta / ?
5. hotel (*m.*) / ?
6. parque (*m.*) / ?

D. **¿Quién es?** Give the male or female counterpart of each of the following persons.

MODELO   Pablo Ortiz es consejero. (Paula Delibes) →
Paula Delibes es consejera también.

1. Camilo es estudiante. (Conchita)
2. Carmen Leal es profesora. (Carlos Ortega)
3. Juan Luis es dependiente. (Juanita)
4. Josefina es mi amiga. (José)

Now identify as many people as you can in your class and on your campus.

E. **Entrevista.** ¿Te gusta… ?

MODELO   comida (*food*) de la residencia →
—¿Te gusta la comida de la residencia?
—Sí, me gusta. (No, no me gusta.)

1. profesor
2. clase de español (de historia, de…)
3. comida de la residencia (en la cafetería, en…)
4. programa *General Hospital* (*All My Children,*…)
5. drama *Dallas* (*Hill Street Blues,*…)

2 ¿Singular o plural?
Nouns and Articles: Plural Forms

	Singular	Plural	
Nouns Ending in a Vowel	**el** libro	**los** libros	*the books*
	la mesa	**las** mesas	*the tables*
	un libro	**unos** libros	*some books*
	una mesa	**unas** mesas	*some tables*
Nouns Ending in a Consonant	**la** universidad	**las** universidad**es**	*the universities*
	un papel	**unos** papel**es**	*some papers*

A. Spanish nouns that end in a vowel form plurals by adding **-s.** Nouns that end in a consonant add **-es.** Nouns that end in the consonant **-z** change the **-z** to **-c** before adding **-es: lápiz → lápices.**

B. The definite and indefinite articles also have plural forms: **el → los, la → las, un → unos, una → unas. Unos** and **unas** mean *some, several,* or *a few.*

C. In Spanish, the masculine plural form of a noun is used to refer to a group that includes both males and females.

los amig**os**   *the friends* (both male and female)

los extranjer**os**   *the foreigners* (males and females)

Práctica

A. Dé la forma plural.

1. la mesa
2. el libro
3. el amigo
4. la oficina
5. un cuaderno
6. un lápiz
7. una extranjera
8. un bolígrafo
9. un edificio

Dé la forma singular.

10. los profesores
11. las secretarias
12. las niñas
13. los lápices
14. unos papeles
15. unas tardes
16. unas residencias
17. unas sillas
18. unos escritorios

B. Identificaciones. Which of the words listed on the right might be used to refer to the person(s) named on the left?

1. Ana María: consejero mujer dependiente estudiante
2. Tomás: niño consejera profesor secretaria
3. Margarita y Juan: extranjeros amigos hombres estudiantes

C. ¿Cómo se dice en español? Express in Spanish these people and buildings that you might see on your campus.

1. the (*male and female*) students
2. some dormitories
3. a (*female*) clerk in the bookstore
4. the foreigners
5. the (*male*) secretaries
6. some (*female*) professors

CH. Identifique las personas, las cosas y los lugares.

MODELO   Hay _____ en _____ . → Hay un libro en la mesa.

1.   2.   3.   4.   5.

D. ¿Qué hay en el cuarto (*room*)? Use el artículo indefinido.

> **MODELOS**   Hay _____ en el cuarto.
> En el escritorio hay _____ .

Ahora describa su propio (*your own*) cuarto.

> **MODELOS**   Hay _____ en mi cuarto.
> En mi escritorio hay _____ .

E. ¿Qué hay en una oficina típica de esta (*this*) universidad? ¿Qué hay en una clase típica? ¿Qué hay en una clase que *no* hay en una oficina?

REPASO

A. Working with your classmates, give as many nouns as you can that fit into these categories. Before you begin, you may wish to review the cognates presented in the explanations and exercises in the **Pasos preliminares**.

1. lugares de la universidad
2. cosas en una librería
3. personas en una librería
4. cosas en una clase típica
5. problemas de los estudiantes

B. Your instructor will name a place and a student will mention a noun at random. React by saying whether or not it is likely that the person or thing would be found in the place mentioned.

> **MODELOS**   cafetería... exámenes... →
> ¡Imposible! (No. Creo que no.) No hay exámenes en la cafetería.
> biblioteca... libros... →
> Sí. Creo que sí. Hay libros en la biblioteca.

Hablando (*Speaking*) **de clases**

—¿Cuántos estudiantes hay en la clase de física?
—Creo que hay quince o dieciséis.
—Y ¿quién es el profesor?
—La doctora Ortega.

Universidad Católica, Santiago, Chile

Katherine A. Lambert/Kay Reese & Assoc.

UN PASO MÁS: Imágenes del mundo hispánico

Antes de leer

Before starting a reading or a photo essay, it is a good idea to try to get a general sense of its content. The more you know about the reading or photo essay before you begin to read, the easier it will seem to you. Here are some things you can do to prepare yourself for readings and photo essays.

1. Make sure you understand the meaning of the title. Think about what it suggests to you and what you already know about the topic.
2. Look at the drawings, photos, or other visual cues that accompany the reading or photo essay. What do they indicate about its content?
3. Read the comprehension questions before starting to read. They will tell you what kind of information you should be looking for.

La juventud°

youth

¿*C*ómo es la juventud (*youth*) del mundo hispánico? ¿Qué le gusta? ¿Cuál es su música favorita? ¿sus diversiones favoritas? La juventud hispana, ¿es muy diferente de la norteamericana?

Los jóvenes hispanos estudian y trabajan (*work*) pero también se divierten (*they have a good time*). Les gusta la música moderna, la nacional y la importada (y hay para todos: Madonna, Duran-Duran, Ray Charles...), la música clásica y la música con raíces tradicionales. Otras diversiones son las discotecas y los cafés. Hay cafés ideales

Madrid, España

Peter Menzel

para hablar (*talking*) con los amigos. ¡Y es tan divertido (*so much fun*)
cantar y tocar la guitarra! También hay exposiciones de arte, y
siempre hay obras de teatro o películas (*movies*) interesantes.

Los días favoritos de muchos jóvenes hispánicos son los fines de
semana. ¿Realmente es muy distinta la juventud hispana?

Madrid, España

Universidad de Costa Rica

David Kupferschmid

VOCABULARIO

LAS PERSONAS

el/la amigo/a friend
el/la cliente client, customer
el/la consejero/a counselor,
  adviser
el/la dependiente/a clerk
el/la estudiante student
el/la extranjero/a foreigner
  el hombre man
  la mujer woman
el/la niño/a child; little boy/girl
el/la profesor(a) professor
el/la secretario/a secretary

LAS COSAS

el bolígrafo (ballpoint) pen
el cuaderno notebook
el diccionario dictionary
el dinero money

el escritorio desk
el lápiz (*pl.* **lápices**) pencil
el libro (de texto) (text)book
la mesa table
el papel paper
la pizarra chalkboard
la silla chair

LOS LUGARES

la biblioteca library
la clase class
el cuarto room
el edificio building
la librería bookstore
la oficina office
la residencia dormitory
la universidad university

OTROS SUSTANTIVOS

el día day
la noche night
el precio price
el problema problem
la tarde afternoon

LOS NÚMEROS 31–100

**cuarenta, cincuenta, sesenta,
setenta, ochenta, noventa, cien**

PALABRAS ADICIONALES

para for; in order to
pero but
ya already

FRASES ÚTILES PARA LA COMUNICACIÓN			
creo que sí	I think so	**creo que no**	I don't think so

¿Qué estudia usted?

VOCABULARIO: PREPARACIÓN

LAS MATERIAS

el comercio

las matemáticas

las ciencias naturales

las ciencias sociales

la historia

las lenguas

la sicología

LAS LENGUAS / LANGUAGES

el alemán German
el español Spanish

el francés French
el inglés English

el italiano Italian
el ruso Russian

Estudiando con un amigo

—¿Cuándo es tu clase de cálculo?
—A las once. ¿Qué hora es?
—Son las diez y veinte.
—¿Estudiamos (*Shall we study*) media hora más (*more*)?
—¡Cómo no! (*Of course!*)

Universidad de Panamá

A. **Asociaciones.** Which words do you associate with the numbered words on the left?

1. las ciencias
2. la sicología
3. la biblioteca
4. el diccionario
5. las lenguas
6. el comercio

las matemáticas	la librería	el papel
la universidad	el dinero	el laboratorio
la mesa	el edificio	el libro
el alemán	naturales	la historia
el secretario	la clase	sociales
el español	el italiano	el inglés

B. Identifique los libros.

MODELO   *Los insectos de Norteamérica* → Es para una clase de ciencias.

1. *El cálculo I*
2. *Romeo y Julieta*
3. *México en crisis*
4. *¿Qué tal?*
5. *Skinner y Freud*
6. *Don Quijote*
7. *Análisis crítico de la economía mexicana*
8. *La caída* (fall) *del imperio romano*

C. **¿Qué estudias?** (*What are you studying?*) The right-hand column lists a number of university subjects. Tell about your academic interests and those of other people by creating sentences using one word or phrase from each column. You will be telling what you study, want to study, need to study, and like to study.

(No) Estudio _____ .
(No) Deseo estudiar _____ .
(No) Necesito estudiar _____ .
(estudiante) estudia _____ .
(No) Me gusta estudiar _____ .

español, francés, inglés,
    alemán, ruso, italiano
arte, filosofía, literatura,
    música
ciencias políticas, historia,
    sicología, sociología
biología, física, química,
    ciencias naturales
comercio, matemáticas

PRONUNCIACIÓN: *d*

Some sounds, such as English [b], are called *stops* because, as you pronounce them, you briefly stop the flow of air and then release it. Other sounds, such as English [f] and [v], pronounced by pushing air out with a little friction, are called *fricatives*.

Spanish **d** has two basic sounds. At the beginning of a phrase or sentence or after **n** or **l,** it is pronounced as a stop [d] (similar to English *d* in *dog*). Like the Spanish [t], it is produced by putting the tongue against the back of the upper teeth. In all other cases, it is pronounced as a fricative [đ], that is, like the *th* sound in English *they* and *another*.

Práctica

A. Practique las siguientes palabras y frases.

1. [d] ¿dónde? el doctor el dinero el domingo diez dos
2. [đ] ¿adónde? la doctora mucho dinero es domingo adiós comida usted

B. Pronuncie.

¿Dónde está el dinero?
David Dávila es doctor.
Dos y diez son doce.
¿Qué estudia usted?

MINIDIÁLOGOS Y ESTRUCTURA

3 ¿Quién?
Subject Pronouns

Singular		Plural	
yo	*I*	**nosotros, nosotras**	*we*
tú	*you* (familiar)	**vosotros, vosotras**	*you* (familiar)
usted (Ud.)	*you* (formal)	**ustedes (Uds.)**	*you* (formal)
él	*he*	**ellos** }	*they*
ella	*she*	**ellas** }	

The *subject* **(el sujeto)** of a sentence is the word or group of words about which something is said or asserted. Usually the subject indicates who or what performs the action of the sentence: *The girl threw the ball.*

Indicate the subjects in the following sentences:

1. Olga is going to write a letter.
2. The car ran off the road.
3. Have Jack and Joyce arrived yet?
4. Love conquers all.

A *pronoun* **(un pronombre)** is a word used in place of a noun: *She (the girl) threw the ball.* What English pronouns would you use in place of the subjects in the preceding four sentences?

Spanish subject pronouns are used as follows:

A. Several subject pronouns have masculine and feminine forms: **nosotros, nosotras; vosotros, vosotras; ellos, ellas.** The masculine plural form is used to refer to a group of males as well as to a group of males and females.

B. Note that, in general, the English subject pronoun *it* has no equivalent in Spanish: **Es para la clase** (*It is for the class*).

C. Spanish has two different words for *you* (singular): **tú** and **usted. Usted** is generally used to address persons with whom the speaker has a formal relationship. Use **usted** with people whom you call by their title and last name **(Sr. Gutiérrez, profesora Hernández),** or with people you don't know very well. Students generally address their instructors with **usted.** In some parts of the Spanish-speaking world, children use **usted** with their parents.

   Tú implies a familiar relationship. Use **tú** when you would address a person by his or her first name, with close friends or relatives, and with children and pets. Students usually address each other as **tú.** If you are unsure about whether to use **tú** or **usted,** it is better to use **usted.** The native speaker can always suggest that you use **tú** if that form is more appropriate.

CH. The plural of **usted** is **ustedes.** In Latin America, as well as in the United States, **ustedes** also serves as the plural of **tú.** In Spain, however, the plural of **tú** is **vosotros/vosotras,** which is used when speaking to two or more persons whom you would call **tú** individually.

Práctica

A. What subject pronoun would you use to speak *about* the following persons?

1. yourself
2. two men
3. a female child
4. yourself (*m.*) and a female friend
5. yourself (*f.*) and a female friend
6. your uncle Jorge
7. your aunts Ana and Elena

B. What subject pronoun would you use to speak *to* the following persons?

1. una profesora
2. unos consejeros
3. un extranjero
4. unas amigas
5. un dependiente
6. un niño
7. un estudiante
8. mamá ·

C. What subject pronoun would you *substitute* for each of the following persons?

1. Eva
2. Luis
3. Fausto y yo (*m.*)
4. tú (*m.*) y Cecilia
5. Vicente y David
6. Graciela y yo (*f.*)

---

4 Expressing Actions
Present Tense of *-ar* Verbs

Una fiesta para los estudiantes extranjeros

CARLOS: ¿No *desean* Uds. *bailar?*
ALFONSO: ¡Cómo no! Yo *bailo* con Mary. Ella *habla* inglés.
TERESA: Yo *hablo* francés y *bailo* con Jacques.
CARLOS: Y yo *bailo* con Gretchen.
GRETCHEN: Sólo si *pagas* las cervezas. ¡*Bailas* muy mal!

Who made—or might have made—each of the following statements?

1. *Yo bailo con Jacques.*
2. *Yo hablo inglés.*
3. *Yo hablo alemán.*
4. *Nosotros hablamos francés.*
5. *Yo bailo con Alfonso.*
6. *¡Yo no bailo mal!*

A party for foreign students. CARLOS: *Don't you want to dance?* ALFONSO: *Of course! I'll dance with Mary. She speaks English.* TERESA: *I speak French and I'll dance with Jacques.* CARLOS: *And I'll dance with Gretchen.* GRETCHEN: *Only if you buy (pay for) the beers! You dance very badly!*

hablar (*to speak*): habl-	
Singular	**Plural**
yo hab**lo**	nosotros/as hab**lamos**
tú hab**las**	vosotros/as hab**láis**
Ud. ⎫	Uds. ⎫
él ⎬ hab**la**	ellos ⎬ hab**lan**
ella ⎭	ellas ⎭

Infinitives and Personal Endings

A. A *verb* (**un verbo**) is a word that indicates an action or a state of being: *We **run**, The house **is** in San Antonio.* The *infinitive* (**el infinitivo**) of a verb indicates the action or state of being with no reference to who or what performs the action, or when it is done (present, past, or future). In English the infinitive is indicated by *to: **to** run, **to** be.* In Spanish all infinitives end in **-ar, -er,** or **-ir.**

B. To *conjugate* (**conjugar**) a verb means to give the various forms of the verb with their corresponding subjects: *I speak, you speak, he (she, it) speaks,* and so on. All regular Spanish verbs are conjugated by adding *personal endings* (**las terminaciones personales**) that reflect the subject doing the action. These are added to the *stem* (**la raíz** or **el radical**): the infinitive minus the infinitive ending (habl**ar** → habl-). These personal endings are added to the stem of all regular **-ar** verbs: **-o, -as, -a, -amos, -áis, -an.**

C. Some important **-ar** verbs in this chapter include:

bailar	to dance	**hablar**	to speak; to talk
buscar	to look for	**necesitar**	to need
cantar	to sing	**pagar**	to pay (for)
comprar	to buy	**practicar**	to practice
desear	to want	**regresar**	to return (*to a place*)
enseñar	to teach	**tomar**	to take; to drink
estudiar	to study	**trabajar**	to work

■ **¡OJO!** *In Spanish the meaning of the English word* for *is included in the verbs* **pagar** *(to pay for) and* **buscar** *(to look for).*

D. As in English, when two Spanish verbs are used in sequence and there is no change of subject, the second verb is usually in the infinitive form.

| Necesito **trabajar.** | *I need to work.* |
| También desean **bailar.** | *They want to dance too.* |

English Equivalents for Present Tense

In both English and Spanish, conjugated verb forms also indicate the *time* or *tense* (**el tiempo**) of the action: *I speak* (present), *I spoke* (past).

The present tense forms of Spanish verbs correspond to four English equivalents.

hablo	*I speak*	Simple present tense
	I am speaking	Present progressive to indicate action in progress
	I do speak	Emphatic present to give special emphasis
	I will speak	Near future action

Note that another word or phrase may indicate future time when the present is used to describe near future actions.

| Hablo con Juan **mañana.** | *I'll speak with John tomorrow.* |
| ¿Estudiamos **por la noche?** | *Shall we study at night?* |

[Práctica A]

Use and Omission of Subject Pronouns

In English, a verb must have an expressed subject (a noun or pronoun): *he/she/the train returns.* In Spanish, an expressed subject is not required; verbs are accompanied by a subject only for clarification, emphasis, or contrast.

1. *Clarification.* When the context does not make the subject clear, the subject pronoun is expressed: *usted/él/ella* **habla;** *ustedes/ellos/ellas* **hablan.**

2. *Emphasis.* Subject pronouns are used in Spanish to emphasize the subject when in English you would stress it with your voice.

   | —¿Quién habla bien? | *"Who speaks well?"* |
   | —**Yo** hablo bien. | *"I speak well."* |

3. *Contrast.* Contrast is a special case of emphasis. Subject pronouns are used to contrast the actions of two individuals or groups.

   | **Ellos** hablan mucho; **nosotros** hablamos poco. | ***They** talk a lot; **we** talk little.* |

Negation

A Spanish sentence is made negative by placing the word **no** before the conjugated verb. No equivalent for the English words *do* or *does* exists in negative sentences.

El señor **no** habla inglés.   *The man doesn't speak English.*
No, **no** necesitamos dinero.   *No, we don't need money.*

[Práctica B–E]

Expressing Preferences

In the **Pasos preliminares** you learned to combine the phrases **me gusta** and **te gusta** with infinitives to express what you like—or don't like—to do. In this chapter, you have seen that verbs like **desear** and **necesitar** can also be followed by infinitives as well. Here are two other verbs to express preferences that are followed by infinitives. Learn their **yo** forms now.

(no) quiero + *infinitive*   *I (don't) want to . . .*
prefiero + *infinitive*   *I prefer to . . .*

Quiero comprar un bolígrafo.   *I want to buy a pen.*
Prefiero estudiar más tarde.   *I prefer to study later.*

[Práctica F]

Práctica

A. Dé oraciones nuevas según las indicaciones. (*Give new sentences according to the cues.*)

En la clase de español

1. *Ud.* estudia mucho.   (*nosotros, yo, ellos, Juan, tú, vosotras*)
2. *Sara* necesita un diccionario.   (*yo, Carlos y tú, tú, nosotras, Ada, vosotros*)

En una fiesta en la residencia

3. *Clara* toma Coca-Cola.   (*tú, Ud., él, Uds., Elena y yo, vosotras*)
4. *Tú* cantas y bailas.   (*nosotros, los amigos, Uds., Eva y Diego, yo, vosotros*)

B. Exprese en forma negativa.

1. Necesito dinero.
2. Cantamos en alemán.

3. Deseo practicar español con Ricardo Montalbán.
4. Yo trabajo todas las noches (*every night*).
5. Hoy los estudiantes enseñan la clase.
6. Los Rockefeller necesitan mucho dinero.
7. Aquí (*Here*) los estudiantes toman cerveza.
8. Julio Iglesias enseña español.
9. Tomo dieciocho clases.

C. Form complete sentences by using one word or phrase from each column. The words and phrases may be used more than once, in many combinations. Be sure to use the correct form of the verbs. Make any of the sentences negative, if you wish.

MODELOS   Jorge y yo regresamos por la noche.
                Ud. trabaja en una oficina.

Jorge y yo		comprar	las cervezas
Ud.		regresar	ruso
tú		buscar	la biblioteca
yo		trabajar	una clase de biología/
el dependiente	(no)	enseñar	sicología
Uds.		pagar	en una oficina
		tomar	por la noche
			lápices en la librería
		desear	hablar bien el español
		necesitar	trabajar más (*more*)
			estudiar más
			comprar unos
			cuadernos

CH. **Escenas universitarias.** ¿Cómo se dice en español?

1. We work in an office.
2. *She* teaches French; *he* teaches English.
3. They're not buying the notebook.
4. John won't pay for the pens tomorrow.
5. *You* (*fam. s.*) are looking for the bookstore.
6. He's singing, but she's working.

D. Tell where these people are (using **está** for singular or **están** for plural) and what they are doing. Note that the definite article is used with titles—**el señor, la señora, la señorita, el profesor, la profesora**—when talking about a person.

MODELO   La Sra. Martínez _____ .
              La señora Martínez está en la oficina.
              Busca un libro, trabaja...

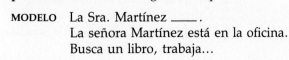

1. Los estudiantes extranjeros _____ .

2. La cliente _____ .

3. La profesora Gil _____ .

4. Los amigos _____ .

5. El Sr. Miranda _____ .

6. Los estudiantes _____ .

E. Preguntas

1. ¿Ud. estudia mucho o poco? ¿Dónde estudia, en casa (*at home*), en la residencia o en la biblioteca? ¿Cuándo estudia, por la tarde o por la noche? ¿Con quién practica español? ¿Con quién desea practicar?

2. Preguntas «indiscretas»: ¿Canta Ud. muy bien o muy mal? ¿Baila muy bien o muy mal? ¿Toma mucho o poco? ¿Regresa a casa (*home*) tarde (*late*) o temprano (*early*)?

3. En una fiesta, ¿qué *no* desean Uds. hacer (*to do*)? ¿Desean estudiar? ¿cantar? ¿trabajar? ¿bailar con el profesor (la profesora)?

4. ¿Qué estudian Uds. en esta (*this*) clase? ¿Qué lengua hablan en clase? ¿Hablan inglés en la clase de español? ¿Desean hablar español muy bien?

5. ¿Cuántas lenguas habla el profesor (la profesora)? ¿Qué lenguas enseña? ¿Trabaja en una oficina de la universidad? ¿Enseña por la mañana o por la tarde?

6. ¿La universidad paga la matrícula (*registration fees*)? ¿Los estudiantes necesitan pagar la matrícula? ¿los libros de texto? ¿Necesitan comprar lápices? ¿un diccionario? ¿Compran libros de texto en la biblioteca?

F. Complete the following sentences by using infinitives you have learned plus any other necessary words.

1. Prefiero _____ temprano. No me gusta _____ tarde.
2. No quiero _____ hoy. Prefiero _____ .
3. Quiero _____ pasado mañana.
4. Me gusta _____ los fines de semana, pero este (*this*) fin de semana necesito _____ .

5 ¿Sí o no?
Asking Yes/No Questions

En una universidad: La oficina de matrícula

ESTUDIANTE: Necesito una clase más. *¿Hay sitio* en la clase de sicología 2?

CONSEJERO: Imposible, señorita. No hay.

ESTUDIANTE: *¿Hay un curso* de historia o de matemáticas?

CONSEJERO: Sólo por la noche. *¿Desea Ud. tomar* una clase por la noche?

ESTUDIANTE: Trabajo por la noche. Prefiero tomar una clase por la mañana.

CONSEJERO: Pues... ¿qué tal el francés 10? Hay una clase a las diez de la mañana.

ESTUDIANTE: *¿El francés 10?* Perfecto. Pero, *¿no necesito tomar* primero el francés 1?

---

1. *¿Necesita la señorita dos clases más?*
2. *¿Hay sitio en la sicología 2?*
3. *¿Hay cursos de historia o de matemáticas por la mañana?*
4. *¿A qué hora es la clase de francés 10?*
5. *¿Cuál es el problema con la clase de francés 10?*

There are two kinds of questions: information questions and yes/no questions. Questions that ask for new information or facts that the speaker does not know often begin with *interrogative words* such as *who, what*, etc. (You learned many interrogative words in the **Pasos preliminares.**) Yes/no questions, however, are those that permit a simple *yes* or *no* answer.

Do you speak French? → No, I don't (speak French).

Rising Intonation

A common way to form yes/no questions in Spanish is simply to make your voice rise at the end of the question.

At a university: The registration office STUDENT: *I need one more class. Is there space in Psychology 2?* COUNSELOR: *Impossible, Miss. There's no room.* STUDENT: *Is there a history or math class?* COUNSELOR: *Only at night. Do you want to take a night course?* STUDENT: *I work at night. I prefer to take a class in the morning.* COUNSELOR: *Well . . . what about French 10? There's a class at 10:00 in the morning.* STUDENT: *French 10? Perfect. But don't I need to take French 1 first?*

Statement

Ud. trabaja aquí todos los días.
You work here every day.

El niño regresa a casa hoy.
*The boy is returning home
     today.*

Question

¿Ud. trabaja aquí todos los días?
Do you work here every day?

¿El niño regresa a casa hoy?
Is the boy returning home today?

There is no Spanish equivalent to English *do* or *does* in questions. Note also the inverted question mark (¿) at the beginning of questions.

Inversion

Another way to form yes/no questions is to invert the order of the subject and verb, in addition to making your voice rise at the end.

Statement: Ud. trabaja aquí todos
     los días.

Question: ¿Trabaja **Ud.** aquí
     todos los días?

El niño regresa a casa hoy.

¿Regresa **el niño** a casa hoy?

Práctica

A. Forme dos preguntas, según el modelo.

MODELO   Irma habla español. → ¿Irma habla español?
                                         ¿Habla Irma español?

1. Ud. regresa a clase mañana.
2. Elvira busca un cuaderno también.
3. Ramón toma café.
4. Ud. paga la matrícula.

5. Uds. enseñan italiano.
6. Ellos bailan todos los días.
7. Ella trabaja mañana.

B. En la librería. Ask the questions that might lead to the following answers you have just overheard. Follow the model.

MODELO   Sí, estudio con él (*him*). → ¿Estudia Ud. con Guillermo?
                                         ¿Estudias (tú) con Guillermo?

1. No, no trabajo aquí todos los días.
2. Sí, ella habla muy bien.
3. No, no regreso a casa hoy.

4. Sí, estudiamos mucho para esa (*that*) clase.
5. Sí, él busca un diccionario español-inglés.
6. No, no necesitamos lápiz.

C. **Entrevista.** Ask another student the following questions about what he or she is going to do tomorrow.

1. ¿Pagas la matrícula mañana?
2. ¿Necesitas comprar el texto en la librería mañana?
3. ¿Practicas el español?
4. ¿Tomas cerveza en clase?
5. ¿Quieres bailar en clase?
6. ¿Regresas a clase?

Now ask your Spanish instructor the last three questions. Begin each question with **Profesor(a)** _____ . Remember to use **usted.**

CH. **Entrevista.** Without taking notes, interview another student by asking the following questions or any others that occur to you. Then present as much of the information as you can to the class.

MODELO   David estudia literatura, trabaja en McDonald's y baila mucho.

1. ¿Cuántas clases tomas este (*this*) semestre/trimestre?
2. ¿Estudias matemáticas? ¿literatura? ¿sicología? ¿alemán?
3. ¿Quieres estudiar ciencias naturales? ¿matemáticas? ¿comercio?
4. ¿Practicas español? ¿Con quién?
5. Por la mañana, ¿prefieres tomar café, té o leche (*milk*)?
6. ¿Trabajas? ¿Dónde? ¿Te gusta el trabajo (*job*)?
7. En una fiesta, ¿bailas o sólo hablas?

REPASO

Las actividades de la universidad. Complete the following paragraph from Tomás Gutiérrez's letter home from college. Give the correct form of the words in parentheses, as suggested by the context. When two possibilities are given in parentheses, select the correct word.

UNIVERSIDAD DEL PRESENTE Y DEL FUTURO

UNIVERSIDAD CENTRAL

Admisión:
- Derecho   (5 años)
- Arquitectura   (6 años)
- Sicología   (6 años)
- Ingeniería Comercial   (5 años)
- Administración Pública   (5 años)
- Educación Parvularia   (4 años)

... Tomo cinco materias, y la que° más° (*me/te*[1]) gusta es (*el/la*[2]) español.   la... *the one / most*
Todos (*los/las*[3]) días estudio español con Jaime y Luisa. (*Nosotros: practicar*[4])
el vocabulario y (*el/la*[5]) pronunciación y hablamos con Micaela, (*un/una*[6])
estudiante de Buenos Aires. Ella (*hablar*[7]) español más rápido que° noso-   más... *faster than*
tros. Micaela, Jaime, Luisa y yo también (*cantar*[8]). Yo (*cantar*[9]) muy mal,
pero Jaime y Micaela (*cantar*[10]) bien.

En este momento° estoy° en la cafetería. A (*los/las*[11]) tres y media quiero   En... *Right now / I am*
regresar a (*una/la*[12]) biblioteca para estudiar. Necesito (*buscar*[13]) un libro para
(*el/la*[14]) clase de sicología. Prefiero no (*comprar*[15]) más° libros, si no es nece-   *any more*
sario.

(*El/La*[16]) viernes por la noche hay (*un/una*[17]) fiesta en la residencia. Los
estudiantes de (*el/la*[18]) universidad trabajan mucho, pero sólo cinco días
por° semana. ¡(*Los/Las*[19]) fines de semana son para divertirse°!   *per / to have a good time*

El horario (*schedule*)

—¿Cuándo regresas a la biblioteca?
—A las dos y media. Necesito estudiar.
—¿No trabajas en la librería por la tarde?
—Sólo los martes y los jueves. Hoy no.

Horario Biblioteca José M. Lázaro
Período exámenes finales 1er Semest. 1985-86

Lunes 2 al jueves 5 de diciembre   7:00 am – 12:00 medianoche
Viernes 6 de diciembre   7:00 am – 10:00 pm
Sábado 7 de diciembre   7:30 am – 6:00 pm
Domingo 8 de diciembre   10:00 am – 7:30 pm
Lunes 9 al jueves 12 de diciembre   7:00 am – 12:00 medianoche
Viernes 13 de diciembre   7:00 am – 10:00 pm
Sábado 14 de diciembre   7:30 am – 4:00 pm
Domingo 15 de diciembre   CERRADO
Lunes 16 al viernes 20 de diciembre   HORARIO ADMINISTRATIVO
(8:00 am – 5:00 pm)

Feliz Navidad

Owen Franken

Universidad de Puerto Rico

UN PASO MÁS: Lectura cultural

Antes de leer

As you learned in **El mundo hispánico (Pasos preliminares),** you can often guess the meaning
of unfamiliar words from the context (the words that surround them) and by using your knowledge about the topic in general. Making "educated guesses" about words in this way will be an
important part of your reading skills in Spanish.

What is the meaning of the underlined words in these sentences?

1. En una lista alfabetizada, la palabra **grande** ocurre antes de la palabra **grotesco.**
2. El edificio no es moderno; es viejo.
3. Me gusta estudiar español, pero detesto la biología. En general, odio las ciencias como
materia.

Some words are underlined in the following reading (and in the readings in subsequent chapters). Try to guess their meaning from context.

Las universidades hispánicas

En el mundo hispánico—y en los Estados Unidos—hay universidades grandes° y pequeñas, públicas, religiosas y privadas, modernas y antiguas. Pero el concepto de «vida° universitaria» es diferente.

    Por ejemplo, en los países° hispánicos la universidad no es un centro de actividad social. No hay muchas residencias estudiantiles. En general, los estudiantes viven en pensiones* o en casas particulares° y llegan a la universidad en coche o en autobús. En algunas° universidades hay un *campus* similar a los de° las universidades de los Estados Unidos. En estos casos se habla° de la «ciudad° universitaria». Otras universidades ocupan sólo un edificio grande, o posiblemente varios edificios, pero no hay zonas verdes.°

    Otra diferencia es que en la mayoría° de las universidades hispánicas no se da° mucha importancia a los deportes. Si los estudiantes desean practicar un deporte—el tenis, el fútbol° o el béisbol—hay clubes deportivos, pero éstos° no forman parte de la universidad.

    Como se puede ver,° la forma y la organización de la universidad son diferentes en las dos culturas. Pero los estudiantes estudian y se divierten° en todas partes.°

large
life
naciones

private
unas
los... *those of*
se... *one speaks / city*
green
majority
se... *is given*
soccer
they
Como... *As you can see*
se... *have a good time*
en... *everywhere*

Comprensión

¿Cierto o falso? Corrija (*Correct*) las oraciones falsas. Todas las oraciones se refieren a la vida universitaria hispánica.

1. Es similar a la de los Estados Unidos.
2. Hay pocas residencias para los estudiantes.
3. Una «ciudad universitaria» es una ciudad grande con una universidad.
4. Siempre (*Always*) hay un equipo (*team*) de fútbol.

Para escribir

In this exercise, you will write a description of your own **vida universitaria.** First, answer the following questions in short but complete sentences.

1. ¿Es grande o pequeña la universidad? (Mi universidad...)
2. ¿Es pública or privada?
3. ¿Cuántas residencias hay en el *campus*?
4. En general, ¿viven (*live*) los estudiantes en residencias, en apartamentos o con su (*their*) familia?

---

*A **pensión** is a boarding house where students rent bedrooms and share a common bathroom with other boarders. Many students take their meals at the **pensión** as well.

5. ¿Cuáles son los dos edificios más grandes (*biggest*)? ¿la biblioteca? ¿la administración? ¿el *student union*?
6. ¿Se da mucha importancia a los deportes?
7. ¿Dónde vive Ud.? (Yo vivo…)
8. ¿Cómo llega Ud. al *campus*? ¿en coche o en autobús? ¿O camina Ud.? (*Or do you walk?*)
9. ¿En qué edificios del *campus* estudia Ud.?
10. ¿Qué materia le gusta más?

Now take your individual answers and form two coherent paragraphs (using items 1–6 and 7–10) with them. Use the following words to make your paragraphs flow smoothly: **y, también, pero,** and **por eso** (*that's why, for that reason*).

VOCABULARIO

VERBOS

bailar to dance
buscar to look for
cantar to sing
comprar to buy
desear to want
enseñar to teach
estudiar to study
hablar to speak; to talk
necesitar to need
pagar to pay (for)
practicar to practice
regresar to return (*to a place*)
  regresar a casa to return home
tomar to take; to drink
trabajar to work

LAS LENGUAS

el alemán German
el español Spanish
el francés French
el inglés English
el italiano Italian
el ruso Russian

OTRAS MATERIAS

las ciencias (naturales, sociales) (natural, social) sciences
el comercio business
la historia history
las matemáticas mathematics
la sicología psychology

OTROS SUSTANTIVOS

la cerveza beer
la fiesta party
la matrícula registration fee

PALABRAS ADICIONALES

aquí here
bien well
con with
mal badly
mucho a lot
muy very
poco little, a little
por (la mañana, la tarde, la noche) in (the morning, afternoon, evening)
pues… well . . .
si if
sólo only
tarde late
temprano early
todos los días every day

FRASES ÚTILES PARA LA COMUNICACIÓN	
¡cómo no!	of course!
prefiero + *inf.*	I prefer to (*do something*)
quiero (no quiero) + *inf.*	I want (I don't want) to (*do something*)

CAPÍTULO 3

La familia

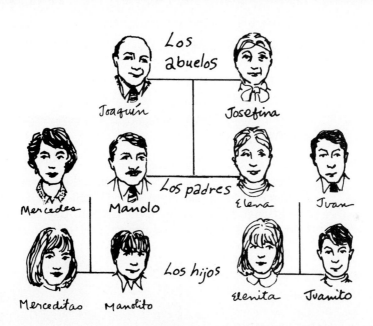

—— **LOS PARIENTES** / RELATIVES ——

la madre (mamá) mother (mom)	**la esposa** wife	**la prima** cousin (female)
el padre (papá) father (dad)	**el esposo** husband	**el primo** cousin (male)
la hija daughter	**la abuela** grandmother	**la tía** aunt
el hijo son	**el abuelo** grandfather	**el tío** uncle
la hermana sister	**la nieta** granddaughter	**la sobrina** niece
el hermano brother	**el nieto** grandson	**el sobrino** nephew

A. **¿Cierto o falso?** Corrija las oraciones falsas.

1. Juan es el hermano de Elena.
2. Josefina es la abuela de Elenita.
3. Merceditas es la sobrina de Joaquín.
4. Merceditas y Juanito son (*are*) primos.
5. Manolo es el tío de Elenita.
6. Juanito es el sobrino de Juan.
7. Elena es la esposa de Manolo.

B. **¿Quiénes son?** Identifique los miembros de cada (*each*) grupo, según el modelo.

MODELO los hijos → el hijo y la hija

1. los abuelos	3. los hermanos	5. los tíos
2. los padres	4. los nietos	6. los sobrinos

C. **¿Quién es?** Complete las oraciones en una forma lógica.

1. La madre de mi* padre es mi_____.
2. El hijo de mi tío es mi_____.
3. La hermana de mi padre es mi_____.
4. El esposo de mi abuela es mi_____.

Ahora (*Now*) defina estas (*these*) personas, según el mismo (*same*) modelo.

5. prima   6. sobrino   7. tío   8. abuelo

CH. **Entrevista.** With a classmate, discuss the members of your family, following the model of the photo caption below. Use **tengo** (*I have*) and **tienes** (*you have*) as in the caption. Use **cuántos** before masculine nouns and **cuántas** before feminine nouns.

Hablando de la familia

—Tienes una familia muy grande. ¿Cuántos son?
—Bueno, tengo seis hermanas y un hermano.
—Y ¿cuántos primos?
—¡Uf! Tengo un montón. Más de veinte.

Cali, Colombia

*Use **mi** to mean *my* with singular nouns and **mis** with plural ones. You will learn more about using words of this type in Grammar Section 11.

Formas del verbo *ser*

In **Paso uno,** you learned the singular forms of the verb **ser.*** Here is the complete conjugation.

ser (*to be*)			
yo	**soy**	nosotros/as	**somos**
tú	**eres**	vosotros/as	**sois**
Ud.⎱		Uds.⎱	
él ⎬	**es**	ellos ⎬	**son**
ella⎰		ellas⎰	

Here are some basic uses of **ser.** You have used many of them already.

- To *identify* people and things

  Yo soy **estudiante.**   **Esto** es **un libro.**
  La doctora Ramos es   **Alicia y yo** somos **amigas.**
     profesora.

- To *describe* people and things

  Soy **sentimental.**   *I'm sentimental (a sentimental person).*

- To *tell time* (**es, son**)

  Es **la una.**   Son **las tres.**

- With **para**, to tell *for whom something is intended*

  La comida es **para Andrés.**   *The food is for Andrés.*

  —¿**Para quién** son los   *"For whom are the presents?"*
     regalos?
  —Son **para el niño.**   *"They're for the child."*

- To express *generalizations* (**es**)

  Es **importante** estudiar.   *It's important to study.*
  No es **necesario** trabajar   *It's not necessary to work every*
     todos los días.   *day.*

---

*There are two Spanish verbs that mean *to be:* **ser** and **estar.** They are not interchangeable; the meaning the speaker wishes to convey determines their use. You will learn some of the uses of **ser** in this chapter and in subsequent ones. Remember to use **está** to express location. You will learn its conjugation and uses later.

A. **Situaciones.** With a partner, choose a fictitious family relationship, imagining that you are cousins, aunts of the same person, and so on. Another student will ask you questions until he or she determines your identity.

MODELO   —¿Son Uds. primos?
          —No, no somos primos.
          —¿Son... ?

B. **¿Para quién son los regalos?** The first column is a list of possible gifts. The second column lists some members of your imaginary family. Decide who should receive which gift and explain why.

MODELO   _____ es para _____ .

el dinero para comprar comida (pagar la matrícula)
el coche, un Mercedes
la cerveza
la silla mecedora (*rocking chair*)
los discos (*records*) de Sade y Bruce Springsteen
el televisor (*TV set*)
los cien mil (*100,000*) dólares
_____?

mis abuelos Ernesto y Lupita: pasan todos los días en casa
mi tío Juan: le gusta mirar los partidos (*games*) de fútbol
mi hermano Raúl y su (*his*) esposa: ¡tienen (*they have*) seis niños!
mi prima Anita: estudia en la universidad
mi primo Marcos: le gusta mucho la música moderna
mi tía Juana: es médica
mis padres: quieren comprar una casa en Phoenix

C. Haga oraciones originales, afirmativas o negativas, con estas palabras.

(No)

Es importante
Es muy práctico
Es necesario
Es tonto (*silly*)
Es fascinante
Es posible

mirar (*to watch*) la televisión todos los días
hablar español en la clase
comer (*to eat*) tres veces (*times*) al día
llegar (*to arrive*) a clase a la hora en punto
tomar cerveza en clase
hablar con los animales/las plantas
escribir cartas (*to write letters*) al presidente

CH. **Una fiesta familiar.** Imagine que Ud. está en una fiesta familiar. ¿A qué hora llegan todos? ¿Qué toman Uds.? ¿Es posible bailar? ¿cantar? ¿hablar con muchos (*many*) parientes? ¿Es necesario ser amable con todos? ¿Le gusta hablar con la familia? ¿A qué hora termina la fiesta?

PRONUNCIACIÓN: *r* and *rr*

Spanish has two *r* sounds, one of which is called a *flap*, the other a *trill*. The rapid pronunciation of *tt* and *dd* in the English words *Betty* and *ladder* produces a sound similar to the Spanish flap **r**: the tongue touches the alveolar ridge (behind the upper teeth) once. Although English has no trill, when people imitate a motor they often produce the Spanish trill, which is a rapid series of flaps.

The trilled **r** is written **rr** between vowels **(carro, correcto)** and **r** at the beginning of a word **(rico, rosa).** Any other **r** is pronounced as a flap. Be careful to distinguish between the flap **r** and the trilled **r**. A mispronunciation will often change the meaning of a word—for example, **pero** (*but*)/**perro** (*dog*).

Práctica

A. inglés: potter   ladder   cotter   meter   total   motor
   español: para   Lara   cara   mire   toro   moro

B. **1.** ruso   **4.** Roberto   **7.** real   **10.** carro
   2. rápido   **5.** reportero   **8.** burro   **11.** barra
   3. roca   **6.** rebelde   **9.** corral   **12.** corro

C. **1.** el hombre correcto   **6.** el precio del cuaderno
   2. las residencias   **7.** Enrique, Carlos y Rosita
   3. una mujer refinada   **8.** Los errores son raros.
   4. Puerto Rico   **9.** Necesitan buscar un carro.
   5. el extranjero   **10.** Soy el primo de Roque Ramírez.

MINIDIÁLOGOS Y ESTRUCTURA

¿Recuerda Ud.?

The personal endings used with **-ar** verbs share some characteristics of those used with **-er** and **-ir** verbs, which you will learn in the next section. Review the endings of **-ar** verbs by telling which subject pronoun you associate with each of these endings.

   1. **-amos**   2. **-as**   3. **-áis**   4. **-an**   5. **-o**   6. **-a**

6 Expressing Actions
Present Tense of *-er* and *-ir* Verbs

El sábado por la tarde, en casa de la familia Robles

EL SR. ROBLES: Paquita, *debes* estudiar más ahora. *Insisto* en eso.

PAQUITA: Pero, papá, *asisto* a todas mis clases y saco buenas notas. Además, todos mis amigos van a un concierto esta noche.

EL SR. ROBLES: Tus amigos no son mis hijos. Nunca *abres* los libros en casa.

PAQUITA: ¡Ay, papá! ¡No me *comprendes*! ¡Eres terrible a veces!

¿Quién...
1. *debe estudiar más hoy?*
2. *insiste en imponer su voluntad (his will, way)?*
3. *asiste a todas las clases?*
4. *nunca abre los libros en casa?*
5. *no comprende la situación?*

comer (*to eat*)		**vivir** (*to live*)	
como	comemos	vivo	vivimos
comes	coméis	vives	vivís
come	comen	vive	viven

The present tense of **-er** and **-ir** verbs is formed by adding personal endings to the stem of the verb (the infinitive minus its **-er/-ir** ending). The personal endings for **-er** and **-ir** verbs are the same except for the first and second person plural.

Remember that the Spanish present tense has a number of present tense equivalents in English and can also be used to express future meaning:

	I eat	Simple present
como	*I am eating*	Present progressive
	I do eat	Emphatic present
	I will eat	Future

Saturday afternoon at the Robles's house MR. ROBLES: *Paquita, you should study more now. I insist on that.* PAQUITA: *But Dad, I go to all of my classes and I get good grades. Besides, all my friends are going to a concert tonight.* MR. ROBLES: *Your friends aren't my children. You never open your books at home.* PAQUITA: *Oh, Dad! You don't understand me! You're terrible sometimes!*

Some important **-er** and **-ir** verbs in this chapter include the following:

aprender	to learn	**abrir**	to open
beber	to drink	**asistir (a)**	to attend, go to
comer	to eat	**escribir**	to write
comprender	to understand	**insistir**	to insist
creer (en)	to think; to believe (in)	**(en** + *inf.*)	(*on doing something*)
deber (+ *inf.*)	should, must, ought to	**recibir**	to receive
	(*do something*)	**vivir**	to live
leer	to read		

Práctica

A. Dé oraciones nuevas según las indicaciones.

Escenas de la sala de clase

1. *Yo* asisto a clase todos los días.   (*tú, nosotros, Ud., todos los estudiantes, Carlos, vosotros*)

2. *Aprendemos* español aquí.   (*yo, Ud., la prima de José, Uds., vosotros*)

Es Navidad (*Christmas*) y hay una fiesta en casa. ¿Qué pasa?

3. *Todos* comen y beben.   (*yo, los tíos, tú, Uds., la prima y yo, Ud., vosotras*)

4. *Los niños* reciben regalos.   (*papá, tú, nosotras, los hijos de Juan, Alicia, los nietos, vosotros*)

B. Form complete sentences using one word or phrase from each column. Be sure to use the correct forms of the verbs. Make any of the sentences negative if you wish.

Ud.	abrir	Coca-Cola, café antes de (*before*) la clase
yo	escribir	un periódico (*newspaper*), un poema, una revista (*magazine*), un
Rosendo	deber	telegrama, una carta, los ejercicios
nosotros (no)	leer	la situación, el problema, la lección, todo (*everything*)
mis abuelos	beber	la puerta (*door*), el regalo
tú	comprender	beber toda (*all*) la cerveza, llegar tarde/temprano, asistir a un
___?___	vivir	concierto, mirar la televisión
		en una casa, en un apartamento, en ___?___
		___?___

C. En clase, ¿qué deben o no deben hacer (*do*) Uds.?

1. llegar a la hora en punto
2. hablar inglés
3. escribir los ejercicios
4. llevar (*bring*) regalos para el profesor (la profesora)
5. aprender las palabras nuevas (*new words*)
6. asistir a clase todos los días
7. terminar los ejercicios

CH. ¿Cómo se dice en español?

1. "Does he understand Italian?" "I don't believe so, and she doesn't understand English." "What language should we speak, then **(entonces)**?"
2. "Where's Julio this year **(este año)**?" "He's living in Caracas and he's speaking Spanish every day!"
3. Anita doesn't believe in Santa Claus.

D. ¿Qué hacen estas (*these*) personas?

E. **¿Cómo usa Ud. su tiempo (*your time*)?** How frequently do you do each of the following things?

todos los días	*every day*
con frecuencia	*frequently*
a veces	*at times*
una vez/dos veces a la semana/al mes	*once/twice a week/month*
casi nunca*	*almost never*
nunca*	*never*

---

*Use these expressions only at the beginning of a sentence. You will learn more about how to use them in **Palabras indefinidas y negativas (Capítulo 10)**.

1. Escribo una carta.
2. Hablo por teléfono.
3. Como con todos los parientes.
4. Leo novelas.
5. Miro la televisión.
6. Bebo Coca-Cola.
7. Leo el periódico.
8. Aprendo palabras nuevas en español.
9. Compro regalos para papá y mamá.
10. Escribo un poema.
11. Insisto en hablar inglés en esta (*this*) clase.
12. Recibo un suspenso (*F*) en un examen.

Now interview another student, asking him or her questions based on the sentences given above. Begin each question with **¿Con qué frecuencia... ?**

MODELO   ¿Con qué frecuencia escribes una carta?

Now use the same phrases to describe the activities of at least one member of your family.

MODELO   Mi padre nunca escribe cartas. Habla por teléfono con frecuencia. ...

F.   **Entrevista.** Hold a brief conversation with a classmate based on the following questions. Note that you will be using the **tú** forms of expressions you learned in **Capítulo** 2.

MODELO   —¿Qué (no) quieres estudiar hoy?
—(No) Quiero estudiar español (filosofía, biología, ruso,...).

1. ¿Qué (no) quieres leer?
2. ¿A qué hora prefieres comer?
3. ¿Prefieres aprender español o alemán?
4. ¿Qué no quieres hacer (*to do*) hoy?
5. ¿Qué (no) debes hacer en clase?
6. ¿Qué te gusta escribir?
7. ¿Quieres asistir a un concierto esta noche?
8. ¿Prefieres hablar inglés o español?

G.   Preguntas

1. ¿Insiste Ud. en hablar inglés en esta (*this*) clase? ¿en comprender todo? ¿en cantar en clase? ¿en aprender todo? ¿en practicar español un poco todos los días? ¿en tomar exámenes todos los días?
2. ¿En qué o en quién cree Ud.? ¿en Santa Claus? ¿en Dios (*God*)? ¿en Alá? ¿en el dólar norteamericano?

Study Hint: Learning Grammar

Learning a language is similar to learning any other skill; knowing *about* it is only part of what is involved. Consider how you would acquire another skill—swimming, for example. If you read all the available books on swimming, you would probably become an expert in talking *about* swimming and you would know what you *should* do in a pool. However, it would take practice in a pool before you could swim well. In much the same way, if you memorize all the grammar rules but spend little time *practicing* them, you will not be able to communicate very well in Spanish.

As you study each grammar point in *¿Qué tal?*, you will learn how the structure works; then you need to put your knowledge into practice. First, read the grammar discussion, then study the examples and **¡OJO!** sections, which will call your attention to problem areas. Then begin to practice. When you are certain that your answers are correct, practice doing each exercise several

times until the answers sound and "feel" right to you. As you do each item, think about what you are conveying and the context in which you could use each sentence, as well as about spelling and pronunciation. Then move on to the more conversational exercises and continue to practice, this time in a situation in which there are no "right" or "wrong" answers.

Always remember that language learning is cumulative. This means that you are not finished with a grammar point when you go on to the next chapter. Even though you are now studying the material in Chapter 3, you must still remember how to conjugate **-ar** verbs and how to form *yes/no* questions, because Chapter 3 builds on what you have learned in Chapters 1 and 2 and in the **Pasos preliminares**. All subsequent chapters will build on the material leading up to them. A few minutes spent each day reviewing "old" topics will increase your confidence—and success—in communicating in Spanish.

7 ¿De quién?, ¿adónde?
Uses of *ser* Plus *de*; Contractions *del* and *al*

Amalia and Emily are describing family customs. Who made each statement?

MODELO   El número ____ es el comentario *de* Amalia/Emily.

1. «Uso el apellido *de* mi padre y también el *de* mi madre.»
2. «Hasta en los documentos oficiales, generalmente la esposa usa sólo el apellido *del* esposo.»
3. «Por lo general, hay un sistema de familia extendida.»
4. «Los niños participan en casi todas las actividades familiares.»

Amalia
Medellín, Colombia

Emily
Iowa City, Iowa
Estados Unidos

---

1. "I use my father's last name and also my mother's (that of my mother)." *2.* "Even in official documents, a wife generally uses only the husband's last name." *3.* "In general, there's an extended family system." *4.* "Children participate in almost all family activities."

Uses of *ser* Plus *de*

Ser is used with the preposition **de** to perform a number of language functions.

- To express possession

Es el dinero **de Carla.**	*It's Carla's money.*
Son los abuelos **de Jorge.**	*They're Jorge's grandparents.*
¿**De quién** es el examen?	*Whose exam is it?*

    Note that there is no *'s* in Spanish.   [Práctica A]

- To express national origin

Soy **de los Estados Unidos.**	*I'm from the United States.*
La niña es **de Panamá.**	*The little girl is from Panama.*

                                              [Práctica B]

Contractions *del* and *al*

A *contraction* (**una contracción**) is the joining of two words that may also be said or written separately. In English, contractions are optional: *Pam is not/isn't a student; They are not/aren't here.*

    In Spanish there are only two contractions, and they are obligatory. The masculine singular article **el** contracts with the prepositions **de** and **a** to form **del** and **al**. No other articles contract with **de** or with **a.**

Es la casa **del** joven.	*It is the young man's house.*
Es la casa **de los** jóvenes.	*It is the young people's house.*
Llego **al** edificio a las dos.	*I'll get to the building at 2:00.*
Llego **a la** oficina a las tres.	*I'll get to the office at 3:00.*

                                           [Práctica C–D]

Práctica

A. Aquí está la familia de Luisa. ¿Quiénes son los parientes de Luisa?

    MODELO   Alfonso es el abuelo de Luisa.

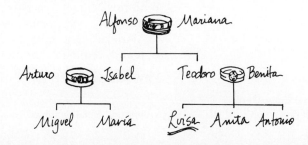

B. ¿De dónde son (*Where are they from*) según los nombres y apellidos?

Francia	Italia	Inglaterra (*England*)
México	los Estados Unidos	Alemania (*Germany*)

1. John Doe   **3.** Graziana Lazzarino   **5.** Claudette Moreau
2. Karl Lotze   **4.** María Gómez   **6.** Timothy Windsor

¿De dónde es Ud.? ¿de los Estados Unidos? ¿De dónde son sus (*your*) padres? (Mis padres...) ¿sus abuelos? (Mis abuelos...)

C. **¿De quién son estas (*these*) cosas?** Answer the following questions, using the names of the people listed.

MODELOS   —¿De quién es el coche?   —Es del tío Julio.
   —¿De quiénes son las cartas? —Son de mamá y papá.

PERSONAS   el tío Julio   mamá y papá
   el actor   los señores Schmidt
   el niño   el estudiante de periodismo (*journalism*)

1. ¿De quién es la casa en Beverly Hills?
2. ¿De quién es la casa en Viena?
3. ¿De quiénes son las niñas?
4. ¿De quién es el perro?
5. ¿De quiénes son las cartas?
6. ¿De quién es el coche elegante?
7. ¿De quién son las revistas *Time* y *Newsweek*?

CH. ¿Adónde (*Where*) necesitan regresar estas (*these*) personas después de comer (*after eating*)?

MODELO   consejero / universidad →
   El consejero necesita regresar a la universidad.

1. médico / hospital (*m.*)   **4.** estudiante / cuarto en la residencia
2. dependiente / librería   **5.** señor Ramos / oficina
3. profesora / biblioteca   **6.** joven (*m.*) / edificio Bolívar

D. ¿Quiénes son, de dónde son y dónde trabajan ahora?

MODELO   Teresa: actriz / de Madrid / en Ohio →
   Teresa es actriz. Es de Madrid. Ahora trabaja en Ohio.

1. Carlos Miguel: doctor / de Cuba / en Milwaukee
2. Maripili: extranjera / de Burgos / en Miami
3. Mariela: dependienta / de Buenos Aires / en Nueva York
4. Juan: dentista* / de Lima / en Los Ángeles

Now tell about a friend of yours, following the same pattern.

---

*A number of professions end in **-ista** in masculine and feminine forms. The article gives gender: **el/la dentista, el/la artista.**

Juana Gómez Arias

—¿Cómo te llamas?
—Mi nombre es Juana y mis apellidos son Gómez Arias.
—Y ¿dónde vive tu (*your*) familia?
—Aquí en la ciudad. Mi padre es profesor en la universidad.

David Kupferschmid

Buenos Aires, Argentina

REPASO

Unas diferencias familiares: Habla Paquita. Complete Paquita's description of some of the members of her family. Give the correct form of the words in parentheses, as suggested by the context. When two possibilities are given in parentheses, select the correct word.

Según° mi padre, los jóvenes (*deber*[1]) asistir (*a/de*[2]) clase todos los días (*del/ de la*[3]) semana. También (*creer*[4]) papá que° nosotros (*necesitar*[5]) estudiar con frecuencia. Papá (*insistir*[6]) en que no es necesario (*mirar*[7]) la televisión. Según él, (*los/las*[8]) periódicos (*ser*[9]) más interesantes. Él sólo (*trabajar*[10]) y (*comer*[11]).

 Yo no (*ser*[12]) como papá. Prefiero mirar (*el/la*[13]) televisión todas las noches. ¡(*Los/Las*[14]) programas son fascinantes! (*Yo: abrir*[15]) los libros a veces y (*leer*[16]) cuando es necesario, pero… tengo muchos amigos y (*creer*[17]) que es más interesante estar con ellos.

 Mi hermana Filis también (*ser*[18]) estudiante, pero ella (*estudiar*[19]) mucho más que° yo. Ya (*hablar*[20]) inglés y (*tomar*[21]) una clase de ruso. Los martes y los jueves (*tomar*[22]) una clase de gimnasia. Trabaja en la librería (*del/de la*[23]) universidad para pagar (*la/una*[24]) matrícula. Regresa a casa sólo para (*comer*[25]) y estudiar. ¡Filis es como papá! Yo prefiero mi vida.

According to

that

más… more than

UN PASO MÁS: Imágenes del mundo hispánico

Los hispanos en los Estados Unidos

Forsyth/Monkmeyer Press Photo Service

Henry Cisneros, en una fiesta en San Antonio, Texas

*T*al vez (*Perhaps*) la contribución más importante de la cultura hispana a los Estados Unidos es la propia población hispana. En la actualidad (*Currently*), personajes como César Chávez, Nancy López o Henry Cisneros (el alcalde [*mayor*] de San Antonio) son ejemplos de las actividades de los hispanos en el país. Pero no es necesario ser famoso. Los anónimos artistas de los barrios (*neighborhoods*) y los niños que aprenden a usar computadoras nos (*to us*) hablan orgullosos (*proud*) del pasado y del futuro.

El deseo de trabajar por un mundo mejor (*better*) tiene un lugar (*place*) importante en la vida norteamericana. Los hispanos, con su identidad étnica también, contribuyen a la realización de ese sueño (*dream*).

J. Schweiker/Photo Researchers, Inc.

Nancy López, en un torneo en Indianápolis, Indiana

Barbara Rios/Photo Researchers, Inc.

Niños hispanos neoyorquinos

VOCABULARIO

VERBOS

abrir to open
aprender to learn
asistir (a) to attend, go to
beber to drink
comer to eat
comprender to understand
creer (en) to think; to believe (in)
deber (+ *inf.*) should, must, ought to (*do something*)
escribir to write
insistir (en + *inf.*) to insist (*on doing something*)
leer to read
llegar to arrive
mirar to look (at); to watch
recibir to receive
ser (*irreg.*) to be
terminar to finish; to end
vivir to live

LOS PARIENTES

el/la abuelo/a grandfather/ grandmother
los abuelos grandparents
el/la esposo/a husband/wife, spouse
la familia family
el/la hermano/a brother/sister
el/la hijo/a son/daughter
los hijos children
la madre (mamá) mother (mom)
el/la nieto/a grandson/ granddaughter
el padre (papá) father (dad)
los padres parents
el/la primo/a cousin
el/la sobrino/a nephew/niece
el/la tío/a uncle/aunt

OTROS SUSTANTIVOS

el apellido last name
la carta letter
la casa house
el coche car
la comida meal; food
el ejercicio exercise
el examen test, exam

el/la joven young man/woman
la palabra word
el periódico newspaper
el perro dog
la puerta door
el regalo gift
la revista magazine

PALABRAS ADICIONALES

a veces at times, sometimes
ahora now
casi almost
con frecuencia frequently
en casa at home
esta noche tonight
familiar (*adj.*) of the family
mi(s) my
nunca never
que that, which
todo everything

FRASES ÚTILES PARA LA COMUNICACIÓN		
¿De dónde es Ud.?	Where are you from?	**tengo/tienes**
Soy de...	I'm from . . .	*I have/you have*

CAPÍTULO 4

¿Cómo eres?

VOCABULARIO: PREPARACIÓN

ALTO   BAJO   GRANDE   PEQUEÑO   TRABAJADOR   PEREZOSO

RUBIO   MORENO   JOVEN   NUEVO   VIEJO

ADJETIVOS

guapo handsome, good-looking
bonito pretty
feo ugly
corto short (*length*)
largo long

bueno good
malo bad
listo smart, clever
tonto silly, foolish
casado married
soltero single

simpático nice, likeable
antipático unpleasant
rico rich
pobre poor
delgado thin, slender
gordo fat

To describe a masculine singular noun, use **alt*o*, baj*o*,** and so on; use **alt*a*, baj*a*,** and so on for feminine singular nouns.

En la residencia

—¿Quién es el joven alto y moreno de la foto?
—Es mi hermano Julio.
—¡Qué guapo es!
—¿Te gustaría (*Would you like*) conocerlo?*
—¡Sí! ¡Claro que sí!

Nicaragua

A. Preguntas. Conteste según los dibujos.

1. Einstein es listo. ¿Y el chimpancé?

2. Pepe es bajo. ¿Y Pablo?

3. Roberto es trabajador. ¿Y José?

4. El ángel es bueno y simpático. También es guapo. ¿Y el demonio?

5. Ramón Ramírez es casado. También es viejo. ¿Y Paco Pereda?

6. El libro es viejo y corto. ¿Y el lápiz?

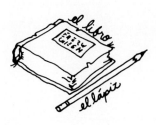

*To use this sentence to talk about a woman, change **-lo** to **-la**: ¿Te gustaría conocer**la**?

7. Elena es gord**a** y moren**a**. ¿Y Marta? (¡OJO!)

8. La familia Pérez es grande y rica. ¿Y la familia Gómez? (¡OJO!)

Marta   Elena

la familia Pérez   la familia Gómez

B. **¿Cómo son?** Your Spanish friend Maripepa is not familiar with these famous personalities. Describe them to her, using as many adjectives as possible. Don't forget to use cognate adjectives you have seen in the **Pasos preliminares** and in previous chapters.

1. Tom Selleck
2. J. R. Ewing
3. la princesa Diana
4. Jane Fonda

¿Verdad?: Tag Questions

Hay de todo aquí, **¿no?/¿verdad?**	*There's a bit of everything here, right? (isn't there?)*
No necesito impermeable hoy, **¿verdad?**	*I don't need a raincoat today, do I? (right?)*

In English and in Spanish, questions are frequently formed by adding tags or phrases to the end of statements. Two of the most common question tags in Spanish are **¿verdad?**, found after affirmative or negative statements, and **¿no?**, usually found after affirmative statements. The inverted question mark comes immediately before the tag question, not at the beginning of the sentence.

A. **Situaciones.** Su (*Your*) amigo Carlos hace (*asks*) muchas preguntas... y a veces son absurdas. Conteste (*Answer*) sus (*his*) preguntas con mucha paciencia, usando **claro que sí/no** (*of course [not]*) y oraciones completas.

1. El presidente vive en Washington, ¿verdad?
2. Los estudiantes beben en clase, ¿verdad?
3. Debo escribir los ejercicios en italiano, ¿no?
4. Muchos actores viven en Pocatella, Idaho, ¿no?
5. Todos los niños creen en Santa Claus, ¿no?
6. Los profesores de aquí insisten en recibir muchos regalos, ¿no?

B. **Entrevista.** Using tag questions, ask your instructor questions based on the following statements. He or she will answer as truthfully as possible.

1. No necesitamos estudiar esta (*this*) lección.
2. Es importante comprender todo en esta clase.
3. Es posible comer en clase.
4. Ud. vive en una casa elegante.
5. Ud. tiene una familia muy grande.
6. Ud. quiere comprar un perro.
7. No hay examen mañana.
8. Ud. pasa todo el día en la biblioteca.

Now make up questions of your own.

PRONUNCIACIÓN: *c* and *qu*

The Spanish [k] sound is like English [k], but is not *aspirated* (released with a small puff of air). The [k] sound is written as **c** before a consonant (**clase, creo**) or the vowels **a, o,** and **u** (**casado, cómico, matrícula**), and as **qu** before **e** or **i** (**que, quien**).

Práctica

1. casa   coche   carro   corto   Cuco   Carmen   cliente
2. quince   que   Quito   quienes   conquistador   practique
3. Creo que sí.
    Quico come aquí.
    La carta es corta.
    Enrique compra el periódico.
    Raquel come con Clara.

En la calle (*street*)

—Oye, **quiero hablar un momento contigo** (*with you*).
—**No puedo ahora... tengo prisa... hablamos después** (*later*), **¿eh?**
—**¡Hombre, nunca descansas!**
—**¡Tú tranquila! ¡Nos vemos** (*We'll see each other*) **mañana!**

San Sebastián, España

Owen Franken

MINIDIÁLOGOS Y ESTRUCTURA

8 Descripciones
Adjectives: Gender, Number, and Position

Un poema sencillo

Amiga	Amigo
Fiel	Fiel
Amable	Amable
Simpática	Simpático
¡Bienvenida!	¡Bienvenido!

According to their form, which of the adjectives below can be used to describe each person?
Which can refer to you?

Marta: *fiel   bienvenido   simpática*
Mario: *amable   simpático   bienvenida*

Segovia, España

An *adjective* (**un adjetivo**) is a word that describes a noun or a pronoun. Adjectives may describe (*large* desk, **tall** woman) or tell how many there are (*a few* desks, **several** women).

Adjectives with *ser*

In Spanish, forms of **ser** are used with adjectives that describe basic, inherent qualities or characteristics of the nouns or pronouns they modify.

Antonio **es interesante.**	*Antonio is interesting. (He's an interesting person.)*
Tú **eres amable.**	*You're nice. (You're a nice person.)*
El diccionario **es barato.**	*The dictionary is inexpensive.*

Forms of Adjectives

Spanish adjectives agree in gender and number with the noun or pronoun they modify. Each adjective has more than one form.

A simple poem *Friend Loyal Kind Nice Welcome!*

Adjectives that end in **-e (inteligente)** or in most consonants **(fiel)** have only two forms, a singular form and a plural form. The plural of adjectives is formed in the same way as that of nouns.

	Masculine	**Feminine**
Singular	amigo inteligent**e** amigo fie**l**	amiga inteligent**e** amiga fie**l**
Plural	amigos inteligentes amigos fiel**es**	amigas inteligentes amigas fiel**es**

Adjectives that end in **-o (alto)** have four forms, showing gender and number.*

	Masculine	**Feminine**
Singular	amigo alt**o**	amiga alt**a**
Plural	amigos alt**os**	amigas alt**as**

[Práctica A–C]

Most adjectives of nationality have four forms:

	Masculine	**Feminine**
Singular	el doctor mexican**o** español alemán inglés	la doctor**a** mexican**a** español**a** aleman**a** ingles**a**
Plural	los doctor**es** mexican**os** español**es** aleman**es** ingles**es**	las doctor**as** mexican**as** español**as** aleman**as** ingles**as**

The names of many languages—which are masculine in gender—are the same as the masculine singular form of the corresponding adjective of nationality: **el español, el inglés, el alemán,** and so on. Note that in

---

* Adjectives that end in **-dor, -ón, -án,** and **-ín** also have four forms: **trabajador**, *trabajadora*, **trabajador***es*, **trabajador***as*.

Spanish the names of languages and adjectives of nationality are not capitalized, but the names of countries are: **español** but **España.**

[Práctica CH]

Forms of This/These

The demonstrative adjective *this/these* has four forms in Spanish.*

es**te** hijo	*this son*	es**ta** hija	*this daughter*
es**tos** hijos	*these sons*	es**tas** hijas	*these daughters*

You have already used the neuter demonstrative **esto.** It refers to something that is as yet unidentified: **¿Qué es esto?**

[Práctica D]

Mucho and poco

Adverbs **(Los adverbios)** are words that modify verbs, adjectives, or other adverbs: *quickly, very smart, very quickly.* In Spanish and in English they are invariable in form. The words **mucho** and **poco** can be used as adjectives or as adverbs.

Adverb
Rosa trabaja **mucho/poco.**   *Rosa works a lot/little.*

Adjective
Rosa tiene **muchas** primas.   *Rosa has a lot of (female)*
                                       cousins.

[Práctica E]

Placement of Adjectives

Adjectives that describe the qualities of a noun generally follow the noun they modify. Adjectives of quantity and demonstratives precede the noun.

Hay **muchos** edificios **altos** en   *There are many tall buildings in*
    esta ciudad.   *this city.*
Necesito **otro** carro.†   *I need another car.*
Hay **cinco** sillas y **un** escritorio.   *There are five chairs and one*
                                               desk.

---

*You will learn all the forms of the Spanish demonstrative adjectives (*this, that, these, those*) in Grammar Section 13.
†**Otro** by itself means *another* or *other.* The indefinite article is not used with **otro.**

The interrogative adjectives **¿cuánto/a?** and **¿cuántos/as?** also precede the noun: **¿cuánto dinero?, ¿cuántas hermanas?**

Bueno, malo, and **grande** may precede the nouns they modify. When **bueno** and **malo** precede a masculine singular noun, they shorten to **buen** and **mal,** respectively.

un recuerdo **bueno** / un **buen** recuerdo	*a good (pleasant) memory*
una niña **buena** / una **buena** niña	*a good girl*

When **grande** appears after a noun, it means *large* or *big.* When it precedes a singular noun—masculine or feminine—it is shortened to **gran** and means *great* or *impressive.*

una ciudad **grande** / una **gran** ciudad	*a big city / a great (impressive) city*
un libro **grande** / un **gran** libro	*a big book / a grea*

Práctica

A. **Descripciones: ¿Cómo son?** Dé oraciones nuevas según las indicaciones.

1. —¿Su (*Your*) familia?   —(No) Es una familia *grande.*   (*interesante, importante, amable, intelectual*)
2. —¿Los perros?   —(No) Son *valientes.*   (*fiel, impaciente, inteligente, importante*)
3. —¿Su (*Your*) universidad?   —(No) Es *nueva.*   (*viejo, grande, pequeño, bueno, famoso, malo*)

B. Complete each sentence with all the adjectives that are appropriate according to form and meaning.

1. La doctora es _____.   (morena / casado / jóvenes / lista / bonito / trabajadora)
2. El hotel es _____.   (viejo / alto / nueva / grande / fea / interesante)
3. Los abuelos son _____.   (rubio / antipático / inteligentes / viejos / religiosos / práctica)
4. Las niñas son _____.   (malo / cortas / sentimental / buenas / casadas / joven)

C. Juan and Juana, fraternal twins, are totally different. Tell what Juana is like.

> Juan es soltero. Es alto. Es guapo. Es moreno. Es perezoso. Es gordo. Es simpático.

CH. Tell what nationality the following persons could be and where they might live: **Portugal, Alemania, Inglaterra, España, Francia, Italia.**

1. Monique habla francés; es _____ y vive en _____ .
2. José habla español; es _____ y vive en _____ .
3. Greta y Hans hablan alemán; son _____ y viven en _____ .
4. Gilberto habla portugués; es _____ y vive en _____ .
5. Gina y Sofía hablan italiano; son _____ y viven en _____ .
6. Winston habla inglés; es _____ y vive en _____ .

D. **En una reunión familiar...** Your friend Julio does not know any of the members of your family. Tell him something about some of your relatives. Begin each sentence with a demonstrative, as in the model, and use the correct form of **ser.**

MODELO   fiesta / para Manolo →
         Esta fiesta es para mi hermano Manolo.

1. parientes / de San Francisco   3. joven morena / mi hermana
2. nietas / de California también   4. primo guapo / profesor

E. **Las necesidades de la vida estudiantil** (*student life*). ¿Qué necesita Ud.? ¿Y qué necesitan hacer (*to do*) Uds.? Dé oraciones nuevas según las indicaciones.

1. Necesito muchos/pocos *textos.* (*lápices, mesas, cuadernos, papel, ideas, dinero, clases,* _?_)
2. Necesitamos *estudiar* mucho/poco. (*trabajar, pagar, aprender, hablar en clase, leer, practicar, escribir,* _?_)

F. **Variaciones.** Create new sentences by inserting the adjectives in parentheses into the sentences, *one at a time.* Can you add any other appropriate adjectives?

1. En la agencia de automóviles: «Busco un coche.»   (pequeño / francés / grande)
2. En la librería: «Por favor, quiero comprar un diccionario.» (completo / barato / nuevo)
3. En la biblioteca: «Estas novelas son buenas.» (alemán, nuevo, mexicano)
4. En la agencia de viajes (*travel agency*): «Buscan una excursión, ¿verdad?» (fascinante / largo / barato)

G. **Vacaciones en Acapulco.** Create new phrases about your last vacation by changing the position of the adjectives. Be sure to use the appropriate form of the adjective.

1. un recuerdo bueno   4. unas fiestas grandes
2. una ciudad grande   5. un hotel malo
3. unos parientes buenos   6. unos niños malos

H. Cambie: Miguel → María.

Miguel es un buen estudiante, pues estudia mucho. Es listo y amable. Es argentino; por eso (*that's why*) habla español. Es alto y guapo; también es muy delgado. ¡Es una persona ideal!

I. **Entrevista.** Ask another student questions that will elicit the following responses. Use adjectives, when appropriate, in your questions and remember that questions can be asked in a number of ways.

MODELO   El profesor (La profesora) es _____ . →
—¿Cómo es la profesora? (¿Es inteligente la profesora? La profesora es simpática, ¿verdad?)
—La profesora es inteligente.

1. El profesor (La profesora) es _____ .
2. Por lo general (*In general*) las mujeres (madres, hermanas) son _____ .
3. Por lo general los hombres (padres, hermanos) son _____ .
4. Los buenos amigos son _____ .
5. Yo soy _____ .
6. Mi mejor (*best*) amigo/a es _____ .

Now compare your classmate's answers with those of other students. Is there general agreement on the adjectives used to complete these sentences?

9 Expressing Actions and States
Tener, venir, preferir, querer, and *poder;* Some Idioms with *tener*

No es por falta de ganas...

MIGUEL: Hola, Mariela. Habla Miguel. ¿No *tienes ganas de* venir a la fiesta?

MARIELA: *Quiero* ir, pero no *puedo. Tengo que* estudiar.

MIGUEL: *¡Tienes que* estudiar! ¿Cómo *puedes* estudiar con una fiesta en el apartamento vecino?

MARIELA: No hay más remedio. Si *quieres, puedes* traerme una Coca o un café. ¡*Tengo sueño!*

It's not that I don't want to . . .   MIGUEL: *Hi, Mariela. It's Miguel. Don't you feel like coming to the party?*   MARIELA: *I want to come (go), but I can't. I have to study.*   MIGUEL: *You have to study! How can you study with a party in the next apartment?*   MARIELA: *It can't be helped. If you want, you can bring me a Coke or some coffee. I'm sleepy!*

Imagine que Ud. es Mariela. ¿Cómo va a completar estas oraciones?
1. *No tengo ganas de* _____ .   3. *Pero tengo que* _____ .
2. *Quiero* _____ .   4. *Quiero tomar* _____ *porque tengo*
                                        _____ .

tener *(to have)*	venir *(to come)*	preferir *(to prefer)*	querer *(to want)*	poder *(to be able, can)*
tengo	vengo	prefiero	quiero	puedo
tienes	vienes	prefieres	quieres	puedes
tiene	viene	prefiere	quiere	puede
tenemos	venimos	preferimos	queremos	podemos
tenéis	venís	preferís	queréis	podéis
tienen	vienen	prefieren	quieren	pueden

You have been using forms of some of these verbs for several chapters.
The **yo** forms of **tener** and **venir** are irregular: **tengo, vengo.** In other
forms of **tener, venir, preferir,** and **querer,** when the stem vowel **e** is
stressed, it becomes **ie**: **ti*e*nes, vi*e*nes, prefi*e*res, qui*e*res,** and so on.
Similarly, the stem vowel **o** in **poder** becomes **ue** when stressed. In
vocabulary lists these changes are shown in parentheses after the
infinitive: **poder (ue).** You will learn more verbs of this type in Grammar
Section 16.

[Práctica A]

Some Idioms with *tener*

An *idiom* (**un modismo**) is a group of words that has meaning to the
speakers of a language but that does not necessarily appear to make
sense when examined word by word. Idiomatic expressions are often
different from one language to another. For example, in English, *to pull
Mary's leg* usually means *to tease her,* not *to grab her leg and pull it.* In
Spanish *to pull Mary's leg* is **tomarle el pelo a María** (literally, *to take
María's hair*).

Many ideas expressed in English with the verb *to be* are expressed in
Spanish with idioms using **tener.** Here are some of them:

tener (18, 20) años	to be (18, 20) years old
tener sueño	to be sleepy
tener miedo (de)	to be afraid (of)
tener prisa	to be in a hurry
tener razón	to be right
no tener razón	to be wrong

Other **tener** idioms include **tener ganas de** (*to feel like*) and **tener que** (*to have to*). The infinitive is always used after these two idiomatic expressions.

Tengo ganas de trabajar.	*I feel like working.*
¿No tienes ganas de descansar?	*Don't you feel like resting?*
Tienen que ser prácticos.	*They have to be practical.*
¿No tiene Ud. que estudiar ahora mismo?	*Don't you have to study right now?*

[Práctica B–F]

Práctica

A. Es la semana de los exámenes. Por eso ocurren las siguientes situaciones. Dé oraciones nuevas según las indicaciones.

1. *Sara* tiene muchos exámenes. (*Pepe, nosotros, Alicia y Carlos, yo, tú, vosotras*)
2. *Ramón* viene a la biblioteca todas las noches. Prefiere estudiar aquí. (*yo, los estudiantes, tú, Uds., nosotras, vosotros*)
3. *Silvia* quiere estudiar más, pero no puede. (*yo, ella, nosotros, todos, tú, vosotros*)

B. Expand the situations described in these sentences by using a related idiom with **tener**.

MODELO   Son las dos de la mañana. → ¡Tengo sueño!

1. ¿Cuántos años? ¿cuarenta? No, yo sólo...
2. Esta calle (*street*) es peligrosa (*dangerous*) de noche. Por eso...
3. ¿Ya son las tres de la mañana? Por eso...
4. ¡Hasta luego! ¡Me voy (*I'm leaving*)!
5. No, mi hijo, dos y dos no son cinco.

C. Conteste según las indicaciones.

1. —¿Qué tiene Ud. que hacer (*to do*) esta noche?
   —Tengo que *llegar a casa temprano* (*early*). (*asistir a una clase a las siete, aprender unas palabras en español, estudiar la Lección 4, leer toda la noche, hablar con un amigo,* __?__)
2. —Pero... ¿qué tiene ganas de hacer?
   —Tengo ganas de *descansar*. (*abrir una botella de vino, mirar la televisión, comer en un buen restaurante, ¡no estudiar más!,* __?__)

CH. Listen as a classmate reads the following paragraphs to you and complete them with the appropriate **tener** idioms.

1. De repente (*Suddenly*) un tigre entra en la clase. Todos tienen _____ .

2. Amanda trabaja todos los días y estudia todas las noches. Es una estudiante fenomenal, pero no descansa mucho y siempre tiene _____ .

3. Ernesto regresa a la universidad. Son las tres menos cinco, y tiene clase de matemáticas a las tres. Ernesto tiene _____ .

4. Hay una fiesta porque hoy es el cumpleaños (*birthday*) de mi primo Antonio. Tiene 29 _____ . Todos tienen _____ de ir (*go*) a la fiesta.

5. Profesor: ¿Y la capital de la Argentina?
   Mariela: Buenos Aires.
   Celia: Cuzco.
   Mariela tiene _____ y Celia no tiene _____ . Celia _____ estudiar.

D. **¿Qué se hace (*are we doing*) esta tarde?** ¿Cómo se dice en español?

1. Alicia feels like singing.
2. We have to study for the exam, but we prefer to talk!
3. I don't feel like watching television. I want to dance!
4. Do you have to return home now? Are you in a hurry?
5. Jorge has to buy another car, doesn't he?

E. **El noticiero (*newscast*) de las seis.** ¿Qué actividades de personas famosas o conocidas (*well known*) puede Ud. anunciar hoy?

1. _____ quiere ser { presidente / gobernador / senador / alcalde (*mayor*) } de este país (*country*)/estado (*state*) de esta ciudad

2. _____ viene a esta universidad a dar (*to give*) { un concierto / una conferencia (*lecture*) }

3. _____ tienen { mucha responsabilidad / mucho poder (*power*) }

F. **¿Cómo eres?** Imagine that the following statements are true for you. Tell what kind of person you are and the things you typically do or want to do.

1. Quiero ser presidente de los Estados Unidos.
2. ¡Siempre tengo prisa!
3. Soy el/la mejor estudiante de la universidad.
4. Quiero ser profesor(a) de lenguas extranjeras.
5. Soy un actor famoso (una actriz famosa).

Study Hint: Studying and Learning Verbs

Knowing how to use verb forms quickly and accurately is one of the most important parts of learning how to communicate in a foreign language. The following suggestions will help you recognize and use verb forms in Spanish.

1. Study carefully any new grammar section that deals with verbs. Are the verbs regular? What is the stem? What are the personal endings? Don't just memorize the endings (**-o, -as, -a,** and so on). Practice the complete forms of each verb (**hablo, hablas, habla,** and so on) until they are "second nature" to you. Be sure that you are using the appropriate endings: **-ar** endings with **-ar** verbs, for example. Be especially careful when you write and pronounce verb endings, since a misspelling or mispronunciation can convey inaccurate information. Even though there is only a one-letter difference between **hablo** and **habla** or between **habla** and **hablan,** for example, that single letter makes a big difference in the information communicated.

2. Are you studying irregular verbs? If so, what are the irregularities? Practice the irregular forms many times so that you "overlearn" them and will not forget them: **tengo, tienes, tiene, tienen.**

3. Once you are familiar with the forms, practice asking short conversational questions using **tú/Ud.** and **vosotros/Uds.** Answer each question, using the appropriate **yo** or **nosotros** form.

¿Hablas español? ⎫
¿Habla español? ⎬ Sí, hablo español.

¿Comen Uds. en clase? ⎫ No, no comemos
¿Coméis en clase? ⎬ en clase.

4. It is easy to become so involved in mastering the *forms* of new verbs that you forget their *meanings.* However, being able to recite verb forms perfectly is useless unless you also understand what you are saying. Be sure that you always know both the spelling *and* the meaning of all verb forms, just as you must for any new vocabulary word. Practice using new verb forms in original sentences to reinforce their meaning.

5. Practice the forms of all new verbs given in the vocabulary lists in each chapter. Any special information that you should know about the verbs will be indicated either in the vocabulary list or in a grammar section.

REPASO

La familia hispánica típica: ¿Existe? Complete the paragraph on the next page with the correct form of the words in parentheses, as suggested by the context. When two possibilities are given in parentheses, select the correct word.

(*Mucho*[1]) personas creen que todas las familias (*hispánico*[2]) son (*grande*[3]), pero no es así.° Como en todas partes (*de/del*[4]) mundo,° el concepto (*del/de la*[5]) familia ha cambiado° mucho últimamente,° sobre todo° en las ciudades (*grande*[6]).

    Es verdad° que la familia campesina° (*típico*[7]) es grande, pero es así en casi (*todo*[8]) las sociedades° rurales del mundo. Ya que° los hijos (*trabajar*[9]) la tierra° con sus° padres, es bueno y (*necesario*[10]) tener muchos niños.

    Pero en los grandes centros (*urbano*[11]), las familias con sólo dos o tres hijos (*ser*[12]) cada día° más comunes. Es caro° mantener a* (*mucho*[13]) hijos en una sociedad (*industrializado*[14]). Cuando la madre (*trabajar*[15]) fuera de° casa, nadie se queda° en casa con los niños. Esto pasa especialmente en las familias de clase (*medio*°[16]) y de clase (*alto*[17]).

    Pero es realmente difícil° (*hablar*[18]) de una sola° familia (*hispánico*[19]). ¿Hay una familia (*norteamericano*[20]) típica?

no… that isn't so / world
ha… has changed / lately / sobre… especialmente
true / country
societies / Ya… Since
land / their

cada… every day / expensive
fuera… outside
nadie… no one stays
middle
difficult / single

UN PASO MÁS: Lectura cultural

Antes de leer

You already know that cognates are words that are similar in form and meaning from one language to another: for example, English *poet* and Spanish **poeta**. The more cognates you can recognize, the more quickly and easily you will read in Spanish.

    The endings of many Spanish words correspond to English word endings according to fixed patterns. Learning to recognize these patterns will increase the number of close and not-so-close cognates that you can recognize. Here are a few of the most common.

-dad → -ty   **-ción** → -tion   **-ico** → -ic, -cal
-mente → -ly   **-sión** → -sion   **-oso** → -ous

What is the English equivalent of these words?

1. unidad
2. reducción
3. explosión
4. frecuentemente
5. dramático
6. estudioso
7. famoso
8. reacción
9. recientemente
10. idéntico
11. religioso
12. vanidad

Try to spot cognates in the following reading, and remember that you should be able to guess the meaning of underlined words from context.

---

*Note the use of the word **a** before a direct object that refers to a specific person or persons. This **a** has no equivalent in English. You will see this usage from time to time in *¿Qué tal?* and will learn to use the word **a** in this way in Grammar Section 18.

Los apellidos hispánicos

En español, generalmente, las personas tienen dos apellidos: el apellido paterno y también el materno. Cuando un individuo usa sólo uno de sus° apellidos, casi siempre° es el paterno.

his / always

Imagine que Ud. tiene una amiga, Gloria Gómez Pereda. El **nombre** de esta persona es «Gloria» y s<u>u</u>s **apellidos** son «Gómez» y «Pereda». «Gómez» es el apellido paterno y «Pereda» es el materno. En situaciones oficiales o formales, ella <u>u</u>sa los dos apellidos. En ocasiones informales, usa solamente el paterno. Cuando uno habla con ella, la llama° «Señorita Gómez» o «Señorita Gómez Pereda», pero nunca «Señorita Pereda».

la... one calls her

Es importante comprender el sistema de apellidos cuando Ud. usa una lista alfabetizada. Lo primero° que determina el orden en la lista es el apellido paterno, y <u>d</u>espués el materno. En una <u>g</u>uía telefónica, el señor Carlos Martínez Aguilar <u>a</u>parece cerca del comienzo° de la lista de todos los Martínez.* <u>S</u>u padre, el señor Alfonso Martínez Zúñiga, aparece cerca del <u>f</u>inal de la lista. En la guía telefónica de la Ciudad de México, hay más <u>d</u>e veinticinco páginas—con más de 8.000° personas— que tienen el apellido paterno «Martínez». Si usted busca el número de teléfono de un señor Martínez y no sabe° <u>s</u>u apellido materno, ¡va a° tener un gran problema!

Lo... The first thing

cerca... close to the beginning

ocho mil

no... you don't know / va... you're going to

Comprensión

Complete las oraciones 1 a 3 según la lectura. Después (*Then*) conteste la pregunta 4.

1. Un hispano tiene dos apellidos: _____ .

   a. el materno y el paterno   **c.** dos maternos
   b. dos paternos

2. En una fiesta de amigos y colegas, un hispano usa _____ .

   a. su apellido materno   **c.** los dos apellidos
   b. su apellido paterno

3. Si Ud. busca el nombre de un amigo en la guía telefónica, necesita saber (*to know*) _____ .

   a. sólo el apellido paterno   **c.** los dos apellidos
   b. sólo el apellido materno

---

*Last names are made plural in Spanish simply by putting the plural definite article in front of the name: **los Martínez** (*the Martínez family*), **los García** (*the Garcías*), and so on.

4. ¿En qué orden aparecen estos nombres en una guía telefónica?

_____ Benito Pérez Galdós   _____ Juan Pereda García
_____ Jaime García Jiménez   _____ Virginia Pérez García
_____ Baldomero Pérez Almena

Para escribir

A. Write a brief paragraph about the Hispanic system of names as it would apply to your own family. Use the following sentences as a guide.

1. Me llamo _____ .
2. Mi apellido paterno es _____ y _____ es mi apellido materno.
3. En situaciones informales me llamo _____ .
4. _____ es el nombre completo de mi padre.
5. _____ es el nombre completo de mi madre.
6. Si me caso con (*If I marry*) Juan(a) García Sandoval, el nombre completo de mi hijo Carlos será (*will be*) Carlos _____ .

B. Continue to describe your family by completing these brief sentences.

1. Mis padres viven en _____ . Son _____ y _____ . Mi padre trabaja (estudia...) _____ ; es una persona _____ . Mi madre _____ ; es _____ .
2. Tengo _____ hermanos. Mi hermano/a _____ vive _____ ; es _____ .
3. Somos una familia _____ .

VOCABULARIO

VERBOS

descansar to rest
poder (ue) to be able to; can
preferir (ie) to prefer
querer (ie) to want, wish
tener (*irreg.*) to have
venir (*irreg.*) to come

SUSTANTIVOS

la ciudad city
el estado state
el recuerdo memory; souvenir

PARA DESCRIBIR LAS PERSONAS

alto/a tall
amable kind, nice
antipático/a unpleasant
bajo/a short (*in height*)
bonito/a pretty
casado/a married
delgado/a thin, slender
feo/a ugly
gordo/a fat
gran(de) big, large; great
guapo/a handsome, good-looking
inteligente intelligent
joven young
listo/a smart, clever
moreno/a brunet(te)
pequeño/a small
perezoso/a lazy
pobre poor
rico/a rich
rubio/a blond(e)
simpático/a nice, likeable
soltero/a single, unmarried
tonto/a silly, foolish
trabajador(a) hard-working
viejo/a old

ADJETIVOS DE NACIONALIDAD

**alemán (alemana), español(a),
francés (francesa), inglés
(inglesa), italiano/a,
mexicano/a, norteamericano/a,
ruso/a**

OTROS ADJETIVOS

barato/a cheap, inexpensive
buen, bueno/a good
corto/a short (*in length*)
este/a this; **estos/as** these
largo/a long
mal, malo/a bad
mejor best
mucho/a a lot of, many
nuevo/a new
otro/a other, another
poco/a little, few
todo/a all

UNOS MODISMOS CON *TENER*

tener...
    __ **años** to be __ years old
    ganas de + *inf.* to feel like
        (*doing something*)
    miedo (de) to be afraid (of)
    prisa to be in a hurry
    que + *inf.* to have to (*do
        something*)
    razón to be right
    sueño to be sleepy

PALABRAS ADICIONALES

por eso that's why
por lo general in general

FRASES ÚTILES PARA LA COMUNICACIÓN

¿Cómo es (____)?	What is (*something or someone*) like?
¿no?	right? isn't that so?
¿verdad?	right? is that right? is that so?
¡claro que sí/no!	of course (not)!

UN POCO DE TODO 1

A. Complete the following story by arranging the last eight sentences in the proper order.

Una noche hay una fiesta en la universidad. Marcos habla mucho con Ana, una estudiante de su (*his*) clase de comercio. Luego (*Then*) los dos cantan y bailan un poco.

_____ Necesita regresar a la biblioteca para estudiar.

_____ Toman una Coca-Cola y bailan un poco más.

_____ Por eso va (*he goes*) a la biblioteca y estudia hasta las tres de la mañana.

_____ Después de bailar (*After dancing*), tienen ganas de tomar una Coca-Cola.

_____ Ana prefiere bailar más. Está en la fiesta hasta las tres.

_____ Marcos no quiere regresar, pero tiene que estudiar—toma seis clases.

_____ Marcos busca la Coca-Cola y regresa adonde está Ana.

_____ A las once Marcos tiene que salir (*leave*).

B. **¿Quién es?** Identifique estos miembros de su (*your*) familia imaginaria, la familia Pérez.

1. Es viejo y retirado. Es casado y es padre de tres hijos. Uno de estos hijos es mi padre. Es mi _____ .

2. Es joven. Es la hija de tío Carlos y tía Matilde. Es mi _____ .

3. Es el hijo de los señores Pérez (mis padres). Hay más hijos en la familia. Es mi _____ .

4. Es el esposo de la Sra. Pérez. Es mi _____ .

5. Es la hija de los abuelos. También, es la hermana de mi padre. Es mi _____ .

C. **Situaciones: ¿De dónde eres tú?** With two other students, ask and answer questions according to the model.

MODELO   Atlanta → ENRIQUETA: ¿De dónde eres tú?

AGUSTÍN: Soy de *Atlanta*.

EVA: Ah, eres *norteamericano*.

AGUSTÍN: Sí, por eso hablo *inglés*.

1. Guadalajara   **3.** Roma   **5.** Madrid   **7.** Berlín

2. París   **4.** San Francisco **6.** Londres   **8.** Moscú

CH. Describe the following persons by telling what they do, what they are like in general, and, if possible, where they work.

1. un secretario   **3.** un estudiante   **5.** Julio Iglesias

2. una profesora   **4.** una actriz   **6.** John Travolta

D. **¿Qué pasa y dónde?** Tell what you and your friends do in each of the following places. Use the verbs you have already learned plus some of those listed here.

escuchar (música, discos, cintas) to listen to (music, records, tapes)   **fumar** to smoke
tocar (la guitarra, el piano, los tambores) to play (the guitar, the piano, the drums)

1. en la biblioteca
2. en una fiesta
3. en casa por la noche
4. en casa durante las vacaciones

5. en el laboratorio de lenguas
6. en un bar estudiantil
7. en el pasillo (*hallway*) antes de (*before*) clase
8. en ___?___

Now tell what is happening in the following scene. Use complete sentences and describe as many details as possible so that a person who has not seen it could visualize it.

MODELO   Dos personas, un hombre y una mujer, cantan.

E. **Situaciones.** Practice accepting and declining invitations by responding to these questions from your friend Alfonso, who is calling from the place or event he mentions. How many different ways can you respond?

MODELO   Vienes a la fiesta, ¿no? → · No puedo porque (*because*) tengo que...
· No tengo ganas de ir esta noche. Tengo que...
· ¡Sí, cómo no! ¿Qué puedo llevar (*bring*)?
· Yo no, pero creo que Anita quiere ir (*to go*).

1. Vienes a la fiesta, ¿no?
2. ¿Qué es esto? ¿No vienes al baile (*dance*)?
3. Vienes al café esta tarde, ¿verdad?
4. Vienes a la biblioteca a estudiar hoy, ¿no?

A propósito...

Las presentaciones. The following phrases are frequently used in making introductions.

Sra. Aguilar, le presento a Adolfo Álvarez Montes. (*formal*)	*Mrs. Aguilar, may I introduce you to Adolfo Álvarez Montes.*
Benito, te presento a Adela. (*informal*)	*Benito, let me introduce you to Adela.*
Mucho gusto. ⎱ Encantado/a. ⎰	*Pleased to meet you.*
Igualmente.	*Likewise.*
Bienvenido/a	*Welcome.*

When introduced, Spanish speakers—both men and women—almost always shake hands.

F. Situaciones. With other students, practice making the following introductions, using **le** (*formal*) or **te** (*informal*), as appropriate. Tell something about the person you are introducing.

1. You are at home, and a good friend stops by for a few minutes. Introduce him or her to your family.
2. You are in the library and happen to run into two of your professors at the circulation desk. Introduce them to each other.
3. You are at a party. Introduce one good friend to another.
4. Introduce the student next to you to another student.

G. Entrevista. You have already learned enough vocabulary and expressions to enable you to find out a lot of information about another person. Use the following cues as a guide to interviewing someone in the class with whom you have *not* spoken very much at all so far this year.

1. nombre
2. lugar de residencia; de dónde es
3. años
4. familia grande
5. número de hermanos, tíos y primos
6. un pariente interesante
7. materias que estudia este semestre (trimestre)
8. materia favorita
9. trabajo (*job*); lugar donde trabaja
10. qué hace (*what does he or she do*) los fines de semana

H. Situaciones de la vida estudiantil. Listen as your instructor role-plays each of the following situations with one or more students. Pay close attention to how your classmates interact with your instructor to see if you would have said or done the same thing. You may have to make some educated guesses about what your instructor says as he or she plays the situation. After you have watched each situation at least once, act out the situations with another student. Try to use as much of the vocabulary that you know as possible.

1. You are a freshman **(Estoy en el primer año...)** at the university and don't know anyone yet. Introduce yourself to the student sitting next to you and try to find out about him.
2. You find yourself waiting in line at the bookstore behind one of your professors. Strike up a conversation with her. Tell her something interesting about yourself and ask her some questions about her family.
3. You have just begun preregistering for next term's classes when you discover that all the Spanish classes are closed. Explain to the secretary why you want to get into one of them.

CAPÍTULO 5

¡Vamos de compras!

VOCABULARIO: PREPARACIÓN

DE COMPRAS / SHOPPING

comprar to buy
gastar to spend (*money*)
regatear to haggle, bargain
vender to sell
venden de todo they sell everything

la ganga bargain
el precio (fijo) (fixed, set) price

barato/a inexpensive
caro/a expensive

el centro downtown
el mercado (al aire libre) (outdoor) market
la tienda store, shop

A. Llene los espacios con las palabras apropiadas.

   1. El _____ es una tienda grande.
   2. En la librería _____ de todo: libros de texto y otros libros, cuadernos, lápices...
   3. Venden aspirinas y otras medicinas en la _____ .
   4. Cuando compramos un coche es necesario _____ mucho. Uno nunca debe pagar el primer (*first*) _____ que da (*offers*) el vendedor.
   5. En el almacén todo tiene _____ .
   6. Hay muchas _____ en un mercado _____ .
   7. En la _____ puedes comprar de todo para escribir.
   8. Venden zapatos (*shoes*) y botas en una _____ .
   9. Necesito un suéter. Hay una _____ en la calle (*street*) Tres de Abril, ¿verdad?

B. Asociaciones. ¿Qué palabras asocia Ud. con estas frases?

   1. dulces (*sweets*) y chocolates
   2. precios muy bajos
   3. la parte céntrica de una ciudad
   4. sin (*without*) regatear
   5. ¡¿cinco mil dólares?!
   6. al aire libre
   7. comprar zapatos
   8. no pagar un precio fijo
   9. cosas buenas y baratas
   10. una calle

¿Cómo se dice... ?: **Impersonal se**

   Se estudia mucho aquí, ¿verdad?   *You (They) study a lot here, right?*

In English several subjects—*you, one, people, they*—can refer to people in general instead of to one person in particular. In Spanish these impersonal subjects are commonly expressed by using the word **se** followed by the third person singular of the verb.* There is no expressed subject.

A. Situaciones. ¿Qué se hace (*is done*) y qué no se hace en... ? Conteste con un compañero (una compañera).

MODELO   la biblioteca →
        —En la biblioteca, se estudia, se lee.... No se habla en voz alta (*loudly*),....
        —Tienes razón. Tampoco (*Neither*) se come en la biblioteca.

---

*Se habla español aquí is a similar construction: *Spanish is spoken here; One speaks Spanish here.*

1. la clase de español
2. un mercado al aire libre
3. una papelería
4. una discoteca

5. una tienda de ropa
6. una fiesta
7. la calle

B. Se usa la expresión **¿Cómo se dice?** cuando se quiere aprender una palabra nueva. Repase Ud. (*Review*) el vocabulario nuevo de esta lección y pregunte (*ask*) a las otras personas de la clase, **¿Cómo se dice _____ en inglés?** o **¿Cómo se dice _____ en español?**

Los números 100 y más

Continúe la secuencia: cien, ciento uno,…
                    mil, dos mil,…
                    un millón, dos millones,…

100	cien, ciento	700	setecientos/as
101	ciento uno/una	800	ochocientos/as
200	doscientos/as	900	novecientos/as
300	trescientos/as	1.000	mil
400	cuatrocientos/as	2.000	dos mil
500	quinientos/as	1.000.000	un millón
600	seiscientos/as	2.000.000	dos millones

- **Ciento** is used in combination with numbers from 1 to 99 to express the numbers 101 through 199: **ciento uno, ciento dos, ciento setenta y nueve,** and so on. **Cien** is used in counting and before numbers greater than 100: **cien mil, cien millones.**

- When the numbers 200 through 900 modify a noun, they must agree in gender: **cuatrocientas niñas, doscientas dos casas.**

- **Mil** means *one thousand* or *a thousand*. It does not have a plural form in counting, but **millón** does. When used with a noun, **millón,** (**dos millones,** and so on) must be followed by **de.** Note the use of a period in numerals where English uses a comma. (Spanish also uses a comma to indicate the decimal where English uses a period: **$10,45.**)

1.899	mil ochocientos noventa y nueve
3.000 habitantes	tres mil habitantes
14.000.000 de habitantes	catorce millones de habitantes

- **Mil** is used to express the year (after 999).

    1987   mil novecientos ochenta y siete

En una librería

—Buscamos un regalo para un estudiante
universitario.
—Pues, en esta tienda venden de todo.
—¿Cuánto es esta novela de García Márquez?
—Doscientos cincuenta y nueve pesos. Es
una ganga.

Madrid, España

A. Practique los números.

1. 2, 12, 20, 200
2. 3, 13, 30, 300
3. 4, 14, 40, 400
4. 5, 15, 50, 500
5. 6, 16, 60, 600

6. 7, 17, 70, 700
7. 8, 18, 80, 800
8. 9, 19, 90, 900
9. 1, 10, 100, 1.000, 1.000.000

B. **¿Cuántos hay?** Practique los números.

MODELO   930 almacenes → Hay novecientos treinta almacenes.

1. 7.354 personas
2. 100 mercados
3. 5.710 tiendas
4. 670 revistas
5. 2.486 mujeres
6. $1.000,00

7. 528 edificios
8. 863 artículos (*items*)
9. 101 niñas
10. $1.000.000,00
11. $6.500.000,00
12. $25.000.000,00

C. Lea los siguientes (*following*) años en español. ¿A qué dato (*fact,
event*) corresponden?

1. 1492
2. 1776
3. 1945
4. 2001
5. 1963
6. 1984
7. _____?

a. el año de mi nacimiento (*my birth*)
b. la Declaración de la Independencia
c. el asesinato de John F. Kennedy
ch. Cristóbal Colón descubre América
d. la bomba atómica
e. una película (*movie*) famosa
f. la novela de George Orwell
g. este año

CH. **Situaciones.** Imagine that you have recently made the following
purchases. With a classmate, ask and answer questions about the
price you paid. Follow the model.

MODELO   —¿Cuánto pagaste (*did you pay*) por la radio?
—Cien dólares.
⎧ —¡Uy! Pagaste demasiado (*too much*). ¡Es caro!
⎨ —¡Es/Fue (*It was*) una ganga!
⎩ —Fue una buena compra (*purchase*).

1. la calculadora   4. la computadora
2. tu (*your*) coche nuevo   5. tu casa nueva
3. tu estéreo   6. tu televisor (*television set*)

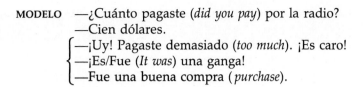

PRONUNCIACIÓN: *j* and *g*

j Spanish **j** never has the sound of English *j*, as in *Jane* or *John*. In some dialects of Spanish it is like the English [h], but in others it has a rougher sound—a fricative—that is produced by tightening the throat muscles. To make it, articulate a [k] sound, but with a light friction in the airflow instead of stopping it: **taco/Tajo, carro/jarro.**

g Spanish **g** before **e** or **i** is pronounced like the **j: general, página.** Spanish **g** before **a, o,** or **u** is pronounced like the **g** in English *go,* [g], at the beginning of a phrase or sentence or after **n: gas, gorila, gusto, inglés.** Elsewhere it is pronounced with a very light friction, [g̶]: **el gas, el gorila, el gusto.**

Práctica

1. jueves   jirafa   fijo   extranjero
   mujer   joven   viejo   consejero

2. general   generoso   inteligente   geografía
   región   religión   sicología   biología

3. [g] grande   tengo   gusto   gracias   guapo   gordo
   ganga

4. [g̶] amiga   delgado   regatear   pagar   diálogo

MINIDIÁLOGOS Y ESTRUCTURA

10 ¿Adónde vas?
Ir; ir + a + infinitive

Un regalo para la «mamá» ecuatoriana

ALLEN: Esta tarde *voy a ir* de compras. ¿Quieres *ir* conmigo?

LORENZO: Sí, con mucho gusto. ¿Qué *vas a comprar*?

ALLEN: Un regalo para mi mamá ecuatoriana... algo bueno pero barato—como una tostadora, por ejemplo.

LORENZO: Los aparatos eléctricos son muy caros, Allen. ¿Por qué no compras una blusa bordada a mano?

ALLEN: Todos los artículos hechos a mano son también muy caros, ¿no?

LORENZO: Pues... no. Normalmente son muy baratos aquí.

¿Qué va a pasar hoy por la tarde? Conteste completando las oraciones.

1. *Allen y Lorenzo van a ir* _____ .
2. *Allen va a buscar* _____ .
3. *Allen no va a comprar* _____ .
4. *Sí va a comprar* _____ *porque* _____ .

ir *(to go)*	
voy	**vamos**
vas	**vais**
va	**van**

The first person plural of **ir, vamos** (*we go, are going, do go*), is also used to express *let's go.*

Vamos a clase ahora mismo.   *Let's go to class right now.*

Ir + a + *infinitive* is used to describe actions or events in the near future.

A gift for one's Ecuadorian "mother"   ALLEN: *I'm going shopping this afternoon. Do you want to go with me?*   LORENZO: *Yes, I'd really like to (lit., with much pleasure). What are you going to buy?*   ALLEN: *A present for my Ecuadorian mother . . . something nice but inexpensive—like a toaster, for example.*   LORENZO: *Electrical appliances are very expensive, Allen. Why don't you buy a hand-embroidered blouse?*   ALLEN: *All handmade things are also very expensive, aren't they?*   LORENZO: *Well . . . no. Normally they're very inexpensive here.*

Voy a estudiar esta tarde.	*I'm going to study this afternoon.*
Van a venir a la fiesta esta noche.	*They're going to come to the party tonight.*

Práctica

A. ¿Adónde van Uds. los viernes después de (*after*) la clase? Haga oraciones completas usando **ir.**

1. yo / residencia
2. Francisca / zapatería para trabajar
3. tú / otra clase
4. Jorge y Carlos / bar (*m.*)
5. nosotros / biblioteca
6. el profesor (la profesora) / __?__

B. **¡Vamos de compras!** Describa la tarde, usando **ir** + **a** + el infinitivo, según el modelo.

MODELO   Raúl compra un regalo para Estela. →
         Raúl va a comprar un regalo para Estela.

1. Llegamos al mercado a las diez de la mañana.
2. Los niños quieren comer algo.
3. Compro chocolates para Lupita.
4. Carlos busca un recuerdo de Bogotá.
5. No gastas mucho dinero, ¿verdad?
6. Tenemos que buscar algo más barato.
7. ¿Puedes ir de compras mañana también?

C. **¡Qué negativos!** Exprese en español, usando **ir** + **a** + el infinitivo.

1. I'll go to the market with you **(Uds.)**, but I'm not going to bargain!
2. We'll sell the old car, but we won't buy another, right?
3. You'll look for bargains, but the things won't be cheap.

CH. **Gustos y preferencias.** ¿Cuántas oraciones puede Ud. formar?

Me gusta	leer	Por eso voy a __?__ .
	bailar	
	regatear	
	comer en restaurantes mexicanos	
	mirar la televisión	
	comer al aire libre	
	ir de compras	
	?	

D. Entrevista: ¿Qué hay en su (*your*) futuro? Complete las oraciones en una forma lógica. Luego úselas (*use them*) para entrevistar a un compañero (una compañera) de clase.

1. Un día voy a tener (ser, comprar, poder) _____ porque (*because*) _____. (¿Qué vas a tener tú? ...)
2. Esta noche voy a estudiar _____. Voy a comer (en) _____. Y voy a mirar _____ en la tele. (¿Qué vas a... ?)
3. Mañana voy a llegar a clase a la(s) _____. Voy a preguntar (*ask*) _____ porque.... (¿A qué hora... ? ¿Qué vas a... ?)

¿Recuerda Ud.?

Before beginning Grammar Section 11, review what you already know about expressing possession. Use **de** + *noun* or **mi(s)**.

¿Cómo se dice en español?

1. Where are (**están**) Dad's shoes?
2. Well, whose shoes are these?
3. I don't have my shoes!
4. Dad's shoes are big and old.

---

11 ¿De quién es?
Possessive Adjectives (Unstressed)

En el periódico

Querida Antonia,

Tengo un problema con *mis* padres. Me gusta ir de compras con *mi* hermana menor, pero *nuestros* padres creen que no se debe gastar dinero. ¡*Nuestra* situación es desesperante! ¿Cuál es *tu* consejo?

Sin Zapatos

In the newspaper *Dear Antonia, I have a problem with my parents. I like to go shopping with my younger sister, but our parents think that one should not spend money. Our situation is desperate! What is your advice?   Shoeless*

Querida Sin Zapatos,

Tu situación es difícil pero no es imposible de solucionar. Debes contraer matrimonio con un ladrón porque casi siempre son ricos y no les importa gastar mucho dinero. Por otro lado, casi siempre tienen un par de esposas... *

Antonia

---

*¿Qué escribe Sin Zapatos, **mi** o **mis**?*

1. _____ padres tienen mucho dinero.
2. _____ hermana también quiere ir de compras.
3. ¡_____ situación es terrible!

*¿Qué contesta Antonia, **tu** o **tus**?*

4. _____ zapatos son muy viejos.
5. _____ padre no tiene razón.
6. _____ problema tiene solución.

You have already learned **mi(s),** one of the possessive adjectives in Spanish. Here is the complete set.

Possessive Adjectives				
my	**mi** libro/mesa **mis** libros/mesas	*our*	nuest**ro** libro nuest**ros** libros	nuest**ra** mesa nuest**ras** mesas
your	**tu** libro/mesa **tus** libros/mesas	*your*	vuest**ro** libro vuest**ros** libros	vuest**ra** mesa vuest**ras** mesas
your, his, *her, its* }	**su** libro/mesa **sus** libros/mesas	*your,* *their* }	**su** libro/mesa **sus** libros/mesas	

In Spanish, the ending of possessive adjectives agrees in form with the person or thing possessed, not with the owner/possessor. Note that unstressed possessive adjectives are placed before the noun.

Son $\left\{ \begin{array}{l} \text{mis} \\ \text{tus} \\ \text{sus} \end{array} \right\}$ zapatos.   Es $\left\{ \begin{array}{l} \text{nuestra} \\ \text{vuestra} \\ \text{su} \end{array} \right\}$ casa.

The possessive adjectives **mi(s), tu(s),** and **su(s)** show agreement in number only with the noun they modify. **Nuestro/a/os/as** and

---

Dear Shoeless, Your situation is difficult but it isn't impossible to solve. You should marry a thief because they're almost always rich and they don't mind spending a lot of money. On the other hand, they almost always have a couple of wives (handcuffs*) . . . Antonia

*The plural form **esposas** means *handcuffs,* as well as *wives.*

vuestro/a/os/as, like all adjectives that end in **-o,** show agreement in both number and gender.

Su(s) can have several different equivalents in English: *your (sing.), his, her, its, your (pl.), their.* Usually its meaning will be clear in context. For example, if you are admiring the car of someone whom you address as **Ud.** and ask, **¿Es nuevo su coche?,** it is clear from the context that you mean *Is your car new?* When context does not make the meaning of **su(s)** clear, **de** and a pronoun are used instead, to indicate the possessor.

el coche
la casa
los libros   de él (de ella, de Ud., de ellos, de ellas, de Uds.)
las mesas

¿Son jóvenes los hijos **de él**?	*Are his children young?*
¿Dónde vive el abuelo **de ellas**?	*Where does their grandfather live?*

Práctica

A. Which nouns can these possessive adjectives modify without changing form?

1. **su:** problema / parientes / ropa / apellido / precios / bolígrafo
2. **tus:** chocolates / cerveza / tienda / primas / exámenes / regalo
3. **mi:** ejercicios / tostadora / problemas / zapato / escritorio / palabras
4. **sus:** lápices / universidad / profesor / mercados / solución / familias
5. **nuestras:** precios / gangas / fiesta / cartas / calle / comidas
6. **nuestro:** perros / ciudad / almacén / farmacia / chocolates / recuerdo

B. ¿Cómo son los parientes de Isabel? Conteste según el modelo.

MODELO   familia / grande → Su familia es grande.

1. primo Julián / antipático	4. hija / pequeño
2. hermana Lucía / delgado	5. abuelas / viejo / ya
3. tíos / feo	6. esposo / muy trabajador

Ahora imagine que Ud. es Isabel y describa a sus parientes, usando las mismas palabras como guía.

MODELO   familia / grande → Mi familia es grande.

C. **¡Propaganda!** Your store has the following characteristics. Explain them to a prospective client, following the model.

MODELO   tienda / extraordinario → ¡Nuestra tienda es
extraordinaria!

1. precios / bajo
2. ropa / elegante

3. dependientes / amable
4. estacionamiento (*parking*) / gratis

CH. **¡Qué confusión!** With another student, ask and answer questions
according to the model.

MODELO   ¿Es la casa de Paco? → —No, no es su casa.
—No, no es la casa de él.

1. ¿Es la revista de Estela?
2. ¿Son los regalos de los niños?
3. ¿Es el mercado del Sr. Fernández?
4. ¿Es el apellido de tu novio?
5. ¿Son las tiendas de los padres de Ud.?

D. **Cosas del mercado.** ¿Cómo se dice en español?

1. Their fixed prices are high.
2. His new department store is very big.
3. Our young clerks are nice and hard-working.
4. My candy store is going to be small.
5. When are you going to open your clothing store?

E. **Entrevista.** You have already learned a great deal about the families
of your classmates and instructor. This interview will help you
gather more information. Use the questions as a guide to
interviewing your instructor or a classmate and take notes on what
he or she says. Then report the information to the class.

1. ¿Cómo es su familia? ¿grande? ¿pequeña? ¿Cuántas personas
viven en su casa?
2. ¿Son norteamericanos sus padres? ¿hispanos? ¿De dónde son?
3. ¿Son simpáticos sus padres? ¿generosos? ¿cariñosos (*affectionate*)?
4. ¿Trabaja su padre (madre)? ¿Dónde?
5. ¿Cuántos hijos tienen sus padres? ¿Cuántos años tienen?
6. ¿Cómo son sus hermanos? ¿listos? ¿traviesos (*mischievous*)?
¿trabajadores? Si son muy jóvenes, ¿prefieren estudiar o mirar la
televisión? Si son mayores (*older*), ¿trabajan o estudian? ¿Dónde?
7. ¿Viven sus padres en una casa o en un apartamento? ¿Cómo es
su casa/apartamento?
8. ¿Sus abuelos/tíos viven también en la casa (el apartamento)?
9. ¿De dónde son sus abuelos? ¿Cuántos años tienen? ¿Cuántos
hijos tienen?
10. ¿Tiene Ud. esposo/a o novio/a (*boyfriend/girlfriend*)? ¿Quién es?
¿Cómo es? ¿Trabaja o estudia?

REPASO

Pero, ¿no se puede regatear? Complete the following paragraphs with the correct form of the words in parentheses, as suggested by the context. When two possibilities are given in parentheses, select the correct word.

Cuando Ud. va (*de/a*¹) compras en (*un/una*²) país hispánico, (*ir*³) a ver° una (*grande*⁴) variedad de tiendas. Hay almacenes (*elegante*⁵) como (*los/las*⁶) almacenes de los Estados Unidos, donde los precios siempre (*ser*⁷) (*fijo*⁸). También hay (*pequeño*⁹) tiendas que se especializan° en un solo° producto. En (*un/una*¹⁰) zapatería, por ejemplo, se venden* solamente zapatos. (*El/La*¹¹) sufijo **-ería** se usa para formar el nombre (*del/de la*¹²) tienda. ¿Dónde (*creer*¹³) Ud. que se vende papel y (*otro*¹⁴) artículos de escritorio? ¿A qué tienda (*ir*¹⁵) Ud. a comprar fruta?

    Si Ud. (*poder*¹⁶) (*pagar*¹⁷) el precio que piden,° (*deber*¹⁸) comprar los recuerdos en (*los/las*¹⁹) almacenes o *boutiques*. Pero si (*tener*²⁰) ganas o necesidad de regatear, tiene (*de/que*²¹) (*ir*²²) a un mercado: un conjunto° de tiendas (*pequeño*²³) o locales° donde el ambiente° es más (*informal*²⁴) que° en los (*grande*²⁵) almacenes. Ud. no (*deber*²⁶) (*pagar*²⁷) el primer precio que menciona (*el/la*²⁸) vendedor°—¡casi siempre va (*de/a*²⁹) ser muy alto!

to see

se... specialize / single

they ask

group
stalls / atmosphere / than

seller

Hablando de compras

—¿Cuánto pagaste por el estéreo?
—Sólo trescientos dólares. ¿Te gusta?
—¡Sí, hombre! Sobre todo (*Especially*) me gusta el precio.
—Fue una ganga, ¿verdad?

Viña del Mar, Chile

David Kupferschmid

---

*In addition to the *one/you/they* construction, the word **se** before a verb form can change the verb's meaning slightly in another way: *Se vende* **papel en una papelería.** *Paper is sold in a stationery store.* **Se venden** **chocolates en una dulcería.** *Chocolates are sold in a candy store.* You will see this construction throughout *¿Qué tal?*, especially in reading passages. Learn to recognize it, for it is frequently used in Spanish.

UN PASO MÁS: Imágenes del mundo hispánico
Barcelona

Rogers/Monkmeyer Press Photo Service

Los originalísimos diseños de Gaudí

Barcelona, en la costa mediterránea, es la segunda ciudad más importante de España. A su puerto (*port*) llegan barcos de todo el mundo. Esta gran ciudad, cosmopolita y moderna, también mantiene sus tradiciones y la lengua de su región, el catalán.

Entre las visitas obligatorias que el turista no puede olvidar (*miss*) en Barcelona están: el Barrio Gótico y la Catedral (frente a la cual [*in front of which*] jóvenes y mayores, ricos y pobres, bailan la sardana todos los domingos); los edificios construidos por el arquitecto Gaudí; el Zoo; y, por supuesto (*of course*), la famosa zona de las «Ramblas», con sus cientos de floristerías. Una moderna tradición en Barcelona, y en el resto de Cataluña, es regalar (*to give*) un libro y una rosa a los amigos el día de San Jordi, el 23 de abril. Las dos cosas se pueden comprar en las «Ramblas».

Britton-Logan/Photo Researchers, Inc.

Floristerías en las «Ramblas»

Stuart Cohen

La Catedral, en el Barrio Gótico

VOCABULARIO

VERBOS

contestar to answer
gastar to spend (*money*)
ir (*irreg.*) to go
preguntar to ask a question
regatear to bargain, haggle
vender to sell

LAS TIENDAS

el almacén department store
la dulcería sweetshop, candy store
la farmacia pharmacy
el mercado market
la papelería stationery store
la tienda de ropa clothing store
la zapatería shoe store

LAS COSAS QUE SE COMPRAN

el chocolate chocolate
los dulces sweets; candy
la ropa clothing
el zapato shoe

OTROS SUSTANTIVOS

la calle street
el centro downtown
la ganga bargain
el país country

ADJETIVO

caro/a expensive

PALABRAS ADICIONALES

¿adónde? where (to)?
al aire libre outdoor(s)
algo something
de todo everything
demasiado too much
más more
por ejemplo for example
por otro lado on the other hand
¿por qué? why?
siempre always
sin without

LOS NÚMEROS 100 Y MÁS

cien(to), doscientos/as, trescientos/as, cuatrocientos/as, quinientos/as, seiscientos/as, setecientos/as, ochocientos/as, novecientos/as, mil, un millón

---

FRASES ÚTILES PARA LA COMUNICACIÓN

¿Quieres ir de compras conmigo?	Do you want to go shopping with me?
Sí. ¡Vamos (al mercado)!	Yes. Let's go (to the market)!
el primer precio	the first price
el precio fijo	the set price
¿Cuánto pagaste por... ?	How much did you pay for . . . ?
Fue una buena compra.	It was a good purchase.

CAPÍTULO 6

¡Es de última moda!

VOCABULARIO: PREPARACIÓN

— LA ROPA / CLOTHING —

llevar to wear; to carry

un par de (zapatos, sandalias, botas, calcetines) a pair of (shoes, sandals, boots, socks)

los *bluejeans* jeans
el cinturón belt

la corbata necktie
la mochila backpack
el traje de baño bathing suit

es de (lana, algodón, seda) it is made of (wool, cotton, silk)

115

A. ¿Qué ropa llevan estas personas? ¿Adónde van?

1. El Sr. Rivera lleva _____ .

2. La Srta. Alonso lleva _____ . El perro lleva _____ .

3. Sara lleva _____ .

4. Alfredo lleva _____ . Debe comprar _____ .

Generalmente, ¿qué artículos de ropa son para los hombres? ¿para las mujeres? ¿para hombres y mujeres?

B. Complete las oraciones en una forma lógica.

1. Para ir a bailar a una discoteca, prefiero llevar _____ .
2. A una fiesta de etiqueta (*formal*), me gusta llevar _____ .
3. Muchos ejecutivos llevan _____ .
4. Muchas ejecutivas llevan _____ .
5. Nunca llevo _____ a clase.
6. En casa casi siempre llevo _____ .
7. Hoy la temperatura está a 30° (grados). Tengo frío (*I'm cold*). Voy a llevar _____ a la universidad.
8. Tengo calor (*I'm hot*). Tengo ganas de llevar _____ .

C. Give advice to the following people who need to make some clothing purchases immediately.

→ ¿No tiene Ud. calor? ¿Por qué no compra… ? También debe comprar…

→ Seguro que (*Undoubtedly*) Ud. tiene frío. ¿Por qué no compra... ?

← ¡Qué horror! Tiene que comprar....
No puede asistir a...

¿De qué color es?					
amarillo/a	yellow	**morado/a**	purple	**rosado/a**	pink
anaranjado/a	orange	**negro/a**	black	**verde**	green
azul	blue	**pardo/a**	brown		
blanco/a	white	**rojo/a**	red	**de cuadros**	plaid
gris	gray			**de rayas**	striped

A. ¿Qué colores asocia Ud. con... ?

¿el dinero? ¿la una de la mañana? ¿una mañana bonita? ¿una mañana fea? ¿el demonio? ¿los Estados Unidos? ¿una jirafa? ¿un pingüino? ¿un limón? ¿una naranja? ¿un elefante? ¿las flores (*flowers*)?

B. **¿De qué color es?** Tell the color of things in your classroom, especially the clothing your classmates are wearing. Describe the clothing in as much detail as you can.

MODELO   El bolígrafo de Anita es amarillo.
Los calcetines de Roberto son azules. Son de lana. Los de Jaime* son pardos, de rayas. Los de Julio...

Now describe what someone is wearing without revealing his or her name. Using your clues, can your classmates guess whom you are describing?

---

*You can avoid repeating the noun **calcetines** just by dropping it and retaining the definite article. Here are some other examples of the same construction: **la camisa de Janet y la camisa de Paula** → **la camisa de Janet y *la de* Paula; el sombrero del niño y el sombrero de Pablo** → **el sombrero del niño y *el de* Pablo.**

¿Dónde está?: Las preposiciones

> Prepositions express relationships in time and space:
>
> The book is *on* the table.   The magazine is *for* you.

• Some common Spanish prepositions you have already used include **a, con, de, en,** and **para.** Here are some others.

cerca de close to	**delante de** in front of
lejos de far from	**detrás de** behind
antes de before	**entre** between, among
después de after	**durante** during
encima de on top of	**a la izquierda (derecha) de**
debajo de below	to the left (right) of

• In Spanish the pronouns that serve as objects of prepositions are identical in form to the subject pronouns, except for **mí** and **ti.**

Ella va a comprar un regalo para **mí.**	*She's going to buy a gift for me.*
Buscamos algo para **ti.**	*We're looking for something for you.*

• The words **conmigo** and **contigo** express *with me* and *with you (fam. sing.).*

No puedo hablar **contigo** ahora.	*I can't talk with you now.*

• Subject pronouns are used after the preposition **entre.**

Entre tú y yo, Horacio es un tipo antipático.
Between you and me, Horace is an unpleasant guy.

A. En una tienda de ropa. With a classmate, locate the following articles of clothing in the drawing.

MODELO   —¿Dónde están los pantalones para señora?
—A la izquierda de las faldas.

1. las camisas
2. los zapatos
3. las medias
4. los calcetines
5. los pantalones para caballero (*men*)
6. las blusas
7. los abrigos
8. las faldas

B. ¿Qué hace Ud. (*do you do*) antes de la clase de español? ¿y después? ¿y durante la clase? ¿Tiene otra clase después de ésta (*this one*)? ¿Adónde va Ud. después de estudiar en la biblioteca toda la tarde?

C. Complete las oraciones en una forma lógica, usando un pronombre apropiado.

1. Sí, sí, Teresa es muy simpática, pero casi nunca hablo con _____ .
2. Sin _____ no puedo vivir, mi cielo (*beloved*). Siempre quiero vivir con _____ .
3. Jaimito no puede ver (*see*) bien porque hay un hombre delante de _____ .
4. —Entre _____ y _____ , no puedo aguantar (*stand*) las fiestas de Paula.
   —No estoy de acuerdo (*I don't agree*) con _____ . ¿Por qué siempre hablas mal de (*about*) _____ ?
5. Declaración de amor: Nunca voy a bailar con otro hombre (otra mujer). Siempre voy a bailar con _____ . Tampoco (*Neither*) voy a cantar para otro/a. Sólo voy a cantar para _____ .

CH. **Situaciones.** You and a friend are discussing what is easy (**fácil**) and difficult (**difícil**) for each of you to do. Ask and answer questions according to the model, adding more information when possible.

MODELO   hablar en público →
          —Para ti, ¿es fácil o difícil *hablar en público*?
          —Para mí es difícil *hablar en público*.
          —Pues, para mí es muy fácil. ¡Me gusta *hablar en público*!

1. asistir a clase todos los días
2. aprender el vocabulario
3. comer menos (*less*)
4. regatear en un mercado
5. estudiar los sábados por la noche
6. gastar menos dinero en (ropa, libros, discos...)

PRONUNCIACIÓN: *b/v*

In Spanish, the pronunciation of the letters **b** and **v** is identical. At the beginning of a sentence or phrase—that is, after a pause—or after **m** or **n**, the letters **b** and **v** are pronounced just like the English stop [b]. Everywhere else they are pronounced like the fricative [ƀ], produced by creating friction when pushing the air through the lips. This sound has no equivalent in English.

Práctica

1. [b]   bueno   viejo   verde   venir   barato   Vicente   bota   viernes   también   hombre   sombrero   bienvenido   hombre

2. [ƀ]   abuelo   llevar   libro   pobre   abrir   abrigo   universidad

3. [b/ƀ]   bueno / es bueno   busca / Ud. busca   bien / muy bien   en Venezuela / de Venezuela   vende / se vende   en Bolivia / de Bolivia

4. [b/ƀ]   beber   bebida   vivir   biblioteca   Babel   vívido

¡Vamos de compras!

—Necesito comprar un abrigo nuevo.
—¿Adónde vas? ¿al centro comercial *Oakwood*?
—Sí. ¿Quieres ir conmigo?
—¡Cómo no! ¿A qué hora vas?
—Pues… a las tres. ¿Qué te parece? (*What do you think?*)

Peter Menzel

Ciudad satélite, Ciudad de México, México

MINIDIÁLOGOS Y ESTRUCTURA

12 ¿Qué estás haciendo?
Estar; Present Progressive: *Estar* + *-ndo*

The sentences in the left-hand column tell what the following persons are able to do. Following the example, tell what they are doing right now (**ahora mismo**).

Dolores baila muy bien.   → Dolores **está bailando** ahora mismo.
Soledad canta muy bien.   → Soledad **está cantando** ahora mismo.
Yo hablo español muy bien.   → Yo **estoy** _____ .
El profesor enseña muy bien.   → Él **está** _____ .

The sentences in the left-hand column tell what the following persons want to do. Following the example, tell what they are doing at the moment.

Santiago quiere comer algo.   → Santiago **está comiendo** algo en este momento.
Nati quiere beber algo.   → Nati **está bebiendo** algo en este momento.
Yo quiero escribir una carta.   → Yo **estoy** _____ .
Tú quieres abrir el regalo.   → Tú **estás** _____ .

Forms and Uses of *estar*

estar (*to be*)	
estoy	estamos
estás	estáis
está	están

¿Dónde **está** el parque?   Where is the park?
¿Cómo **está** Ud.?   How are you?
Estoy bien (mal, enfermo).   I'm fine (not well, sick).

Forms of **estar** are used to tell where someone or something is, and to talk about how someone is feeling, one's condition or state of health.

Estar de acuerdo (con) means *to be in agreement (with).*

¿No **están** Uds. **de acuerdo con**   Don't you agree with Pablo?
Pablo?

[Práctica A–B]

Formation of the Progressive

In English the *present progressive* is formed with the verb *to be* and the *present participle*, the verb form that ends in -ing: *I **am** walking, we **are** driving, she **is** studying.*

The Spanish present progressive **(el progresivo)** is formed with **estar** plus the present participle **(el gerundio),** which is formed by adding **-ando** to the stem of **-ar** verbs and **-iendo** to the stem of **-er** and **-ir** verbs.* The present participle never varies; it always ends in **-o.**

tomar   → **tomando**   *taking; drinking*
comprender   → **comprendiendo**   *understanding*
abrir   → **abriendo**   *opening*

When an unstressed **-i-** occurs between two vowels, it becomes a **-y-.**

leer   → **leyendo**   *reading*
creer   → **creyendo**   *believing*

Use of the Progressive

Ramón **está comiendo** ahora mismo.   *Ramón is eating right now.*
Compramos la casa mañana.   *We're buying the house*
                                          tomorrow.

Ella **estudia** química este semestre.   *She's studying chemistry this*
                                          semester.

In Spanish, the present progressive is used primarily to describe an action that is actually in progress, as in the first sentence above. The simple Spanish present is used to express other English usages of the present progressive: to tell what is going to happen (the second sentence) and to tell what someone is doing over a period of time but not necessarily at this very moment (the third sentence).

[Práctica C–F]

---

*__Ir, poder, preferir__, and **venir**—as well as several other verbs that you will learn later—have irregular present participles: **yendo, pudiendo, prefiriendo, viniendo.** However, these four verbs are seldom used in the progressive.

Práctica

A. ¿Cómo están Uds. hoy? Haga oraciones según las indicaciones.

1. yo / muy bien
2. tú / bien / ¿no?
3. el profesor (la profesora) / muy bien

4. nosotros / no / enfermo
5. Julio / mal / ¿verdad?
6. Uds. / bien / también

B. ¿Dónde están las siguientes ciudades? ¿Están cerca o lejos la una de la otra?

1. ¿Amarillo? ¿Los Ángeles? ¿San Agustín? ¿Toledo? ¿Santa Fe? ¿Reno?
2. ¿Managua? ¿Guadalajara? ¿Buenos Aires? ¿La Habana? ¿Quito? ¿La Paz? ¿Bogotá?

C. **El sábado por la noche.** Dé oraciones nuevas según las indicaciones.

— Todos los amigos de Ud. están en una fiesta. Ud. quiere asistir también. ¿Por qué?
— Todos están *bailando.* (*cantar, beber, comer, abrir botellas de champán, hablar mucho,* __?__)
— Pero Ud. no puede ir. ¿Por qué no?
— Estoy *estudiando.* (*trabajar, escribir los ejercicios, leer el periódico, mirar un programa muy interesante, aprender el vocabulario nuevo,* __?__)

CH. **¡Esta noche es diferente!** What is happening that makes tonight different from other evenings? Answer by completing each sentence with the progressive form of the verb in parentheses. Then expand each situation if you can.

1. Generalmente miro la televisión por la noche, pero esta noche… (leer un libro)
2. María Cristina prepara la cena (*dinner*) casi siempre, pero esta noche ella y su esposo Juan Carlos… (comer en un restaurante)
3. Generalmente los niños estudian por la noche, pero ahora mismo… (descansar)
4. Por lo general comemos a las seis. Esta noche… (comer a las cinco)
5. Mi esposa generalmente trabaja en casa por la noche, pero en este momento… (escribir cartas)
6. Casi todas las noches los nietos visitan a sus abuelos, pero esta noche… (visitar a sus tíos)

D. **Situaciones: ¿Qué vamos a hacer?** With another student, form sentences that tell where you are and one thing that you are going to do there. Follow the model.

MODELO   en la clase → Estamos en la clase.
Vamos a cantar en español.

1. en una tienda de ropa   3. en casa
2. en el parque   4. en un restaurante (bar)

Now reverse the situation. Tell what you're doing, then tell where you are.

MODELO   cantando en español →
Estamos cantando en español.
Estamos en la cafetería con unos amigos colombianos.

1. leyendo   3. comiendo unos tacos
2. celebrando una fiesta   4. hablando por teléfono

E. ¿Con qué o con quién está Ud. de acuerdo?

(No) Estoy de acuerdo con la política de... (el presidente, los republicanos, los demócratas, el senador _____, Karl Marx, los capitalistas, __?__)

F. ¡Lógico! With a classmate, describe situations and draw logical conclusions from them, according to the model. When possible, use **tener** idioms that you learned in **Capítulo 4** as well as the ones you have learned in this chapter: **tener frío** and **tener calor**. Use **estar bien** to express *to be comfortable* (neither hot nor cold). Here are two more useful expressions.

Estoy $\begin{cases} \text{poniéndome (}\textit{putting on}\text{) el/la...} \\ \text{quitándome (}\textit{taking off}\text{) el/la...} \end{cases}$

MODELO   poniéndome otro suéter →
—Estoy poniéndome otro suéter.
—Ah, tienes frío, ¿no?

1. quitándome la ropa de calle (**la playa** = *beach*)
2. poniéndome el traje de baño (**nadar** = *to swim*)
3. poniéndome el pijama
4. esquiando
5. (no) quitándome el suéter

¿Recuerda Ud.?

You have already learned the forms of **este** (*this*), one of the Spanish demonstrative adjectives. Review them by describing the color of articles that are close to you and the clothing you are wearing. You can also tell what things are made of.

MODELO   Esta camisa es de rayas. Estos cuadernos son de papel...

13 ¿Éste, ése o aquél?
Demonstrative Adjectives and Pronouns

En la sección de suéteres

CLIENTE: Quiero ver algo diferente, algo fuera de serie... tal vez uno de *esos* suéteres amarillos.

DEPENDIENTA: Muy buena selección, señora. *Este* color está de moda este año.

CLIENTE: (Mirando el suéter de cerca.) Quizás, pero... realmente no me gusta el color. ¿Puedo ver uno de *aquéllos*?

DEPENDIENTA: Cómo no, señora. Los suéteres de *ese* modelo también son muy elegantes.

CLIENTE: Sí... ¡y probablemente son demasiado caros para mí!

¿Quién habla, la cliente o la dependienta?

1. Creo que prefiero aquellos suéteres amarillos.
2. Ese color se vende mucho este año.
3. Ahora no me gusta este color.
4. ¡Ay, estos clientes!

Demonstrative Adjectives		
this	est**e** libro	est**a** mesa
these	est**os** libros	est**as** mesas
that	es**e** libro aqu**el** libro (allí)	es**a** mesa aqu**ella** mesa (allí)
those	es**os** libros aqu**ellos** libros (allí)	es**as** mesas aqu**ellas** mesas (allí)

Demonstrative Adjectives

Demonstrative adjectives **(los adjetivos demostrativos)** are used to point out or indicate a specific noun or nouns. In Spanish, demonstrative adjectives precede the noun they modify. They also agree in number and gender with the noun.

In the sweater section CUSTOMER: *I want to see something different, something unique . . . perhaps one of those yellow sweaters.* CLERK: *Very good choice, madam. This color is in style this year.* CUSTOMER: *(Looking closely at the sweater.) Maybe, but . . . I really don't like the color. Could I see one of those over there?* CLERK: *Of course, madam. Sweaters in that style are also very elegant.* CUSTOMER: *Yes . . . and probably too expensive for me!*

A. Este, esta, estos, estas (*this, these*)

Este coche es de Francia.	*This car is from France.*
Estas señoritas son argentinas.	*These women are Argentinean.*

Forms of **este** are used to refer to nouns that are close to the speaker in space or time.

B. Ese, esa, esos, esas (*that, those*)

Esas blusas son baratas.	*Those blouses are cheap.*
Ese hombre (cerca de Ud.) es abogado.	*That man (close to you) is a lawyer.*

Forms of **ese** are used to refer to nouns that are *not* close to the speaker. Sometimes nouns modified by forms of **ese** are close to the person addressed.

C. Aquel, aquella, aquellos, aquellas (*that* [over there], *those* [over there])

Aquel coche (allí en la calle) es rápido.	*That car (there in the street) is fast.*
Aquella casa (en las montañas) es del hermano de Ramiro.	*That house (in the mountains) belongs to Ramiro's brother.*

Forms of **aquel** are used to refer to nouns that are even farther away.

Note that Spanish speakers use forms of **ese** and **aquel** interchangeably to indicate nouns that are at some distance from them; **esa/aquella casa en las montañas; esa/aquella ciudad en Sudamérica.** However, if a form of **ese** has been used to indicate a distant noun, a form of **aquel** is normally used to indicate a noun that is even farther away in comparison: **esa señora allí y aquel hombre en la calle.**

[Práctica A–B]

Demonstrative Pronouns

In English and in Spanish, the demonstrative adjectives can be used as pronouns, that is, in place of nouns. Note the use of the accent mark to distinguish demonstrative pronouns (**éste, ése, aquél**) from demonstrative adjectives (**este, ese, aquel**).

Necesito este diccionario y **ése.**	*I need this dictionary and that one.*
Estas señoras y **aquéllas** son profesoras, ¿verdad?	*These women and those (over there) are professors, right?*

[Práctica C]

Neuter Demonstratives

The neuter demonstratives **esto, eso,** and **aquello** mean *this, that* (not close), and *that* (farther away), respectively.

¿Qué es **esto?**   *What is this?*
Eso es todo.   *That's all.*
¡Aquello es terrible!   *That's terrible!*

They refer to a whole idea, concept, situation, or statement, or to an as yet unidentified object. They never refer to a specific noun. Compare **este libro y ése, esa mesa y aquélla,** and so on.

[Práctica CH–D]

Práctica

A. ¿De qué color es la ropa que todos llevan hoy? Dé oraciones completas usando la forma apropiada del demostrativo **ese.**

MODELO   falda / azul → Esa falda es azul.

1. sombrero / negro
2. blusa / amarillo
3. pantalones / gris
4. calcetines / blanco
5. sandalias / pardo
6. suéter / verde

B. Situaciones. Imagine that you were in Mexico recently and had a good trip. With another student, ask and answer the following questions, using the cues in parentheses. Follow the model.

MODELO   —¿Recuerdas (*Do you remember*) cómo es el restaurante la Independencia?   (excelente)
—¡Ah, aquel restaurante es excelente!

1. ¿Recuerdas si es cara la ropa del Mercado de la Merced? (barata)
2. ¿Recuerdas cómo son los periódicos de la capital? (magníficos)
3. Y el Hotel Libertad, ¿recuerdas qué tal es? (fenomenal)
4. ¿Y los dependientes del hotel? (simpáticos)
5. ¿Recuerdas si se puede regatear en los almacenes? (precios fijos)

C. Comentarios en la tienda de la señora Estévez. Forme dos oraciones según el modelo.

MODELO   Esta blusa es cara. (barato) →
Esta blusa es cara y ésa es barata.
Ésta es cara y ésa es barata.

1. Este traje es de Francia. (Inglaterra)
2. Estos pantalones son elegantes. (muy feo)
3. Estas botas son prácticas. (muy bonito)
4. Este dependiente es mi amigo. (el amigo de Tina)
5. Estas medias son largas. (demasiado corto para mí)

CH. Match the questions or statements in the left-hand column with the situations described on the right.

1. ¿Qué es esto?
2. ¿Todo eso?
3. Eso es terrible.
4. ¿Qué es aquello?

a. En la montaña hay una cosa que Ud. no puede ver (*see*) muy bien.
b. El profesor dice (*says*), «Uds. tienen que estudiar para un examen mañana y tienen que escribir una composición para el lunes».
c. Ud. abre el regalo y descubre una cosa interesante y curiosa.
ch. La hermana de un amigo está en el hospital por (*because of*) un accidente de carro.

D. **Situaciones.** Help Alicia decide what to buy in each situation.

MODELO   Pues me gusta mucho aquel abrigo rojo. Pero también me gusta este gris.* ¿Qué te parece? →

· Debes comprar el rojo.* Va muy bien con tu personalidad.
· Vas a comprar el rojo, ¿verdad? Es más barato.
· A mí me gusta más el gris porque es más elegante.

1. Hay una camisa azul que me gusta. Pero aquella amarilla también es bonita.
2. Aquí venden un diccionario inglés-alemán muy barato, pero en aquella tienda tienen otro que sólo cuesta dos dólares más... y es más grande.
3. Aquí hay unas plantas grandes que son muy bonitas. Aquéllas son más pequeñas.
4. Estas blusas de seda son elegantes. Aquellas otras, de algodón, son mucho más baratas.

---

*Note the *article* + *adjective* or *demonstrative* + *adjective* combination that can be used as a noun: **la camisa roja** (*the red blouse*) → **la roja** (*the red one*); **aquellos pantalones azules** (*those blue pants*) → **aquellos azules** (*those blue ones*).

LISTA	BATAS - Robes	22.-	
	CALCETINES - Socks	5.-	
DE	CALZONCILLOS - Drawers	8.-	
	CAMISAS - Shirts	14.-	
LAVANDERIA	CAMISAS SPORT O DE SEDA Sport or Silk Shirts	22.-	
	CAMISETAS - Undershirts	8.-	
	PANTALON - Algodón, Lino - Cotton or Linen Slacks	22.-	
	PAÑUELOS - Handkerchiefs	3.-	
	PIJAMAS - Pajamas	22.-	
	TRAJES DE BAÑO - Bathing Suits	14.-	
	SHORTS	14.-	

	FALDAS - Skirts	21.-	
	BLUSAS - Blouses	20.-	
	BRASSIERES - Brassieres	9.-	
	CAMISONES - Nightgowns	22.-	
	FONDOS - Slips	17.-	
	PANTALETAS - Panties	9.-	
	VESTIDOS - Dresses	22.-	
	PANTALON - Slack's	21.-	
	SERVICIO URGENTE – Quick service		
	4% Impuesto - 4% Tax		

REPASO

Cuando voy de compras… Complete the following paragraphs with the correct form of the words in parentheses, as suggested by the context. When two possibilities are given in parentheses, select the correct word.

(*Me/Mí*[1]) gusta ir de (*comprar/compras*[2]) con mi amiga Margarita cuando ella tiene (*gastar/ganas*[3]) de acompañarme.° Este fin de semana, necesito (*buscar*[4]) unos regalos para los hijos (*del/de el*[5]) Sr. Suárez, que (*trabajar*[6]) con mi madre en el hospital. (*Mi*[7]) padres y los Suárez son muy (*bueno*[8]) amigos, aunque° no (*estar*[9]) siempre de acuerdo con sus opiniones (*político*[10]), y la familia Suárez (*venir*[11]) a (*nuestro*[12]) casa con frecuencia.

go with me

although

Este mes° todos los niños Suárez (*celebrar*[13]) su cumpleaños.° Por (*ese/eso*[14]) tengo que (*ir*[15]) de compras antes (*de/en*[16]) su visita. Ana, (*el/la*[17]) mayor,° es una chica muy simpática. (*Yo: querer*[18]) comprarle° un vestido de cuadros o de rayas si encuentro° uno bonito en el centro. Ya tiene (*dos/doce*[19]) años y está (*comenzar*° [20]) a tener interés en la ropa elegante. (*Su*[21]) hermanos son muy niños todavía°—casi siempre (*llevar*[22]) camisetas y pantalones cortos. Por eso no (*yo: ir*[23]) a comprarles° ropa; creo que (*ellos: tener*[24]) más interés en los juguetes.°

month / birthday

eldest / buy her
I find
to begin
still
buy them
toys

(Más tarde, por teléfono)

—¿Diga?°

—Margarita, ¿eres tú?

—Sí, chica. ¿Qué hay?° ¿Cómo (*estar*[25])?

—Muy bien. Oye,° ¿qué (*estar*[26]) haciendo° en este momento?

—Ahora mismo estoy (*leer*[27]) una novela para la clase de literatura (*inglés*[28]). ¿Qué pasa?

—¿Qué te parece si (*ir*[29]) al centro? Hay (*mucho*[30]) gangas en las tiendas (*este*[31]) días y tengo que comprar (*los/unos*[32]) regalos.

—¡(*Encantado*[33])! En este momento (*estar*[34]) poniéndome el abrigo.

Hello? (on the telephone)

¿Qué… What's up?
Listen / doing

Es cuestión de gustos

—¿Cuánto pagaste por esa camiseta?
—Fue muy barata... sólo cuatro dólares. ¿Te gusta?
—Sí, me gusta mucho.
—¿Verdad? Pues... yo creo que el color no me va (*doesn't suit me*) muy bien.
—¡Qué va! (*Nonsense!*) Te va estupendamente.

Peter Menzel

Barcelona, España

UN PASO MÁS: Lectura cultural

Antes de leer

When reading Spanish, it's easy to "get lost" in long sentences. Here is a way to get around that difficulty. First omit the words and information set off by commas; then concentrate on the main verb and its subject. Try this strategy in the following sentence:

> En muchos lugares del mundo hispánico, especialmente en las tierras templadas o frías, los hombres casi siempre llevan una camisa con corbata y una chaqueta.

Once you have located the subject and verb **(los hombres, llevan),** you can read the sentence again, adding more information to the framework provided by the phrase *men wear.* . . . Men from what part of the world? What, specifically, do they wear? Try the strategy again in this sentence:

> Aunque mi mamá parece tímida, es una mujer independiente con ideas fijas, que no tiene miedo de ofrecer su opinión.

Now apply the strategy as you do the following reading.

Las modas

Por lo general, los hispanos desean lucir bien.° Claro que° los *bluejeans* son muy populares entre los jóvenes de todo el mundo. Pero para casi toda ocasión los hispanos se visten° con más esmero que° los norteamericanos. Cuando uno está en la calle, es decir,° cuando no está en casa, es preferible estar elegante.

En muchos lugares del mundo hispánico, especialmente en las tierras templadas o frías, los hombres por lo general llevan camisa con corbata y una chaqueta. Los colores preferidos para los pantalones y las chaquetas son azul, negro o gris, y las camisas son casi siempre blancas. En cambio, las mujeres usan ropa de colores vivos y alegres.°

lucir... *look nice* / Claro... *Of course*

se... *dress* / con... *more carefully than*
es... *that is*

vivos... *living and happy*

En los climas cálidos, el estilo de ropa se relaciona con el tiempo.° En ciudades como Cartagena, Veracruz o Guayaquil, por ejemplo, no todos los hombres llevan siempre chaqueta y corbata. Es muy común en estos lugares llevar una guayabera* para ir a la oficina o la universidad. Las guayaberas pueden ser muy elegantes; hay algunas muy bonitas, bordadas a mano.° También son muy cómodas.°

weather

bordadas... hand-embroidered
comfortable

Si usted va a visitar un país hispánico, debe llevar ropa apropiada. Así° usted siempre va a hacer una buena impresión.

That way

Comprensión

¿Cierto o falso? Corrija las oraciones falsas.

1. Los hispanos tienen poco interés en lucir bien.
2. A veces el clima determina el tipo de ropa que una persona lleva.
3. Al hombre hispano típico le gusta llevar ropa de colores vivos.
4. Cartagena y Veracruz son ciudades con un clima templado.
5. La guayabera es una camisa que se lleva solamente en casa.

Para escribir

A. Complete el siguiente párrafo sobre las modas en los Estados Unidos.

En los Estados Unidos la individualidad es importante en las modas. Por ejemplo, los estudiantes llevan ____, pero los profesores ____ . También son diferentes los estilos de los jóvenes y los viejos. Las madres llevan ____ y los padres ____ . Pero yo, cuando bailo en una discoteca (estudio en la biblioteca, trabajo en casa), llevo ____ .

B. Use the following phrases as a guide to describe an imaginary shopping excursion in Madrid. Form complete sentences and add as many details as you can.

1. ir al centro en (coche, autobús,...)
2. llegar a (un almacén, una tienda pequeña,...)
3. buscar la sección de/para...
4. no poder creer los precios porque...
5. querer regatear pero...
6. por fin decidir comprar...
7. pagar ____ pesetas por el/la...

---

*A **guayabera** is a man's shirt made to wear outside the trousers, not tucked in.

VOCABULARIO

VERBOS

estar (*irreg.*) to be
llevar to wear; to carry

LA ROPA

el abrigo overcoat
los *bluejeans* jeans
la blusa blouse
la bolsa handbag, purse
la bota boot
los calcetines socks
la camisa shirt
la camiseta T-shirt
la cartera wallet
el cinturón belt
la corbata necktie
la chaqueta jacket
la falda skirt
el impermeable raincoat
las medias stockings
la mochila backpack
los pantalones pants, trousers
el par pair
la sandalia sandal
el suéter sweater
el traje (de baño) (bathing) suit
el vestido dress

OTRO SUSTANTIVO

el parque park

PARA DESCRIBIR

amarillo/a yellow
anaranjado/a orange
azul blue
blanco/a white
gris gray
morado/a purple
negro/a black
pardo/a brown
rojo/a red
rosado/a pink
verde green

de cuadros plaid
de rayas striped

de lana, algodón, seda (made) of
    wool, cotton, silk

OTROS ADJETIVOS

aquel(la), aquellos/as that, those
    (over there)
difícil hard, difficult
enfermo/a sick
ese/a, esos/as that, those
fácil easy

PREPOSICIONES

a la izquierda (derecha) de to the
    left (right) of
antes de before
cerca de close to, near
debajo de under, below
delante de in front of
después de after
detrás de behind
durante during
encima de on top of, above
entre between, among
lejos de far from

PALABRAS ADICIONALES

ahora mismo right now
allí there
conmigo/contigo with me/with
    you
estar de acuerdo (con) to be in
    agreement (with), to agree
estar de moda to be in style
generalmente generally
¿qué te parece? what do you
    think?

FRASES ÚTILES PARA LA COMUNICACIÓN

tener frío	to be cold, chilly
tener calor	to be hot, warm
estar bien	to be comfortable (*temperature*)
estoy {**poniéndome** / **quitándome**}	I am {putting on / taking off}

La vida social

VOCABULARIO: PREPARACIÓN

la amistad

la cita

el amor

el noviazgo

la boda

la luna de miel

el matrimonio

el divorcio

LAS RELACIONES SENTIMENTALES

el novio boyfriend; fiancé; groom
la novia girlfriend; fiancée; bride

el esposo husband
la esposa wife

cariñoso/a affectionate

A. Definiciones. Match these words with their definitions.

1. el matrimonio
2. el amor
3. el divorcio
4. la boda
5. la amistad

   a. relación cariñosa entre dos amigos
   b. posible resultado de un matrimonio desastroso
   c. relación sentimental y especial entre dos personas
  ch. una ceremonia (religiosa o civil) en que la novia a veces lleva un vestido blanco
   d. relación legal entre dos personas

B. Complete las oraciones en una forma lógica.

1. Mi abuelo es el _____ de mi abuela.
2. Muchos novios tienen un largo _____ antes del matrimonio.
3. María y Julio tienen _____ el viernes para comer en un restaurante y luego (*then*) van a bailar.
4. La _____ de Juan y Marta es el domingo a las dos de la tarde, en la iglesia (*church*) de San Martín.
5. En una _____, ¿quién debe pagar o comprar los boletos (*tickets*), el hombre o la mujer?
6. La _____ entre estos exesposos es imposible. No pueden ser amigos.
7. Ramón tiene miedo del _____; no quiere tener esposa.

Una cita para esta noche

—Oye (*Hey*), tengo dos boletos para el concierto de Madonna esta noche. ¿Quieres ir?
—¡Sí! Realmente tenía ganas (*I really wanted*) de asistir a ese concierto.
—Paso por ti a las siete, ¿vale?
—¡De acuerdo!

Estados Unidos

Don Smetzer/Click/Chicago

C. ¿Cierto o falso? Conteste **cierto, falso** o **depende**.

1. El amor verdadero (*real*) no existe.
2. El matrimonio es una institución social necesaria.
3. Un novio/una novia es una limitación.
4. Las bodas grandes y formales son una tontería (*foolish thing*).
5. Un novio debe ser alto, moreno y guapo.
6. Las mujeres rubias no son muy inteligentes.
7. Los esposos deben trabajar; las esposas deben estar en casa con los niños.
8. Vivir con el novio/la novia es una alternativa del matrimonio.
9. La luna de miel es un concepto anticuado.

Summary of Interrogative Words

¿Cómo?	How?	**¿Quién(es)?**	Who?
¿Cuándo?	When?	**¿De quién(es)?**	Whose?
¿A qué hora?	At what time?	**¿Dónde?**	Where?
		¿De dónde?	From where?
¿Qué?	What? Which?	**¿Adónde?**	Where (to)?
¿Cuál(es)?	What? Which one/ones?		
		¿Cuánto/a?	How much?
¿Por qué?	Why?	**¿Cuántos/as?**	How many?

¿Qué? Versus ¿cuál?

¿Qué? asks for a definition or an explanation.

¿Qué es esto?	*What is this?*
¿Qué quieres?	*What do you want?*
¿Qué tocas?	*What do you play?*

¿Qué? can be directly followed by a noun.*

¿Qué traje necesitas?	*What (Which) suit do you need?*
¿Qué anillo te gusta más?	*What (Which) ring do you like most?*
¿Qué instrumento musical tocas?	*What (Which) musical instrument do you play?*

¿Cuál(es)? expresses *what?* or *which?* in all other cases.

¿Cuál es la clase más grande?	*What (Which) is the biggest class?*
¿Cuáles son tus actrices favoritas?	*What (Which) are your favorite actresses?*
¿Cuál es la capital de Uruguay?	*What is the capital of Uruguay?*

¿Por qué?

¿Por qué?, written as two words and with an accent mark, means *why?* **Porque,** written as one word and with no accent, means *because.*

—**¿Por qué** no escuchas?	*"Why don't you listen?"*
—**Porque** no quiero.	*"Because I don't want to."*

---

*¿Cuál(es)? is not generally used as an adjective.

¿Cuál de los dos anillos quieres? *Which of the two rings do you want?* BUT **¿Qué anillo** quieres? *Which (What) ring do you want?*

A. ¿Qué? o ¿cuál(es)?

1. —¿ _____ es esto? —Un peso mexicano.
2. —¿ _____ es Sacramento? —Es la capital de California.
3. —¿ _____ es tu clase preferida? —Pues, yo creo que es la de psicología.
4. —¿ _____ piano vas a tocar? —El de Juanita.
5. —¿ _____ son los cines más modernos? —Los del centro.
6. —¿ _____ camisa debo llevar? —La azul.
7. —¿ _____ es un anillo de boda? —Es un símbolo del amor.
8. —¿ _____ es el novio de Alicia? —Es el hombre moreno.

B. ¿Quién?, ¿quiénes? o ¿de quién?

1. —¿ _____ es Shirley MacLaine? —Es una actriz muy famosa.
2. —¿ _____ son las damas de honor (*maids of honor*)? —Son mis hermanas.
3. —¿ _____ son estas sandalias? —Son de Pepita.
4. —¿ _____ son los dueños (*owners*) de aquellos coches? —Esos dos hombres.
5. —¿ _____ están en la iglesia ahora? —Sólo la novia y sus parientes.

C. ¿Dónde?, ¿de dónde? o ¿adónde?

1. —¿ _____ son los Chevalier? —De Francia.
2. —¿ _____ van Uds. después de la boda? —¡A Puerto Vallarta!
3. —¿ _____ quieres viajar (*travel*)? —Quiero ir a Colombia.
4. —¿ _____ está el cine? —Creo que está en el centro.
5. —¿ _____ hay muchas personas de habla española (*Spanish-speaking*)? —En New Jersey, por ejemplo.
6. —¿ _____ está su casa? —Está muy lejos de aquí.
7. —¿ _____ vienen los novios? —De la iglesia.

CH. ¿Cuándo?, ¿a qué hora?, ¿cuánto/a? o ¿cuántos/as?

1. —¿ _____ vestidos de rayas hay? —Hay más de (*than*) catorce.
2. —¿ _____ llegamos? —A las diez de la noche.
3. —¿ _____ dinero tienes? —Pues, creo que tengo cuatro dólares.
4. —¿ _____ personas hay delante de la iglesia? —Hay quince.
5. —¿ _____ vamos a viajar a Ciudad Juárez? —Después del fin de semana.
6. —¿ _____ es la película (*movie*)? —A las ocho.
7. —¿ _____ cuestan los boletos? —Diez dólares.

D. Entrevista. Without taking notes, interview another student by asking the following questions or any others like them that occur to you. Then present as much of the information as you can to the class.

1. ¿De dónde eres? ¿Dónde vives ahora? ¿Por qué vives allí?
2. ¿Adónde quieres viajar algún día (*some day*)?
3. ¿Qué materias tienes este semestre (trimestre)? ¿Por qué?
4. ¿Cuántos hermanos tienes? ¿cuántos primos? ¿cuántos tíos?
5. ¿Qué tipo de persona eres?
6. ¿Qué instrumento musical tocas? (el piano, la guitarra, la trompeta, los tambores [*drums*]...)
7. ¿Cuál es tu color favorito? ¿Tienes mucha ropa de ese color?
8. ¿Tienes novio/a (esposo/a)? ¿Cómo es?
9. ¿Con quién te gusta salir (*to go out*) los sábados? ¿Adónde van?

Después de clase

—¿Tienes tiempo ahora para tomar un café?
—Gracias, pero no puedo. Tengo un examen mañana y tengo que estudiar. (Ya tengo otros planes. Lo siento. / Estoy citado/a con unos amigos en la biblioteca. / Tengo que estar en el centro a las tres hoy.)
—Tal vez (*Perhaps*) mañana.
—Sí, cómo no.

Universidad de Puerto Rico

Owen Franken

PRONUNCIACIÓN: *p* and *t*

English [p] and [t] sounds at the beginning of a word or syllable are *aspirated* (released with a small puff of air). Spanish [p] and [t] are never aspirated. Spanish [t] differs from English [t] in another way. The English [t] is pronounced with the tip of the tongue on the alveolar ridge, just behind the upper teeth. The Spanish [t] is a *dental* sound (pronounced with the tongue against the back of the upper teeth).

Práctica

1. pasar   padre   programa   palabra   puerta   prisa
2. tienda   todos   traje   todavía   tener   televisión
3. una tía trabajadora   un tío tonto   tres tristes tigres
   unos pantalones pardos   pasar por la puerta
   un perro   perezoso
4. Tomás toma tu té.   También toma tu café.
   Papá paga el papel.   Pero Pablo paga el periódico.

MINIDIÁLOGOS Y ESTRUCTURA

14 ¿Ser o estar?
Summary of Uses of *ser* and *estar*

Una conversación telefónica con un esposo (una esposa) que *está* en un viaje de negocios.

Aló... ¿Cómo *estás*, mi amor?... ¿Dónde *estás* ahora?... ¿Qué hora *es* ahí? ¡Uyy!, *es* muy tarde. Y el hotel, ¿cómo *es*?... ¿Cuánto cuesta por noche?... *Es* bien barato. Oye, ¿qué *estás* haciendo ahora?... Ay, pobre, lo siento. *Estás* muy ocupado/a. ¿Con quién *estás* citado/a mañana?... ¿Quién *es* el dueño de esa compañía?... Ah, él *es* de Cuba, ¿verdad?... Bueno, mi vida, ¿adónde vas luego?... ¿Y cuándo vas a regresar?... *Está* bien, querido/a. Hasta luego, ¿eh?... Adiós.

¿Qué contesta la otra persona?
Aló... → **Aló.** → *¿Cómo estás, mi amor?... etcétera.*

Summary of the Uses of *ser*	
· To *identify* people and things	Ella **es doctora.**
· To express *nationality;* with **de** to express *origin*	**Son cubanos. Son de** la Habana.
· With **de** to tell of what *material* something is made	Este bolígrafo **es de plástico.**
· With **para** to tell *for whom something is intended*	El regalo **es para** Sara.
· To tell *time*	**Son las once. Es la una y media.**
· With **de** to express *possession*	**Es de Carlota.**
· With *adjectives* that describe *basic, inherent characteristics*	Ramona **es inteligente.**
· To form many *generalizations*	**Es necesario** llegar temprano. **Es importante** estudiar.

A phone conversation with a husband/wife who is on a business trip   *Hello . . . How are you, dear? . . . Where are you now? . . . What time is it there? . . . My, it's very late. And how's the hotel? . . . How much is it per night? . . . It's very inexpensive. Hey, what are you doing now? . . . Poor dear, I'm sorry. You're very busy. Whom do you have an appointment with tomorrow? . . . Who is the owner of that company? . . . Ah, he's from Cuba, isn't he? . . . Well, dear, where are you going next? . . . And when are you coming home? . . . OK, dear. Talk to you soon . . . 'Bye.*

Summary of the Uses of *estar*	
· To tell *location*	El libro **está en la mesa.**
· To form the *progressive*	**Estamos tomando** un café ahora.
· To describe *health*	Paco **está enfermo.**
· With *adjectives* that describe *conditions*	**Estoy** muy **ocupada.**
· In a number of *fixed expressions*	**(No) Estoy de acuerdo. Está bien. Está claro.**

Ser *and* estar *with Adjectives*

Ser is used with adjectives that describe the fundamental qualities of a person, place, or thing.

La amistad es **importante.**	*Friendship is important.*
Son **cariñosos.**	*They are affectionate (people).*
Esta mujer es muy **baja.**	*This woman is very short.*

Estar is used with adjectives to express conditions or observations that are true at a given moment, but that do not describe inherent qualities of the noun.

furioso/a	furious	**sucio/a**	dirty
nervioso/a	nervous	**limpio/a**	clean
cansado/a	tired	**abierto/a**	open
ocupado/a	busy	**cerrado/a**	closed
aburrido/a	bored	**triste**	sad
preocupado/a	worried	**alegre, contento/a**	happy

Many adjectives can be used with either **ser** or **estar,** depending on what the speaker intends to communicate. In general, when *to be* implies *looks, tastes, feels,* or *appears,* **estar** is used. Compare the following pairs of sentences:

Daniel **es** guapo.	*Daniel is handsome. (He is a handsome person.)*
Daniel **está** muy guapo esta noche.	*Daniel looks very nice (handsome) tonight.*
Este plato mexicano **es** muy rico.	*This Mexican dish is very delicious.*
Este plato mexicano **está** muy rico.	*This Mexican dish is (tastes) great.*
—¿Cómo **es** Amalia? —**Es** simpática.	*"What is Amalia like (as a person)?" "She's nice."*
—¿Cómo **está** Amalia? —**Está** enferma todavía.	*"How is Amalia (feeling)?" "She's still feeling sick."*

Práctica

A. Cambie por antónimos los adjetivos indicados.

1. Estoy muy *enfermo.*
2. La falda de la novia está *sucia.*
3. ¿Está *cerrada* la iglesia?
4. Daniel está *triste,* ¿no?
5. El novio está muy *tranquilo* ahora.

B. Haga oraciones completas con una palabra o frase de cada grupo.

1. ¿Qué puede decir de (*you say about*) este regalo de boda?

El florero (*vase*) es / está del Almacén Carrillo / de cristal / alto / verde / limpio / en mi apartamento / en una caja (*box*) / para Alicia / un regalo caro / también un regalo bonito

2. Fotografía familiar: ¿quiénes son los dos jóvenes?

Los jóvenes son / están nuestros primos argentinos / de Buenos Aires / visitando a nuestra familia / a la derecha de los abuelos en la foto / simpáticos / en San Francisco esta semana / muy contentos con el viaje / un poco cansados ahora / tocando la guitarra ahora

C. Forme oraciones completas, usando las palabras entre paréntesis y la forma correcta de **ser** o **estar,** según el modelo.

MODELO ¿El vestido de la novia? (muy elegante) →
       Es muy elegante.

1. ¿John? (norteamericano)
2. ¿Mi escritorio? (sucio)
3. ¿Los Hernández? (ocupados esta noche)
4. ¿Yo? (muy bien hoy)
5. ¿Su abuelo? (viejo, muy viejo)
6. ¿Este problema? (muy difícil)
7. ¿Esa clase? (muy interesante)
8. ¿Maricarmen? (de acuerdo con nosotros)
9. ¿Los hijos de Francisco? (cariñosos)
10. ¿La tienda? (abierta esta tarde)

CH. Describa este dibujo de un cuarto típico de una residencia. Invente los detalles necesarios. ¿Quiénes son las dos compañeras de cuarto? ¿De dónde son? ¿Cómo son? ¿Dónde están en este momento? ¿Qué hay en el cuarto? ¿En qué condición está el cuarto?

D. **Escenas de la primera** (*first*) **cita.** ¿Cómo se dice en español?

1. These flowers (**flores,** *f.*) are for you.
2. I'm a little nervous.
3. You look very pretty tonight!
4. It's necessary to be home by (**a**) 12:00. Is that clear?
5. Oh, the restaurant is closed.
6. These tacos are (taste) good!
7. The movie is excellent, isn't it?
8. It's 11:00, but I'm not tired yet.

E. **Sentimientos.** Complete the following sentences by telling how you feel.

1. Cuando recibo una A en un examen, estoy _____ .
2. Cuando trabajo mucho, estoy _____ .
3. Cuando no puedo estar con mis amigos, estoy _____ .
4. Cuando estoy en clase, _____ .

F. **Entrevista.** Assume the identity of a famous person (television or movie personality, recording artist, or sports figure, for example). Your classmates will ask you *yes/no* questions in order to determine your identity. They may ask about your place of origin, your basic personal characteristics, your nationality, and so on. Here are some possible questions.

1. ¿Es Ud. hombre? ¿mujer? ¿niño/a?
2. ¿Es Ud. viejo/a? ¿joven? ¿guapo/a? ¿rubio/a? ¿moreno/a? ¿casado/a? ¿soltero/a?
3. ¿Es de los Estados Unidos? ¿del Canadá?

   4. ¿Está en (lugar) ahora?
   5. ¿Está muy ocupado/a ahora? ¿muy contento/a con su vida?
   6. ¿Está visitando esta ciudad esta semana?

Study Hint: Practicing Spanish Outside of Class

The few hours you spend in class each week are not enough time for practicing Spanish. But once you have done your homework and gone to the language lab (if one is available to you), how else can you practice your Spanish outside of class?

1. Practice "talking to yourself" in Spanish as you walk across campus, wait for a bus, and so on. Have an imaginary conversation with someone you know, or simply practice describing what you see or what you are thinking about at a given moment. Write notes to yourself in Spanish.

2. Hold a conversation hour—perhaps on a regular basis—with other students of Spanish. Or make regular phone calls to practice Spanish with other students in your class. It is difficult to communicate on the phone, as you can't rely on gestures and facial expressions, but it's an excellent way to improve your skill.

3. See Spanish-language movies when they are shown on campus or in local movie theaters. Check local bookstores, libraries, and record stores for Spanish-language newspapers, magazines, and music. Read the radio and television listings. Are there any Spanish-language programs or any stations that broadcast partially or exclusively in Spanish?

4. Practice speaking Spanish with a native speaker—either a Hispanic American or a foreign student. Is there an international students' organization on campus? An authentic Hispanic restaurant in your town? Spanish-speaking professors at your university? Try out a few phrases—no matter how simple—every chance you get. Every bit of practice will enhance your ability to speak Spanish.

---

15 Más descripciones: Comparisons

Tipos y estereotipos

Adolfo es muy atlético y extrovertido, pero estudia poco.

- Es una persona **más** atlética **que** Raúl y Esteban.
- Es **menos** estudioso **que** Raúl.
- Es **tan** extrovertido **como** Esteban.

Y Raúl, ¿cómo es?

- Es menos extrovertido que _____ .
- Es más estudioso que _____ .
- No es una persona tan atlética como _____ .

Esteban trabaja en la cafetería y también estudia—tiene cinco clases este semestre.

- Tiene **tantas** clases **como** Raúl.
- No tiene **tanto** tiempo libre (free) **como** Adolfo.
- Tiene **más** amigos **que** Raúl pero **menos** amigos **que** Adolfo.

Y Adolfo, ¿cómo es?

- No tiene tantas clases _____.   • Tiene más tiempo libre _____.   • Tiene más amigos _____.

Regular Comparisons of Adjectives

Alicia es **más perezosa que** Marta.	_Alicia is lazier than Marta._
Julio es **menos listo que** Pablo.	_Julio is less bright than Pablo._
Enrique es **tan trabajador como** Alicia.	_Enrique is as hard-working as Alicia._

The _comparative_ (**el comparativo**) of most English adjectives is formed by using the adverbs _more_ or _less_ (**more** intelligent, **less** important), or by adding -er (tall**er**, long**er**).

In Spanish, unequal comparisons are usually expressed with **más** (more) + adjective + **que** or **menos** (less) + adjective + **que.**

Equal comparisons are expressed with **tan** + adjective + **como.**

[Práctica A–B]

Irregular Comparative Forms

Spanish has the following irregular comparative forms:

mejor(es)	better		**mayor(es)**	older
peor(es)	worse		**menor(es)**	younger

Estos dulces son **buenos,** pero ésos son **mejores.**	_These candies are good, but those are better._

[Práctica C]

Comparison of Nouns

Alicia tiene **más/menos** bolsas **que** Susana.	_Alicia has more/fewer purses than Susana._
Nosotros tenemos **tantas** revistas **como** ellas.	_We have as many magazines as they (do)._

Nouns are compared with the expressions **más/menos** + *noun* + **que** and **tanto/a/os/as** + *noun* + **como. Más/menos** *de* are used when the comparison is followed by a number: **Tengo más** *de un* **hijo. Tanto** must agree in gender and number with the noun it modifies.

[Práctica CH–E]

Práctica

A. Conteste según el dibujo.

1. Emilia, ¿es más alta o más baja que Sancho?
2. ¿Es tan tímida como Sancho? ¿Quién es más extrovertido?
3. Sancho, ¿es una persona tan atlética como Emilia?
4. ¿Quién es más intelectual? ¿Por qué cree Ud. eso?
5. ¿Es Emilia tan estudiosa como Sancho? ¿Es tan trabajadora?
6. ¿Quién es más listo? ¿Por qué cree Ud. eso?

B. Opiniones. Cambie, indicando su opinión personal: **tan... como →
más/menos... que.**

1. Hoy estoy tan alegre como el profesor (la profesora).
2. Siempre estoy tan ocupado/a como mi mejor amigo/a.
3. Mi coche está tan sucio como el del profesor (de la profesora).
4. Esta clase es tan interesante como la clase de geografía.
5. El dinero es tan importante como la amistad.
6. El matrimonio es tan importante como el amor.

C. Complete, haciendo una comparación.

1. La comida italiana es buena, pero la mexicana es _____ .
2. Las pruebas (*quizzes*) son malas, pero los exámenes son _____ .
3. Pepito tiene dieciséis años. Demetrio, que tiene veinte años, es su hermano _____ .
4. Luisita es muy joven; el bebé de la familia es su hermano _____ .
5. La Argentina es grande, pero el Brasil es _____ .
6. El elefante es grande. El chimpancé es _____ .

CH. Conteste, comparando las cosas de Alfredo con las de Graciela.

1. ¿Cuánto dinero tiene Alfredo?
2. ¿Cuánta cerveza tiene Graciela?
3. ¿Cuántos libros tiene Alfredo?
4. ¿Cuántos bolígrafos tiene Graciela?
5. ¿Cuántos cuadernos tiene Alfredo?
6. ¿Cuántas cartas tiene Graciela?

D. Más opiniones. Cambie, indicando su opinión personal: **tanto...
como → más/menos... que,** o vice versa.

1. Los profesores trabajan más que los estudiantes.
2. En esta universidad las artes son tan importantes como las ciencias.
3. Aquí el béisbol es tan importante como el fútbol.
4. Hay más hombres que mujeres en esta clase.
5. Hay tantos exámenes en la clase de español como en la clase de historia.
6. Yo bebo menos cerveza que el profesor (la profesora).
7. Las mujeres pueden practicar tantos deportes (*sports*) como los hombres.

E. ¿Cómo se dice en español?

1. more than $10
2. fewer than 100 students
3. fewer than 20 seats
4. Are you over 18 years old?
5. She's over 90 years old!
6. I'm younger than she is.

F. Conteste las preguntas en una forma lógica.

¿Es Ud....
1. tan guapo/a como Tom Selleck/Kate Jackson?
2. tan rico/a como los Rockefeller?
3. tan fiel como su mejor amigo/a?
4. tan inteligente como Einstein?
5. tan cariñoso como su novio/a (esposa/a, amigo/a)?

¿Tiene Ud....
6. tanto dinero como los Ford?
7. tantos tíos como tías?
8. tantos amigos como amigas?
9. tantas buenas ideas como _____?
10. tantos años como su profesor(a)?

REPASO

Actividades sociales. Complete the following descriptions with the correct form of the words in parentheses, as suggested by the context. When two possibilities are given in parentheses, select the correct word.

LAS FIESTAS: Las fiestas (*ser/estar*[1]) populares (*en/entre*[2]) los jóvenes de todas partes. (*Este*[3]) diversión ofrece una (*bueno*[4]) oportunidad para (*ser/estar*[5]) con los amigos y conocer° a (*nuevo*[6]) personas. Imagine que Ud. (*ser/estar*[7]) en una fiesta hispánica en (*este*[8]) momento: todos (*ser/estar*[9]) comiendo, hablando y (*bailar*[10])... ¡y van a seguir° así° hasta (*mucho/muy*[11]) tarde!

to meet

to continue / that way

EL PASEO: (*Este*[12]) actividad social *no* (*ser/estar*[13]) típica de los Estados Unidos, pero sí (*ser/estar*[14]) una importante costumbre° (*hispánico*[15]) en los pueblos (*pequeño*[16]). Todos los (*domingo*[17]) por (*el/la*[18]) tarde los (*joven*[19])— y también (*muy/muchos*[20]) otras personas—van a la plaza principal donde (*caminar*° [21]) y (*conversar*[22]) con (*su*[23]) amigos. A veces (*ser/estar*[24]) posible escuchar° un concierto. En muchas ciudades, (*este*[25]) costumbre (*ser/estar*[26]) una actividad diaria° que tiene lugar° por (*el/la*[27]) tarde.

custom (f.)

to walk
to hear

daily / tiene… takes place

LA PANDILLA:° Ahora en (*el/la*[28]) mundo hispánico no (*ser/estar*[29]) necesario tener chaperona. Muchas de (*los/las*[30]) actividades sociales de los jóvenes se dan° en grupos. Si Ud. (*ser/estar*[31]) miembro de una pandilla, (*su*[32]) amigos (*ser/estar*[33]) el centro de (*su*[34]) vida social y Ud. y (*su*[35]) novio o novia salen° frecuentemente con otras parejas° o personas del grupo.

group of friends

se… ocurren
go out
couples

La Avenida 9 de Julio

Allan Cash/Rapho/Photo Researchers, Inc.

El Teatro Colón

David Kupferschmid

UN PASO MÁS: Imágenes del mundo hispánico

Buenos Aires

David Kupferschmid

*L*a capital de la Argentina, Buenos Aires es la ciudad más grande de Suramérica. Los «porteños», sus habitantes, consideran su ciudad la capital del hemisferio sur.

Además de las grandes avenidas, sus modernos edificios y barrios populares (como la «Boca»), sus calles comerciales, el puerto… Buenos Aires tiene una gran tradición artística. Hay que triunfar en Buenos Aires para ser realmente famoso en Hispanoamérica. Numerosos escritores argentinos describen esta multicolor ciudad en sus obras, entre ellos, Jorge Luis Borges, Julio Cortázar y Manuel Puig. Los tres son famosos en todo el mundo por sus novelas y cuentos (*short stories*).

Buenos Aires, la ciudad que nunca duerme (*sleeps*), está llena de sabor europeo. Sin duda, la mejor comida italiana – fuera de (*outside of*) Italia – está aquí. ¡Chau!

Gisèle Freund / Photo Researchers, Inc.

La Calle Florida

Jorge Luis Borges, 1899–1986

VOCABULARIO

VERBOS

tocar to play (*a musical instrument*)
viajar to travel

**LOS MOMENTOS DE
UNA RELACIÓN SENTIMENTAL**

la **amistad** friendship
el **amor** love
la **boda** wedding
la **cita** date
el **divorcio** divorce
la **luna de miel** honeymoon
el **matrimonio** marriage
el **noviazgo** engagement

OTROS SUSTANTIVOS

el **anillo** ring
el **boleto** ticket (*for a performance*)
el **cine** movie (theater)
el/la **dueño/a** owner
la **iglesia** church
el/la **novio/a** boyfriend/girlfriend;
    fiancé(e); groom/bride
la **película** movie

ADJETIVOS PARA PERSONAS

aburrido/a bored
alegre happy
cansado/a tired
cariñoso/a affectionate
contento/a happy
furioso/a furious
libre free, unoccupied
mayor older
menor younger
nervioso/a nervous
ocupado/a busy, occupied
preocupado/a worried
querido/a dear, beloved
triste sad

ADJETIVOS PARA COSAS

abierto/a open
cerrado/a closed
limpio/a clean
mejor better
peor worse
sucio/a dirty

PALABRAS ADICIONALES

está claro it's clear/obvious
luego later, next, then
porque because
todavía still, yet

FRASES ÚTILES PARA LA COMUNICACIÓN	
oye...	hey . . . listen . . .
lo siento	I'm sorry
estoy citado/a	I've got a prior engagement; I'm busy

Las estaciones del año y el tiempo

VOCABULARIO: PREPARACIÓN

Hace frío. Hace calor. Hace viento. Hace sol.

Está muy nublado. Llueve. Está lloviendo. Nieva. Está nevando. Hay mucha contaminación.

— EL TIEMPO / THE WEATHER —

Hace (mucho) frío (calor, viento, sol). It's (very) cold (hot, windy, sunny).
Hace fresco. It's cool.
Hace (muy) buen/mal tiempo. It's (very) good/bad weather. The weather is (very) good/bad.

Gustos y preferencias

—De todas las estaciones, ¿cuál es tu favorita?
—Creo que el otoño.
—¿El otoño? ¿Por qué?
—Porque hace calor durante el día y fresco durante la noche. Y porque llueve... ¡Me gusta la lluvia!

Aranjuez, España

A. Diga qué tiempo hace, según la ropa de cada persona.

1. San Diego: María lleva pantalones cortos y una camiseta.
2. Madison: Juan lleva suéter, pero no lleva chaqueta.
3. Toronto: Roberto lleva suéter y chaqueta.
4. Guanajuato: Ramón lleva impermeable y botas y también tiene paraguas (*umbrella*).
5. Buenos Aires: Todos llevan abrigo, botas y sombrero.

B. **¿Dónde debe vivir Joaquín?** Joaquín es de Valencia, España. El clima allí es moderado y hace mucho sol. Hay poca contaminación. Va a venir a los Estados Unidos y quiere vivir en un lugar con un clima similar. ¿Dónde debe—o *no* debe—vivir?

MODELO   Joaquín, (no) debes vivir en ____ porque allí ____.

1. Seattle   3. Phoenix   5. Buffalo
2. Los Ángeles   4. New Orleans   6. __?__

C. **¿Tienen frío o calor? ¿Están bien?** Describe the following weather conditions and tell how the people pictured are feeling.

1.   2.   3.   4.   5.   6.   7.

Los meses y las estaciones° del año   *seasons*

se(p)tiembre ⎫
octubre ⎬ **el otoño**
noviembre ⎭

marzo ⎫
abril ⎬ **la primavera**
mayo ⎭

diciembre ⎫
enero ⎬ **el invierno**
febrero ⎭

junio ⎫
julio ⎬ **el verano**
agosto ⎭

La fecha°   *date*

¿Cuál es la fecha de hoy?	What is today's date?
(Hoy) Es el primero de abril.	(Today) It is the first of April.
(Hoy) Es el cinco de febrero.	(Today) It is the fifth of February.

The ordinal number **primero** is used to express the first day of the month. Cardinal numbers (**dos, tres,** and so on) are used for the other days. The definite article **el** is used before the date. However, when the day of the week is expressed, **el** is omitted: **Hoy es jueves, tres de octubre.**

A. ¿Qué día de la semana es el 12 (1, 20, 16, 11, 4, 29) de noviembre?

B. Exprese estas fechas en español.

1. March 7
2. August 24
3. December 1
4. June 5
5. September 19, 1988
6. May 30, 1842
7. January 31, 1660
8. July 4, 1776

C. ¿Cuándo se celebran?

1. el Día de la Raza (*Columbus Day*)
2. el Día del Año Nuevo
3. el Día de los Enamorados (de San Valentín)
4. el Día de la Independencia de los Estados Unidos
5. el Día de los Inocentes (*Fools*) en los Estados Unidos
6. la Navidad (*Christmas*)

CH. Preguntas

1. ¿Cuál es la fecha de su cumpleaños (*birthday*)? ¿del cumpleaños de su mejor amigo/a? ¿de su novio/a (esposo/a)? ¿Cuándo se celebran los cumpleaños de Lincoln y Washington?
2. ¿Cuándo tenemos el examen final en esta clase? ¿en su clase de ___ ? ¿Cuál es la fecha del próximo examen de español? ¿Tiene Ud. una prueba (*quiz*) mañana? ¿pasado mañana?
3. ¿Cuándo entra el verano? ¿el invierno? ¿y la primavera? ¿Cuál es su estación favorita? ¿Por qué?

D. ¿Cómo se siente Ud. (*do you feel*) **cuando... ?** Complete las oraciones en una forma lógica.

1. En otoño generalmente estoy ____ porque ____ .
2. Cuando hace frío (calor) estoy ____ porque ____ .
3. En verano estoy ____ porque ____ .
4. Cuando llueve (nieva) estoy ____ porque ____ .

Expressing Actions: *Hacer, poner,* **and** *salir*

hacer *(to do; to make)*		poner *(to put; to place)*		salir *(to leave; to go out)*	
hago	hacemos	pongo	ponemos	salgo	salimos
haces	hacéis	pones	ponéis	sales	salís
hace	hacen	pone	ponen	sale	salen
haciendo		poniendo		saliendo	

Pero, niñõs, ¿qué hacen?

- *hacer:* ¿Por qué no **haces** los ejercicios?   *Why aren't you doing the exercises?*

Two common idioms with **hacer** are **hacer un viaje** (*to take a trip*) and **hacer una pregunta** (*to ask a question*).

Quieren hacer un viaje al Perú.   *They want to take a trip to Peru.*
Los niños siempre hacen muchas preguntas.   *Children always ask a lot of questions.*

- *poner:* Siempre **pongo** mucho azúcar en el café.   *I always put a lot of sugar in my coffee.*

With appliances, **poner** means *to turn on.*

Voy a **poner** el televisor.   *I'm going to turn on the TV.*

- *salir:* **Salen de** la clase ahora.   *They're leaving class now.*

Note that **salir** is always followed by **de** to express leaving a place. **Salir para** expresses destination. **Salir con** can mean *to go out with, to date.*

Salimos para la playa mañana.   *We're leaving for the beach tomorrow.*
Salgo con el hermano de Cecilia.   *I'm going out with Cecilia's brother.*

A. ¿Qué hacemos por la noche? Dé oraciones nuevas según las indicaciones.

1. *Alfonso* hace ejercicio en el gimnasio. (*tú, Raúl, yo, Lilia y yo, Uds., vosotros*)
2. *Susana* sale de clase a las ocho. (*yo, tú, nosotros, Ud., Ernesto, vosotros*)
3. Ponemos el televisor a las nueve. (*Gabriela, yo, tú, nosotras, Uds., vosotras*)

B. **Consecuencias lógicas.** ¿Qué puede pasar si se dan (*exist*) estas condiciones? Use las siguientes frases en su respuesta.

poner el aire acondicionador/   salir de/para…
   la calefacción (*heat*)   hacer un viaje a…
poner el televisor/la radio   hacer una pregunta

1. Me gusta esquiar. Por eso…
2. Tengo frío y hace frío afuera (*outside*). Por eso…
3. Tenemos calor y hace calor afuera. Por eso…
4. Hay un programa interesante en la televisión.
5. ¡Estoy cansada de trabajar!
6. Estamos aburridos.
7. Quiero escuchar (*to listen to*) música y bailar.
8. No comprendo.

C. Preguntas

1. ¿Qué pone Ud. en el café? ¿en el té? ¿en una limonada? ¿Pone Ud. hielo (*ice*) en los refrescos (*soft drinks*) en invierno? ¿en verano?

En la biblioteca: Hablan dos compañeras de cuarto.

—¿Hace mucho frío hoy, ¿verdad?
—Sí. Hace dos horas que nieva.
—¿Por qué no regresamos a la residencia temprano esta tarde?
—Lo siento, pero no puedo. Tengo que estudiar más.

Peter Menzel/Stock, Boston

2. ¿Qué hace Ud. en verano? ¿en invierno? ¿el día de su cumpleaños? ¿en setiembre? ¿los sábados?

3. ¿Qué quiere Ud. hacer esta noche? ¿Qué necesita hacer? ¿Qué va a hacer? ¿Va a salir con sus amigos? ¿Adónde van?

4. ¿A qué hora sale Ud. de la clase de español? ¿de otras clases? ¿A veces sale tarde de clase? ¿Por qué? ¿Le gusta salir temprano? ¿Siempre sale Ud. temprano para la universidad? ¿Sale tarde a veces?

PRONUNCIACIÓN: ñ

The consonant **ñ** is called a *palatal* because it is produced with the middle of the tongue against the hard palate (the roof of the mouth). The **ñ** resembles the [ny] sound of English *canyon* and *union*, but it is a single sound, not an [n] followed by a [y].

Práctica

A. cana/caña   mono/moño   sonar/soñar   tino/tiño   pena/peña
una/uña   lena/leña   cena/seña

B. año   señora   cañón   español   pequeña   compañero

C. El señor Muñoz es de España.
Los niños pequeños no enseñan español.
La señorita Ordóñez tiene veinte años.

MINIDIÁLOGOS Y ESTRUCTURA

¿Recuerda Ud.?

The change in the stem vowels of **querer** and **poder** (**e** and **o,** respectively) follows the same pattern as that of the verbs in the next section. Review the forms of **querer** and **poder** before beginning that section.

querer: **e** → ?		poder: **o** → ?	
qu__ro	queremos	p__do	podemos
qu__res	queréis	p__des	podéis
qu__re	qu__ren	p__de	p__den

16 Expressing Actions
Present Tense of Stem-changing Verbs

Haciendo planes

PADRE: Mira, Esteban, *empiezo* a perder la paciencia contigo.
No comprendo por qué no *quieres* hacer este viaje a
Sudamérica con nosotros.

ESTEBAN: Estoy muy bien aquí...

MADRE: Pero, hijo, aquí *nieva* todos los días y allí hace muy buen
tiempo ahora. ¡Con lo que a ti te gusta nadar... !

ESTEBAN: Pero es que aquí *jugamos* al básquetbol en invierno y si
nosotros no *volvemos* hasta febrero *pierdo* el campeonato.
Prefiero no ir.

PADRE: Lo *siento*,* Esteban, pero no *pensamos* dejarte aquí. ¡Y se acabó!

1. ¿Adónde va la familia?
2. ¿Qué tiempo hace este mes donde viven? ¿Y en Sudamérica?
3. ¿A qué juegan los amigos de Esteban en invierno?
4. ¿Qué va a perder Esteban si acompaña a sus padres?
5. En la opinión de Ud., ¿qué va a decir (say) ahora Esteban?
   · Bueno, está claro que no tengo alternativa.
   · ¿No puedo volver un poco antes que Uds.?
   · ¡No quiero ir y no voy!

e → ie	o (u) → ue	e → i
pensar (ie) *(to think)*	**volver (ue)** *(to return)*	**pedir (i)** *(to ask for, order)*
pienso pensamos piensas pensáis piensa piensan pensando	vuelvo volvemos vuelves volvéis vuelve vuelven volviendo	pido pedimos pides pedís pide piden pidiendo

---

Making plans   *FATHER: Look, Esteban, I'm starting to lose patience with you. I don't understand why you don't want to take this trip to South America with us.*   ESTEBAN: *I'm just fine here . . .*   MOTHER: *But son, here it's snowing every day, and there the weather is very nice now. Considering how much you like to swim . . . !*   ESTEBAN: *But it's just that we play basketball here in the winter and if we don't come back until February, I'll miss the championship game. I'd rather not go.*   FATHER: *I'm sorry, Esteban, but we don't intend to leave you here. And that's that!*

***Siento** is the first-person singular form of the stem-changing verb **sentir** *(to regret)*. You will learn to use other forms of **sentir** in later chapters of *¿Qué tal?*.

A. You have already learned three *stem-changing verbs* **(los verbos que cambian el radical): querer, preferir,** and **poder.** In these verbs the stem vowels **e** and **o** become **ie** and **ue,** respectively, in stressed syllables. The stem vowels are stressed in all present-tense forms except **nosotros** and **vosotros.** All three classes of stem-changing verbs follow this regular pattern in the present tense. In vocabulary lists the stem change will always be shown in parentheses after the infinitive: **volver (ue).**

Some stem-changing verbs practiced in this chapter include the following.

e → ie		o (u) → ue		e → i	
cerrar (ie)	*to close*	almorzar (ue)	*to have lunch*	pedir (i)	*to ask for, order*
empezar (ie)	*to begin*	dormir (ue)	*to sleep*	servir (i)	*to serve*
pensar (ie)	*to think*	jugar (ue)*	*to play (a game, sports)*		
perder (ie)	*to lose; to miss (a function)*	volver (ue)	*to return*		

[Práctica A–C]

B. When used with an infinitive, **empezar** is followed by **a.**

Uds. **empiezan a hablar** muy
   bien el español.

*You're beginning to speak
   Spanish very well.*

When followed directly by an infinitive, **pensar** means *to intend, plan to.*

¿Cuándo **piensas contestar** la carta?

*When do you intend to
   answer the letter?*

C. The stem vowels in the present participle of **-ir** stem-changing verbs also show a change. When listed in the vocabulary, all **-ir** stem-changing verbs will show two stem changes in parentheses: **dormir (ue, u).** The first stem change occurs in the present tense, the second in the present participle.

dormir (ue, **u**) → durmiendo   preferir (ie, **i**) → prefiriendo
pedir (i, **i**) → pidiendo   servir (i, **i**) → sirviendo

[Práctica CH–E]

Práctica

    A. Es verano y hace buen tiempo. ¿Cuáles son las actividades de todos? Dé oraciones nuevas según las indicaciones.

*****Jugar** is the only **u** → **ue** stem-changing verb in Spanish. **Jugar** is often followed by **al** when used with the name of a sport: **Juego** *al* **tenis.** Some Spanish speakers, however, omit the **al.**

1. *Sara y Anita* almuerzan en el patio. (*Ud., nuestros hijos, nosotros, tú, yo, vosotros*)
2. *Felipe* pide un refresco. (*yo, nosotros, ellos, Lisa, tú, vosotras*)
3. *Yo* prefiero descansar en la playa (*beach*). (*Sergio, nosotros, Ana, ellas, tú, vosotras*)
4. *El equipo* (*team*) pierde muchos partidos (*games*). (*ellos, yo, Fernando, tú, los niños, vosotros*)
5. *Los González* vuelven de su viaje el sábado. (*yo, nosotras, mis primas, Manuel, tú, vosotros*)

B. ¿Qué prefieren?

MODELO   Ignacio pide café, pero nosotros *pedimos* un refresco. →

1. Tomás y Julia piensan viajar a Sudamérica este otoño, pero nosotros ⎯⎯ viajar a España.
2. Tú vuelves a la estación (*station*) mañana, pero nosotros ⎯⎯ allí el jueves.
3. Nosotros empezamos a trabajar a las ocho, pero Reynaldo ⎯⎯ a las nueve.
4. Nosotros dormimos ocho horas todas las noches, pero Lucía sólo ⎯⎯ seis horas.
5. Nosotros servimos comida mexicana en casa y Susana también ⎯⎯ comida mexicana, especialmente en las fiestas.
6. Nosotros jugamos al tenis hoy y Paula ⎯⎯ con nosotros.
7. Tú cierras la tienda a las ocho, pero nosotros no ⎯⎯ hasta las diez.
8. María y Teresa prefieren esquiar en Vail, pero nosotros ⎯⎯ ir a Aspen.

C. Using the following verbs as a guide, tell about a visit to a restaurant. Use **yo** as the subject except where otherwise indicated.

1. pensar comer comida española
2. entrar en un restaurante en la calle Bolívar
3. pedir el menú
4. preferir comer paella, un plato español
5. no servir comida española (ellos)
6. pedir tacos y un refresco
7. servir la comida en diez minutos (ellos)
8. comer y volver a casa
9. dormir la siesta porque hacer calor

CH. Hace frío hoy y hay mucha nieve. Por eso todos están en casa. Son las tres de la tarde. ¿Qué están haciendo estas personas? Haga oraciones según las indicaciones.

1. niños / mirar la televisión
2. papá / pedir la comida
3. Pepito y Carlos / jugar / en sus cuartos
4. el perro / dormir en el sofá
5. mamá / empezar / perder la paciencia

D. ¿A qué hora...
1. se cierra la biblioteca?
2. se cierran las tiendas en los Estados Unidos?
3. empieza Ud. a estudiar todas las noches?
4. empieza Ud. a comer?
5. vuelve Ud. a casa?
6. almuerza Ud., por lo general?
7. piensa Ud. almorzar hoy?

E. Situaciones. Ask two other students the following questions. They should decide on an answer between them and reply using the **nosotros** form.
1. ¿Qué prefieren Uds., las clases fáciles o las difíciles? ¿hacer preguntas o contestar en clase? ¿hablar en español o en inglés?
2. ¿Prefieren Uds. la tequila con limón o sin limón? ¿el café con azúcar o sin azúcar? ¿la Coca-Cola con hielo o sin hielo? ¿beber agua (*water*) o cerveza cuando hace mucho calor? ¿la comida norteamericana o la extranjera? ¿la mexicana o la italiana?
3. ¿Qué prefieren Uds., viajar en autobús o en tren? ¿tomar las vacaciones en verano o en invierno?
4. ¿Mañana juegan Uds. al golf o al fútbol? ¿al tenis o al béisbol?
5. ¿Qué piensan Uds. de (*about*) la clase de español? (**Pensamos que** [*that*]...) ¿del profesor (de la profesora)? ¿de su universidad?
6. ¿Prefieren Uds. los perros grandes o los pequeños? ¿los gatos siameses o los persas?
7. ¿Prefieren los coches americanos o los extranjeros? ¿los japoneses o los italianos?
8. ¿Prefieren la música clásica o la moderna? ¿las películas dramáticas o las cómicas?

17 El infinitivo
Preposition + Infinitive: Another Use of the Present Tense

Una diferencia de opinión

ELLA: ...y luego, *después de almorzar*, podemos *volver a esquiar*.

ÉL: Pero, Angélica, hace cuatro horas que esquiamos... Ya me caí cuatro veces... *Acabo de perder* un guante... *Empieza a nevar* otra vez... ¡Sólo *tengo ganas de descansar*!

ELLA: Pero, hombre, ¡hay que aprovechar cada momento! ¿Cuándo *vamos a estar* aquí otra vez?

ÉL: Pues... si me salgo con la mía... ¡nunca!

A difference of opinion SHE: . . . and then, after having lunch, we can go skiing again. HE: But, Angélica, we've been skiing for four hours . . . I've already fallen four times . . . I've just lost a glove . . . It's starting to snow again . . . I only feel like resting! SHE: But my goodness, we have to take advantage of every moment! When are we going to be here again? HE: Well . . . if I have my way about it . . . never!

La opinión de él	La opinión de ella
1. ¡Ay, acabo de perder _____ !	**1.** ¡Qué gusto! Empieza a _____ .
2. Antes de esquiar más, tengo ganas de _____ .	**2.** Después de almorzar, quiero volver a _____ .
3. ¡Nunca vamos a _____ !	**3.** Para las próximas vacaciones, vamos a _____ .

Preposition + Infinitive

The infinitive is the only verb form that can follow a preposition in Spanish. You have already learned to use the following constructions in which prepositions are followed by infinitives: **ir a, empezar a,** and **tener ganas de.** Two other important expressions with prepositions are **acabar de** + *infinitive* (*to have just done something*) and **volver a** + *infinitive* (*to do something again*).

Acabamos de almorzar con Tina.	*We've just eaten lunch with Tina.*
Acabo de perder mi anillo.	*I've just lost my ring.*
Vuelven a cerrar las puertas.	*They're closing the doors again.*
La niña **vuelve a pedir** dulces.	*The little girl is asking for candy again.*

Remember to use the infinitive after the temporal prepositions **antes de** and **después de**. Note that the English equivalent of the infinitive after these prepositions is often *-ing*.

Antes de esquiar, vamos a descansar.	*Before skiing, let's rest.*
Después de estudiar, vamos al cine.	*After studying, let's go to the movies.*

Another Use of the Present Tense

As you saw in the minidialogue, you can use **hace** + *period of time* + **que** + *the present tense* in Spanish to express an action that has been going on over a period of time and is still going on.

Hace dos horas que nieva.	*It's been snowing for two hours.*
Hace ocho semanas que estudio español.	*I've been studying Spanish for eight weeks.*
¿Cuánto tiempo hace que vives aquí?	*How long have you been living here?*

There are no exercises in this section that specifically practice the preceding construction. It will be used, however, in dialogues and in questions where its use is natural. Be alert to occurrences of the construction and simply follow the lead of the dialogue or question when you formulate your answer.

Práctica

A. Es verano y todos están de vacaciones. ¿Qué acaba de pasar? Haga oraciones según las indicaciones.

MODELO   los Gutiérrez / salir de viaje →
Los Gutiérrez acaban de salir de viaje.

1. Benjamín y su hermana / llegar desde (*from*) Salt Lake, ¿verdad?
2. Felipe y yo / jugar al béisbol
3. mis abuelos / escribir que vienen a visitarme
4. Silvia / salir para la playa con Ernesto
5. ¿tú / volver del centro?
6. yo / comprar un traje de baño nuevo

B. **Reacciones.** Ud. está en los siguientes lugares o situaciones. ¿Qué quiere volver a hacer?

MODELO   Ud. está en una discoteca con unos amigos. Están hablando ahora, pero empiezan a tocar una música encantadora. → ¡Quiero volver a bailar!

1. Ud. está en las montañas. Hace cuatro horas que esquía. Está descansando ahora, pero empieza a nevar.
2. Ud. está en la playa. Acaba de nadar (*to swim*) un poco, pero ahora está tomando el sol. ¡Hace mucho calor!
3. Ud. está en la cama (*bed*). Son las seis de la mañana y acaba de sonar (*to ring*) el despertador (*alarm clock*). Ud. todavía tiene sueño.
4. Ud. está en la clase de historia y acaba de sacar (*to receive*) una D en un examen.
5. Ud. está mirando un programa interesante en la tele y su amigo Julio llama por teléfono. Ud. contesta.
6. Ud. está en un restaurante con unos amigos. Acaban de comer unos platos estupendos.

C. **Entrevistas.** Pregúntele a otro/a estudiante...

• qué acaba de hacer si sale de los siguientes lugares.

MODELO   un restaurante →
—Si sales de un restaurante, ¿qué acabas de hacer?
—Acabo de comer.

1. una playa   3. una librería   5. un mercado
2. una discoteca 4. una tienda de ropa

- dónde está si acaba de hacer las siguientes cosas.

MODELO almorzar → —¿Dónde estás si acabas de almorzar?
                    —Estoy en la cafetería.

1. ver (*to see*) una película
2. escribir los ejercicios de español
3. escuchar música en la radio
4. dormir ocho horas
5. hacer una pregunta en español
6. salir para la universidad

CH. Complete las oraciones en una forma lógica.
  1. Después de estudiar, siempre me gusta_____ .
  2. Antes de hablar bien una lengua extranjera, es necesario_____ .
  3. Después de bailar mucho, a veces tengo ganas de_____ .
  4. Después de tomar un examen, me gusta_____ .
  5. Antes de ir al cine, siempre prefiero_____ .
  6. Después de comer en un restaurante, es necesario_____ .

REPASO

Dos hemisferios. Complete the following paragraphs with the correct form of the words in parentheses, as suggested by the context. When two possibilities are given in parentheses, select the correct word.

Hay (*mucho*[1]) diferencias entre el clima del hemisferio norte y el del hemisferio sur. Cuando (*ser/estar*[2]) invierno en los Estados Unidos, por ejemplo, (*ser/estar*[3]) verano en la Argentina, en Bolivia, en Chile…. Cuando yo (*salir*[4]) para la universidad en enero, con frecuencia tengo que (*llevar*[5]) abrigo y botas. En (*los/las*[6]) países del hemisferio sur, un estudiante (*poder*[7]) asistir (*a/de*[8]) clases en enero llevando sólo pantalones (*corto*[9]), camiseta y sandalias. En muchas partes de los Estados Unidos, cuando (*nosotros: ser/estar*[10]) (*de/en*[11]) vacaciones en diciembre, casi siempre (*hacer*[12]) frío y a veces (*nevar*[13]). En (*grande*[14]) parte de Sudamérica, al otro lado del ecuador, hace calor y (*muy/mucho*[15]) sol durante (*ese*[16]) mes. A veces en enero hay fotos, en los periódicos, de personas que están (*tomar*[17]) el sol y (*nadar*[18]) en las playas latinoamericanas.

Tengo un amigo que acaba de (*hacer/tomar*[19]) un viaje a Buenos Aires. Él me dice° que allí la Navidad (*ser/estar*[20]) una fiesta de verano y que todos (*llevar*[21]) ropa como la que° llevamos nosotros en julio. Parece increíble, ¿verdad?

Él… *He tells me*
la… *that which*

Study Hint: Using a Bilingual Dictionary

A Spanish-English/English-Spanish dictionary or vocabulary list is an excellent study aid, but one that should be used carefully. Follow these guidelines to minimize the pitfalls.

1. If you are looking for a Spanish word in the Spanish-English part of the dictionary, remember that in the Spanish alphabet the letters **ch, ll,** and **ñ** follow the letters **c, l,** and **n,** respectively. The word **coche** is found after the word **cocina; calle** comes after **calma;** and **caña** follows **candidato.**

2. When you look in the English-Spanish section for the Spanish equivalent of an English word, keep in mind the part of speech—noun, verb, adjective, and so on—of the word you are looking for. By doing so, you will avoid many mistakes. Imagine the confusion that would arise if you chose the wrong word in the following cases:

light: **luz** (noun, *electric light, daylight*) but **ligero** (adjective, *light, not heavy*) and **claro** (adjective, *light in color*)

can: **lata** (noun, *tin can*) but **poder** (verb, *can, to be able*)

3. If the Spanish word that you find is unfamiliar to you, or if you simply want to check its meaning and usage, look up the new word in the Spanish-English section of the dictionary. Do the English equivalents given there correspond to the meaning you want to convey?

4. Remember that there is rarely a one-to-one equivalency between Spanish and English words. **Jugar** means *to play* a sport or game, but the verb **tocar** must be used to talk about playing a musical instrument. **Un periódico** is a paper (a *news*paper) and **un papel** is a *sheet* of paper.

5. Minimize the number of "dictionary words" you use when writing in Spanish. Limit yourself to words you know because you have used them in class. When you do have to use the dictionary, try to check your word choice with your instructor or someone else who knows Spanish.

UN PASO MÁS: Lectura cultural

Antes de leer

Guessing the meaning of a word from context is easier if it has a recognizable root or a relation to another word that you already know. For example, if you know **estudiar,** you should be able to guess the meaning of **los estudios** and **estudioso/a** quite easily in context. Can you guess the meaning of these words?

la pobreza	La pobreza es un problema muy grave en muchas partes de la India y de Latinoamérica.
la enseñanza	Muchos datos indican que la calidad de la enseñanza en los Estados Unidos es inferior a la del año 1960.
lluvioso	En las zonas tropicales el clima es lluvioso.

If you know the meaning of the following words, you will be able to guess the meaning of the words related to them that you will encounter in the reading: **división, llover** and **lluvioso, variación, nevar, respiración, duración, alto.**

La geografía y el clima de Hispanoamérica

El hemisferio occidental se divide en dos continentes: América del Norte y América del Sur. La América Central no es un continente. Es parte de la América del Norte. Las Antillas, cadena° de islas en el Mar Caribe, también forman parte de la América Central. *chain*

En las diferentes zonas del mundo hispánico, hay también climas diferentes. En los extremos geográficos (México al norte, la Argentina y Chile al sur) hay cuatro estaciones: primavera, verano, otoño e° invierno. En los países tropicales (desde la parte central de México hasta la parte norte de Chile) el clima alterna entre temporadas° lluviosas y secas. Es común en Latinoamérica llamar a la temporada de lluvias «invierno», y a la temporada seca «verano». En este sentido,° «el invierno» en Guayaquil, Ecuador llega dos veces: una vez en mayo y otra vez en octubre. En el trópico la temperatura no varía con los meses del año sino° con la altura. Hay tierras cálidas,° templadas y frías.
y
estaciones
sense
but rather
hot

La cordillera de los Andes bordea el Océano Pacífico a todo lo largo° de la América del Sur. Es una zona sísmica muy activa. Los Andes son la mayor cadena de montañas del mundo. Algunos picos son tan altos que están cubiertos de nieve todo el año, aunque° algunos de ellos están muy cerca de la línea ecuatorial. El punto más alto del hemisferio occidental es el pico del Aconcagua, en la Argentina, a 6959 metros° sobre el nivel del mar.
a... the whole length
although
22.834 pies

Si usted viaja a una de las ciudades más altas de Sudamérica y no está acostumbrado a vivir en estas alturas, al principio le va a ser difícil a su organismo° acomodarse a la altitud. Si usted camina° a paso normal dos o tres cuadras,° va a sentir° que su cuerpo necesita más oxígeno y que le es difícil respirar bien. También va a notar más el efecto del alcohol sobre su cuerpo. Pero estos efectos no duran más que dos o tres semanas. Luego usted puede hacer todo: caminar, bailar y practicar deportes.
al...it's going to be hard at first for your body / walk
blocks / feel

Comprensión

¿Probable o improbable?

1. Un turista de Nueva York puede esquiar y nadar desde el principio de sus vacaciones en los Andes.
2. La gente (*people*) que vive en los Andes tiene pulmones (*lungs*) más grandes que los de los habitantes de Los Ángeles.
3. El clima no varía mucho en lugares como la Argentina y Chile.
4. Muchos geólogos (personas que estudian geología) tienen mucho interés en la zona de los Andes.

Para escribir

A. Write a brief paragraph introducing a Latin American to the geography and climate of the United States. You may want to give an overview, or you may prefer to describe the area in which you live. Some of the following questions may help you to organize your ideas.

1. ¿Hay mucha variedad geográfica en los Estados Unidos?
2. ¿Cuáles son algunos diferentes fenómenos geográficos de los Estados Unidos? ¿Dónde están situados? En su opinión, ¿uno de estos fenómenos es más interesante (hermoso [*beautiful*], importante) que los otros? ¿Cuál es? ¿Por qué?
3. ¿Cómo es el clima de los Estados Unidos? ¿Hay mucha variedad? ¿Dónde hay extremos de clima?
4. ¿Qué tiempo hace en el estado en el que (*which*) vive? ¿Cuándo llegan las diferentes estaciones?
5. ¿Cómo afectan las estaciones la vida en las diferentes regiones del país?
6. ¿Prefiere Ud. vivir en su estado o en otra parte del país? ¿Por qué?

B. Write a brief paragraph about your favorite season by completing the following sentences. Describe your attitudes and activities during this season, as well as the weather.

Yo prefiero _____ porque _____ . Durante esta estación _____ .

8-1 © King Features Syndicate, Inc., 1978. World rights reserved.

Te digo,° Mabel, que es necesario un día como éste para saber° apreciar la vida.

Te... *I tell you*
to know how to

VOCABULARIO

VERBOS

almorzar (ue) to have lunch
cerrar (ie) to close
dormir (ue, u) to sleep
empezar (ie) (a) to begin
escuchar to listen to
esquiar to ski
hacer (*irreg.*) to do; to make
jugar (ue) to play (*a game, sport*)
llover (ue) to rain
nadar to swim
nevar (ie) to snow
pedir (i, i) to ask for, order
pensar (ie) to think; to intend, plan to
perder (ie) to lose; to miss (*a function*)
poner (*irreg.*) to put; to place; to turn on (*lights or appliances*)
salir (*irreg.*) **(de)** to leave; to go out
servir (i, i) to serve
volver (ue) to return

LOS MESES DEL AÑO

enero, febrero, marzo, abril, mayo, junio, julio, agosto, se(p)tiembre, octubre, noviembre, diciembre

LAS ESTACIONES DEL AÑO

el invierno winter
el otoño fall
la primavera spring
el verano summer

LA FECHA

¿cuál es la fecha de hoy? what is today's date?
es el primero (dos,...) de it's the first (second, . . .) of

EL TIEMPO

está lloviendo it's raining
está nevando it's snowing
está nublado it's cloudy, overcast
hace...
 (muy) buen/mal tiempo it's (very) good/bad weather
 calor/frío/fresco it's hot/cold/cool
 sol it's sunny
 viento it's windy
hay (mucha) contaminación there's (a lot of) pollution
¿qué tiempo hace? what's the weather like?

LOS SUSTANTIVOS

el azúcar sugar
el cumpleaños birthday
el hielo ice
la Navidad Christmas
la playa beach
el refresco soft drink
el televisor television set
la vez (*pl.* **veces**) time, occasion

PALABRAS ADICIONALES

acabar de + *inf.* to have just (*done something*)
afuera outside
estar de vacaciones to be on vacation
hacer un viaje to take a trip
hacer una pregunta to ask a question
volver a + *inf.* to (*do something*) again

FRASES ÚTILES PARA LA COMUNICACIÓN

¿Qué piensas de... ?	What do you think about . . . ?
Pienso que...	I think that . . .
¿Cuánto tiempo hace que (vives aquí)?	How long have you been (living here)?
Hace dos años que (vivo aquí).	I've been (living here) for two years.

UN POCO DE TODO 2

A. **En esta foto familiar...** Imagine that the following persons are in a family photograph. Identify them and give one detail about them according to the model, using either **ser** or **estar**.

MODELO   abuelo: México → Éste es mi abuelo. Es de México.

1. madre: doctora
2. padre: una persona muy generosa
3. tías Elena y Eugenia: en España este año
4. novio/a: mirando fotos conmigo
5. abuela: muy vieja pero simpática
6. perro: contento porque está con la familia

B. **¿Qué llevas en tu maleta (*suitcase*)?** With another student, ask and answer questions based on the places listed below. Follow the model, providing appropriate weather information.

MODELO   San Francisco / impermeable →
          —¿Piensas hacer un viaje a <u>San Francisco</u>?
          —Sí, salgo para allí el ____ .
          —¿Cuánto tiempo hace que planeas el viaje?
          —Un año.
          —¿No hace (mucho) ____ allí en ____ ?
          —Sí, por eso pienso llevar mi <u>impermeable</u>.

1. Mallorca / traje de baño
2. el Polo Norte / suéteres
3. San Juan, Puerto Rico / camisetas
4. Vermont / abrigo
5. Acapulco / raqueta de tenis

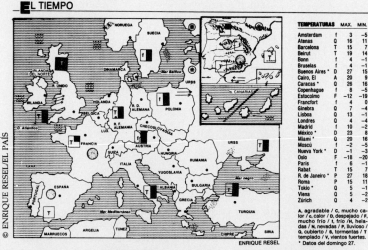

TEMPERATURAS		MAX.	MIN.
Amsterdam	f	3	−5
Atenas	Q	16	11
Barcelona	T	15	7
Beirut	T	19	14
Bonn	f	4	−1
Bruselas	f	4	−1
Buenos Aires *	D	27	15
Cairo, El	A	20	9
Caracas *	Q	26	16
Copenhague	f	8	−5
Estocolmo	F	−12	−19
Francfort	f	4	0
Ginebra	Q	7	−4
Lisboa	Q	13	−1
Londres	Q	4	−4
Madrid	f	10	−2
México *	D	23	8
Miami *	Q	20	16
Moscú	f	−2	−5
Nueva York *	D	−1	−3
Oslo	F	−18	−20
París	f	6	−1
Rabat	T	15	7
R. de Janeiro *	P	27	18
Roma	P	15	11
Tokio *	Q	5	−1
Viena	Q	5	−2
Zúrich	Q	4	−2

A, agradable / C, mucho calor / c, calor / D, despejado / F, mucho frío / t, frío /H, heladas / N, nevadas / P, lluvioso / Q, cubierto / 8, tormentas / V, templado / V, vientos fuertes.
* Datos del domingo 27.

© ENRIQUE RESEL/EL PAÍS

ENRIQUE RESEL

Subirán ligeramente las temperaturas

C. **¿Somos tan diferentes?** Answer the following questions. Then ask the same question of other students in the class to find at least one person who answered a given question the way you did.

1. ¿A qué hora almuerzas generalmente, y dónde?
2. ¿Adónde piensas ir hoy después de la clase?
3. ¿Estás triste cuando llueve? ¿Qué haces cuando llueve?
4. ¿Qué estación del año prefieres? ¿Por qué?
5. ¿Qué día prefieres, el lunes o el sábado? ¿Por qué?
6. ¿Cuánto tiempo hace que vives en esta ciudad?
7. Generalmente, ¿cuántas horas duermes todas las noches?
8. ¿Cuántos hermanos tienes en total? ¿Son mayores o menores que tú?

CH. Entrevista: Los deportes. How interested are you and your classmates in sports? Are you active participants or do you prefer to watch? Use the following questions to interview another student. Take notes and report what you learn to the class.

1. ¿Juegas al béisbol? ¿al vólibol? ¿al básquetbol? ¿al fútbol norteamericano? ¿al fútbol? De estos deportes, ¿cuál es tu favorito? ¿Con quiénes practicas este deporte?
2. ¿Juegas al tenis? ¿al ping pong? ¿al golf? ¿Cuál prefieres?
3. En invierno, ¿qué prefieres, jugar en la nieve, patinar (*skate*) o esquiar?
4. ¿Te gusta correr (*run*)? ¿pasear en bicicleta? ¿nadar? ¿Cuál prefieres?
5. ¿Qué deportes se ven en la televisión? ¿Cuáles miras tú con frecuencia? ¿Cuál es tu favorito?
6. En tu opinión, ¿uno de los deportes es más peligroso (*dangerous*) que los otros? ¿Cuál? ¿Uno es más violento que los otros? ¿más interesante? ¿más aburrido? ¿más sano (*healthful*) que los otros?

A propósito...

Here are a number of phrases that will be useful when you go shopping.

Vendedor(a):

¿Qué desea Ud.?	
¿En qué puedo servirle?	*Can I help you?*
Dígame.	
¿Qué talla necesita?	*What size do you need? (clothing)*
¿Qué número necesita?	*What size do you need? (shoes)*
¿De qué color?	*What color?*
No hay. No tenemos.	*We don't have any.*
Lo siento.	*I'm sorry.*
No nos quedan.	*We don't have any left.*

Cliente:

Deseo comprar un regalo para...	*I want to buy a gift for . . .*
¿Tienen Uds...?	*Do you have . . . ?*
¿Cuánto es/son? ¿Cuánto vale(n)?	*How much is it/are they?*
¿Qué precio tiene(n)?	
Es muy caro/a.	*It's very expensive.*
Necesito algo más barato.	*I need something cheaper.*
¿Se aceptan tarjetas de crédito?	*Do you take credit cards?*

D. De compras. Although it is often possible—and lots of fun— to bargain over the price of an item in a shop or open-air market, merchandise is normally sold at a fixed price in many, if not most, Hispanic stores.

With your instructor acting as the salesperson, try to make the purchases described in one of the following situations. Use the phrases and expressions from **A propósito...** as a model. Not everyone will get the chance to act out a shopping scene, so pay close attention to how your classmates interact with the salesperson to see if you would have said or done the same thing. You may have to make some educated guesses about what the native-speaking salesperson says.

1. Ud. está en un almacén de Bogotá (Colombia). Desea comprar un suéter para su mamá. Quiere un color y un estilo específicos.
2. Ud. está en un almacén de Madrid. Necesita comprar un traje elegante/un vestido de noche para asistir a una fiesta muy elegante.
3. Ud. está en un almacén de la Ciudad de México. Necesita comprar los siguientes objetos, pero no sabe (*you don't know*) las palabras en español.
   a. shoelaces   **b.** an umbrella   **c.** a bow tie   **ch.** tennis shoes

Now, with another student, take the roles of customer and salesperson in the following situations. Use the phrases from **A propósito...** as well as strategies that you learned from the preceding dialogues.

4. En la librería de la universidad: Ud. desea comprar dos cuadernos pequeños.
5. En una tienda pequeña: Ud. desea comprar una blusa azul para su hermana (madre, amiga, tía).
6. En un almacén: Ud. quiere comprar un regalo para un amigo.
7. En una tienda de flores: Ud. necesita comprar seis rosas rojas.

E. Situaciones sociales. Listen as your instructor role-plays each of the following situations with one or more students. Pay close attention to how your classmates interact with your instructor to see if you would have said or done the same thing. You may have to make some educated guesses about what your instructor says as he or she plays the situation. After you have watched each of the situations at least once, act out the situations with another student. Try to use as much of the vocabulary that you know as possible.

1. Your best friend has just invited you to go downtown with him or her. Find out what time you will leave, where you will go, what you will do, and all other pertinent information.
2. You have gone to a department store to buy some clothing. Explain to the salesclerk exactly what you are looking for.
3. You have become friendly in class with a person of the opposite sex, but you have never dated that person. Now you want to invite him or her to a party at your dormitory or home next Saturday night. Arrange a time and place to meet and discuss the kind of clothing to wear.
4. You are a travel agent (**un[a] agente de viajes**) in the northern part of Spain. A customer comes to you in January asking for information about the weather in New York, Buenos Aires, and Acapulco.

CAPÍTULO 9

¿Qué vamos a pedir?

La comida

las bebidas

el café   el té   el refresco   el jugo (de fruta)
la leche   la cerveza   el vino blanco   el vino tinto

la carne

el jamón   el pollo
el bistec   las chuletas
la hamburguesa   (de cerdo)

los mariscos

los camarones
la langosta
el pescado

las verduras

las papas (fritas)   la zanahoria   los frijoles   las arvejas

otros platos y comidas

la ensalada (de lechuga y tomate)   la sopa   los huevos
el arroz   el pan   el queso   el sándwich

la fruta

la manzana   la naranja   la banana

los postres

el pastel   el helado   el flan   la galleta

169

Después de la cena

—Camarero, para mí el pastel con helado de chocolate.
—Muy bien, señora. ¿Y para Ud., señor?
—Voy a probar (*try*) el flan.
—Muy bien, señor. Está muy rico* hoy.

Toledo, España

A. **Definiciones.** ¿Qué es esto?

1. Un líquido caliente (*hot*) que se toma† con cuchara (*spoon*)
2. Un plato de lechuga y tomate
3. Una bebida alcohólica blanca o roja
4. Una verdura anaranjada
5. La carne típica para barbacoa en los Estados Unidos
6. Una comida muy común en la China y el Japón
7. La comida favorita de los ratones
8. Una verdura frita que se come con las hamburguesas
9. Una fruta roja o verde
10. Una fruta amarilla de las zonas tropicales
11. Un líquido de color blanco que se sirve especialmente a los niños
12. La bebida tradicional de los ingleses
13. Se usa para preparar sándwiches
14. Un postre muy frío
15. Un postre que se sirve en las fiestas de cumpleaños
16. Una cosa que se come y que tiene el centro amarillo y el resto blanco

B. ¿Qué se debe (*should one*) comer o beber...

1. cuando se quiere comer algo ligero (*something light*)?
2. cuando se quiere comer algo fuerte (*something heavy*)?
3. antes del plato (*dish*) principal?
4. después del plato principal?
5. cuando se tiene mucha sed (*thirsty*)?
6. cuando se está a dieta (*on a diet*)?
7. cuando se es vegetariano?
8. cuando se está en Maine o Boston?
9. cuando se está enfermo?

---

*When used with foods, **rico** (*rich*) means *especially good* or *tasty*.

†Remember that placing **se** before a verb form can change its English equivalent slightly: **usa** (*he/she/it uses*) → **se usa** (*is used*).

C. Asociaciones. ¿Qué palabras asocia Ud. con estas frases y oraciones?

   1. comer bien
   2. un bistec
   3. cenar
   4. engordar (*to gain weight*)
   5. el desayuno
   6. el almuerzo
   7. Acabo de comer pero todavía tengo hambre (*hungry*).
   8. ¡Nunca voy a volver a comer ese plato!

CH. Entrevista. Use the following patterns to find out what several classmates had to eat last night. Take notes on what you learn.

   MODELO —¿Qué **comiste** anoche?
   —**Comí** una hamburguesa con papas fritas.

   Now use this pattern to report what you learned to the class and to add information about what you had to eat.

   MODELO Juanita **comió** una hamburguesa con papas fritas anoche.
   Yo **comí** pescado.

Las comidas

desayunar: el desayuno	to have breakfast: breakfast
almorzar (ue): el almuerzo	to have lunch: lunch
cenar: la cena	to have dinner: dinner

   ■ **¡OJO!** *The Spanish equivalents for* breakfast/lunch/dinner *given here do not express exactly the U.S. concept of these meals, nor are the meals eaten at the same time of day. See the **Lectura cultural** in **Capítulo 10** for more information about mealtimes in Hispanic countries.*

Invitaciones. Su amigo/a acaba de invitarlos (*invited you*) a comer en su casa. Con un compañero (una compañera), invite y conteste según el modelo.

   MODELO 8:30 A.M. →
   —¿Por qué no llegan a las ocho de la mañana?
   —Ah, ¿nos invitas (*you're inviting us*) a desayunar? ¡Con mucho gusto!

   1. 7:00 P.M.   **3.** 6:45 A.M.
   2. 12:30 P.M.   **4.** 10:00 P.M.

Después de comer, felicite (*congratulate*) a su amigo/a por la excelente comida.

   MODELO ¡Qué (*What a*) desayuno más delicioso!

Expressing Actions: *Oír, traer,* **and** *ver*

oír (to hear)	traer (to bring)	ver (to see)
oigo oímos oyes oís oye oyen oyendo	traigo traemos traes traéis trae traen trayendo	veo vemos ves veis ve ven viendo

- *oír:* No oigo bien por el ruido.   *I can't hear well because of the noise.*

English uses *listen!* or *hey!* to attract someone's attention. In Spanish the command forms of **oír** are used: **oye (tú), oiga (Ud.), oigan (Uds.).**

    Oye, Juan, ¿vas a la fiesta así?   *Hey, Juan, are you going
    to the party like that?*

- *traer:* —¿Qué podemos llevar?   *What can we bring?*
       —Pueden traer el vino.   *You can bring the wine.*

- *ver:* No veo bien por la contaminación.   *I can't see well because of the pollution.*

A. ¡No vamos a volver a ese restaurante! Dé oraciones nuevas según las indicaciones.

1. ¡Hay tanto ruido! No oigo la música. (*Juan y yo, tú, Uds., yo, Paula, vosotros*)
2. ¡Hay poca luz (*light*)! No veo bien el menú. (*Ud., nosotros, Andrés, los clientes, yo, tú, vosotras*)
3. ¡Qué desgracia! ¡No traigo dinero! (*tú, Eduardo, Uds., nosotros, vosotros*)

B. Un *picnic* en la playa. ¿Cómo se dice en español?

1. We've just brought the chairs from the car.
2. I see the ice cream, but I can't see the cookies.
3. Pablo is bringing the beer and wine now.
4. Why are you looking at the dog like that?
5. I'm listening to the radio, but I can't hear well because of (**por**) the waves (**olas**).

C. Los estudiantes van a hacer una comida todos juntos (*together*) en la clase. Pregunte Ud. a varios compañeros, **Oye, ¿qué vas a traer?**

CH. Muchas personas ven la televisión o van al cine con frecuencia. Pregunte Ud. a otros estudiantes de la clase, **¿Qué programa ves con frecuencia y por qué? ¿Qué película(s) nueva(s) quieres ver y por qué?**

PRONUNCIACIÓN: *y* and *ll*

The consonant **ñ (Capítulo 8)** is not the only palatal in Spanish; **y** and **ll** also fall in this category.

y   In Spanish, the **y** at the beginning of a syllable **(yo, papaya)** resembles English *y* (*yo-yo, papaya*), except that the tongue is closer to the palate. The result is a sound with some palatal friction, in between English *y* and the *zh* sound of *measure*. In some dialects, when the speaker is emphatic, **y** at the beginning of a word has even more friction, sounding like the *j* in the English *Joe:* **—¿Quién? —¡Yo!**

ll   In most parts of the Spanish-speaking world, **ll** is pronounced exactly like **y**;* therefore, pronunciation alone will not tell you whether a word is spelled with **y** or **ll**.

Práctica

A. llamo   llamas   llueve   yogurt   yo-yó   yanqui   yoga

B. ellas   tortilla   millón   calle   villa   mayo   papaya

C. El anillo de Yolanda Carrillo es de Sevilla.
¿Llueve o no llueve allí en Yucatán?
Ella ya no lleva una silla a la playa.

---

*In many areas of Spain, **ll** is a sound made with the middle of the tongue against the palate. This resembles the [ly] sound of English *million,* but is one sound, not an [l] plus a [y].

MINIDIÁLOGOS Y ESTRUCTURA

18 ¿Qué sabes y a quién conoces?
Saber and *Conocer*; Personal *a*

Delante de un restaurante

AMALIA: ¿Dónde vamos a almorzar?
ERNESTO: (entrando en el restaurante) ¿Por qué no aquí mismo?
AMALIA: ¿*Conoces* este restaurante?
ERNESTO: Sí, lo *conozco* y *sé* que es excelente.
AMALIA: ¿Y cómo *sabes* que es tan bueno?
ERNESTO: *Conozco* muy bien a la dueña. ¡Es mi tía! ¿Nos sentamos?

México

1. *¿Qué hora es, aproximadamente?*
2. *¿Conoce Ernesto el restaurante?*
3. *¿Cuál es su opinión del restaurante?*
4. *¿Cómo sabe Ernesto que el restaurante es muy bueno?*
5. *¿Por qué conoce a la dueña del restaurante?*

Saber and *conocer*

saber (*to know*)	**conocer** (*to know*)
sé sabemos	conozco conocemos
sabes sabéis	conoces conocéis
sabe saben	conoce conocen
sabiendo	conociendo

Saber means *to know facts or pieces of information.* When followed by an infinitive, **saber** means *to know how to do something.*

No **saben** el teléfono de Alejandro.   *They don't know Alejandro's phone number.*

¿**Saben** Uds. dónde vive Carmela?   *Do you know where Carmela lives?*

¿**Sabes** nadar?   *Do you know how to swim?*

In front of a restaurant   AMALIA: *Where are we going to have lunch?*   ERNESTO: *(entering the restaurant) Why not right here?*   AMALIA: *Do you know (Are you familiar with) this restaurant?*   ERNESTO: *Yes, I know it, and I know that it's excellent.*   AMALIA: *And how do you know it's so good?*   ERNESTO: *I know the owner very well. She's my aunt! Shall we sit down?*

Conocer means *to know* or *to be acquainted (familiar) with a person, place, or thing.* It can also mean *to meet.* Note the **a** used before a specific person.

No **conocen** a la nueva estudiante todavía.	*They don't know the new student yet.*
¿**Conocen** Uds. el restaurante mexicano en la calle Goya?	*Are you familiar with (Have you been to) the Mexican restaurant on Goya Street?*
¿Quieren **conocer** a aquel joven?	*Do you want to meet that young man?*

[Práctica A–CH]

Personal *a*

A. In English and in Spanish, the *direct object* (**el complemento directo**) of a sentence answers the question *what?* or *whom?* in relation to the subject and verb.

Ann is preparing dinner. $\left\{\begin{array}{l}\text{Ann is preparing } \textit{what?} \\ \textit{What} \text{ is Ann preparing?}\end{array}\right\}$ *dinner*

They can't hear the baby. $\left\{\begin{array}{l}\text{They can't hear } \textit{whom?} \\ \textit{Whom} \text{ can't they hear?}\end{array}\right\}$ *the baby*

Indicate the direct objects in the following sentences:

1. I don't see Betty and Mary here.
2. Give the dog a bone.
3. No tenemos dinero.
4. ¿Por qué no pones la sopa en la mesa?

B. In Spanish, the word **a** immediately precedes the direct object of a sentence when the direct object refers to a specific person or persons. This **a,** called the **a personal,** has no equivalent in English.*

Vamos a visitar **al profesor.**	*We're going to visit the professor.*
but	
Vamos a visitar **el museo.**	*We're going to visit the museum.*
Necesitan **a la camarera.**	*They need the waitress.*
but	
Necesitan **la cuenta.**	*They need the bill.*

---

*The personal **a** is not generally used with **tener: Tengo cuatro hijos.**

■ **¡OJO!** *The verbs* **esperar** *(to wait for),* **escuchar** *(to listen to),* **mirar** *(to look at), and* **buscar** *(to look for) include the sense of the English prepositions* for, to, *and* at. *These verbs take direct objects in Spanish (not prepositional phrases, as in English).*

Estoy buscando **mi abrigo.**	*I'm looking for my overcoat.*
Estoy esperando **a mi hijo.**	*I'm waiting for my son.*

C. The personal **a** is used before the interrogative words **¿quién?** or **¿quiénes?** when these words function as direct objects.

¿A quién debemos llamar?	*Whom should we call?*
¿A quiénes ves?	*Whom do you see?*

[Práctica D–G]

Práctica

A. La familia de Julita. Dé oraciones nuevas según las indicaciones.

1. Conocemos muy bien a Julita. (*yo, Uds., Juan y yo, Raúl y Mario, vosotros*)
2. Sabemos que su familia es de Chile. (*ellos, yo, Elvira, Uds., Ana y tú, vosotros*)

B. Describe what these well-known people know how to do.

José Feliciano		jugar al béisbol
Mikhail Baryshnikov		hacer ejercicios gimnásticos
Pete Rose		cantar en español
Mary Lou Retton	sabe	cocinar (*to cook*) bien
James Michener		jugar al tenis
Chris Evert Lloyd		escribir novelas
Julia Child		bailar

C. Can you match these famous couples?

Adán		Marta
Archie Bunker		Cleopatra
Romeo		Eva
Rhett Butler	conoce a	Julieta
Antonio		Scarlett O'Hara
Jorge Washington		Edith

CH. Complete las siguientes oraciones con **conozco** o **sé**.

1. _____ al nuevo novio de Marta pero no _____ de dónde es.
2. _____ un excelente restaurante chino pero no _____ en qué calle está.
3. Sí, sí, _____ a Julio pero no _____ su teléfono.
4. _____ jugar muy bien al tenis pero no _____ a ningún otro jugador (*any other players*) en esta residencia.

5. No ____ muy bien la Ciudad de México pero ____ que quiero regresar este verano.

6. ¡Qué problema! ____ que hay una prueba (*quiz*) en esa clase mañana pero no ____ sobre qué capítulo es y no ____ a nadie (*no one*) de la clase que me pueda informar (*who can tell me*)...

D. En este momento... Dé oraciones nuevas según las indicaciones.

1. —¿A quién o qué ve? —Veo *el texto*. (*profesor, pizarra, estudiantes, mesa, mi amigo/a, puerta*)

2. —¿A quién o qué busca? —Estoy buscando *a mi amigo José*. (*mi libro, Felipe, el amigo de Tomás, el profesor, un cuaderno*)

E. Preparativos para cenar fuera (*eat out*) con los amigos. ¿Cómo se dice en español?

1. We're going to call Miguel.
2. They're inviting Rosario.
3. Whom are you looking at like that?
4. Why don't you listen to Jorge? It's not a good restaurant!
5. I'm waiting for Benjamín. *He* knows that restaurant.

F. Preguntas

1. ¿Qué restaurantes conoce Ud.? ¿Cuál es su restaurante favorito? ¿Es buena la comida de ese restaurante? ¿Qué sirven allí? ¿Come Ud. allí con frecuencia? ¿Conoce a los dueños del restaurante? ¿Son simpáticos?

2. ¿Conoce Ud. a una persona famosa? ¿Quién es? ¿Cómo es? ¿Qué detalles (*details*) sabe Ud. de su vida?

3. En clase, ¿sabe Ud. todas las respuestas? ¿todos los verbos? ¿todas las palabras nuevas?

4. ¿Sabe Ud. jugar al tenis? ¿a otro deporte? ¿Sabe tocar un instrumento musical? ¿bailar? ¿cantar? ¿hablar otra lengua?

5. ¿Qué platos sabe Ud. preparar? ¿tacos? ¿enchiladas? ¿pollo frito? ¿hamburguesas (con queso)?

A la hora de pedir

—¿Qué tal las chuletas aquí?
—No lo sé. Nunca las pido.
—¿Y qué tal el pollo frito?
—¡Estupendo! (¡Riquísimo!) Esto es lo que (*what*) voy a pedir. ¿Y tú?
— ____ ?

Madrid, España

Peter Menzel

G. Ud. ya conoce a los otros estudiantes de la clase y sabe mucho de ellos. Describa Ud. a varios de sus compañeros de clase.

Conozco a _____ . Sé que él/ella _____ .

19 Expressing What or Whom
Direct Object Pronouns

¿Dónde vamos a comer?

AGUSTÍN: Estoy empezando a tener hambre. ¿Qué te parece si cenamos fuera esta noche?

MARIELA: ¡Buena idea! A propósito, ¿conoces a los Velázquez?

AGUSTÍN: Claro que sí. Hace años que *los* conozco. ¿Por qué me *lo* preguntas? Estamos hablando de comidas.

MARIELA: Pues acabo de oír que tienen un restaurante en la Avenida Bolívar.

AGUSTÍN: ¡Qué suerte! ¡A ver si *nos* invitan* a comer!

1. *¿Quién tiene hambre?*
2. *¿Quién conoce a los Velázquez?*
3. *¿Por qué habla Mariela de ellos?*
4. *¿Quiere pagar la comida Agustín?*

Direct Object Pronouns			
me	*me*	**nos**	*us*
te	*you* (fam. sing.)	**os**	*you* (fam. pl.)
lo†	*you* (form. sing.), *him, it* (m.)	**los**	*you* (form. pl.), *them* (m., m. + f.)
la	*you* (form. sing.), *her, it* (f.)	**las**	*you* (form. pl.), *them* (f.)

Where are we going to eat? AGUSTÍN: *I'm starting to get hungry. What do you think about eating out tonight?* MARIELA: *Great! By the way, do you know the Velázquezes?* AGUSTÍN: *Of course I do. I've known them for years. Why do you ask? We're talking about food (meals).* MARIELA: *Well, I've just heard that they have a new restaurant on Bolivar Avenue.* AGUSTÍN: *What luck! Let's see if they invite us to a free meal!*

*¡OJO! **Invitar** is a cognate that has somewhat different connotations in Spanish and in English. In English, *to invite* someone is a request for that person's company. In Spanish **te invito, nos invitan,** and similar phrases imply that the person who is inviting will also pay.

†In Spain and in other parts of the Spanish-speaking world, **le** is frequently used instead of **lo** for the direct object pronoun *him*. This usage will not be followed in *¿Qué tal?*.

A. Like direct object nouns, *direct object pronouns* (**los pronombres del complemento directo**) answer the questions *what?* or *whom?* in relation to the subject and verb. Direct object pronouns are placed before a conjugated verb and after the word **no** when it appears. Direct object pronouns are used only when the direct object noun has already been mentioned.

Ellos **me** ayudan.	*They're helping me.*
¿El libro? Diego no **lo** necesita.	*The book? Diego doesn't need it.*
¿Dónde están la revista y el periódico? **Los** necesito ahora.	*Where are the magazine and the newspaper? I need them now.*

B. The direct object pronouns may be attached to an infinitive or a present participle.

Las tengo que leer. ⎱ Tengo que leer**las**. ⎰	*I have to read them.*
¿**Nos** están buscando? ⎱ ¿Están buscándo**nos**? ⎰	*Are you looking for us?*

When a pronoun object is attached to a present participle, a written accent is needed on the stressed vowel: **buscándonos.**

[Práctica A–D]

C. The direct object pronoun **lo** can refer to actions, situations, or ideas in general. When used in this way, **lo** expresses English *it* or *that.*

Lo comprende muy bien.	*He understands it (that) very well.*
No **lo** creo.	*I don't believe it (that).*
Lo sé.	*I know (it).*

[Práctica E–H]

Práctica

A. Situaciones. Imagine that you have not clearly heard the following questions. For that reason, you will verify your comprehension by repeating part of the question before answering it.

1. —¿Busca Ud. *el bolígrafo* ahora?
   —¿El bolígrafo? No, no *lo* necesito ahora. (*el menú, los platos, la silla, el carro, las cuentas, los lápices*)
2. —¿Tienen Uds. que preparar *el ejercicio* para mañana?
   —¿El ejercicio? Sí, tenemos que prepararlo para mañana. (*la sopa, los postres, el flan, la lección, las papas, la cena, el almuerzo*)
3. —¿Pides *cerveza*?
   —¿Cerveza? Sí, estoy pidiéndola ahora. (*queso, carne, helado, verduras, papas fritas, huevos, la cuenta*)

B. Escenas en un restaurante. Cambie: complementos directos →
pronombres.

1. El camarero pone los vasos (*glasses*) en la mesa.
2. Los niños están leyendo el menú ahora.
3. Voy a pedir la ensalada esta noche.
4. ¿Por qué no pagas tú la cuenta?
5. ¿El dinero? No tengo dinero.
6. Queremos esos dos pasteles, señor.
7. El dueño está preparando la cuenta en este momento, señor.
8. Los camareros están abriendo las botellas de champán.

C. Más invitaciones. Con otro/a estudiante, haga y conteste preguntas
según el modelo.

MODELO   comer en tu casa →
          —¿Cuándo me invitas a comer en tu casa?
          —Te invito a comer el sábado.

1. cenar en tu casa   4. ver una película
2. almorzar contigo   5. ir contigo a la playa
3. nadar en tu piscina (*pool*)

Ahora repita el ejercicio en plural, según el modelo.

MODELO   comer en tu casa →
          —¿Cuándo nos invitas a comer en tu casa?
          —Los invito a comer el sábado.

CH. ¿Comiste tacos anoche? Con otro/a estudiante, haga y conteste
preguntas según el modelo.

MODELO   tacos → —¿Comiste tacos anoche?
                —Sí, los comí. (No, no los comí.)

1. jamón   4. pastel
2. zanahorias   5. enchiladas
3. papas fritas   6. helado

D. Your roommate **(compañero/a de cuarto)** is constantly suggesting
things for you to do, but you've always just finished doing them.
How will you respond to each of the following suggestions? Follow
the model.

MODELO   —¿Por qué no escribes la composición para la clase de
             español?
          —¡Porque *acabo de* escribirla!

1. ¿Por qué no estudias la lección ahora?
2. ¿Por qué no visitas el museo conmigo?
3. ¿Por qué no aprendes las palabras nuevas?

4. ¿Por qué no compras el periódico de hoy?
5. ¿Por qué no pagas las cervezas?
6. ¿Por qué no preparas las arvejas?
7. ¿Por qué no compras agua mineral?
8. ¿Por qué no me ayudas más?

E. Situaciones. Ud. y sus amigos están muy negativos hoy. ¿Cómo van a responder a las preguntas siguientes?

MODELO   ¿Creen Uds. eso? → ¡No, no lo creemos!

1. ¿Prefieren Uds. eso?   **4.** ¿Piensan Uds. eso?
2. ¿Comprenden Uds. eso?   **5.** ¿Aceptan Uds. eso?
3. ¿Desean Uds. eso?   **6.** ¿Esperan Uds. eso?

F. Preguntas

1. ¿Quién lo/la invita a cenar con frecuencia? ¿a tomar café? ¿a salir? ¿a bailar?
2. Todos necesitamos la ayuda (*help*) de alguien, ¿verdad? ¿Sus padres los ayudan a Uds.? **(Sí, nuestros padres...)** ¿Quién más? ¿sus amigos? ¿sus compañeros de cuarto? ¿sus profesores? ¿sus consejeros? ¿sus ____ ?
3. Imagine que Ud. es actor/actriz en un drama de la universidad. Todos sus amigos y parientes vienen a verlo/la. ¿Quién lo/la mira en este momento? ¿su padre? ¿su madre? ¿sus hermanos? ¿Quién lo/la escucha?

G. Este sábado Ud. va a dar (*to have*) una fiesta y puede invitar a una persona famosa. ¿A quién va a invitar Ud.?

Voy a invitar a ____ . Lo/La quiero invitar porque ____ .

H. ¿A quién va a llamar Ud. esta noche? ¿Por qué?

Voy a llamar a ____ . Necesito llamarlo/la porque ____ .

¿Y quién lo/la va a llamar a Ud.? ¿Por qué?

Creo que ____ me va a llamar. Necesita llamarme porque ____ .

REPASO

Gustos y preferencias. Survey some of the members of your class to determine their tastes and preferences in food. Tabulate the responses to find the most/least popular foods, restaurants, and so on.

1. ¿Prefieres cenar en casa, en un restaurante o en la cafetería de los estudiantes?
2. ¿Qué días no desayunas? ¿no cenas?
3. ¿Prefieres comer en McDonald's (o en otro restaurante donde sirven la comida rápidamente) o en un restaurante de lujo (*deluxe*)?
4. ¿Qué comes—y dónde—cuando tienes mucha prisa?
5. ¿Qué comes—y dónde—cuando tienes mucho dinero? ¿poco dinero?
6. ¿Qué platos comes con frecuencia? ¿Qué platos debes comer más frecuentemente? ¿Qué platos no comes nunca? ¿Qué platos tienes que comer en casa de tus padres?
7. ¿Qué bebida prefieres cuando hace mucho calor y tienes mucha sed? ¿cuando estás estudiando? ¿cuando sales con los amigos por la noche?
8. Cuando tienes hambre a las tres de la tarde, ¿qué prefieres comer o tomar? ¿un yogurt? ¿galletas y leche? ¿zanahorias? ¿un jugo de tomate? ¿chocolate? ¿un sándwich y una cerveza? ¿un pastel y un vaso de leche? ¿otra cosa?
9. ¿Qué comes cuando tienes hambre a las once de la noche?
10. ¿Qué comiste anoche? ¿Dónde lo comiste?

UN PASO MÁS: Imágenes del mundo hispánico

España: De la prehistoria a la reconquista

*L*a historia de España comienza hace (*ago*) cientos de años, en los oscuros días de la Prehistoria. Las pinturas rupestres que todavía se conservan en varios sitios de la Península Ibérica, nos muestran (*show*) la vida y las costumbres de aquel tiempo.

Desde siempre la historia de España está marcada por el ir y venir de distintos pueblos y diferentes culturas. Griegos, fenicios, cartagineses, romanos, godos y árabes van a dejar sus huellas (*leave traces*) en la tierra que hoy se llama España.

Los romanos llegan a la Península en el siglo III a. de C. Traen el latín, sus leyes (*laws*) y sus costumbres, que se mantienen incluso después de la invasión visigótica

(siglo V d. de C.).

Los árabes conquistan fácilmente la Península en el siglo VIII. Durante setecientos años van a vivir en España y a dejar en la cultura hispana una influencia muy particular. Durante los siglos IX, X y XI no hay en Europa ningún otro centro cultural de mayor importancia que del imperio árabe en la Península.

Se llama «Reconquista» al largo período de guerras que termina con la expulsión de los árabes (1492). El héroe más popular de la Reconquista es Rodrigo Díaz de Vivar, «El Cid», personaje del siglo XI del que hablan numerosos romances (*ballads*) y leyendas.

(Continúa en el Capítulo 11.)

La estatua de El Cid Campeador, Burgos

Mark Antman/Image Works

Monkmeyer Press Photo Service

El Patio de los Leones, La Alhambra, Granada

Rogers/Monkmeyer Press Photo Service

Pinturas rupestres, Los Caballos

Stuart Cohen

La Mezquita de Córdoba

Stuart Cohen

El acueducto romano de Segovia

VOCABULARIO

VERBOS

ayudar to help
cenar to have dinner
conocer (conozco) to know; to be acquainted with; to meet
desayunar to have breakfast
esperar to wait (for)
invitar to invite
llamar to call
oír (*irreg.*) to hear
saber (*irreg.*) to know; (+ *inf.*) to know how (*to do something*)
traer (*irreg.*) to bring
ver (*irreg.*) to see

LA COMIDA

el arroz rice
la ensalada salad
el huevo egg
el pan bread
las papas (fritas) (french-fried) potatoes
el queso cheese
la sopa soup

LAS VERDURAS

las arvejas peas
los frijoles beans
la lechuga lettuce
el tomate tomato
la zanahoria carrot

LA CARNE

el bistec steak
la chuleta (de cerdo) (pork) chop
la hamburguesa hamburger
el jamón ham
el pollo chicken

LOS MARISCOS

los camarones shrimp
la langosta lobster
el pescado fish

LA FRUTA

la banana banana
la manzana apple
la naranja orange

LOS POSTRES

el flan custard
la galleta cookie
el helado ice cream
el pastel cake; pie; pastry

LAS BEBIDAS

el café coffee
el jugo (de fruta) (fruit) juice
la leche milk
el té tea
el vino (blanco, tinto) (white, red) wine

LAS COMIDAS

el almuerzo lunch
la cena dinner
el desayuno breakfast

OTROS SUSTANTIVOS

el/la camarero/a waiter/waitress
la cuenta bill, check
el plato plate; dish
el restaurante restaurant
el ruido noise
el vaso glass

PALABRAS ADICIONALES

así thus, so; like this/that
por because of

FRASES ÚTILES PARA LA COMUNICACIÓN

tener hambre	to be hungry
tener sed	to be thirsty
¿Qué comiste anoche?	What did you eat last night?
Comí...	I ate . . .

CAPÍTULO 10

En un restaurante mexicano

VOCABULARIO: PREPARACIÓN

RESTAURANTE EL CHARRO
Desayuno (de 8:00 a 11:00) precio fijo ___

Frutas o jugo extra
Pan dulce o Pan tostado (Sweet rolls or toast)
Café   Té   chocolate

Huevos rancheros (eggs with tomatoes, onions, and chiles) o Huevos con jamón

Comida (de 1:00 a 4:00) precio fijo ___

Antojitos (appetizers):
   Guacamole (avocado dip) o Cóctel de camarones (shrimp cocktail)

Sopas:
   Sopa de albóndigas (meatball soup) o sopa de tortillas

Bebidas: café, Té Leche Refrescos
   Agua* mineral
   Cerveza o vino (blanco, tinto, o rosado) extra

Postres: Helado o pastel de chocolate

Platos fuertes (main courses):
• Tacos «El Charro» con salsa picante ("El Charro" special-tacos with hot sauce)
• Bistec con papas* fritas
• Mole poblano de guajolote (turkey in a spicy sauce of chiles and chocolate)
• Pescado veracruzano† (fish in a spicy sauce of tomatoes, chiles, onions, and green olives)

   Tortillas o Bolillos (rolls)

---

*In Hispanic America, **papas** means *potatoes;* in most parts of Spain, the word **patatas** is used. Similarly, the word **camarones** means *shrimp* in most parts of Hispanic America, while **gambas** is used in Spain.

†This style of preparing fish is typical of the Mexican coastal city of Vera Cruz.

‡The noun **agua** (*water*) is feminine, but the masculine articles are used with it in the singular: **el agua.** This phenomenon occurs with all feminine nouns that begin with a stressed **a** sound: **el ama de casa** (*the homemaker*).

Oiga, señor...

—Camarero, esta sopa está fría.
—No es posible, señor. Acaban de
  prepararla.
—De todas maneras, está fría.
—Lo siento (Disculpe), señor. Le traigo otro
  plato inmediatamente.

David Kupferschmid

Buenos Aires, Argentina

A. Explique el menú de «El Charro» a su amigo Luis, llenando los espacios en blanco con las palabras apropiadas.

1. Para el desayuno se puede escoger (*to choose*) entre el pan tostado y el ＿＿ ＿＿ .
2. Con los huevos se puede pedir ＿＿ . También hay fruta o ＿＿ de fruta.
3. Para la comida, se puede escoger entre las tortillas o los ＿＿ .
4. El ＿＿ ＿＿ es un plato mexicano que se hace con guajolote, chiles y chocolate.
5. Se sirve el bistec con ＿＿ ＿＿ .
6. El guacamole y el cóctel de camarones son ＿＿ .
7. Hay sopa de tortillas y de ＿＿ .
8. Se sirve una salsa ＿＿ con los tacos «El Charro».
9. Las bebidas no alcohólicas que se sirven son el café, el té, la ＿＿ , los ＿＿ y el ＿＿ mineral.
10. De postre, hay ＿＿ o ＿＿ ＿＿ ＿＿ .

¿Qué va a pedir Ud. para el desayuno? ¿para la comida?

B. Situaciones. El menú, por favor. Using the menu and the phrases in the model, answer the following questions that a waiter/waitress would ask. Try to answer each question in several different ways.

MODELO   ¿Qué desea Ud. de postre? →
          —Para mí, fruta.
          —Me trae un helado, por favor.
          —Favor de traerme un helado.
          —¿Todavía hay flan?
          —¿Qué tal los pasteles?
          —No quiero nada, gracias.

1. ¿Qué antojitos desea Ud.?
2. ¿Va a tomar sopa?
3. ¿Qué desea Ud. de plato principal?
4. ¿Y para beber?

5. ¿Qué quiere de postre?
6. ¿Prefiere Ud. té o café?
7. ¿Traigo la cuenta con el café?

Palabras indefinidas y negativas

algo	something, anything	**nada**	nothing, not anything
alguien	someone, anyone	**nadie**	no one, nobody, not anybody
algún (alguno/a/os/as)	some, any	**ningún (ninguno/a)**	no, none, not any
siempre	always	**nunca, jamás**	never
también	also	**tampoco**	neither, not either

- **Double negative:** When a negative word comes *after* the main verb, Spanish requires that another negative word—usually **no**—be placed before the verb. When a negative word precedes the verb, **no** is not used.

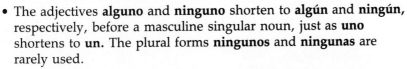

¿**No** estudia **nadie?** ⎱	*Isn't anyone studying?*
¿**Nadie** estudia? ⎰	
No estás en clase **nunca.** ⎱	*You're never in class.*
Nunca estás en clase. ⎰	
No hablan árabe **tampoco.** ⎱	*They don't speak Arabic either.*
Tampoco hablan árabe. ⎰	

- The adjectives **alguno** and **ninguno** shorten to **algún** and **ningún**, respectively, before a masculine singular noun, just as **uno** shortens to **un**. The plural forms **ningunos** and **ningunas** are rarely used.

—¿Tiene Ud. **algunos** amigos hispanos?	*"Do you have any Hispanic friends?"*
—No, no tengo **ningún** amigo hispano.	*"No, I don't have any Hispanic friends."*

- The personal **a** is used before **alguien** and **nadie** when these words function as direct objects.

¿Vas a invitar **a alguien?**	*Are you going to invite someone?*
—¿A quién llamas?	*"Whom are you calling?"*
—No llamo **a nadie.**	*"I'm not calling anyone."*

A. ¡Por eso no come nadie allí! Exprese negativamente, usando el negativo doble.

1. Hay algo interesante en el menú.
2. Tienen algunos platos típicos.
3. El profesor cena allí también.

4. Mis amigos siempre almuerzan allí.
5. Preparan algo especial para grupos grandes.
6. Siempre hacen platos nuevos.
7. Y también sirven guajolote.

B. Answer these questions by following the example and cues given. Then, if you can, expand each response by explaining the situation. Some model explanations are given in parentheses below.

1. ¿Hay **algo** en la pizarra? (palabras)   ¿en la calle? (carro)
   ¿en la mesa? (periódico)   ¿en la montaña? (pueblo)

Sí, hay **algo.** Hay
unas **palabras**
en la pizarra.
(Hay clase hoy
en esta sala [*room*]).

No, no hay **nada.**
(**No** hay
ninguna clase
aquí hoy.)

2. ¿Hay alguien en el cine? (muchas personas)
   ¿en el restaurante? (varias familias)
   ¿en el parque? (niños)
   ¿en la biblioteca? (muchos estudiantes)

Sí, hay **alguien.**
Hay **muchas**
personas. (Hay
una película muy
buena hoy.)

No, no hay **nadie.**
(¡La película es
muy mala!)

C. ¿Cómo se dice en español?

A la hora de la cena

1. Is there anything special tonight?
2. They serve dinner at six at **(en)** their house, too.
3. No one is eating at home tonight, right?
4. We don't want to order anything right now.
5. There's no restaurant on that street.

En la residencia, antes del examen

1. No one understands that.
2. Marcos can't write this sentence either.
3. You never study with Carmen. Why not?
4. No one is as tired as I am!
5. Isn't anybody sleepy yet?

CH. Rosa es una persona muy positiva, pero su hermano Rodolfo tiene ideas muy negativas. Aquí hay unas oraciones que expresan las ideas de Rosa. ¿Cómo puede reaccionar Rodolfo?

1. Tengo hambre; quiero comer algo.
2. Alguien puede hacer un pastel para la fiesta.
3. Siempre salgo con mis amigos.
4. Hay algo interesante en la televisión.
5. Hay algunos estudiantes excelentes en mi clase de sicología.
6. Hay algunas personas muy listas en esta clase.
7. Vamos a beber algo.
8. Se sirven algunos platos estupendos aquí.

D. **Ningún cumpleaños es perfecto.** Using the words and phrases given under **Posibilidades** and some of the negative words you have just learned, tell someone about a terrible birthday.

MODELO   cartas → No hay ninguna carta para mí.
              bailar → Nadie quiere bailar conmigo.

POSIBILIDADES: regalos, tarjetas (*cards*), cena especial, telegramas, flores, platos especiales, llamarme, cenar, salir, cantar para mí

E. Preguntas

1. ¿Vamos a vivir en la luna (*moon*) algún día? ¿y en los otros planetas? ¿Dónde va Ud. a vivir algún día?
2. ¿Hay algo más importante que el dinero? ¿la amistad? ¿el amor?
3. ¿Algunos de sus amigos son de habla española? ¿De dónde son?
4. En clase, ¿hay alguien más inteligente que el profesor (la profesora)? ¿más estudioso/a que Ud.? ¿más rico/a que Ud.?
5. Hay algo en la mesa en este momento? ¿en el suelo (*floor*)? ¿debajo de su silla (escritorio)?

PRONUNCIACIÓN: *s, z, ce,* and *ci*

Spanish **s** and **z** are usually pronounced like the [s] in English *class* and *Sue*. The letter **c** before **e** and **i** also produces an [s] sound; **cine, once.*** Except in a few words borrowed from other languages **(zigzag),** the letter **z** never occurs before an **e** or **i** in Spanish. For this reason, spelling changes sometimes occur: **lápiz → lápices; vez → veces.**

Práctica

A. 1. pescado   pastel   vaso   sopa   mariscos   langosta
   2. cenar   piscina   ciudad   sucio   cita   cine   cerrado
   3. arroz   actriz   azul   razón   perezoso   noviazgo
   4. estación   solución   situación   calefacción   acción

*In many parts of Spain, the letter **z,** as well as **c** before **e** and **i,** is pronounced like *th* in English *thin.*

B. Siempre salgo a cenar con Zoila.
Ese sitio muy sucio está en esta ciudad.
No conozco a Luz Mendoza de Pérez.
La preparación del gazpacho es difícil.
Los zapatos de Celia son azules.

MINIDIÁLOGOS Y ESTRUCTURA

20 Expressing to Whom or for Whom
Indirect Object Pronouns: *Dar* and *decir*

Una comida casera

BETO: Quiero preparar*te* una cena especial. ¿Cuál es tu plato favorito?

SARA: Realmente *me* gusta casi todo.

BETO: ¡Estupendo! Una típica comida mexicana, pues. Primero *te* voy a *dar* un poco de guacamole...

SARA: Bueno, en realidad *te* debo *decir* que no *me* gusta mucho el aguacate... ni la cebolla... ni la salsa picante... ni los tomates... ni...

BETO: ¡Qué «casi» más curioso! Creo que *te* voy a servir un bistec, ¿qué *te* parece?

Barbara Alper/Stock, Boston

¿Qué dicen Beto y Sara, **me** *or* **te***?*

Sara

1. _____ *gusta casi todo.*
2. *Ahora* _____ *voy a decir la verdad (*truth*).*
3. *¡*_____ *gusta más el bistec!*

Beto

1. _____ *voy a preparar una comida especial.*
2. _____ *gusta la comida mexicana.*
3. _____ *voy a servir el bistec.*

Indirect Object Pronouns

me	*to, for me*	**nos**	*to, for us*
te	*to, for you* (fam. sing.)	**os**	*to, for you*
le	*to, for you* (form. sing.), *him, her, it*	**les**	*to, for you* (form. pl.), *them* (m., f.)

A home-cooked meal BETO: *I want to make a special dinner for you. What is your favorite dish?* SARA: *I like almost everything, really.* BETO: *Great! A typical Mexican meal, then. First I'll give you a little guacamole . . .* SARA: *Well, I really should tell you that I don't like avocados very much . . . or onion . . . or hot sauce . . . or tomatoes . . . or . . .* BETO: *What a strange "almost"! I think I'm going to serve you a steak. What do you think about that?*

A. *Indirect object* nouns and pronouns usually answer the questions *to whom?* or *for whom?* in relation to the verb. The word *to* is frequently omitted in English. Note that indirect object pronouns have the same form as direct object pronouns, except in the third person: **le, les.**

Indicate the direct and indirect objects in the following sentences.

1. I'm giving her the present tomorrow.
2. Could you tell me the answer now?
3. El profesor nos va a hacer algunas preguntas.
4. ¿No me compras el librito ahora?

B. Like direct object pronouns, *indirect object pronouns* **(los pronombres del complemento indirecto)** are placed immediately before a conjugated verb. They may be attached to a present participle—with the addition of an accent mark—or to an infinitive.

No, no **te** presto el coche.	*No, I won't lend you the car.*
Están preparándo**nos** unos antojitos. **Nos** están preparando unos antojitos.	*They're preparing some appetizers for us.*
Voy a mandar**te** un pastel de chocolate. **Te** voy a mandar un pastel de chocolate.	*I'm going to send you a chocolate cake.*

C. Since **le** and **les** have several different equivalents, their meaning is often clarified or emphasized with the preposition **a** and the pronoun objects of prepositions (see **Capítulo 6**).

Vamos a regalar**le** una camiseta **a Ud. (a él, a ella).**	*We're going to give you (him, her) a T-shirt.*
Estoy haciéndo**les** una comida **a Uds. (a ellos, a ellas).**	*I'm making you (them) a meal.*

CH. When there is an indirect object noun in a sentence, the indirect object pronoun is almost always used in addition. This construction is very common in Spanish.

Vamos a decir**le** la verdad **a Juan.**	*Let's tell Juan the truth.*
Estamos mandándo**les** un regalo **a Mateo** y **Marta.**	*We're sending Mateo and Marta a gift.*

[Práctica A (1 y 2)]

D. Verbs frequently used with indirect objects include **dar** (*to give*), **decir** (*to say; to tell*), **escribir, explicar, hablar, mandar, pedir,**

preguntar, preparar, prestar, regalar (*to give as a gift*), **servir,** and **traer.**

Dar and *decir*

dar (*to give*)	
doy	damos
das	dais
da	dan
dando	

decir (*to say, tell*)	
digo	decimos
dices	decís
dice	dicen
diciendo	

¿Cuándo me das el dinero?

¿Por qué no me dice Ud. la verdad, señor?

When will you give me the money?

Why don't you tell me the truth, sir?

▨   **¡OJO!** *In Spanish it is necessary to distinguish between the verbs* **dar** (to give) *and* **regalar** (to give as a gift). *Do not confuse* **decir** (to say *or* to tell) *with* **hablar** (to speak).

[Práctica A (3 y 4)–F]

Práctica

A. **En casa durante la cena.** Dé oraciones nuevas según las indicaciones.

1. *Les* sirvo guacamole *a los chicos* (*kids*). (*a ti, a Ud., a Andrés, a Uds., a Alicia, a vosotros*)
2. Ahora estoy preparándo*le* la sopa *a Jorge*. (*a Sergio y Víctor, a ti, a Eva, a Uds., a Martín y Rosa*)
3. Esteban *les* dice algo *a todos*. (*yo, ellos, tú, nosotros, Uds., vosotras*)
4. Rosalinda *les* da algo de postre. (*tú, nosotros, yo, Uds., ellos*)

B. **¿Qué va a pasar?** Dé varias respuestas.

1. Su amiga Elena está en el hospital. Todos le mandan... Le escriben...
2. Es Navidad. Los niños les prometen (*promise*) a sus padres... Les piden... Los padres les mandan... a sus amigos. Les regalan...
3. Mi coche no funciona bien. Mi amigo Julio me presta... Mis padres me dan...

C. Hoy es el cumpleaños de Marcos. ¿Qué le dice Ud. (a él)? ¿Qué le regala Julio? ¿Ana? ¿Ernesto? ¿María? ¿Qué les dice Marcos a todos? ¿Le da Ud. algunos regalos a Marcos? ¿Por qué no? ¿No lo conoce Ud.? Y a Ud., ¿qué le van a regalar sus amigos este año el día de su cumpleaños?

- un libro
- un regalo grande
- una radio portátil
- una camisa

CH. Hoy es el aniversario de los Sres. González. ¿Qué les dice Ud. a ellos? ¿Qué les regala Inés? ¿Irma? ¿Pepe? ¿Rodolfo? ¿Qué les va a regalar Ud. a sus padres para su aniversario?

- un televisor
- unos boletos (*tickets*) para un viaje
- una pintura bonita
- un regalo de sorpresa

D. Your little cousin Benjamín has never eaten in a restaurant before. Explain to him what will happen, filling in the blanks with the appropriate indirect object pronoun.

Primero el camarero _____ indica una mesa desocupada. Luego tú _____ pides el menú al camarero. También _____ haces preguntas sobre los platos y las especialidades de la casa y _____ dices tus preferencias. El camarero _____ trae la comida. Por fin papá _____ pide la cuenta al camarero. Si tú quieres pagar, _____ pides dinero a papá y _____ das el dinero al camarero.

E. Complete las oraciones en una forma lógica.

1. Mi amigo/a (novio/a) siempre me manda _____ para mi cumpleaños.
2. Mis padres me pagan _____ .
3. Quiero darle a _____ un(a) _____ porque _____ .
4. ¿Deben los hombres abrirles la puerta a _____ ?
5. En casa les sirvo _____ a mis amigos.
6. Para el cumpleaños de mi mejor amigo/a, voy a hacerle _____ .
7. En _____ , mi restaurante favorito, les recomiendo a Uds. _____ .
8. Nunca le presto a nadie mi(s) _____ .

F. **Entrevista.** With another student, find out to whom or for whom he or she does the following things.

MODELO   darle consejos (*advice*) → —¿A quién le das consejos?
　　　　　　　　　　　　　　　　　—Le doy consejos a...

1. escribirle cartas románticas (tarjetas postales)
2. pedirle ayuda académica (dinero)
3. prestarle la ropa (el coche, dinero)
4. mandarle flores (dulces)
5. decirle secretos (mentiritas [*little white lies*])
6. hacerle favores (regalos especiales)
7. darle consejos (dinero)

¿Recuerda Ud.?

¿You have already used forms of **gustar** to express your likes and dislikes **(Paso dos).** Review what you know by answering the following questions. Then use them, changing their form as needed, to interview your instructor.

1. ¿Te gusta el café (el vino, el té,...)?
2. ¿Te gusta jugar al béisbol (al golf, al vólibol, al...)?
3. ¿Te gusta viajar en avión (en tren, en coche,...)?
4. ¿Qué te gusta más, estudiar o ir a fiestas (trabajar o descansar, cocinar [*to cook*] o comer)?

---

21 Gustos y preferencias: *Gustar*

1. *Al hombre de la derecha, ¿le gusta fumar (to smoke)?*
2. *¿Qué cosa no le gusta al hombre de la izquierda?*
3. *¿A Ud. le gusta fumar?*
4. *¿Les gusta a todos el humo de los cigarrillos?*

Parece que a Ud. no le gusta el humo.

Constructions with *gustar*

Spanish	Literal Equivalent	English
Me gusta la playa.	The beach is pleasing to me.	*I like the beach.*
No le gustan sus cursos.	His courses are not pleasing to him.	*He doesn't like his courses.*
Nos gusta vivir aquí.	Living here is pleasing to us.	*We like to live here.*

The verb **gustar** is used to express likes and dislikes, but **gustar** does not literally mean *to like*. **Gustar** means *to be pleasing* (to someone).

Gustar is always used with an indirect object pronoun: someone or something is pleasing *to* someone else. It is most commonly used in the third-person singular or plural **(gusta/gustan),** and must agree with its subject, which is the person or thing liked, *not* the person whose likes are being described. Note that an infinitive (**vivir** in the final sentence on page 194) is viewed as a singular subject in Spanish.

A mí me gustan los tacos.	*I like tacos.*
A Ud. no **le** gustan, ¿verdad?	*You don't like them, do you?*
¿A ellos les gusta leer?	*Do they like to read?*

As in the preceding sentences, **a mí (a ti, a Ud.,** and so on) may be used in addition to the indirect object pronouns for clarification or emphasis.

The indirect object pronoun *must* be used with **gustar** even when an indirect object noun is expressed. A common word order is as follows:

(*A* + **pronoun/noun**)	**indirect object pronoun**	*gustar* + **subject**
A Juan	le	gustan las fiestas.
(A ellas)	Les	gusta esquiar.

Would Like/Wouldn't Like

What one *would* or *would not* like to do is expressed with the form **gustaría*** + *infinitive* and the appropriate indirect objects.

A mí me gustaría viajar a Colombia.	*I would like to travel to Colombia.*
Nos gustaría almorzar contigo hoy.	*We would like to eat lunch with you today.*

Práctica

A. Gustos y preferencias. ¿Le gusta o no le gusta? Siga los modelos.

MODELOS ¿el café? → (No) Me gusta el café.
¿los pasteles? → (No) Me gustan los pasteles.

---

*This is one of the forms of the conditional of **gustar.** You will study all of the forms of the conditional in **Capítulo 24.**

1. ¿el vino?
2. ¿los niños pequeños?
3. ¿la música clásica?
4. ¿los discos de Barbra Streisand?
5. ¿el invierno?
6. ¿probar (*to try*) platos nuevos?
7. ¿las clases que empiezan a las ocho?
8. ¿el chocolate?
9. ¿las películas de horror?
10. ¿cocinar?
11. ¿las clases de este semestre?
12. ¿la gramática?
13. ¿los postres?
14. ¿bailar en las discotecas?

B. Los miembros de la familia Soto no están de acuerdo sobre el lugar donde van a cenar esta noche. Describa las preferencias de todos, según el modelo.

MODELO   padre / comida japonesa→
    Al padre le gusta la comida japonesa.

1. mí / mariscos
2. Ernesto / tacos con salsa picante
3. niños / comida mexicana
4. mamá / verduras
5. nosotros / helado de chocolate
6. Elena / pescado veracruzano

C. Seleccionando una pizza. ¿Cómo se dice en español?

1. My father likes anchovies **(las anchoas),** but he doesn't like sausage **(el chorizo).**
2. My mother likes sausage, but she doesn't like cheese much.
3. My brothers like cheese, but they don't like mushrooms **(los champiñones).**
4. I like everything **(todo),** and I would like to order that pizza right now!

Escriba Ud. en español un párrafo parecido (*similar*) sobre los gustos y preferencias de los miembros de su familia (sus compañeros de clase, de la residencia, etcétera).

CH. ¿Qué te gusta? ¿Qué odias (*do you hate*)? Almost every situation has aspects that one likes or dislikes—even hates. React to the following situations by telling what you like or don't like about them. Follow the model and the cues, but add your own words as well and expand your responses, using **me gustaría** if you can.

MODELO   En la playa: el agua, el sol, nadar, la arena (*sand*) →
    · Me gusta mucho el agua pero no me gusta nada el sol. Por eso no me gustaría pasar todo el día en la playa.
    · Me gusta nadar pero odio la arena. Por eso me gustaría más nadar en una piscina (*pool*).

1. En un avión: viajar en avión, la comida, las películas, la música
2. En una discoteca: la música, bailar, el ruido, el humo

3. En un parque: los animales, los insectos, las flores, la hierba (*grass*)
4. En un coche: manejar (*to drive*), el tráfico, los camiones (*trucks*), los policías, el límite de velocidad
5. En un hospital: las inyecciones, los médicos, los enfermeros (las enfermeras) (*nurses*), los visitantes, recibir flores

OTROS SITIOS: En una fiesta; En la biblioteca; En clase; En una cafetería; En un gran almacén; En casa, con sus padres

D. **Entrevista: ¿Qué te gusta más?** Use the following cues to determine what another student likes or dislikes about the topics, asking him or her to give reasons, if possible. When the interview is over, report the most interesting information you have learned to the class.

MODELO   el rojo, el azul o el verde →
　　　　　—¿Qué color te gusta más—el rojo, el azul o el verde?
　　　　　—Pues… yo creo que me gusta más el azul.
　　　　　—¿Puedes explicarme por qué te gusta más ese color?
　　　　　—Sí, me gusta porque es el color de los ojos (*eyes*) de mi novio/a.

1. el cine o la televisión
2. el verano, el invierno, el otoño o la primavera
3. vivir solo/a (*alone*) o vivir con un compañero (una compañera)
4. viajar en clase turística o en primera clase
5. viajar en avión, en tren, en autobús o en coche
6. vivir en la residencia o en un apartamento
7. las fiestas grandes o las pequeñas
8. las fiestas improvisadas o las bien organizadas
9. comer en casa o salir a comer en un restaurante
10. ir de compras en un almacén o en un mercado

¿Dónde vamos a comer?

—Vamos a «Las Tres Marías».
—No conozco ese restaurante.
—Pues allí sirven un mole delicioso.
—¿Y no es muy caro?
—Al contrario. Los precios son muy razonables.
—¡Eso espero! ¡A comer! ¡Tengo hambre!

Guadalajara, México

Peter Menzel

REPASO

Comentarios de un camarero. Complete the following paragraphs with the correct form of the words in parentheses, as suggested by the context. When two possibilities are given in parentheses, select the correct word.

(*Yo: ser/estar*[1]) camarero en un restaurante mexicano excelente que se llama «El Charro». El dueño del restaurante (*ser/estar*[2]) mi tío Rodrigo. (*Él: llegar*[3]) al restaurante cada° mañana (*son/a*[4]) las ocho en punto.° (*Nada/Nunca*[5]) puede llegar tarde porque él tiene (*que/de*[6]) (*abrir*[7]) las puertas y (*hacer*[8]) los preparativos para el día. Entra en la oficina y (*cerrar*[9]) la puerta tan pronto como llega. Nunca (*le/lo*[10]) veo salir antes de (*los/las*[11]) once y media.

    every / en… on the dot

Pasa tres horas y media (*preparar*[12]) el menú del día. Todo depende de° los productos disponibles° en el mercado. En primavera y verano, por ejemplo, hay más verduras y frutas frescas (*como/que*[13]) en las otras estaciones. Durante el otoño se (*vender*[14]) mucho guajolote o carne de res.° Los vendedores° del mercado (*lo/le*[15]) venden a mi tío lo mejor de todo porque (*conocer/saber*[16]) que (*nosotros/nuestros*[17]) clientes esperan lo mejor que hay.

    on
    available

    carne… beef
    salespeople

Durante todas las estaciones del año (*nosotros: ofrecer*[18]) platos tradicionales de (*nuestro*[19]) país: tacos con salsa picante, mole poblano, enchiladas de pollo, guacamole… Estos platos (*los/les*[20]) (*gustar*[21]) a todos. Si los clientes (*ser/estar*[22]) satisfechos, nosotros (*ser/estar*[23]) contentos. ¡Nuestro trabajo nos (*dar*[24]) mucha satisfacción!

UN PASO MÁS: Lectura cultural

Antes de leer

It is easy to "get off the track" while reading if you assign the wrong meaning to a word that has multiple English equivalents. The word **como** can cause confusion because it can mean *how, like, the way that, as, since,* and *I eat,* depending on the context in which it occurs. Other common words with multiple meanings include **que** (*what, that, who*), **clase** (*class meeting, course, kind,* or *type*), and **esperar** (*to wait for, to hope, to expect*).

    You must rely on the context to determine which meaning is appropriate. Practice by telling what **como** means in each of the following sentences.

1. En España, como en Francia, se come mucho pescado.
2. No me gusta como habla el profesor; debe hablar más despacio.
3. Como tú no deseas estudiar, ¿por qué no tomamos una cerveza?

Las comidas en el mundo hispánico

En algunas partes del mundo hispánico, como en México y España, «la comida» se come al mediodía. En otras partes, como en el Perú, Chile y Nicaragua, «la comida» se come por la noche. Pero en casi todas partes la comida del mediodía es la comida fuerte.°   *principal*

En las grandes ciudades el sistema está cambiando° poco a poco. Es cada vez más° común no almorzar en casa, sobre todo° cuando uno vive muy lejos de su trabajo. En este caso, el almuerzo tiende a ser un poco más ligero, y la comida de la noche es la principal. En algunas partes es costumbre comer cinco veces al día: la jornada° se interrumpe una vez por la mañana y otra vez por la tarde.   *changing* / cada... *increasingly* / sobre... *especialmente* / día laboral

Como en todas partes del mundo, en los países hispánicos hay muchos restaurantes buenos y variados. El único problema es que a veces el horario de los restaurantes no corresponde a lo que° por costumbre se espera. En Buenos Aires, por ejemplo, los buenos restaurantes se abren por la noche a las siete u° ocho, o incluso más tarde. Los turistas norteamericanos acostumbran a cenar más temprano.   lo... *what* / *o*

Una de las características más interesantes de los restaurantes en la América Latina es que los camareros casi no charlan° con los clientes; son mucho más reservados. En cambio, en los Estados Unidos no es nada raro° hablar un rato° con la persona que sirve la comida.   *hablan* / no... *it isn't unusual* / breve período de tiempo

---

Comprensión

Indique si es una costumbre (*custom*) hispana o norteamericana. Explique su respuesta en cada caso.

1. comer a las seis
2. no hablar con el camarero
3. tomar la comida más fuerte durante el día
4. salir a cenar en un restaurante a las nueve de la noche
5. tomar un almuerzo ligero a las doce del día
6. tomar un breve descanso por la mañana, aun (*even*) si se trabaja en una oficina

Para escribir

A. Create your own composition about eating and drinking habits in the United States by completing the sentences of the following paragraph.

En los Estados Unidos no damos gran importancia a las comidas. La vida norteamericana es tan rápida que _____. Muchas veces el padre o la madre _____ y no puede _____ . También los niños _____ . Por eso cada miembro de la familia norteamericana _____ .

B. Write a brief paragraph about your eating preferences or those of your family. Use the following questions as a guide in developing your paragraph.

1. ¿Cuántas veces comen al día? ¿A qué hora?
2. ¿Comen juntos?
3. ¿Quién(es) prepara(n) la comida?
4. ¿Qué prepara(n)? ¿Es excelente la comida? ¿buena? ¿mala? ¿regular?
5. ¿Qué comida prefieren cuando comen en un restaurante? ¿comida china? ¿mexicana? ¿italiana? ¿hamburguesas? ¿En qué restaurantes comen?
6. ¿Comen allí con frecuencia? ¿Cuántas veces al año? ¿Cuándo van a volver?

VOCABULARIO

VERBOS

dar (*irreg.*) to give
decir (*irreg.*) to say; to tell
gustar to like
mandar to send
odiar to hate
preparar to prepare
prestar to lend
regalar to give (*as a gift*)

MÁS COMIDAS Y BEBIDAS

el agua (*f.*) **(mineral)** (mineral) water
las albóndigas meatballs
los antojitos appetizers
el bolillo (hard) roll

el cóctel (de camarones) (shrimp) cocktail
el guacamole avocado dip
el guajolote turkey
el mole poblano chocolate sauce (*for meat, poultry*)
el pan dulce sweet rolls
el pan tostado toast
la salsa (picante) (hot) sauce

OTROS SUSTANTIVOS

el consejo advice; piece of advice
el/la chico/a boy/girl; guy, kid
la flor flower
el humo smoke
la tarjeta card
la verdad truth

PALABRAS INDEFINIDAS Y NEGATIVAS

alguien someone, anyone
algún (alguno/a/os/as) some, any
jamás never
nada nothing
nadie no one, nobody, not anybody
ningún (ninguno/a) no, none, not any
tampoco neither, not either

FRASES ÚTILES PARA LA COMUNICACIÓN	
¿Qué te (le,...) parece?	What do you think? How does that strike you?
Me (Te,...) gustaría...	I (You, . . .) would (really) like . . .

CAPÍTULO 11

De vacaciones

VOCABULARIO: PREPARACIÓN

EN EL AEROPUERTO / AT THE AIRPORT

el asiento seat
el boleto/billete*de ida (y vuelta) one-way (round-trip) ticket
la demora delay
estar atrasado/a to be late
guardar (un puesto) to save (a place)

hacer escalas to have/make stopovers
hacer la(s) maleta(s) to pack one's suitcase(s)
ir/estar de vacaciones to go/be on vacation

la llegada arrival
el maletero porter
el pasaje ticket, fare
la salida departure
subir al/bajar del avión to get on/off the plane
el vuelo flight

IR EN TREN, EN AUTOBÚS / GOING BY TRAIN, BY BUS

la estación (de trenes, de autobuses) (train, bus) station

*Throughout Spanish America, **boleto** is the word used for a *ticket for travel*. **Billete** is commonly used in Spain. The words **entrada** and **localidad** are used to refer to tickets for movies, plays, or similar functions.

En el aeropuerto

—Perdón, ¿sabe Ud. si el vuelo 638 va a salir a tiempo?

—Sí, eso dicen. A las tres y cuarto.

—Pues, ¡qué bien! Así tengo tiempo para tomar algo.

—Si quiere, deje (*leave*) sus cosas aquí. Le puedo guardar el puesto.

—Muchísimas gracias. ¿Quiere que le traiga algo?

—No, nada. Gracias.

Puerto Vallarta, México

A. ¿Cuántas cosas y acciones puede Ud. identificar o describir en este dibujo?

B. Ud. va a hacer un viaje en avión. El vuelo sale a las siete de la mañana. Usando los números de **1** a **9**, indique en qué orden van a pasar las siguientes cosas.

_____ Subo al avión.

_____ Voy a la sala de espera.

_____ Hago cola para comprar el boleto de ida y vuelta y facturar el equipaje.

_____ Llego al aeropuerto a tiempo (*on time*) y bajo del taxi.

_____ Se anuncia la salida del vuelo.

_____ Estoy atrasado/a. Salgo para el aeropuerto en taxi.

_____ La azafata me indica el asiento.

_____ Pido asiento en la sección de no fumar.

_____ Hay demora. Por eso todos tenemos que esperar el vuelo allí antes de subir al avión.

C. ¿Qué va Ud. a hacer en estas situaciones?

1. Ud. no tiene mucho dinero. ¿Qué clase de pasaje va a comprar?
   a. clase turística   b. primera clase   c. un pasaje en la sección
   de fumar
2. Ud. quiere pedir dos pasajes—uno para Ud., el otro para su
   amigo/a. Él/Ella tiene alergia a los cigarrillos. ¿Qué pide Ud.?
   a. Dos boletos, sección de fumar, por favor.
   b. Dos pasajes, sin escala, por favor.
   c. Dos asientos, sección de no fumar, por favor.
3. Ud. es una persona muy nerviosa y tiene miedo de viajar en
   avión. Necesita ir desde Nueva York a Madrid. ¿Qué pide Ud.?
   a. un vuelo con muchas escalas
   b. un vuelo sin escalas
   c. un boleto de tren
4. Ud. tiene muchas maletas. Pesan (*They weigh*) mucho y no puede
   llevarlas. ¿Qué hace Ud.?
   a. Compro boletos.   b. Guardo un asiento.   c. Facturo el
   equipaje.
5. Su vuelo está atrasado, pero Ud. está tranquilo/a. ¿Qué dice Ud.?
   a. Azafata, insisto en hablar con el capitán.
   b. Una demora más... no importa.
   c. Si no llegamos dentro de (*within*) diez minutos, bajo del avión.

CH. ¿A quién se describe, a don Gregorio, vicepresidente de la IBM, o a
Harry, típico estudiante universitario?

1. Siempre viaja en clase turística porque es más económica.
2. No le importan nada las demoras; no tiene prisa.
3. Nunca hace cola para comprar el boleto porque su secretaria le
   arregla (*arranges*) todo el viaje.
4. Cuando viaja en avión, es porque está de vacaciones.
5. Por lo general, prefiere viajar en autobús porque es más
   económico.
6. Muchas veces no lleva equipaje porque hace viajes de un solo
   día.
7. Siempre que (*Whenever*) viaja, lleva traje y corbata.

D. Preguntas

1. Cuando Ud. está de vacaciones, ¿le gusta viajar o prefiere no salir
   de su ciudad? ¿Cuáles son las actividades que Ud. normalmente
   asocia con las vacaciones?
2. Cuando Ud. viaja, ¿prefiere ir solo/a (*alone*), con un amigo (una
   amiga) o con un grupo de personas? ¿Le gusta ir de vacaciones
   con su familia?

3. ¿Prefiere Ud. viajar en avión, en tren o en autobús? ¿Cuál es más rápido? ¿más económico? ¿Cuál de ellos hace más escalas?
4. Cuando Ud. va a viajar en avión, ¿pide boletos de primera clase o de clase turística? ¿Por qué? ¿Pide Ud. asiento en la sección de fumar o en la de no fumar? ¿Cómo paga Ud. el pasaje? ¿con cheque? ¿con tarjeta de crédito? ¿Paga al contado (*cash*) a veces?
5. Cuando Ud. viaja, ¿prefiere salir por la mañana o por la noche? ¿Lleva muchas o pocas maletas? ¿Lo/La ayuda el maletero? ¿Cómo reacciona Ud. si la aerolínea pierde su equipaje?

PRONUNCIACIÓN: *x*

The letter **x** is usually pronounced as [ks], as in English. Before a consonant, however, the [k] is often dropped and the resulting sound is simply an [s] sound, as in **texto** and **extranjero.**

Práctica

A. [ks] léxico sexo axial existen examen

B. [s] explique extraordinario sexto extremo extraterrestre

MINIDIÁLOGOS Y ESTRUCTURA

22 Telling Someone to Do Something: Formal Commands

En el avión

AZAFATA: *Pase Ud.*, señor. Bienvenido a bordo.
PASAJERO: Gracias. Éste es mi asiento, ¿verdad?
AZAFATA: Sí, es el 24A. *Tome* asiento y *no olvide* el cinturón de seguridad.
PASAJERO: ¿Puedo fumar?
AZAFATA: Ésta es la sección de fumar, pero *no fume Ud.* ahora, por favor. Vamos a despegar pronto para Quito.
PASAJERO: ¿Para Quito? Pero… ¿el vuelo ciento doce no va a Cuzco?
AZAFATA: Sí señor, pero éste es el vuelo ciento dos. *¡Baje Ud.* ahora mismo—todavía hay tiempo!

On the plane FLIGHT ATTENDANT: *Come in, sir. Welcome aboard.* PASSENGER: *Thank you. This is my seat, isn't it?* FLIGHT ATTENDANT: *Yes, it's (number) 24A. Take your seat and don't forget the seatbelt.* PASSENGER: *May I smoke?* FLIGHT ATTENDANT: *This is the smoking section, but don't smoke now, please. We're going to take off for Quito right away.* PASSENGER: *For Quito? But ... doesn't Flight 112 go to Cuzco?* FLIGHT ATTENDANT: *Yes, sir, but this is Flight 102. Get off right now—there's still time!*

1. *¿Qué dice la azafata cuando el pasajero entra en el avión?*
2. *¿El pasajero encuentra (finds) su asiento? ¿Cuál es?*
3. *¿Por qué no debe fumar ahora el pasajero?*
4. *¿Cuál es el error del pasajero?*
5. *¿Qué debe hacer el pasajero?*

Commands (imperatives) are verb forms used to tell someone to do something. In this section you will learn the *formal commands* **(los mandatos formales),** that is, the commands used with people whom you address as **Ud.** or **Uds.**

Formation of Formal Commands

Regular Verbs		Stem	Singular	Plural	English Equivalent
hablar:	hablø →	habl-	hable (Ud.)	hablen (Uds.)	*speak*
comer:	comø →	com-	coma (Ud.)	coman (Uds.)	*eat*
escribir:	escribø →	escrib-	escriba (Ud.)	escriban (Uds.)	*write*

A. **Ud./Uds.** commands are formed by dropping the final **-o** from the first-person singular of the present tense and adding **-e/-en** for **-ar** verbs and **-a/-an** for **-er** and **-ir** verbs. Using **Ud.** or **Uds.** after the command forms makes the command somewhat more formal or more polite.

B. Formal commands of stem-changing verbs will show the stem change, since these commands are based on the **yo** form.

   pi**e**nse Ud.   v**ue**lva Ud.   p**i**da Ud.

C. Verbs ending in **-car, -gar,** and **-zar** require a spelling change in the command form in order to preserve the **-c-, -g-,** and **-z-** sounds.

   buscar: bus**que** Ud.   pagar: pa**gue** Ud.   empezar: empie**ce** Ud.

CH. The **Ud./Uds.** commands for verbs that have irregular **yo** forms will reflect the irregularity.

conocer:	conozcø	→ **conozca Ud.**	salir:	salgø	→ **salga Ud.**
decir:	digø	→ **diga Ud.**	tener:	tengø	→ **tenga Ud.**
hacer:	hagø	→ **haga Ud.**	traer:	traigø	→ **traiga Ud.**
oír:	oigø	→ **oiga Ud.**	venir:	vengø	→ **venga Ud.**
poner:	pongø	→ **ponga Ud.**	ver:	veø	→ **vea Ud.**

D. A few verbs have irregular **Ud./Uds.** command forms.

dar: **dé Ud.**   ir: **vaya Ud.**   saber: **sepa Ud.**
estar: **esté Ud.**   ser: **sea Ud.**

[Práctica A–B]

Position of Object Pronouns with Formal Commands

Direct and indirect object pronouns must follow affirmative commands and be attached to them. In order to maintain the original stress of the verb form, an accent mark is added to the stressed vowel if the original command has two or more syllables.

Léalo Ud.	*Read it.*
Búsquele el bolígrafo.	*Look for the pen for him.*

Direct and indirect object pronouns must precede negative commands.

No lo lea Ud.	*Don't read it.*
No le busque el bolígrafo.	*Don't look for the pen for him.*

[Práctica C–G]

Práctica

A. El Sr. Casiano no se siente (*feel*) bien. ¿Qué *no* debe hacer para estar mejor? Déle mandatos negativos según el modelo, usando los verbos indicados o cualquier (*any*) otro.

MODELO   comer tanto → Sr. Casiano, no coma tanto.

1. trabajar tanto
2. cenar demasiado
3. fumar
4. beber tanto
5. volver tarde a casa
6. almorzar tanto
7. jugar al fútbol todas las tardes
8. salir tanto por la noche
9. ir a discotecas
10. ser tan impaciente

B. Imagine que Ud. es el profesor (la profesora) hoy. ¿Qué mandatos debe dar a la clase?

MODELO   hablar español → Hablen Uds. español.

1. llegar a tiempo
2. leer la lección
3. escribir una composición
4. abrir los libros
5. pensar en español
6. estar en clase mañana
7. traer los libros a clase
8. __?__

C. Con otro estudiante, haga recomendaciones sobre lo que (*what*) se debe o no se debe comer o beber si se está a dieta.

MODELOS   ensalada → —¿Ensalada?   postres → —¿Postres?
       —Cómala.   —No los coma.

1. alcohol (*m.*)   6. hamburguesas con queso
2. verduras   7. fruta
3. pan   8. carne
4. dulces   9. pollo
5. leche   10. refrescos dietéticos

CH. La Sra. Medina quiere tener solamente clases fáciles este semestre. ¿Debe o no debe tomar las siguientes clases?

MODELO   la física → —¿Física?
         —No, no la tome.

1. Inglés 1   5. Cálculo 1
2. Ciencias políticas 6. Comercio
3. Historia de Latinoamérica 7. Español 2
4. Química orgánica   8. ?

D. Give a singular command (affirmative or negative, as appropriate) in response to each exclamation.

MODELO   ¡Qué canción más bonita! (*What a pretty song!*) → Cántela.
                     Tóquela.
                     Escúchela.

1. ¡Qué canción más fea!   5. ¡Qué libro más aburrido!
2. ¡Qué vestido más elegante! 6. ¡Qué maleta más bonita!
3. ¡Qué abrigo más caro!   7. ¡Qué ciudad más interesante!
4. ¡Qué viaje más interesante! 8. ¡Qué viaje más largo!

E. Preparativos para un viaje. ¿Cómo se dice en español?

1. Pack your bags.   7. Wait in line.
2. Don't forget your wallet. 8. Give your ticket to the flight
3. Go to the airport.   attendant.
4. Don't be (**llegar**) late.   9. Get on the plane.
5. Buy your round-trip ticket. 10. Find your seat.
6. Check your bags.

F. ¿Qué le aconseja? Dé mandatos afirmativos o negativos a la persona que dice lo siguiente.

1. Estoy cansado.   6. Necesito más dinero.
2. Tengo sed.   7. Mis padres quieren saber cómo
3. Tengo hambre.   estoy.
4. No puedo dormir.   8. No puedo encontrar mi libro de
5. No entiendo el ejercicio.   español.

G. Situaciones. You are a clerk at an airport ticket counter (**el**

mostrador) and someone asks you how to get to the waiting room **(sala de espera).** Give him or her directions in Spanish.

Frases útiles

ir: vaya Ud.	go	todo derecho	straight ahead
doblar: doble Ud.	turn	a la derecha	to the right
seguir (i, i): siga Ud.	continue	a la izquierda	to the left
pasar: pase Ud. por	pass through/by	el pasillo	the hall, corridor

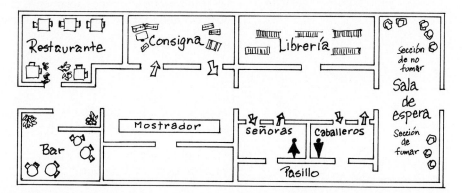

If you are in	Tell someone how to get to
1. la sala de espera	el bar
2. la consigna (*baggage claim area*)	la librería
3. el restaurante	los servicios (*restrooms*)

23 Another Verbal System
The Subjunctive: An Introduction

Al aeropuerto, por favor. ¡Tenemos prisa!

ESTEBAN: ¡Qué temprano sale el avión! ¡Ojalá que *lleguemos* a tiempo!

CARLOTA: ¿Quieres que te *ayude* con las maletas?

ESTEBAN: No. Quiero que *subas* al taxi. Estamos atrasados. ¡No quiero que *perdamos* el vuelo!

CARLOTA: ¡Y yo quiero que tú *tomes* un calmante! Si el avión despega sin nosotros, ¿qué más da? Tomamos el próximo vuelo y ya está.

To the airport, please. We're in a hurry!   ESTEBAN: *What an early flight this is! (lit., How early the plane is leaving!) I hope we get there on time!*   CARLOTA: *Do you want me to help you with the bags?*   ESTEBAN: *No. I want you to get into the cab. We're late. I don't want us to miss the flight!*   CARLOTA: *And I want you to take a tranquilizer! If the plane takes off without us, so what? We'll take the next flight, that's all.*

Describa los deseos de Esteban.

1. *Esteban quiere que (ellos)...*
  a. *lleguen a tiempo.* **b.** *lleguen en dos horas.*
2. *Quiere que Carlota...*
  a. *suba al taxi.* **b.** *suba al autobús.*
3. *No quiere que Carlota...*
  a. *lo ayude con las maletas.* **b.** *lo ayude con el taxista.*
4. *No quiere que (ellos)...*
  a. *pierdan el taxi.* **b.** *pierdan el vuelo.*

Subjunctive: An Overview

The present tense forms you have already learned are part of a verb system called the *indicative mood* (**el indicativo**). The **Ud.** and **Uds.** command forms that you learned in Grammar Section 22 are part of another verb system called the *subjunctive mood* (**el subjuntivo**).

In both English and Spanish, the indicative is used to state facts and ask questions. It is used to express objectively most real-world actions or states of being.

> She's writing the letter.
> We are already there!

The subjunctive is used to express more subjective or conceptualized actions or states: things we want to happen, things we try to get other people to do, and events that we are reacting to emotionally.

> I recommend that she **write** the letter immediately.
> I wish (that) we **were** already there.*

In later sections you will learn more about the concepts associated with the Spanish subjunctive. This section focuses on the forms of the subjunctive and on the structure of a type of sentence in which it is used.

Subjunctive: Sentence Structure

Each of the preceding English sentences with the subjunctive has two clauses: an independent clause with a conjugated verb and subject that can stand alone (*I recommend, I wish*), and a dependent (subordinate) clause that cannot stand alone (*that she write, that we were there*). The subjunctive is used in the dependent clause.

---

*The use of the subjunctive has lessened in modern English, and many English speakers no longer use it.

Indicate the independent and dependent clauses in the following sentences.

1. I don't think (that) they're very nice.
2. We feel (that) you really shouldn't go.
3. He suggests (that) we be there on time.
4. We don't believe (that) she's capable of that.

The Spanish subjunctive also occurs primarily in *dependent clauses* **(las cláusulas subordinadas).** Note that each clause has a different subject.

Independent Clause		Dependent Clause
first subject + *indicative*	(that)	second subject + *subjunctive*
Quiero	**que**	subas al taxi.
No quiero	**que**	perdamos el vuelo.

Forms of the Present Subjunctive

The personal endings of the present subjunctive are added to the first-person singular of the present indicative minus its **-o** ending. As with **Ud./Uds.** commands, **-ar** verbs add endings with **-e**, while **-er/-ir** verbs add endings with **-a**.

PRESENT SUBJUNCTIVE OF REGULAR VERBS					
hablar: **hablø → habl-**		**comer:** **comø → com-**		**vivir:** **vivø → viv-**	
hable	hablemos	coma	comamos	viva	vivamos
hables	habléis	comas	comáis	vivas	viváis
hable	hablen	coma	coman	viva	vivan

The irregularities that you learned with **Ud./Uds.** commands occur in all forms of the present subjunctive.

Present subjunctive of verbs with spelling changes:

-car: c → **qu**	buscar:	bus**qu**e, bus**qu**es,...
-gar: g → **gu**	pagar:	pa**gu**e, pa**gu**es,...
-zar: z → **c**	empezar:	empie**c**e, empie**c**es,...

*Present subjunctive of verbs with irregular indicative **yo** form:*

conocer: **conozca, conozcas, conozca, conozcamos, conozcáis, conozcan**

decir: **diga,...**	poner: **ponga,...**	traer: **traiga,...**
hacer: **haga,...**	salir: **salga,...**	venir: **venga,...**
oír: **oiga,...**	tener: **tenga,...**	ver: **vea,...**

Irregular present subjunctive forms:

dar:	**dé, des, dé, demos, deis, den**

estar:	**esté,**...	saber:	**sepa,**...
haber (hay):	**haya**	ser:	**sea,**...
ir:	**vaya,**...		

Present subjunctive of stem-changing verbs:

-Ar and **-er** stem-changing verbs follow the stem-changing pattern of the present indicative.

pensar (ie): p**ie**nse, p**ie**nses, p**ie**nse, pensemos, penséis, p**ie**nsen
poder (ue): p**ue**da, p**ue**das, p**ue**da, p**o**damos, p**o**dáis, p**ue**dan

-Ir stem-changing verbs show the first stem change in four forms and the second stem change in the **nosotros** and **vosotros** forms.

dormir (ue, u): d**ue**rma, d**ue**rmas, d**ue**rma, d**u**rmamos, d**u**rmáis,
d**ue**rman
preferir (ie, i): pref**ie**ra, pref**ie**ras, pref**ie**ra, pref**i**ramos, pref**i**ráis,
pref**ie**ran

Meanings of the Present Subjunctive; Use with *querer*

Like the present indicative, the Spanish present subjunctive has several English equivalents: **(yo) hable** can mean *I speak, I am speaking, I do speak, I may speak,* or *I will speak.* The exact English equivalent of the Spanish present subjunctive depends on the context.

An English infinitive is frequently used to express the Spanish subjunctive.

Quieren que **estemos** allí a las dos.	*They want us **to be** there (that we be there) at 2:00.*
Quiero que **hables** con él en seguida.	*I want you **to speak** to him immediately.*

The use of the verb **querer** in the independent clause is one of the cues for the use of the subjunctive in the dependent clause. In this section you will practice the forms of the subjunctive mainly with **querer.** You will learn additional frequent uses of the subjunctive in the remaining sections of this book, and see yet other instances of the Spanish subjunctive wherever appropriate, though you may not know the rule or generalization that governs a particular occurrence. Now that you know how the subjunctive is formed, however, you will always be able to recognize it and understand its general meaning.

Práctica

A. Haga oraciones según las indicaciones. **¡OJO!** Cambie sólo el verbo de la cláusula subordinada.

1. Quiero que (tú)... (*bailar, cenar, mirar esto, llegar a tiempo, buscar a Anita*)
2. ¿Quieres que el niño...? (*aprender, escribir, leer, responder, asistir a clases*)
3. Ud. quiere que (yo)..., ¿verdad? (*empezar, jugar, pensarlo, servirlo, pedirlo*)
4. No quieren que (nosotros)... (*pedir eso, almorzar ahora, perderlos, dormir allí, cerrarla*)
5. Queremos que Uds.... (*conocerlo, hacerlo, traerlo, saberlo, decirlo*)
6. Yo no quiero que Ana... (*venir, salir ahora, ponerlo, oírlo, ser su amiga*)
7. ¿Quieres que (yo)...? (*tenerlo, verlo, estar allí, dar una fiesta, ir al cine contigo*)

B. ¿Qué desea cada una de las siguientes personas que hagamos? Haga oraciones según el modelo.

MODELO   profesora: hablar mejor el español →
         La profesora quiere que **hablemos** mejor el español.

1. Fred: no tener muchos exámenes
2. Betty: no tener que escribir más composiciones
3. Sally: aprender a expresarnos (*ourselves*) mejor
4. profesor: contestar bien todas las preguntas en el examen final

C. **Más sugerencias para las vacaciones.** ¿Adónde quieren todos que vayamos? Haga oraciones según el modelo.

MODELO   Papá: ir a la playa → Papá quiere que **vayamos** a la playa.

1. Mamá: visitar la ciudad de Santa Fe
2. Laura: hacer varias excursiones cortas
3. niños: ir a Miami
4. Guillermo: volver a una casita (*cabin*) en las montañas
5. tú: estar en casa todo el verano

CH. **Trabajo del guía** (*guide*). ¿Cómo se dice en español?

1. I want him to buy the tickets.
2. Do you want him to check the bags?
3. He doesn't want us to stand in line.
4. He doesn't want us to be late.

D. La palabra **ojalá** significa *I wish* o *I hope;* nunca cambia de forma. Se usa con el subjuntivo para expresar deseos.

- **Ojalá que** haya paz (*peace*) en el mundo.
- **Ojalá que** todos estén bien.

Imagine que Ud. tiene tres deseos. Puede desear cualquier (*any*) cosa para cualquier persona. ¿Qué desea Ud.? Empiece sus deseos con **Ojalá que....**

E. ¿Qué quiere Ud. que hagan los demás (*others*)? Complete la oración en una forma lógica, haciendo todas las oraciones posibles.

Quiero que mi(s) (padres, novio/a, esposo/a, mejor amigo/a) _____ .

---

24 Expressing Desires and Requests
Use of the Subjunctive in Noun Clauses: Willing

Noun Clauses

The use of the subjunctive is associated with the presence, in the independent clause, of a number of concepts or conditions—willing, emotion, and doubt—that trigger the use of the subjunctive in the dependent clause.

- *What does the boss **want**?*
  Quiere que los empleados lleguen a tiempo.   (*direct object*)

- *What does the boss **like**?*
  Le gusta que los empleados lleguen a tiempo.   (*subject*)

- *What does the boss **doubt**?*
  Duda que los empleados siempre lleguen a tiempo.   (*direct object*)

These uses of the subjunctive fall into the general category of the subjunctive in noun clauses. The clause in which the subjunctive appears functions like a noun (subject or direct object) in the sentence as a whole.

Willing

Independent Clause		Dependent Clause
first subject + *indicative* (expression of willing)	**que**	second subject + *subjunctive*
La empresa **quiere** que los empleados **estén** contentos.		*The company wants the employees to be happy.*
¿**Prefieres** (tú) que (yo) **haga** un flan o un pastel?		*Do you prefer that I make a flan or a cake?*
Es necesario que Álvaro **estudie** más.		*It's necessary that Álvaro study more.*

A. Expressions of willing are those in which someone, directly or indirectly, tries to influence what someone else does or thinks: *I suggest that you be there on time; It's necessary that you be there.* In Spanish, expressions of willing, however strong or weak, are followed by the subjunctive mood in the dependent clause.

B. Some verbs of willing include **decir, desear, insistir (en), mandar** (*to order* or *to send*), **pedir (i, i), permitir** (*to permit*), **preferir (ie, i), prohibir** (*to prohibit* or *forbid*), **querer (ie),** and **recomendar (ie).** Because it is impossible to give a complete list of all Spanish verbs of willing, remember that verbs that convey the sense of willing—not just certain verbs—are followed by the subjunctive.

> ¡OJO! *The subjunctive is used in the dependent clause after **decir** and **insistir en** when they convey an order. The subjunctive is* not *used when they convey information. Compare the following:*

Carolina nos dice que **lleguemos** a las siete en punto.	*Carolina says (that) we should arrive at 7:00 sharp.*
Carolina dice que **son** simpáticos.	*Carolina says (that) they're nice.*

C. Remember to use the infinitive—not the subjunctive—after verbs of willing when there is no change of subject: *Desean cenar ahora.* but *Desean que Luisa y yo cenemos ahora.*

CH. As you know, generalizations are followed by infinitives. **Es necesario estudiar.** When a generalization of willing is personalized (made to refer to a specific person), it is followed by the subjunctive in the dependent clause: **Es necesario** *que estudiemos.* Other generalizations of willing include **es urgente, es preferible,** and **es preciso** (*necessary*).

Práctica

A. **Sugerencias y recomendaciones.** Dé oraciones nuevas según las indicaciones.

1. En clase: El profesor no permite que *Uds.* fumen. (*yo, nosotros, tú, los estudiantes, Lupe, vosotros*)
2. En casa, el día antes de la fiesta: Es necesario que alguien *llame a nuestros amigos.* (*comprar los refrescos, buscar unos discos nuevos, invitar a nuestros amigos, traer la comida, cocinar*)

B. ¿Qué le piden a Ud. siempre sus amigos?

Mis amigos siempre me piden que _____ . (*estudiar con ellos, salir con ellos, explicarles la gramática, ir al cine, no tomar tanto café,* _____*?*___)

C. Complete las oraciones, usando el subjuntivo de los verbos indicados.

1. No nos gusta *pagar* los impuestos (*taxes*), pero es preciso que (nosotros) los _____ .
2. Quiero *ir* a Albania, pero nuestro gobierno prohíbe que los ciudadanos (*citizens*) de los Estados Unidos _____ a ese país.
3. Quiero *tomar* seis clases este semestre, pero el consejero no permite que _____ tantas.
4. Amanda no le quiere *regalar* nada a su primo, pero su madre insiste en que le _____ algo.

CH. De viaje. Your friends the Padillas, from Guatemala, need help arranging for and getting on their flight back home. Explain who will help them, using the cues as a guide. Form two-clause sentences, as in the model.

MODELO   los Padilla: querer [tú: comprarles los boletos] →
Los Padilla quieren que tú les compres los boletos.

1. es necesario [Juan: llamarles un taxi]
2. yo: insistir [el maletero: bajar (*to carry down*) las maletas]
3. ellos: preferir [yo: facturarles el equipaje]
4. es preferible [tú: guardarles un puesto en la cola]
5. es preciso: [el señor Padilla: buscar los pasaportes]
6. la azafata: recomendar [ellos: subir al avión]
7. por fin, es preciso [nosotros: decirles adiós]

¡Por fin estamos de vacaciones!

—¿Cuántos días te dan de vacaciones?
—Este año, tres semanas.
—¿Vas a ir a algún lugar?
—¡Claro! Es posible que vayamos a la playa.

Stuart Cohen

Macuto, Venezuela

D. Oiga, por favor... ¿Cómo se dice en español?

1. Buy the tickets. Buy them the tickets, please. They insist that you buy them the tickets.
2. Save the seat. Save me the seat, please. I prefer that you save me the seat.
3. Check the bags. Check the bags for us, please. We recommend that you check the bags for us.

E. ¿Qué quieren estas personas?

1. El cliente_____. El dependiente_____. Yo creo que es importante _____.

2. La madre _____. Los niños _____. Yo creo que es necesario _____. Los padres siempre _____.

3. La jefa (*boss*) _____. La empleada _____. Parece que es urgente _____. Los jefes siempre _____.

REPASO

Recomendaciones para las vacaciones. Complete the following vacation suggestion with the correct form of the words in parentheses, as suggested by the context. When two possibilities are given in parentheses, select the correct word.

(*Les/Los*¹) quiero decir (*algo/nada*²) sobre (*el/la*³) ciudad de Machu Picchu. ¿Ya (*lo/la*⁴) (*saber/conocer*⁵) Uds.? (*Ser/Estar*⁶) situada en los Andes, a unos ochenta kilómetros° de la ciudad de Cuzco (Perú). Machu Picchu es conocida° como (*el/la*⁷) capital escondida° de los incas. Se (*decir*⁸) que (*ser/estar*⁹) una de las manifestaciones (*más/tan*¹⁰) importantes de la arquitectura incaica. Era° refugio y a la vez ciudad de vacaciones de los reyes° (*incaico*¹¹).

Yo (*querer*¹²) que Uds. la (*visitar*¹³) porque (*ser/estar*¹⁴) un sitio inolvidable.° (*Ir*¹⁵) Uds. a Machu Picchu en primavera o verano—son las (*mejor*¹⁶) estaciones para visitar este lugar. Pero (*comprar*¹⁷) Uds. los boletos pronto, porque (*mucho*¹⁸) turistas de todos los (*país*¹⁹) del mundo (*visitar*²⁰) este sitio extraordinario. ¡(*Yo: saber/conocer*²¹) que a Uds. (*los/les*²²) va a (*gustar*²³) el viaje!

50 millas
known / hidden

It was
kings

unforgettable

UN PASO MÁS: Imágenes del mundo hispánico
España: De la Edad Media (Middle Ages) *al Siglo de Oro*

Heide/Monkmeyer Press Photo Service

"El Entierro del Conde de Orgaz", obra
de El Greco

Bernard Silberstein/Monkmeyer Press Photo Service

Antiguas murallas (*walls*) de la ciudad de Ávila

*E*l culto al apóstol Santiago (*St. James*) tiene
una gran influencia en la historia de la
Península. Durante la Edad Media
numerosos peregrinos (*pilgrims*) vienen de
toda Europa a visitar la tumba del apóstol en
la ciudad de Santiago de Compostela, en el
noroeste. Traen con ellos sus costumbres y
su cultura, y así los reinos (*kingdoms*) de la
Península van integrándose en la tradición
europea.

En 1492 los Reyes Católicos, Isabel y
Fernando, expulsan definitivamente a los
musulmanes (árabes) de la Península.
Empieza entonces la época moderna de
España. Se descubre América, se inician los
viajes de exploración y de conquista y, en
unas décadas, España pasa a ser un gran
imperio. «En mis tierras nunca se pone (*sets*)
el sol», dice el emperador Carlos V. San
Lorenzo de El Escorial, el colosal monasterio

Mark Antman/The Image Works

El Escorial, cerca de Madrid

mandado (*ordered*) construir por Felipe II, es
uno de los símbolos de la grandeza imperial.

Se llama Siglo de Oro al siglo XVII. El
poder politicoeconómico de España ya no es
el mismo (*the same*) pero artísticamente es
una época excepcional. En la pintura, es el

siglo de Velázquez, El Greco y Zurbarán, entre otros. En la literatura hay que hablar de Lope de Vega, el Shakespeare español, autor de más de 400 comedias. Pero sobre todo es el siglo de Miguel de Cervantes, autor de *Don Quijote de la Mancha*. Sus

personajes presentan toda la complejidad no sólo del espíritu hispánico sino del ser humano en general. *El Quijote* es efectivamente la primera novela moderna.
(Continúa en el Capítulo 13.)

VOCABULARIO

VERBOS

bajar (de) to go down (from); to get off (of)
despegar to take off (*plane*)
encontrar (ue) to find
facturar to check (*luggage*)
fumar to smoke
guardar to keep, hold (*a seat, place*)
mandar to order
olvidar to forget
pasar (por) to pass (through, by)
permitir to permit
prohibir to forbid, prohibit
recomendar (ie) to recommend
subir (a) to go up (onto); to get on

LOS VIAJES

el asiento seat
el billete/boleto de ida (y vuelta) one-way (round-trip) ticket

la demora delay
el equipaje luggage
la estación (de trenes, de autobuses) (bus, train) station
la llegada arrival
el maletero porter
el pasaje ticket, fare
el/la pasajero/a passenger
el puesto place, position
la sala de espera waiting room
la salida departure

VIAJANDO EN AVIÓN

el aeropuerto airport
el avión plane
la azafata stewardess
el/la camarero/a flight attendant
la sección de (no) fumar (no-) smoking section
el vuelo flight

ADJETIVOS

atrasado/a late, behind schedule
solo/a alone

LAS SUGERENCIAS

es preciso it's necessary
es preferible it's preferable
es urgente it's urgent

PALABRAS ADICIONALES

a tiempo on time
hacer cola to stand in line
hacer escalas to have/make stopovers
hacer la(s) maleta(s) to pack one's suitcase(s)
ir de vacaciones to go on vacation

FRASES ÚTILES PARA LA COMUNICACIÓN	
¡Ojalá!	I wish!
¡Ojalá que... !	I hope that... !
¡Qué más da!	What difference does it make!

CAPÍTULO 12

En busca de un puesto

VOCABULARIO: PREPARACIÓN

DIRECCIÓN DE PERSONAL

caerle bien a la entrevistadora

graduarse*

llenar las solicitudes

escribir a máquina

─────── **DURANTE LA ENTREVISTA** / DURING THE INTERVIEW ───────

caer (caigo) to fall
caerle bien/mal a alguien to make a good/bad impression on someone
cambiar (de puesto) to change (jobs)
conseguir (i, i) to get, obtain

dejar to quit; to leave (behind)
renunciar (a) to resign (from)
solicitar to apply for
el/la aspirante candidate, applicant

EN LA OFICINA / AT THE OFFICE

el/la director(a) manager, director
el/la empleado/a employee
el/la jefe/a boss

despedir (i, i) to fire
funcionar to function

ganar to earn; to win
quitar to take out, withhold

el aumento raise, increase
la carrera career
el cheque check

la empresa corporation, business
los impuestos taxes
el negocio business
el puesto job, position
el sueldo salary
el trabajo job, work

─────────────

*Although you have probably guessed that **graduarse** means *to graduate*, **graduarse** is a type of Spanish verb that you have not yet learned how to use. You will see the **yo (me gradúo)** and **tú (te gradúas)** forms in this chapter, as well as a special form used to talk about your eventual graduation: **Cuando me gradúe...** Some past forms will also be introduced, as needed.

¿Cuándo te gradúas?

—¿Qué hace tu hermano? Se graduó (*He graduated*) el año pasado, ¿verdad?

—Sí, se graduó de abogado, pero no tiene trabajo todavía. Mis padres quieren que solicite un puesto con el gobierno.

—Y tú, ¿cuándo te gradúas?

—Espero que en junio.

Víctor Englebert/Photo Researchers, Inc.

Cali, Colombia

A. ¿Qué acción o descripción corresponde a los sustantivos de la izquierda?

1. el gobierno (*government*)
2. el empleado
3. la jefa
4. el puesto
5. los impuestos
6. el aumento
7. los consejos
8. el sueldo

a. Trabaja en una oficina.
b. Puede tener prestigio e* interés o puede ser algo regular y monótono.
c. Quita impuestos de nuestros cheques.
ch. Parte del sueldo que se paga al gobierno.
d. Es necesario si el empleado va a poder combatir la inflación.
e. Puede despedir a los empleados no satisfactorios.
f. Se dan gratis porque «no cuestan nada».
g. Nos pueden dar esto semanal (una vez a la semana), bi-semanal o mensualmente.

Ahora, siguiendo el modelo de las oraciones anteriores (*preceding*), describa estos sustantivos de una manera sencilla.

1. el aspirante   2. la entrevista   3. la solicitud   4. la secretaria

B. Escoja (*Choose*) el mejor consejo para cada problema; luego justifique su respuesta.

1. Su jefe es muy antipático.
   a. Cambie de puesto, porque los jefes no cambian nunca.
   b. Sea muy simpático/a con él para ver si empieza a ser simpático con Ud.
2. Los empleados llegan tarde todos los días.
   a. Por cada minuto de retraso (*tardiness*), quíteles un dólar de su cheque.
   b. Dígales que va a anunciar sus puestos como vacantes y empiece a organizar entrevistas.

---

*Y (*and*) becomes **e** before a word that begins with **i** or **hi: Isabel y Fernando**, but **Fernando *e* Isabel; hijos y padres**, but **padres *e* hijos**.

3. Ud. gana un sueldo muy bajo.
   a. Explíquele su situación al director (a la directora) y pídale un aumento.
   b. Consiga un trabajo extra por las noches.
4. Un empleado habla mucho por teléfono con sus amigos.
   a. Cuando Ud. ve que llama a alguien, déle algo que hacer.
   b. Cuando llegue la cuenta telefónica, déjela en el escritorio del empleado.
5. Le quitan muchos impuestos del cheque.
   a. Renuncie Ud. y no busque otro trabajo. Así no tiene que pagar nada al gobierno.
   b. Declare en el formulario *W-4* que Ud. tiene cinco hijos.

C. ¿Quién lo dijo (*said*)? ¿La directora, el empleado o los dos? Explique su respuesta.

1. Siempre les doy buenos consejos, pero no me escuchan nunca.
2. Este negocio no funciona bien. Voy a renunciar a mi trabajo.
3. La voy a despedir si no escribe a máquina mejor.
4. Me gusta mucho la responsabilidad de dirigir (*running*) la empresa.
5. Creo que los jefes ganan mucho más que nosotros.
6. Es necesario caerle bien al jefe. Si no, te despide.
7. ¡Es tan aburrido leer solicitudes!—todas son iguales.
8. Quieren que pensemos solamente en el trabajo. ¿No tenemos vida privada?

Profesiones y oficios°   *trades*

el/la abogado/a	lawyer
el/la comerciante	merchant, shopkeeper
el/la criado/a	servant
el/la enfermero/a	nurse
el hombre/la mujer de negocios	businessman/woman
el/la ingeniero/a	engineer
el/la médico/a	doctor
el/la obrero/a	worker, laborer
el/la periodista	journalist
el/la plomero/a	plumber
el/la siquiatra	psychiatrist

You will see the preceding names of professions throughout *¿Qué tal?*. Learn to use those that are particularly important or interesting to you. The entire list will not be considered "active" vocabulary that you will be expected to say or write spontaneously.

A. ¿A quién necesita Ud. en estas situaciones? ¿A quién va a llamar?

1. Hay problemas con la tubería (*pipes*) en la cocina (*kitchen*).
2. Ud. acaba de tener un accidente con el coche; la otra persona dice que Ud. tiene la culpa (*fault*).
3. Por las muchas tensiones y presiones, Ud. tiene serios problemas afectivos (*emotional*).
4. Ud. está en el hospital y quiere que alguien le dé una aspirina.
5. Ud. quiere que alguien le ayude con el trabajo doméstico porque no tiene mucho tiempo para hacerlo.
6. Ud. quiere que alguien le haga unos arreglos (*repairs*) en la casa.
7. Ud. conoce todos los detalles de un escándalo en la administración local.

B. ¿Qué profesiones asocia Ud. con estas frases? Consulte la lista anterior y la siguiente.

actor/actriz	carpintero/a	poeta
ama de casa (*homemaker*)	consejero/a	policía
arquitecto/a	cura/pastor(a)/rabino	político
azafata/camarero	dentista	presidente/a
barman	maestro/a (*teacher*)	profesor(a)
camarero/a	pintor(a)	secretario/a

1. intelectual/aburrido
2. muchos/pocos años de preparación
3. sensible (*sensitive*)
4. mucho/poco dinero
5. mucho/poco poder (*power*)
6. mucha/poca responsabilidad
7. mucho/poco prestigio
8. mucha/poca prisa
9. mucho/poco peligro (*danger*)
10. mucho/poco trabajo
11. «de las nueve a las cinco»

C. Hablando de carreras. Complete las oraciones en una forma lógica.

1. Cuando me gradúe, quiero ser_____. Mis padres quieren que sea_____.
2. Tengo un pariente que es_____. Creo que su trabajo es_____.
3. Creo que los médicos (abogados, periodistas, plomeros,...)_____.
4. Ninguno de mis amigos tiene ganas de ser_____porque_____.

PRONUNCIACIÓN: *i* and *u* with Other Vowels

When unstressed **u** and **i** occur next to another vowel, they always form diphthongs. For this reason, the words **bueno** and **siete** have two syllables each; the **u** and the **i** form diphthongs with the following vowel and are pronounced [w] and [y], respectively: [bwe-no], [sye-te].

When **u** and **i** have written accent marks, they do not form diphthongs. Thus, **dios** has one syllable, while **días** has two syllables; **continuo** has three syllables, and **continúo** has four.

Unaccented **i** represents [y] in the participle ending **-iendo:**
comiendo, viviendo. Unaccented **i** between two vowels becomes **y:**
oyendo, leyendo, cayendo.

Práctica

A. ai/aí   uo/úo   ia/ía   au/aú
ue/úe   ie/íe   io/ío   ua/úa

B. viaje   experiencia   historia   bien   tierra
radio   idioma   ciudad   traigo   aire
seis   veinte   treinta   oigo   ciudadano   ruido

C. Guadalajara   suave   puedo   fueron   antiguo
cuota   causa   bautizo   Europa   europeo

CH. país   paraíso   oímos   sociología   energía
período   río   gradúa   continúe   acentúo

MINIDIÁLOGOS Y ESTRUCTURA

El mundo laboral

ÁLVARO: ¡Marcos! El jefe acaba de decirme que pase por su oficina. *Temo que quiera* despedirme.

MARCOS: ¡Hombre, *dudo que haga* eso! ¿*No es posible que* te *quiera* dar un aumento de sueldo?

ÁLVARO: No, *no creo que piense* hacer eso. *Es obvio que no está* contento conmigo.

MARCOS: Pues, ¡ojalá *que no tengas* razón! *Es lástima que* le *tengas* tanto miedo.

1. ¿Qué acaba de hacer el jefe de la empresa?
2. ¿De qué tiene miedo Álvaro?
3. Según Marcos, ¿qué puede pasar?
4. ¿Por qué piensa Álvaro que no va a recibir un aumento de sueldo?

The working world *ÁLVARO: Marcos! The boss just told me to stop by (come by) his office. I'm afraid he wants to fire me. MARCOS: Come on, I doubt that he'll do that! Isn't it possible that he wants to give you a raise? ÁLVARO: No, I don't think he intends to do that. It's obvious that he isn't happy with me. MARCOS: Well, I hope you're not right! It's a shame you're so afraid of him.*

25 Expressing Feelings
Use of the Subjunctive in Noun Clauses: Emotion

Independent Clause		Dependent Clause
first subject + *indicative* (expression of emotion)	**que**	second subject + *subjunctive*
Esperamos que Ud. **pueda** asistir.		*We hope (that) you'll be able to come.*
Tengo miedo (de) que mi abuelo **esté** muy enfermo.		*I'm afraid (that) my grandfather is very ill.*
Es lástima que no **den** aumentos este año.		*It's a shame they're not giving raises this year.*

A. Expressions of emotion are those in which speakers express their feelings: *I'm glad you're here; It's good that they can come.* Such expressions of emotion are followed by the subjunctive mood in the dependent clause.

B. Some expressions of emotion are **esperar, gustar, sentir (ie, i)** (*to regret* or *feel sorry*), **me** (**te, le,** and so on) **sorprende** (*it is surprising to me, you, him/her*), **temer** (*to fear*), and **tener miedo (de).** Since not all expressions of emotion are given here, remember that any expression of emotion—not just certain verbs—is followed by the subjunctive.

C. When generalizations of emotion are personalized, they are followed by the subjunctive in the dependent clause. Some generalized expressions of emotion are **es terrible, es ridículo, es mejor/bueno/malo, es increíble** (*incredible*), **es extraño** (*strange*), **¡qué extraño!** (*how strange!*), **es lástima** (*shame*), and **¡qué lástima!** (*what a shame!*).

Práctica

A. Sentimientos. ¿Cuáles son algunas de las cosas que le gustan o que le dan miedo a Ud.?

1. Me gusta mucho que _____ . (*estar contentos mis amigos, funcionar bien mi coche, venir todos a mis fiestas, estar bien mis padres, __?__*)
2. Tengo miedo de que _____ . (*haber mucho trabajo en la oficina mañana, no venir nadie a mi fiesta, haber una prueba* [quiz] *mañana, ocurrir una crisis internacional, no darme el jefe un aumento, __?__*)

B. Chismes (*Gossip*) de la oficina. Haga oraciones completas de dos cláusulas, según el modelo.

MODELO   Juan / no gustar / tenemos que trabajar los fines de
semana →
A Juan no le gusta que tengamos que trabajar los fines de
semana.

1. Sara / esperar / le dan un aumento
2. ¿a ti / sorprender / hay tantos puestos vacantes?
3. Armando / temer / lo despiden
4. (nosotros) sentir / nos quitan tanto del cheque para los impuestos
5. a mí / no gustar / nos dan sólo dos semanas de vacaciones
6. todos / tener miedo / no hay aumentos este año

C. Complete las oraciones con la forma apropiada del verbo entre paréntesis.

1. Dicen en la agencia que mi carro nuevo es muy económico. Por eso me sorprende que (*usar tanta gasolina*). Temo que el coche (*no funcionar totalmente bien*).
2. ¡Qué desastre! El jefe dice que me va a despedir. ¡Es increíble que (*despedirme*)! Es terrible que (yo) (*tener que buscar otro puesto*). Espero que (él) (*cambiar de idea*).
3. Generalmente nos dan un mes de vacaciones, pero este año sólo tenemos dos semanas. Es terrible que sólo (*darnos dos semanas*). No nos gusta que (*ser tan breves las vacaciones*). Es lástima que (*no poder ir a ningún sitio*).
4. A los padres de Soledad no les cae bien su novio. Siento que Soledad (*estar tan triste*). ¡Qué lástima que a sus padres (*caerles mal el novio*). Espero que los dos (*poder resolver la situación*).

CH. Noticias familiares. ¿Cómo se dice en español?

1. I'm sorry your daughter is sick.
2. It's incredible that Johnny is already twelve years old!
3. What a shame that Julio isn't feeling well.
4. How strange that Jorge never calls you.
5. I'm glad (It pleases me) that you're going to invite John to the wedding.

D. Profesiones y oficios. Express your feelings about the following situations by restating them, beginning with one of the following phrases or any others you can think of: **es bueno/malo que, es extraño/increíble que, es lástima que.**

1. Muchas personas buscan trabajo hoy en día.
2. Los salarios no aumentan al mismo ritmo (*same pace*) que la inflación.

3. Los plomeros ganan mucho por hora.
4. Muchos obreros ganan más que los maestros.
5. Hay muchos/pocos cursos comerciales en esta universidad.
6. Uno tiene que estudiar diez años para ser médico.
7. Los siquiatras nunca descubren (*reveal*) los secretos de sus pacientes.
8. Las mujeres no siempre ganan tanto como los hombres cuando hacen el mismo trabajo.

26 Expressing Uncertainty
Use of the Subjunctive in Noun Clauses: Doubt and Denial

Independent Clause		Dependent Clause
first subject + *indicative* (expression of doubt or denial)	**que**	second subject + *subjunctive*

No creo que **sean** estudiantes.
No están seguros de que Roberto **tenga** razón.
Es imposible que ella **esté** con él.

I don't believe they're students.
They're not sure that Roberto is right.
It's impossible for her to be with him.

A. Expressions of doubt and denial are those in which speakers express uncertainty or negation: *I doubt he's right; It's not possible for her to be here.* Such expressions, however strong or weak, are followed by the subjunctive in the dependent clause in Spanish.

B. Expressions of doubt and denial include **no creer, dudar** (*to doubt*), **no estar seguro/a**, and **negar (ie)** (*to deny*). Not all Spanish expressions of doubt are given here. Remember that any expression of doubt is followed by the subjunctive in the dependent clause.

C. When generalizations of doubt are personalized, they are followed by the subjunctive in the dependent clause. Some generalizations of doubt and denial are **es posible, es imposible, es probable, es improbable, no es verdad, no es cierto** (*certain*), and **no es seguro** (*sure*).*

---

*Generalizations that express certainty are not followed by the subjunctive: *Es verdad* que *funciona* bien; *No hay duda* de que el director lo *paga*.

Indicative versus Subjunctive

No creer, dudar, no estar seguro, and **negar** are followed by the subjunctive. However, **creer, no dudar, estar seguro,** and **no negar** are usually followed by the indicative, since they do not express doubt, denial, or negation. Compare the following:

No niego (No dudo) que **es** simpático.	*I don't deny (doubt) that he's nice.*
Niego (Dudo) que **sea** simpático.	*I deny (doubt) that he's nice.*
Estamos seguros (Creemos) que el examen **es** hoy.	*We're sure (believe) the exam is today.*
No estamos seguros (No creemos) que el examen **sea** hoy.	*We're not sure (We don't believe) that the exam is today.*

Práctica

A. **¡La máquina de escribir no funciona!** Dé oraciones nuevas según las indicaciones.

1. Dudo que *Luis* sepa mucho de máquinas. (*tú, el jefe, Uds., Ud., vosotros*)
2. *No creo* que sea un problema serio. (*creo, dudo, estoy seguro/a, niego, no dudo, no estoy seguro/a*)
3. Es *necesario* que Ud. compre otra máquina. (*mejor, posible, seguro, probable, verdad, imposible*)

B. **¿Lo cree o lo duda Ud.?** Give your response to the following statements, repeating them with one of the suggested phrases.

(No) Creo que…	Es (im)posible que…
(No) Dudo que…	Es (im)probable que…
(No) Niego que…	(No) Es verdad que…
(No) Estoy seguro/a de que…	

1. Es necesario vivir en una casa enorme.
2. Los casados están más contentos que los solteros.
3. Hay vida en los otros planetas.
4. Es bueno manejar (*to drive*) a 55 millas por hora.
5. El español se habla en todas partes del mundo.
6. Juan sale todas las noches, no estudia nunca y recibe buenas notas.
7. Hay una guerra nuclear.
8. Los profesores ganan bastante (*enough*) dinero.

C. ¿Qué va a pasar en clase mañana? ¿Cómo se dice en español?

1. There's a quiz, but I'm not sure that it's tomorrow.
2. I doubt that the subjunctive is **(entrar)** on the test.
3. Is it possible there will be commands?
4. I don't think it will be easy!
5. It's probable that John won't come to class!

CH. ¿Cómo van a contestar estas personas las preguntas? ¿Y cómo contesta Ud.?

1. ¿El carro es económico?

2. ¿El niño tiene catorce años?

3. ¿El hombre puede volar (*to fly*) por el aire?

4. ¿Cuatro y cuatro son nueve?

D. Algunos creen que las oraciones siguientes describen el mundo de hoy. ¿Qué cree Ud.? Reaccione Ud. a estas oraciones, empezando con una de estas expresiones:

Dudo que...   Es bueno/malo que...
(No) Es verdad que...   Es lástima que...
No hay duda que...   Es increíble que...
Es probable que...   (No) Me gusta que...

1. Los niños miran la televisión seis horas al día.
2. Hay mucha pobreza (*poverty*) en el mundo.
3. En los Estados Unidos, gastamos (*we use*) mucha energía.
4. Hay mucho sexo y violencia en la televisión y en las películas.
5. Se come poco y mal en muchas partes del mundo.
6. Los niños de habla española reciben una buena educación en los Estados Unidos.
7. Hay mucho interés en la exploración del espacio.
8. El fumar no es malo para la salud (*health*).

9. Las mujeres reciben menos apoyo (*support*) financiero que los hombres para practicar deportes (*sports*).
10. No se permite el uso de la marihuana.

Indique Ud. soluciones para algunos de los problemas. Empiece las soluciones con estas frases:

Es urgente que...   Es necesario que...
Es preferible que...   Es importante que...
Quiero que...   Insisto en que...

¿Recuerda Ud.?

Review the direct (Grammar Section 19) and indirect (Grammar Section 20) object pronouns before beginning Grammar Section 27. Remember that direct objects answer the questions *what?* or *whom?* and that indirect objects answer the questions *to whom?* or *for whom?* in relation to the verb.

DIRECT: me   te   **lo/la**   nos   os   **los/las**
INDIRECT: me   te   **le**   nos   os   **les**

Identifique los complementos directo e indirecto en las siguientes oraciones.

1. Nos mandan los libros.
2. ¿Por qué no los compras mañana?
3. ¿Me puedes leer el menú?
4. Léalo ahora, por favor.

5. Juan no te va a dar el dinero hoy.
6. No lo va a tener hoy.
7. Sí, claro que te veo.
8. Hábleme ahora, por favor.

---

27 Expressing Direct and Indirect Objects Together
Double Object Pronouns

¡Tráigamelo!
¡Mándenselas!
¡No se lo digan!
¡No nos la solicite!

Match these requests with the boss's commands.
· *No quiero que les digan el verdadero problema.*
· *Quiero que me traiga el contrato.*

· *Prohíbo que nos solicite otra entrevista.*
· *Es necesario que le manden las cuentas.*

A. When both an indirect and a direct object pronoun are used in a sentence, the indirect object pronoun **(I)** precedes the direct **(D): ID.** Note that nothing comes between the two pronouns. The position of double object pronouns with respect to the verb is the same as that of single object pronouns.

¿Por qué no **nos lo** dices?	*Why don't you tell it to us?*
Acaba de dár**melas.**	*He's just given them to me.*
Me lo está sirviendo ahora.	*She's serving it to me now.*

[Práctica A–B]

B. When both the indirect and the direct object pronouns begin with the letter **l,** the indirect object pronoun always changes to **se.** The direct object pronoun does not change.

Le → Se	compra unos zapatos. los compra.	*He's buying her some shoes.* *He's buying them for her.*
Les → Se	mandamos la blusa. la mandamos.	*We'll send you the blouse.* *We'll send it to you.*

Since **se** stands for **le** (*to/for you* [sing.], *him, her*) and **les** (*to/for you* [pl.], *them*), it is often necessary to clarify its meaning by using **a** plus the pronoun objects of prepositions.

Se lo escribo **a Uds. (a ellos, a ellas).**	*I'll write it to you (them).*
Se las doy **a Ud. (a él, a ella).**	*I'll give them to you (him, her).*

[Práctica C–CH]

C. The position of double object pronouns in relation to formal commands is the same as that of single object pronouns (Grammar Section 22). The pronouns must follow and be attached to affirmative commands, and precede negative ones.

Págue**melo.** No **me lo** pague.	*Pay it for me. Don't pay it for me.*
Díga**selo.** No **se lo** diga.	*Tell it to them. Don't tell it to them.*

[Práctica D–F]

Práctica

A. Ud. todavía tiene hambre. Pida más comida, según el modelo. Fíjese en (*Note*) el uso del tiempo presente como sustituto para el mandato.

MODELO   ensalada → ¿Hay más ensalada? Me la pasas, por favor.

1. pan **2.** tortillas **3.** tomates **4.** fruta **5.** vino **6.** jamón

B. La casa de su amigo Raúl es un desastre. Dígale Ud. cómo lo va a ayudar a ponerla en orden, usando el verbo **lavar** (*to wash*).

MODELO   coche → ¿El coche? Te lo lavo mañana.

1. ventanas   **2.** refrigerador (*m.*)   **3.** platos   **4.** ropa

C. Answer the questions, basing your answers on what you observe happening in the drawings. Use double object pronouns.

1. ¿El empleado le vende el carro a María? (→ *No, no se lo vende a ella.*) ¿a los Sres. Benítez? ¿a Ud.? ¿a Esteban?

2. ¿El camarero le sirve una cerveza a Carlos? ¿a los hermanos? ¿a Uds.? ¿a Emilia?

3. ¿Carmen les recomienda los tacos a Raúl y Celia? ¿a Estela? ¿a Ud.? ¿a Lucas?

CH. **En el aeropuerto.** Cambie: sustantivos → pronombres.

1. Acaban de decirme la hora de la salida.
2. Sí, quiero que Ud. me lea el horario (*schedule*), por favor.
3. No, no tiene que darle los boletos ahora.
4. Estoy guardándole el equipaje.
5. ¿No quieres que te compre los pasajes?
6. ¿Nos pueden guardar el puesto en la cola?
7. Le recomiendo la clase turística, señor.

D. **Mandatos de la oficina.** Con otro/a estudiante, haga y conteste las preguntas según el modelo.

MODELO   traer un café → —¿Quiere que le traiga un café?
                           —Sí, tráigamelo, por favor.

1. buscar las solicitudes
2. firmar (*to sign*) las cartas
3. comprar el boleto
4. hacer las reservaciones
5. escribir el contrato
6. preparar el inventario
7. llenar la solicitud
8. conseguir una entrevista

Ahora repita el ejercicio, contestando negativamente.

MODELO   traer un café → —¿Quiere que le traiga un café?
                              —No, no me lo traiga todavía.

E. **Se lo di a...** (*I gave it to...*) Con otro/a estudiante, haga y conteste preguntas, según el modelo.

MODELO   disco de Santana →
                 —Oye, ¿me prestas (*lend*) tu disco de Santana?
                 —Lo siento, pero no puedo. Se lo di a (Roberto).

1. discos de Menudo
2. bicicleta vieja
3. libro de francés
4. máquina de escribir vieja
5. maleta vieja
6. televisor viejo

F. **Situaciones.** Someone has just mentioned the following items to you. Give as many commands as you can, based on them. Be creative! And remember to give negative as well as affirmative commands.

MODELO   la novela *Guerra y Paz* →
                 ¡No me la lea!
                 Désela a mi hermano, por favor. A él le gusta leer.
                 Mándemela, por favor. Me gustan las novelas largas.

1. un millón de dólares
2. un coche usado del año sesenta
3. dos entradas (*tickets*) para un concierto de la orquesta sinfónica
4. unas flores
5. unos dulces
6. la cuenta

Hablando del trabajo

—¿Cuánto tiempo llevas en tu nuevo empleo?
—Casi dos meses.
—¿Y cómo te va? (*How's it going?*)
—No muy bien. Me piden que trabaje los fines de semana..., y no le caigo bien al jefe.
—Me imagino que vas a renunciar, ¿no?
—Sí. Sólo espero que termine el mes para hacerlo.

San José, Costa Rica

Katherine A. Lambert/Kay Reese & Assoc.

REPASO

Conversaciones en la oficina. Complete the following conversations with the correct form of the words in parentheses, as suggested by the context. When two possibilities are given in parentheses, select the correct word.

VENDEDORES(AS) Y SUPERVISOR
SUELDO BASE MAS COMISIONES

Empresa internacional requiere los servicios de (15) vendedores(as) para promover servicios educativos. Indispensable: Experiencia mínima de dos años en el ramo, buena presentación e iniciativa personal.
Interesados enviar currículum con fotografía reciente a la

CASILLA 3357, CORREO CENTRAL, SANTIAGO

JEFE: Tenemos (de/que[1]) trabajar (el/los[2]) sábado, señores, y tal vez (el/los[3]) domingo. (Ser/Estar[4]) necesario que el inventario (estar[5]) listo° (el/los[6]) lunes. *ready*

EMPLEADO: ¡Ay! (Mi[7]) planes para (el/la[8]) fin de semana... ¡Ojalá que el jefe (cambiar[9]) de idea!

EMPLEADA: ¡Lo más probable° es que tú (tener[10]) que cambiar (de/a[11]) planes! *¡Lo... It's more likely*

ANITA: ¿Qué tal el tráfico en la carretera° (este[12]) mañana? *freeway*

CARLOS: ¡Un desastre total! Dos horas al volante° y ahora (el/la[13]) coche no (funcionar[14]) como (deber[15]). *wheel*

ANITA: ¡Hombre, hace años que (tú: tener[16]) problemas de este tipo! Me (sorprender[17]) que no (tú: comprar[18]) una casa más cerca de la oficina.

JEFA: Señor Torres, necesito (ver[19]) los archivos° de los impuestos de los últimos diez años. (Tráigamelas/Tráigamelos[20]) en seguida,° por favor. *files* / *en... inmediatamente*

TORRES: ¿(Saber/Conocer[21]) Ud. dónde están, señora?

JEFA: (Buscarlos[22]) Ud. en la caja° que (ser/estar[23]) encima del escritorio en mi oficina. (El/La[24]) de 1984 es el más importante. No (perderlo[25]), por favor. *box*

UN PASO MÁS: Lectura cultural

Antes de leer

In upcoming chapters of *¿Qué tal?* you will learn a number of different verb tenses. But even before you know the actual verb forms you should be able to make educated guesses about when an action takes place by examining the context that surrounds the verb. Pay particular attention to the time cues in the following sentences. Can you guess what the verbs mean?

1. Pagaré la matrícula mañana. Y tú, ¿cuándo la pagarás?
2. El año pasado los Ramírez viajaron a Colombia en junio.
3. Anoche Raúl estaba leyendo mientras (*while*) su esposa preparaba la cena.

In the following reading, a number of verb forms end in **-ó**. This is part of the third-person ending for a past tense that you will study in the next chapter. If you recognize the infinitive, you should be able to determine the meaning of the unglossed verb forms that end in **-ó: habló** = *he/she, you* (form.) *spoke,* **vivió** = *he/she, you* (form.) *lived.*

La educación en el mundo hispánico

Para describir el sistema educativo de muchos países hispanos, tomemos° como ejemplo el caso de Josué, un arquitecto colombiano que acaba de graduarse en la Universidad Nacional de Bogotá. Josué entró en la escuela primaria a los seis años de edad. Asistió a una escuela privada para varones° dirigida por padres jesuitas. Después de terminar los seis años de primaria, entró en otra escuela privada para hacer los seis años de colegio.° Allí siguió diez cursos al año: ciencias, matemáticas, religión, filosofía, dibujo, inglés, francés, latín, literatura y economía. Luego empezó a estudiar en la Universidad Nacional—la matrícula allí era° más barata que en las universidades privadas. Terminó su programa de estudios en seis años en vez de cuatro porque hubo° mucha actividad política durante aquel tiempo. Además de° varias huelgas° estudiantiles, el gobierno cerró la universidad en varias ocasiones.

    El programa educativo de Josué es un ejemplo de la educación que reciben muchos de los estudiantes hispanos. Por lo general, el sistema hispano impone un programa más rígido que el de las escuelas de los Estados Unidos, y lo mismo sucede en el colegio y en la universidad. En los planes de estudios hispánicos hay menos cursos «optativos». Por sus esfuerzos° en el colegio los estudiantes reciben el título de Bachiller después de aprobar° los exámenes de bachillerato. En la universidad se preparan para una profesión específica en alguna de las facultades distintas como Ingeniería, Medicina, Arquitectura, Derecho° o Filosofía.

let's take

niños

escuela secundaria

was

there was
Además... In addition to / strikes

efforts

passing

Law

Otra diferencia entre los dos sistemas es que el hispano es más tradicional que el norteamericano. En los Estados Unidos se da más importancia a la discusión que a las conferencias° y lo que° se lee fuera de clase. Por ejemplo, para muchos profesores norteamericanos, un factor muy importante en la nota° que se da al estudiante es su activa participación en la clase durante el semestre. En cambio, en las universidades hispánicas es más corriente° que hable sólo el profesor durante la hora de clase.

lectures / lo... what

grade

common

Comprensión

¿De quién se habla, de un estudiante hispano o de un norteamericano?

1. Estudia en la escuela secundaria cuatro años.
2. Con frecuencia se interrumpen los estudios porque los estudiantes protestan por algo.
3. Estudia una lengua extranjera porque es uno de los cursos optativos.
4. Entra en una facultad profesional inmediatamente después de graduarse en la secundaria.
5. Para él, es más importante escuchar al profesor que participar en las clases.
6. En la secundaria, estudia muchas materias clásicas.

Para escribir

A. Complete the following paragraph about your chosen career.

Estudio para ser _____ porque _____ . Después de graduarme, quiero _____ . En esta profesión se puede _____ .

B. Haga una comparación entre dos clases de su universidad: su clase de español y otra. Incluya las respuestas de estas preguntas en la comparación.

1. ¿En qué clase participan más los estudiantes? ¿Por qué?
2. ¿En qué clase se da más importancia a las conferencias? ¿a la participación activa de los estudiantes?
3. ¿Cuántos días a la semana es obligatorio asistir a clase?
4. ¿Es un curso optativo o es obligatorio?
5. ¿Qué clase le gusta más a Ud.? ¿Por qué?

VOCABULARIO

VERBOS

caer (*irreg.*) to fall
cambiar (de) to change
conseguir (i, i) to get, obtain
dejar to quit; to leave (behind)
despedir (i, i) to fire (*someone*)
dudar to doubt
funcionar to function; to work (*a thing*)
ganar to earn; to win
llenar to fill out (*a form*)
negar (ie) to deny
quitar to take out, withhold
renunciar (a) to resign (from)
sentir (ie, i) to regret
solicitar to apply for (*a job*)
sorprender to surprise
temer to fear

EN LA OFICINA

el aumento raise, (salary) increase

el cheque check
la empresa corporation; business
la entrevista interview
la máquina de escribir typewriter
el negocio business
el puesto job, position
la solicitud application (form)
el sueldo salary
el trabajo job, work

LAS PERSONAS

el/la aspirante candidate, applicant
el/la director(a) manager, director
el/la empleado/a employee
el/la entrevistador(a) interviewer
el/la jefe/a boss

OTROS SUSTANTIVOS

la carrera career
el disco record (*musical*)

el gobierno government
los impuestos taxes
la prueba quiz

EXPRESIONES DE SORPRESA Y DUDA

es cierto it's certain
es extraño/¡qué extraño! it's strange/how strange!
es increíble it's incredible
es lástima/¡qué lástima! it's a shame/what a shame!
es seguro it's certain
estar seguro/a to be certain, sure

PALABRAS ADICIONALES

caerle bien/mal a alguien to make a good/bad impression on someone
escribir a máquina to type

FRASES ÚTILES PARA LA COMUNICACIÓN

graduarse:

Cuando me gradúe...	When I graduate . . .
yo me gradúo	I (will) graduate
Ud./él/ella se gradúa	you/he/she graduate(s)

UN POCO DE TODO 3

A. Con dos estudiantes haga y conteste preguntas según el modelo.

> MODELO   BLANCA: ¿Ves al profesor en este momento?
> EDUARDO: No, no lo veo. (Sí, lo veo.)
> BENI: Yo no lo veo tampoco. (Yo también lo veo.)

1. ¿Ves a_____?
2. ¿Conoces al rector (*president*) de la universidad?
3. ¿Sabes todo el vocabulario para la prueba de hoy?
4. ¿Me oyes (ves) bien?
5. ¿Siempre aprendes todas las palabras nuevas?
6. ¿Vas a traer a tus padres a la universidad algún día?
7. ¿Sabes la dirección (*address*) de mi casa? ¿mi teléfono?

B. Acciones y reacciones. React to each situation, then resolve it by giving advice according to the model.

> MODELO   SITUACIÓN: Su profesor(a) de español les pone muchos
> exámenes.
> REACCIÓN: Eso (no) me gusta. Quiero que nos ponga
> más/menos exámenes.
> SOLUCIÓN: Profesor(a), pónganos más/menos exámenes, por
> favor.

1. Su profesor(a) les habla muy rápidamente en español.
2. No hay asientos en la sección de no fumar y Ud. tiene que tomar un asiento al lado de (*next to*) un señor que fuma mucho.
3. Su vecino/a (*neighbor*) pone el estéreo por la mañana mientras Ud. trata de (*are trying to*) estudiar.
4. Sus padres siempre van al mismo (*same*) sitio todos los veranos.
5. Sus compañeros de cuarto sólo preparan hamburguesas.

C. Ud. es director(a) de una oficina. Hoy un empleado (una empleada) viene a la oficina por primera vez. ¿Qué le va a decir? ¿Qué consejos le va a dar?

Le recomiendo que Ud...	trabajar juntos aquí
Ojalá que los otros empleados...	llegar puntualmente por la mañana
Es necesario que Ud...	no usar el teléfono en exceso
Me gusta que todos...	no dejar para mañana el trabajo de hoy
Prefiero que...	ayudarlo/la a acostumbrarse (*to get used*) a la rutina
	siempre estar de acuerdo con el jefe

CH. Necesito comprar... Imagine that you need to buy the following items but do not know—or have forgotten—the words in Spanish. Try to get your idea across to a Spanish-speaking clerk by paraphrasing, using synonyms, telling what the item is like, what it is used for, what it is made of, and so on.

MODELO a suitcase → Necesito comprar algo para mi viaje. Lo uso para llevar mi ropa y mis otras cosas. Cuando tengo demasiada ropa y demasiadas cosas, otra persona me ayuda a cerrarlo.

1. Kleenex
2. motion-sickness pills
3. a bread box
4. a music box
5. a hammock
6. postcards
7. a briefcase
8. a wallet

D. Situaciones. Con otro/a estudiante, planee un viaje de vacaciones para este verano. Primero, hágale preguntas al compañero (a la compañera) para descubrir sus preferencias. Luego, pónganse de acuerdo (*agree*) sobre el itinerario. Use las siguientes preguntas como guía.

1. ¿Quieres que vayamos a las montañas o a la playa? (¿al mar o al campo [*country*]?)
2. ¿Prefieres que pidamos hoteles de lujo (*deluxe*) o de clase turística?
3. ¿Es mejor que vayamos en avión o en barco? ¿en coche?
4. ¿Qué lugares esperas que visitemos?
5. ¿Cómo quieres que paguemos? ¿con tarjetas de crédito o al contado (*in cash*)?

Ahora describa el itinerario para la clase.

E. Por favor. How would you go about getting the following information? Using the suggestions in **A propósito...**, prepare a series of short statements and questions that will help you get all the information you need. Your instructor will play the role of ticket seller, travel agent, or flight attendant.

MODELO You need to buy two first-class tickets on Tuesday's 10:50 A.M. train for Guanajuato. → Dos boletos para Guanajuato, por favor. Para el martes, el tren de las 10:50. De primera clase, por favor.

1. You need to buy two second-class train tickets for today's 2:50 P.M. train for Barcelona.
2. You are at the train station and need to find out how to get to the university—which you understand is quite some distance away—by 10:00 A.M.
3. You want to find out from your travel agent what you need to do before taking your first trip abroad. In what order should things be done?
4. The flight you are on is arriving late, and you will probably miss your connecting flight to Mexico City. You want to explain your situation to the flight attendant and find out how you can get to Mexico City by 7:00 this evening.
5. You are talking to a travel agent and want to fly from Santiago, Chile, to Quito, Ecuador. You are traveling with two friends who prefer to travel first class, and you need to arrive in Quito by Saturday afternoon.

F. Situaciones prácticas. Listen as your instructor role-plays each of the following situations with one or more students. Pay close attention to how your classmates interact with your instructor to see if you would have said or done the same thing. You may have to make some educated guesses about what your instructor says as he or she plays the situation. After you have watched each of the situations at least once, act out the situations with another student. Try to use as much of the vocabulary that you know as possible.

1. You meet someone at a college party and learn that he or she is a graduate of your high school **(Me gradué en... ¿Cuándo te graduaste?)**. It's possible that you know many of the same people. Ask each other questions about teachers and students at your high school.
2. You go to a French/Mexican/American restaurant. The other student will take the role of waiter. Ask for a table near a window **(ventana)**, away from the kitchen **(cocina)**, and order a meal.
3. You are the personnel manager of a large office. Today you are interviewing a candidate for a secretarial position. Find out all you can about the applicant: education, experience, ambition, interests, family, and so on.

A propósito...

Communicating with a minimum of words. In class you are frequently asked to use complete sentences. But when you speak Spanish outside the classroom, you don't always speak in complete sentences—sometimes because you do not know or cannot remember how to say something. And when you try to say a long sentence, such as *"Would you be so kind as to tell me how I can get to the train station?,"* it is easy to get tongue-tied, to omit something, or to mispronounce a word. When this happens, the listener often has trouble understanding. A shorter, more direct phrase or sentence often yields more effective results. A simple **perdón** or **por favor** followed by **¿la estación de trenes?** is both adequate and polite.

To accomplish something more complicated, such as buying two first-class tickets on Tuesday's 10:50 A.M. train for Guanajuato, you might begin by saying **"Dos boletos para Guanajuato, por favor."** After that, you can add other information, often in response to the questions that the ticket agent will ask you. By breaking the message down into manageable bits of information, you simplify the communication process for both parties.

A word of caution is in order, however. While you may streamline your message, native speakers may answer using complex sentences and words that are unfamiliar to you. Be prepared to guess, relying on context and on real-world information. You can also use the following strategies.

Repita, por favor. No comprendo.	*Repeat, please. I don't understand.*
Por favor, repita ____ .	*Please, repeat ____ . (if you can repeat or approximate the word or phrase you didn't understand)*
Más despacio, por favor.	*More slowly, please.*
¿Me lo escribe, por favor?	*Would you write it down for me, please?*

CAPÍTULO 13

La vida doméstica

VOCABULARIO: PREPARACIÓN

despertar (ie) a los padres

bañar al bebé

divertir (ie, i) al bebé

vestir (i, i) a los niños

sentar (ie) a la niña

quitarle los anteojos a la abuela

levantar al bebé

afeitar a papá

acostar (ue) a los niños

LA RUTINA DIARIA / THE DAILY ROUTINE

la bañera bathtub
la cama bed

la cuna crib, cradle
el despertador alarm clock

el juguete toy
la pelota ball

*The masculine noun **el bebé** is used to refer to both male and female babies.

A. Describa Ud. los distintos momentos en la vida de los Hernández que se ven en los dibujos de la página 240. ¿Quién despierta al bebé? ¿Quién baña al bebé? ¿Quién lo divierte?

B. Ahora conteste estas preguntas sobre la vida diaria de la familia en los dibujos.

1. ¿Por qué no necesitan los Hernández un despertador?
2. ¿Dónde duermen los hijos? ¿Dónde es necesario que duerma la niña?
3. ¿Cuáles son los «juguetes» del bebé?
4. ¿Qué parece ser el centro de la vida doméstica de la familia?

C. Complete las oraciones en una forma lógica, usando estas palabras o cualquier otra.

- el televisor, el ruido, una buena película, el sol, la clase de español, el despertador, el estéreo

- mi compañero/a, la enfermera, el camarero, el barbero, el dueño, el padre, la esposa, un estudiante

1. _____ me despierta.
2. _____ me divierte.
3. _____ baña al bebé.
4. _____ nos sienta en el restaurante.
5. _____ nos afeita en la barbería.

6. _____ acuesta a los niños en el hospital.
7. _____ quita los platos después de la comida.
8. _____ viste a los niños.
9. _____ levanta la mano (*hand*).

¿Dónde vive Ud.? ¿Dónde quiere vivir?

alquilar	to rent	**el/la inquilino/a**	tenant, renter
		la luz	light; electricity
las afueras	outskirts; suburbs	**la piscina**	swimming pool
el alquiler	rent	**el/la portero/a**	building manager; doorman
el campo	country	**el/la vecino/a**	neighbor
el centro	downtown	**la vista**	view
la dirección	address		
el/la dueño/a	owner; landlord, landlady	**la planta baja**	ground floor
		el (primer, segundo, tercer) piso	the (second, third, fourth) floor*
el garaje	garage		
el gas	gas; heat		

---

*The Spanish equivalents of *second* (*third, fourth,* . . .) *floor* correspond to English *first* (*second, third,* . . .) *floor,* respectively. Thus, **el primer piso** (literally, *the first floor*) refers to what English speakers call *the second floor,* and so on.

A. ¿Qué prefiere Ud.?

1. ¿vivir en una casa o vivir en un edificio de apartamentos?
2. ¿vivir en el centro o en las afueras? ¿o tal vez (*perhaps*) en el campo?
3. ¿alquilar una casa/un apartamento o comprar una casa?
4. ¿pagar el gas y la luz—o pagar un alquiler más alto con el gas y la luz incluidos?
5. ¿ser el dueño del apartamento o ser el inquilino?
6. ¿que el portero/la portera lo arregle (*fix*) todo o arreglarlo todo Ud. mismo/a (*yourself*)?
7. ¿tener un garaje o una piscina?
8. ¿vivir en la planta baja o en un piso más alto?
9. ¿un apartamento pequeño con unas vistas magníficas o un apartamento más grande sin vistas?
10. ¿un apartamento pequeño con una dirección elegante o un apartamento grande con una dirección más modesta?
11. ¿conocer muy bien a los vecinos o mantenerse a distancia (*keep your distance*)?

B. Definiciones

MODELO   la piscina → Allí nadamos. (Se nada en una piscina.)

| 1. el inquilino | 3. el garaje | 5. el vecino |
| 2. el centro | 4. el portero | 6. el dueño |

PRONUNCIACIÓN: More on Stress and the Written Accent

Some English words are distinguished from each other solely by the position of stress: *objéct* (*to express disagreement*), or *óbject* (*thing*); *súspect* (*one who is suspected*) or *suspéct* (*to be suspicious*). The same is true in Spanish: **tomas** (*you take*) or **Tomás** (*Thomas*). As you will soon learn, many past-tense verb forms are accented on the last syllable, so it is important to pay special attention to stress in verbs: **hable** (*speak*) versus **hablé** (*I spoke*); **hablo** (*I speak*) versus **habló** (*he spoke*). Note that the addition of an object pronoun to a verb form or of an ending to nouns and adjectives often affects accent marks: **usando** → **usándolo**; **ambición** → **ambiciones**; **francés** → **franceses**.

Práctica

A. Pronounce the following groups of words. Stress is the only difference in pronunciation.

1. tomas, Tomás   esta, está   papa, papá   halla, allá
2. hablo, habló   trabajo, trabajó   estudio, estudió   llego, llegó
3. baile, bailé   termine, terminé   cante, canté   compre, compré
4. continuo, continúo, continuó   intérprete, interprete, interpreté

B. Explain why accents are needed or not needed on the following words.

1. joven, jóvenes
2. francés, franceses
3. orden, órdenes
4. examen, exámenes

5. nación, naciones
6. dando, dándonos, dándonoslo
7. diga, dígame, dígamelo
8. hagan, háganlos, hágonselos

MINIDIÁLOGOS Y ESTRUCTURA

28 Expressing *-self/-selves:* Reflexive Pronouns

Un día típico

1. *Me llamo* Alicia; mi esposo *se llama* Miguel. **2.** *Me despierto* y *me levanto* temprano, a las seis. Él también *se levanta* temprano. **3.** *Nos bañamos* y *nos vestimos.* **4.** Luego yo pongo la mesa y él prepara el desayuno. **5.** Después él hace la cama y yo lavo los platos. **6.** ¡Por fin! Estamos listos para salir para la oficina. **7.** Pero... un momentito. ¡Es sábado! ¿Es demasiado tarde para *acostarnos* otra vez?

Imagine que Ud. es Alicia y complete las oraciones.

1. _____ llamo Alicia y mi esposo _____ llama Miguel.
2. _____ levanto a las seis y Miguel _____ levanta a las seis y diez.
3. _____ baño; luego él _____ baña.
4. _____ visto y él _____ viste al mismo tiempo (at the same time).

Ahora imagine que Ud. es Miguel y complete las oraciones describiendo las acciones de los dos.

5. Alicia y yo _____ levantamos temprano.
6. _____ bañamos y _____ vestimos con prisa (quickly) por la mañana.
7. Casi siempre _____ acostamos temprano también.

A typical day   *1. My name is Alicia; my husband's name is Miguel. 2. I wake up and get up early, at 6:00. He also gets up early. 3. We bathe and get dressed. 4. Then I set the table and he prepares breakfast. 5. Afterward he makes the bed and I wash the dishes. 6. Finally! We're ready to leave for the office. 7. But ...wait a minute. It's Saturday! Is it too late to go back to bed (to go to bed again)?*

Uses of Reflexive Pronouns

bañarse (to take a bath)		
(yo)	**me** baño	I'm taking a bath
(tú)	**te** bañas	you're taking a bath
(Ud.) (él) (ella)	**se** baña	you're taking a bath he's taking a bath she's taking a bath
(nosotros)	**nos** bañamos	we're taking baths
(vosotros)	**os** bañáis	you're taking baths
(Uds.) (ellos) (ellas)	**se** bañan	you're taking baths they're taking baths they're taking baths

In Spanish, whenever the subject does anything to or for him/her/itself, a *reflexive pronoun* (**un pronombre reflexivo**) is used. The Spanish reflexive pronouns are **me, te,** and **se** in the singular; **nos, os,** and **se** in the plural. English reflexives end in *-self/-selves: myself, yourself,* and so on.

The pronoun **se** at the end of an infinitive indicates that the verb is used reflexively. When the verb is conjugated, the reflexive pronoun that corresponds to the subject must be used: **(yo)** *me* **baño, (tú)** *te* **bañas,** and so on.

Spanish frequently uses reflexive pronouns with verbs to express ideas that are not reflexive or are not expressed reflexively in English: *I'm taking a bath* → *Me* **baño** (literally, *I'm bathing myself*).

The following Spanish verbs, which you have already used nonreflexively, are also frequently used with reflexive pronouns.* Many of them are stem-changing.

acostarse (ue) to go to bed
afeitarse to shave
bañarse to take a bath
despertarse (ie) to wake up
divertirse (ie, i) to have a good time, enjoy oneself
dormirse (ue, u) to fall asleep
lavarse to wash oneself, get washed

levantarse to get up; to stand up
llamarse to be named, called
ponerse to put on (*clothing*)
quitarse to take off (*clothing*)
sentarse (ie) to sit down
vestirse (i, i) to get dressed

¡OJO! *After* **ponerse** *and* **quitarse,** *the definite article—not the possessive—is used with articles of clothing.*

---

*Compare: **Juan se lava.** (*John gets washed.*) **Juan lava la ropa.** (*John washes the clothing.*) **Juan la lava.** (*John washes it.*)

| Se pone **el** abrigo. | *He's putting on his coat.* |
| Se quitan **el** sombrero. | *They're taking off their hats.* |

Placement of Reflexive Pronouns

Like direct and indirect object pronouns, reflexive pronouns are placed before a conjugated verb but after the word **no** in a negative sentence: **No se bañan.** They may either precede the conjugated verb or be attached to an infinitive or present participle.

Me tengo que levantar temprano. ⎫	
Tengo que levantar**me** temprano. ⎭	*I have to get up early.*
¿**Te** estás divirtiendo? ⎫	
¿Estás divirtiéndo**te**? ⎭	*Are you having a good time?*

■ **¡OJO!** *Regardless of its position, the reflexive pronoun reflects the subject of the sentence.*

[Práctica A–C]

Reflexive pronouns are attached to affirmative commands, but they precede the verb in negative commands. When a reflexive and another object pronoun are used together, the reflexive comes first.

Quíte**se** el suéter.	*Take off your sweater.*
Quíte**selo** Ud.	*Take it off.*
No **se** ponga esa blusa.	*Don't put on that blouse.*
No **se la** ponga Ud.	*Don't put it on.*

[Práctica CH–E]

Reciprocal Actions with Reflexive Pronouns

Reciprocal actions are usually expressed in English with *each other* or *one another*. The plural reflexive pronouns **nos, os,** and **se** can be used to express *reciprocal actions* (**las acciones recíprocas**) in Spanish.

Nos queremos.	*We love each other.*
¿**Os** ayudáis?	*Do you help one another?*
Se miran.	*They're looking at each other.*

[Práctica F–H]

Nos queremos

Se miran

There are no exercises in this section that specifically practice this construction. It will be used, however, in dialogues and in questions where its use is natural. Be alert to occurrences of the construction and simply follow the lead of the dialogue or question when you formulate your answer.

Práctica

A. **Hace calor.** ¿Qué hacemos? Dé oraciones nuevas según las indicaciones.

—*Ellos* se quitan el suéter. (*yo, Carolina, nosotros, tú, todos, vosotros*)

B. **Hábitos y costumbres.** ¿Qué hacemos todos los días? Use el sujeto pronominal cuando sea necesario.

1. yo / levantarse / a las siete
2. Ud. / levantarse / más tarde
3. nosotros / bañarse / por la mañana
4. Roberto / bañarse / por la noche
5. tú / vestirse / antes de desayunar
6. los niños / vestirse / después de desayunar
7. mi padre / acostarse / temprano
8. yo / acostarse / temprano / también

C. Complete las oraciones, usando la forma correcta de los verbos de la derecha.

1. En la escuela primaria los niños ＿＿ en el suelo (*floor*) con frecuencia. Generalmente los maestros prefieren ＿＿ en una silla.
2. ¡Hace calor! Yo voy a ＿＿ el abrigo. ¿No vas a ＿＿ la chaqueta?
3. Voy a ＿＿ antes de acostarme esta noche. Mi esposo/a, en cambio, ＿＿ en la mañana.
4. Nosotros ＿＿ muy temprano, a las seis de la mañana. Y tú, ¿a qué hora te gusta ＿＿?
5. Hace un poco de frío. En este momento yo estoy ＿＿ una chaqueta. Alfredo prefiere ＿＿ un suéter.
6. ¡Tú siempre ＿＿ en las fiestas! ¿Por qué no estás ＿＿ ahora?

lavarse
sentarse
despertarse
ponerse
quitarse
divertirse

¡Me gusta tu casa!

—¿Hace mucho tiempo que vives aquí?
—Casi tres años. ¿Te gusta?
—¡Sí! ¡Es un apartamento fenomenal!
—Pues lo decoré yo misma y casi no gasté nada.

Lima, Perú

Barbara Rios/Photo Researchers, Inc.

CH. Dé Ud. consejos a una persona que es muy perezosa y descuidada (*careless*). Déle consejos basados en estos verbos.

MODELO afeitarse → Es necesario que se afeite. ¡Aféitese!

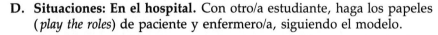

1. despertarse más temprano
2. levantarse más temprano
3. no acostarse tan tarde
4. vestirse mejor
5. no divertirse tanto
6. quitarse esa ropa sucia y ponerse ropa limpia
7. bañarse más

D. Situaciones: En el hospital. Con otro/a estudiante, haga los papeles (*play the roles*) de paciente y enfermero/a, siguiendo el modelo.

MODELO los zapatos →
   —¿Quiere Ud. que me quite los zapatos ahora?
   —Sí, quíteselos, por favor.

1. el suéter   4. la camiseta
2. la camisa/la blusa   5. los calcetines/las medias
3. los pantalones   6. toda la ropa

¿Qué otros mandatos le puede dar la enfermera (el enfermero) al paciente?

E. Escenas domésticas. ¿Cómo se dice en español?

¡**OJO!** *No se usan pronombres reflexivos en todas las oraciones.*

1. I'm going to put Johnny to bed now.
2. I'll go to bed later.
3. Wake up now!
4. And wake up the kids, too!
5. Their son's name is Agustín.
6. He always calls his parents on weekends.
7. They're putting on their shoes now.
8. They're putting the toys in the garage.

F. Preguntas

1. ¿Prefiere Ud. bañarse por la mañana o por la noche? ¿Es necesario que los hombres se afeiten todos los días? ¿Se afeita Ud. todos los días? ¿Prefiere no afeitarse los fines de semana? ¿Cuántos años hace que se afeita?
2. ¿Dónde le gusta a Ud. sentarse para leer, en un sofá, en un sillón (*armchair*) o en la cama? ¿Es buena idea sentarse en la cama para estudiar? ¿Por qué sí o por qué no? ¿Es mejor que uno se siente a estudiar en un escritorio? ¿Dónde le gusta sentarse en las clases? ¿cerca o lejos del profesor? ¿cerca o lejos de la puerta?

3. ¿Le gusta a Ud. vestirse elegantemente? ¿informalmente? ¿Qué ropa se pone cuando quiere estar elegante? ¿cuando quiere estar muy cómodo/a (*comfortable*)? ¿Qué se pone para ir a las clases?

4. ¿A qué hora tiene que levantarse todos los días? ¿Es necesario que alguien lo/la despierte? ¿A qué hora se acuesta? ¿Cuál es la última cosa que hace antes de acostarse? ¿Cuál es la última cosa en que piensa antes de dormirse?

5. ¿Ud. se duerme fácilmente o con dificultad? ¿Qué hace cuando no puede dormirse? ¿Es necesario que Ud. piense en cosas agradables para poder dormir? ¿Qué hace cuando tiene sueño pero no debe dormirse?

6. ¿Cómo se llama el dueño (la dueña) de su casa de apartamentos? ¿el portero (la portera)? ¿Cómo se llama su vecino favorito (vecina favorita)? ¿Por qué le cae tan bien?

7. ¿Con qué frecuencia se ven Ud. y su novio/a (esposo/a, mejor amigo/a)? ¿Cuánto tiempo hace que se conocen? ¿Con qué frecuencia se dan regalos? ¿se escriben? ¿se telefonean? ¿Le gusta a Ud. que se vean tanto (tan poco)? ¿Es lástima que no se vean con más frecuencia?

G. **En el espejo (*mirror*).** Describa lo que pasa en el dibujo. Use oraciones cortas, pero sea imaginativo/a.

1. ¿Quiénes son las personas del dibujo? ¿Cómo se llaman?
2. ¿Dónde están y qué hacen?
3. ¿Quién intenta (*tries*) mirarse en el espejo?
4. ¿Se puede ver? ¿Por qué sí o por qué no?

H. **Entrevista.** Using the following verbs as a guide, ask another student what he or she does during a typical day, and, when appropriate, where. Note the answers; then tell the class about his or her day.

MODELO   despertarse → ¿Se despierta Ud. temprano? ¿tarde? ¿fácilmente? ¿A qué hora se despierta Ud.?

1. despertarse	8. asistir a las clases	15. sentarse para ver la televisión
2. levantarse	9. almorzar	16. quitarse la ropa
3. bañarse	10. divertirse	17. acostarse
4. afeitarse	11. volver a casa	18. dormirse
5. vestirse	12. cocinar	19. dormir ____ horas
6. desayunar	13. cenar	
7. salir para la universidad	14. lavar los platos	

Study Hint: Listening

When you are listening to someone speaking Spanish, try to pick out cognates and guess the meaning of unfamiliar words from context, just as you do when you are reading. The following suggestions will also help you understand more of what you hear in Spanish.

1. Remember that it is not necessary to understand every word in order to get the gist of the conversation. You may feel uncomfortable if you cannot understand absolutely everything, but chances are good that you will still be able to handle the conversational situation.

2. Watch the speaker's facial expressions and gestures—they will give you a general idea about what he or she is saying. For example, if there is a pause and the speaker is looking at you expectantly, it is reasonable to guess that he or she has just asked you a question.

3. Use brief pauses in the conversation to digest the words that you have just heard.

4. The more familiar you are with the vocabulary being used, the easier it will be to understand what you are hearing. Listen for familiar words—and be flexible: they may appear with a different meaning in a new context. Listen also for specific clues, such as the following:

a. *the gender of nouns and adjectives:* Is the speaker talking about **un chico alto** or **una chica alta**? Here you have three chances—with the article, the noun itself, and the adjective—to catch the gender of the person being described.

b. *verb endings:* Who did what to whom? As you will learn in the next grammar section, if you hear **habló,** you know that the speaker is not talking about himself or herself, since the **-ó** ending signals a third person.

c. *object pronouns:* The sentence **La voy a ver en el restaurante** can only refer to a woman or to a feminine noun.

ch. *intonation:* Did you hear a question or a statement?

Above all, if you really have not understood what someone said to you, react: ask questions, admit that you haven't understood, and ask him or her to repeat.

¿Qué hiciste hoy?

—¿A qué hora te levantaste esta mañana?
—A las siete. Me bañé y me vestí rápidamente y luego fui al centro.
—¿Qué hiciste allí? ¿Fuiste de compras?
—No. Busqué trabajo, pero no encontré nada.

Buenos Aires, Argentina

Stuart Cohen

29 Talking About the Past (1)
Preterite of Regular Verbs and of *dar*, *hacer*, *ir*, and *ser*

Un problema con la agencia de empleos

SRA. GÓMEZ: ¡La criada que Uds. me *mandaron* ayer *fue* un desastre!

SR. PARDO: ¿Cómo que *fue* un desastre? ¿Qué *hizo*?

SRA. GÓMEZ: Pues, no *hizo* nada. *Pasó* todo el día en la casa, pero no *lavó* los platos, no *limpió* la bañera, ni *recogió* los juguetes de los niños. Y cuando *salió* a las tres, me *dio* las buenas tardes como si nada.

SR. PARDO: Trate de comprender, señora; cada persona tiene sus más y sus menos. Por lo menos esta criada *fue* mejor que la otra que le *mandamos* anteayer... que ni *llegó*.

Imagine que Ud. es la Sra. Gómez y describa para el Sr. Pardo las acciones de la criada. Use el diálogo como guía.

1. Ella no... (lavar los platos, limpiar la bañera, recoger los juguetes)

2. Pero (ella) sí... (llegar temprano por la mañana, pasar todo el día en casa, salir a las tres)

3. Total que (ella)... (no hacer nada, ser un desastre)

¿Quiere la Sra. Gómez que esta criada vuelva mañana? ¿Va a querer que esta agencia le mande otra criada?

In Spanish two simple tenses (tenses formed without an auxiliary or "helping" verb) are used to talk about the past: the preterite and the imperfect.* The *preterite* (**el pretérito**) has several equivalents in English. For example, **hablé** can mean *I spoke* or *I did speak*. The preterite is used to report finished, completed actions or states of being in the past. If the action or state of being is viewed as completed—no matter how long it lasted or took to complete—it will be expressed with the preterite.

A problem with the employment agency   MRS. GÓMEZ: *The maid you sent me yesterday was a disaster!*   MR. PARDO: *What do you mean, a disaster? What did she do?*   MRS. GÓMEZ: *Well, she didn't do anything. She spent all day at the house, but she didn't wash the dishes, clean the bathtub, or pick up the kids' toys. And when she left at 3:00, she said, "Good afternoon," as if nothing were wrong.*   MR. PARDO: *Try to understand, madam; everyone has his or her good and bad points. At least this maid was better than the other one we sent you the day before yesterday—who didn't even arrive.*

*The forms of the preterite are presented in this section and in **Capítulo 14**. The imperfect is presented in **Capítulo 15**.

Preterite of Regular Verbs

hablar		comer		vivir	
hablé	*I spoke (did speak)*	comí	*I ate (did eat)*	viví	*I lived (did live)*
hablaste	*you spoke*	comiste	*you ate*	viviste	*you lived*
habló	*you/he/she spoke*	comió	*you/he/she ate*	vivió	*you/he/she lived*
hablamos	*we spoke*	comimos	*we ate*	vivimos	*we lived*
hablasteis	*you spoke*	comisteis	*you ate*	vivisteis	*you lived*
hablaron	*you/they spoke*	comieron	*you/they ate*	vivieron	*you/they lived*

Note the accent marks on the first- and third-person singular of the preterite tense. These accent marks are dropped in the conjugation of **ver: vi, vio.**

Verbs that end in **-car, -gar,** and **-zar** show a spelling change in the first-person singular of the preterite.

buscar: bus**qué**, buscaste,...
pagar: pa**gué**, pagaste,...
empezar: empe**cé**, empezaste,...

-Ar and **-er** stem-changing verbs show no stem change in the preterite: **desperté, volví. -Ir** stem-changing verbs do show a change.*

As in the present participle, an unstressed **-i-** between two vowels becomes **-y-.**

creer: cre**y**ó, cre**y**eron   leer: le**y**ó, le**y**eron

Irregular Preterite Forms

dar		hacer		ir/ser	
di	dimos	hice	hicimos	fui	fuimos
diste	disteis	hiciste	hicisteis	fuiste	fuisteis
dio	dieron	hizo	hicieron	fue	fueron

The preterite endings for **dar** are the same as those used for regular **-er/ir** verbs in the preterite, except that the accent marks are dropped. The third-person singular of **hacer—hizo—**is spelled with a **z** to keep the [s] sound of the infinitive. **Ser** and **ir** have identical forms in the preterite. Context will make the meaning clear.

Fui profesora.   *I was a professor.*
Fui al centro anoche.   *I went downtown last night.*

---

*You will practice the preterite of most stem-changing verbs in **Capítulo 14.**

Práctica

A. **Preparativos para el examen de química.** Dé oraciones nuevas según las indicaciones.

1. *Pepe* estudió hasta muy tarde. (*yo, Uds., tú, Graciela, nosotros, vosotros*)
2. *Tú* escribiste todos los ejercicios. (*Rodrigo, yo, nosotras, ellas, Uds., vosotros*)
3. *Julio* fue al laboratorio. (*yo, Paula, tú, nosotros, Estela y Clara, vosotras*)
4. *Ana* hizo los experimentos. (*yo, nosotros, Uds., tú, Adolfo, vosotros*)

B. **Escenas del edificio de apartamentos.** ¿Qué pasó ayer? Haga oraciones según las indicaciones. Use el sujeto pronominal cuando sea necesario.

1. dueño / no / pagar / gas
2. tú / llamar / dueño
3. alguno / inquilinos / salir / de viaje
4. portera / alquilar / tres / apartamento
5. electricista / arreglar / luz
6. Ud. / limpiar / piscina / ¿verdad?
7. yo / ir / garaje / para / buscar / cajas (*boxes*)
8. nosotros / levantar / alfombra (*rug*) / para / limpiar / suelo

C. **¿Qué pasó?** Cambie los verbos indicados al pretérito.

1. *Regreso* tarde a casa. Mi compañero *prepara* la cena y *cenamos* juntos. Luego *empiezo* a estudiar, pero mi compañero *sale* con unos amigos a ver una película.
2. *Paso* un semestre estudiando en México. Mis padres me *pagan* el vuelo y *trabajo* para tener dinero para la matrícula y para los otros gastos (*expenses*). En México *vivo* con una encantadora familia mexicana y *aprendo* mucho. *Voy* a muchos lugares interesantes. Mis amigos me *escriben* muchas cartas. Yo les *compro* recuerdos a todos.
3. ¡La fiesta de cumpleaños de la Sra. Sandoval *es* un desastre! Alicia le *hace* un pastel pero no lo *come* nadie. Y a la señora no le *gustan* los regalos que le *dan*. Todos *salen* descontentos. *Deciden* no dar nunca otra fiesta para la Sra. Sandoval.

CH. **¿Qué hicieron ayer?** Dé oraciones completas, usando los verbos en el pretérito.

1. **Julián:** hacer cola para comprar una entrada de cine / comprarla por fin / entrar en el cine / ver la película / gustarle mucho / regresar a casa tarde

2. **mis hermanos:** regresar temprano a casa / ayudar a mamá / limpiar la casa / recoger todos los juguetes / prepararlo todo para la fiesta de esta noche
3. **yo:** llegar a la universidad a las __?__ / asistir a clases / ir a la cafetería / almorzar / estudiar en la biblioteca / darle un libro a un amigo / __?__

D. **¿Qué hicieron estas personas ayer?** ¿Qué piensa Ud.? Invente los detalles necesarios.

Personas	**Acciones**
Dan Rather	dar un discurso *(speech)*
el presidente	leer las noticias *(news)*
Julio Iglesias	cocinar
Julia Child	cantar
el profesor (la profesora)	enseñar
	no hacer nada
__?__	__?__

E. Preguntas

1. ¿Qué le dio Ud. a su mejor amigo/a (esposa/a, novio/a) para su cumpleaños el año pasado? ¿Qué le regaló a Ud. esa persona para su cumpleaños? ¿Alguien le mandó a Ud. flores el año pasado? ¿Le mandó Ud. flores a alguien? ¿Le gusta a Ud. que le traigan chocolates? ¿otras cosas?
2. ¿Dónde y a qué hora comió Ud. ayer? ¿Con quiénes comió? ¿Le gustaron todos los platos que comió? ¿Quién se los preparó? Si comió fuera, ¿quién pagó?
3. ¿Cuándo decidió Ud. estudiar el español? ¿Cuándo lo empezó a estudiar? ¿Cuánto tiempo hace que lo estudia ahora? ¿Va a seguir estudiándolo el semestre (trimestre) que viene?
4. ¿Qué hizo Ud. ayer? ¿Adónde fue? ¿Con quién(es)? ¿Ayudó a alguien a hacer algo? ¿Lo/La llamó alguien? ¿Llamó Ud. a alguien? ¿Lo/La invitaron algunos amigos a hacer algo especial? Y anteayer, ¿qué hizo? ¿Lo mismo?
5. ¿Qué programa de televisión vio Ud. anoche? ¿Qué película vio la semana pasada? ¿Qué libro/novela leyó el año pasado? El año pasado, ¿pasó Ud. más tiempo leyendo o viendo la televisión? ¿trabajando o estudiando? ¿estudiando o viajando? Si hizo algún viaje, ¿adónde fue? ¿Qué tal fue el viaje?

F. **Entrevista: Preguntas indiscretas.** Using the following phrases as a guide, ask a classmate about his or her activities. Note the answers; then tell the class about your classmate's activities.

1. a qué hora: despertarse esta mañana
2. a qué hora: volver a casa anoche
3. por cuánto tiempo: mirar la televisión ayer
4. con quién: cenar ayer
5. qué: comer anoche
6. a qué hora: acostarse anoche
7. cuánto: pagar de gas (luz) el mes pasado
8. de quién: enamorarse (*to fall in love*) el año pasado

REPASO

Los anuncios. Complete the following paragraphs with the correct form of the words in parentheses, as suggested by the context. When two possibilities are given in parentheses, select the correct word. Use the preterite of infinitives indicated with an asterisk.

Hay anuncios publicitarios por (*todo*[1]) partes (*del/de la*[2]) mundo° y los hay° de (*todo*[3]) tipos. Algunos (*aparecer*[4])* primero en los Estados Unidos, pero ahora (*ser/estar*[5]) internacionales.   *world / los… there are some*

· (*Beber*[6]) Ud. Coca-Cola, (*delicioso*[7]) y refrescante.
· ¿No (*ser/estar: tú*[8]) contento de usar Dial?
· La (*nuevo*[9]) sonrisa° Colgate…   *smile*

Un estadounidense° que (*viajar*[10]) por Latinoamérica o España (*poder*[11]) (*tener*[12]) la impresión de que (*cada*[13]) hombre (*afeitarse*[14]) con Gillette y que todos (*bañarse*[15]) y (*lavarse*[16]) los dientes° con productos norteamericanos.   *persona que vive en los Estados Unidos*   *teeth*

Hay un caso famoso en el mundo de la propaganda° que (*demostrar* [*ue*][17]) el peligro° de vender un producto en el extranjero° (*con/sin*[18]) considerar bien su nombre. Se trata° (*del/de la*[19]) coche norteamericano *Nova*, que (*alguno*[20]) latinoamericanos malpensados° (*cambiar*[21])* en **No va.**° Ya que° (*este*[22]) nombre realmente no (*animar*[23]) al comprador de habla española, los fabricantes° lo (*cambiar*[24])* a *Caribe*.   *advertising*   *danger / en… abroad*   *Se… It's the case*   *wicked / No… It doesn't run*   *Ya… Since*   *manufacturers*

En los países hispanos también hay muchos anuncios de lotería. Allí, como aquí, (*ser/estar*[25]) probable que tales anuncios nos (*prometer*°[26]) un futuro mejor: *to promise*

· Juan Fernández (*ganar*[27])* un millón de pesos en la lotería nacional.

(*Ser/Estar*[28]) el sueño de todos comprar un décimo° o un billete entero° y ganar el premio gordo.°   *tenth / billete… whole sheet*   *premio… first prize*

UN PASO MÁS: Imágenes del mundo hispánico
La España moderna

Bernard Pierre Wolff/Photo Researchers, Inc.

Un café de «La Gran Vía», **Madrid**

Hiller/Monkmeyer Press Photo Service

Pueblo de la Costa Brava

*E*spaña es en la actualidad (*currently*) un país que guarda sus tradiciones y que también forma parte de la historia democrática europea. La constitución de 1978 es fundamental para comprender la transición de la época de Franco a la monarquía constitucional de Juan Carlos de Borbón y las características del nuevo período. España forma parte de la Comunidad Económica Europea y de la Organización del Tratado del Atlántico Norte (OTAN) y, además, mantiene muy buenas relaciones con los países de Hispanoamérica.

Por su belleza y su clima, España es un país muy favorecido por el turismo. Hay numerosos lugares de veraneo (*summer vacations*) que ofrecen todo lo necesario para el descanso y para disfrutar las diversiones más cosmopolitas. También existen rincones (*corners*) maravillosos llenos de sabor popular. Es muy difícil viajar por España sin encontrar monumentos, museos, restos artísticos de diferentes períodos y, por supuesto, las comodidades (*comforts*) de la vida moderna.

El español es sobre todo un pueblo comunicativo. Le gusta divertirse como a todo el mundo, pero le gusta especialmente divertirse con los demás (*others*). Por este motivo en las calles de las ciudades y pueblos hay mucho movimiento y animación durante las veinticuatro horas del día.

VOCABULARIO

VERBOS

acostar (ue) to put to bed;
  acostarse to go to bed
afeitar to shave; **afeitarse** to
  shave oneself
alquilar to rent
arreglar to fix, repair
bañar to bathe; **bañarse** to bathe
  oneself
despertar (ie) to wake;
  despertarse to wake up
divertir (ie, i) to amuse, entertain;
  divertirse to have a good time,
  enjoy oneself
dormirse (ue, u) to fall asleep
lavar to wash; **lavarse** to wash
  oneself, get washed
levantar to raise, lift;
  levantarse to get up, stand up
limpiar to clean
llamarse to be named, called

ponerse to put on (*clothing*)
quitarse to take off (*clothing*)
recoger (recojo) to gather, pick up
sentar (ie) to seat; **sentarse** to sit
  down
vestir (i, i) to get dressed;
  vestirse to dress oneself

¿DÓNDE VIVE UD.?

  las afueras outskirts; suburbs
  el alquiler rent
  el campo country
  la dirección address
  el garaje garage
  el gas gas; heat
el/la inquilino/a tenant, renter
  la luz (*pl.* **luces**) light;
    electricity
  la piscina swimming pool
  el piso floor, story
  la planta baja ground floor

el/la portero/a building manager;
  doorman
el/la vecino/a neighbor
  la vista view

OTROS SUSTANTIVOS

  los anteojos (eye)glasses
  la bañera bathtub
  la cama bed
el/la criado/a servant/maid
  la cuna crib, cradle
  el despertador alarm clock
  el juguete toy
  la mano hand
  la pelota ball
  la vida life

ADJETIVOS

cada (*invariable*) each, every
diario/a daily
doméstico/a domestic

FRASES ÚTILES PARA LA COMUNICACIÓN	
anoche, anteayer, ayer	last night, the day before yesterday, yesterday
el (fin de semana, mes, año) pasado	last (weekend, month, year)
la semana pasada	last week

CAPÍTULO 14

En casa: La rutina diaria y los días festivos

LOS APARATOS DOMÉSTICOS

LOS QUEHACERES DOMÉSTICOS / DOMESTIC TASKS

hacer la cama to make the bed
lavar (las ventanas, los platos) to wash (the windows, dishes)
limpiar la casa (entera) to clean the (whole) house

pasar la aspiradora to vacuum
poner la mesa to set the table
preparar la comida/cocinar to prepare food/to cook
sacar la basura to take out the trash
sacudir los muebles to dust the furniture

257

¿A quién le toca? *(Whose turn is it?)*

—¿Quieres poner el televisor? Hay una
película estupenda esta noche.

—Espérate. ¿A ti no te toca lavar los platos?

—A mí, no. Creo que le toca a Julio.

—Pero Julio no está. Ya salió.

—Vamos a dejarlos hasta que regrese.

Barcelona, España

Entrevista. ¿Es Ud. buen(a) ama de casa *(housekeeper)*? ¿Con qué
frecuencia hace Ud. los siguientes quehaceres? Si Ud. no los hace, ¿a
quién le toca? Otro/a estudiante lo/la va a entrevistar para evaluar sus
hábitos domésticos. Si Ud. vive en una residencia estudiantil, imagine
que vive en una casa o en un apartamento.

MODELO   lavar las ventanas →
    —¿Con qué frecuencia lavas las ventanas?
    —Nunca me toca lavarlas. Me las lava la criada. (Las lavo
       frecuentemente. No me gusta que estén sucias.)

0 = nunca   **1** = a veces   **2** = frecuentemente   **3** = todos los días

_____ 1. lavar las ventanas   _____ 6. lavar los platos
_____ 2. hacer las camas   _____ 7. limpiar la casa entera
_____ 3. poner la mesa   _____ 8. sacar la basura
_____ 4. preparar la comida   _____ 9. pasar la aspiradora
_____ 5. sacudir los muebles   _____ 10. limpiar el horno *(oven)*

_____ TOTAL

Interpretaciones

0–7 puntos: ¡Cuidado *(Careful)*! Ud. estudia demasiado. Por
                favor, ¡limpie su casa! O, por lo menos, haga que
                alguien se la limpie.

8–14 puntos: Ud. puede vivir en su casa, pero no debe invitar a
                otras personas si no la limpia bien primero.

15–23 puntos: Su casa, aunque *(although)* no está perfecta, está
                limpia. Es un buen modelo para todos.

24–30 puntos: ¡Ud. es una maravilla y tiene una casa muy, muy
                limpia! Pero, ¿pasa Ud. todo el día limpiándola?
                ¿Tiene Ud. una criada? ¿Le pide a la criada que se
                lo limpie todo?

Las partes de una casa

la alcoba (el dormitorio)
  bedroom
el baño bathroom
la cocina kitchen

el comedor dining room
el garaje garage
el patio patio; yard
la sala living room

la sala de recreo recreation
  room, family room
el sótano basement

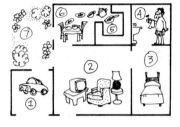

A. ¿En qué cuarto o parte de la casa se puede hacer las siguientes
  actividades?

1. Se hace la cama en _____ .
2. Se pone la mesa en _____ .
3. Se saca la basura de _____ y se pone en _____ .
4. Se prepara la comida en _____ .
5. Se sacude los muebles de _____ .
6. Se duerme en _____ .
7. Uno se baña en _____ . Se baña al perro en _____ .
8. Se mira la televisión en _____ .
9. Se pasa la aspiradora en _____ y en _____ .
10. Se lava el coche en _____ .

B. ¿Para qué se usan los siguientes productos? Explíqueselo a su amigo
  hispano, que no los conoce.

1. Windex
2. Mr. Coffee
3. Endust
4. Glad Bags
5. Joy
6. Cascade
7. Tide
8. Lysol

Los días festivos y las fiestas

la Noche Vieja New Year's
  Eve
el Día del Año Nuevo
  New Year's Day
la Pascua Passover
la Pascua (Florida) Easter
el Día de los Muertos All
  Souls' Day

el Día de Gracias
  Thanksgiving
la Nochebuena Christmas Eve
la Navidad Christmas

felicitaciones
  congratulations
dar/hacer una fiesta to give/
  have a party

llorar to cry
pasarlo bien/mal to have a
  good/bad time
recordar (ue) to remember
reírse (i, i) to laugh
sentirse (ie, i) feliz/triste to
  feel happy/sad
sonreír (i, i) to smile

■ **¡OJO!** *You will see the preceding holidays throughout **¿Qué tal?**. Learn to use those that are
particulary important or interesting to you. The entire list will not be considered "active" vocabulary
that you will be expected to say or write spontaneously.*

A. ¿Qué palabra corresponde a estas definiciones?

1. El día en que se celebra el nacimiento (*birth*) de Jesús

2. El día en que los hispanos visitan el cementerio para honrar la memoria de los difuntos (*deceased*)
3. Reacción emocional cuando se reciben muy buenas noticias (*news*) (tres respuestas)
4. Reacción emocional cuando se recibe la noticia de una tragedia (dos respuestas)
5. La noche en que se celebra el paso de un año a otro

B. Explique cómo se divierte Ud. en estas fiestas y en otras ocasiones. ¿Qué hace para pasarlo bien? ¿Qué quiere Ud. que ocurra, idealmente?

1. El día de su cumpleaños
2. Durante las vacaciones de invierno o de primavera
3. En una fiesta que dan sus padres (sus hijos)... y los amigos de ellos están presentes
4. Los viernes por la noche
5. El Día de Gracias
6. La Navidad/La Pascua

Ahora describa una situación típica en la que Ud. lo pasa mal.

MINIDIÁLOGOS Y ESTRUCTURA

30 Talking About the Past (2): Irregular Preterites

Un sábado por la tarde

JORGE: Mujer, ¿dónde *estuviste* toda la mañana?
LUCÍA: *Tuve* que ir a la oficina a terminar un trabajo.
JORGE: ¿Por qué no me lo *dijiste* antes de irte?
LUCÍA: Estabas durmiendo, pero te lo *dije* anoche.
JORGE: Posiblemente, pero se me olvidó.
LUCÍA: ¿*Vinieron* tus padres?
JORGE: Sí, y los chicos y yo *tuvimos* que arreglar la sala. ¡Qué lata!
LUCÍA: No te quejes. Tú también puedes hacer algunos de los quehaceres.
JORGE: ¿Por qué? Nunca los *hice* en casa de mis padres y no quiero empezar ahora.

One Saturday afternoon   JORGE: *Woman, where were you all morning?*   LUCÍA: *I had to go to the office to finish a job.*   JORGE: *Why didn't you tell me before you left (before going)?*   LUCÍA: *You were sleeping, but I told you last night.*   JORGE: *Maybe, but it slipped my mind.*   LUCÍA: *Did your folks come?*   JORGE: *Yes, and the kids and I had to pick up the living room. What a pain!*   LUCÍA: *Don't complain. You can do some of the housework too.*   JORGE: *Why? I never did it at my parents' house and I don't want to start now.*

1. *¿Por qué no estuvo Lucía en casa·esta mañana?*
2. *¿Arregló la casa antes de irse?*
3. *¿Quiénes vinieron de visita?*
4. *¿Quiénes tuvieron que arreglar la sala?*
5. *¿Por qué se está enojando (getting angry) Jorge?*
6. *¿Quiere compartir (to share) Jorge algunos de los quehaceres domésticos con Lucía? ¿Por qué sí o por qué no?*

You have already learned the irregular preterite forms of **dar, hacer, ir,** and **ser.** The following verbs are also irregular in the preterite. Note that the first- and third-person singular endings, which are the only irregular ones, are unstressed, in contrast to the stressed endings of regular preterite forms.

estar:	**estuv-**	
poder:	**pud-**	-e
poner:	**pus-**	-iste
querer:	**quis-**	-o
saber:	**sup-**	-imos
tener:	**tuv-**	-isteis
venir:	**vin-**	-ieron

estar	
estuve	**estuvimos**
estuviste	**estuvisteis**
estuvo	**estuvieron**

decir:	**dij-**	-e, -iste, -o, -imos, -isteis, **-eron**
traer:	**traj-**	

When the preterite verb stem ends in **-j-,** the **-i-** of the third-person plural ending is omitted: **dijeron, trajeron.**

The preterite of **hay (haber)** is **hubo** (*there was/were*).

Several of these Spanish verbs have an English equivalent in the preterite tense that is different from that of the infinitive.

saber:	Ya lo sé.	*I already know it.*
	Lo **supe** ayer.	*I found it out (learned it) yesterday.*
conocer:	Ya la conozco.	*I already know her.*
	La **conocí** ayer.	*I met her yesterday.*
querer:	Quiero hacerlo hoy.	*I want to do it today.*
	Quise hacerlo ayer.	*I tried to do it yesterday.*
	No quise hacerlo anteayer.	*I refused to do it the day before yesterday.*
poder:	Puedo leerlo.	*I can (am able to) read it.*
	Pude leerlo ayer.	*I could (and did) read it yesterday.*
	No pude leerlo anteayer.	*I couldn't (did not) read it the day before yesterday.*

Práctica

A. La fiesta del Día del Año Nuevo. ¿Qué pasó? Dé oraciones nuevas según las indicaciones.

1. *Todos* estuvieron en casa de Mario. (*yo, Raúl, Uds., tú, nosotros, vosotras*)
2. *Muchos* vinieron con comida y bebidas. (*Ud., nosotros, tú, Rosalba, Uds., vosotros*)
3. *Todos* dijeron que la fiesta estuvo estupenda. (*tú, Anita, Uds., yo, ellas, vosotros*)

B. ¿Qué pasó en casa de los Ramírez durante la Nochebuena? Haga oraciones según las indicaciones. Use el sujeto pronominal cuando sea necesario.

1. nosotros / poner / mucho / regalos / debajo / árbol
2. niños / querer / dormir / pero / no / poder
3. ellos / tener / preparar / mucho / comida
4. haber / cena / para / mayores
5. alguno / amigos / venir / a / cantar / villancicos (*carols*)
6. a / doce / yo / les / decir / «¡Feliz Navidad!» / todos

C. A Ernesto le toca ayudar hoy con los quehaceres de la casa, pero se le olvidó (*he forgot*) hacer ciertas cosas. Hágale preguntas según el modelo.

MODELO　estar: garaje / sacar la basura →
　　　　　Estuviste en el garaje. ¿Por qué no sacaste la basura?

1. estar: comedor / poner la mesa
2. ir: sótano / sacar la ropa de la secadora
3. pasar por: alcoba / hacer las camas
4. estar: sala / poder pasar la aspiradora
5. ir: cocina / poner el lavaplatos

CH. ¿Qué pasó anoche? Cambie por el pretérito.

1. Ana y su nieto *vienen* a visitarnos. Ana *trae* su perro y lo *ponemos* en el garaje, donde *ladra* (*he barks*) durante toda la visita. Los dos *están* en casa sólo una hora y luego *tienen* que regresar a casa. Se *van* a las nueve y media.
2. Los Sres. Torres *hacen* la cena y *ponen* la mesa a las seis. Luego *tienen* que lavar los platos. No *pueden* ir al cine hasta muy tarde.
3. *Quiero* estudiar pero no *puedo* porque mi amigo Octavio *viene* a casa con un amigo ecuatoriano. *Tengo* que ver las fotos que *traen*.

D. Describa Ud. estos hechos (*events*) históricos, usando una palabra o frase de cada columna. Use el pretérito de los verbos.

en 1969 los	traer	un hombre en la luna
estadounidenses	saber	en Valley Forge con sus
Adán y Eva	conocer	soldados
George Washington	decir	«que coman (*let them eat*)
los europeos	estar	pasteles»
Stanley	poner	que las serpientes son malas
María Antonieta		a Livingston en África
		el caballo (*horse*) al Nuevo
		Mundo

E. Preguntas

1. ¿En qué mes conoció Ud. al profesor (a la profesora) de español?
    ¿A quién(es) más conoció ese mismo día? ¿Tuvo Ud. que hablar
    español el primer día de clase? ¿Cuánto tiempo hace que lo
    habla? ¿Qué les dijo a sus amigos después de esa primera clase?
    ¿Qué les va a decir hoy?

2. ¿Hubo una prueba ayer en la clase de español? ¿Cuándo hubo
    examen? ¿Le fue difícil a Ud. aprenderlo todo para ese último
    examen? ¿Cuánto tiempo estudió Ud.? ¿Qué dijo cuando supo la
    nota que tuvo en ese examen? ¿Cuándo va a haber otra prueba en
    esta clase? ¿Le gusta a Ud. que haya tantas pruebas?

3. ¿Dónde estuvo Ud. el fin de semana pasado? ¿Con quiénes
    estuvo? ¿Adónde fue con ellos? ¿Qué hicieron? ¿Lo pasaron bien?
    ¿Dónde estuvo Ud. la última Noche Vieja? ¿el último Día de
    Gracias? ¿Dónde piensa estar este año para celebrar esos días
    festivos?

4. ¿Le dio alguien a Ud. una fiesta de cumpleaños este año? ¿Qué le
    trajeron sus amigos? ¿Qué le regalaron sus padres? ¿Le hizo
    alguien un pastel? ¿Qué le dijeron todos? ¿Y qué les dijo Ud.?
    ¿Quiere que le den otra fiesta este año?

5. ¿Dónde puso su coche ayer? ¿Lo puso en el garaje o lo dejó en la
    calle? ¿Dónde puso el abrigo cuando se lo quitó? ¿Dónde puso los
    libros cuando llegó a casa? ¿Olvida a veces dónde pone las cosas?
    ¿Qué otra cosa olvida Ud. a veces?

F. **Entrevista.** With another student, ask and answer questions to
    determine the first and/or last time the following situations occurred.

    MODELO   ¿Cuándo fue la última vez (la primera vez) que tú... ?

    1. decir algo muy interesante
    2. estar muy contento/a
    3. estar enfermo/a
    4. traer diez dólares a clase
    5. tener que pedirle ayuda a
        alguien

    6. dar una fiesta
    7. ir al mercado
    8. hacer un viaje en avión
    9. enojarse

31 Talking About the Past (3) Preterite of Stem-changing Verbs

El cumpleaños de Mercedes

Siguiendo las indicaciones, invente Ud. una descripción de la fiesta de sorpresa que se celebró para Mercedes el año pasado.

1. Llegaron todos a ___(hora)___ .

2. Mercedes $\begin{cases} \text{sonrió} \\ \text{se rió} \\ \text{empezó a llorar} \end{cases}$ cuando los vio.

3. Sus amigos le trajeron muchos regalos. Su amigo Raúl le regaló un disco. Su prima Julita le regaló un diccionario de español. Su hermano _____ .

4. Mercedes $\begin{cases} \text{sonrió} \\ \text{se rió} \\ \text{le dijo} \_\_\_\_ \end{cases}$ cuando abrió el regalo de _____ .

5. Su compañera de cuarto sirvió (¿un pastel? ¿helado?) .

6. Se despidieron (*said goodbye*) todos a ___(hora)___ , y Mercedes se durmió, muy contenta, a ___(hora)___ .

Ahora repita Ud. algunos de los detalles, pero desde el punto de vista de Mercedes.

1. *Yo* $\begin{cases} \text{sonreí} \\ \text{me reí} \\ \text{empecé a llorar} \end{cases}$ *cuando llegaron todos.*

2. *Cuando _____ me dio _____ , (yo)* $\begin{cases} \text{sonreí} \\ \text{me reí} \\ \text{le dije} \_\_\_\_ . \end{cases}$

3. *Comí _____ y bebí _____ .*

4. *Me dormí, muy contenta, a ___(hora)___ .*

-Ar and **-er** stem-changing verbs have no stem change in the preterite.

recordar (ue)		perder (ie)	
recordé	recordamos	perdí	perdimos
recordaste	recordasteis	perdiste	perdisteis
recordó	recordaron	perdió	perdieron

-Ir stem-changing verbs have a stem change in the preterite, but only in the third-person singular and plural, where the stem vowels **e** and **o** change to **i** and **u,** respectively. This is the same change that occurs in the present participle of **-ir** stem-changing verbs.

pedir (i, i)		**dormir (ue, u)**	
pedí	pedimos	dormí	dormimos
pediste	pedisteis	dormiste	dormisteis
pidió	pidieron	durmió	durmieron

The **-ir** stem-changing verbs that you already know or have seen are the following.

conseguir (i, i)   pedir (i, i)   servir (i, i)
despedir(se) (i, i)   preferir (ie, i)   sonreír (i, i)*
divertir(se) (ie, i)   reír(se) (i, i)*   vestir(se) (i, i)
dormir(se) (ue, u)   sentir(se) (ie, i)

Another **-ir** stem-changing verb is **morirse (ue, u)** (*to die*).

Práctica

A. Todos pasaron un día fatal ayer. ¿Qué les pasó? Dé oraciones nuevas según las indicaciones.

1. *Dormimos* muy mal anoche. (*yo, los inquilinos, Irma, tú, Uds., vosotros*)
2. No *recordaste* sacar la basura. (*Raúl, nosotros, Ud., ellos, vosotros*)
3. *Raúl* perdió la cuenta de la luz. (*tú, los vecinos, yo, Ud., vosotras*)
4. *Pedimos* mariscos pero no había (*they were out of them*). (*yo, Jacinto, tú, Uds., vosotros*)
5. *Todos* se rieron mucho de Nati. (*nosotros, el portero, yo, Uds., vosotras*)

B. **¿Qué pasó ayer?** Cambie los verbos indicados por el pretérito. Luego continúe las historias con más acciones.

1. Juan se *sienta* en un restaurante. *Pide* una cerveza. El camarero no *recuerda* su pedido (*order*) y le *sirve* una Coca-Cola. Juan _____ .
2. Rosa se *acuesta* temprano y se *duerme* en seguida. *Duerme* bien y se *despierta* temprano, a las siete. Se *viste* y *sale* para la universidad. Rosa _____ .

---

*Note the simplification: **ri-ió** → **rió**; **ri-ieron** → **rieron**; **sonri-ió** → **sonrió**; **sonri-ieron** → **sonrieron**.

3. Yo me *visto*, *voy* a una fiesta, me *divierto* mucho y *vuelvo* tarde a casa. Mi compañero de cuarto *decide* quedarse (*to stay*) en casa y *ve* la televisión toda la noche. No se *divierte* nada. *Pierde* una fiesta excelente y lo *siente* mucho. Yo ____ .

C. Describa Ud. estos hechos (*events*) pasados, usando una palabra o frase de cada columna. Use el pretérito de los verbos.

durante la primavera pasada	llover	buenos puestos despúes de graduarse
Romeo	recordar	
la segunda guerra (*war*) mundial	divertirse	en Acapulco
	dormir	en 1939
	morirse	por Julieta
Rip Van Winkle	empezar	muchos años
los turistas	conseguir	todo el vocabulario en el último examen
mis amigos	nevar	mucho

CH. Preguntas

1. ¿Dónde almorzó Ud. ayer? ¿Qué pidió? ¿Quién se lo sirvió? ¿Quién pagó la cuenta? ¿Cuánto dejó Ud. de propina (*tip*)? La última vez que cenó en un restaurante, ¿qué pidió? ¿Prefiere Ud. que otra persona pague en un restaurante elegante?

2. ¿A qué hora se acostó Ud. anoche? ¿Cuántas horas durmió? ¿Durmió bien? ¿Se sintió descansado/a (*rested*) cuando se despertó? ¿Cómo se vistió esta mañana, elegante o informalmente? ¿Se levantó con el pie izquierdo (*on the wrong side of the bed*)?

3. ¿Qué película o programa de televisión le divirtió más el año pasado? ¿Se rió Ud. mucho cuando vio ____ ? ¿Les gustó también a sus amigos? ¿Qué película quieres ver este mes? ¿Es posible que se ría mucho o es más probable que llore?

D. **Entrevista.** Ask another student **preguntas indiscretas** based on these cues. He or she should invent equally outrageous answers. Then report what you have learned to the class.

MODELO   dormirse → —¿A qué hora te dormiste anoche?
—Me dormí a las tres de la mañana... y me levanté a las siete, muy descansada.
—Alicia se durmió a las tres... y se levantó a las siete, muy descansada.

1. dormir(se): ¿a qué hora? ¿dónde?
2. servir: ¿qué, en su última (fiesta, cena)? ¿quién? ¿a quién?
3. despedirse: ¿de quién, anoche? ¿a qué hora?
4. perder: ¿qué cosa? ¿cuánto dinero? ¿dónde?

REPASO

Los días festivos. Complete the following dialogue and paragraphs with the correct form of the words in parentheses, as suggested by context. When two possibilities are given in parentheses, select the correct word. Use the preterite of infinitives indicated with an asterisk.

La Navidad

Carol (*ser/estar*[1]) hablando con Elena, su amiga (*español*[2]). Hace un año que Elena (*vivir*[3]) en los Estados Unidos con su esposo y (*su*[4]) tres hijos.

CAROL: ¿Qué esperan tus niños que (*los/les*[5]) (*traer*[6]) Santa Claus este año?

ELENA: ¿Santa Claus? Mis niños no (*lo/la*[7]) (*saber/conocer*[8]). En nuestro hogar° son los Reyes Magos° quienes (*los/les*[9]) traen los regalos (*a/de*[10]) los niños.   *household*
Reyes... Three Kings

CAROL: ¿Ah, sí?

ELENA: Sí, pero no (*llegar*[11]) en la Nochebuena sino° (*el/la*[12]) seis de enero, el Día de los Reyes Magos.   *but rather*

La fiesta de la Virgen de Guadalupe

En (*alguno*[1]) países hispánicos los días de (*cierto*[2]) santos (*ser/estar*[3]) fiestas nacionales. El día 12 (*de/del*[4]) diciembre se (*conmemorar*[5]) a la santa patrona de México, la Virgen de Guadalupe. (*Mucho*[6]) mexicanoamericanos celebran (*este*[7]) fiesta también. Se (*creer*[8]) que la Virgen María se le (*aparecer*[9])* (*a/de*[10]) Juan, un humilde pastor,° en el pueblo (*a/de*[11]) Guadalupe. La Virgen (*dejar*[12])* su imagen en un rebozo° que todavía se puede (*ver*[13]) en la Catedral de la Ciudad de México.   *shepherd*
shawl

La fiesta de San Fermín

No (*todo*[1]) las fiestas hispánicas (*ser/estar*[2]) religiosas. Esta fiesta de Pamplona (España) lleva (*el/la*[3]) nombre de un santo y (*ser/estar*[4]) de origen religioso, pero es esencialmente secular. Durante diez días—entre (*el/la*[5]) 7 y (*el/la*[6]) 17 de julio—se interrumpe la rutina diaria (*del/de la*[7]) ciudad. (*Llegar*[8]) personas de todas partes de España e inclusive de (*otro*[9]) países para beber, cantar, bailar... y (*pasarlo*[10]) bien en general. Todas las mañanas se (*permitir*[11]) que algunos toros (*correr*° [12]) sueltos° por (*el/la*[13]) calle de la Estafeta, en dirección (*al/a la*[14]) plaza de toros. (*Alguno*[15]) jóvenes atrevidos° (*correr*[16]) delante de ellos. No (*haber*[17]) duda que (*este*[18]) demostración de brío° (*ser/estar*[19]) bastante peligrosa.° Luego por (*el/la*[20]) tarde se celebra una corrida° en la famosa plaza de toros que (*describir*[21])* Ernest Hemingway en (*su*[22]) novela *The Sun Also Rises*. En Pamplona todavía (*ser/estar*[23]) posible (*hablar*[24]) con personas que (*saber/conocer*[25])* a este famoso escritor estadounidense que (*tener*[26])* tanto interés por las culturas (*hispánico*[27]).   *to run / free*
daring

courage / dangerous
bullfight

La Nochebuena

—¿Cómo pasaste la Nochebuena?
—Estuve bailando en casa de unos amigos.
 Lo pasamos muy bien. ¿Y tú?
—Tuve una invitación de mis tíos y fui a
 cenar con ellos.
—¿Te divertiste?
—Sí. Comí, bailé y me reí mucho.

Peter Menzel

Ciudad de México, México

UN PASO MÁS: Lectura cultural

Antes de leer

Before beginning a reading, it is sometimes helpful to think about the information the reading might contain in order to review important background information you already know about the topic. For example, if you are reading a newspaper account of a traffic accident, what kinds of information and details would you expect to find in it? What kinds of information would you find in a magazine article about drugs? In a manual for the owner of a car or a computer?

   Working with a partner, spend three minutes "brainstorming" about ideas and information you think will be discussed in «**Hogar, dulce hogar**» (*"Home, Sweet Home"*). You can talk in English or in Spanish. Then, working as a class, share your ideas and select the ten most frequently mentioned ideas. How many of the ideas actually appear in the reading?

«Hogar, dulce hogar»

Una casa es una casa, ¿verdad? Pues, eso depende de la persona y también de su cultura. Es verdad que hasta cierto punto la vida en una casa hispana es como en una norteamericana: la gente duerme por la noche y por la mañana se despierta; se levanta, se baña, se viste y desayuna. Pero hay también diferencias interesantes, algunas físicas y otras en cuanto al° uso de ciertos cuartos, sobre todo el de la alcoba y el del baño.

    °en... *concerning*

   Por ejemplo, la típica alcoba hispánica en las casas tradicionales probablemente no tiene un clóset. Pero sí tiene un ropero° grande donde se

    °*large, freestanding closet*

guarda no solamente la ropa sino medicinas, pañuelos,° la cartera y otros   *handkerchiefs*
objetos de uso personal: toallas, jabón,° artículos para afeitarse, maquillaje,   *soap*
perfumes y un cepillo° para el pelo. ¿Por qué no están estas cosas en el   *brush*
baño? Porque el baño es considerado un área común compartida por todos.
Es preferible dejar el baño completamente desocupado después de usarlo.
Así las demás personas de la casa pueden entrar y encontrarlo listo° para   *ready*
ellas. Por eso, si algún día Ud. se encuentra en una casa hispana, ¡no deje
sus cosas personales en el baño! Llévelas todas a su alcoba. La toalla
mojada° también se cuelga° en el ropero o afuera en el patio.   *damp / se… is hung*

   Otro aspecto un poco desconcertante en cuanto al uso de la alcoba es
que es muy común encontrar el televisor en la alcoba de los señores de la
casa, sobre todo en casas de la clase media. Cuando los jóvenes invitan a
sus amigos a ver un programa de televisión, todos van a la alcoba a verlo.
Otras veces se reúne allí toda la familia para ver su programa favorito—una
comedia, el noticiario° o quizá° un partido de fútbol. Pero también es fre-   *news / perhaps*
cuente encontrar el televisor en el comedor, donde toda la familia se reúne
para comer y ver la tele al mismo tiempo.

Comprensión

¿Dónde está Ud., en una casa hispana, en una norteamericana o en las
dos?

1. Hay una botella de champú y varios cepillos en el lavabo (*sink*) del
   cuarto de baño.
2. Ud. está colgando una camisa en el ropero.
3. Ud. se lleva siempre la toalla a su cuarto para colgarla allí.
4. Toda la familia se sienta en la sala para mirar la tele.
5. Hay un jabón que usa toda la familia.
6. Después de usar la pasta dental, Ud. la deja en el cuarto de baño.

Para escribir

Write two short paragraphs about your living accommodations. The first
should give information about where you live: whether in a house,
apartment, or dormitory; the number of rooms; a description of the
furniture; and so on. You might also want to write about what you like
or do not like about where you live. The second paragraph should
include information about those you live with and about their and your
personal habits: who gets up first, who takes care of domestic chores,
who does or doesn't smoke, and so on.

VOCABULARIO

VERBOS

cocinar to cook
despedirse (i, i) (de) to say goodbye (to)
enojarse to get angry
haber *infinitive form of* **hay** (there is/are)
llorar to cry
morirse (ue, u) to die
recordar (ue) to remember
reírse (i, i) to laugh
sentirse (ie, i) to feel
sonreír (i, i) to smile

LOS APARATOS DOMÉSTICOS

el (aire) acondicionador air conditioner
la aspiradora vacuum cleaner
la cafetera coffeepot
el congelador freezer
la estufa stove

la lavadora washing machine
el lavaplatos dishwasher
el refrigerador refrigerator
la secadora clothes dryer
la tostadora toaster

LOS QUEHACERES DOMÉSTICOS

hacer la cama to make the bed
pasar la aspiradora to vacuum
poner la mesa to set the table
preparar la comida to prepare food
sacar la basura to take out the garbage
sacudir los muebles to dust the furniture

LAS PARTES DE UNA CASA

la alcoba (el dormitorio) bedroom
el baño bathroom

la cocina kitchen
el comedor dining room
el patio patio; yard
la sala living room
la sala de recreo recreation room, family room
el sótano basement
la ventana window

ADJETIVOS

descansado/a rested
entero/a whole, entire
feliz (*pl.* **felices**) happy

PALABRAS ADICIONALES

dar/hacer una fiesta to give/have a party
felicitaciones congratulations
pasarlo bien/mal to have a good/bad time

FRASES ÚTILES PARA LA COMUNICACIÓN

¿A quién le toca... ?	Whose turn is it to . . . ?
(A mí) me toca...	It's my turn to . . .
Se me olvidó (+ *inf.*).	I forgot (to _____).

¡Huy! ¡Perdón!

VOCABULARIO: PREPARACIÓN

¡POBRE SR. MARTÍNEZ!

Le duele la cabeza.

la cabeza

Está distraído.

la mano

el brazo

DAMAS

el pie

la pierna

Se equivoca.

Se hace daño en el pie.

ALGUNAS PARTES DEL CUERPO

ME LEVANTÉ CON EL PIE IZQUIERDO / I GOT UP ON THE WRONG SIDE OF THE BED

acordarse (ue) de to remember

apagar to turn off (*lights or an appliance*)

caerse (me caigo) to fall down

cambiar de lugar to move (*something*)

doler (ue) to hurt

Me duele la cabeza. I have a headache.

equivocarse to be wrong, make a mistake

hacerse daño to hurt oneself

pegar to hit, strike

romper to break

sufrir muchas presiones to be under a lot of pressure

tropezar (ie) con to bump into

Fue sin querer. It was unintentional. I (he, we . . .) didn't mean to do it.

¡Qué mala suerte! What bad luck!

las aspirinas aspirin

la llave key

distraído/a absentminded

torpe clumsy

Discúlpeme, por favor.

—Perdone, fue sin querer.
—No se preocupe.
—De verdad, no lo vi. Déjeme ayudarlo.
—No, si no es nada. Estoy bien.

Madrid, España

L. H. Mangino/The Image Works

A. Match each response from column B with the appropriate statement from column A.

A	B
A	**B**

A

1. ¡Ay, estoy sufriendo muchas presiones en el trabajo!
2. Anoche no me acordé de poner el despertador.
3. ¡Ay! ¡Me pegaste!
4. Nunca miro por donde camino (*I'm going*). Esta mañana me caí otra vez.
5. Lo siento, señores, pero ésta no es la casa de Lola Pérez.
6. No cambié de lugar el coche y el policía me puso una multa (*fine*).
7. Anoche en casa de unos amigos rompí su lámpara favorita.

B

a. ¿Vas a comprarles otra?
b. Perdón, señora. Nos equivocamos de casa.
c. ¿Otra vez? ¡Qué distraído eres! ¿Te hiciste daño?
ch. Huy, perdón. Fue sin querer.
d. ¿Te olvidaste otra vez? ¿A qué hora llegaste a la oficina?
e. ¡Qué mala suerte! ¿Cuánto tienes que pagar?
f. ¿Sí? ¿Por qué no te tomas unos días de vacaciones?

B. Asociaciones. ¿Qué verbos asocia Ud. con estas palabras?

la llave	el brazo	la luz
la pierna	las aspirinas	los pies
la mano	la cabeza	el despertador

Posibilidades: despedirse, doler, apagar, caminar (*to walk*), levantar, correr (*to run*), preguntar, pegar, escribir, pensar, tomar, caerse, hacerse daño, poner, tropezar, perder

C. ¿De cuántas maneras diferentes puede Ud. reaccionar en cada situación? Describa sus reacciones.

1. A Ud. le duele mucho la cabeza.
2. Ud. se equivoca en un asunto (*matter*) importante / en un pequeño detalle (*detail*).
3. Ud. le pega a otra persona sin querer.
4. Ud. se olvida del nombre de otra persona.
5. Ud. está muy distraído/a.
6. Ud. se hace daño en la mano/el pie.

CH. ¿Se refieren a Ud. estas oraciones? Conteste diciendo «**Sí, así soy**» o «**No, no soy así**».

1. Se me caen (*I drop*) las cosas de las manos con facilidad en el trabajo y en casa.
2. Con frecuencia no me acuerdo de hacer la tarea (*homework*) para la clase de español.
3. Cuando oigo el despertador, lo apago y me duermo otra vez.
4. Rompo los platos y los vasos cuando los lavo.
5. Se me pierden (*I misplace*) ciertos objetos, como las llaves, los cuadernos, la cartera…
6. Con frecuencia tropiezo con los muebles.
7. Algunas veces me hago daño en las manos mientras (*while*) preparo la cena.
8. En las fiestas, me olvido de los nombres de las personas que acabo de conocer.

Study Hint: False Cognates

Not all Spanish and English cognates are identical in meaning. Here are a few important "traps" to be aware of: **sano** is *healthy*; **renta**, *income*; **pariente**, *relative*; **gracioso**, *funny*; **actual**, *current, up-to-date*; **fábrica**, *factory*; **colegio**, *elementary* or *secondary school*; **una molestia**, *a bother*; **sopa**, *soup*; **ropa**, *clothing*; **real**, *real* or *royal*; **sensible**, *sensitive*; **éxito**, *success*—and **constipado** means *suffering from a head cold*. These words are *false*, or misleading, *cognates* (**amigos falsos**).

Occasionally such words can lead to communication problems. The American tourist who, feeling embarrassed, describes himself or herself as **embarazado/a** may find people chuckling at the remark, since **embarazada** means not *embarrassed* but *pregnant*.

Expresando emociones

enojarse	to get angry	**olvidarse (de)**	to forget (about)
llorar	to cry	**portarse bien/mal**	to behave well/badly

To Become (Get)

¿Por qué **te pones** tan furioso?

Vamos a **ponernos** muy tristes.

Se hizo } directora de
Llegó a ser } la companía.

Quiere { **hacerse**
        { **llegar a ser** } rico.

Why are you getting (becoming) so angry?

We're going to get (become) very sad.

She became director of the company.

He wants to become rich.

Ponerse + *adjective* is used to indicate physical, mental, or emotional changes. **Hacerse** and **llegar a ser** + *noun* indicate a change as the result of a series of events or as the result of effort. They are also frequently used with the adjective **rico**.

A. ¿Cómo reacciona o cómo se pone Ud. en estas situaciones? Use estos adjetivos o cualquier otro, y también los verbos que describen las reacciones emocionales.

Me pongo...

serio/a	feliz/triste	avergonzado/a (*embarrassed*)
nervioso/a	furioso/a	contento/a

me enojo   río
lloro   me olvido de...
sonrío

1. Es Navidad y alguien le regala a Ud. un reloj (*watch*) muy muy caro.
2. Es Navidad y sus padres se olvidan de regalarle algo.
3. En una fiesta, alguien acaba de contarle (*to tell you*) un chiste (*joke*) muy cómico.
4. Ud. está completamente aburrido/a en una fiesta que sus amigos le están dando. Tiene ganas de estar en otro sitio, pero no quiere ofender a sus amigos.
5. Ud. está dando una fiesta pero la gente no lo está pasando bien, es decir, no se ríen, no sonríen, no cuentan chistes, etcétera.
6. Hay un examen muy importante esta mañana, pero Ud. no estudió nada anoche.
7. Ud. acaba de terminar un examen difícil (fácil) y cree que lo hizo bien (mal).
8. En un examen de química, Ud. se olvida de una fórmula muy importante.

    9. Sin querer, Ud. se portó en una forma muy descortés con un buen amigo.

   10. Se acaban (*run out*) los refrescos durante su fiesta de Noche Vieja, y sólo son las diez de la noche.

B. ¿Qué ambiciones tiene Ud.? Complete las oraciones en una forma lógica. (No se olvide de la lista de los nombres de profesiones y oficios, página 221.) Luego explique sus decisiones.

Yo quiero hacerme _____ algún día.
No quiero nunca llegar a ser _____ .

Talking About How Things Are Done: Adverbs

You already know some of the most common Spanish *adverbs* (**los adverbios**): **bien, mal, mejor, peor, mucho, poco, más, menos, muy, pronto, a tiempo, tarde, temprano, siempre, nunca, sólo.** The form of adverbs is invariable.

Adverbs that end in *-ly* in English usually end in **-mente** in Spanish. The suffix **-mente** is added to the feminine singular form of adjectives. Adverbs ending in **-mente** have two stresses: one on the adjective stem and the other on **-mente.** The stress on the adjective stem is the stronger of the two.

Adjective	Adverb	English
rápido	**rápidamente**	*rapidly*
fácil	**fácilmente**	*easily*
valiente	**valientemente**	*bravely*

In Spanish, adverbs modifying a verb are placed as close to the verb as possible. When they modify adjectives or adverbs, they are placed directly before them.

Hablan **estupendamente** el español.	*They speak Spanish marvelously.*
Ese libro es **poco** interesante.*	*That book is not very interesting.*
Vamos a llegar **muy tarde.**	*We're going to arrive very late.*

---

*Note that the Spanish equivalent of *not very* + *adjective* is **poco** + *adjective*.

A. Complete Ud. estas oraciones con adverbios basados en los siguientes adjetivos.

directo	posible	puntual	constante
inmediato	rápido	tranquilo	
paciente	fácil	total	

1. La familia está esperando _____ en la cola.
2. Hay examen mañana y tengo que empezar a estudiar _____ .
3. Se vive _____ en aquel pueblo en la montaña.
4. ¿Las enchiladas? Se preparan _____ .
5. ¿El hombre va a vivir en la luna algún día? Mi hermana contesta, «_____».
6. ¿Qué pasa? Estoy _____ confundido.
7. Un vuelo que hace escalas no va _____ a su destino.
8. Cuando mira la tele, mi hermanito cambia el canal _____ .
9. Es necesario que las clases empiecen _____ .

B. El pianista del dibujo (página 275). Contesta las preguntas.

1. Según el pianista, ¿la pieza se toca fácil o difícilmente?
2. ¿Cree Ud. que la tocó lenta or rápidamente?
3. ¿Toca maravillosamente este pianista?
4. ¿Toca Ud. algún instrumento musical? ¿Cómo lo toca?

En busca de la casa de unos amigos

—¡Ay! Se nos quedó la dirección en casa.
—Pero ¿no la recuerdas? Acabas de buscarla en la guía telefónica.
—Es verdad, pero siempre se me olvidan esas cosas.
—No hay tiempo para volver. Ojalá que podamos reconocer la casa.

Ciudad de México, México

Stuart Cohen

MINIDIÁLOGOS Y ESTRUCTURA

32 Descriptions and Habitual Actions in the Past Imperfect of Regular and Irregular Verbs

La nostalgia

MATILDE: ...y todos los hijos *eran* chiquitos. *Entraban* y *salían* de casa como locos. ¡Qué ruido *había* siempre! ¿Te acuerdas?

ARMANDO: Sí, sí, sí, aquéllos *eran* otros tiempos.

MATILDE: Y luego en verano *íbamos* siempre a la playa con todos los tíos y tus padres y dos criados y los amigos de los niños. *Teníamos* aquella casita tan linda... ¡Casi la puedo ver! ¿No la ves?

ARMANDO: Sí, sí, sí, aquéllos *eran* otros tiempos.

MATILDE: Dime una cosa, Armando. De verdad, ¿qué prefieres, aquella época o estos tiempos más tranquilos?

ARMANDO: Sí, sí, sí, aquéllos *eran* otros tiempos.

MATILDE: Ay, querido, parece que las cosas nunca cambian. ¡Tampoco me *escuchabas* en aquel entonces!

Rick Windsor/Woodfin Camp & Assoc.

España

1. *¿Qué hacían los niños de Matilde y Armando?*
2. *¿Su casa estaba muy tranquila?*
3. *¿Adónde iban siempre en verano? ¿Iban solos?*
4. *¿Qué pregunta Matilde a Armando? ¿Cómo responde?*
5. *¿Armando escucha bien a Matilde? Y antes, ¿la escuchaba?*

The *imperfect* (**el imperfecto**) is another past tense in Spanish. In contrast to the preterite, which views actions or states of being as finished or completed, the imperfect tense views past actions or states of being as habitual or as "in progress." The imperfect is also used for descriptions.

The imperfect has several English equivalents. For example, **hablaba,** the first-person singular of **hablar,** can mean *I spoke, I was speaking, I used to speak,* or *I would speak* (when *would* implies a repeated

---

Nostalgia   MATILDE: *. . . and all the kids were little. They went in and out of the house like mad. There was always so much noise! Remember?*   ARMANDO: *Yes, yes, yes, those were different times.*   MATILDE: *And then in the summer we would go to the beach with all the uncles and aunts and your parents and two servants and the kids' friends. We used to have that pretty little house . . . I can almost see it! Don't you see it?*   ARMANDO: *Yes, yes, yes, those were different times.*   MATILDE: *Tell me something, Armando. Honestly, which do you prefer—those times or these more peaceful times?*   ARMANDO: *Yes, yes, yes, those were different times.*   MATILDE: *Well, dear, I guess things never change. You never used to listen to me back then, either!*

action). Most of these English equivalents indicate that the action was still in progress or was habitual, except *I spoke,* which can correspond to either the preterite or the imperfect.

Forms of the Imperfect

hablar		comer		vivir	
hablaba	hablábamos	comía	comíamos	vivía	vivíamos
hablabas	hablabais	comías	comíais	vivías	vivíais
hablaba	hablaban	comía	comían	vivía	vivían

Stem-changing verbs do not show a change in the imperfect: **almorzaba, perdía, pedía.** The imperfect of **hay** is **había** (*there was, there were, there used to be*).

Only three verbs are irregular in the imperfect: **ir, ser,** and **ver.**

ir		ser		ver	
iba	íbamos	era	éramos	veía	veíamos
ibas	ibais	eras	erais	veías	veíais
iba	iban	era	eran	veía	veían

Uses of the Imperfect

The imperfect is used for the following.

A. To describe *repeated habitual actions* in the past

> Siempre **nos quedábamos** en aquel hotel.
> *We always stayed (used to stay, would stay) at that hotel.*
> Todos los veranos **iban** a la costa.
> *Every summer they went (used to go, would go) to the coast.*

B. To describe an *action that was in progress*

> **Pedía** la cena.
> *She was ordering dinner.*
> **Buscaba** la llave.
> *He was looking for the key.*

C. To describe two *simultaneous actions in progress,* with **mientras**

> Tú **leías mientras** Juan **escribía** la carta.
> *You were reading while John was writing the letter.*

CH. To describe ongoing *physical, mental, or emotional states* in the past

> **Estaban** muy confundidos.
> *They were very confused.*
> La **quería** muchísimo.
> *He loved her a lot.*

D. To tell *time* in the past and to express *age* with **tener**

Era la una.	*It was one o'clock.*
Eran las dos.	*It was two o'clock.*
Tenía dieciocho años.	*She was eighteen years old.*

■ **¡OJO!** *Just as in the present, the singular form of the verb **ser** is used with one o'clock, the plural form from two o'clock on.*

E. To form a *past progressive:* imperfect of **estar** + *present participle**

Estábamos cenando a las diez.	*We were having dinner at 10:00.*
¿No **estabas estudiando**?	*Weren't you studying?*

Práctica

A. Dé oraciones nuevas según las indicaciones.

En la escuela primaria...

1. *Tina* estudiaba y jugaba mucho. (*yo, Uds., tú, nosotros, Julio, vosotros*)
2. *Todos* bebían leche y dormían la siesta. (*Tina, tú, nosotros, Alicia, yo, vosotros*)

¿Qué hacían Uds. anoche a las doce?

3. *Ceci* veía un programa interesante. (*tú, yo, Uds., Pablo, ellas, vosotros*)
4. *Mis padres* iban a acostarse. (*tú, yo, nosotros, Hernando, ellas, vosotros*)
5. Yo (no) estaba _____ . (*leer, mirar la televisión, escribir una carta, dormir, llorar, comer, apagar las luces, __?__*)

B. ¿Cómo eran o qué hacían estas personas de (*as*) niños?

O. J. Simpson	ser	con frecuencia/
todos	cantar	siempre
Michael Jackson	tocar	fútbol americano/
Elizabeth Taylor (no)	estudiar	béisbol/tenis
Fernando	jugar al	música moderna
Valenzuela	creer en	mucho/poco
Chris Evert	acostarse	el piano/la guitarra
Lloyd	equivocarse	temprano/tarde
yo	levantarse	guapo/a
Ann Landers	dar	con el pie izquierdo
Tom Selleck	caerse	Santa Claus/los
__?__		Reyes Magos
		pobre, rico/a
		consejos
		__?__

---

*A progressive tense can also be formed with the preterite of **estar**: *Estuvieron* **cenando hasta las doce.** The progressive with the preterite of **estar,** however, is relatively infrequent, and it will not be practiced in *¿Qué tal?*.

C. ¿Qué pasaba? Cambie los verbos indicados por el imperfecto.

1. Olga *va* a la universidad todos los días. Siempre *asiste* a sus clases. *Pregunta* mucho porque *es* inteligente. Sus profesores *están* muy contentos con ella.
2. Yo *trabajo* para el gobierno. Mi jefe, que se *llama* Ángel, nos *hace* trabajar mucho. Siempre *almorzamos* juntos en el mismo restaurante y a veces *jugamos* al básquetbol por la tarde.
3. *Vivo* en Sacramento. Siempre *llueve* mucho en invierno y en primavera, pero me *gusta* mucho el clima. Además (*Besides*), las montañas *están* cerca y *puedo* esquiar.

CH. Una noche tranquila en casa. ¿Cómo se dice en español?

It was eight o'clock, and I was reading while my friend was writing a letter. There was little noise, and it was snowing outside. We weren't expecting **(esperar)** anyone, and we thought that it was going to be a quiet evening. We intended to stay home.

D. Entrevista. Using the following questions as a guide, interview another student about his or her childhood. Then report the information to the class.

1. ¿Dónde vivías y con quién? ¿Tenías un apodo (*nickname*)?
2. ¿Cómo se llamaba tu escuela primaria? ¿y tu maestro/a en el primer grado?
3. ¿Cuál era tu materia favorita? ¿Por qué?
4. ¿Cómo se llamaba tu mejor amigo/a? ¿Dónde vivía? ¿Siempre se llevaban bien (*did you get along*)?
5. ¿Perdías o rompías muchas cosas? ¿Eras un niño distraído (una niña distraída)?
6. ¿Practicabas algunos deportes? **(Sí, jugaba al _____ .)**
7. ¿Te caías con frecuencia? ¿Siempre te hacías daño?
8. ¿Tenías un perrito? ¿un gato (*cat*)? ¿Cómo se llamaba?
9. ¿Cómo era la casa o el apartamento en que vivías?
10. ¿Cómo era tu cuarto? ¿Tenías allí un objeto muy especial?
11. ¿Qué bebías (comías) cuando eras niño/a que ahora no bebes?
12. ¿Qué programas de televisión veías que ahora no ves?

E. Complete estas oraciones, usando un verbo en el pretérito para describir una acción.

1. La semana pasada yo estaba muy ocupado/a (preocupado/a). Por eso yo (no) _____ .
2. Era tarde y tenía que estudiar más todavía. Por eso yo _____ .
3. Eran las cuatro de la mañana cuando mi amigo/a _____ .
4. Yo estaba manejando (*driving*) mi carro a setenta millas por hora. Por eso el policía _____ .
5. El carro estaba en un lugar mercado «Prohibido estacionarse». Por eso yo lo _____ .

6. Me dolían los pies. Por eso yo _____ .

7. Todos tenían mucha sed. Por eso yo les _____ .

8. Me dolía la cabeza. Por eso yo _____ .

---

33 Expressing Unplanned or Unexpected Events
Another Use of *se*

Se me cayó el vaso.
I dropped the glass. (The glass fell
from my hands.)

A Mario se le perdieron los
libros.
Mario lost his books. (Mario's
books were lost to him.)

Unplanned or unexpected events (*I dropped, we lost, you forgot*) are
frequently expressed with **se** and the third person of the verb. The
occurrence is viewed as happening *to* someone—the unwitting
performer of the action. Thus the victim is indicated by an indirect
object pronoun, often clarified by **a** + *noun* or *pronoun*. In such
sentences, the subject (the thing that is dropped, broken, forgotten, and
so on) usually follows the verb.

(*A* + *noun* or *pronoun*)	*Se*	*Indirect object pronoun**	*Verb*	*Subject*
(A mí)	Se	me	cayó	el vaso.
A Mario	se	le	perdieron	los libros.

The verb agrees with the grammatical subject of the Spanish sentence (**el
vaso, los libros**), not with the indirect object pronoun. **No** immediately
precedes **se: A Mario** *no se* **le perdieron los libros.**

---

*While the verb form is always third-person singular or plural in this construction, all of the indirect object pronouns can be used:
¿A Uds. *se les* **perdió todo el dinero?; A los niños** *se les* **perdió el perro.** However, the exercises in *¿Qué tal?* will focus on sentences
containing **se me...** and **se le...** .

As with **gustar,** the clarification of the indirect object pronoun is optional. But the indirect object pronoun itself is always necessary whether or not the victim is named: *A la mujer* **se** *le* **rompió el plato.** Some verbs frequently used in this construction include the following.

acabar	to finish; to run out of	**perder (ie)**	to lose
caer	to fall	**quedar**	to leave behind
olvidar	to forget	**romper**	to break

Práctica

A. **¡Qué distraídos estuvimos todos ayer!** Dé oraciones nuevas según las indicaciones.

1. A *Pablo* se le olvidó la cartera.   (*mí, Julio*)
2. ¡Se *te* perdieron las llaves otra vez!   (*Ernesto, mí, Anita*)
3. María fue la persona que estuvo más distraída que nadie. Se le olvidó/olvidaron _____.   (*tomar el desayuno, las gafas* [glasses], *estudiar para el examen, los cheques, venir a clase*)

B. **Anteayer fue aun peor que ayer.** Describa lo que pasó, usando el **se** reflexivo según el modelo.

MODELO   Marcial olvidó los discos. → A Marcial se le olvidaron los discos.

1. Jorge rompió las tazas (*cups*).
2. Roberto se olvidó de llenar el tanque de gasolina.
3. Olvidé tomar las aspirinas.
4. Dejé los billetes en casa. (quedar)
5. Juanita perdió las llaves.
6. Rompí varias cosas.
7. El camarero no pudo servir más pan. (acabar)

C. **Al mono más vivo se le cae la banana de vez en cuando.** (*Even the brightest monkey drops his banana sometimes.*) ¿Qué desastres le han ocurrido (*have happened*) a Ud.? Después de completar las oraciones, use sus propias respuestas como guía para entrevistar a un compañero (una compañera) de clase.

1. Una vez se me cayó/cayeron _____.
2. Es posible que se me olvide(n) _____, pero nunca se me olvida(n) _____.
3. Una vez se me rompió/rompieron _____ y me enojé.
4. Hoy se me quedó/quedaron _____ en casa.
5. El año pasado se me perdió/perdieron _____.

REPASO

Me levanté con el pie izquierdo. Hay días en que nada sale a derechas, como dice el paracaidista (*parachutist*) del dibujo. Usando las siguientes preguntas como guía, describa Ud. un día en la vida de una persona que se levantó con el pie izquierdo. Puede describir un día en su propia (*own*) vida o en la vida de otra persona—un amigo (una amiga), un hombre/una mujer de negocios, una ama de casa, el presidente, etcétera.

A mí... nada me sale a derechas.°
sale... *turns out right*

1. ¿A qué hora se despertó? ¿Se levantó inmediatamente? ¿Se sentía bien?
2. ¿Tuvo tiempo para comer y vestirse bien? ¿Le faltaba (*Were you missing*) algo? ¿Qué no podía encontrar?
3. ¿Había problemas con los otros miembros de la familia? ¿con el coche?
4. ¿Qué tiempo hacía? ¿Llovía? ¿Nevaba?
5. ¿Dónde estaba por la mañana? ¿por la tarde? ¿Qué le pasó en cada lugar?
6. ¿Se le perdió algo?
7. ¿Había problemas con los amigos (el jefe, los empleados, los niños)?
8. ¿Recordó todo lo que tenía que hacer ese día? ¿Se le olvidó algo?

UN PASO MÁS: Imágenes del mundo hispánico
Centroamérica y el Caribe

Peter Menzel

Ruinas mayas de Tikal, Guatemala

*E*l puente entre América del Norte y América del Sur es Centroamérica, tierra poblada por los indios mayas* en la época precolombina. Esta región está dividida ahora en siete pequeños países: Belice, Guatemala, Honduras, El Salvador, Nicaragua, Costa Rica y Panamá. Cada uno de ellos tiene características propias. Belice, por ejemplo, de habla inglesa, se independizó de Gran Bretaña en 1981, y Panamá fue una región de Colombia hasta 1903.

La situación política y el nivel de desarrollo (*development*) económico también diferencian a estos países. Su comercio exterior depende en la mayoría de los casos de un solo producto—café, bananas o algodón—lo que no les permite tener una economía muy fuerte y estable.

Guatemala, Honduras, El Salvador y

Nicaragua en particular están sufriendo grandes tensiones sociales y políticas en los últimos años. Estas tensiones se agudizan (*are intensified*) por las presiones y la intervención de fuerzas exteriores. ¡Ojalá se resuelvan pronto sus problemas!

Las islas del Caribe son un gran mosaico, verdaderamente variado y multicolor. Aunque todas fueron parte del imperio español, en la actualidad sólo la República Dominicana y especialmente Cuba y Puerto Rico pertenecen (*belong*) al mundo hispánico. La organización politicoeconómica de estos países no tiene características comunes. Pero todos sí comparten la simpatía de su gente, un clima ideal y unas playas estupendas.

---

*See also photo essay, Chapter 17.

Manifestación en contra de la intervención estadounidense en Nicaragua

La Playa de Luquillo, Puerto Rico

VOCABULARIO

VERBOS

acabar to finish; to run out of
acordarse (ue) (de) to remember
apagar to turn off (*lights or appliances*)
caerse (me caigo) to fall down
contar (ue) to tell
doler (ue) to hurt
equivocarse to be wrong, make a mistake
hacerse to become
llegar a ser to become
olvidarse (de) to forget (about)
pegar to hit, strike
ponerse to become
portarse bien/mal to behave well/badly

quedar to remain, be left
quedarse to stay (*in a place*)
romper to break
sufrir to suffer
tropezar (ie) con to bump into

ALGUNAS PARTES DEL CUERPO

el brazo arm
la cabeza head
el pie foot
la pierna leg

OTROS SUSTANTIVOS

las aspirinas aspirin
el chiste joke
el desastre disaster
la llave key
la presión pressure
la tarea homework

ADJETIVOS

avergonzado/a embarrassed
confundido/a confused
distraído/a absentminded
torpe clumsy

PALABRAS ADICIONALES

cambiar de lugar to move (*something*)
hacerse daño to hurt oneself
levantarse con el pie izquierdo to get up on the wrong side of the bed
mientras while

FRASES ÚTILES PARA LA COMUNICACIÓN	
Fue sin querer.	It was unintentional. I (he, we . . .) didn't mean to do it.
¡Qué mala suerte!	What bad luck!
Aquéllos eran otros tiempos.	It was different back then. Things were different then.
Los tiempos cambian.	Times change.

¿Cómo se encuentra Ud. hoy?

VOCABULARIO: PREPARACIÓN

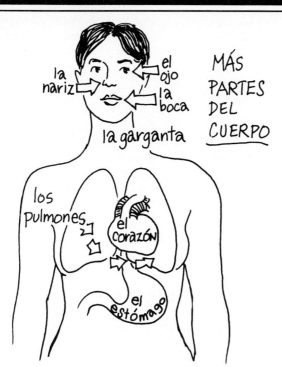

la nariz
el ojo
la boca
la garganta

MÁS PARTES DEL CUERPO

los pulmones
el corazón
el estómago

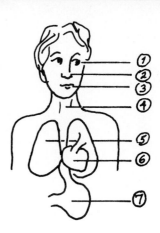

① ② ③ ④ ⑤ ⑥ ⑦

¿Cómo se llaman
estas partes del cuerpo?

--- **LA SALUD Y EL BIENESTAR** / HEALTH AND WELL-BEING ---

caminar to walk
comer bien to eat well
correr to run
cuidarse to take care of oneself
dejar de + *inf.* to stop (*doing something*)

dormir lo suficiente to get enough sleep
hacer ejercicio to exercise, get exercise
llevar una vida tranquila (sana) to lead a calm (healthy) life
practicar deportes to participate in sports

A. Imagine que Ud. es Richard Simmons y explique cada una de las siguientes oraciones.

MODELO   Se debe comer bien. →
RICHARD: ¡Sí, eso es! Eso quiere decir (*means*) que es necesario comer muchas verduras, que...

1. Se debe dormir lo suficiente todas las noches.
   RICHARD: ¡Exacto! Esto significa que... También...
2. Hay que hacer ejercicio.
3. Es necesario llevar una vida tranquila.
4. En general, uno debe cuidarse mucho.

B. Entrevista. Use las siguientes frases como guía para entrevistar a un compañero (una compañera) de clase. ¿Cree él/ella que estas acciones son buenas o malas para la salud? Pídale que explique su punto de vista. ¿Tienen algún beneficio para la salud de uno? ¿Hacen algún daño? ¿En qué parte del cuerpo?

1. Fumar tres o cuatro cigarrillos al día
2. Fumar dos paquetes de cigarrillos al día
3. Preocuparse mucho y no descansar
4. Gritar (*To shout*) y enojarse con frecuencia
5. Leer con poca luz
6. Hacer ejercicio sin llevar zapatos
7. Salir sin chaqueta cuando hace frío
8. Beber uno o dos vasos de vino al día
9. Dejar de tomar bebidas alcohólicas por completo
10. Dejar de comer por completo para adelgazar (*to lose weight*)

En el consultorio° del médico   *office*

el/la enfermero/a nurse	**enfermarse** to get sick	**tener dolor (de)** to have a pain (in)
el/la paciente patient	**guardar cama** to stay in bed	**tener fiebre** to have a fever
congestionado/a congested, stuffed-up	**ponerle una inyección** to give someone a shot	**tomarle la temperatura** to take someone's temperature
mareado/a nauseated; dizzy	**resfriarse** to get/catch a cold	**toser** to cough
el antibiótico antibiotic	**respirar** to breathe	
el jarabe (cough) syrup	**sacar la lengua** to stick out (the tongue)	
la pastilla pill		
la receta prescription		
el resfriado cold		
la tos cough		

A. Describa Ud. la situación de estas personas. ¿Dónde están y con quiénes? ¿Qué síntomas tienen? ¿Qué les recomienda Ud.?

1. Anamari está muy bien de salud. Nunca le duele(n) _____. Nunca tiene _____. Siempre _____. Es bueno que _____.

2. Martín tiene resfriado. Le duele(n) _____. Tiene _____. El médico le dice que _____. Es mejor que _____.

3. Inés tiene apendicitis. Le duele(n) _____. Tiene _____. Debe _____. El médico y la enfermera mandan que _____. Es necesario que _____.

B. ¿Qué partes del cuerpo asocia Ud. con las siguientes palabras?
1. un ataque   **2.** la digestión   **3.** comer   **4.** respirar
5. congestionado   **6.** ver   **7.** mareado

C. Ud. no se siente bien y va al consultorio del médico. Complete el diálogo entre Ud. y el médico.

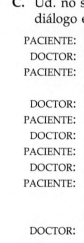

PACIENTE: Buenas tardes, doctor.

DOCTOR: Buenas tardes. ¿Qué le pasa? ¿Qué tiene?

PACIENTE: Es que me _____ muy mal. Me _____ la cabeza y tengo una _____ muy alta.

DOCTOR: Entonces, ¿tiene resfriado?

PACIENTE: Bueno, Ud. es el médico.

DOCTOR: ¿Se tomó la temperatura antes de venir?

PACIENTE: No, pero la _____ me la tomó y tenía 38,5.

DOCTOR: ¿Tiene dolor de estómago? ¿Se siente _____?

PACIENTE: No, pero respiro sólo con dificultad; estoy muy _____. Toso tanto que me duelen también los _____. Es que me duele el _____ entero.

DOCTOR: Vamos a ver. Abra Ud. la _____, por favor, y _____ la lengua. Humm... tiene la _____ bastante (*rather*) inflamada. Ahora la respiración... _____ Ud. profundamente... Me parece que está bien. ¿Tiene alergia a los antibióticos?

PACIENTE: No, no creo.

DOCTOR: Bueno, aquí tiene Ud. una _____. Vaya a la farmacia y compre este _____ para la tos. Tómelo cuatro veces al día. Para la fiebre, tome un par de _____ cada cuatro horas y compre este _____ para combatir la infección. También recomiendo que _____ cama uno o dos días. Si todavía se siente mal la semana que viene, venga a verme otra vez. Y cuídese, ¿eh?

PACIENTE: Muchas gracias, doctor. Adiós.

MINIDIÁLOGOS Y ESTRUCTURA

34 Narrating in the Past: Preterite and Imperfect

No es para tanto...

CARMEN: Yo no *sabía* lo que *tenía*, pero la doctora me lo *diagnosticó* en seguida.

PILAR: ¿Y qué te *dijo* que *tenías*?

CARMEN: Pues... que tengo insomnio... y que tengo los ojos muy irritados... Pero de todos modos todavía tengo que terminar las investigaciones para un proyecto que necesitan discutir mañana en la oficina. ¡Eso es lo peor!*

---

1. ¿Quién acaba de tener una consulta con la doctora?
2. ¿Pudo la doctora diagnosticar la enfermedad?

3. ¿Qué dijo la doctora que tenía Carmen?

Ahora invente respuestas para las siguientes preguntas.

4. ¿Cuánto tiempo hace que no duerme bien Carmen?
5. ¿Por qué tiene los ojos muy irritados?
6. ¿Qué recomienda la doctora que haga?

7. ¿Qué quiere el jefe que Carmen haga?
8. ¿Qué cree Ud. que va a hacer?

When speaking about the past in English, you choose which past tense forms to use in a given context: *I wrote letters, I did write letters, I was writing letters, I used to write letters,* and so on. Usually only one or two of these options will convey exactly the idea you want to express. Similarly, in some Spanish sentences either the preterite or the imperfect can be used, but the meaning of the sentence will be different, depending on which tense you use. The choice between the preterite and imperfect depends on the speaker's perspective: how does he or she view the action or state of being?

A. The PRETERITE is used to report *completed* actions or states of being in the past, no matter how long they lasted or took to complete; if the action or state is viewed as finished or over, the preterite is used. The IMPERFECT is used, however, if the *ongoing or habitual nature* of the action is stressed, with no reference to its termination.

It's not that serious . . .   CARMEN: *I didn't know what I had, but the doctor diagnosed it for me immediately.*   PILAR: *And what did she say you had?*   CARMEN: *Well . . . that I have insomnia . . . and that my eyes are very irritated . . . But in any case I still have to finish the research for a project (that) they need to discuss at the office tomorrow. That's the worst part!*

*Note that **lo** + the masculine singular form of an adjective expresses *the (best, worst, good, interesting . . .) thing/part*.

Escribí las cartas.	*I wrote (did write) the letters.*
Escribía las cartas cuando...	*I was writing the letters when . . .*
Carlos **fue** estudiante.	*Carlos was a student (and no longer is).*
Carlos **era** estudiante.	*Carlos was (used to be) a student.*
Anita **estuvo** nerviosa.	*Anita was nervous (and no longer is).*
Anita **estaba** nerviosa.	*Anita was (used to be) nervous.*

B. *A series of completed actions that take place in sequence* will be expressed in the PRETERITE (unless it refers to habitual actions).

Me **levanté,** me **vestí** y **desayuné.**	*I got up, got dressed, and ate breakfast.*

Actions or states *in progress* are expressed with the IMPERFECT. The IMPERFECT is also used to express most *descriptions; physical, mental, and emotional states; the time;* and *age.*

Escribía las cartas **mientras** Ana **leía.**	*I was writing letters while Ana was reading.*
Estaban cansados.	*They were tired.*
Eran las ocho.	*It was eight o'clock.*
Tenía ocho años.	*She was eight years old.*

C. Certain words and expressions are frequently associated with the preterite, others with the imperfect.

Words often associated with the preterite:

ayer, anteayer, anoche
una vez (*once*), dos veces
   (*twice*), etcétera

el año pasado, el lunes
   pasado, etcétera
de repente (*suddenly*)

Words often associated with the imperfect:

todos los días, todos los lunes, etcétera
siempre, frecuentemente
mientras
de niño/a (*as a child*), de joven
was ____-*ing, were* ____-*ing* (in English)
used to, would (when *would* implies *used to* in English)

▌ **¡OJO!** *These words do not automatically cue either tense, however. The most important consideration is the meaning that the speaker wishes to convey.*

Ayer cenamos temprano.	*Yesterday we had dinner early.*
Ayer cenábamos cuando Juan llamó.	*Yesterday we were having dinner when Juan called.*

De niño jugaba al fútbol.   *He played football as a child.*
De niño empezó a jugar al   *He began to play football as a*
fútbol.   *child.*

[Práctica A–B]

CH. Remember the special English equivalents of the preterite forms of
saber, conocer, poder, and **querer: supe** (*I found out*), **conocí** (*I met*),
pude (*I could and did*), **no pude** (*I failed*), **quise** (*I tried*), **no quise** (*I
refused*).

[Práctica C]

D. The preterite and the imperfect frequently occur in the same
sentence.

Miguel **estudiaba** cuando   *Miguel was studying when the*
  sonó el teléfono.   *phone rang.*
Olivia **comió** tanto porque   *Olivia ate so much because she*
  tenía mucha hambre.   *was very hungry.*

In the first sentence the imperfect tells what was happening when
another action—conveyed by the preterite—broke the continuity of
the ongoing activity. In the second sentence, the preterite reports
the action that took place because of a condition, described by the
imperfect, that was in progress or in existence at that time.

E. The preterite and imperfect are also used together in the
presentation of an event. The preterite narrates the action while the
imperfect sets the stage, describes the conditions that caused the
action, or emphasizes the continuing nature of a particular action.

[Práctica CH–G]

Práctica

A. Give the preterite or the imperfect of the verbs in parentheses,
basing your decision on the clues in the sentences.

1. Cuando (*ser*) niños, Jorge y yo (*vivir*) en la Argentina. Siempre (*ir*)
   al Mar del Plata para pasar la Navidad. Allí casi siempre (*quedarse*)
   en el Hotel Fénix.
2. ¡(*Ser*) las once de la noche cuando de repente se nos (*apagar*)
   todas las luces de la casa!
3. Antonio (*trabajar*) en aquella farmacia todos los lunes. ¿No lo (*ver*)
   tú allí alguna vez?
4. La tía Anita (*resfriarse*) la semana pasada, pero (*guardar cama*) y
   ahora se siente mucho mejor.
5. ¡Qué mala suerte tengo! El año pasado (*enfermarse*) durante las
   vacaciones. (*Estar*) muy mal durante todo el viaje.

6. El niño (*toser*) mientras la enfermera le (*hablar*). La madre del niño (*esperar*) pacientemente. Por fin (*venir*) la doctora. Le (*tomar*) la temperatura, le (*examinar*) la garganta y le (*dar*) un jarabe.

B. **Situaciones.** With another student, ask and answer questions based on the model. Ask the questions in the preterite (**P**) and answer them in the imperfect (**I**), as indicated. Use subject pronouns only when needed.

MODELO
P: por qué / quedarse / tú / en casa anoche
I: saber / que / no / ir / gustar / la / película
USTED: ¿Por qué te quedaste en casa anoche?
COMPAÑERO: Porque sabía que no me iba a gustar la película.

1. P: por qué / pedir / Ud. / tanto / restaurante
   I: tener / mucha hambre
2. P: por qué / dormirse / ellos / en clase
   I: tener / sueño
3. P: por qué / se les / olvidar / Uds. / apagar / luz
   I: estar / distraído / por / examen
4. P: por qué / reírse / tú / tanto
   I: Horacio / portarse / como / un loco
5. P: por qué / se te / caer / vaso
   I: pensar / en / otro / cosa
6. P: por qué / equivocarse / Uds. / tanto / en / detalles
   I: no / saber / bien / fórmulas

C. **Los hijos de los Quintero.** ¿Cómo se dice en español?

1. When I met Mr. and Mrs. Quintero, I already knew their son.
2. He knew how to read when he was five.
3. And he could play the piano before starting (to go to) school (**escuela**).
4. They tried to teach their daughter to play when she was five.
5. But she refused to practice ten hours a (**al**) day.
6. How did you find all of that (**todo eso**) out?

CH. Explain the reasons for the use of the preterite or the imperfect for each verb in the following paragraph.

Hacía mucho frío. Éster cerró con cuidado todas las ventanas y puertas, pero todavía tenía frío. Se preparó una taza de té y se puso otro suéter, pero todavía temblaba de frío. Eran las once de la noche cuando sonó el teléfono. Era su esposo. Entre otras cosas, dijo que hacía mucho frío afuera. Éster ya lo sabía.

Which Spanish past tense should be used to express each verb in the following paragraph? Explain why in each case.

We were walking down Fifth Street when we caught sight of him. He looked very tired and his clothes were very dirty. He said he was hungry and he asked us for money. We gave him all the money we had because he was an old friend.

D. Read the following paragraph at least once to familiarize yourself with the sequence of events in it. Then read it again, giving the proper form of the verbs in parentheses in the preterite or the imperfect, according to the needs of each sentence and the context of the paragraph as a whole.

Rubén (*estar*) estudiando cuando Soledad (*entrar*) en el cuarto. Le (*preguntar*) a Rubén si (*querer*) ir al cine con ella. Rubén le (*decir*) que sí porque se (*sentir*) un poco aburrido con sus estudios. Los dos (*salir*) en seguida (*immediately*) para el cine. (*Ver*) una película muy cómica y (*reírse*) mucho. Luego, como (*hacer*) frío, (*entrar*) en «El Gato Negro» y (*tomar*) un chocolate. (*Ser*) las dos de la mañana cuando por fin (*regresar*) a casa. Soledad (*acostarse*) inmediatamente porque (*estar*) cansada, pero Rubén (*empezar*) a estudiar otra vez.

Answer the following questions based on the paragraph about Rubén and Soledad. ■ **¡OJO!** *A question is not always answered in the same tense as that in which it is asked.*

1. ¿Qué hacía Rubén cuando Soledad entró?
2. ¿Qué le preguntó Soledad a Rubén?
3. ¿Por qué dijo Rubén que sí?
4. ¿Les gustó la película? ¿Por qué?
5. ¿Por qué tomaron un chocolate?
6. ¿Regresaron a casa a las tres?
7. ¿Qué hicieron cuando llegaron a casa?

E. Read the following paragraphs once for meaning. Then read them again, giving the proper form of the verbs in parentheses in the present, preterite, or imperfect.

Durante mi segundo (*second*) año en la universidad, yo (*conocer*) a Roberto en una clase. Pronto nos (*hacer*) muy buenos amigos. Roberto (*ser*) una persona muy generosa que (*organizar*) una fiesta en su apartamento todos los viernes. Todos nuestros amigos (*venir*). (*Haber*) muchas bebidas y comida, y todo el mundo (*cantar*) y (*bailar*) hasta muy tarde.

Una noche algunos de los vecinos de Roberto (*llamar*) a la policía y (*decir*) que nosotros (*hacer*) demasiado ruido. (*Venir*) un policía al apartamento y le (*decir*) a Roberto que la fiesta (*ser*) demasiado ruidosa. Nosotros no (*querer*) aguar (*to spoil*) la fiesta, pero ¿qué (*poder*) hacer? Todos nos (*despedir*) aunque (*ser*) solamente las once de la noche.

Aquella noche Roberto (*aprender*) algo importantísimo. Ahora cuando (*hacer*) una fiesta, siempre (*invitar*) a sus vecinos.

F. Dé Ud. sus impresiones del primer día de su primera clase universitaria. Use estas preguntas como guía.

1. ¿Qué hora era cuando llegó Ud. a la universidad? ¿Por qué llegó tan tarde/temprano?
2. ¿Cuál fue la clase? ¿A qué hora era la clase y dónde era *(was it taking place)*?
3. ¿Vino Ud. a clase con alguien? ¿Ya tenía su libro de texto o lo compró después?
4. ¿Qué hizo Ud. después de entrar en la sala de clase? ¿Qué hacía el profesor (la profesora)?
5. ¿A quién conoció Ud. aquel día? ¿Ya conocía a algunos miembros de la clase? ¿A quiénes?
6. ¿Aprendió Ud. mucho durante la clase? ¿Ya lo sabía todo?
7. ¿Le cayó bien o mal el profesor (la profesora)? ¿Por qué? ¿Cómo era?
8. ¿Cómo se sentía durante la clase? ¿nervioso/a? ¿aburrido/a? ¿cómodo/a? ¿Por qué?
9. ¿Les dio tarea el profesor (la profesora)? ¿Pudo Ud. hacerla fácilmente?
10. ¿Cuánto tiempo estudió Ud. la materia antes de la próxima clase?
11. Su primera impresión de la clase y del profesor (de la profesora), ¿fue válida o la cambió luego? ¿Por qué?

En la sala de urgencia (de emergencias)

—¿Qué le ocurre?
—Me caí por la escalera (*staircase*) y ahora me duele mucho el tobillo (*ankle*).
—A ver... Lo tiene bastante inflamado... pero no parece que haya fractura.
—Lo peor es que no lo puedo mover.
—Bueno, lo voy a mandar a radiología para que le saquen una radiografía.

Stuart Cohen

Caracas, Venezuela

G. Describa Ud. su última enfermedad. Use estas preguntas como guía.

1. ¿Cuándo empezó Ud. a sentirse mal? ¿Dónde estaba Ud.? ¿Qué hacía?
2. ¿Cuáles eran sus síntomas? ¿Cómo se sentía? ¿Estaba mareado/a? ¿congestionado/a? ¿Le dolía alguna parte del cuerpo? ¿Tenía fiebre? ¿Se tomó la temperatura?

3. ¿Qué hizo? ¿Regresó a casa? ¿Se quitó la ropa? ¿Tosía mucho? ¿Se acostó?

4. ¿Fue al consultorio del médico? ¿Lo/La examinó? ¿Cuál fue su diagnóstico?

5. ¿Le puso una inyección el médico? ¿Le dio una receta? ¿Llevó Ud. la receta a la farmacia? ¿Cuánto le costó la medicina?

6. ¿Cuándo se sintió bien por fin? ¿Empezó a cuidarse más?

¿Qué tenías?

—¿Es cierto que estuviste enferma ayer?

—Sí, me dolía todo el cuerpo y no pude dormir nada anoche.

—Bueno, por lo menos ya estás mejor.

—¡Qué va! Esta mañana todavía tenía fiebre.

Salamanca, España

Beryl Goldberg

REPASO

Un accidente que salió bien. Complete the following paragraphs with the correct form—preterite or imperfect—of the verbs in parentheses as suggested by the context. When two possibilities are given in parentheses, select the correct word.

Cuando yo (*tener*[1]) doce años, (*caerse*[2]) de la bicicleta en que (*montar*[3]) y se me (*romper*[4]) el brazo derecho. (*Los/Las*[5]) personas que (*ver*[6]) el accidente (*llamar*[7]) una ambulancia (*que/qué*[8]) me (*llevar*[9]) al hospital. Me (*doler*[10]) mucho el brazo y (*tener*[11]) mucho miedo, pero no (*querer*[12]) portarme como un niño. Por fin, cuando (*ver*[13]) la sala de urgencia, (*empezar*[14]) a llorar.

La recepcionista (*llamar*[15]) a mi madre, pero ella no (*estar*[16]) en casa; (*trabajar*[17]) en la oficina. Cuando por fin la (*localizar*[18]), ella les (*dar*[19]) permiso para tratarme. Yo (*dejar*[20]) de llorar muy pronto porque los médicos me (*contar*[21]) chistes mientras me (*examinar*[22]) el brazo. Lo (*más/muy*[23]) divertido° fue cuando ellos (*cubrirse*°[24]) de yeso° al° ponerme la enyesadura.°

(*Ser*[25]) las siete de la noche y ya (*estar*[26]) oscuro cuando mi madre y yo (*llegar*[27]) a casa. Yo (*tener*[28]) mucha hambre y (*querer*[29]) comer, pero mi mamá no (*sentirse*[30]) muy bien. Utilizando sólo el brazo sano, le (*hacer*[31]) una taza de té y me (*preparar*[32]) un sándwich.

¿Qué fue lo bueno del accidente? Pues que ahora soy completamente ambidextro.

Llamadas de emergencia
Emergency phone

POLICIA   FEDERAL — Tel.   101

ATENCION MEDICA DE URGENCIA—
Tel. 34-1001.

SERVICIO SACERDOTAL DE
URGENCIA — Tel. 84-2000.

AEROPUERTO   INTERNACIONAL
DE EZEIZA — Tel.   620-0217.

amusing

to get covered / plaster / when / cast

Study Hint: Writing

You can develop a more mature writing style in Spanish by using transitional words to link shorter sentences. Follow these suggestions.

1. Write a first draft of your composition, trying to express your ideas in short, simple sentences. Be sure that each sentence contains at least a subject and a verb.

2. Determine which sentences have a logical relationship and can be linked together. Choose transition words that show these relationships.

3. Rewrite the composition, adding the transition words and making changes, if necessary. For example, if you link the following sentences together with **cuando,** the word **ella** will not be necessary.

Vimos a Jacinta. Ella estaba en la cafetería. →

Cuando vimos a Jacinta, estaba en la cafetería.

Remember to use words familiar to you because you have used them before. Use the dictionary only when necessary. (*Study Hint,* page 162).

Transition Words

además	*besides*	pero	*but*
así	*thus, so*	por ejemplo	*for example*
cuando	*when*	por eso	*therefore, for that reason*
de vez en cuando	*from time to time*	por fin	*at last, finally*
en cambio	*on the other hand*	puesto que	*since*
es decir	*that is*	sin embargo	*nevertheless*
luego	*then, next*	también	*also*
mientras	*while*		

UN PASO MÁS: Lectura cultural

La salud y la medicina

Una de las preocupaciones que todos tenemos es «¿Qué me va a pasar si me pongo enfermo cuando estoy en un lugar desconocido?» Afortunadamente, si usted está en una ciudad de Latinoamérica o España, no tiene por qué preocuparse, puesto que, por lo general, la calidad del servicio médico es muy alta. El sistema está organizado de forma que permite dar una atención más personal al paciente que en los Estados Unidos.

En muchos países hispánicos, es muy común que los médicos, como parte obligatoria de su <u>entrenamiento</u>, pasen hasta un año prestando servicio en las áreas rurales. Como resultado de esta experiencia, los médicos jóvenes aprenden a curar a la gente sin la ayuda de tantos aparatos como los que tienen los hospitales urbanos, y se hacen expertos en la diagnosis y en el tratamiento de las enfermedades.

En cuanto a los hospitales, claro que están equipados con modernos aparatos médicos, farmacias, enfermeras, y todo lo que° uno espera en un buen hospital. Pero están organizados de acuerdo con las necesidades personales de los pacientes. Por ejemplo, en muchos centros hospitalarios existe la posibilidad de que alguno de los familiares del paciente pueda quedarse—a veces en el mismo cuarto—mientras que el enfermo se mejora. Lógicamente, esto ayuda mucho al paciente y le hace mucho más tolerable su estancia en el hospital.

Otra ventaja del sistema médico hispánico es que es fácil y barato conseguir los servicios de una enfermera particular° que cuide del enfermo, ya sea en la casa o en el hospital. Hay cierta abundancia de enfermeras en la América Latina, ya que el entrenamiento que se requiere no es tan riguroso como en este país. Estas enfermeras no tienen tanto conocimiento teórico como las enfermeras en los Estados Unidos, pero tienen mucha experiencia en su campo y saben cuidar al enfermo.

lo... that

privada

Comprensión

¿Cierto o falso? Corrija las oraciones falsas.

1. Las enfermeras hispanas estudian más años que sus colegas norteamericanas.
2. Por lo general, la medicina en Latinoamérica está bastante avanzada y es de muy buena calidad.
3. Como parte de su preparación profesional, algunos médicos jóvenes prestan sus servicios primero en zonas rurales.
4. En casi todos los hospitales hispanos, es imposible que un pariente se quede con el enfermo.
5. Es difícil conseguir la ayuda de enfermeras en los países hispanos a causa del alto costo de sus servicios.

Para escribir

Answer these questions about your last visit to the doctor with as many details as possible. Use the words in *Study Hint: Writing* and any others you know to join the sentences to form three coherent paragraphs.

Paragraph A
1. ¿Cuándo fue la última vez que Ud. consultó con un médico?
2. ¿Por qué lo hizo? ¿Cuáles eran sus síntomas?

Paragraph B
1. En el consultorio, ¿tuvo Ud. que esperar mucho tiempo? ¿Esperaban también otros pacientes?

2. Cuando por fin entró en el consultorio, ¿cuánto tiempo duró la consulta? ¿Qué actitud mostró el médico? ¿compasión? ¿humor? ¿preocupación? ¿indiferencia?

3. ¿Le recetó alguna medicina? ¿Qué otras recomendaciones le dio? ¿Las siguió Ud.? ¿Por qué sí o por qué no?

Paragraph C

1. ¿Cuándo se mejoró Ud. por fin?
2. ¿Qué hace ahora para mantenerse en buen estado de salud?

VOCABULARIO

VERBOS

caminar to walk

correr to run

cuidarse to take care of oneself

dejar de + *inf.* to stop (*doing something*)

enfermarse to get sick

resfriarse to get/catch a cold

respirar to breathe

sonar (ue) to ring (*telephone*)

toser to cough

MÁS PARTES DEL CUERPO

la boca mouth

el corazón heart

el estómago stomach

la garganta throat

la lengua tongue

la nariz (*pl.* **narices**) nose

el ojo eye

los pulmones lungs

EN EL CONSULTORIO DEL MÉDICO

el antibiótico antibiotic

el/la enfermero/a nurse

el jarabe (cough) syrup

el/la paciente patient

la pastilla pill

la receta prescription

el resfriado cold

la salud health

el síntoma symptom

la tos cough

ponerle una inyección to give someone a shot, injection

tener dolor (de) to have a pain (in)

tener fiebre to have a fever

tomarle la temperatura to take someone's temperature

EL BIENESTAR FÍSICO

guardar cama to stay in bed

hacer ejercicio to exercise, get exercise

llevar una vida tranquila (sana) to lead a calm (healthy) life

practicar deportes to participate in sports

ADJETIVOS

congestionado/a congested, stuffed-up

mareado/a nauseated; dizzy

PALABRAS ADICIONALES

bastante (*adv.*) rather

de niño/a (joven) as a child (young person)

de repente suddenly

en seguida immediately

lo suficiente enough

FRASES ÚTILES PARA LA COMUNICACIÓN

¿Qué le ocurre (pasa)? **¿Qué tiene?**	What do you have?
tener + *noun* + *adj.*	
Tengo los ojos irritados.	My eyes are irritated.
Tengo la garganta inflamada.	My throat is swollen.
lo + *adj.*	
lo bueno (malo, interesante, mejor,...)	the good (bad, interesting, best . . .) thing/part/news

UN POCO DE TODO 4

A. Use Ud. estos verbos en el presente para describir un día típico en la vida de Domingo Meléndez. Luego diga lo que (*what*) Ud. hizo ayer, usando el pretérito.

> ¡**OJO!** *Hay verbos de todos tipos en la lista: regulares (Sección 29), irregulares (Secciones 29 y 30) y verbos que cambian el radical (Sección 31). Haga un repaso del pretérito antes de empezar esta actividad.*

despertarse	divertirse con los amigos	no poder estudiar
apagar el despertador	despedirse de ellos	mirar la televisión
levantarse	estudiar en la biblioteca	decirles buenas noches a ____
bañarse	volver a casa	quitarse la ropa
vestirse	preparar la cena	acostarse
hacer la cama	poner la mesa	leer un poco
desayunar	cenar	poner el despertador
ir a la universidad	lavar los platos	dormirse pronto
asistir a clases	sacar la basura	
almorzar	quedarse en casa toda la noche	

B. Entrevista. Use the following questions to interview another student about his or her childhood and about specific events in the past, as well as what is currently happening in his or her life. Report the most interesting information to the class.

1. ¿A qué escuela asistías (cuando tenías ____ años)? ¿Asististe a esta universidad el año pasado? ¿Cuánto tiempo hace que estudias aquí?
2. ¿Qué lenguas estudiabas? ¿Estudiaste latín en la secundaria? ¿Cuánto tiempo hace que estudias español?
3. ¿Qué hacías cuando te enfermabas? ¿Cuántas veces te resfriaste el año pasado? ¿Es necesario que empieces ahora a llevar una vida más sana?
4. ¿Qué películas te gustaban más? ¿Te gustó la última película que viste? ¿Qué nueva película quieres ver este mes?
5. En la secundaria, ¿qué era lo más importante de tu vida? ¿Qué cosa importante te pasó el año pasado? ¿Qué esperas que pase este año?
6. ¿Qué hacías durante los veranos? ¿Qué hiciste el verano pasado? ¿Qué vas a hacer este verano?

out of bed, up
sacar de encima to get rid of: me he sacado *I got rid*

C. **¿Te importa tu salud?** What steps do you take to stay healthy? With another student, ask and answer the following questions.

1. ¿Cuántas horas duermes cada noche? ¿Duermes bien?
2. ¿Comes bien? ¿Comes muchos dulces? ¿muchas proteínas? ¿mucha ensalada? ¿muchas verduras? ¿mucha fruta?
3. ¿Comes comidas «instantáneas» o prefieres comidas «naturales»?
4. ¿Tomas mucho café, mucho té o mucha Coca-Cola? ¿bebidas alcohólicas?
5. ¿Fumas? ¿mucho o poco? ¿Cuándo fumas? ¿Quieres dejar de fumar?
6. ¿Consultas a tu médico por lo menos una vez al año?
7. ¿Llevas una vida con muchas presiones? ¿Tienes muchas responsabilidades?
8. ¿Tienes tiempo para pensar, meditar o simplemente descansar?
9. ¿Caminas mucho o siempre vas en coche (tomas el autobús, etcétera)?
10. ¿Haces mucho ejercicio? ¿Corres? ¿Practicas algún deporte?

CH. **Estereotipos sobre la salud.** Su amigo hispano es muy observador... por lo menos así lo cree él. Le gusta mirar a la gente y después hacer comentarios sobre ella. Hace un año que observa las costumbres de los estadounidenses referentes a la comida y la salud. ¿Qué le va a decir Ud. cuando él haga los siguientes comentarios?

A propósito...

It is important to be able to communicate accurately when you are in need of medical or dental attention. English-speaking doctors and dentists are available in most large cities in Spanish-speaking countries. But if you do need to speak Spanish with medical personnel, the following words and phrases will be useful.

¿Cuánto tiempo hace que Ud. está enfermo/a?	*How long have you been ill?*
Hace (dos días) que estoy enfermo/a.	*I've been sick for (two days).*
¿Cuándo se enfermó?	*When did you get sick?*
¿Padece de algo más?	*Is anything else wrong?*
Sí, padezco de _____ .	*Yes, I'm also suffering from _____ .*
¿Ha tenido Ud. _____ ?	*Have you had _____ ?*
Sí, he tenido/No, no he tenido _____ .	*Yes, I've had/No, I haven't had _____ .*
¿Toma Ud. alguna medicina?	*Are you taking any medicine?*
Vamos a sacar los rayos equis/las radiografías.	*We're going to take X-rays.*
Voy a ponerle una inyección.	*I'm going to give you a shot.*
Tenemos que sacarle el diente (la muela).	*We have to pull the tooth (molar).*

Remember that any temperature above 37 degrees Centigrade (98.6 degrees Fahrenheit) constitutes a fever.

1. «Uds. los norteamericanos tienen una verdadera manía por el *jogging*.»
2. «Creo que las comidas favoritas de los norteamericanos son el yogurt y el *wheat germ*.»
3. «Uds. los norteamericanos trabajan demasiado. No saben descansar y divertirse. La jornada de las nueve a las cinco es una tontería (*silly*).»
4. «¿Por qué toman Uds. tantas vitaminas? Vitamina C, vitaminas de alta potencia... ¿Es realmente tan mala la comida de este país?»

D. Dramas médicos. Con su profesor(a), haga los papeles de paciente (Ud.) y doctor(a) o enfermero/a (su profesor[a]) en las siguientes situaciones.

1. Ud. está en el consultorio del médico. Le duele muchísimo la garganta.
2. Ud. visita al médico porque tiene dolor de cabeza desde hace (*for*) una semana. Tampoco respira bien—le es casi imposible bajar y subir las escaleras (*stairs*).
3. Ud. visita al dentista porque hace varios días que tiene dolor de muela. Pero Ud. es cobarde y no quiere que el dentista se la saque.
4. Ud. lleva a su hijo para consultar con la doctora. Tiene fiebre y vomita con frecuencia.
5. Ud. está en el hospital, en la sala de urgencia (*emergency*). Acaba de tener lo que parece ser un ataque de apendicitis y lo/la van a operar. Habla con una enfermera.

E. Situaciones de la vida diaria. With another student act out the following role-play situations as fully as possible. Try to use as much of the vocabulary that you know as possible.

1. A journalist (**un reportero/una reportera**) from another country is interviewing you about the everyday lives of students at your university. Tell him or her in detail what you normally do from the moment you get up to the moment you go to bed, stressing things that are special to your university.
2. A journalist from another country is interviewing a young professional who also has a spouse and two young children. Play the role of the professional, answering the journalist's questions about how you and your spouse handle the responsibilities of your personal and professional lives.
3. Your roommate (spouse, friend) has just found a marvelous apartment in the city and is very excited about it. Ask him or her questions about its location, how big it is, what it looks like, what kinds of public transportation are available, what the neighborhood (**el barrio**) is like, how much the rent is, if light and heat are included in the rent, if you can have a dog, and so on.
4. You run into a friend who is obviously feeling out of sorts, since his or her eyes are red and he or she can barely talk. Ask questions to find out why your friend is in such bad shape. Your friend should invent details of the "problem": an illness, a term paper (**un informe**) written and then lost before it was handed in, a problem in the family or with a class, and so on.

En la estación de gasolina

VOCABULARIO: PREPARACIÓN

LOS COCHES / CARS

el camino street, road
la carretera highway
la circulación, el tráfico traffic
el conductor/la conductora driver
la esquina (street) corner
la licencia (de manejar, conducir) driver's license
el semáforo traffic light

la estación de gasolina, la gasolinera gas station
los frenos brakes
una llanta desinflada a flat tire
el taller (repair) shop

arrancar to start up (*a car*)
arreglar to fix, repair
contener (*like* **tener**) to contain
chocar (con) to run into, collide (with)

doblar to turn
estacionar to park
gastar (mucha gasolina) to use (a lot of gas)
manejar, conducir (conduzco) to drive
parar to stop
seguir (i, i) (todo derecho) to keep on going; to go (straight ahead)

Un servicio rápido y completo

—Buenas. ¿Qué desea?

—Necesito que me arreglen la rueda de repuesto (*spare tire*).

—Puede dejarla y pasar mañana a recogerla (*to pick it up*).

—Pero... es que salgo de viaje ahora mismo... y pensé que tal vez (*perhaps*)...

—De acuerdo. Se lo hacemos en seguida.

Stuart Cohen

Mérida, Venezuela

A. Definiciones. Busque Ud. la definición de las palabras de la columna de la derecha.

1. Se pone en el tanque.
2. Se llenan de aire.
3. Lubrica el motor.
4. Es necesaria para arrancar el carro.
5. Cuando se llega a una esquina hay que hacer esto o seguir todo derecho.
6. No contiene aire y por eso es necesario cambiarla.
7. Es un camino público ancho (*wide*) donde los coches circulan rápidamente.
8. Se usan para parar el coche.
9. El policía nos la pide cuando nos para en el camino.
10. Allí se revisan y se arreglan los carros.

a. los frenos
b. doblar
c. la carretera
ch. la batería
d. el taller
e. una llanta desinflada
f. la gasolina
g. las llantas
h. el aceite
i. la licencia

Ahora, siguiendo el modelo de las definiciones anteriores, ¿puede Ud. dar una definición de las siguientes palabras?

11. el semáforo
12. la circulación
13. estacionarse
14. gastar gasolina
15. la gasolinera
16. el tanque

B. Mientras Ud. conducía... Invente los detalles para explicar lo que (*what*) pasó en las siguientes situaciones. ¿Qué necesitaba o qué debía hacer Ud.? ¿Qué hizo?

1. De repente Ud. oyó un *flop flop*.
2. El coche de Ud. se paró y no volvió a arrancar.
3. Ud. llegó a una esquina donde había otro coche parado (*stopped*) a la derecha.
4. En una esquina, Ud. vio dos coches, una ambulancia y varios policías.

5. Ud. manejó solamente 20 millas y gastó un cuarto de tanque de gasolina.

C. **En la gasolinera.** Describa Ud. las cosas y acciones que se ven en el dibujo.

CH. **Entrevista.** Usando las siguientes frases como guía, entreviste a un compañero (una compañera) de clase para determinar con qué frecuencia hace las siguientes cosas.

1. Dejar la licencia en casa cuando va a manejar
2. Acelerar (*To speed up*) cuando ve a un policía
3. Manejar después de beber alcohol
4. Respetar o exceder el límite de velocidad
5. Estacionar el coche donde dice «Prohibido estacionarse»
6. Revisar el aceite y la batería
7. Seguir todo derecho a toda velocidad cuando no sabe llegar a su destino
8. Adelantar (*To pass*) tres carros a la vez

Ahora, según lo que Ud. averiguó (*learned*), describa la forma de manejar de su compañero/a. ¿Es un buen conductor (una buena conductora)?

¿Recuerda Ud.?

Before beginning the next section in **Vocabulario: Preparación,** review the comparison of adjectives (Grammar Section 15).

¿Cómo se dice en español?
1. I'm taller than John.
2. This highway is longer than that one.
3. This repair shop is better than that one.
4. My car is older than Raúl's (**el de Raúl**).

Más descripciones: **Superlatives**

article + noun + **más/menos** + adjective + **de**
article + **mejor/peor** + noun + **de**

> David es **el** estudiante **más inteligente de** la clase.
> Son **los mejores** doctores **de** aquel hospital.

> *David is the smartest student in the class.*
> *They're the best doctors at that hospital.*

¡Es la calle más peligrosa° de la ciudad!   *dangerous*

The *superlative* (**el superlativo**) is formed in English by adding *-est* to adjectives or by using expressions such as *the most, the least,* and so on, with the adjective. In Spanish, this concept is expressed in the same way as the comparative, but is always accompanied by the definite article. In this construction **mejor** and **peor** tend to precede the noun; other adjectives follow. *In* or *at* is expressed with **de.**

A. Expand the information in these sentences, according to the model.

> MODELO   Carlota es una estudiante muy inteligente. (la clase) →
> En efecto, es la estudiante más inteligente de la clase.

En la oficina

1. Olga y Paula son unas empleadas muy trabajadoras. (la oficina)
2. La Sra. Gómez es una aspirante muy buena. (la lista)
3. Es una oficina muy eficiente. (la empresa)

En la excursión

4. Es una plaza muy pequeña. (la ciudad)
5. Son ciudades muy grandes. (el estado)
6. Es un metro muy rápido. (el mundo [*world*]).

En la universidad

7. Son capítulos muy importantes. (el texto)
8. Es una residencia muy buena. (la universidad)
9. ¡Es una clase muy mala! (la universidad)

B. Usando oraciones completas, dé Ud. el nombre de...

1. el/la mejor estudiante de la clase
2. la persona más pobre de su familia
3. el profesor (la profesora) más paciente de la universidad
4. la empresa/el negocio más importante de esta cuidad
5. el mejor coche de este año

MINIDIÁLOGOS Y ESTRUCTURA

¿Recuerda Ud.?

Ud. and **Uds.** commands (Grammar Section 22) are the third persons (singular and plural) of the present subjunctive. Object pronouns (direct, indirect, reflexive) must follow and be attached to affirmative commands; they must precede negative commands.

AFFIRMATIVE:	Háblele Ud.	Duérmase.	Dígaselo Ud.
NEGATIVE:	No le hable Ud.	No se duerma.	No se lo diga Ud.

¿Cómo se dice en español?

1. Bring me the book. **(Uds.)**
2. Don't give it to her. **(Uds.)**
3. Sit here, please. **(Ud.)**
4. Don't sit in that chair! **(Ud.)**
5. Tell them the truth. **(Uds.)**
6. Tell it to them now! **(Uds.)**
7. Never tell it to her. **(Uds.)**
8. Follow that street. **(Ud.)**
9. Follow it. **(Ud.)**
10. Listen to me. **(Ud.)**

35 Telling Someone to Do Something
Informal Commands

En la escuela primaria: Frases útiles para la maestra

—Maritere, *toma* tu leche; *no tomes* la de Carlos.
—Cristina, *escribe* las oraciones en la pizarra; *no las escribas* en la pared.
—Joaquín, *escucha*; *no hables* tanto.
—Esteban, *siéntate* en tu silla; *no te sientes* en el suelo.
—Silvia, *quítate* el abrigo; *no te quites* el suéter.
—Graciela, *dale* el cuaderno a Ernesto; *no se lo des* a Joaquín.
—Mario, *ponte* el abrigo; *no olvides* tu calculadora.
—Ramón, *ten* cuidado; *no corras*; *no te caigas*.
—Juana, *no hagas* eso; *tráeme* el papel.

In grade school: Useful phrases for the teacher *Maritere, drink your milk; don't drink Carlos's. Cristina, write the sentences on the board; don't write them on the wall. Joaquín, listen; don't talk so much. Esteban, sit in your chair; don't sit on the floor. Silvia, take off your coat; don't take off your sweater. Graciela, give the notebook to Ernesto; don't give it to Joaquín. Mario, put on your coat; don't forget your calculator. Ramón, be careful; don't run; don't fall. Juana, don't do that; bring me the paper.*

1. *¿Qué dice la maestra cuando Maritere no toma su leche? ¿cuando alguien debe escribir en la pizarra? ¿no escucha? ¿no se sienta en la silla? ¿no se quita el abrigo? ¿no le da el cuaderno a Ernesto? ¿no se pone el abrigo? ¿no tiene cuidado? ¿no trae el papel?*

2. *¿Por qué da la maestra los mandatos negativos? Por ejemplo, ¿por qué le dice la maestra a Maritere «no tomes la leche de Carlos»?*

   a. Porque Maritere tomó la leche de Carlos.
   b. Porque no está tomando su propia (own) leche.
   c. Porque la maestra no quiere que Maritere la tome.

Informal commands (**los mandatos informales**) are used with persons whom you address as **tú**.

Negative *tú* Commands

-ar Verbs		-er/-ir Verbs	
No hables.	Don't speak.	**No comas.**	Don't eat.
No cantes.	Don't sing.	**No escribas.**	Don't write.
No juegues.	Don't play.	**No pidas.**	Don't order.

Like **Ud.** commands (Grammar Section 22), the negative **tú** commands are expressed with the present subjunctive: **no hable Ud., no hables tú.** The pronoun **tú** is used only for emphasis.

  No cantes **tú** tan fuerte.   *Don't you sing so loudly.*

As with negative **Ud.** commands, object pronouns—direct, indirect, and reflexive—precede negative **tú** commands.

  No lo mires.   *Don't look at him.*
  No les escribas.   *Don't write to them.*
  No te levantes.   *Don't get up.*
                                                    [Práctica A–B]

Affirmative *tú* Commands*

-ar Verbs		-er/-ir Verbs	
Habla.	Speak.	**Come.**	Eat.
Canta.	Sing.	**Escribe.**	Write.
Juega.	Play.	**Pide.**	Order.

---

*Affirmative **vosotros** commands are formed by substituting **-d** for the final **-r** of the infinitive: **hablar** → **hablad**; **comer** → **comed**; **escribir** → **escribid**. There are no irregular affirmative **vosotros** commands. Negative **vosotros** commands are expressed with the present subjunctive: **no habléis/comáis/escribáis**. Placement of object pronouns is the same as with all other command forms: **Decídmelo; No me lo digáis.**

Unlike the other command forms you have learned, most affirmative **tú** commands have the same form as the third-person singular of the present *indicative*.

Only the following verbs have irregular affirmative **tú** command forms.

decir:	**di**	poner:	**pon**	tener:	**ten**
hacer:	**haz**	salir:	**sal**	venir:	**ven**
ir:	**ve**	ser:	**sé**		

■ **¡OJO!** *The affirmative **tú** commands for **ir** and **ver** are identical: **ve**. Context will clarify meaning.*

| ¡**Ve** esa película! | *See that movie!* |
| **Ve** a casa ahora mismo. | *Go home right now.* |

As in affirmative **Ud.** commands, object and reflexive pronouns follow affirmative **tú** commands and are attached to them. Accent marks are necessary except when a single pronoun is added to a one-syllable command.

Dile la verdad.	*Tell him the truth.*
Léela, por favor.	*Read it, please.*
Póntelos.	*Put them on.*

[Práctica C–E]

Práctica

A. Un viaje con Raúl. Durante un viaje en coche, su amigo Raúl insiste en hacer cosas que a Ud. no le gustan. Dígale que no las haga, según el modelo.

MODELO   Raúl estaciona el carro en medio (*middle*) de la calle. →
Raúl, no lo estaciones aquí, por favor.

1. Raúl gasta mucho dinero en gasolina.
2. Raúl maneja muy rápidamente.
3. Cierra la ventana.
4. Dobla en una esquina.
5. Para en una esquina.
6. Lee el mapa.
7. Sigue todo derecho.
8. Dice que Uds. van a llegar tarde.
9. Es muy descortés con Ud.
10. Arranca muy rápidamente.

B. Dé Ud. mandatos informales para continuar estos comentarios que Ud. hace a unos miembros de su familia. Siga el modelo.

MODELO   *Hablaste* tanto ayer. → No hables tanto hoy, por favor.
Dejaste tu ropa en el suelo ayer. →
No la dejes allí hoy, por favor.

1. *Dejaste* tus libros en el suelo también.
2. Ayer *regresaste* tarde a casa.
3. No quiero que *conduzcas* mi coche.
4. No es bueno que *corras* y *juegues* en la calle.
5. No es necesario que *vayas* al parque todos los días.
6. No es bueno que *mires* la televisión constantemente.
7. Siempre le *dices* mentiras (*lies*) a Papá.
8. Siempre *te olvidas* de sacar la basura.
9. ¿Por qué *comes* en tu cuarto?
10. *Eres* tan mala.

C. Haga mandatos informales afirmativos para cada situación, usando las frases como guía.

Lo que (*What*) Ud. le dice a su amigo Teodoro

1. estudiar / química / con / nosotros
2. ayudarme / con / español
3. venir / a mi casa / noche
4. almorzar / conmigo hoy

Lo que (*What*) la maestra le dice a Lilia, una estudiante de primaria

5. escribir / problema / pizarra
6. quitarse / abrigo / ahora
7. leerlo / y / aprenderlo / para / examen
8. sentarse / y / callarse (*to be quiet*)

CH. Imagine que sus amigos hacen las siguientes cosas. Ayúdelos con lo que deben de hacer, según el modelo.

MODELO   Carlos escribe la carta con lápiz.   (bolígrafo) →
                Carlos, escríbela con bolígrafo; no la escribas con lápiz.

1. Anita habla inglés en la entrevista.   (español)
2. Gilberto lee un periódico.   (una novela)
3. Nati le pregunta a Carmen la dirección.   (Lorenzo)
4. Santiago revisa las llantas.   (los frenos)
5. Maricarmen nos está comprando tres boletos.   (cuatro)
6. Julio dobla en la primera esquina.   (la tercera)
7. Dolores trae cerveza.   (vino)
8. Silvia estaciona el carro en el estacionamiento (*parking lot*).   (en la calle Bolívar)
9. Mariela llena la solicitud amarilla.   (la verde)
10. Jaime se pone *bluejeans* para la entrevista.   (un traje)

D. Su amigo Carlos tiene una entrevista para un trabajo que le interesa mucho y quiere caerle bien al entrevistador. Déle Ud. consejos sobre la entrevista en forma de mandatos informales.

MODELO   Llega a la hora en punto, Carlos.

E. Dé Ud. mandatos informales para las siguientes situaciones.

· Para ser un esposo (una esposa) feliz
· Para ser el compañero (la compañera) de cuarto ideal
· Para tener buena salud

---

36 El infinitivo
Verb + Infinitive; Verb + Preposition + Infinitive

Ventajas (*Advantages*) y desventajas de la era de la tecnología

Algunos de los inventos del siglo (*century*) XX nos traen problemas a la vez (*at the same time*) que nos facilitan otros aspectos de la vida. Mire el dibujo y lea el comentario del señor. Luego, usando las frases como guía, invente la historia de este señor, que es víctima del progreso. Use infinitivos con cada frase.

Yo quería ir a su oficina a pagar la tasa de estacionamiento,° pero no pude hacerlo porque no encontré sitio para estacionar.

tasa... *parking fee*

1. Este señor tenía que...
2. Quería...
3. Cuando llegó a la oficina, trató de (he tried to)...
4. Pero no pudo...
5. Por eso tuvo que...
6. Una vez en casa, decidió...
7. En este momento, acaba de...
8. El señor con quien habla va a...

As you have already learned, when two verbs occur in a series, the second verb is usually in the infinitive form. The infinitive is also the only verb form that can follow a preposition. You have already used many of the constructions that are presented in this section.

A. Many Spanish verbs require no preposition before an infinitive.

Prefieren poner la mesa.   *They prefer to set the table.*

deber	gustar	**preferir (ie)**
decidir	necesitar	**querer (ie)**
desear	pensar (ie) (*to intend*)	**saber**
esperar	poder (ue)	

B. Some Spanish verbs require a preposition or **que** before an infinitive.

1. Some verbs require **a** before an infinitive.

La profesora nos **enseña a bailar.**   *The professor is teaching us to dance.*

aprender a	enseñar a	venir (ie) a
ayudar a	invitar a	volver (ue) a
empezar (ie) a	ir a	

2. Other verbs or verb phrases require **de** before an infinitive.

Siempre **tratamos de llegar**   *We always try to arrive on time.*
   puntualmente.

acabar de	**olvidarse de**
acordarse (ue) de	**tener ganas de**
dejar de	**tratar de**

3. One frequently used verb requires **en** before an infinitive.

Insisten en venir esta noche.   *They insist on coming over*
                                              tonight.

insistir en

4. Two verbs require **que** before an infinitive.

Hay que sacar la basura.   *It's necessary to take out the*
                                         garbage.

haber que   tener que

Práctica

A. Dé oraciones nuevas según las indicaciones.

1. Con frecuencia mis amigos me invitan a _____. (*jugar al tenis, cenar, salir con ellos, visitarlos, bailar en un club, __?__*)
2. Las máquinas modernas nos ayudan a _____. (*tener más tiempo libre, mantener más limpia la casa, ir de un lugar a otro más rápidamente, comunicarnos con los amigos que viven lejos, __?__*)
3. Para salir bien (*succeed*) en esta clase, hay que _____. (*conjugar muchos verbos, escuchar con atención, saber el vocabulario, estar siempre alerta, __?__*)

B. Complete las siguientes descripciones, usando **a, de, en** o **que** (si es necesario) y un infinitivo.

1. El mecánico tiene _____.
2. Los novios van _____.
3. En el avión, la azafata insiste _____.
4. Un niño de seis años empieza _____ y aprende _____. Le gusta _____.
5. Un profesor de español nos enseña _____. Sin duda sabe _____.
6. Los invitados vienen a casa _____. No vienen _____. Esperan _____.
7. Un estudiante de baile tiene ganas _____. Trata _____.
8. Si un estudiante sale de la biblioteca a las once de la noche, acaba _____. Piensa _____. No va a volver _____.

C. Preparativos para un viaje en carro. ¿Qué tiene Ud. que hacer en las siguientes situaciones? Use las palabras que Ud. ya sabe y las que se dan a continuación (*below*). Use también **a, de, en** o **que,** si es necesario.

Palabras útiles

las cadenas (*chains*)
el filtro del aire (del aceite, del combustible)
hacer una revisión de _____

los limpiaparabrisas (*windshield wipers*)
la llanta de repuesto (*spare*)
el radiador

1. Pienso viajar durante la época de las lluvias. Por eso debo _____ .
2. Quiero hacer un viaje por las montañas de Colorado en el mes de diciembre. Por eso tengo _____ .
3. Vamos al desierto a hacer *camping* este fin de semana. Parece que una de las llantas está un poco desinflada. Por eso hay _____ .
4. Antes de empezar un viaje largo, debo consultar con _____ . Él/Ella va _____ .
5. Yo no sé _____ . Por eso siempre me lo/la cambia _____ .

Pidiendo información

—Dígame, por favor, ¿cómo puedo llegar al parque San Marcos?
—Siga todo derecho en esta calle por dos cuadras (*blocks*). Luego doble a la derecha en el semáforo y siga una cuadra más. Allí lo va a encontrar.
—Gracias, y perdone la molestia.
—No hay de qué.

Ciudad de México, México

REPASO

Incidentes automovilísticos. Complete the dialogue with the correct form of the infinitives. In the dialogue, begin with the present tense; then give the correct form required by context throughout.

En la gasolinera, con el nuevo coche

Margarita, una joven de unos veinticinco años, (*acabar*[1]) (*de/que*[2]) comprarse un carro nuevo. Está con ella su amigo Alberto.

EMPLEADO: ¿En qué puedo servirle, señorita?

MARGARITA: (*Llenarme*[3]) el tanque, por favor.

EMPLEADO: ¿(*Querer*[4]) que le (*revisar*[5]) las llantas y (*el/la*[6]) aceite?

MARGARITA: Sí, por favor, y (*el/la*[7]) agua de la batería y del radiador.

ALBERTO: Temo que tu coche (*ser/estar*[8]) gastando mucha gasolina.

MARGARITA: Lo (*calcular: yo*[9]) la semana pasada y estoy segura de que en la carretera no llego a los diez kilómetros por litro° que me (*prometer*[10]) el vendedor. Y temo que en la ciudad (*gastar*[11]) aún° más…

diez… *22.6 miles a gallon*

even

UN PASO MÁS: Imágenes del mundo hispánico

México: Período precolombino

Bajorrelieves y jeroglíficos mayas

La llegada de Cortés in Tenochtitlán, mural de Diego Rivera

Stuart Cohen

La Pirámide del Sol, Teotihuacán, cerca de la Ciudad de México

*N*umerosas civilizaciones vivieron en el territorio del México actual antes de la llegada de los españoles. Las dos más importantes son la maya y la azteca.

Los mayas, de origen todavía poco claro, vivieron en pleno esplendor durante los siglos I al X d. de C. En México quedan construcciones mayas en la Península del Yucatán: Chichén Itzá y Uxmal.* Se sabe que, además de construir tan impresionantes edificios, tuvieron conocimientos de astronomía muy avanzados y que también fueron matemáticos, ingenieros y artistas admirables. Las causas de su desaparición son tan enigmáticas como su origen. Parece que las ciudades mayas fueron abandonadas en el siglo X sin razones aparentes.

Los aztecas levantaron su imperio en los tres siglos anteriores al descubrimiento de América en 1492. Su capital, Tenochtitlán, construida sobre el lago salado (*salt*) de Texcoco, asombró (*amazed*) extraordinariamente a los españoles. Antes de la llegada de los conquistadores, los aztecas, pueblo mucho más guerrero que los mayas, llegaron a dominar gran parte del Golfo de México y Centroamérica. También desarrollaron la artesanía, el comercio y la ingeniería. Por desgracia la gran ciudad de Tenochtitlán fue destruida en 1521 durante la guerra contra Hernán Cortés y sus soldados.

(Continúa en el Capítulo 19.)

---

*See also photo essay, Chapter 15.

VOCABULARIO

VERBOS

arrancar to start up (*a car*)
conducir (conduzco) to drive
contener (like *tener*) to contain
chocar (con) to run into, collide (with)
estacionar to park
gastar to use (*gas*)
manejar to drive
parar to stop
revisar to check, inspect
seguir (i, i) to keep on, continue
tratar de + *inf.* to try to (*do something*)

LAS PARTES DE UN COCHE

la batería battery
los frenos brakes
la llanta (desinflada) (flat) tire
el parabrisas windshield
el tanque (gas) tank

LO NECESARIO PARA CONDUCIR

el aceite oil
la gasolina gasoline
la licencia (de manejar, conducir) (driver's) license

EN LA CIUDAD

el camino street, road
la carretera highway
la circulación traffic

el/la conductor(a) driver
la esquina (street) corner
la estación de gasolina gas station
la gasolinera gas station
el semáforo traffic light
el taller (repair) shop
el tráfico traffic

OTRO SUSTANTIVO

el mundo world

PALABRAS ADICIONALES

todo derecho straight ahead

FRASES ÚTILES PARA LA COMUNICACIÓN	
¿Cómo puedo llegar a... ?	How can I get to . . . ?
hay que + *inf.*	it is necessary to (*do something*)
no hay de qué	you're welcome

CAPÍTULO 18

La tecnología

el monitor
la pantalla
la impresora
el teclado
el disco
el monitor
las teclas
la máquina de escribir

LAS COMPUTADORAS/LOS ORDENADORES / COMPUTERS

la informática data processing
el lenguaje (computer) language
el manejo/uso operation, use (*of a machine*)
la memoria memory
la microcomputadora microcomputer
el ordenador personal personal computer, PC
el sistema system

archivar la información to store information
diseñar programas to design, write programs
editar textos to do word processing
escribir a máquina to type
manejar/usar to use, operate (*a machine*)

316

A. ¿Cómo se llaman las partes de la computadora que se ven en el dibujo?

B. ¿Está Ud. de acuerdo con las ideas siguientes? Defienda sus opiniones.

1. Saber manejar una computadora es un requisito indispensable para conseguir un buen empleo hoy en día.
2. Es difícil aprender a manejar un ordenador. Es mucho más fácil escribir a máquina.
3. La informática es una ciencia muy útil. Saber algo de informática debe ser un requisito para graduarse en esta universidad.
4. El precio de los microordenadores personales baja todos los años. Por eso no pienso comprarme uno todavía.
5. Las computadoras nos controlan a nosotros; nosotros no las controlamos a ellas.
6. Es bueno que tengamos acceso a información médica, bancaria y educativa por medio (*means*) de las computadoras.

C. Definiciones. Dé Ud. una definición de estas palabras.

MODELO   la memoria → Es lo que (*what*) se archiva en un ordenador.

1. la pantalla	3. el disco	5. el lenguaje
2. las teclas	4. la impresora	6. el programador

CH. Preguntas

De niño/a, ¿tenía Ud. mucho contacto con las computadoras? ¿Aprendió a manejar una computadora en la escuela primaria? ¿en la secundaria? ¿Es necesario que aprenda la informática en la universidad? ¿Qué lenguajes sabe Ud.? ¿Pascal? ¿BASIC? ¿Tiene una computadora personal? ¿Cuánto le costó? ¿Cuándo la usa?

Más descripciones: **Adjetivos ordinales**

primer(o)	first	**cuarto**	fourth	**séptimo**	seventh	**décimo**	tenth
segundo	second	**quinto**	fifth	**octavo**	eighth		
tercer(o)	third	**sexto**	sixth	**noveno**	ninth		

Ordinal numbers are adjectives and must agree in number and gender with the nouns they modify.* Ordinals usually precede the noun: **la cuarta lección, el octavo ejercicio.**

Like **bueno,** the ordinals **primero** and **tercero** shorten to **primer** and **tercer,** respectively, before masculine singular nouns: **el primer niño, el tercer mes.**

---

*Ordinal numbers are frequently abbreviated with superscript letters that show the adjective ending: **las 1ªˢ lecciones, el 1ᵉʳ grado, el 5° estudiante.**

A. ¿En qué grado están estos niños?

1. Manuel—5°   **3.** Eduardo—7°   **5.** Pablo—10°
2. Teresa—3ᵉʳ   **4.** Jesús—1ᵉʳ   **6.** Evangelina—2°

B. Conteste las preguntas según el dibujo.

1. ¿Quién es la décima persona? ¿la quinta? ¿la tercera? ¿la novena? ¿la segunda?

2. ¿En qué posición está Ángela? ¿Cecilia? ¿Juan? ¿Simón? ¿Linda?

C. ¿En qué orden de importancia coloca Ud. (*do you put*) los distintos factores al tomar las siguientes decisiones? ¿Por qué?

MODELO   El primer factor sería (*would be*)… El segundo sería…

1. Ud. tiene que elegir (*to choose*) los cursos para el próximo semestre.
 _____ la hora de la clase
 _____ el profesor (la profesora)
 _____ la materia del curso
 _____ la necesidad de usar una computadora
 _____ la posibilidad de sacar una buena nota

2. Ud. tiene que escoger (*to choose*) entre dos puestos.
 _____ el sueldo
 _____ el prestigio de la empresa
 _____ la ciudad
 _____ la posibilidad de ascenso (*promotion*)
 _____ la personalidad del jefe (de la jefa)
 _____ las condiciones físicas de la oficina
 _____ las computadoras disponibles (*available*)

En una tienda de computadoras

—Quiero comprar una computadora personal, pero no sé cuál. ¿Puede recomendarme alguna?
—¿Tiene experiencia?
—Realmente no.
—Entonces le sugiero que compre este modelo. Es fácil de manejar y tiene muchas funciones.

México

Más descripciones: **Absolute Superlatives**

Esos ejercicios son
  facilísimos.
Esa mujer es **inteligentísima.**

*Those exercises are very, very
  easy.*
*That woman is extremely
  intelligent.*

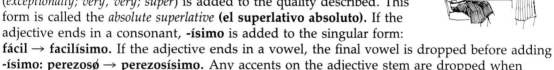

¡Es facilísimo de manejar!

When **-ísimo/-a/-os/-as** is used with an adjective, the concept *extremely*
(*exceptionally; very, very; super*) is added to the quality described. This
form is called the *absolute superlative* **(el superlativo absoluto).** If the
adjective ends in a consonant, **-ísimo** is added to the singular form:
fácil → facilísimo. If the adjective ends in a vowel, the final vowel is dropped before adding
-ísimo: perezos → **perezosísimo.** Any accents on the adjective stem are dropped when
-ísimo is added: **difícil → dificilísimo.**

Spelling changes occur when the final consonant of an adjective is **c, g,** or **z:**
rico → ri*qu*ísimo; largo → lar*gu*ísimo; feliz → feli*c*ísimo.

A. En la tienda de computadoras. Un cliente le hace las siguientes
preguntas. Contéstele según el modelo, haciendo el papel (*role*) de
vendedor(a). Use el adjetivo indicado en la pregunta o el antónimo,
según el contexto.

MODELO ¿Son *caros* los discos? (baratos) → No, son baratísimos.

1. ¿Es *fácil* aprender a manejar este modelo?
2. ¿Es *grande* la memoria?
3. ¿Las palabras en la pantalla salen *claras*?
4. ¿Es *barato* el precio en comparación con el de otras computadoras?
5. ¿Hay *muchos* nuevos programas disponibles todos los meses?
6. ¿Gasta *mucha* energía? (poca)
7. ¿Se ofrece un servicio *completo* en esta tienda?

B. Usando oraciones completas, dé Ud. el nombre de...

1. una persona riquísima
2. un coche baratísimo y otro rapidísimo
3. un coche pequeñísimo y otro grandísimo
4. una persona famosa viejísima
5. una computadora personal buenísima

C. Entrevista. With another student, ask and answer questions based
on the following phrases. Then report your opinions to the class.
Report any disagreements as well.

1. Un libro interesantísimo y otro pesadísimo (*very boring*)
2. Un plato riquísimo y otro malísimo
3. Un programa de televisión interesantísimo y otro aburridísimo
4. Un lugar tranquilísimo y otro peligrosísimo (*very dangerous*)

MINIDIÁLOGOS Y ESTRUCTURA

37 Expressing Willing, Emotion, and Doubt
Uses of the Subjunctive in Noun Clauses: A Summary*

Una computadora: ¿Una compra (*purchase*) esencial?

Si Ud. quiere comprar una computadora para su uso personal, tiene que ir a una tienda especializada en electrónica. Allí va a ver todos los nuevos modelos. *Ud. va a querer que* el dependiente...

- le *enseñe* los últimos modelos
- le *explique* cómo funciona cada computadora
- le *diga* cuáles son las ventajas y desventajas de cada modelo

Claro está que Ud. va a aprender mucho. *Le va a sorprender que...*

- las computadoras *cuesten* tan poco hoy día
- *sean* tan fáciles de manejar
- *haya* tantos sistemas diferentes y tantos programas

Después de examinar muchas computadoras, *es probable que* Ud. por fin *decida* comprar una. Si no puede pagar al contado (*in cash*), *es posible que* el dependiente...

- le *proponga* (*suggest*) un plan para pagar a plazos (*in installments*)
- le *pida* su tarjeta de crédito
- le *diga* que *espere* hasta el mes que viene, pues va a haber muchas gangas

Si Ud. decide pagar a plazos, firme los papeles necesarios y ya puede tener su computadora nueva. ¡Buena suerte!

Use la narración anterior como guía para explicar lo que pasa cuando uno va a comprar un aparato eléctrico.

COLEGIO DE INGENIEROS TÉCNICOS
DE OBRAS PÚBLICAS
ZONA DE MADRID

**CURSOS DE
MICROORDENADOR
EN LOS LENGUAJES
PASCAL, FORTH
LOGOS Y ADA**

- **PASCAL:** Comienzo, 6 de febrero.
- **FORTH:** Comienzo, 27 de febrero.
- **LOGOS:** Comienzo, 26 de marzo.
- La duración de los cursos es de 24 horas, y corresponde al primer nivel de estos lenguajes.
- Precio: 12.000 pesetas. Colegiados de colegios oficiales: 25% descuento.
- Diploma del Colegio de Ingenieros Técnicos de Obras Públicas.
- Curso especial de sábados.
- Abierta la matrícula para dichos cursos.

**CURSO ESPECIAL PARA JÓVENES
(E.G.B., B.U.P. y F.P.)**

- Duración: 24 horas en 8 sábados.
- Precio: 5.000 pesetas.
- Comienzo: 28 de enero.

INFORMACIÓN: Secretaría del Colegio
San Hermenegildo, 3
MADRID-8. Teléfono 448 59 98

Independent Clause		Dependent Clause
first subject + *indicative*	**que**	second subject + *subjunctive*
expression of $\begin{cases} \text{willing} \\ \text{emotion} \\ \text{doubt, denial} \end{cases}$		

---

*See Grammar Sections 24, 25, and 26 for a more detailed presentation of the uses of the subjunctive in noun clauses.

A. Remember that, in Spanish, the subjunctive occurs primarily in two-clause sentences with a different subject in each clause. If there is no change of subject, an infinitive follows the first verb. Compare the following:

Quiero ⎱ que él revise
Es necesario ⎰ la impresora.

I want ⎱ him to check
It's necessary for ⎰ the printer.

Quiero ⎱ revisar
Es necesario ⎰ la impresora.

I want ⎱ to check
It's necessary ⎰ the printer.

The independent clause, in addition to fulfilling the preceding condition, must contain an expression of willing, emotion, or doubt in order for the subjunctive to occur in the dependent clause. If there is no such expression, the indicative is used. Compare the following:

Dicen que Uds. archiven la información.

They say that you should (for you to) store the information.

Dicen que el secretario no sabe archivar la información; por eso quieren que Uds. la archiven.

They say that the secretary doesn't know how to store information; that's why they want you to store it.

B. Some verbs of willing are frequently used with indirect object pronouns.

Nos dicen
Nos piden ⎬ que **vayamos.**
Nos recomiendan

They tell us to
They ask us to ⎬ *go.*
They recommend that we

The indirect object indicates the subject of the dependent clause, as in the sentences above: **nos** → **vayamos.**

Práctica

A. En esta era de los avances tecnológicos, hay máquinas para todo. Imagine que Ud. tiene en casa un robot de último modelo. Complete las oraciones según las indicaciones.

1. Quiero que el robot (me) _____. (*lavar los platos, hacer las camas, mantener el carro en buenas condiciones, pagar las cuentas, __?__*)
2. Me alegro de (*I'm glad*) que el robot _____. (*ayudarme tanto, funcionar bien casi siempre, no quejarse* [to complain] *nunca, no pedirme un aumento de sueldo, __?__*)
3. Me sorprende que el robot _____. (*hablar tan bien y tan lógicamente, ser tan inteligente, parecer tan humano, saberlo todo, __?__*)

4. Dudo que los robots _____ algún día.   (*reemplazar* [to replace] *a los seres humanos, controlarlo todo, llegar a ser muy comunes,* __?__)

B. **El viernes, en la oficina.** ¿Qué recomendaciones le hace la directora? Haga oraciones según el modelo, usando el pronombre sujeto donde sea necesario.

MODELO   recomendar / Paco / trabajar el sábado →
             La directora le recomienda a Paco que trabaje el sábado.

1. recomendar / yo / no hablar tanto por teléfono
2. mandar / Alicia / llegar a tiempo el lunes
3. recomendar / Ud. / buscar otro puesto
4. decir / todos / ser más cuidadosos (*careful*) con los detalles
5. pedir / Uds. / tener el inventario preparado para el miércoles
6. prohibir / tú / hablar con el presidente de la empresa
7. pedir / nosotros / archivar la información con cuidado
8. decir / todos / aprender a manejar el nuevo sistema de computadoras

C. **Situaciones.** Ud. es mecánico/a y encuentra muchos problemas en el coche de un cliente. ¿Cuáles son? Ud. y el cliente pueden hablar de los frenos de disco, la transmisión, el aire acondicionado, las llantas, la batería, el radiador, el aceite, etcétera. Use estas palabras como guía. ¿Cuántas oraciones puede Ud. inventar?

Temo que	revisarme _____
Recomiendo que	su _____ estar roto (*broken*)
Me sorprende que	no funcionar bien _____
¿Cómo es posible que... ?	poner un(a) _____ nuevo/a
Quiero que	arreglar _____
	ir a costarle _____
	usar un(a) _____ reconstruido/a (*rebuilt*)
	no hay _____ en _____
	_____?

CH. **Entrevista.** ¿Qué espera Ud. de la tecnología? Complete the following sentences in a logical fashion; then ask other students how they responded (**¿Qué esperas de las computadoras?, etcétera),** until you find some who share your own hopes and/or uncertainties.

1. Espero que las computadoras _____ .
2. Estoy seguro/a de que el progreso _____ .
3. Dudo que los robots _____ .
4. Prefiero que la gente (*people*) _____ .
5. Me alegro de que la tecnología _____ .
6. Tengo miedo de que los seres humanos _____ .
7. Creo que la velocidad de la comunicación _____ .

38 Que, quien(es), lo que
Relative Pronouns

Lo que dijo el técnico

ISABEL: ¿Y qué más te dijo este técnico *que* tanto sabe?
BEATRIZ: Que lo más importante es tener la computadora en un sitio apropiado y no tocar nunca los discos con los dedos.
ISABEL: Mira, la próxima vez *que* tengas un problema con tu computadora, la primera persona con *quien* debes hablar es conmigo. Te digo lo mismo... ¡y sin cobrar!

1. *La persona con quien habla Isabel es _____ .*
2. *La persona de quien hablan es _____ .*
3. *El técnico recomienda que Beatriz _____ .*
4. *Isabel le recomienda que _____ .*
5. *Yo creo que lo que debe hacer Beatriz es _____ .*

There are four principal relative pronouns in English: *that, which, who,* and *whom.* They are usually expressed in Spanish by the following relative pronouns.

A. Que = *that, which, who*

Tuve una cita con el médico **que** duró una hora.	*I had an appointment with the doctor that lasted an hour.*
Es un buen médico **que** sabe mucho.	*He's a good doctor who knows a lot.*

B. Lo que = *what, that which*

No entiendo **lo que** dice.	*I don't understand what he is saying.*
Lo que no me gusta es su actitud hacia los pobres.	*What I don't like is his attitude toward poor people.*

The antecedent of **lo que** is always a sentence, a whole situation, or something that hasn't been mentioned yet: **Lo que necesito es estudiar más.**

C. Quien(es) = *who/whom* after a preposition or as an indirect object

La mujer con **quien** hablaba es mi hermana.	*The woman with whom I was talking is my sister.*

What the technician said   ISABEL: *And what else did this technician who knows so much tell you?*   BEATRIZ: *That the most important thing is to have the computer in an appropriate place and never to touch the disks with your fingers.*   ISABEL: *Look, the next time you have a problem with your computer, the first person you should talk to is me. I'll tell you the same thing . . . and without charging!*

Éste es el hombre de **quien** te hablaba.	*This is the man about whom I was talking to you.*
¿A **quién** no le gustan las tortillas?	*Who doesn't like tortillas?*

Práctica

A. Situaciones. Imagine que Ud. es un médico (una médica). Explíquele a la enfermera lo que Ud. necesita.

MODELO   bisturí (*m., scalpel*) / mesa →
      —Lo que necesito es el bisturí.
      —¿Cuál?
      —El bisturí que está en la mesa.

1. termómetro / armario (*closet*)
2. jarabe / consultorio
3. frasco (*bottle*) / bolsa
4. bolsa / escritorio
5. teléfono del especialista / mi agenda
6. nombre del hospital / ese pueblo

B. En el taller. ¿Cómo se dice en español?

1. Who was the man that brought this computer here?
2. Where are the printers that arrived yesterday?
3. They found the addresses of the men with whom we used to design programs.
4. I need the name of the disks that they were using.
5. What we did wasn't very good.

C. Complete las oraciones en una forma lógica.

1. Lo que más me gusta/molesta de esta clase es/son _____ .
2. Lo que (no) me gusta de la vida universitaria es/son _____ .
3. Lo que más necesito en este momento es/son _____ .
4. Lo que (no) me gusta de nuestro actual (*current*) presidente es/son _____ .

CH. Problemas y consejos. Dé varios consejos a la persona que tiene los siguientes problemas. Use estas frases como guía.

· La persona con quien debes hablar es...
· Lo que debes hacer es...
· Lo que creo es que debes...

1. Tengo un resfriado terrible.
2. Necesito descansar y tengo tres días libres la semana que viene.
3. Tengo ganas de comer comida china esta noche.
4. No sé qué clases debo tomar el semestre que viene.

5. ¡Sufro tantas presiones en mi vida privada!
6. Vivo muy lejos de la universidad. Pierdo una hora en ir y venir todos los días.
7. Se me cayó el vaso favorito de mi abuela y se rompió, pero no se lo dije cuando pasó.
8. Tardo mucho en (*It takes me a long time to*) escribir mis informes (*reports*) a máquina.

Ahora invente Ud. problemas semejantes (*similar*) y pídales consejos a sus compañeros de clase.

REPASO

Los sentimientos «robóticos». Complete the following paragraph with the correct form of the words in parentheses, as suggested by the context. When two possibilities are given in parentheses, select the correct word. Begin with the present indicative.

Yo (*ser/estar*¹) uno de los robots de una fábrica de juguetes.° (*Preferir: yo*²) (*trabajar*³) aquí porque me (*gustar*⁴) (*ayudar*⁵) a la gente (*a/de*⁶) (*fabricar*⁷) juguetes (*bueno*⁸) y duraderos.° Los empleados (*del/de la*⁹) fábrica tratan (*que/de*¹⁰) (*mantener*¹¹) mi cuerpo en (*bueno*¹²) condiciones; (*poner: ellos*¹³) aceite en (*mi*¹⁴) junturas° y (*limpiar*¹⁵) el abrigo de metal (*que/lo que*¹⁶) llevo. Pero a mí me (*molestar*¹⁷) que ellos no (*hacer*¹⁸) absolutamente nada más. Sólo tienen (*que/de*¹⁹) (*empujar*°²⁰) los botones y esperan que yo (*hacer*²¹) todo el trabajo. Insisten (*de/en*²²) que yo (*funcionar*²³) veinticuatro horas al día. No me dejan (*ir*²⁴) a la cafetería con ellos y no me (*dar*²⁵) vacaciones. No (*creer*²⁶) que yo (*cansarse*°²⁷) de vez en cuando° y dudan que yo (*tener*²⁸) sentimientos. Tampoco me permiten que (*hablar*²⁹) con (*los/las*³⁰) demás° robots.

fábrica... *toy factory*

long-lasting

joints

to push

to grow tired / de... *from time to time*
other

UN PASO MÁS: Lectura cultural

Los países en vías de desarrollo°

El nivel de vida de los países no industrializados no puede compararse con el de los Estados Unidos. Pero tampoco quiere decir que todos esos pueblos viven en la miseria. Es importante reconocer que aun entre los países generalmente llamados «países en vías de desarrollo», y particularmente entre los que forman la América Latina, existen diferentes niveles de desarrollo. Hay países cuya° economía se basa principalmente en la agricul-

en... *developing*

whose

tura, pero también hay otros bastante industrializados, como demuestran las siguientes noticias.

PANAMÁ SE BENEFICIA CON EL TRANSBORDADOR ESPACIAL

El transbordador espacial de los Estados Unidos, Columbia, va a ayudar a Panamá a realizar un inventario de sus recursos naturales. El sistema de Imágenes por Radar del transbordador actúa como un ojo en el cielo. El país tiene grandes extensiones de selva° que no pueden examinarse fácilmente.   *jungle*

IMPORTANCIA ECONÓMICA DEL TABACO

El tabaco ocupa el séptimo lugar entre los cultivos más difundidos° del mundo, después del trigo,° el arroz, la soja,° el algodón y el café. Los Estados Unidos y el Brasil, que duplicaron° sus exportaciones de tabaco en la última década, son los principales productores y exportadores de Occidente.   *widespread* / *wheat* / *soybeans* / *doubled*

EL METRO EN EL TRANSPORTE URBANO

El metro de la ciudad de México, que es el más utilizado del continente, transportó más de 1.000 millones de pasajeros el año pasado. Durante más de 50 años, Buenos Aires tuvo el único sistema de transporte subterráneo de la América Latina. Pero el éxito° del metro mexicano, inaugurado en 1968 para los Juegos Olímpicos, ayudó a convencer a otras naciones con problemas de tráfico de la ventaja de construir sus propios sistemas subterráneos.   *success*

DESARROLLO DEL VALLE DEL CAUCA

La Corporación del Valle del Cauca (CVC), una de las entidades° de desarrollo regional de más éxito de la América Latina, celebró su trigésimo° aniversario en 1984. La organización fue fundada en 1954 siguiendo el modelo del Tennessee Valley Authority. Es una entidad pública y autónoma que ha desarrollado° el valle más rico de Colombia mediante° el control de inundaciones y el suministro° de energía hidroeléctrica.   *empresas* / *treinta* / ha... *has developed* / por medio de / *providing*

(Adaptado de *Américas*)

Comprensión

¿Cierto o falso? Corrija las oraciones falsas.

1. La mayoría de los países latinoamericanos forman parte del grupo de los países desarrollados.
2. Los países latinos son países del tercer mundo, muy poco industrializados y con pocos recursos naturales.
3. La economía de los países latinoamericanos está basada en uno o dos productos o industrias.
4. Hay pocos metros en Latinoamérica.

5. El Brasil es el principal productor y exportador de trigo del Occidente.
6. Se produce mucha energía hidroeléctrica en Colombia.

Para escribir

Hay un debate constante sobre el siguiente tema: ¿Deben ayudar o no los Estados Unidos a los «países en vías de desarrollo» (al gobierno, a las empresas nacionales y las del sector privado, a la comunidad científica…)? ¿Qué piensa Ud.? Si dice que sí, ¿qué forma debe tomar esta ayuda? Conteste en un párrafo breve, usando las siguientes frases como guía. Haga las modificaciones necesarias.

Creo que los Estados Unidos (no) deben ayudar a los «países en vías de desarrollo». Es muy importante que _____. Si nosotros los ayudamos, entonces _____. En mi opinión, estos países _____. También tenemos que considerar _____. En fin, (no) es buena idea ayudarlos.

VOCABULARIO

VERBOS
alegrarse (de) to be happy (about)
archivar to store
controlar to control
diseñar to design
editar textos to do word processing
manejar to use, operate (*a machine*)
reemplazar to replace
usar to use; to use, operate (*a machine*)

LA TECNOLOGÍA
la computadora computer (*Latin America*)
el disco disk
la impresora printer
la información information
la informática data processing

el lenguaje (computer) language
la memoria memory
el monitor monitor
el ordenador computer (*Spain*)
la pantalla screen
el programa program
el/la programador(a) programmer
el sistema system
el teclado keyboard
las teclas keys

LAS MÁQUINAS
el manejo operation, use (*of a machine*)
el robot robot
el/la técnico/a technician

OTROS SUSTANTIVOS
la desventaja disadvantage

la gente people
el requisito requirement
el ser humano human being
la ventaja advantage

ADJETIVOS
disponible available
micro- micro-
peligroso/a dangerous
pesado/a boring

LOS ADJETIVOS ORDINALES
primer (primero/a), segundo/a, tercer (tercero/a), cuarto/a, quinto/a, sexto/a, séptimo/a, octavo/a, noveno/a, décimo/a

PALABRAS ADICIONALES
lo que what; that which
quien who; whom

FRASES ÚTILES PARA LA COMUNICACIÓN	
(el primer factor) sería...	(the first factor) would be . . .

CAPITULO 19

En mis ratos libres

LOS PASATIEMPOS / PASTIMES

dar un paseo to take a walk
esquiar to ski
hacer *camping* to go camping
hacer planes para + *inf.* to
  make plans to (*do something*)
ir al teatro/a ver una
  película to go to the
  theater/to see a movie
jugar (ue) a las cartas/al
  ajedrez to play cards/chess
nadar to swim

pasarlo bien, divertirse
  (ie, i) to have a good time
patinar to skate
practicar un deporte to
  participate in a sport
ser aficionado/a a to be a fan
  of
ser divertido/a to be fun
tomar el sol to sunbathe
visitar un museo to visit a
  museum

la butaca seat (*in a theater*)
el cine movie theater
la comedia play
la película (doblada) (dubbed)
  movie
la trama plot

los ratos libres free time

---

*The words **billete** and **boleto** can designate *tickets* for travel or theater tickets. **Entrada** can mean only *theater tickets*.

La vida de la gran ciudad

—¿Cómo pasas tus ratos libres aquí en la
capital?
—A veces voy al teatro o a ver una película.
Soy muy aficionado al cine.
—¿No te gusta visitar los museos?
—Eso también. Sobre todo el Museo de Arte
Moderno.

Ciudad de México, México

1.

2.

3.

4.

A. Describa Ud. los dibujos, contestando las preguntas. Invente los
detalles necesarios.

1. VOCABULARIO: el fútbol (*soccer*)
   ¿Qué hacen los hombres? ¿En qué país viven? ¿Qué tiempo hace
   hoy? ¿Qué estación del año es? ¿Cómo lo sabe Ud.? ¿Quiénes son
   las personas que observan?

2. VOCABULARIO: la pantalla, tener lugar (*to take place*)
   ¿Dónde tiene lugar esta escena? ¿Por qué están de pie esas dos
   personas? ¿En qué país se hizo esta película? ¿Está doblada? ¿Por
   qué sí o por qué no? ¿Quiénes son el actor y la actriz? Cuente
   Ud. un poco de la trama.

3. VOCABULARIO: la plaza central
   ¿Tiene lugar esta escena en los Estados Unidos? Explique su
   respuesta. ¿Qué hace la familia? ¿Qué planes tiene para esta
   tarde? ¿Qué hace el resto de la gente? ¿Lo pasan bien o no?

4. VOCABULARIO: el río, el valle, el bosque (*forest*)
   ¿Qué hace esta familia? ¿Dónde están? ¿De dónde son? ¿Cuánto
   tiempo van a pasar aquí? ¿Por qué les gusta esta actividad?

5.

5. VOCABULARIO: la pareja (*couple*), la exposición de arte
¿En qué tipo de edificio está la pareja? ¿Dónde viven? ¿Por qué cree Ud. esto? ¿Qué día de la semana es, probablemente? ¿Por qué está aquí la pareja?

B. Mire Ud. los dibujos de nuevo (*again*) y compare los pasatiempos que se ven. ¿Cuál le parece a Ud. (*seems to you*) el más divertido? **(Me parece que...)** ¿aburridísimo? ¿peligrosísimo? ¿el más barato? ¿el más caro?

C. Asociaciones. ¿Qué actividades asocia Ud. con... ?

1. el verano
2. la primavera
3. el otoño
4. el invierno
5. una cita especial con (su novio/a, su esposo/a,...)
6. un día lluvioso
7. un día feriado (*holiday*) cuando no hay clases

CH. Ud. quiere ir al cine. Usando los números **1** a **9,** indique en qué orden va a hacer las cosas siguientes.

_____Llamo a mi amigo/a para ver si quiere acompañarme.
_____Cuando hago planes para ir al cine, lo primero que hago es consultar el periódico.
_____Compramos las entradas en la taquilla.
_____Subo al autobús para ir al centro, donde está el cine.
_____Buscamos buenas butacas para poder ver bien.
_____Compramos refrescos para tomar durante la película.
_____Me fijo en (*I pay attention to*) la trama para adivinar (*to guess*) cómo va a terminar la película.
_____Espero a mi amigo/a en la acera delante de la taquilla.
_____Después de la función, vamos a tomar algo a un café.

D. Es un día perfecto de verano y Ud. y unos amigos están haciendo planes para hacer una excursión. Exprese sus preferencias y haga sugerencias para que resulte una tarde ideal. Piense sólo en sus propios (*own*) deseos.

MODELO   —Prefiero que vayamos a la playa porque quiero tomar el sol. Temo que haga fresco si vamos a las montañas.
—Juanita, haz los sándwiches, ¿qué te parece? Carlos, trae tu radio...

MINIDIÁLOGOS Y ESTRUCTURA

39 No hay nadie que...
Subjunctive After Nonexistent and Indefinite Antecedents

En la plaza central

Describa lo que pasa y lo que *no* ocurre en esta escena de una plaza de un pueblo mexicano.

· *Hay personas* que *conversan* con los amigos, que *pasan* aquí sus ratos libres todos los días, que... (jugar al ajedrez, vender/comprar periódicos/comida, tomar el sol, __?__)

· *Hay niños* que *toman* helados, que... (jugar en la acera, dar un paseo con sus padres, __?__)

· *No hay nadie* que *lleve* ropa de invierno, que *pasee* en bicicleta, que... (ser aficionado al golf, ser de los Estados Unidos, escuchar la radio, __?__)

In English and in Spanish, an adjective clause is a dependent clause that modifies a noun or a pronoun: *I have a car **that gets good gas mileage;** I need a house **that is closer to the city.*** The noun or pronoun that precedes the adjective clause and is modified by it is called the *antecedent* **(el antecedente)** of the clause.

In Spanish, when the antecedent of an adjective clause refers to someone (something, someplace, and so on) that does not exist, the subjunctive must be used in the adjective clause.

EXISTENT ANTECEDENT:	**Hay algo** aquí que me **interesa.**	*There is something here that interests me.*

NONEXISTENT ANTECEDENT:	**No hay nada** aquí que me **interese.**	*There is nothing here that interests me.*

Similarly, when the existence of the antecedent is indefinite or uncertain, the subjunctive is used.

DEFINITE ANTECEDENT:	**Tenemos un portero** que lo **arregla** todo.	*We have a manager who fixes everything.*
INDEFINITE ANTECEDENT:	**Necesitamos un portero** que lo **arregle** todo.	*We need a manager who will (can) fix everything.*

The personal **a** is not used with direct object nouns that refer to hypothetical persons.* Compare the following:

Busco **un señor** que lo **sepa.**   *I'm looking for a man who knows that.*

Busco **al señor** que lo **sabe.**   *I'm looking for the man who knows that.*

Note that the subjunctive is used when the antecedent is unknown to the questioner, but the indicative is used if the antecedent is known to the answerer.

—**¿Hay algo** aquí que te **guste?**   *Is there something here that you like?*

—**Sí, hay mucho** que me **gusta.**   *Yes, there is lots that I like.*

Práctica

A. Dé oraciones nuevas según las indicaciones.

1. Aquí hay unas personas que hablan español y que son de Costa Rica. No hay nadie aquí que hable inglés, que sea de los Estados Unidos, que _____. (*llamarse Smith, ser rubio, vivir en Kansas, tener parientes en Cincinnati*)
2. Los Sres. Alonso tienen un apartamento que es bonito y que está en el centro. Los Sres. Alonso buscan una casa que sea más grande, que esté en el campo, que _____. (*no costar mucho, tener un patio enorme, tener una terraza, ser elegante*)
3. Acabo de mudarme (*to move*) a esta ciudad. Quiero tener amigos que _____. (*ir al cine con frecuencia, jugar a las cartas, practicar algún deporte, desear esquiar, __?__.*)

*Remember that **alguien** and **nadie** always take the personal **a** when they are used as direct objects: **Busco a alguien que lo sepa. No veo a nadie que sea norteamericano.**

4. Las habilidades de los miembros de esta clase son sorprendentes (*surprising*), pero no hay nadie aquí que _____ . (*ser actor/actriz, hablar chino, saber tocar la viola, coleccionar insectos, saber preparar comida turca, __?__*)

B. Contradict the speakers in the following situations, using the cues in parentheses.

- Ud. y su amigo Rodolfo están perdidos (*lost*) en un camino rural, por la noche. Además, parece que el coche empieza a fallar (*sputter*).

  RODOLFO: **1.** Seguramente hay alguien en aquella casa que conoce el camino. (No, hombre, no hay nadie…)
  2. Sin duda hay alguien en aquella gasolinera que puede arreglar el coche. (No, no hay nadie…)

- En una oficina: son las cinco de la tarde y hay mucho trabajo que hacer todavía. Ud. habla con el jefe.
  JEFE: **3.** Necesito al secretario que sabe español. (Pero, señor, aquí no tenemos ningún…)
  4. Claro que hay alguien que lo puede terminar para mañana. (Siento decírselo, pero no hay…)

- En la tienda de muebles: su esposo/a busca muebles para su casa.
  ESPOSO/A: **5.** Pues, sí, aquí hay algunas cosas que me gustan. (No hay nada…)
  6. Necesitamos un sillón que sea un poco más grande. (Pero si ya tenemos dos…)

C. ¿Cómo se dice en español?

1. "I have a friend who goes camping with me every summer. Now I want to meet someone who knows how to ski." "I don't know anyone who skis, but there are many people who want to learn the sport."
2. "I know three guys who play cards, but I don't know anyone who plays chess." "I just met someone who plays chess! Do you want to meet her?"

CH. Complete las oraciones en una forma lógica.

1. Tengo un carro que es _____ .
2. Necesito un carro que _____ .
3. Tengo un apartamento que está _____ .
4. Busco un apartamento que _____ .
5. En mi familia hay alguien que _____ , pero no hay nadie que _____ .

6. En clase hay algo que _____ , pero no hay nada que _____ .

7. En clase hay alguien que _____ , pero no hay nadie que _____ .

D. Entrevista. With another student, ask and answer the following questions. Then report what you have learned to the class.

1. ¿Hay alguien que te quiera más que tus padres?
2. ¿Hay algo que te importe más que los estudios universitarios?
3. ¿Buscas una especialización (*major*) que sea interesante? ¿útil? ¿que lleve a un puesto bien remunerado?
4. Para el semestre que viene, ¿qué clases buscas? ¿una que empiece a las ocho de la mañana?
5. ¿Deseas vivir en un apartamento (una casa) que tenga piscina?
6. ¿Conoces a alguien que sepa patinar muy bien? ¿bailar muy bien? ¿nadar muy bien?
7. ¿Hay alguien en tu familia que sepa manejar una computadora? ¿que sea programador(a)?

40 Aunque no lo creas...
Indicative and Subjunctive After *aunque*

Delante del cine

EMILIO: Hola, Armando. ¿Tú también vienes a ver «El museo de Drácula»?

ARMANDO: No, Emilio. Voy a ver «El sol de Acapulco».

EMILIO: ¿Por qué no nos acompañas? Está con nosotros Marisa, la prima de Carlos. *Aunque* no la *conoces*, sé que los dos se llevarían bien.

ARMANDO: Lo siento, Emilio. Voy a encontrarme con Elena Ortega, y *aunque* a ti te *parezcan* maravillosas las películas de horror, a mí me caen pesadísimas.

EMILIO: Hasta luego, entonces. Que lo pases bien.

ARMANDO: Chau, Emilio. ¡Que se diviertan!

1. *¿Dónde se ven Armando y Emilio?*
2. *¿Adónde van los dos?*
3. *¿Qué quiere Emilio que Armando haga? ¿A quién quiere que conozca?*
4. *¿Por qué no quiere Armando acompañarlos?*

In front of the movie theater   EMILIO: *Hi, Armando. Have you also come to see Dracula's Museum?*   ARMANDO: *No, Emilio. I'm going to see Acapulco Sun.*   EMILIO: *Why don't you come with us? Marisa, Carlos's cousin, is with us. Although you don't know her, I know that the two of you would get along well.*   ARMANDO: *I'm sorry, Emilio. I'm going to meet Elena Ortega, and although you may think horror movies are wonderful, I can't stand them.*   EMILIO: *See you later then. Have a good time.*   ARMANDO: *Ciao, Emilio. Enjoy yourselves!*

When you want to convey doubt, uncertainty, or disbelief, use the subjunctive after the conjunction **aunque** (*although, even though*). When there is no doubt or uncertainty, use **aunque** with the indicative. Compare the following:

No me gusta **aunque sea** amigo de Rita.

I don't like him although he may (might) be Rita's friend.

No me gusta **aunque es** amigo de Rita.

I don't like him even though he is Rita's friend.

Práctica

A. Dé oraciones nuevas según las indicaciones. Fíjense en (*Note*) el contraste entre la primera oración y la segunda.

1. Hoy está nevando mucho. Los niños están inquietos y quieren hacer algo, pero no saben qué hacer. Su mamá les hace unas sugerencias. ¿Qué les dice?
—Aunque _____, pueden jugar a las cartas. (*ser imposible dar un paseo, nevar muchísimo, no haber nada en la televisión, __?__*)

2. La madre sigue haciendo sugerencias, pero los niños no tienen interés en nada, y ella se pone impaciente. ¿Qué les dice por fin?
—Aunque _____, ¡salgan fuera a jugar! (*seguir nevando, hacer mucho frío, enfermarse Uds., no tener botas, __?__*)

Un fin de semana en la ciudad

—¿Qué hacen Uds. los fines de semana?
—Nos encanta pasear por la mañana, cuando hay poco tráfico.
—Sí, y a veces visitamos alguna exposición de arte y después tomamos el aperitivo en un café.
—¿Me invitan a ir con Uds. alguna vez?
—¡Encantados!

Madrid, España

B. **Las diversiones.** ¿Cómo se dice en español?

1. I won't go camping with him, although it might be fun.
2. You should buy tickets for the show now, even though it's early.
3. Although they may be good seats, I don't want them.
4. Even though they may be sports fans, they aren't going to have a good time.
5. Even though she already knows how to skate, she can learn something from you.

C. **El arte de decir que no.** Complete estas oraciones en una forma lógica.

1. No les voy a acompañar en el viaje a la Antártida, aunque _____ .
2. No vuelvo a quedarme en ese hotel, aunque _____ .
3. No vuelvo a tomar otro curso de informática, aunque _____ .
4. No vamos a comprar ese coche, aunque _____ .
5. No pienso comentar este problema con el jefe, aunque _____ .

REPASO

Hablando de películas... Complete the following dialogue and movie reviews with the correct form of the words in parentheses, as suggested by the context. When two possibilities are given in parentheses, select the correct word. Use the preterite or imperfect of infinitives indicated with an asterisk. Adjectives that end in **-do** are the equivalent of English past participles: **cerrar → cerrado** (*closed*). See if you can guess their meaning in context.

Saliendo del cine

—Bueno, ¿qué (*pensar*[1])* tú de la película? Te gustó?

—Pues, (*ser/estar*[2])* muy divertida, pero quizás° un poco superficial.   *maybe*

—Ah, ¿sí? ¿Por qué (*reírse*[3])* (*tan/tanto*[4])?

—Hombre, no hay (*alguien/nadie*[5]) que no lo (*pasar*[6]) bien viendo una de estas historietas° de vez en cuando.° Pero (*que/lo que*[7]) yo realmente (*preferir*[8]) son las películas sobre temas más (*profundo*[9]). Como, por ejemplo, (*ese*[10]) película francesa (*que/lo que*[11]) (*nosotros: ver*[12])* la semana pasada.   *insignificant stories / de... from time to time*

—Bueno, la próxima vez quiero que tú (*seleccionar*[13]) la película; pero no (*llevarme*[14]) a ver (*alguna/ninguna*[15]) película doblada, ¿eh? Ya (*sabes/conoces*[16]) que no me (*gustar*[17]) nada esas películas.

«El regreso del Jedi»

Esta película (*ser*/*estar*[18]) la (*tercero*[19]) parte de una serie muy famosa que se (*iniciar*[20])* con «La guerra de las galaxias» y (*continuar*[21])* con «El imperio (*contraatacar*[22])». El rasgo° principal de «El regreso del Jedi» (*ser*/*estar*[23]) la acción emocionante, caracterizada por complejos efectos (*especial*[24]). En «Jedi», los personajes° principales, (*que*/*lo que*[25]) representan la Alianza Rebelde, (*volver*[26]) para enfrentarse° con las Fuerzas Imperiales de la Oscuridad, encabezadas° por el malévolo Darth Vader.

characteristic, trait

characters

to confront

headed

«Superman II»

Este film (*contar*[27]) las peripecias° (*que*/*lo que*[28]) el (*tímido*[29]) periodista Clark Kent (*tener*[30]) que afrontar° para defender el bien.° Obligado por las circunstancias, Kent (*transformarse*[31]) en el mitológico héroe Superman para luchar° contra tres supercriminales (*que*/*quienes*[32]) tratan (*de*/*en*[33]) conquistar el mundo, ayudados por Lex Luthor, el «archienemigo» de Superman.

perils

to face / good

to fight

UN PASO MÁS: Imágenes del mundo hispánico

México: Período colonial, independencia, revolución

Stuart Cohen

Benito Juárez, al frente del movimiento liberal

Gruber/Monkmeyer Press Photo Service

El castillo de Chapultepec, donde vivieron Maximiliano y Carlota

La ciudad colonial de Taxco

El «Grito de Dolores», mural de Orozco

*P*ocos países cuentan con una historia tan bellamente descrita como México. En numerosos edificios públicos, en las estaciones del metro, los museos, construcciones oficiales... existen hermosos murales que describen distintos episodios de la historia de la nación.

México fue nombrado Virreinato de Nueva España o México en 1534. Poco después Hernán Cortés mandó reconstruir la capital, que se llamó Ciudad de México. Desde aquí la corona de España extendió su influencia por América del Norte. Con el paso de los años, los abusos de los gobernadores y la rigidez de las leyes (*laws*)

que regulaban todas las actividades de la colonia despertaron un fuerte sentimiento independentista. Pero no va a ser hasta 1810 que comienzan verdaderamente, con el «Grito de Dolores» del Padre Hidalgo, las luchas (*struggles*) en favor de la Independencia. Este proceso termina en 1821 con un acuerdo entre los insurgentes y los representantes del poder establecido.

Así se inicia un largo período de inestabilidad y guerras, no sólo internas sino también contra diversas potencias extranjeras (*foreign powers*). Hay que destacar (*emphasize*) los enfrentamientos con los Estados Unidos y Francia. Además de estas guerras en las que va a perder Texas, California, Nevada, Utah, Arizona, Nuevo México y parte de Colorado, México pasó por un breve período monarquía, bajo el emperador francés Maximiliano y una guerra civil. Benito Juárez, presidente durante este período de tumulto, dirigió (*led*) la lucha contra los franceses. No es hasta 1876, con el dictador Porfirio Díaz, que México disfrutó de un período de tranquilidad y cierto progreso económico. Sin embargo, los abusos del poder y la falta de una distribución equitativa de la tierra llevan inevitablemente a la Revolución mexicana de principios del siglo XX.

(Continúa en el Capítulo 21.)

VOCABULARIO

VERBOS

acompañar to accompany, go with
parecer (*like* **gustar**) to seem; to appear
patinar to skate
visitar to visit

EN EL TEATRO

la acera sidewalk
la butaca seat (*in a theater*)
la comedia play
la entrada ticket

la función show, performance
la taquilla ticket window
la trama plot

OTROS PASATIEMPOS

el ajedrez chess
las cartas (playing) cards
el deporte sport
el museo museum

ADJETIVOS

divertido/a amusing, fun
doblado/a dubbed

PALABRAS ADICIONALES

aunque although, even though
dar un paseo to take a walk
hacer *camping* to go camping
hacer planes para + *inf.* to make plans to (*do something*)
los ratos libres free time
ser aficionado/a (a) to be a fan (of)
tener (*irreg.*) **lugar** to take place
tomar el sol to sunbathe

FRASES ÚTILES PARA LA COMUNICACIÓN	
Me parece que...	I think that . . .
¡Que lo {**pases**/**pasen**} **bien!**	Have a good time!
¡Que se diviertan!	Enjoy yourselves!

CAPÍTULO 20

¿Le gustan los deportes?

VOCABULARIO: PREPARACIÓN

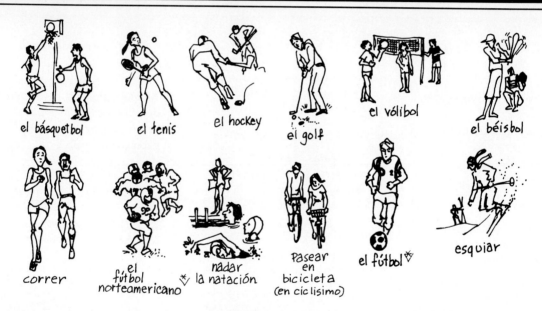

el básquetbol · el tenis · el hockey · el golf · el vólibol · el béisbol

correr · el fútbol norteamericano · nadar / la natación · pasear en bicicleta (en ciclismo) · el fútbol* · esquiar

LOS DEPORTES / SPORTS

ganar to win
jugar (ue) (al) to play (*sports*)
perder (ie) to lose

el jugador, la jugadora player

el equipo team
el estadio stadium
el juego play (*in a game*);
   (card, board) game
el partido game, match

la cancha (tennis) court
los esquís skis
la pelota ball
la pista (race)track
la raqueta racket
la red net
el traje de baño bathing suit

---

*El fútbol (*Soccer*) is a popular spectator and participation sport in Hispanic countries. The game called *football* in the United States is usually called **el fútbol (norte)americano** in Spanish.

¡Malas noticias!

—Lo siento, pero tu equipo volvió a perder.
—No me hables. 3 a 0... ¡y en casa!
—Si siguen así, es posible que pierdan la liga (*division title*).
—¡La culpa es de los árbitros!
—¡Claro! Siempre que pierde tu equipo, la culpa es del árbitro.

David Kupferschmid

Buenos Aires, Argentina

A. ¿Qué palabra o frase no pertenece al grupo? Explique por qué.

1. la cancha   la raqueta   la pista   la piscina
2. el ciclismo   el correr   el juego   la natación
3. el traje de baño   la pelota   el jugador   la raqueta
4. la red   los esquís   la bicicleta   el equipo
5. la pista   el equipo   los aficionados   los jugadores

B. ¿Dónde y cuándo se practican estos deportes? ¿Cómo es el jugador típico de cada deporte? ¿Qué tipo de persona es? ¿Le gusta jugar con un equipo o practicar el deporte individualmente? ¿Le interesa la competencia o prefiere competir consigo mismo (*with himself*)? ¿Cómo es el aficionado típico? Conteste estas preguntas sobre uno o dos de los siguientes deportes.

1. el golf
2. el fútbol norteamericano
3. el correr
4. el béisbol
5. el básquetbol
6. la natación
7. el ciclismo
8. el esquiar

¿Cuáles son sus deportes favoritos? ¿Por qué?

C. **¿Es Ud. deportista? ¿O es más aficionado/a a otra clase de diversiones?** What are you most likely to do on each of these occasions? Mark your answers and score yourself. (The scoring system is at the bottom of page 342.) Then refer to the **Interpretaciones** that follow the test. Does the interpretation of your score describe you accurately?

1. El lunes por la noche cuando realmente quiero pasarlo bien,
_____ .

    a. miro «El partido de la semana» (fútbol norteamericano)
    b. escucho música
    c. juego al vólibol con mis amigos

2. En verano en mis ratos libres _____ .

a. tomo el sol pero no nado
b. corro o paseo en bicicleta
c. paso horas debajo de un árbol (*tree*) leyendo una novela

3. Es sábado y ya terminé las cosas que tenía que hacer. Ahora voy
a _____ .
a. jugar al tenis
b. leer una revista de deportes
c. organizar una barbacoa con unos amigos

4. Es un día de invierno y son las cuatro de la tarde. Hace mucho
frío y está nevando. Prefiero _____ .
a. esquiar, patinar o jugar en la nieve (*snow*)
b. invitar a varios amigos a hacer una cena informal en mi casa
c. mirar los Juegos Olímpicos en la televisión

5. Es el 4 de julio y la temperatura es de unos 40 grados (*104°F*) a la
sombra (*shade*). Voy a _____ .
a. tomar limonada
b. jugar al béisbol
c. hablar de deportes con mis parientes

6. Estoy mirando el *Super Bowl* en la televisión. Estoy _____ .
a. contento/a
b. descontento/a; prefiero estar en el estadio
c. aburridísimo/a

_____ TOTAL

Interpretaciones

0–3 puntos   Ud. tiene poco interés en los deportes. Para Ud.
son quizá (*perhaps*) una pérdida de tiempo.

4–8 puntos   Ud. tiene cierto interés en los deportes. A Ud. le
gusta ver, leer y hablar de deportes, pero participa
muy poco.

9–12 puntos   Ud. sí es un verdadero deportista. Debe ser una
persona muy activa.

CH. Definiciones. Make up definitions of sports terms and present them
orally to your classmates, who will guess the term defined.

MODELOS   Hay nueve jugadores en un equipo.
Es un deporte que se practica individualmente; no se
juega en equipo.
Se juega en una cancha con una raqueta y una pelota.

Scoring

6-a; 0: 1-b, 2-c, 3-c, 4-b, 5-a, 6-c

2 puntos: 1-c, 2-b, 3-a, 4-a, 5-b, 6-b; **1 punto:** 1-a, 2-a, 3-b, 4-c, 5-c,

MINIDIÁLOGOS Y ESTRUCTURA

41 Expressing Contingency and Purpose
The Subjunctive After Certain Conjunctions

Unos verdaderos aficionados

SARA: No quiero ir al partido *a menos que juegue* el equipo de David.
CARLOS: Estoy de acuerdo. *Antes de que compres* los boletos, pregunta si van a jugar.
JULIO: Y *en caso de que* no *jueguen*, ¿qué?
CARLOS: ¡Hombre, pues entonces mejor nos quedamos en casa! Hay un estupendo partido en la televisión. Aquí tenemos cerveza y bocadillos y cojines y... ¡Y además está empezando a llover! ...¿No es hora de poner la tele?

Busque en el diálogo el equivalente de estas frases.

1. *No voy al partido si no juega el equipo de David.*
2. *Antes de comprar los boletos, quiero saber quién juega.*
3. *¿Qué hacemos si no juegan?*

¿Son verdaderos deportistas Sara y Carlos? ¿Les interesa más el deporte o su amigo David? ¿Les interesa más el deporte o su propia comodidad (own comfort)?

In Spanish the subjunctive always occurs in dependent clauses introduced by these *conjunctions* (**las conjunciones**):

a menos que	unless	**en caso de que**	in case
antes (de) que	before	**para que**	so that
con tal que	provided (that)	**sin que**	without

Voy **con tal que** ellos me acompañen.

En caso de que llegue Juan, dile que ya salí.

I'm going, provided (that) they go with me.

In case Juan arrives, tell him that I already left.

Note that these conjunctions introduce dependent clauses in which the events have not yet materialized; the events are conceptualized, not real-world events. When there is no change of subject in the dependent

---

Some real fans SARA: *I don't want to go to the game unless David's team is playing.* CARLOS: *I agree. Before you buy the tickets, ask if they're going to play.* JULIO: *And if (in case) they're not playing, what shall we do?* CARLOS: *Well, then it's better to stay home! There's a great game on TV. We've got beer and snacks and cushions here . . . And besides, it's starting to rain! . . . Isn't it time to turn on the TV?*

clause, Spanish more frequently uses the prepositions **antes de, para,** and **sin** plus an infinitive, instead of the corresponding conjunctions plus the subjunctive. Compare the following:

PREPOSITION:	Estoy aquí **para** **aprender.**	*I'm here to (in order to)* *learn.*
CONJUNCTION:	Estoy aquí **para que** **Uds. aprendan.**	*I'm here so that you will* *learn.*
PREPOSITION:	Voy a comer **antes de** **salir.**	*I'm going to eat before* *leaving.*
CONJUNCTION:	Voy a comer **antes (de)** **que salgamos.**	*I'm going to eat before we* *leave.*

Práctica

A. Dé oraciones nuevas según las indicaciones.

1. —¿De veras es tan importante esa llamada (*call*) de Luis?
   —¡Claro que sí! No salgo esta tarde _____ me llame Luis.   (*sin que, a menos que, antes de que*)

2. —¿Por qué quieres que lleguemos al estadio tan temprano?
   —Pues, para que (nosotros) _____ . ¡Es un equipo buenísimo!   (*no perder el partido, poder comprar entradas, conseguir buenos asientos, ver el primer juego*)

B. Un fin de semana en las montañas. Hablan Manuel y su esposa Marta. Use la conjunción entre paréntesis para unir las dos oraciones. Haga todos los cambios necesarios.

1. Voy a aprender a esquiar. Tú me enseñas.   (con tal que)
2. Vamos a salir para la sierra esta tarde. Nieva mucho.   (a menos que)
3. No salgo a esquiar. Dejamos a los niños en casa.   (a menos que)
4. Yo también prefiero que vayamos solos. Pasamos un rato (*a little while*) sin ellos.   (para que)
5. Tu hermano Juan quiere acompañarnos, pero no quiere salir. Termina el partido de fútbol.   (antes de que)
6. No podemos esperar más. Dejemos un recado. (*Let's leave a message.*) (Juan) llama.   (en caso de que)
7. Es importante que lleguemos a la cabaña. Empieza a nevar.   (antes de que)
8. Compra leña (*firewood*) aquí. No hay leña en la cabaña.   (en caso de que)

C. Una tarde en el parque. ¿Cómo se dice en español?

1. We go there to have fun.
2. We also go there so that the kids can play baseball.

3. They're going to swim before eating (they eat).
4. Are they going to swim before *we* eat?
5. Don't go without talking to your mother.
6. And don't leave without your father giving you money.

CH. Cualquier acción humana puede justificarse. Explique Ud. las siguientes situaciones tan lógicamente como sea posible.

1. Cuando la familia es muy grande, los padres trabajan mucho para (que)...
2. Los profesores les dan tarea a los estudiantes para que...
3. Tenemos que pagar los impuestos federales para que...
4. Los dueños de los equipos profesionales pagan mucho a algunos jugadores para (que)...
5. Les compramos juguetes a los niños para que...
6. Se doblan las películas extranjeras para (que)...
7. Cambiamos de lugar los muebles de vez en cuando (*from time to time*) para (que)...
8. Los padres castigan (*punish*) a los niños para (que)...

D. Complete las oraciones en una forma lógica.

1. Voy a graduarme en ____ a menos que ____ .
2. Este verano voy a ____ a menos que ____ .
3. Voy a seguir viviendo en esta ciudad con tal que ____ .
4. Nunca estudio sin (que) ____ .
5. Siempre me baño antes de (que) ____ .
6. Siempre llevo impermeable cuando voy a un partido de fútbol norteamericano en caso de que ____ .

42 Más descripciones: Past Participle Used As an Adjective

Unos refranes y dichos en español

1. En boca *cerrada* no entran moscas.

2. *Aburrido* como una ostra.

3. Cuando está *abierto* el cajón, el más *honrado* es ladrón.

A few Spanish proverbs and sayings   *1. Into a closed mouth no flies enter.   2. As bored as an oyster.   3. When the drawer is open, the most honest person is (can become) a thief.*

1. *A veces, ¿es mejor no decir nada? ¿Qué le puede pasar a uno cuando tiene la boca abierta?*
2. *¿Llevan una vida muy interesante las ostras? ¿Sufren de muchas presiones?*
3. *¿Cometen todos los delitos (crimes) los criminales? ¿Es posible que una persona honrada llegue a ser un criminal?*

Forms of the Past Participle

hablar	comer	vivir
habl**ado** (*spoken*)	com**ido** (*eaten*)	viv**ido** (*lived*)

The past participle of most English verbs ends in *-ed*: for example, *to walk → walked; to close → closed.* However, many English past participles are irregular: *to sing → sung; to write → written.* In Spanish the *past participle* (**el participio pasado**) is formed by adding **-ado** to the stem of **-ar** verbs, and **-ido** to the stem of **-er** and **-ir** verbs. An accent mark is used on the past participle of **-er/-ir** verbs with stems ending in **-a, -e,** or **-o.**

caído   creído   leído   oído   (son)reído   traído

The following Spanish verbs have irregular past participles.

abrir:	**abierto**	escribir:	**escrito**	resolver:	**resuelto**
decir:	**dicho**	hacer:	**hecho**	romper:	**roto**
cubrir (*to cover*):	**cubierto**	morir:	**muerto**	ver:	**visto**
descubrir:	**descubierto**	poner:	**puesto**	volver:	**vuelto**

The Past Participle Used As an Adjective

In both English and Spanish, the past participle can be used as an adjective to modify a noun. Like other Spanish adjectives, the past participle must agree in number and gender with the noun modified.

Tengo una bolsa **hecha** en El Salvador.
I have a purse made in El Salvador.

El español es una de las lenguas **habladas** en los Estados Unidos.
Spanish is one of the languages spoken in the United States.

The past participle is frequently used with **estar** to describe conditions that are the result of a previous action.

La puerta **está abierta.**
The door is open.

Todos los lápices **estaban rotos.**
All the pencils were broken.

◼ **¡OJO!** *English past participles often have the same form as the past tense:*
I **closed** the book. The thief stood behind the **closed** door. *The Spanish
past participle is never identical in form or use to a past tense. Compare the
following:*

Cerré la puerta.	*I **closed** the door.*
Ahora la puerta está **cerrada**.	*Now the door is **closed**.*

Práctica

A. Identifique los objetos que se encuentran en la sala, según las
indicaciones. Use el participio pasado de los verbos.

MODELO   flores / mandar / Anita → Son flores mandadas por Anita.

1. el sillón / usar / papá
2. regalos / mandar / abuelos
3. revistas / leer / niños
4. un libro / recomendar / la vecina
5. una figurita / hacer / en Colombia
6. vasos / comprar / en el Brasil

B. Describa Ud. las condiciones en estas situaciones, siguiendo el
modelo.

MODELO   La nieve va a *cubrir* la tierra. →
         La tierra no está cubierta de nieve todavía.

1. Natalia tiene que *escribir* una carta.
2. Los Sres. García tienen que *abrir* la tienda.
3. David y Marta van a *casarse* (*to get married*) mañana.
4. Pablo tiene que *cerrar* la ventana.
5. Los turistas tienen que *facturar* el equipaje.
6. Delia tiene que *poner* la mesa.
7. Es posible que *descubran* el error.
8. Tenemos que *resolver* este problema.

C. Describa Ud. el siguiente dibujo, tratando de mencionar todos los
detalles que han ocasionado (*have caused*) la situación presentada.
Use participios pasados donde sea posible.

MODELO   Todo está preparado para la fiesta…

CH. Preguntas

1. ¿Tiene Ud. algo (ropa, perfume, un auto,…) hecho en Francia? ¿en un país latinoamericano? ¿en España? ¿en el Japón? ¿algo hecho a mano?
2. ¿Sabe Ud. el título de un libro escrito por un autor latinoamericano? ¿por un autor español?
3. En su casa o garaje, ¿hay algo roto? ¿algo sucio?
4. En su casa, ¿el televisor está puesto constantemente? ¿el estéreo? ¿la radio?
5. ¿El Nuevo Mundo ya estaba descubierto en 1700? ¿La penicilina ya estaba descubierta en 1960?

D. Dé Ud. el nombre de las cosas siguientes.

1. Algo contaminado
2. Una persona bien/mal organizada
3. Una persona cansada
4. Un edificio bien/mal construido
5. Un grupo/humano explotado
6. Algo que pueda estar cerrado o abierto
7. Un curso acelerado
8. Un servicio necesitado por muchas personas
9. Un tipo de transporte usado por muchas personas
10. Algo deseado por muchas personas
11. Un programa visto por muchas personas
12. Un problema resuelto por un árbitro

REPASO

El partido del campeonato (*championship*). Complete the following paragraphs with the correct form of the words in parentheses, as suggested by the context. When two possibilities are given in parentheses, select the correct word. Give the preterite or imperfect of all verb forms, except those marked with an asterisk, which require either the present or the past participle.

Cuando yo (*ser/estar*[1]) joven, (*practicar*[2]) (*mucho*[3]) deportes con mis amigos. En invierno, cuando la tierra (*ser/estar*[4]) (*cubrir**[5]) de nieve, nos (*gustar*[6]) ir a las montañas a esquiar; también (*nadar*[7]) en la piscina de la escuela secundaria. Durante el verano siempre (*nosotros: pasear*[8]) en bicicleta o (*jugar*[9]) al béisbol cuando (*hacer*[10]) buen tiempo. A veces (*ser/estar*[11]) posible ganar un poco de dinero (*ayudar**[12]) a los jugadores de golf en un club que (*ser/estar*[13]) cerca de mi casa. También (*ser/estar*[14]) populares los partidos de vólibol (*organizar**[15]) por los salvavidas° en la playa.

lifeguards

El incidente que recuerdo con más intensidad fue cuando nuestro equipo de básquetbol (*ganar*[16]) el campeonato de todo el estado. Aquel año yo (*tener*[17]) sólo dieciséis años. (*Ir*[18]) al gimnasio todas las tardes para practicar con mi equipo y casi todos los sábados (*nosotros: ir*[19]) a otras ciudades a jugar contra los equipos de otras escuelas. Por fin (*llegar*[20]) el día en el que° (*nosotros: ir*[21]) a la capital para el campeonato. Durante el último (*partido/ juego*[22]), yo (*realizar*°[23]) un par de jugadas° importantes y gracias a (*eso/esa*[24]) ¡(*ganar*[25]) nosotros el campeonato! Yo (*ser/estar*[26]) un héroe ese día. Cuando el gobernador del estado nos (*presentar*[27]) el trofeo, me (*lo/la*[28]) dio a mí. (*Todo*[29]) mis parientes (*ser/estar*[30]) en el auditorio y yo (*poder*[31]) oírlos gritar° mi nombre. ¡(*Ser/Estar*[32]) uno de los (*mejor*[33]) momentos (*de/en*[34]) mi vida!

el... which

to do, complete / plays

to shout

Una tarde de verano

—Hace mucho que no paseo en bicicleta.
—Pues, si quieres, puedes usar la de mi hermano.
—¿Qué te parece si vamos hasta el lago?
—¡Estupendo! ...y podemos llevar una merienda (*snack*).

Bogotá, Colombia

UN PASO MÁS: Lectura cultural

Las diversiones

En el mundo hispánico, las diversiones son tan variadas y numerosas como en los Estados Unidos. Las actividades pueden variar según la clase social y el lugar, pero hay aficiones que gozan de° gran aceptación popular en todos los rincones° del mundo hispánico: el cine, el baile, las visitas y los deportes.

gozan... enjoy
corners

Las visitas a los familiares ocupan una parte importante del tiempo libre. Los fines de semana sobre todo, los hijos ya casados, con sus hijos, visitan la casa de sus padres. Generalmente los hombres terminan hablando en una parte de la casa y las mujeres en otra, con los niños jugando en el patio. Otra actividad familiar muy popular es salir al campo para comer y a veces para jugar un poco al fútbol, al vólibol o al bádminton.

Entre los jóvenes, las actividades más populares son las fiestas y los bailes. Lo más común es reunirse con los amigos en la casa de alguien para hablar y bailar hasta muy tarde. A casi todo el mundo le gusta también ir al cine. A veces un grupo de jóvenes va al cine temprano, después va a la casa de alguien a cenar y con frecuencia termina organizando una fiesta allí. También van con frecuencia a los clubes <u>nocturnos</u> y las discotecas.

Las personas de las clases acomodadas° suelen ir° a un club deportivo donde practican el golf, el tenis, la natación e incluso el polo. También hay centros en los que se reúnen miembros de diferentes <u>colonias</u> de extranjeros (la alemana, la libanesa, la norteamericana, la italiana, etcétera). En estos centros hay de todo: billar, cartas, exhibiciones de arte, bailes y comidas formales y muchas otras diversiones.   *well-off* /suelen... tienden a ir

El ciclismo, el boxeo y el fútbol son los deportes más populares. Y en México, las islas del Caribe y Venezuela, el béisbol es una locura. Hay muchísimos jugadores latinoamericanos que juegan en las <u>ligas</u> mayores de béisbol en los Estados Unidos. Quizás en este momento el más famoso de éstos es Fernando Valenzuela, el famoso <u>lanzador</u> de los Dodgers de Los Ángeles.

En la América Latina y España, no se televisan los partidos y otras actividades deportivas con la misma frecuencia que en los Estados Unidos, pero hay excepciones: las Olimpíadas, los Juegos Panamericanos y los Juegos Bolivarianos—y sobre todo la Copa Mundial° de fútbol. La Copa Mundial es un <u>torneo</u> que se celebra cada cuatro años, y casi todos los países del mundo hispánico tienen equipos que participan en esta competición. Cuando juega el equipo nacional, todos tratan de estar delante del televisor y, si éste gana, siempre hay grandes fiestas y celebraciones por todo el país.   *World*

Comprensión

Según la lectura, las siguientes observaciones sobre el mundo hispánico *no* son válidas. Explique brevemente por qué.

1. Después de casarse, los hijos se olvidan de sus padres.
2. Durante las visitas familiares, los hombres y las mujeres se quedan en el comedor jugando a las cartas o conversando.
3. Los padres no les permiten a los hijos que salgan mucho de noche.
4. Muchas personas de las clases humildes pertenecen (*belong*) a clubes deportivos.
5. El béisbol es un deporte desconocido en Latinoamérica.
6. Es posible ver un espectáculo deportivo en la televisión todos los fines de semana.

Para escribir

Describa la última fiesta a la que Ud. fue. Su breve párrafo debe incluir los siguientes detalles.

1. si había allí muchas personas cuando Ud. llegó
2. lo que todos hicieron durante la fiesta
3. si Ud. se divirtió o no
4. a qué hora salió Ud. de la fiesta y si volvió a casa en seguida
5. si Ud. se levantó tarde o temprano al día siguiente
6. cómo se sentía al levantarse

VOCABULARIO

VERBOS

cubrir to cover
descubrir to discover
interesar (*like* **gustar**) to interest, be of interest
resolver (ue) to solve, resolve
volar (ue) to fly

LOS DEPORTES

el básquetbol basketball
el béisbol baseball
el ciclismo cycling
el fútbol soccer
el fútbol (norte)americano football
el golf golf
el hockey hockey

la natación swimming
pasear en bicicleta cycling
el tenis tennis
el vólibol volleyball

OTROS SUSTANTIVOS

la cancha (tennis) court
el equipo team
los esquís skis
el estadio stadium
el juego play (*in a game*); (card, board) game
el/la jugador(a) player
la nieve snow
el partido game, match
la pista (race)track
la raqueta racket
el rato short period of time
la red net
el tiempo time

ADJETIVO

deportista sports-minded

LAS CONJUNCIONES

a menos que unless
antes (de) que before
con tal que provided (that)
en caso de que in case
para que so that
sin que without

PALABRAS ADICIONALES

de vez en cuando from time to time
quizá perhaps

FRASES ÚTILES PARA LA COMUNICACIÓN	
es hora de + *inf.*	it's time to (*do something*)

UN POCO DE TODO 5*

A. ¿Qué haces para pasarlo bien? No todos nos divertimos de la misma manera. A veces el dinero y el tiempo imponen restricciones y otras veces es sencillamente una cuestión de gustos: lo que a alguna persona le gusta mucho tal vez no le guste a Ud.… y vice versa. ¿Qué cree Ud. que hacen para pasarlo bien las siguientes personas en un sábado típico? Use su imaginación pero entre los límites de lo que es posible en el mundo real de cada persona o grupo.

1. Una persona rica que vive en Nueva York
2. Un grupo de buenos amigos que trabajan todos en una fábrica (*factory*) en Michigan
3. Un matrimonio joven con poco dinero y dos niños pequeños
4. Un niño de ocho años que vive en el centro de una ciudad grande
5. Dos amigas de mediana edad (*middle-aged*) que viven en los suburbios de Los Ángeles
6. Un matrimonio viejo—él de ochenta años y ella de ochenta y dos—que vive en Texas

B. Entrevista. Use the following questions to interview another student about his or her childhood and about specific events in the past, as well as what is currently happening in his or her life. Report the most interesting information to the class.

1. ¿A qué escuela asistías (cuando tenías _____ años)? ¿Asististe a esta universidad el año pasado? ¿Cuánto tiempo hace que estudias aquí?
2. ¿Qué lenguas estudiabas? ¿Estudiaste latín en la secundaria? ¿Cuánto tiempo hace que estudias español?
3. ¿Qué hacías cuando te enfermabas? ¿Cuántas veces te resfriaste el año pasado? ¿Es necesario que empieces ahora a llevar una vida más sana?
4. ¿Qué películas te gustaban más? ¿Te gustó la última película que viste? ¿Qué nueva película quieres ver este mes?
5. En la secundaria, ¿qué era lo más importante de tu vida? ¿Qué cosa importante te pasó el año pasado? ¿Qué esperas que pase este año?
6. ¿Qué hacías durante los veranos? ¿Qué hiciste el verano pasado? ¿Qué vas a hacer este verano?
7. ¿Qué tipo de coche tenían tus padres cuando estabas en la escuela primaria? ¿Cuál fue el primer coche que compraron? ¿Qué coche es posible que tú compres en diez años?
8. ¿Sabías manejar una computadora cuando estabas en la primaria? ¿Cuándo aprendiste a manejar una computadora? ¿Es necesario que uses una computadora para escribir tus trabajos para la universidad?

C. ¿Qué se debe decir? What would you say to be especially courteous in each of the following situations? Use words and phrases from **A propósito…**

1. You need to return an article of clothing to a department store because it is the wrong size **(una talla equivocada).** You want the clerk to help you select the right size.
2. You know that you need to catch the number 17 bus to get to the **Museo de Arte,** but you don't know where to catch it. You ask a police officer on the street corner.

---

*This is the last regular review section in *¿Qué tal?* Beginning with **Capítulo 23,** there will be a review section (called **Repaso general**) incorporated into each chapter.

3. You have lost the key to your hotel room and need to tell the clerk **(el recepcionista).** You also need to get another key.
4. The waiter has just brought you a cup of coffee. You ordered tea.
5. Something is wrong with your car. You want the mechanic to fix it as quickly and as cheaply as possible.
6. You have gone to the doctor with a routine ailment. After he or she has examined you and you have received a prescription, you discover that you have left your money and checkbook **(libreta)** at home and cannot pay at this moment.

CH. **Situaciones sociales.** With another student act out the following role-play situations as fully as possible. Try to use as much of the vocabulary that you know as possible.

1. Your car is almost out of gas and needs some repair work. Ask a pedestrian where you can find a gas station and a repair shop.
2. You are the parent of a small child. Your child is playing outside when it begins to rain. Call the child in and help him or her find something else to do.
3. You meet a new neighbor who has just moved to your city. He or she is very interested in learning from you what activities are available and what activities you personally participate in.
4. You invite a friend to go to a movie with you. Discuss with him or her what film you want to see, where it's showing, how you will get there, how much tickets cost, etc.
5. You are a tour guide for prospective students at your college. One person on your tour is especially interested in the sports program. Discuss his or her interests and explain the campus sports options.

A propósito...

Más sobre la cortesía.   When you are searching for words to express the exact nature of a problem or situation, it is possible to sound abrupt or impolite, even though that is not your intention. The use of phrases such as **por favor, perdón,** and **con permiso** will show that you want to be polite, even when you may not be able to express yourself as precisely or as eloquently as a native speaker of Spanish.

Other phrases that will help you to communicate respect and politeness include the following.

Quisiera hablar con el Sr. Jiménez.	*I would like to talk to Mr. Jiménez.*
Me gustaría comprar una blusa azul.	*I would like to buy a blue blouse.*
Me trae otro café, **si fuera tan amable.**	*Bring me another cup of coffee, if you would be so kind.*
Es Ud. muy amable.	*You are very kind.*
Mil gracias. Ud. me ha ayudado muchísimo.	*Thanks a million (a thousand thanks). You have helped me a lot.*
Ha sido un placer hablar con Ud.	*It has been a pleasure to talk with you.*

Both **quisiera** and **me gustaría** (*I would like*) are more polite than **quiero** (*I want*). This usage parallels that of English.

CAPÍTULO 21

¿Dónde prefieres vivir?

VOCABULARIO: PREPARACIÓN

el campesino / la campesina

trabajar en la finca

el caballo

montar a caballo

el gallo

madrugar

el ranchero

la vaca

la gallina

LA CIUDAD Y EL CAMPO / THE CITY AND THE COUNTRY

bello/a beautiful
denso/a dense
puro/a pure

encantar to enchant
me encanta(n) I like very
  much
madrugar to get up early
recorrer to pass through;
  to cover (*territory, miles, etc.*)

el árbol tree
la autopista freeway
el delito crime
la escasez shortage, lack
la naturaleza nature
el pájaro bird
la población population

el rascacielos skyscraper
**el ritmo (acelerado) de la
  vida** (fast) pace of
  life, living
los servicios públicos
  public services
la soledad solitude
el transporte (means of)
  transportation
la vivienda housing

De vacaciones

—El mes que viene vamos al campo.

—¿Cuánto tiempo piensan pasar allí?

—Una semana y media. Vamos a montar a caballo todos los días.

—Eso es lo que más les gusta a los niños, ¿verdad?

—Sí. Les encantan los animales.

—Pues, ¡que se diviertan todos!

Mathias T. Oppersdorff/Photo Researchers, Inc.

Entre Salamanca y Ávila, España

A. De las siguientes oraciones, ¿cuáles corresponden al campo? ¿a la ciudad?

1. El aire es más puro y hay menos contaminación.
2. La naturaleza es más bella.
3. El ritmo de la vida es más acelerado.
4. Hay menos autopistas y menos tráfico.
5. Los delitos son más frecuentes.
6. Los servicios financieros y legales son más asequibles (*available*).
7. Hay pocos transportes públicos.
8. La población es menos densa.
9. Hay escasez de viviendas.
10. Hay más árboles y pájaros.
11. Casi nunca se oye el canto (*song*) de un gallo.
12. Mucha gente madruga para dar de comer a las gallinas y otros animales.

B. Definiciones. Dé Ud. una definición de estas palabras.

MODELO   ranchero → Es el dueño de una finca (un rancho).

1. autopista   3. delito   5. naturaleza   7. rascacielos
2. campesino   4. finca   6. población   8. pájaro

El medio ambiente°			medio... *environment*
la energía	energy	**conservar**	to save, conserve
el parque	park	**construir***	to build
los recursos naturales	natural resources	**contaminar**	to pollute
		desarrollar	to develop
acabar	to run out of; to	**destruir***	to destroy
	use up completely	**proteger (protejo)**	to protect

*Note the present indicative conjugation of **construir: construyo, construyes, construye, construímos, construís, construyen.** **Destruir** is conjugated like **construir.**

A. ¿Está Ud. de acuerdo con las ideas siguientes? Explique sus opiniones.

1. Para conservar energía debemos bajar la calefacción en invierno y usar menos el aire acondicionado en verano.
2. Es mejor calentar la casa con una estufa de leña (*woodstove*) que con gas o electricidad.
3. Debemos proteger nuestras «zonas verdes» y abrir más parques públicos para las futuras generaciones.
4. Es más importante explotar los recursos naturales que proteger el medio ambiente.
5. Para gastar menos gasolina, debemos tomar el autobús, caminar más y formar *car pools*.
6. No debemos importar petróleo de otros países a menos que se acaben nuestras propias (*own*) reservas.
7. El gobierno debe poner multas (*fines*) muy fuertes a las compañías y a los individuos que contaminen el aire.

B. Situaciones. Pancho cree que la vida del campo es ideal. Para él, vivir en la ciudad no ofrece ni una sola ventaja. Gabriela, la amiga de Pancho, es una mujer muy cosmopolita. Le encanta la ciudad y no puede decir nada bueno de la vida del campo. ¿Quién dijo las siguientes oraciones? ¿Qué ventaja o desventaja puede citar la otra persona en cada caso?

1. No hay buenos servicios públicos.
2. Hay más actividades culturales—teatro, conciertos y museos.
3. Aquí es posible vivir en paz y en tranquilidad.
4. No me gusta levantarme temprano; allí hay que madrugar para terminar el trabajo.
5. Me encanta recorrer las autopistas de la ciudad por la noche.
6. Necesito vivir en contacto con la naturaleza.
7. Cuando la nieve cubre las calles, las ciudades están paralizadas.

Ahora adopte el punto de vista de Pancho o de Gabriela. ¿Qué va Ud. a decir sobre los siguientes temas?

8. el ritmo de la vida
9. la explotación de la tierra
10. la gente/los vecinos
11. el gobierno

C. Complete estas oraciones de una forma lógica, adoptando el punto de vista de la persona que diría (*would say*) cada una.

1. «Estamos cansados de vivir en Nueva York. Buscamos un lugar (en) que _____ .»
2. «Estamos aburridos del campo. Queremos mudarnos (*to move*) a un lugar que _____ .»

MINIDIÁLOGOS Y ESTRUCTURA

43 ¿Qué has hecho? Perfect Forms: Present Perfect Indicative and Present Perfect Subjunctive

Una cuestión de perspectiva

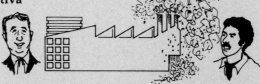

El dueño de la fábrica

No creo que *hayan construido* una fábrica mejor en todo el mundo.
Es posible que nuestra explotación de la zona *haya hecho* algún daño... pero no creo que *haya sido* irrevocable.

El defensor del medio ambiente

Han construido una fábrica que contamina no sólo el aire sino también el agua de la zona. El daño que *han hecho* al medio ambiente no puede repararse. La actitud de algunos industriales *ha sido* irresponsable.

¿Quién cree...
1. *que la fábrica es una maravilla de la tecnología moderna?*
2. *que la fábrica destruye el medio ambiente?*
3. *que la protección del medio ambiente es más importante que el progreso industrial?*
4. *que importa poco el medio ambiente en comparación con el desarrollo económico?*
5. *que los recursos naturales son inagotables (endless)?*
6. *que hay que conservar los recursos naturales, no explotarlos?*

Present Perfect Indicative

he hablado	*I have spoken*	**hemos** hablado	*we have spoken*
has hablado	*you have spoken*	**habéis** hablado	*you (pl.) have spoken*
ha hablado	*you have spoken, he/she has spoken*	**han** hablado	*you (pl.) have spoken, they have spoken*

A question of perspective THE FACTORY OWNER *I don't think they've built a better factory anywhere in the world. It's possible that our development of the area has done some damage . . . but I don't think it's anything irreversible.* THE ENVIRONMENTALIST *They've built a factory that not only pollutes the air but the water in the area as well. The damage they've done to the environment can't be reversed. The attitude of some industrialists has been irresponsible.*

In English, the present perfect is a compound tense consisting of a present-tense form of the verb *to have* plus the past participle: *I have written, you have spoken,* and so on.

In the Spanish *present perfect* (**el presente perfecto**) the past participle is used with present-tense forms of **haber,** the equivalent of English *to have* in this construction. **Haber,** an auxiliary verb, is not interchangeable with **tener.**

In general, the use of the Spanish present perfect parallels that of the English present perfect.

No **hemos estado** aquí antes.	*We haven't been here before.*
Me he divertido mucho.	*I've had a very good time.*
Ya **le han escrito** la carta.	*They've already written her the letter.*

The form of the past participle never changes with **haber,** regardless of the gender or number of the subject. The past participle always appears immediately after the appropriate form of **haber** and is never separated from it. Object pronouns and **no** are always placed directly before the form of **haber.**

The present perfect of **hay** is **ha habido** (*there has/have been*).

■ **¡OJO!** *Remember that* **acabar** + **de** + infinitive—*not the present perfect tense—is used to state that something* has just *occurred.*

Acabo de mandar la carta.	*I've just mailed the letter.*

[Práctica A–C]

Present Perfect Subjunctive

haya hablado	**hayamos** hablado
hayas hablado	**hayáis** hablado
haya hablado	**hayan** hablado

The *present perfect subjunctive* (**el perfecto del subjuntivo**) is formed with the present subjunctive of **haber** plus the past participle. It is used to express *I have spoken* (*written,* and so on) when the subjunctive is required. Although its most frequent equivalent is *I have + past participle,* its exact equivalent in English depends on the context in which it occurs.

Es posible que lo **haya hecho.**	*It's possible (that) he may have done (he did) it.*
Me alegro de que **hayas venido.**	*I'm glad (that) you have come (you came).*
Es bueno que lo **hayan construido.**	*It's good that they built (have built) it.*

Note that the English equivalent of the present perfect subjunctive can
be expressed as a simple or as a compound tense: *did/have done;
came/have come; built/have built.*

[Práctica CH–E]

Práctica

A. Ud. y su amigo/a visitan un rancho. Es el segundo día de su visita.
¿Qué han hecho Uds.? Dé oraciones basadas en las siguientes
palabras.

1. recorrer la finca entera **2.** ver las vacas y los toros **3.** montar a
caballo **4.** hablar con los campesinos **5.** respirar el aire puro
6. ver los efectos del desarrollo industrial

B. Entrevista. Con otro/a estudiante, haga y conteste preguntas con
estos verbos. La persona que contesta debe decir la verdad.

MODELO   visitar México →
—¿Has visitado México?
—Sí, he visitado México una vez. (No, no he visitado
México nunca. Sí, he visitado México durante las últimas
vacaciones.)

1. comer en un restaurante hispánico   **7.** actuar en una comedia
2. estar en Nueva York   **8.** ver un monumento
3. manejar un Alfa-Romeo   histórico
4. correr en un maratón   **9.** conocer a una persona
5. abrir hoy tu libro de   famosa
español   **10.** romperte la pierna alguna
6. escribir un poema   vez

C. Situaciones. Margarita lo/la llama a Ud. por teléfono. Quiere saber lo
que Ud. está haciendo. Con otro/a estudiante, haga y conteste
preguntas, según el modelo.

MODELO   cenar → MARGARITA: Estás cenando, ¿no?
UD.: No, ya he cenado.

1. cocinar   **4.** leer el periódico
2. descansar   **5.** poner la mesa
3. lavar los platos

Ahora Margarita tiene unos recados (*messages*) de Jorge. **¡OJO!** *Use
el presente del subjuntivo para lo que dice Margarita.*

MODELO   llamarlo → MARGARITA: Jorge dice que lo llames.
UD.: Pero ya lo he llamado.

6. mandarle una invitación a Pablo
7. hablar con Concepción
8. ir a su casa
9. ver (película)
10. escribir la composición esta tarde

CH. Imagine que se descubrió el año pasado un caso de contaminación ambiental en su ciudad. ¿Qué ha dicho la gente sobre el caso? Haga oraciones completas según las indicaciones. Use **Uds.** como sujeto y el perfecto del subjuntivo en la cláusula dependiente.

1. es probable: ya estudiar el problema
2. no creo: descubrir la solución todavía
3. es posible: ya consultar con unos expertos
4. es dudoso: ya arreglar la situación
5. espero: ya reconocer la necesidad de evitar (*to avoid*) situaciones parecidas en el futuro

D. Indique algo inolvidable (*unforgettable*) que Ud. ha hecho en el pasado, usando los siguientes verbos.

MODELO   oír → He oído un concierto de Bruce Springsteen.

1. ver   3. romper   5. leer
2. comer   4. hacer un viaje 6. olvidar

E. Con otro/a estudiante, reaccione a las siguientes oraciones. La persona que reaccione debe empezar con frases como **Lo siento, (nombre), pero dudo que...** ; **No, es imposible que...** ; **Estoy seguro/a que...** ; **Es obvio que...** ; etcétera.

MODELO   —Anoche hice un viaje a la luna.
           —Lo siento, Harry, pero dudo que hayas hecho un viaje a la luna.

1. Escribí una novela este fin de semana.
2. Leí *Lo que el viento se llevó* (*Gone with the Wind*) en veinte minutos.
3. Anoche salí con Robert Redford/Kate Jackson/Billy Dee Williams/Madonna.
4. Vi un OVNI (objeto volador no identificado) esta mañana.
5. Tom Selleck/Jessica Lange me mandó una carta de amor.
6. Hice algo estúpido en una ocasión.
7. En mi otra vida fui rey/reina de Inglaterra.
8. Anoche tomé ocho botellas de cerveza y una de vino.

44 ¿Nunca habías hecho esto?
Past Perfect Indicative

Cambio de ritmo

RAFAEL: Antes de mudarme al campo, yo siempre *había usado* el carro para todo. Nunca *había tenido* tiempo de apreciar la naturaleza. Y nunca *había madrugado* tanto.

LINDA: Pues, antes de mudarme a la ciudad, yo siempre *había vivido* en una finca. Nunca *había visto* tantas autopistas. Y nunca *había visitado* museos.

RAFAEL: La ciudad tiene muchas ventajas.... Pero yo me siento más a gusto ahora.

LINDA: ¡Y yo estoy más a gusto en la ciudad! Como dicen, ¡no hay nada escrito sobre gustos!

1. *¿Quién no había vivido antes en la ciudad?*
2. *¿Quién no había apreciado las flores y las montañas?*
3. *¿Quién había tenido acceso a manifestaciones culturales?*
4. *¿Quién no se había levantado temprano con frecuencia?*
5. *¿Quién no había visto tantas autopistas en un solo lugar?*
6. *¿Quién había manejado mucho?*
7. *¿Dónde se siente más a gusto Linda? ¿y Rafael?*

Forms of the Past Perfect Indicative			
había hablado	*I had spoken*	**habíamos** hablado	*we had spoken*
habías hablado	*you had spoken*	**habíais** hablado	*you (pl.) had spoken*
había hablado	*you had spoken, he/she had spoken*	**habían** hablado	*you (pl.) had spoken, they had spoken*

The English past perfect consists of the past tense of *to have* plus the past participle: *I had written, you had written,* and so on.

In Spanish the *past perfect* (**el pluscuamperfecto**) is formed with the imperfect of **haber** plus the past participle.

Change of pace   RAFAEL: *Before I moved to the country, I had always used the car for everything. I had never had time to appreciate nature. And I had never gotten up early so often.*   LINDA: *Well, before I moved to the city, I had always lived on a farm. I had never seen so many freeways. And I had never visited museums.*   RAFAEL: *The city has a lot of advantages. . . . But I'm more comfortable now.*   LINDA: *And I'm more at home in the city! As they say, there's no accounting for tastes!*

Ya **había cenado** cuando llegó Juan.	*I had already eaten dinner when Juan arrived.*
Habíamos visto aquella película antes de 1980.	*We had seen that movie before 1980.*

The past perfect tense is used to emphasize the fact that an action (**había cenado, Habíamos visto**) took place before another action, event, or moment in the past (**llegó Juan, 1980**).

Práctica

A. Jaimito es un niño acusón (*tattletale*). Siempre le dice a su madre las cosas que ha hecho—y que *no* ha hecho—Laura, su hermana mayor. ¿Qué le dijo a su madre ayer? Dé oraciones nuevas según las indicaciones.

—Jaimito le dijo que Laura *había dicho una mentira (lie)*. (*mirar la televisión toda la tarde, no estudiar, perder sus libros, romper un plato, faltar [miss] a clase, comer todo el pastel, pegarle, ___?___*)

B. ¿Qué cosas habían hecho—o *no* habían hecho—Uds. antes de 1985? Dé oraciones nuevas según las indicaciones.

1. Antes de 1985 (no) habíamos... (*estudiar español, asistir a esta universidad, graduarnos en la escuela superior, escuchar un concierto, ver una comedia española, comer flan, ___?___*)

¿Qué cosas no habían hecho... y no han hecho todavía?

2. No habíamos... ¡Y no lo hemos hecho todavía! (*visitar la Patagonia, viajar a Moscú, aprender ruso, conocer a Julio Iglesias, ___?___*)

C. Situaciones. Con otro/a estudiante, haga y conteste   según el modelo.

MODELO   leer la lección para hoy →
      —Ayer, cuando llamaste, no pude hablar contigo. Lo siento.
      —Estabas *leyendo la lección para hoy*, ¿no?
      —No, ya *la* había *leído*. Estaba *durmiendo*.

1. escuchar el noticiero (*newscast*)
2. bañarse
3. preparar la cena
4. hacer las maletas
5. mirar (programa de televisión)

CH. Describa Ud. su juventud (*youth*). Antes de cumplir dieciocho años, ¿qué había hecho? ¿Qué no había hecho?

D. Complete las oraciones en una forma lógica.

1. Antes de 1492 Cristóbal Colón no _____ .
2. Antes de 1938 la Segunda Guerra Mundial no _____ .
3. Antes de 1500 Shakespeare no _____ .
4. Antes de 1950 mis padres (no) _____ .
5. Antes de 1975 yo (no) _____ .

Ventajas y desventajas

—¿Prefieres vivir en el campo o en la ciudad?

—Me encantan las ciudades... el bullicio
(*hubbub*), la animación...

—También tienen sus inconvenientes, ¿no?

—¡Por supuesto! Por eso... vivo en el campo.

Cuzco, Perú

Stuart Cohen

REPASO

Cambio de ritmo. Complete the following paragraphs with the correct form of the words in parentheses, as suggested by the context. When two possibilities are given in parentheses, select the correct word.

Ayer yo pasé un rato recorriendo mi nueva finca. Toda la vida he (*admirar*[1]) la naturaleza, pero creo que fue (*la primera vez/el primer tiempo*[2]) que (*ver*[3]) (*tan/tanto*[4]) belleza° en (*tan/tanto*[5]) poco tiempo. En el lago había unos patitos° y dos patos (*les/los*[6]) estaban (*enseñar*[7]) a nadar. La buganvilla, que (*haber florecer*[8]) la semana pasada, estaba (*cubrir*[9]) de flores de colores (*brillante*[10]). (*Oír: yo*[11]) el canto° de un pájaro y (*ver: yo*[12]) que uno (*haber construir*[13]) su nido° en el árbol cerca del lago.

  (*Pasar: yo*[14]) todo el día a caballo hasta (*la hora/el tiempo*[15]) de cenar y luego, después de (*comer*[16]), (*descansar*[17]) (*un rato/una vez*[18]) bajo los árboles. Antes de (*mudarnos*[19]) al campo, (*haber hablar: nosotros*[20]) de las ventajas del aire puro y del ritmo lento de la vida, pero no (*haber pensar*[21]) en la tranquilidad y la belleza de las cosas (*cotidiano*°[22]). Ahora (*ser/estar: nosotros*[23]) (*tan/tanto*[24]) contentos que no es posible que nuestra decisión (*haber ser*[25]) un error.

beauty
ducklings

song

nest

daily

UN PASO MÁS: Imágenes del mundo hispánico

México: La época moderna

Víctor Englebert/Photo Researchers, Inc.

La Plaza de las Tres Culturas: La indígena, la colonial y la moderna

*S*e puede decir que el México moderno nace con la Revolución Mexicana, movimiento que se convirtió en una sangrienta (*bloody*) guerra civil durante 1910–1920. Esta revolución permitió la creación de una constitución más radical que ninguna de su tiempo.

En la actualidad, y a pesar de las dificultades económicas por las que atraviesa (*she is passing*), México es un país abierto al futuro, preocupado por mantener sus tradiciones y superar (*overcome*) los problemas socioeconómicos que se le plantean (*that she is faced with*). Uno de ellos es el urbano. En la capital, el llamado «D.F.» (México, Distrito Federal), cuenta con casi el 25% del total de la población del país; es una de las ciudades más grandes del mundo.

Aunque en algunos lugares de la ciudad la vida sea caótica, se trata de una capital llena de actividad, de parques maravillosos, grandes avenidas y zonas residenciales. Sus museos, galerías de arte y, por supuesto, sus universidades, son reconocidos y respetados en todo el mundo.

Debido en parte a su proximidad con los Estados Unidos, México recibe cientos de turistas—no sólo norteamericanos—deseosos de disfrutar de sus paisajes (*scenery*), sus playas, su clima, su comida y la hospitalidad de su población. ¿Quién no ha oído hablar de las playas de Acapulco y Cancún, de las ciudades coloniales de Taxco, Guanajuato y Mérida o de las monumentales ruinas de Tenochtitlán, Uxmal y Chichén Itzá?

«Zona Rosa», uno de los barrios más elegantes de México, D. F.

VOCABULARIO

VERBOS

acabar to use up completely
conservar to save, conserve
construir (*irreg.*) to build
contaminar to pollute
desarrollar to develop
destruir (*like* **construir**) to destroy
encantar (*like* **gustar**) to enchant
madrugar to get up early
montar a caballo to ride (a horse)
mudarse to move (*change residence*)
proteger (protejo) to protect
recorrer to pass through, cover
  (*territory, miles, etc.*)

LOS ANIMALES

el caballo horse
la gallina chicken
el gallo rooster
el pájaro bird
la vaca cow

EL CAMPO Y LA CIUDAD

la autopista freeway
el/la campesino/a peasant,
  country person
el delito crime
la fábrica factory
la finca farm
el/la ranchero/a rancher
el rascacielos skyscraper
el ritmo (acelerado) de la vida
  (fast) pace of life, living
los servicios públicos public
  services
la soledad solitude

el transporte (means of)
  transportation
la vivienda housing

EL MEDIO AMBIENTE

el árbol tree
la energía energy
la escasez shortage, lack
la naturaleza nature
la población population
los recursos naturales natural
  resources

ADJETIVOS

bello/a beautiful
denso/a dense
puro/a pure

FRASES ÚTILES PARA LA COMUNICACIÓN

(Necesito) Un cambio de ritmo.   (I need) A change of pace.
Estoy (Me siento) a gusto.   I am (I feel) at home, comfortable.

CAPÍTULO 22

El dinero

CUENTAS CORRIENTES

la cajera

cobrar un cheque

CUENTAS DE AHORROS

el cajero

EN EL BANCO

UNA CUESTIÓN DE DINERO / A MONEY MATTER

el alquiler rent
la cuenta corriente checking account
la cuenta de ahorros savings account
la cuenta/factura bill, invoice
los gastos expenses
el préstamo loan
el presupuesto budget
la tarjeta de crédito credit card

ahorrar to save (*money*)
aumentar to increase
cargar (a la cuenta de uno) to charge (to one's account)
cobrar to cash (*a check*); to charge (*someone for an item or service*)
devolver (ue) to return (*something*)

economizar to economize
gastar to spend (*money*)
pagar al contado/con cheque/a plazos to pay cash/by check/in installments
prestar to lend
quejarse (de) to complain (about)

Entre amigos

—Oye, ¿me puedes prestar cien dólares?

—¡Hombre! Bueno... si me los devuelves lo antes posible.

—Cómo no. Pasado mañana a más tardar (*at the latest*).

—¿Para qué necesitas tanto dinero?

—Hay unas cuentas atrasadas (*late*) que quisiera (*I would really like*) pagar.

España

A. ¿Quiénes son estas personas? ¿Dónde están? ¿Qué van a comprar? ¿Cómo van a pagar?

 1.  2.  3.

B. Definiciones. Dé Ud. una definición de estas palabras en español.

1. el presupuesto   3. el préstamo   5. el alquiler
2. economizar   4. la factura   6. pagar a plazos

Ahora explique la diferencia entre una cuenta corriente y una cuenta de ahorros.

C. Indique una respuesta para cada pregunta o situación. Luego invente un contexto para cada diálogo. ¿Dónde están las personas que hablan? ¿en un banco? ¿en una tienda? ¿Quiénes son? ¿clientes? ¿cajeros? ¿dependientes?

1. ¿Cómo prefiere Ud. pagar?
2. ¿Hay algún problema?
3. Me da su pasaporte, por favor. Necesito verlo para poder cobrar su cheque.
4. ¿Quisiera (*Would you like*) usar su tarjeta de crédito?
5. ¿Va a depositar este cheque en su cuenta corriente o en su cuenta de ahorros?
6. ¿Adónde quiere Ud. que mandemos la factura?
7. ¿Puedes prestarme tu blusa de seda amarilla?

a. En la cuenta de ahorros, por favor.
b. Me la manda a la oficina, por favor.
c. Sí, pero devuélvemela pronto, ¿eh?
ch. No, prefiero pagar al contado.
d. Sí, señorita, Ud. me cobró demasiado por el jarabe.
e. Aquí lo tiene Ud.
f. Cárguelo a mi cuenta, por favor.

MINIDIÁLOGOS Y ESTRUCTURA

45 Talking about the Future and Expressing Conjecture
Future Verb Forms

¡Hay que reducir los gastos! ¿Qué vamos a hacer?

MADRE: *Tomaré* el autobús en vez de usar el carro.
ANDRÉS: *Comeremos* más ensalada y menos carne y pasteles.
PADRE: Los niños no *irán* al cine con tanta frecuencia.
JULIETA: Yo *dejaré* de fumar.
MADRE: Los niños *gastarán* menos en dulces.
PADRE: Y yo no *cargaré* nada a nuestras cuentas. Lo *pagaré* todo al contado.
JULIETA: *Bajaremos* la calefacción.
GABRIELA: Y yo me *iré* a vivir con los abuelos. Allí *habrá* de todo como siempre, ¿verdad?

1. *¿Quién dejará de usar el carro? ¿de fumar?*
2. *¿Qué comerá la familia? ¿Qué no comerá?*
3. *¿Cómo gastará menos dinero el padre? ¿y los niños?*
4. *¿Adónde irá a vivir Gabriela? ¿Por qué?*

hablar		comer		vivir	
hablar**é**	hablar**emos**	comer**é**	comer**emos**	vivir**é**	vivir**emos**
hablar**ás**	hablar**éis**	comer**ás**	comer**éis**	vivir**ás**	vivir**éis**
hablar**á**	hablar**án**	comer**á**	comer**án**	vivir**á**	vivir**án**

Talking About the Future

Future actions or states of being can be expressed with the
ir + **a** + *infinitive* construction (Grammar Section 10) or with the future.
In English the future is formed with the auxiliary verbs *will* or *shall*: *I
will/shall speak*. The *future* (**el futuro**) of most Spanish verbs is formed by
adding the future endings to the infinitive: **-é, -ás, -á, -emos, -éis, -án.**
No auxiliary verbs are needed.

It's necessary to cut down on expenses! What are we going to do? MOTHER: *I'll take the bus instead of using the car.* ANDRÉS: *We'll
eat more salad and less meat and cake.* FATHER: *The kids won't go to the movies so much.* JULIETA: *I'll stop smoking.* MOTHER: *The kids will
spend less on candy.* FATHER: *I won't charge anything. I'll pay for everything in cash.* JULIETA: *We'll turn down the heat.* GABRIELA: *And
I'll go to live with our grandparents. There they'll have (there will be) everything as usual, right?*

The following verbs add the future endings to irregular stems.

decir: **dir-**
hacer: **har-**
poder: **podr-**   **-é**
poner: **pondr-**   **-ás**
querer: **querr-**   **-á**
saber: **sabr-**   **-emos**
salir: **saldr-**   **-éis**
tener: **tendr-**   **-án**
venir: **vendr-**

decir	
diré	diremos
dirás	diréis
dirá	dirán

The future of **hay** is **habrá** (*there will be*).*

■ **¡OJO!** *Remember that indicative and subjunctive present-tense forms can be used to express the immediate future. Compare the following:*

Llegaré a tiempo.   *I'll arrive on time.*
Llego a las ocho mañana. ¿Vienes   *I arrive at 8:00 tomorrow. Will*
  a buscarme?   *you pick me up?*
No creo que Pepe **llegue** a   *I don't think Pepe will arrive on*
  tiempo.   *time.*

■ **¡OJO!** *When English* will *refers not to future time but to the willingness of someone to do something, Spanish uses a form of the verb* **querer,** *not the future.*

¿Quieres cerrar la puerta, por   *Will you please close the door?*
  favor?
¿Quisieras† cerrar la puerta?   *Would you close the door?*

[Práctica A–C]

Expressing Conjecture

¿Dónde **estará** Cecilia?
I wonder where Cecilia is.
(Where can Cecilia be?)

Estará en la carretera.
She is probably (must be) on
  the highway. (I bet she's on
  the highway.)

---

*The *future perfect tense* (**el futuro perfecto**) is formed with the future of the auxiliary verb **haber (habré, habrás, habrá, habremos, habréis, habrán)** plus the past participle. It is used to express what will have occurred at some point in the future.

Para mañana, ya **habré hablado** con Miguel.   *By tomorrow, I will already have talked with Miguel.*

†The forms **quisiera(s)** are the first, second, and third persons singular of the imperfect subjunctive of **querer.** You will learn more about the imperfect subjunctive and its uses in Grammar Section 47. For now, learn to use **quisiera(s)** to be especially polite when making a request.

The future may indicate future actions or express probability or conjecture in the present. This construction is called the *future of probability* (**el futuro de probabilidad**). English *probably*, *I guess*, *I bet*, and *I wonder* are not directly expressed in Spanish; their sense is contained in the future form of the verb used.

[Práctica CH–D]

Práctica

A. ¿Qué pasará durante el viaje a Guatemala? Haga oraciones según las indicaciones.

1. yo: hablar sólo español, leer periódicos en español
2. tú: levantarse temprano todos los días, comer arroz y frijoles
3. nosotros: cambiar mucho dinero, escribir muchas tarjetas postales
4. Uds.: no usar las tarjetas de crédito, querer pagarlo todo al contado
5. Gustavo: tratar de seguir un presupuesto rígido, prometer no gastar todo su dinero
6. vosotros: comprar recuerdos en el mercado indio, divertirse mucho

B. Son las tres de la tarde, un viernes, y todos han recibido el cheque semanal (*weekly*). Claro que todos tratarán de cobrar el cheque antes de que se cierren los bancos, pero... ¿qué harán después? Conteste según las indicaciones.

Algunos comprarán algo. Otros _____. (*pagar las cuentas, volver a hacer un presupuesto, depositar un poco en la cuenta de ahorros, quejarse porque nunca tienen suficiente, decir que ya no usarán las tarjetas de crédito, __?__*)

C. Ud. es astrólogo/a y puede predecir (*predict*) el futuro. ¿Qué predicciones puede Ud. formar usando una palabra o frase—en su forma correcta—de cada columna? Use el futuro de los verbos.

yo	conseguir	pagar todas las cuentas algún día
el/la profesor(a)	querer	casarse (*to get married*),
mi amigo/a (no)	tener	mudarse a _____, retirarse
(nombre)	poder	un aumento de sueldo por fin
mis padres	ser	en un país hispano, en _____
__?__	vivir	casado/a, soltero/a, rico/a,
		famoso/a
		ahorrar dinero para comprar_____
		muchos/pocos/ningún hijo(s)
		médico/a, abogado/a, _____
		__?__

CH. Los nuevos vecinos. ¿Cómo se dice en español? Use el futuro de probabilidad.

1. He's probably a teacher, and she must be a doctor.
2. I wonder where she works.
3. I wonder which one earns more money.
4. They're probably from a big city.
5. They probably have a lot of kids.
6. They must be asking questions about **(acerca de)** us, too!

D. Para conseguir más dinero. What can you do to get extra cash or to save money? Some possibilities are shown in the drawings. What are the advantages and disadvantages of each plan?

MODELO   dejar de tomar cafe →
Si dejo de tomar café estaré menos nervioso/a, pero será más difícil despertarme por la mañana. ¡Pero realmente quisiera dejar de tomar café!

1. pedirles dinero a mis amigos
2. cometer un robo
3. alquilar un cuarto de mi casa a otras personas
4. dejar de fumar
5. buscar un trabajo de tiempo parcial
6. ___?___

¿Recuerda Ud.?

Review the forms and uses of possessive adjectives (Grammar Section 11) before beginning Grammar Section 46.

SINGULAR:	mi	tu	su	nuestro/a	vuestro/a	su
PLURAL:	mis	tus	sus	nuestros/as	vuestros/as	sus

Son **mis** libros.   *They're my books.*
Es **su** gobierno.   *It's his (her, your, their) government.*
Son **nuestras** casas.   *They're our houses.*

¿Cómo se dice en español?

1. It's their checking account.
2. What about (¿Y...) my loan?
3. These are your bills.
4. Their teller hasn't helped them.
5. Your expenses are too high!
6. Our house is beautiful.
7. The peasants will lose their farms soon.
8. They are our natural resources, too!

46 ¿Es mío o es tuyo?
Stressed Possessive Adjectives and Possessive Pronouns

En el banco

EL DR. MÉNDEZ: Perdone, señora, pero esta libreta que Ud. me ha dado no es *mía.*

LA CAJERA: ¿No es *suya?* ¿No es Ud. el doctor Méndez?

EL DR. MÉNDEZ: Sí, soy yo, pero esta libreta no es *mía.* Ud. todavía tiene *la mía.* Está allí a la derecha.

LA CAJERA: Ah, me equivoqué. Ésta es de los señores Palma. Aquí tengo la de Ud. ¡Cuánto lo siento!

1. *¿Qué ha hecho la cajera, según el Dr. Méndez?*

2. *¿Quién tiene la libreta del doctor?*

3. *¿De quiénes es la libreta que la cajera le ha dado?*

4. *¿Cuál ha sido la equivocación de la cajera?*

Stressed Possessive Adjectives

Forms of the Stressed Possessive Adjectives			
mío/a/os/as	*my, (of) mine*	**nuestro/a/os/as**	*our, (of) ours*
tuyo/a/os/as	*your, (of) yours*	**vuestro/a/os/as**	*your, (of) yours*
suyo/a/os/as	*your, (of) yours; his, (of) his; her, (of) hers; its*	**suyo/a/os/as**	*your, (of) yours; their, (of) theirs*

Stressed forms (**las formas tónicas**) of the possessive are, as the term implies, more emphatic than the *unstressed forms* (**las formas átonas**), discussed in Grammar Section 11. The stressed forms are used when in English you would emphasize the possessive with your voice, or when you want to express English *of mine* (*of yours, of his,* and so on).

Es **mi** amigo.	*He's my friend.*
Es **un** amigo **mío.**	{ *He's **my** friend.* / *He's a friend of mine.* }
Es **su** perro.	*It's her dog.*
Es **un** perro **suyo.**	{ *It's **her** dog.* / *It's a dog of hers.* }

At the bank   DR. MÉNDEZ: *Excuse me, ma'am, but this bank book that you've given me isn't mine.*   TELLER: *It isn't yours? Aren't you Dr. Méndez?*   DR. MÉNDEZ: *Yes, that's me, but this bank book isn't mine. You still have mine. It's there, to the right.*   TELLER: *Oh, I made a mistake. This one belongs to Mr. and Mrs. Palma. Here's yours. I'm very sorry!*

The stressed forms of the possessive adjective follow the noun, which must be preceded by a definite or indefinite article or by a demonstrative adjective. The stressed forms agree with the noun modified in number and gender.

Possessive Pronouns

Éste es mi **banco.** ¿Dónde está **el suyo?**	*This is my bank. Where is yours?*
Sus **bebidas** están preparadas; **las nuestras,** no.	*Their drinks are ready; ours aren't.*
No es el **pasaporte** de Juan; es **(el) mío.**	*It isn't Juan's passport; it's mine.*

The stressed possessive adjectives—but not the unstressed possessives—can be used as possessive pronouns: **la maleta suya → la suya.** The article and the possessive form agree in gender and number with the noun to which they refer. The definite article is frequently omitted after forms of **ser: Es suya.**

Práctica

A. Ud. trata de encontrar una serie de objetos perdidos. ¿Son suyos los objetos que le ofrecen? Con un compañero (una compañera), haga y conteste preguntas según los modelos.

> MODELO   —Esta tarjeta, ¿es *de Ud.?*
> —No, no es mía.

1. de Juan   **2.** de Uds.   **3.** de Alicia   **4.** de Ud.   **5.** tuya

> MODELO   —¿Esta *radio?*
> —No, no es mía. La mía es más pequeña.

6. despertador   **8.** llave   **10.** pastillas
7. zapatos   **9.** televisor   **11.** anillo

B. **Situaciones.** Con un compañero (una compañera) haga y conteste preguntas según el modelo.

> MODELO   —Voy a lavar mi carro esta tarde. ¿Y tú? →
> —Ya lavé el mío.

1. Necesito pagar mis facturas esta semana. ¿Y tú?
2. Voy a hacer mis reservaciones para junio. ¿Y Juan?
3. Tienen que comprar sus libros. ¿Y Uds.?
4. Necesitamos encontrar nuestras llaves. ¿Y ellos?
5. Vas a informar a tus padres, ¿no? ¿Y ellos?

6. Vamos a cobrar nuestro cheque. ¿Y Uds.?
7. Voy a pedir un préstamo para la matrícula. ¿Y tú?
8. Vamos a devolver nuestros libros a la biblioteca ahora. ¿Y Úrsula?

C. **Los problemas financieros de la familia Gutiérrez.** ¿Cómo se dice en español?

1. I need a credit card. Would you lend me yours, Mom?
2. My husband, Ricardo, has his checking account and I have mine.
3. The children have spent all their money and now they want to spend yours, Ricardo.
4. We cashed their check when we cashed ours.
5. Let's charge this to our account; she can charge those things to hers.

CH. **Entrevista.** Con otro/a estudiante, haga y conteste las siguientes preguntas.

1. ¿Qué clases tienes este semestre (trimestre)? ¿Son interesantes? ¿Cuáles son más interesantes, mis clases o las tuyas? ¿Qué clases quisieras tener?
2. ¿Cómo es tu horario (*schedule*) este semestre (trimestre)? ¿Cuál es más fácil, mi horario o el tuyo? ¿Qué horario quisieras tener?
3. ¿Tienes coche? ¿Cómo es? ¿Prefieres mi coche o el tuyo?
4. ¿Vives en un apartamento? ¿Cuánto pagas al mes? ¿Cuál es más barato, mi apartamento o el tuyo?
5. ¿Cuántas personas hay en tu familia? ¿Cuál es más grande, mi familia o la tuya?
6. ¿Trabajas? ¿Dónde? ¿Te gusta el trabajo? ¿Cuál es mejor, mi puesto o el tuyo?

REPASO

En el extranjero (*abroad*). Complete the following paragraph with the correct form of the words in parentheses, as suggested by the context. When two possibilities are given in parentheses, select the correct word.

El cambio de la moneda°

El... *The Exchange Rate*

Un aspecto problemático de (*los/las*[1]) viajes al extranjero es el cambio de la moneda: el valor del dinero (*del/de la*[2]) país extranjero en comparación con (*el/la*[3]) dólar. (*Muchos ratos/Muchas veces*[4]), especialmente cuando el cambio (*ser/estar*[5]) muy «favorable», el turista tiende a considerar que el dinero extranjero no (*ser/estar*[6]) realmente dinero, es decir,° que (*ser/estar*[7]) «dinero de juguete». (*Por/Para*[8]) ejemplo, en 1984 el peso mexicano (*valer*[9]) más o menos dos tercios° de un centavo estadounidense; es decir, con un dólar estadounidense se podía comprar (*cien/ciento*[10]) cincuenta pesos mexicanos.

es... *that is*

dos... *two-thirds*

Así, si (*algo/alguno*[11]) (*costar*[12]) 2.550 pesos, en los Estados Unidos costaba $17. Como la diferencia es (*tan/tanto*[13]) enorme, es (*muy/mucho*[14]) fácil creer que el peso no vale (*algo/nada*[15]). Si usted no tiene cuidado, (*poder*[16]) comenzar (*de/a*[17]) gastar su dinero—es decir, (*su*[18]) pesos—más de lo que° debe.   de... *than*

¡La vida es cara!

—No sé qué pasa. El dinero nunca me
alcanza. (*I never have enough money.*)

—¿En qué lo gastas?

—Pues... en el alquiler, en la luz, en la
comida, en libros, en casettes, en el cine...

—Yo creo que tengo menos gastos que tú.

—Sí, porque tu todavía vives con tus padres.
Yo hace un año que tengo mi propio
apartamento.

Stuart Cohen

Ciudad de México, México

UN PASO MÁS: Lectura cultural

La urbanización en el mundo hispánico

Parece que en todas partes coexisten la riqueza y la pobreza, y los Estados Unidos no son ninguna excepción. En nuestro país, la población con escasos° recursos económicos tiende a desplazarse° a las ciudades, mientras   pocos / mudarse
que la clase media prefiere irse al campo o a las afueras de la ciudad. La tendencia de los pobres a dirigirse° a las grandes ciudades es aún más   ir
marcada en los países del mundo hispánico.

     Tomemos° como ejemplo la familia Raquejo, que se despide de su casita   *Let's take*
en el campo y de sus vecinos para empezar el largo viaje a la capital del país. Para los Raquejo, la ciudad ofrece la esperanza de una nueva vida, de un buen trabajo, la oportunidad de vivir en una casa decente, y de proporcionarles° a sus hijos una buena educación. El campo les ha dado su   darles
aire fresco y la tranquilidad de la naturaleza, pero también un trabajo duro y mal pagado. Ha llegado la hora de cambiar de ambiente, de mudarse a la capital para mejorar las condiciones de vida.

     Esta llegada de los campesinos a la ciudad es uno de los problemas urbanos más graves que tiene Hispanoamérica. En muchos países, especialmente en Venezuela y en México, esto se ha debido a la intensa actividad económica provocada por el descubrimiento de grandes

yacimientos° de petróleo. Ante las nuevas perspectivas que ofrecía tal des-   *deposits*
cubrimiento, los gobiernos inauguraron grandes proyectos para la con-
strucción de edificios, carreteras y puertos.° Mucha gente pensó que los   *ports*
campesinos podrían° proporcionar la mano de obra° que la nueva ola° de   *would be able to* / mano… *working*
prosperidad necesitaba.   *force / wave*

Desgraciadamente no todo salió tal como lo habían soñado los gobiernos. Debido a la <u>baja</u> en la demanda y en el precio del petróleo, los
campesinos tuvieron que enfrentarse con el <u>desempleo</u> y la falta de viviendas adecuadas suficientes. Además, con frecuencia no tenían la preparación necesaria para obtener buenos puestos. Estas familias, que aun en la
actualidad° siguen siendo numerosas, cocinan y duermen en viviendas de   *en… currently*
un solo cuarto en los barrios pobres de las ciudades. Para ganar dinero, el
esposo, con frecuencia, vende cigarrillos o billetes de lotería por las calles,
la esposa lava ropa o trabaja de criada, y los niños—que raras veces pueden
asistir a la escuela—limpian zapatos en el centro comercial de la ciudad.

Junto a esta pobreza, el lujo y la grandeza también están presentes en
Hispanoamérica. Desde la ciudad de México hasta Buenos Aires hay ciudades modernas llenas de rascacielos y de barrios elegantes. En las afueras
hay casas modernas y lujosas° con todas las comodidades.° Grandes sis-   *luxurious / comforts*
temas de autopistas conectan los distintos barrios de las ciudades que,
como toda ciudad moderna, sufren los efectos de la contaminación del aire
y del tráfico incontrolable. Como los demás países del mundo, las naciones
hispanoamericanas van a tener que <u>esforzarse</u> para hacer de sus metrópolis
lugares apropiados para la vida de <u>todos</u> sus habitantes.

Comprensión

Haga oraciones completas, combinando las frases de la columna A con
las de la columna B.

A	B
1. La urbanización significa…	a. tienen la esperanza de una vida mejor y buenos puestos
2. Muchas personas pobres emigran a la ciudad porque…	b. lujo y grandeza
3. Los campesinos encontraron… en la ciudad.	c. un movimiento del campo hacia la ciudad
4. Al llegar al centro urbano, la mayoría de los campesinos… ; por eso les era difícil encontrar buenos puestos.	ch. no tenían suficiente preparación
5. A causa de su pobreza, es típico que los niños…	d. trabajen y que no asistan a la escuela
6. A pesar de la pobreza en Latinoamérica, también hay…	e. muchos obstáculos

Para escribir

Describa la ciudad más grande que Ud. conoce. Su descripción debe incluir los siguientes detalles.

1. dónde está
2. su importancia nacional e internacional
3. población: tamaño (*size*), grupos étnicos o culturales

4. lugares de interés
5. industrias
6. política
7. si le gustaría a Ud. vivir allí y por qué (no)

VOCABULARIO

VERBOS

ahorrar to save (*money*)
aumentar to increase
cargar to charge (*to an account*)
casarse (con) to marry
cobrar to cash (*a check*); to charge (*someone for an item or service*)
devolver (ue) to return (*something*)
economizar to economize
quejarse (de) to complain (about)

EN EL BANCO

el/la cajero/a cashier
    la cuenta corriente checking account
    la cuenta de ahorros savings account
    la factura bill, invoice
    los gastos expenses
    el préstamo loan

el presupuesto budget
la tarjeta de crédito credit card

PALABRAS ADICIONALES

pagar a plazos to pay in installments
pagar al contado to pay cash
pagar con cheque to pay by check

FRASES ÚTILES PARA LA COMUNICACIÓN	
Quisiera + *inf.*	I (he, she, you) would really like to (*do something*)
¿Quisiera... ? ⎫ **¿Quisieras... ?** ⎭	Would you like to . . . ? Would you be so kind as to . . . ?

CAPÍTULO 23

El individuo y la sociedad

VOCABULARIO: PREPARACIÓN

Peter Menzel

León, Nicaragua

David Kupferschmid

Ciudad de México, México

EL INDIVIDUO Y LA RESPONSABILIDAD CÍVICA

el bienestar well-being
la cárcel jail, prison
el castigo punishment
el/la ciudadano/a citizen
el deber responsibility, obligation
los demás other people
el derecho (civil) right
la dictadura dictatorship
el egoísmo selfishness

la ley law
la libertad freedom
la manifestación public protest, demonstration
la política politics; policy
la república republic

castigar to punish
garantizar to guarantee
gobernar (ie) to govern

merecer (merezco) to deserve
obedecer (obedezco) to obey
protestar to protest
tomar en cuenta to take into account, keep in mind
votar to vote

es cuestión de, se trata de it's a matter of

A. María y Carmen son dos activistas políticas. Una es conservadora, la otra es liberal. Complete el diálogo entre ellas.

MARÍA: No, no estoy de acuerdo. No debemos ____ a los criminales con la pena de muerte (*death penalty*).

CARMEN: Entonces, ¿cómo vamos a proteger a los inocentes si dejamos libres a los asesinos?

MARÍA: Yo no digo que un criminal no ____ (¡**OJO!** *subjuntivo*) ningún ____. Sólo digo que éste no debe ser demasiado fuerte (*severe*).

CARMEN: Oye, María. Tú tienes que tomar en ____ que se ____ de un acto muy violento. ¡Es ____ de vida o muerte! ¿No crees tú que todos deben ____ la ley?

MARÍA: Sí, pero la pena de muerte no garantiza nada. Es una violación de los ____ humanos más básicos. Creo que sería (*it would be*) mejor poner a los criminales en la ____ .

CARMEN: ¡Ajá! ¿Y quién paga todo eso? ¡La sociedad! No es el individuo que paga el delito, sino (*but rather*) la ____ . No es justo, María.

MARÍA: Ay, Carmen, siempre te refieres a lo económico cuando hablamos de los conflictos entre el individuo y la sociedad.

B. Asociaciones. ¿Con quién asocia Ud. las siguientes ideas?

1. El individuo debe trabajar para el bienestar del estado; el estado es más importante que el individuo.
2. La dictadura es la única manera de gobernar a las masas.
3. Todos tenemos que protestar contra la discriminación de las minorías.
4. La prensa (*press*) es la voz (*voice*) del pueblo, no del gobierno.
5. Para protestar contra la represión de nuestros derechos, estoy en huelga (*strike*) de hambre.
6. Es evidente que el rey (*king*) no toma en cuenta los derechos de los que vivimos aquí en las colonias.
7. Támbien tenemos que garantizar los derechos y la libertad personal de las mujeres.

    a. Martin Luther King
    b. Ghandi
    c. Karl Marx
    ch. William Randolph Hearst
    d. Thomas Jefferson
    e. Gloria Steinem
    f. Adolf Hitler

MINIDIÁLOGOS Y ESTRUCTURA

47 ¡Ojalá que pudiéramos hacerlo!
Past Subjunctive

Aquéllos eran otros tiempos...

«¡Parece imposible que yo *dijera* eso! ¡Qué egoísmo!»

«¡No es posible que *lucháramos* tanto! Nos llevamos tan bien ahora... »

Hace treinta años, era difícil que don Jorge y don Gustavo *hablaran* de las elecciones sin pelearse. Era imposible que se *pusieran* de acuerdo en política. ¡Qué lástima que *hubiera* tanta enemistad entre ellos!

Ahora es probable que no se acuerden de todas las peleas del pasado. También es posible que sus convicciones políticas sean menos fuertes... o simplemente que ahora tengan otras cosas de que hablar.

VIEJOS VOTANTES. ¿Recuerda cuánto tuvimos que discurrir° usted y yo antes de votar hace treinta años°?

to discuss
hace... 30 years ago

Hace diez años...

1. *¿de qué era difícil que Ud. hablara con sus padres?*
2. *¿con quién era imposible que Ud. se pusiera de acuerdo?*
3. *¿con quién era imposible que Ud. se llevara bien?*
4. *¿contra qué órdenes de sus padres era común que Ud. protestara?*

Cuando Ud. era niño/a...

5. *¿con quién era probable que discutiera* (you argued) *en la escuela primaria?*
6. *¿dónde le prohibían sus padres que jugara?*
7. *¿qué era obligatorio que comiera o bebiera?*
8. *¿de qué temía que sus padres se enteraran* (would find out)*?*

Those were the days . . .   *"It seems impossible that I said that. How selfish!"   "It's not possible that we fought that much! We get along so well now . . ." Thirty years ago it was difficult for don Jorge and don Gustavo to talk about elections without fighting. It was impossible for them to come to any agreement about politics. What a shame that there was so much bad feeling between them!*

Now it's probable that they don't remember all the fights of the past. It's also possible that their political convictions are less intense . . . or just that they have other things to discuss now.

¿Recuerda Ud.?

To learn the forms of the past subjunctive (presented in this section), you will need to know the forms of the preterite well, especially the third-person plural. Regular **-ar** verbs end in **-aron** and regular **-er/-ir** verbs in **-ieron** in the third-person plural of the preterite. Stem-changing **-ir** verbs show the second change in the third person: **servir (i, i)** → **sirvieron; dormir (ue, u)** → **durmieron.** Verbs with a stem ending in a vowel change the **i** to **y: leyeron, cayeron, construyeron.** Many common verbs have irregular stems in the preterite: **quisieron, hicieron, dijeron,** and so on. Four common verbs are totally irregular in this tense: **ser/ir** → **fueron; dar** → **dieron; ver** → **vieron.**

Cambie por la tercera persona del plural del pretérito.

1. habla	5. pierde	9. estoy	13. traigo	17. digo
2. como	6. dormimos	10. tenemos	14. dan	18. construimos
3. vives	7. río	11. vamos	15. sé	19. creo
4. juegan	8. leemos	12. visten	16. puedo	20. consiguen

In Spanish, although there are two simple indicative past tenses (preterite and imperfect), there is only one simple subjunctive past tense, **el imperfecto del subjuntivo** (*past subjunctive*). Its exact English equivalent depends on the context in which it is used.

Forms of the Past Subjunctive

PAST SUBJUNCTIVE OF REGULAR VERBS*					
hablar: hablar\u00f8\u0144		**comer: comier\u00f8\u0144**		**vivir: vivier\u00f8\u0144**	
hablara	habláramos	comiera	comiéramos	viviera	viviéramos
hablaras	hablarais	comieras	comierais	vivieras	vivierais
hablara	hablaran	comiera	comieran	viviera	vivieran

The past subjunctive endings **-a, -as, -a, -amos, -ais, -an** are identical for **-ar, -er,** and **-ir** verbs. These endings are added to the third-person plural of the preterite indicative, minus its **-on** ending. For this reason, the forms of the past subjunctive reflect the irregularities of the preterite.

Stem-changing Verbs

-Ar and **-er** verbs: no change

---

*An alternate form of the past subjunctive (used primarily in Spain) ends in **-se: hablase, hablases, hablase, hablásemos, hablaseis, hablasen.** This form will not be practiced in *¿Qué tal?*

empezar (ie):   empezar~~on~~ → **empezara, empezaras,** etc.
volver (ue):   volvier~~on~~ → **volviera, volvieras,** etc.

-Ir verbs: all persons of the past subjunctive reflect the vowel change in the third-person plural of the preterite.

dormir (ue, u):   durmier~~on~~ → **durmiera, durmieras,** etc.
pedir (i, i):   pidier~~on~~   → **pidiera, pidieras,** etc.

Spelling Changes

All persons of the past subjunctive reflect the change from **i** to **y** between two vowels.

   i → y (caer, construir, creer, destruir, leer, oír)

creer: creyer~~on~~ →
creyera, creyeras, creyera, creyéramos, creyerais, creyeran

Verbs with Irregular Preterites

dar: dier~~on~~   → **diera, dieras, diera, diéramos, dierais, dieran**

decir:	dijer~~on~~	→ **dijera**	**poner:**	pusier~~on~~	→ **pusiera**
estar:	estuvier~~on~~	→ **estuviera**	**querer:**	quisier~~on~~	→ **quisiera**
ir:	fuer~~on~~	→ **fuera**	**saber:**	supier~~on~~	→ **supiera**
haber:	hubier~~on~~	→ **hubiera**	**tener:**	tuvier~~on~~	→ **tuviera**
hacer:	hicier~~on~~	→ **hiciera**	**venir:**	vinier~~on~~	→ **viniera**
poder:	pudier~~on~~	→ **pudiera**	**ser:**	fucr~~on~~	→ **fuera**

Uses of the Past Subjunctive

The past subjunctive usually has the same applications as the present subjunctive, but is used for past events.

Quiero que **jueguen** por la tarde.	*I want them to play in the afternoon.*
Quería que **jugaran** por la tarde.	*I wanted them to play in the afternoon.*
Siente que no **estén** allí.	*He's sorry (that) they aren't there.*
Sintió que no **estuvieran** allí.	*He was sorry (that) they weren't there.*
Dudamos que se **equivoquen.**	*We doubt that they will make a mistake.*
Dudábamos que se **equivocaran.**	*We doubted that they would make a mistake.*

Remember that the subjunctive is used (1) after expressions of *willing, emotion,* and *doubt;* (2) after *nonexistent* and *indefinite antecedents;*

(3) after certain *conjunctions:* **a menos que, antes (de) que, con tal que, en caso de que, para que, sin que;** and (4) after **aunque** to imply doubt or uncertainty.

[Práctica A–C]

Softened Requests and Statements

The past subjunctive forms of **deber, poder,** and **querer** are used to soften a request or statement.

Debieras estudiar más.	*You really should study more.*
¿Pudieran Uds. traérmelo?	*Could you bring it for me?*
Quisiéramos hablar con Ud. en seguida.	*We would like to speak with you immediately.*

[Práctica CH–E]

Práctica

A. Recuerdos. Dé oraciones nuevas según las indicaciones.

1. —Cuando Ud. estudiaba en la secundaria, ¿qué le gustaba?
   —Me gustaba que nosotros _____ . (*estudiar idiomas, leer libros interesantes, ver películas en la clase de historia, hacer experimentos en la clase de física, bailar durante la hora del almuerzo, divertirnos después de las clases, __?__*)

2. —De niño/a, ¿cómo era su vida?
   —Mis padres querían que yo _____ . (*ser bueno/a, estudiar mucho, creer en Santa Claus, ponerse la ropa vieja para jugar, no jugar en las calles, no comer tantos dulces, tener amigos que se portaran bien, __?__*)

B. Cuando es cuestión de dinero, todos los años son iguales. Cambie por el pasado.

1. Papá insiste en que ahorremos más.
2. Preferimos que no uses tanto las tarjetas de crédito.
3. Me alegro de que Ud. empiece a economizar.
4. Siento que no le podamos proporcionar (*grant*) el préstamo.
5. Dudamos que en esa tienda cobren tanto por necesidad.
6. El jefe no cree que me queje con razón.
7. Necesito un empleo donde me paguen lo que merezco.
8. Es necesario que no lo cargue a la cuenta.
9. No es probable que tenga fondos en mi cuenta de ahorros ni en la cuenta corriente.
10. No hay nadie que gaste el dinero como Ramón.

C. El comienzo y el fin del delito perfecto. Combine las oraciones, usando las conjunciones entre paréntesis y haciendo otros cambios necesarios.

1. El ladrón (*thief*) no pensaba entrar en la casa. No oía ningún ruido.   (a menos que)
2. No iba a molestar a los dueños. Encontraba dinero y objetos de valor.   (con tal que)
3. Un amigo lo acompañaba. Había alguna dificultad.   (en caso de que)
4. El amigo rompió la ventana. El ladrón pudo entrar.   (para que)
5. El ladrón entró silenciosamente. Los dueños no se despertaron.   (para que)
6. Salió. Los dueños pudieron llamar a la policía.   (antes de que)

CH. La situación es delicada... ¿Cómo se dice en español?

1. You really should drive more slowly.
2. Couldn't you think about others this time?
3. We would like you to consider your obligations.
4. How would you like to pay, madam?
5. We really should protect their welfare first.
6. They really should punish him, although he does have a family.

D. Su tía Laura, quien asistió a la universidad durante los años cincuenta, le describe cómo eran entonces las normas de conducta. ¿Cuáles de estas normas todavía están vigentes (*viable*) en las universidades de los años ochenta? Explíquenle a Laura las diferencias. ¿Hay algunas antiguas normas que le parezcan a Ud. mejores que las modernas? ¿Cuál(es)? ¿Por qué?

1. Era necesario que los hombres y las mujeres vivieran en distintas residencias, como si (*as if*) fuera necesario separarlos.
2. Para entrar en la cafetería de la universidad a cenar, era necesario que los hombres llevaran corbata y las mujeres, falda.
3. Había «horas de visita» en las residencias. Los hombres sólo podían visitar a sus amigas durante esas horas, y vice versa.
4. Era necesario que cada estudiante volviera a su propia residencia a una hora determinada de la noche (a las once, por ejemplo).

E. Preguntas

1. ¿De qué tenía Ud. miedo cuando era pequeño/a? ¿Era posible que ocurrieran las cosas que Ud. temía? ¿Era probable que ocurrieran? ¿A veces temía que lo/la castigaran sus padres? ¿Lo merecía a veces? ¿Era necesario que Ud. los obedeciera siempre? ¿Va a querer que sus propios niños lo/la obedezcan de la misma manera? ¿Cree Ud. que lo harán? ¿Por qué sí o por qué no?
2. ¿Qué quería el gobierno que hicieran los ciudadanos el año pasado? ¿Quería que gastaran menos gasolina? ¿que usaran menos energía? ¿que pagaran los impuestos? ¿que votaran en todas las elecciones? ¿que fueran ciudadanos responsables? ¿Hizo

Verás, quisiera un vaso de agua. Pero no te molestes, porque ya no tengo sed. Sólo quisiera saber si, en el caso de que tuviese otra vez sed, podría venir a pedirte un vaso de agua.

Ud. todo eso? ¿Por qué sí o por qué no? ¿Qué hizo por Ud. el gobierno?

3. ¿Qué buscaban los primeros inmigrantes que vinieron a los Estados Unidos? ¿un lugar donde pudieran practicar su religión? ¿un lugar donde fuera posible escaparse de las obligaciones financieras? ¿donde hubiera abundancia de recursos naturales? ¿menos gente? ¿más espacio?

Hablando de política

—**Nunca creí que hubiera alguien que apoyara (*would support*) a ese candidato.**

—**Ya lo ves. No les importó su postura (*position*) sobre la pena de muerte (la liberación de la mujer, el desarme nuclear, el derecho al aborto, la censura de las canciones *rock,* el terrorismo internacional...).**

—**¿Qué le vamos a hacer, pues?**

—**Bueno... esperar las próximas elecciones y... seguir trabajando.**

David Kupferschmid

Costa Rica

REPASO GENERAL

A. Las revoluciones hispanoamericanas. Complete the following paragraphs with the correct form of the words in parentheses. No hints are given for verb tense or mood except the context of the sentence. Remember that past participles can be used as adjectives. When two possibilities are given in parentheses, select the correct word.

Cuando los conquistadores (*llegar*¹) al Nuevo Mundo, (*instalar*²) (*uno*³) sistema de gobierno directamente (*controlar*⁴) desde España. Este gobierno (*durar*°⁵) casi doscientos años. Durante los (*primero*⁶) años del siglo° XIX, (*haber*⁷) un movimiento general en las Américas con el fin° de (*independizarse*⁸) de España. (*Estallar*°⁹) guerras de independencia desde México hasta la Argentina.

En México el padre° Miguel Hidalgo (*empezar*¹⁰) la revolución con el grito° de independencia el día 16 de septiembre de 1810. Los soldados°

to last / century

goal

to break out

priest

shout, cry / soldiers

españoles (*fusilarlo*°[11]) un año después sin que (*ver*[12]) realizado su sueño.°   *to shoot him / dream*
(*Haber*[13]) héroes en (*todo*[14]) (*los/las*[15]) países, pero el hombre al que todos los
sudamericanos (*reconocer*[16]) como «El Libertador» es Simón Bolívar. Bolívar
es para Sudamérica (*que/lo que*[17]) Jorge Washington es para los norteamericanos: el verdadero padre de la independencia.

Aunque las guerras de independencia (*tener*[18]) éxito y las colonias
(*conseguir*[19]) su independencia, todavía (*haber*[20]) luchas en Hispanoamérica.
En el siglo XX, los dos guerrilleros más (*conocer*[21]) (*haber*[22]) sido Ernesto
«Che» Guevara de la Argentina, (*que/lo que*[23]) (*participar*[24]) intensamente en
la revolución cubana, y Camilo Torres, sacerdote° colombiano que (*morir*[25])   *priest*
en una batalla contra el ejército° del gobierno de su país en 1965. La revo-   *army*
lución moderna que (*haber durar*[26]) más tiempo es la mexicana, que
(*comenzar*[27]) en 1910 y que según algunos mexicanos todavía (*seguir*[28]).
(*Ese*[29]) revolución (*traer*[30]) consigo° la nacionalización de la tierra y una   *with it*
constitución que todavía (*estar*[31]) en vigor.°   *en... in effect*

B. Entrevista. With another student, react to the following statements
by telling whether you believe them to be possible or not. Use the
present perfect indicative or subjunctive, as needed.

MODELO   —Hoy tuve que madrugar. Me levanté a las cinco.
—Bueno, yo creo que te has levantado hoy a las cinco.
(No, no te creo. Es imposible/No es probable que te
hayas levantado hoy a las cinco.)

1. A veces digo cosas estúpidas y absurdas.
2. Nunca digo cosas estúpidas y absurdas.
3. Nunca duermo.
4. Hoy me levanté a las tres de la mañana.
5. Puedo leer quince libros en una hora.
6. He leído muchos libros este año.
7. Mis padres me mandaron mil dólares la semana pasada.
8. Fui al Japón el año pasado.
9. Fui al Japón ayer.
10. Siempre salgo bien en los exámenes difíciles.

A propósito...

Carrying on a conversation in a second language requires effort. When you are speaking to someone in Spanish, you may be making such an effort to understand everything or to formulate even simple answers that you forget to say the things that you would automatically say in English.

A conversation is somewhat like a tennis game: it is important to keep the ball moving. But to keep a conversation going, you need to do more than just answer the other person's questions mechanically. If you volunteer a comment or ask a question in return, you not only provide more information but let the other person know that you are interested in continuing the conversation. For example, in answer to the question **¿Juegas al béisbol?,** the words **Sí** or **Sí, juego al béisbol** do little more than hit the ball back. They are factually and grammatically correct, but since they provide no more new information, they return the burden of carrying the conversation to the other person. Answers such as **Sí, soy el pícher** or **Sí, ¿a ti te gusta también? ¿Quieres jugar con nosotros el domingo?** or **No, pero juego al tenis** demonstrate your willingness to keep on talking.

C. **Dime más** *(Tell me more).* With another student, ask and answer the following questions. After answering the questions with a minimal amount of information, volunteer an additional comment or ask your partner a follow-up question. Using the suggestions in the **A propósito...** section, keep each conversation going for a minimum of three or four exchanges before going on to the next question.

1. ¿A ti te gusta bailar el chachachá?
2. ¿Conoces la ciudad de Nueva York?
3. ¿Dónde vive tu familia?
4. ¿Tienes coche?
5. ¿Por qué estudias español?
6. ¿Cuál es tu programa de televisión favorito?
7. ¿Quieres viajar por México?
8. ¿Qué hiciste el verano pasado?

CH. **Situaciones.** Con su profesor(a) o con otro/a estudiante, haga uno de los siguientes papeles.

1. Ud. está de vacaciones en Lima, Perú. Allí conoce a un peruano (una peruana) que tiene muchas preguntas sobre la vida y la política estadounidense. Contéstele lo mejor posible en español.
2. Ud. es un agricultor (una agricultora) *(farmer)* que acaba de llegar a Buenos Aires. Allí conoce a alguien que dice que los que viven en el campo son tontos y sin cultura. Esa persona no comprende por qué Ud. prefiere vivir tan lejos de la ciudad. ¿Cómo le responde Ud.?

UN PASO MÁS: Imágenes del mundo hispánico

Sudamérica: Época precolombina

Balsas modernas de estilo antiguo en el lago Titicaca

*E*n Sudamérica, especialmente en una ancha (*wide*) región del suroeste del continente, también se desarrollaron importantes civilizaciones indígenas antes del descubrimiento de América.

En Tiahuanaco, cerca del lago Titicaca, en los Andes bolivianos, pueden admirarse las ruinas de una ciudad aimará, anterior al siglo VI d. de C. Poco se sabe de estos pueblos, pues no han dejado documentos escritos que nos informen sobre su historia o costumbres. Pueblos de esa época son el mochica o el nazca, entre otros. Numerosos objetos de oro, tejidos (*weavings*) y vasijas (*urns*) han llegado a nuestros días, enterrados en tumbas de sacerdotes (*priests*), guerreros o personajes importantes.

Restos de murallas construidas por los incas en Sacsahuamán, Perú

Machu Picchu, Perú

Sin embargo, la cultura más famosa de Sudamérica es la incaica. El reino inca aparece en el siglo XII d. de C. «Incas» es el nombre que reciben los diversos pueblos que habitaron los Andes y que tenían un jefe común. Este gobernante era el «Inca», «varón de sangre real». En el siglo XV, los incas se habían convertido en un gran imperio. Poco a poco fueron conquistando a los pueblos vecinos. Su poder se extendió desde el sur de Colombia a la región central de Chile, hasta que fueron conquistados por Francisco Pizarro en 1532.

La cultura incaica tenía una organización social muy desarrollada, con clases sociales y leyes que fijaban (*established*) las obligaciones y derechos de los ciudadanos con todo detalle. Los incas construyeron magníficas edificaciones como las que se pueden admirar en Machu Picchu. Además de valientes guerreros y hábiles constructores, fueron también expertos agricultores. Todavía hoy se usan los métodos que ellos emplearon para cultivar las difíciles tierras de la región andina.

(Continúa en el Capítulo 25.)

VOCABULARIO

VERBOS

castigar to punish
comunicarse (con) to communicate (with)
garantizar to guarantee
gobernar (ie) to govern
merecer (merezco) to deserve
obedecer (obedezco) to obey
protestar to protest
votar to vote

LOS CONCEPTOS

el deber responsibility, obligation
el derecho (civil) right
el egoísmo selfishness
la guerra war
la huelga strike
la ley law

la libertad liberty
la pena de muerte death penalty
la responsabilidad responsibility

LA POLÍTICA

el/la ciudadano/a citizen
la dictadura dictatorship
el individuo individual
la manifestación public protest, demonstration
la república republic

OTROS SUSTANTIVOS

la cárcel jail, prison
el castigo punishment
los demás other people

ADJETIVOS

cívico/a civic
fuerte strong; severe

PALABRAS ADICIONALES

es cuestión de, se trata de it's a matter of; it has to do with
llevarse bien/mal con to get along well/badly with
ponerse de acuerdo to reach an agreement
tomar en cuenta to take into account

FRASES ÚTILES PARA LA COMUNICACIÓN

hace...	(*period of time*) ago
Lo conocí hace dos años.	I met him two years ago.
Se descubrió América hace cinco siglos.	America was discovered five centuries ago.

CAPÍTULO 24

¡Qué catástrofe!

VOCABULARIO: PREPARACIÓN

 Y ahora, el canal 45 les ofrece a Ud. el NOTICIERO 45...
...con las últimas novedades del mundo...

Asesinato de un dictador

Huelga de obreros en Alemania

Guerra en el Oriente Medio

"Erupción de un volcán en Centroamérica"

"Choque de trenes"

"Bombas en un avión"

LAS NOTICIAS / NEWS

el acontecimiento event
la prensa press
el/la reportero/a reporter
el testigo witness

el barrio neighborhood
el camión truck
el choque collision
el desastre disaster
la (des)igualdad (in)equality
la esperanza hope
el ferrocarril railroad (track)
la paz peace
el petróleo oil, petroleum

durar to last, endure
enterarse (de) to find out, learn (about)
informar to inform

390

Las noticias de hoy

—¿Has oído las noticias de las cinco?
—No. ¿Qué pasó? Nada malo, espero.
—Pues, hubo un terremoto (*earthquake*) en
California, pero no fue muy malo.
—¡Gracias a Dios! Siempre esperamos lo peor
de los desastres naturales.

Ciudad de México, México

A. Definiciones. ¿Qué palabra se asocia con cada definición?

1. Un programa que nos informa de lo que pasa en nuestro mundo
2. La persona que está presente durante un acontecimiento y lo ve todo
3. Un medio importantísimo de comunicación
4. La persona que nos informa de las novedades
5. La persona que gobierna un país de una forma absoluta
6. La persona que emplea la violencia para cambiar el mundo según sus deseos
7. Un sistema de transportes
8. La frecuencia en que se transmiten y se reciben los programas de televisión

a. el noticiero
b. la prensa
c. el/la terrorista
ch. el/la dictador(a)
d. el canal
e. el/la testigo
f. el/la reportero/a
g. el ferrocarril

B. Entrevista. With another student, exchange opinions about the news media and television in general. Tell whether you agree or disagree with the following statements and give examples to support your point of view. Then make suggestions for improvement, as appropriate.

1. Los reporteros de la televisión nos informan imparcialmente de los acontecimientos.
2. Por lo general ofrecen los programas más interesantes en el canal _____.
3. En este país la prensa es irresponsable.
4. Las telenovelas (*soap operas*) reflejan la vida exactamente como es.
5. Los anuncios son sumamente (*extremely*) informativos y más interesantes que muchos programas.
6. Me gusta que los reporteros y meteorólogos cuenten chistes durante el noticiero.

C. Algunos creen que las siguientes oraciones describen el mundo actual. ¿Qué cree Ud.? Reaccione Ud., empezando con una de estas expresiones:

(No) Dudo que...   Es lástima que...
(No) Es verdad que...   Es increíble que...
Es probable que...   (No) Me gusta que...
Es bueno/malo que...

1. Usamos demasiado petróleo actualmente (*currently*).
2. El terrorismo es un gran peligro para los viajeros.
3. Hay demasiados camiones en las autopistas de nuestro país.
4. Los tornados nunca destruyen nada en los Estados Unidos.
5. Hay más catástrofes naturales actualmente que hace 50 años.
6. Es buena idea asesinar a todos los dictadores del mundo.
7. No hay esperanzas de una paz mundial.
8. Hay huelgas en todos los países capitalistas.
9. En los Estados Unidos creemos en la igualdad legal de todos los ciudadanos.
10. En el futuro, las guerras mundiales sólo durarán un año, más o menos.

MINIDIÁLOGOS Y ESTRUCTURA

48 Expressing What You Would Do
Conditional Verb Forms and Conditional Sentences

En la dirección del Canal 45

EL JEFE: *¿Qué haría Ud. si hubiera* un choque entre un camión y un tren?

EL ASPIRANTE A REPORTERO: *Yo hablaría* con todos los testigos.

EL JEFE: *¿Y sí explotara* una bomba terrorista en Israel?

EL ASPIRANTE A REPORTERO: *Iría* al país y *me enteraría* de todos los detalles de la situación.

EL JEFE: ¿Y si aquí *hubiera* un terremoto?

EL ASPIRANTE A REPORTERO: *Me escondería* debajo de mi escritorio.... ¡Los terremotos me inspiran más terror que los terroristas!

At Channel 45 headquarters *THE BOSS: What would you do if there were a collision between a truck and a train?* *THE ASPIRING REPORTER: I would talk with all the witnesses.* *THE BOSS: And if a terrorist bomb exploded in Israel?* *THE ASPIRING REPORTER: I would go to the country and find out all the details of the situation.* *THE BOSS: And if there were an earthquake here?* *THE ASPIRING REPORTER: I would hide under my desk. . . . Earthquakes scare me more than terrorists!*

1. *¿Qué haría el aspirante si hubiera un choque?*
2. *¿Adónde viajaría después de la explosión de una bomba en Israel?*
3. *¿Qué haría después de llegar allí?*
4. *¿Qué pasaría durante un terremoto en su ciudad?*

hablar		comer		vivir	
hablaría	hablaríamos	comería	comeríamos	viviría	viviríamos
hablarías	hablaríais	comerías	comeríais	vivirías	viviríais
hablaría	hablarían	comería	comerían	viviría	vivirían

Conditional actions or states of being are expressed with the conditional. In English the conditional uses the auxiliary verb *would: I would speak.* The Spanish *conditional* **(el condicional)** is formed by adding the conditional endings to the infinitive: **-ía, -ías, -ía, -íamos, -íais, -ían.** No auxiliary verb is needed.

Verbs that form the future on an irregular stem use the same stem to form the conditional.

decir: **dir-** ⎫
hacer: **har-** ⎪   **-ía**
poder: **podr-** ⎪   **-ías**
poner: **pondr-** ⎬   **-ía**
querer: **querr-** ⎪   **-íamos**
saber: **sabr-** ⎪   **-íais**
salir: **saldr-** ⎪   **-ían**
tener: **tendr-** ⎪
venir: **vendr-** ⎭

decir	
diría	diríamos
dirías	diríais
diría	dirían

The conditional of **hay** is **habría** (*there would be*).*

Uses of the Conditional

A. The conditional expresses what you would do in a particular situation, given a particular set of circumstances.

—¿**Hablarías** francés en México?   *"Would you speak French in Mexico?"*

—No, **hablaría** español.   *"No, I would speak Spanish."*

---

*The *conditional perfect tense* **(el condicional perfecto)** is formed with the conditional of the auxiliary verb **haber** (**habría, habrías, habría, habríamos, habríais, habrían**) plus the past participle. It expresses what would have happened at some time in the past.

Habríamos tenido que buscarla en el aeropuerto.   *We would have had to pick her up at the airport.*
¿Qué **habría hecho** Ud.?   *What would you have done?*

▪ **¡OJO!** *When* would *implies* used to *in English, Spanish uses the imperfect.*

Íbamos a la playa todos los veranos.	*We would go (used to go) to the beach every summer.*

[Práctica A–B]

B. The conditional is often used in Spanish to express probability or conjecture about past events or states of being, just as the future is used to indicate probability or conjecture about the present. This use of the conditional is called **el condicional de probabilidad.**

—¿Dónde **estaría** Cecilia?	*"I wonder where Cecilia was."* *(Where could Cecilia have been?)*
—**Estaría** en la carretera.	*"She was probably on the highway."*

[Práctica C]

C. DEPENDENT CLAUSE: *SI* CLAUSE   INDEPENDENT CLAUSE

Si + *imperfect subjunctive,*	*conditional.*
Si yo **fuera** tú, no **haría** eso.	*If I were you, I wouldn't do that.**
Si se levantaran más temprano, **podrían** llegar a tiempo.	*If they got up earlier, they would be able to arrive on time.*
Iría a las montañas **si tuviera** tiempo.	*He would go to the mountains if he had the time.*

When a clause introduced by **si** (*if*) expresses a contrary-to-fact situation, **si** is always followed by the past subjunctive. In such sentences, the verb in the independent clause is usually in the conditional, since the sentence expresses what one *would do or say* if the **si** clause were true.

When the **si** clause is in the present tense, the present indicative is used—not the present subjunctive.

Si tiene tiempo, va a las montañas.	*If he has time, he goes to the mountains.*

[Práctica CH–D]

Práctica

A. Es necesario mejorar (*improve***) el mundo.** Cambie por el condicional.

---

*English speakers frequently use the subjunctive after *if* (*If I were you . . .*) in conditional sentences, but this usage, like the use of the subjunctive in general, is inconsistent in contemporary English speech.

1. «Yo sé eliminar el hambre de los países subdesarrollados.»
2. «Quiero enterarme por completo de la tecnología más avanzada.»
3. «Tenemos que eliminar las causas de la guerra.»
4. «La prensa es totalmente libre en todo el mundo.»
5. «Los reporteros nos informan de todo.»
6. «Nadie debe matar (*kill*) a nadie, ni siquiera (*not even*) a los criminales.»
7. «Los obreros nunca hacen huelgas.»
8. «¿Qué hacen Uds. para mejorar nuestro mundo?»

B. ¿Cómo sería el mundo si Ud. pudiera controlarlo todo? Haga oraciones con una palabra o frase de cada columna.

yo	usar	(las) guerras
la gente	tener	(las) bombas
el gobierno (no)	quejarse de	atómicas
nosotros	vivir en	(la) (des)igualdad
los terroristas	ser	un gobierno
alguien	eliminar	mundial
(no) habría que	desarrollar	(el) petróleo, (la)
	matar	gasolina, otros
	destruir	tipos de energía
		(la) esperanza para
		un futuro mejor
		todos los dictadores
		(las) tarjetas de
		crédito

C. Lea el siguiente párrafo.

Había una mujer detrás de un mostrador (*counter*). Vino un hombre que llevaba una maleta porque iba a hacer un viaje. El hombre parecía nervioso y la maleta parecía pesar (*to weigh*) mucho. El hombre habló con la mujer y luego sacó dinero de su cartera. Se lo dio a la mujer, quien le dio un papel. El hombre le dio a la mujer la maleta y fue a sentarse. Parecía muy agitado. Escuchaba los avisos (*announcements*) que se oían periódicamente mientras que escribía rápidamente una tarjeta postal. Al escuchar un aviso en particular, el hombre se levantó y...

¿Qué pasaría aquí? Conteste, usando el condicional de probabilidad. Si quiere, puede inventar más detalles.

1. ¿Dónde estarían el hombre y la mujer?
2. ¿Quién sería la mujer? ¿y el hombre?
3. ¿Por qué estaría nervioso el hombre?
4. ¿Qué tendría el hombre en la maleta?
5. ¿Qué preguntaría el hombre a la mujer?
6. ¿Por qué le daría dinero a la mujer?
7. ¿Qué le daría la mujer al hombre?
8. ¿Por qué le daría el hombre la maleta a la mujer?
9. ¿Cómo serían los avisos? ¿Qué dirían?
10. ¿A quién le escribiría el hombre?
11. ¿Qué haría el hombre después de levantarse?
12. ¿Qué pasaría después?

CH. ¿Qué haría Ud.? ¿Adónde iría? Complete las oraciones en una forma lógica.
1. Si necesitara comprar comida, iría a _____ .
2. Si necesitara un libro, lo compraría en _____ .
3. Si tuviera que emigrar, iría a _____ .
4. Si tuviera sed, tomaría _____ .
5. Si yo _____ , comería un sándwich.
6. Si quisiera ir a _____ , iría en avión.
7. Si quisiera tomar _____ , esperaría en la estación.
8. Si _____ , compraría un coche nuevo.

D. Complete las oraciones en una forma lógica.

1. Si yo fuera presidente/a, yo _____ .
2. Si yo estuviera en _____ , _____ .
3. Si tuviera un millón de dólares, _____ .
4. Si yo pudiera _____ , _____ .
5. Si yo fuera _____ , _____ .
6. Si _____ , (no) me casaría con él/ella.
7. Si _____ , estaría contentísimo/a.
8. Si _____ , estaría enojadísimo/a.

REPASO GENERAL

A. **El noticiero de las seis.** Complete the following news flashes with the correct form of the words in parentheses, as suggested by the context. When two possibilities are given in parentheses, select the correct word.

TRENTON, ESTADOS UNIDOS.   Se reveló ayer que los comandantes de las bases navales de los Estados Unidos han (*recibir*[1]) órdenes «supersecretas» de (*intensificar*[2]) las medidas de seguridad.° Se cree que terroristas (*cubano*[3])   medidas... *security measures* (*pensar*[4]) sabotear instalaciones norteamericanas. Estas órdenes, (*emitir*°[5]) por el jefe de operaciones navales, (*mandar*[6]) que los comandantes (*aumentar*[7]) la seguridad para que no (*ocurrir*[8]) otra tragedia como el ataque contra el cuartel° de los marinos en Beirut.

to issue / *barracks*

MOSCÚ. Hoy todo Moscú se está (*preguntar*[9]) si el jefe del Estado y del Partido Comunista, Yuri Andrópov, (*asistir*[10]) mañana sábado (*por/de*[11]) la tarde a la solemne reunión (*organizar*[12]) por el Kremlin para (*celebrar*[13]) el aniversario (*del/de la*[14]) revolución bolchevique. Hace varios meses que el señor Andrópov no (*aparecer*[15]) en público y es posible que (*ser/estar*[16]) gravemente enfermo. Hasta este momento, claro, la prensa soviética no (*haber decir*[17]) nada al respecto.° Mañana sábado, a las 17 horas, no sólo el cuerpo° diplomático y los periodistas (*extranjero*[18]) sino° también la población soviética (*ser/esta*[19]) ante° los televisores para (*ver*[20]) si la directiva° del Partido hace su entrada° en la Sala de Congreso del Kremlin.

al... *about it* / *corps* / *but* / *in front of* / *leadership* / *entrance*

SANTIAGO, CHILE. Al final del próximo febrero, seis familias chilenas (*viajar*[21]) a la Antártida. Allí (*vivir*[22]) por un período de dos años (*cómo/como*[23]) parte (*del/de la*[24]) programa de exploración y colonización del territorio antártico (*que/lo que*[25]) lleva a cabo la Fuerza Aérea Chilena. Las seis familias (*vivir*[26]) en casas especialmente (*diseñar*[27]) y (*construir*[28]) por la Fuerza Aérea. También se (*construir*[29]) un centro comunitario donde los niños tendrán (*alguno*[30]) diversiones. Para poder participar en la colonización de la Antártida, fue necesario que los profesionales (*estar*[31]) casados, (*tener*[32]) hijos (*pequeño*[33]) y (*viajar*[34]) con su familia. El mayor de los niños (*que/quien*[35]) viaja a la Antártida (*tener/estar*[36]) actualmente siete años.

(Adaptado de *Américas*)

B. ¿Cómo responde Ud.? Un amigo (Una amiga) o un miembro de la familia pregunta o declara las siguientes opiniones. Ud. no está de acuerdo, pero no quiere ofender a la otra persona. ¿Cómo va a responder? Use algunas de las frases que aparecen en **A propósito....**

MODELO —Jorge trabaja mucho y debe recibir un aumento desalario. →
—Puede ser, pero hay otros empleados que trabajan más que él y por eso ellos van a recibir el aumento. (Pues no sé. Me dicen que es un hombre muy simpático, pero, ¿de veras trabaja bien?)

1. Es más interesante ir al teatro que ir al cine, ¿no crees?
2. Barbra Streisand es una actriz excelente. Me gusta mucho.
3. Para descansar, no hay nada como sentarse delante del televisor.
4. Para echar raíces (*to settle down*), las ciudades grandes son mejores que las pequeñas.
5. Me encanta la comida japonesa, sobre todo el *sushi.*
6. No sé qué les pasa a los jóvenes de hoy. ¡Son tan descorteses!
7. Creo que es mejor *no* tener hijos.

8. No me caen bien los gatos. Los perros son infinitamente superiores.

C. **Situaciones.** Con su profesor(a) o con otro/a estudiante, haga uno de los siguientes papeles.

1. Ud., un norteamericano (una norteamericana) joven, asiste a un congreso internacional en favor de la paz. Allí conoce a un ruso (una rusa) joven que ha venido al mismo congreso. Por suerte, tienen una lengua común: el español. Uds. empiezan a hablar de lo peligroso que es el mundo y de qué podrán hacer los jóvenes para mejorarlo.

2. Ud. tiene un amigo que ha estado muy enfermo últimamente y no sabe nada de los acontecimientos mundiales. Explíquele lo que ha pasado en los Estados Unidos y en el resto del mundo.

3. Ud. quiere conseguir trabajo con el Canal 44. Vaya a ver al director (a la directora) de personal y trate de convencerlo/la de que Ud. es el mejor candidato para el puesto de reportero/a.

A propósito...

In English we often use vocalized pauses ("uh," "um") and filler words ("well now," "okay") when we don't know what to say or are looking for the right words. When you need a few seconds to collect your thoughts in Spanish, use one of the following expressions:

este	uh, um	**bueno**	well, OK	**a ver**	let's see
pues	well	**bien**	well, OK	**ahora bien**	well now

When you want to avoid taking a position on an issue, perhaps to avoid an argument, use one of these phrases:

En mi opinión...	In my opinion . . .	**Puede ser.**	That might be.
Depende.	It depends.	**Posiblemente.**	Possibly.
No sé.	I don't know.	**A veces.**	At times.
Tal vez. Quizá(s).	Perhaps.	**¿Ud. cree?**	Do you think so?
Es posible.	It's possible.	**¿Tú crees?**	

Hablando de política

—¿Qué consejos te gustaría darles a los líderes de los países del mundo?

—Lo primero, acabar con las guerras y las injusticias.

—¡Como si (*As if*) eso fuera posible!

—¿Por qué dices eso?

—Porque los políticos no escuchan.

Buenos Aires, Argentina

UN PASO MÁS: Lectura cultural

El pasado y el futuro económicos de Hispanoamérica

Por lo general, cuando hablamos del sistema económico de los países hispanoamericanos, pensamos en economías basadas en un solo producto: el café colombiano o el plátano de las repúblicas centroamericanas. Esta situación procede de la explotación económica de los productos latinos más deseables y valiosos° por los intereses internacionales.

de gran valor

Esta historia comenzó en la época de la Conquista, cuando España explotaba el oro y la plata de sus colonias americanas. Después de conseguir la independencia de España en el siglo XIX, las nuevas naciones hispanoamericanas—políticamente débiles°—fueron lugares de fácil explotación económica para los países industrializados europeos y para los Estados Unidos. Los casos clásicos son la explotación intensiva del cobre° chileno, del petróleo venezolano y de la fruta centroamericana.

weak

copper

Actualmente los hispanoamericanos tienen una clara conciencia° de este pasado de explotación extranjera e insisten cada vez más° en su derecho a tener voz en su propio destino económico. Por lo tanto,° cabe° hacer la siguiente pregunta: ¿Serán algún día los países de Hispanoamérica una de las regiones económicamente más importantes del mundo? Cuando se considera la gran cantidad de recursos naturales que quedan aún por aprovechar° y desarrollar, es muy fácil decir que sí.

awareness
cada... *more and more*
Por... *Por eso* / *es apropiado*

to utilize

Para realizar° tal desarrollo económico, sin embargo, habrá que resolver los muchos problemas internos que son, en gran parte, el resultado de un proceso histórico caracterizado por el predominio político y económico de un reducido grupo de personas y la pobreza de la gran mayoría. Para un norteamericano, en cuyo° país la clase media es la predominate, es muy difícil entender la dinámica de una sociedad en la cual° la clase media es la menos numerosa.

to bring about

whose
la... *which*

El descubrimiento de petróleo en México es sólo un ejemplo de la riqueza natural que posee Hispanoamérica. En esta época de continuas crisis de energía, esta riqueza hispanoamericana tiene muchísimo valor. Además del petróleo, las tierras hispanoamericanas cuentan con grandes depósitos de cobre, plata, hierro,° plomo,° estaño° y tungsteno. Todos éstos son productos que necesitará el mundo del futuro.

iron / lead / tin

Será importante también el aprovechamiento de la riqueza agrícola y pesquera. Con sus vastos territorios cultivables y con la pesca—en especial a lo largo de la costa del Pacífico—las naciones hispanoamericanas, con un desarrollo apropiado, podrán producir comida para su propio consumo y también para la exportación.

Comprensión

¿Cierto o falso? Corrija las oraciones falsas.

1. En los Estados Unidos se conoce la economía latinoamericana por la variedad de los productos que fabrica.
2. Hispanoamérica ha tenido una historia de constante explotación económica.
3. Ya no hay muchos recursos naturales que explotar en Hispanoamérica.
4. Los países hispanoamericanos tienen una clase media muy numerosa que domina el sistema económico.
5. El futuro económico de Latinoamérica depende de sus metales y minerales, del petróleo y de la agricultura, según el autor de la lectura.

Para escribir

Escriba un párrafo sobre el siguiente tema: ¿Cómo será la situación económica de los Estados Unidos en el año 2000? Conteste las siguientes preguntas en el párrafo.

1. ¿Habrá una crisis de energía? ¿Qué clase de energía será la más común en el futuro, la energía nuclear o la solar?
2. ¿Qué países extranjeros serán los más importantes para nuestra economía nacional?
3. ¿Qué grupo político controlará el gobierno? ¿Será un gobierno de tipo conservador o progresista?

VOCABULARIO

VERBOS
durar to last, endure
enterarse (de) to find out, learn (about)
informar to inform
matar to kill
mejorar to improve

LO POLÍTICO Y LO SOCIAL
el asesinato murder, assassination
el barrio neighborhood
la catástrofe catastrophe

la **(des)igualdad** (in)equality
el/la **dictador(a)** dictator
la **esperanza** hope
el/la **obrero/a** worker
la **paz** (*pl.* **paces**) peace

LOS RESULTADOS DEL DESARROLLO
el camión truck
el choque collision, crash
el ferrocarril railroad (track)
el petróleo oil, petroleum

LA PRENSA
el acontecimiento event
el canal channel
las **noticias** news
el noticiero news broadcast
las **novedades** news
el/la **reportero/a** reporter
el testigo witness

ADJETIVOS
actual present
mundial world; worldwide
último/a latest

FRASES ÚTILES PARA LA COMUNICACIÓN	
como si + *past subjunctive*	as if
Habla como si lo supiera todo.	He/She talks as if he/she knew it all.

CAPÍTULO 25

Los hispanos en los Estados Unidos

VOCABULARIO: PREPARACIÓN

emigrar

llevar todos los bienes

establecerse

aprender un nuevo idioma

LOS INMIGRANTES

el/la ciudadano/a citizen
la costumbre custom
la cultura culture
el «choque cultural» culture shock
el/la exiliado/a person in exile, expatriate
la patria native land, homeland
las raíces (la raíz) roots
el/la refugiado/a refugee
la tierra natal native land, place of birth

bilingüe bilingual
por necesidad out of necessity

acostumbrarse (a) to get used (to)
añorar to long for
asimilarse to assimilate, blend in
emigrar to emigrate
establecerse (establezco) to establish oneself
mantener (ie) (mantengo) to support (*a family, and so on*)
sufrir altibajos to have ups and downs

Hablando de nuestras raíces

—¿Son inmigrantes Uds.?
—Bueno, mi familia vino de México, pero nosotros nacimos en Texas.
—¿Todavía tienen parientes en México?
—Sí. Algunos en Guanajuato y otros en Taxco. Los visitamos de vez en cuando, y nos escribimos con frecuencia.

David Kupferschmid

"East Los," Estados Unidos

A. Definiciones. Dé la palabra que corresponde a cada definición.

1. pagar todos los gastos de una familia
2. adaptarse poco a poco
3. el país natal de una persona
4. un individuo que ha dejado su país por razones políticas
5. tener la habilidad de hablar dos idiomas
6. salir de un país para vivir en otro
7. el conflicto que una persona experimenta (*experiences*) en una nueva cultura
8. tener unos ratos alegres y otros tristes
9. la propiedad y los objetos que uno tiene
10. la herencia cultural y familiar de una persona

Ahora, siguiendo el modelo de las definiciones anteriores, dé una definición de las siguientes palabras.

11. el ciudadano
12. una costumbre
13. una cultura
14. añorar
15. establecerse en un país nuevo

B. ¿Cuánto sabe Ud. de la gente de origen hispánico que vive en los Estados Unidos? En cada grupo de oraciones, dos no describen al grupo étnico indicado. ¿Cuáles son las oraciones falsas? Las respuestas se dan al pie de la página.

Los chicanos son personas de descendencia mexicana o mexicanoamericana que viven en los Estados Unidos.

1. Los chicanos viven solamente en California y Texas.
2. Muchos de los chicanos del oeste son descendientes de mexicanos que se establecieron allí en el siglo XIX o antes.
3. Todos los chicanos con apellidos hispanos hablan el idioma español.

Los chicanos: 1. Falso. Los chicanos se han establecido en casi todas partes de los Estados Unidos.   2. Cierto. 3. Falso. Algunos chicanos son bilingües, pero otros son monolingües. 4. Cierto. 5. Cierto.

4. Como sus raíces culturales proceden de México, muchos chicanos comen comidas mexicanas como pan dulce y chocolate, tacos y tortillas, frijoles y arroz.
5. El Cinco de Mayo es una fiesta mexicana celebrada por muchos chicanos.

Los puertorriqueños son personas que proceden—o sus antepasados (*ancestors*)—de la isla de Puerto Rico, en el Mar Caribe.

6. Los puertorriqueños son ciudadanos de los Estados Unidos.
7. Un 15 por ciento de la población de la ciudad de Dallas es de origen puertorriqueño.
8. Puerto Rico es un Estado Libre Asociado (*Commonwealth*).
9. Muchos platos típicos puertorriqueños se preparan con guayaba (*guava*), una fruta tropical.
10. Puerto Rico fue una colonia de los Estados Unidos durante 400 años.

Los cubanos son personas que proceden—o sus antepasados—de la isla de Cuba, que también está en el Mar Caribe, cerca de la Florida.

11. La mayoría de los cubanos que han venido a los Estados Unidos han emigrado por gusto.
12. Los cubanos se han establecido sólo en el estado de la Florida.
13. Un plato típico de los cubanos se llama «moros y cristianos».
14. Los cubanos han influido mucho en la vida política, económica y cultural de algunas regiones de los Estados Unidos.
15. Muchos de los primeros inmigrantes cubanos eran personas con una buena preparación profesional.

C. Javier Ochoa y Bill Moore son dos extranjeros recién llegados a los Estados Unidos, pero hay una gran diferencia entre ellos. Bill es del Canadá y desea estudiar medicina en este país; no está casado. Javier es un estudiante graduado en bioquímica. Es de Madrid y viene con su familia (su esposa que no habla inglés y dos hijos pequeños). ¿En qué cree Ud. que se diferenciarán sus dos primeros años en los Estados Unidos?

CH. Preguntas

1. ¿Cuál es su tierra natal, su patria? ¿y la de sus padres? ¿la de sus abuelos? ¿Son diferentes algunas de las costumbres de este país y las de la tierra natal de su familia? ¿Hay personas bilingües en su familia? ¿Qué idiomas hablan? ¿Qué costumbres todavía conservan?

Los puertorriquenos: 6. Cierto. 7. Falso. Un 15 por ciento de la población de la ciudad de Nueva York es de origen puertorriqueño. 8. Cierto. 9. Cierto. 10. Falso. Puerto Rico fue una colonia de España.

Los cubanos: 11. Falso. La mayoría ha venido por necesidad, por razones políticas. 12. Falso. Hay colonias cubanas en muchas partes de los Estados Unidos, aunque sí hay que reconocer que muchos se concentran en la Florida. 13. Cierto. Consiste en frijoles negros («moros») y arroz («cristianos»). 14. Cierto. 15. Cierto.

2. ¿De qué países proceden muchas de las personas que han emigrado a los Estados Unidos? ¿De qué países han venido muchos refugiados políticos? ¿Conoce Ud. a algún refugiado? ¿Ha podido traer sus bienes o los tuvo que dejar en su tierra natal? ¿Dónde se ha establecido esta persona? ¿Añora su patria? ¿Tiene raíces muy profundas en su cultura?

3. ¿Conoce Ud. a alguien que haya salido de los Estados Unidos? ¿Emigran con frecuencia los estadounidenses? ¿Por qué saldrían? ¿A qué países podrían acostumbrarse fácilmente? ¿Por qué?

MINIDIÁLOGOS Y ESTRUCTURA

49 ¿Por o para?
A Summary of Their Uses

Entre abuelo y nieta

NIETA: Abuelito, ¿por qué vivimos aquí en Nueva York?

ABUELO: Porque perdí mi finca, hija, y entre la falta de trabajo en Puerto Rico y la posibilidad de un trabajo bien pagado aquí, tu abuela y yo optamos *por* emigrar.

NIETA: Entonces, ¿*por* qué dices a veces que preferirías vivir allí todavía?

ABUELO: Mira, es que somos de otra cultura, de otra lengua.... Pero tú has nacido aquí; *para* ti es diferente. *Para* nosotros Puerto Rico es nuestra patria. No salimos *por* gusto sino *por* necesidad.

1. *¿De dónde son los abuelos?*
2. *¿Por qué salieron?*
3. *¿Dónde preferirían vivir ahora? ¿Por qué?*
4. *¿Por qué es diferente la actitud de la nieta?*

Por

The preposition **por** has the following English equivalents.

1. *By, By means of*

Vamos **por avión** (**tren, barco,** etcétera).	*We're going by plane (train, ship, and so on).*
Le voy a hablar **por teléfono.**	*I'll talk to him by phone.*

Between grandfather and granddaughter *GRANDDAUGHTER: Grandad, why do we live here in New York?* *GRANDFATHER: Because I lost my farm, little one, and between the lack of work in Puerto Rico and the possibility of a well-paying job here, your grandmother and I chose to emigrate.* *GRANDDAUGHTER: Then why do you sometimes say that you would still prefer to live there?* *GRANDFATHER: Look, we're from another culture, of another language. . . . But you were born here; for you it's different. For us, Puerto Rico is our native land. We didn't leave because we wanted to, but because we had to.*

2. *Through, Along*

¿No quieres caminar **por el parque**?

Don't you want to walk through the park?

Recomiendan que caminemos **por la playa**.

They suggest that we walk along the beach.

3. *During, In* (the morning, afternoon, and so on)

Por la mañana jugamos al tenis.

We play tennis in the morning.

4. *Because of*

Estoy nervioso **por la entrevista**.

I'm nervous because of the interview.

5. *For*, when *for* means the following:
   a. *In exchange for*

¿Cuánto me das **por este sombrero?**

How much will you give me for this hat?

Gracias por el regalo.

Thanks for the gift.

   b. *For the sake of, On behalf of*

Lo voy a hacer **por ti**.

I'm going to do it for you (for your sake).

   c. *In order to get, In search of*

Van **por pan**.

They're going for (going to get) bread.

   ch. *For a period of time*

Elena manejó **(por)** tres horas esta tarde.

Elena drove for three hours this afternoon.

Many native speakers of Spanish do not use **por** in this and similar sentences; **tres horas** implies *for three hours*.

Por is also used in a number of fixed expressions.

por Dios	for heaven's sake	**por lo general**	generally, in general
por ejemplo	for example		
por eso	that's why	**por lo menos**	at least
por favor	please	**por primera/**	for the first/last
por fin	finally	**última vez**	time
		por si acaso	just in case

[Práctica A]

Para

The preposition **para** has many English equivalents, including *for*. Underlying all of them is the reference to a goal or a destination.

1. *In order to* + infinitive

Se quedaron en Andorra **para esquiar**.	*They stayed in Andorra to (in order to) ski.*
Sólo regresaron **para cenar**.	*They only came back to have dinner.*
Ramón estudia **para (ser) abogado**.	*Ramón is studying to be a lawyer.*

2. *For,* when *for* means the following:

a. *Destined for, To be given to*

Le regalé un libro **para su hijo**.	*I gave him a book for his son.*
Todo esto es **para ti**.	*All of this is for you.*

b. *For (By) a specified future time*

Para mañana estudien Uds. la página 72.	*For tomorrow, study page 72.*
Lo tengo que terminar **para la semana que viene.**	*I have to finish it by next week.*

c. *Toward, In the direction of*

Salieron **para Acapulco** ayer.	*They left for Acapulco yesterday.*

ch. *To be used for*

Es un vaso **para agua**.	*It's a water glass (a glass for water).*

¡**OJO!** *Compare the above with the following:*

Es un vaso **de agua**.	*It's a glass (full) of water.*

d. *Compared with others, In relation to others*

Para mí el español es fácil.	*For me Spanish is easy.*
Para (ser) extranjera habla muy bien el inglés.	*She speaks English very well for a foreigner.*

e. *In the employ of*

Trabajan **para ese hotel**.	*They work for that hotel.*

[Práctica B–C]

Para and *por*

Sometimes either **por** or **para** can be used in a given sentence, but there will always be a difference in meaning depending on which one is used.

Compare the following pairs of sentences.

Vamos **para** las montañas.	*Let's head toward the mountains.*
Vamos **por** las montañas.	*Let's go through the mountains.*
Déle el dinero **para** el carro.	*Give her the money for (so that she can buy) the car.*
Déle el dinero **por** el carro.	*Give her the money for (in exchange for) the car. (Buy the car from her.)*
Es alto **para** su edad.	*He's tall for his age (compared to others of the same age).*
Es alto **por** su edad.	*He's tall because of his age. (He's no longer a child.)*

[Práctica CH–D]

Práctica

A. Conteste Ud. en oraciones completas, usando **por** y las expresiones entre paréntesis.

1. Supongamos que Uds. son muy ricos. ¿Cómo prefieren viajar? ¿y si tienen que ahorrar? (avión, autobús)
2. ¿Cómo se entera Ud. de lo que pasa en otros países? ¿de las noticias del barrio? ¿y de lo que les pasa a sus amigos? (televisión, teléfono)
3. ¿Por dónde les gusta a los hispanos dar paseos? (las plazas, el centro)
4. ¿Cuándo le gusta a Ud. estudiar?   ¿ver la tele? (la tarde, la noche)
5. ¡Qué nervioso está Julio hoy! ¿Por qué será? (el examen, la cita con el dentista)
6. ¿Cuánto tiempo estudia su compañero/a de cuarto todos los días? (tres horas, a veces sólo media hora)
7. ¿Cuánto pagó Ud. por este coche? (menos de lo que Ud. piensa, $2.000)
8. ¿Por quiénes se sacrifican los padres? (los niños, todos los demás)
9. En una conferencia de prensa, ¿por quién hablan los periodistas? (los periódicos que representan, los lectores)
10. ¿Por qué volvieron Uds. a la tienda? (pan, vino)

B. ¿Para dónde salieron estas personas? Haga oraciones según las indicaciones.

MODELO   Ponce de León salió para la Florida.

1. Colón / el Oriente	3. Lewis y Clark / el oeste
2. los astronautas / la luna	4. Hernán Cortés / México

C. Conteste Ud. negativamente, según las indicaciones.

1. Para mañana, ¿hay que leer el vocabulario? (el diálogo)
2. Para Ud., las ciencias son muy interesantes, ¿verdad? (aburridas)
3. ¿Busca Ud. el texto para la clase de comercio? (matemáticas)
4. Para ser principiantes, nosotros pronunciamos muy mal, ¿verdad? (bien)
5. Para la semana que viene, ¿tenemos que repasar el pretérito? (subjuntivo)
6. Ud. está en la biblioteca para conversar, ¿no? (leer un libro)

CH. Complete las oraciones con **por** o **para**.

1. Salieron _____ el Perú ayer. Van _____ avión, pero luego piensan viajar en carro _____ todo el país. Van a estar allí _____ dos meses en total.
2. Pagué veinte dólares _____ esta blusa _____ Clara. Es un regalo de cumpleaños, ¿sabes?
3. Buscamos un regalo de boda _____ nuestra nieta. ¿No tienen Uds. unos vasos de cristal _____ vino?
4. Graciela quiere estudiar _____ (ser) doctora. _____ eso trabaja _____ un médico _____ la mañana; tiene clases _____ la tarde.
5. —No dejes los estudios _____ mañana, ¿eh? —No te preocupes, mamá. Hoy _____ la tarde voy a estudiar _____ el examen.
6. —Sé que tienes mucho que hacer _____ la boda mañana. ¿Te puedo traer o preparar algo _____ la fiesta después? —Pues sí. ¿Me haces el favor de ir a la tienda _____ vino?
7. —¿_____ qué están Uds. aquí todavía? Yo pensaba que iban a dar un paseo _____ el parque. —Íbamos a hacerlo, pero _____ fin no fuimos _____ la nieve.

D. Situaciones. Con un compañero (una compañera), haga y conteste preguntas sobre el dibujo, usando oraciones con **por** o **para** donde sea posible.

MODELO   ¿Cómo se llama la niña?
¿Para quién canta?
Para ser una niña pequeña, ¿canta bien o mal?
¿Cuántos años tendrá?
¿Es muy alta para su edad?
¿Para qué se han reunido todas estas personas?
¿Por qué está sentada la gente?

REPASO GENERAL

A. Un exiliado cubano. Complete the following story with the correct form of the words in parentheses, as suggested by the context. When two possibilities are given in parentheses, select the correct word.

Miguel García es un médico excelente que vive y trabaja en Miami. Emigró de Cuba después de la revolución de Fidel Castro. Miguel (*querer*[1]) mucho a su patria, (*pero/sino*[2]) no le (*gustar*[3]) el nuevo sistema político. Así (*salir: él*[4]) de Cuba en 1963 y (*llegar*[5]) con su familia a los Estados Unidos. El gobierno cubano no les permitió que (*traer: ellos*[6]) muchos bienes personales; (*también/tampoco*[7]) les (*dejar*[8]) sacar dinero del país.

Ser un refugiado político significa empezar una nueva vida. Al° establecerse en los Estados Unidos, Miguel (*experimentar*[9]) muchos cambios difíciles. (*El/La*[10]) idioma, (*por/para*[11]) ejemplo, (*representar*[12]) un obstáculo para él. Ya (*saber*[13]) bastante° gramática (*inglés*[14]) porque la (*haber estudiar*[15]) en el colegio en Cuba, (*pero/sino*[16]) nunca (*haber aprender*[17]) a hablar inglés con facilidad. También tuvo muchos problemas en comprender (*al/a la*[18]) gente. Aunque Miguel (*haber ser*[19]) médico en Cuba, le fue difícil encontrar trabajo. Tuvo que trabajar en una fábrica (*por/para*[20]) mantener a su mujer y a sus tres hijos. Mientras tanto,° hizo la residencia en un hospital y (*examinarse*[21]) en el estado de Florida. (*Por/Para*[22]) fin (*conseguir*[23]) un (*bueno*[24]) puesto en un hospital de Miami.

Además, era necesario que los García (*acostumbrarse*[25]) a una vida y a una cultura completamente diferentes. (*Decidir: ellos*[26]) adoptar una vida bilingüe: el español es (*que/lo que*[27]) usan en la casa, (*pero/sino*[28]) hablan inglés en el trabajo y en (*el/la*[29]) calle.

Hoy, después de muchos años de exilio, Miguel y su familia se (*haber acostumbrar*[30]) a la forma de vida en los Estados Unidos. (*Ser/Estar: ellos*[31]) ciudadanos de (*este/esto*[32]) país, aunque muchas veces (*añorar*[33]) su tierra natal. Sin embargo, saben que si no (*haber emigrar*[34]), su vida en Cuba seguramente (*haber ser*[35]) muy diferente.

Upon

a fair amount of

Mientras... Meanwhile

B. Un episodio de la niñez. Form complete sentences based on the words given in the order given. Conjugate the verbs in the preterite or the imperfect and add other words if necessary. Use subject pronouns only when needed. ■ **¡OJO!** *The lo + adjective construction is used several times.*

1. cuando / yo / ser / niño / pensar / que / mejor / de / estar enfermo / ser / quedarse / en cama
2. peor / ser / que / con frecuencia / yo / resfriarse / durante / vacaciones
3. una vez / yo / ponerme / muy / enfermo / durante / Navidad / y / mi / madre / llamar / a / médico / con / quien / tener / confianza
4. Dr. Vega / venir / casa / y / darme / antibiótico / porque / tener / mucho / fiebre
5. ser / cuatro / mañana / cuando / por fin / yo / empezar / respirar / sin dificultad
6. desgraciadamente / día / de / Navidad / yo / tener / tomar / jarabe / y / no / gustar / nada / sabor (*taste*)
7. bueno / de / este / enfermedad / ser / que / mi / padre / tener / dejar / fumar / mientras / yo / estar / enfermo

C. Situaciones. Con su profesor(a) o con otro/a estudiante, haga Ud. uno de los siguientes papeles.

1. Ud. acaba de conocer a un hispano (una hispana) joven que asiste a clases en su universidad. Ud. tiene mucho interés en su vida y especialmente quiere saber cuándo y por qué vino a Estados Unidos.
2. Ud. es el profesor (la profesora) de una clase de inglés para extranjeros. Es la primera noche del curso y hay un hombre (una mujer) en la clase que sólo habla español. Discutan Uds. por qué él/ella necesita aprender inglés.
3. Ud. es el padre (la madre) de una familia colombiana que vive en Bogotá. Piensan mudarse a Los Ángeles, pero no todos están de acuerdo. Trate de convencer a su hijo/a de que sería una buena decisión emigrar.

Más sobre las raíces

—¿Por qué emigró tu familia?
—Por necesidad. La situación política de mi país era intolerable.
—Para ser extranjera hablas muy bien el inglés.
—¿Ves? La necesidad es la mejor maestra.

Alan Carey/The Image Works

Miami, Florida

UN PASO MÁS: Imágenes del mundo hispánico

Sudamérica: Sus gentes

Joven shipibo de la jungla amazónica, Perú

Niño quechua de la región andina de Ecuador

*S*udamérica es un continente lleno de contrastes. La desigualdad socioeconómica que ya existía bajo la dominación española no ha desaparecido. La inestabilidad ha sido constante en la historia política de casi todos estos países. Sus gentes, sin embargo, miran al futuro con esperanza, aunque su hoy sea difícil y a veces incierto.

Además de las diferencias políticas y socioeconómicas, tanto entre los distintos países como dentro del mismo país, están las diferencias raciales. Sudamérica es también un «crisol» (*melting pot*), incluso mayor y con más tradición que el famoso crisol estadounidense. Con la llegada de los españoles se inicia una etapa fundamental en la evolución de la población. Tanto los españoles, como los portugueses en el Brasil, se mezclaron (*intermarried*) con los indios. Pronto llegaron los negros, con lo que las variedades raciales se multiplicaron. Desde entonces, distintas oleadas de inmigrantes se han establecido en el continente: italianos, alemanes, irlandeses...

En Ecuador, Perú y Bolivia, hay una población mayoritariamente india y mestiza. En cambio, Uruguay y Argentina presentan un elevadísimo índice de población blanca de origen europeo en su mayoría. Es indudable que las distintas proporciones y combinaciones étnicas, así como el desarrollo económico y político de cada lugar, nos permite adivinar (*guess*) algo de la organización social de estos países y de la forma de vivir de sus gentes. Los deseos y posibilidades profesionales no son iguales en Buenos Aires que en un pueblo de los Andes bolivianos. El papel de la mujer en el sistema social es distinto, por ejemplo, en Bogotá que en cualquier comunidad indígena del mismo país. Lo mismo sucede con la forma de celebrar las fiestas, con las diversiones y pasatiempos, la dieta alimenticia, las inquietudes culturales, la forma de entender el progreso. Esta infinidad de rasgos y caracteres y el hecho de que (*the fact that*) coexistan a la vez puede apreciarse en la genial novela *Cien años de soledad* del Gabriel García Márquez, ganador del Premio Nóbel Colombiano de Literatura en 1982.

(Continúa en el Capítulo 27.)

Una madre argentina con sus hijos, Buenos Aires

Gabriel García Márquez

VOCABULARIO

VERBOS

acostumbrarse (a) to get used (to)
añorar to long for
asimilarse to assimilate, blend in
emigrar to emigrate
establecerse (establezco) to establish oneself
experimentar to experience
mantener (ie) (mantengo) to support (*a family, and so on*)

LOS INMIGRANTES

la costumbre custom
la cultura culture
el «choque cultural» culture shock

el/la exiliado/a person in exile, expatriate
el idioma language
la patria native land, homeland
las raíces (la raíz) roots
el/la refugiado/a refugee
la tierra natal native land, place of birth

ADJETIVO

bilingüe bilingual

PALABRAS ADICIONALES

llevar todos los bienes to carry (take) all of one's belongings
por Dios for heaven's sake
por fin finally
por gusto/necesidad out of desire/necessity
por lo menos at least
por primera/última vez for the first/last time
por si acaso just in case
sino but (rather)
sufrir altibajos to have ups and downs

FRASES ÚTILES PARA LA COMUNICACIÓN	
optar por + *inf.*	to choose, opt for (*doing something*)

CAPÍTULO 26

¿Tiene Ud. algo que declarar?

VOCABULARIO: PREPARACIÓN

CRUZAR LA FRONTERA

el viajero

DECLARAR LAS COMPRAS

la inspectora (de aduanas)

REGISTRAR LAS MALETAS

PAGAR LOS DERECHOS/UNA MULTA

— DE VIAJE / TRAVELING —

ir al extranjero to go abroad
tener algo que (declarar, decir, hacer) to have something to (declare, say, do)
viajar al/en el extranjero to travel abroad

la aduana customs
los derechos de aduana customs duty
la multa fine, penalty
la nacionalidad nationality
el pasaporte passport
la planilla (de inmigración) (immigration) form

En la aduana

—¿Tiene Ud. algo que declarar? ¿alcohol, tabaco, frutas, verduras... ?

—No, nada.
—Está bien. Pase.

—Sólo unas cositas que compré en Cartagena.
—Lo siento, pero tendré que registrar sus maletas.

Sevilla, España

A. **Definiciones.** Dé una definición de las siguientes palabras.

1. la aduana
2. el pasaporte
3. los derechos de aduana
4. la frontera
5. la multa
6. registrar
7. la planilla de inmigración

B. **Pasando por la aduana.** ¿Qué dice o pregunta el inspector en este diálogo?

INSPECTOR: ¿_____?
   VIAJERA: Soy española, de Toledo.
INSPECTOR: ¿_____?
   VIAJERA: Aquí lo tiene, señor.
INSPECTOR: ¿_____?
   VIAJERA: Solamente estos libros y estos cigarrillos para uso personal.
INSPECTOR: ¿_____?
   VIAJERA: Espere Ud. un momento. Mi esposo trae la llave.
INSPECTOR: ¡_____!
   VIAJERA: ¡Oh, no! ¡No sabía que $\begin{cases} \text{tenía que declararlo!} \\ \text{era ilegal!} \end{cases}$
INSPECTOR: _____.
   VIAJERA: ¿Cuánto tengo que pagar, pues?
INSPECTOR: _____.

C. Explíquele a su amigo Paul, que nunca ha viajado al extranjero, lo que pasa cuando uno toma un vuelo internacional. Empiece desde el momento de subir al avión hasta el momento de salir de la Oficina de Inmigración. Si Ud. nunca ha hecho un viaje al extranjero, hágale preguntas a su profesor(a) para saber los detalles.

MINIDIÁLOGOS Y ESTRUCTURA

50 Expressing Future or Pending Actions
Subjunctive and Indicative After Conjunctions of Time

Uno, dos, tres...

Describa Ud. lo que está pasando—y lo que va a pasar—en este dibujo. Use las preguntas como guía.

1. ¿Quién es el viajero? ¿Cómo es?
2. ¿Quiénes lo esperan?
3. ¿Cómo es el inspector?
4. ¿Qué problema va a haber?
5. ¿Cómo va a resolverse (*to be resolved*) el problema?

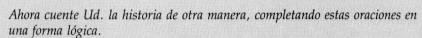

Ahora cuente Ud. la historia de otra manera, completando estas oraciones en una forma lógica.

1. *El viajero cree que tan pronto como* (as soon as) *pase por* _____, *(él)* _____ .
2. *En cuanto* (As soon as) *el inspector vea* _____, *(él)* _____ .
3. *Aunque el viajero sea* _____, *va a tener que* _____ .
4. *Después de que el viajero pague* _____, *el inspector* _____ .

In a dependent clause after a conjunction of time, the subjunctive is used to express a future action or state of being, that is, one that is still pending or has not yet occurred from the point of view of the main verb. The events in the dependent clauses are conceptualized—not real-world—events. Conjunctions of time include the following.

cuando	when	**hasta que**	until
después (de) que	after	**tan pronto como**	as soon as
en cuanto	as soon as		

PENDING ACTION (SUBJUNCTIVE):

Saldremos **en cuanto llegue** Felipe.

We'll leave as soon as Felipe arrives.

Anoche, íbamos a salir **en cuanto llegara** Felipe.

Last night we were going to leave as soon as Felipe arrived.

The indicative, however, is used after conjunctions of time to describe a habitual action or a completed action in the past.

HABITUAL ACTION (INDICATIVE):

Siempre salimos **en cuanto llega**
    Felipe.

We *always leave as soon as*
    Felipe arrives.

PAST ACTION (INDICATIVE):

Anoche, salimos **en cuanto llegó**
    Felipe.

Last *night, we left as soon as*
    Felipe arrived.

The subject and verb are frequently inverted in the subordinate clause
following conjunctions of time.

¡OJO! *Even though it is a time conjunction,* **antes de que** *always requires*
the subjunctive (Grammar Section 39).

Práctica

A. Use la conjunción entre paréntesis para unir las dos oraciones. Haga
   todos los cambios necesarios.

¡OJO! *No se usa el subjuntivo en todas.*

Escenas en el aeropuerto

1. Voy a llamarlos. Paso por la aduana.   (en cuanto)
2. Juan va a decidirlo. El avión aterriza (*lands*).   (después de que)
3. No digas nada. Julio paga los derechos.   (hasta que)
4. El inspector va a registrar la maleta. Mi esposo se la entrega
   (*hands it over*).   (en cuanto)

Se trata de bodas

5. Julio y Ana se casaron. Sus padres volvieron a Colombia.   (antes
   de que)
6. Te lo dije. Lo supe.   (en cuanto)
7. Los padres se sorprendieron. Escucharon lo que les dijo su hijo.
   (cuando)
8. Los novios iban a salir de viaje. Terminó el semestre.   (tan
   pronto como)
9. Les íbamos a dar una fiesta. Regresaron de su luna de miel.
   (después de que)

B. Describa Ud. los dibujos, completando las oraciones. Luego,
   describa Ud. su propia vida.

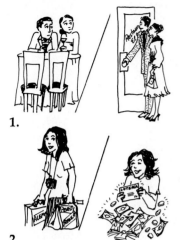

1.

2.

1. Los señores Castro van a cenar tan pronto como _____ .

Esta noche voy a cenar tan pronto como _____ .
Siempre ceno tan pronto como _____ .
Anoche iba a cenar tan pronto como _____ .

2. Lupe va a viajar al extranjero en cuanto _____ .

Voy a _____ en cuanto _____ .
Siempre _____ en cuanto _____ .
De niño/a, _____ en cuanto _____ .

C. Preguntas

1. ¿Qué piensa Ud. hacer después de graduarse en la universidad? ¿Qué le van a regalar sus padres/amigos cuando Ud. se gradúe? ¿Qué recibió Ud. cuando se graduó en la escuela secundaria?
2. Cuando Ud. tenga el tiempo y el dinero, ¿adónde va a ir? ¿Adónde fue Ud. el año pasado cuando estaba de vacaciones? Cuando todavía vivía Ud. con su familia, ¿adónde iban Uds. de vacaciones?

REPASO GENERAL

A. El primer viaje a Guadalajara. Complete the following story with the correct form of the words in parentheses, as suggested by the context. When two possibilities are given in parentheses, select the correct word.

El día que salí para México, (*ser/estar*[1]) nublado. Iba a la Universidad de Guadalajara (*por/para*[2]) presentarme a un examen oral (*por/para*[3]) entrar en la Facultad de Medicina. Yo me (*haber preparar*[4]) con cuidado y (*esperar*[5]) saber todas las respuestas. Aunque en el pasado siempre (*haber sacar*[6]) buenas notas en ciencias, (*saber/conocer*[7]) que los profesores mexicanos (*ser/estar*[8]) muy exigentes.° (*Tener: yo*[9]) miedo (*a/de*[10]) que me (*hacer: ellos*[11]) alguna pregunta difícil. Yo realmente (*querer*[12]) (*posponer*[13]) la entrevista (*pero/sino*[14]) no (*ser/estar*[15]) posible y a las diez (*por/de*[16]) la mañana (*subir: yo*[17]) (*en el/al*[18]) avión.   °demanding

Cuando (*llegar: yo*[19]) a Guadalajara, (*llover*[20]) ligeramente.° (*Ir: yo*[21]) al hotel y (*empezar*[22]) a repasar todas mis notas. (*Leer*[23]) hasta las tres, cuando (*por/para*[24]) fin (*acostarse*[25]). (*Ser/Estar*[26]) tan cansada que (*dormirse*[27]) casi inmediatamente.   °lightly

Al día siguiente, después (*de/que*[28]) vestirme con cuidado, (*tomar*[29]) un taxi (*por/para*[30]) la Facultad. Los examinadores ya (*ser/estar*[31]) allí esperándome.

—(*Sentarse*[32]) Ud. aquí y no (*tener*[33]) miedo, me (*decir*[34]) ellos. —Aquí todos (*ser/estar: nosotros*[35]) amigos. Y con esas palabras todos me (*sonreír*[36]).

Fue como si (*tomar*[37]) un tranquilizante. (*Empezar*[38]) el examen y (*contestar: yo*[39]) como si (*tener*[40]) los libros (*abrir*[41]) en la mesa. Después, ellos me (*decir*[42]) que yo (*haber hacer*[43]) muy buen examen y que todos (*esperar*[44]) verme allí al año siguiente. (*Regresar: yo*[45]) al hotel como si (*volar*[46]), casi sin que los pies (*tocar*[47]) el suelo. ¡Qué felicidad! ¡Y cómo (*brillar*[48]) el sol!

> **B. La aduana.** As you are going through customs, the inspector asks you the questions or makes the comments given on the following page. Give as many appropriate responses as possible.
>
> MODELO   INSPECTOR: Su pasaporte, por favor. →
>   VIAJERO/A: Sí, cómo no.
>   Claro.
>   Aquí tiene mi pasaporte.
>   Un momento, por favor. Está en esta maleta.

A propósito...

Command forms and indirect requests with the subjunctive are not always the best way of getting someone to do something. Often a greater degree of politeness is necessary in order not to offend the person you are addressing.

Here are some examples of how to initiate a request that someone do—or stop doing—something.

Por favor, ¿puede/pudiera Ud.... ?
        ¿quiere/quisiera Ud.... ?
Por favor, ¿me trae... ?   ¿me pasa... ?   ¿me da... ?   ¿me dice/explica... ?

The last series of questions can also be declarative statements: **Por favor, me trae el periódico.** To be even more polite, you could also add **...si (Ud.) es tan amable** to the end of the sentence.

The other side of making a request is responding to one. When someone asks a favor of you, you may or may not want—or even be able—to comply. Here are a few ways to indicate your willingness to help.

¡Sí, sí!   Sí, no hay problema.   ¡Por supuesto!
¡Cómo no!   ¡Claro!   ¡Con mucho gusto!

If the favor is not one that you can grant, use phrases such as the following.

Lo siento. Realmente quisiera hacerlo, pero no puedo por(que)...
(Desgraciadamente) No es posible ahora por(que)...

1. ¿Ciudadanía?
2. ¿Algo que declarar?
3. Hmm. Ud. trae muchos cigarrillos americanos.
4. ¿Son suyas todas estas maletas?
5. ¿Qué lleva en la pequeña?
6. ¿Cuánto tiempo va Ud. a estar en nuestro país?
7. Doscientos pesos, por favor.

C. **¿Me hace el favor de... ?** Here are situations in which you need to ask for something or in which someone makes a request of you. What might you say in each situation? Offer several different responses, and use phrases from **A propósito.**

1. Sus padres le han mandado un cheque desde los Estados Unidos, pero Ud. no lo ha recibido todavía. Ud. necesita un poco de dinero y habla con su amigo Jaime.
2. Ud. se encuentra en una esquina de Madrid y no sabe dónde está. Con el mapa en la mano, Ud. para a dos personas y pregunta...
3. Su amiga Marta le pregunta si Ud. le puede prestar unos discos para una fiesta. Marta tiene fama de olvidarlo todo.

CH. **Situaciones.** Con su profesor(a) o con otro/a estudiante, haga Ud. uno de los siguientes papeles.

1. Ud. es inspector(a) de aduanas en la frontera entre México y Texas. Un día un hombre sospechoso (*suspicious-looking*) (una mujer sospechosa) pasa por la aduana. Ud. le dice que quiere registrar su equipaje y su coche.
2. Ud. es estudiante en la Universidad de Salamanca en España. Acaba de hacer un viaje a Francia y, de regreso a España, cruza ahora la frontera. El inspector (La inspectora) le pregunta por qué fue Ud. a Francia, qué hizo y qué trae en las maletas.
3. Ud. regresa a su universidad después de pasar un año en el extranjero. Dígale a su amigo/a por qué fue una experiencia maravillosa y por qué él/ella debe hacer lo mismo.

Preocupaciones del viajero

—Tengo la sensación de haber olvidado algo...
—A ver. ¿Llevas el pasaporte, el billete, el dinero?
—Sí, aquí va todo. ¡Ah, ya lo tengo! (*I figured it out!*)
—¿Qué?
—¡Dejé la maleta en tu coche!

Madrid, España

Stuart Cohen

UN PASO MÁS: Lectura cultural

En el extranjero

Miles de norteamericanos viajan al extranjero todos los años y regresan después a su país con un nuevo conocimiento de sí mismos, basado en toda una serie de experiencias personales, culturales y académicas. Pero algunos no aprovechan la oportunidad de aprender, y regresan con los mismos horizontes limitados que tenían antes de salir. Veamos° unos ejemplos.   *Let's see*

• Brian va a pasar el verano estudiando en el extranjero, digamos° en México. Se viste para ir a la UNAM° como si estuviera pasando el verano en su propia universidad: sandalias, pantalones cortos, camiseta. Cuando su compañero de cuarto, un mexicano, trata discretamente de informarle de las costumbres locales, Brian lo escucha atentamente. Después contesta insistiendo en su derecho a vestirse como le dé la gana,° ya que su única responsabilidad consiste en pagar las cuentas y en sacarle provecho al programa académico. Naturalmente, terminado el verano, vuelve a los Estados Unidos y comenta con sus amigos lo fríos y antisociales que son los jóvenes mexicanos. Realmente nunca los llegó a conocer.

let's say
Universidad Nacional Autónoma de México

como... however he wants

• El señor Baker tiene 66 años; su esposa tiene 67. Toda la vida habían querido viajar al extranjero pero no pudieron. Primero, tuvieron que establecerse; después, sus hijos necesitaban su ayuda. Ahora, sus hijos han crecido° y el señor Baker se ha jubilado. Han ahorrado durante cinco años para hacer un viaje, y quieren que todo resulte perfecto. Por fin hacen una excursión a Madrid: se quedan en una pensión; comen la mayoría de sus comidas en la pensión o en los pequeños restaurantes del centro; hacen todo lo posible por enterarse de las costumbres locales; las aceptan—aunque a veces les parecen muy «diferentes»—y se adaptan a ellas; tratan de conocer a muchas personas. Cuando regresan a los Estados Unidos, dicen que nunca se habían divertido tanto.

grown up

Para disfrutar una experiencia en el extranjero, basta con darse cuenta de° que conocer una cultura nueva es como conocer a una persona nueva. Las dos tienen su personalidad, sus cualidades y defectos. Lo importante es querer conocerlas.

basta... it's enough to realize

Comprensión

¿Quién lo diría, Brian o el señor Baker?

1. «No me importa lo que digan los otros.»
2. «Conocer a muchas personas es una buena manera de llegar a conocer una cultura.»
3. «Así me visto en verano, así soy. No voy a cambiar.»
4. «Siempre trato de hablar español, aunque no lo hablo muy bien.»
5. «Estoy aquí para aprender, no para preocuparme de sus ideas ni de sus tradiciones anticuadas.»
6. «No es fácil acostumbrarse a cenar a las diez de la noche, pero estoy haciendo un esfuerzo.»

Para escribir

Escríbale una carta a un amigo mexicano que piensa estudiar inglés en los Estados Unidos el verano que viene. Debe tratar de ayudarlo a evitar el «choque cultural» que pudiera experimentar. Use los siguientes temas como guía.

1. Ropa que llevar para ir de compras, asistir a clases, salir por la noche a una discoteca
2. Normas de conducta para los que fuman
3. Cómo saludar y despedirse de los amigos y conocidos
4. Comportamiento en clase y con los profesores
5. Comportamiento en un autobús (tren, avión)

VOCABULARIO

VERBOS
aterrizar to land
cruzar to cross
declarar to declare
entregar to hand over; to hand in
registrar to search, inspect

EN LA FRONTERA
la aduana customs

los derechos de aduana customs duty
el/la inspector(a) inspector
la multa fine, penalty
la nacionalidad nationality
el pasaporte passport
la planilla (de inmigración) (immigration) form
el/la viajero/a traveler

CONJUNCIONES
después (de) que after
en cuanto as soon as
hasta que until
tan pronto como as soon as

FRASES ÚTILES PARA LA COMUNICACIÓN	
tengo algo que + *inf.*	I have something to . . .
no tengo nada que + *inf.*	I have nothing to . . .

CAPÍTULO 27

¿Dónde nos quedamos?

el hotel de lujo

el hotel de primera (segunda) clase

la pensión

EN EL HOTEL O EN LA PENSIÓN

confirmar to confirm
quedarse to remain, stay (*as a guest*)
reservar to reserve

los cheques de viajero traveler's checks
la habitación room
  para una persona single

con/sin baño/ducha with/without bath/shower
la pensión boarding house
la pensión completa room and full board (all meals)
la media pensión room with breakfast and one other meal
la propina tip

con (____ días de) anticipación (____ days) in advance
desocupado/a vacant, unoccupied, free

A. **¿El Hotel María Cristina o la Pensión Libertad?** De estas oraciones, ¿cuáles describen un hotel grande e internacional? ¿una pensión pequeña y modesta?

1. Tiene todas las comodidades (*comforts*) que se encuentran en los mejores hoteles.
2. Los botones llevan el equipaje a la habitación.
3. Muchos de los huéspedes y del personal hablan solamente una lengua, el español, por ejemplo.
4. Hay que reservar una habitación con muchos días de anticipación.
5. Los dependientes confirman la reservación del huésped.
6. Generalmente se puede llegar sin reservaciones y encontrar una habitación desocupada.
7. Hay que gastar mucho dinero en propinas.
8. Los huéspedes suben (*carry up*) su equipaje, o el dueño los ayuda a subirlo.
9. Hablan muchos idiomas en la recepción.
10. Todas las habitaciones tienen ducha y, a veces, baño completo con ducha.
11. Se puede pedir una habitación con todas las comidas incluidas (pensión completa).
12. Generalmente es necesario compartir (*to share*) el baño con otros huéspedes.
13. Tiene un comedor grande y elegante.
14. Es posible que los huéspedes coman con la familia, en el comedor o en la cocina.

En la recepción

—¿Cuál es la tarifa de una habitación con pensión completa?
—¿Con o sin baño?
—Con baño privado, si es posible.
—Mil trescientos pesos la noche, señor.
—Está bien. Quisiéramos quedarnos dos noches.
—Muy bien, señor.

Ciudad de México, México

Stuart Cohen

B. **¿Qué se puede hacer?** Si Ud. se encuentra en estas situaciones, ¿cómo va a resolver el problema? Hay más de una respuesta posible.

1. Ud. reservó una habitación, pero el recepcionista no puede encontrar la reservación.

   a. Me voy a otro hotel.
   b. Insisto en hablar con el gerente (*manager*).
   c. Me quejo en voz alta mientras el recepcionista la sigue buscando.
   ch. ___?___

2. Ud. llega al único hotel del pueblo y encuentra que la única habitación desocupada cuesta muchísimo más de lo que quiere pagar.

   a. Regateo con el hotelero, pidiéndole que baje el precio.
   b. Busco a alguien para compartir el cuarto.
   c. Duermo en el coche.
   ch. ___?___

3. Ud. está viajando con un amigo. Ud. quiere quedarse en un hotel de lujo con todas las comodidades—con aire acondicionado, televisor y refrigerador en la habitación— pero su amigo quiere quedarse en una pensión y prefiere una habitación sin baño porque es más barata.

   a. Lo dejo lo más pronto posible.
   b. Voy a la pensión pero me pongo de muy mal humor.
   c. Insisto en que nos quedemos en un hotel de lujo, pero pago más de la mitad (*half*) de la cuenta.
   ch. ___?___

4. Ud. quiere pagar su cuenta y salir, pero sólo tiene cheques de viajero. El hotel no los acepta. Además, es domingo y los bancos están cerrados.

   a. Me quedo un día más.
   b. Salgo sin pagar.
   c. Le pido al gerente que me haga el favor de aceptar los cheques de viajero y lloro tanto que no me lo puede negar.
   ch. ___?___

5. La pensión en que Ud. quiere quedarse ofrece tres posibilidades. ¿Cuál va a escoger?

   a. habitación sin comida
   b. pensión completa
   c. media pensión

Preparaciones para un año en el extranjero

If you are planning a trip abroad, it is a good idea to find out as much as possible about the country and city where you will be staying.

The following letter is a response to a letter of inquiry from an American student planning to spend a year studying in Madrid. The numbered references are to the **comentario cultural** section, page 426.

Madrid, 4 de julio

Querida Patti,

Me alegro muchísimo de que vengas a pasar el año entero aquí en Madrid. Hace mucho tiempo que no nos vemos y estaré contentísima de verte de nuevo°—esta vez en mi país. Me hiciste muchas preguntas y quiero contestarlas todas para que no tengas muchas sorpresas cuando llegues. | *de... again*

Primero, el alojamiento.° Podrías vivir en un colegio mayor,° pero yo, por mi parte, prefiero una pensión.[1] Si te interesa, puedes quedarte en la misma donde yo vivo. La gente y la señora son muy amables y la pensión está muy bien situada en la Moncloa—la zona estudiantil—muy cerca de la Ciudad Universitaria.[2] Es un sitio° estupendo, con restaurantes y bares divertidísimos por todas partes—y también hay pastelerías excelentes; te lo digo porque te conozco y sé lo golosa que eres.° Y desde allí se llega fácilmente al centro, porque está situada entre la boca° del metro y las paradas de los autobuses. | *lodging* / colegio... *dormitory* ... *place* ... *lo... what a sweet tooth you have* / *entrance*

Hablando de comida, debo decirte que las tres comidas están incluidas en el precio de la habitación. La comida es casera,° pero riquísima. Seguro que te gustará. Sin embargo, si algún día te apeteciera° una hamburguesa y un batido, podrías ir—¿adónde crees?—¡pues al Burger King de la calle Princesa, que está muy cerca! | *home cooked* / *te... you felt like (eating)*

Con respecto a tu segunda pregunta—qué debes traer y qué no debes traer—te voy a dar algunos consejos. Recuerda que no vas a estar en la Costa del Sol sino en Madrid, y si no traes ropa de invierno te vas a congelar.° El clima aquí va de un extremo al otro y empieza a hacer frío en el mes de octubre. Se dice que en Madrid hay nueve meses de invierno y tres de infierno... y por algo lo dirán.° | *to freeze* ... *por... they must have a reason for saying it*

En cuanto a las otras cosas que piensas traer, yo te aconsejaría que no trajeras ningún aparato eléctrico, porque la corriente aquí es diferente a la de los EE.UU. Todas las cosas que vas a necesitar las puedes comprar cuando llegues. Hay muchas tiendas—papelerías, estancos, librerías, farmacias y más—cerca de la pensión, y también hay quioscos donde puedes comprar el último número del *Time* si te cansas° del español. | *te... you grow tired*

También me hiciste varias preguntas sobre tus cursos. De verdad no sé mucho de los cursos que vas a tomar. Tu plan de estudios ha sido preparado por el Centro[3] para estudiantes norteamericanos. Es probable que tengas clases por la mañana y, quizá, también por la tarde, como las tienen muchos de los otros programas para extranjeros. Lo que sí sé es que el Centro queda muy cerca de la Moncloa y podrás ir caminando a tus clases y volver a comer al mediodía° sin problema.

midday

Me dijiste que llegas por la mañana el día 20 de agosto. Si hay cambio de vuelo, no dejes de avisarme,° pues pienso ir a buscarte al aeropuerto. Y por ahora nada más. Si tienes cualquier otra pregunta, no dejes de escribirme. Esperando verte muy pronto, recibe un saludo muy afectuoso de

let me know

tu amiga,

Maripepa

Comentario cultural

1. Hispanic students must make individual arrangements for accommodations, since most Spanish and Latin American universities do not provide living quarters, cafeterias, or restaurants for students. Some students rent rooms and eat at nearby restaurants. Others live in **pensiones,** where the cost of the room includes meals and limited maid service. The **colegios mayores** mentioned in the dialogue are similar to United States dormitories, but they are often privately owned and operated.
2. **La Moncloa** is the district of Madrid where the University of Madrid is located. The campus itself is called **la Ciudad Universitaria.**
3. The **Centro Iberoamericano de Cooperación y Desarrollo,** located on the edge of the **Ciudad Universitaria,** sponsors cultural events and also organizes programs for foreign students **(cursos para extranjeros).** Many foreign university programs hold their classes in its facilities.

¿Qué necesita Ud. saber?

Siguiendo el modelo de la carta de Maripepa, escriba una de las siguientes cartas:

1. Ud. es un estudiante latinoamericano (una estudiante latinoamericana) que viene a los Estados Unidos por primera vez a pasar un año, como mínimo. Escriba una carta a la familia con la cual (*with which*) va a vivir. Preséntese y pida informes sobre el país—el clima, las costumbres, etcétera—y sobre la familia. ¿Qué debe traer? ¿Qué no debe traer? ¿Qué debe saber del lugar donde va a vivir? ¿de los estudiantes de su universidad?

2. Ud. es miembro de la familia con la cual un estudiante extranjero (una estudiante extranjera) va a pasar un año. Escríbale, dándole los informes que pueda necesitar.

3. Ud. es un estudiante norteamericano (una estudiante norteamericana) que va a pasar el próximo año académico en Latinoamérica o en España. Escriba una carta a un amigo que está estudiando allí este año. Pídale informes sobre el país y sobre la vida de un estudiante, es decir, sobre todo lo que Ud. necesita saber para prepararse para el año.

REPASO GENERAL

A. Problemas del viajero. Con otro/a estudiante o con el profesor (la profesora), hagan los papeles de viajero y recepcionista en la siguiente situación. El viajero (la viajera) debe contestar sin leer primero las preguntas. Hagan el diálogo dos veces: primero en un hotel de lujo, luego en una pensión u hotel de tercera categoría. Usen frases de **A propósito...** (páginas 428–429).

En la recepción: El viajero (la viajera) busca una habitación y quiere pagar con cheque.

RECEPCIONISTA: Sí, señor(a). ¿En qué puedo servirlo/la?
VIAJERO/A: _____ .
RECEPCIONISTA: ¿La prefiere Ud. con ducha o con baño?
VIAJERO/A: _____ .
RECEPCIONISTA: Muy bien. Tenemos una habitación en el tercer piso. ¿Necesita ayuda con el equipaje?
VIAJERO/A: _____ .
RECEPCIONISTA: ¿Cómo va Ud. a pagar, por favor?
VIAJERO/A: _____ .
RECEPCIONISTA: Lo siento, pero no las aceptamos. Aceptamos cheques de viajero, si Ud. tiene documentación.

Una conversación telefónica: ¿Cómo responde Ud. en estas situaciones?

1. Ud. llama a su amigo Pepe a su casa. La mamá de él contesta, diciendo «¿Diga?».

2. Cuando Ud. llama a su jefe, su secretaria le pregunta «¿De parte de quién?»

3. Ud. pregunta por Consuelo y la persona que contesta dice: «Perdón, pero aquí no vive ninguna Consuelo.»

Ahora, con otro/a estudiante o con el profesor (la profesora), invente una conversación telefónica. Imagine que Ud. es un(a) turista en la ciudad de México. Busca habitación y llama al Hotel Fénix para pedir información sobre las tarifas y las habitaciones disponibles. Quiere reservar una habitación para dos personas si puede pagar lo que piden. Sea cortés y trate de conseguir toda la información que necesita.

B. **Situaciones.** Con su profesor(a) o con otro/a estudiante, haga Ud. uno de los siguientes papeles.

1. Ud. va a hacer un viaje al Perú y quiere que un(a) agente de viajes le haga las reservaciones. Pero cuando Ud. habla con él/ella, descubre que ha planeado un viaje imposible para Ud. Le sugiere que se quede en hoteles de lujo y que alquile un coche por todo un mes. Explíquele que Ud. no tiene tanto dinero y que es preciso que le arregle algo más barato.
2. Después de seis horas buscando alojamiento (*lodging*) en la capital de Costa Rica, Ud. entra en el Hotel La Paz con sus tres perros. El/La recepcionista le explica que sí tienen habitaciones pero que no permiten que los animales se queden en el hotel. ¿Qué le dice Ud.?
3. Ud. pasó una mala noche en un cuarto de la Pensión Fuentes. Por la mañana baja a la recepción para explicarles por qué Ud. está tan descontento/a con la habitación.

A propósito...

The following phrases—most of which you already know—will be useful to you in arranging for lodging in a Spanish-speaking country.

Frases útiles para el hotel

un hotel de lujo	*a deluxe hotel*
un hotel de primera (segunda) clase	*a first-class (second-class) hotel*
una habitación para una persona (dos personas)	*a single (double) room*
con baño (ducha)	*with a bath (shower)*
sin baño	*without a bath*
para una noche (dos noches)	*for one night (two nights)*
¿Necesita Ud. mi pasaporte?	*Do you need my passport?*
¿Aceptan Uds. cheques de viajero (tarjetas de crédito)?	*Do you accept traveler's checks (credit cards)?*

Frases útiles para la pensión

pensión completa	*room and full board (all meals included)*
media pensión	*breakfast and one other meal included*

While staying in a hotel or pension, you may need to make a phone call or answer one. Here are some typical expressions that are part of phone courtesy.

Contestando

¿Diga?	
¿Aló?	*Hello?*
¿Sí?	
¿De parte de quién?	*Who's calling?*
¿Quiere dejar un recado?	*Would you like to leave a message?*
Adiós.	*Goodbye.*

Llamando

Habla Juan Ordás.	*This is Juan Ordás.*
¿Está Cecilia Hernández, por favor?	*Is Cecilia Hernández there (at home), please?*
Sí, quisiera saber…	*Yes, I would like to know . . .*
Perdón. Marqué mal el número.	*Pardon me. I dialed the wrong number.*

UN PASO MÁS: Imágenes del mundo hispánico

Sudamérica: La actualidad del continente

Sudamérica es un continente lleno de riquezas y de posibilidades. Cuando los españoles llegaron en el siglo XV se maravillaron por la exuberancia de la naturaleza. Se encontraron con selvas, montañas y ríos impresionantes, con animales de infinita variedad, y también con cultivos y frutas totalmente desconocidos en Europa: la patata, el tomate, el maíz, el cacao… ¿Puede imaginarse la vida sin estos productos? Algunos de estos cultivos siguen siendo la base altimenticia y económica de la mayoría de los indios de Sudamérica. Por lo general se trata de una agricultura de subsistencia, pero también hay países cuya economía es fuertemente agrícola. En Colombia, el café es el principal producto de exportación mientras que las bananas y el cacao los son de Ecuador.

Desde el siglo XV, la búsqueda de metales y piedras preciosas ha sido uno de los principales motores para la colonización. Hoy en día la explotación del cobre (*copper*) es fundamental para la economía de Perú y Chile, y lo mismo sucede con el estaño (*tin*) en Bolivia. El sueño (*dream*) de muchos aventureros de encontrar infinitas riquezas escondidas (*hidden*) se ha hecho finalmente realidad con el descubrimiento del famoso «oro negro»: el petróleo. Venezuela es el principal país exportador de petróleo de Sudamérica y también tiene importantes depósitos de mineral de hierro (*iron*).

Durante la últimas décadas Sudamérica ha estado tratando de aumentar su actividad industrial y tecnológica. Esto le permitirá una menor dependencia de otros países más desarrollados. En muchos aspectos, sigue sin descubrir. Sus riquezas y posibilidades darán mucho que hablar en los próximos años.

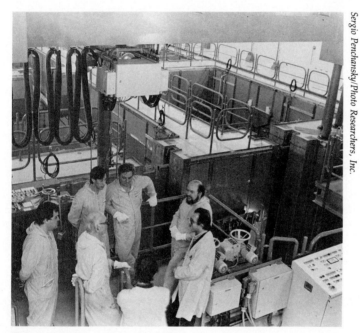

Sergio Penchansky/Photo Researchers, Inc.

Planta nuclear de Atucha, Argentina

Vautier/Decool/Click/Chicago

Cadena de montaje en una fábrica de automóviles argentina

VOCABULARIO

VERBOS

compartir to share
confirmar to confirm
reservar to reserve

EN EL HOTEL

el botones/el mozo bellhop
la comodidad comfort
el cheque de viajero traveler's
    check

la ducha shower
la habitación room (*in a hotel*)
el/la huésped(a) guest
la pensión boarding house
la pensión completa room and
    full board (all meals)
la media pensión room with
    breakfast and one other
    meal
la propina tip
la recepción reception desk

ADJETIVO

desocupado/a unoccupied

PALABRAS ADICIONALES

con (____ días de) anticipación
    (____ days) in advance
de lujo deluxe
para una persona single

CAPÍTULO 28

¿Cuándo vas al extranjero?

VOCABULARIO: PREPARACIÓN

EN EL EXTRANJERO

el champú shampoo
el jabón soap
la pasta dental toothpaste

los fósforos matches
el papel para cartas stationery
el paquete package
la revista magazine
el sello stamp
el sobre envelope
la tarjeta postal postcard

el estanco tobacco stand, shop

el batido drink similar to a milkshake
una copa/un trago (alcoholic) drink
el pastelito small pastry

431

De compras

—Necesito comprar jabón y champú.
¿Quieres acompañarme?
—Cómo no. ¿Adónde vas?
—Hay una farmacia cerca, ¿no?
—Es cierto. Queda muy cerca de aquí, en la
esquina.

Katherine A. Lambert/Kay Reese & Assoc.

Guadalupe, Costa Rica

Even though the places in the drawing on p. 431 may look familiar,
what they have for sale may be very different in another country. The
following letter will show you one aspect of culture shock as it was
experienced by an American university student.

Madrid

Querido Joe:

¡Cuánto siento que no hayas podido venir con nosotros en este viaje
a España! Para que sigas practicando el español, te escribo en este
idioma.

Quiero contarte el «choque cultural» que estoy pasando. Por
ejemplo: en las farmacias no venden la variedad de cosas—dulces,
tarjetas postales, etcétera—que se venden en las farmacias de los
EE.UU.* Esta mañana, cuando fui a una farmacia para comprar postales,
me enteré de que allí sólo venden medicinas y productos de higiene
personal: jabón, pasta dental, champú, etcétera.

Después necesitaba sellos para mandar unas cartas y le pregunté a
un señor que esperaba en la parada del autobús dónde estaba el correo
para poder comprarlos. Me dijo que no tenía que ir hasta el correo
porque los sellos también se venden en los estancos. Como había un
estanco enfrente, entré. Allí no sólo vendían fósforos, cigarrillos y puros
(*cigars*) sino también sellos, sobres y tarjetas postales.

También quería comprar una revista y no tuve que ir lejos porque en
la misma calle había un quiosco. Aquí hay muchas de estas tiendecitas
donde se venden cosas como periódicos, libros, revistas, etcétera. Claro
que también se pueden comprar estas cosas y más—lápices, papel para
cartas, etcétera—en las papelerías.

Bueno, Joe, después de hacer todas estas compras, estaba muy
cansado. Como era la una de la tarde, empezaron a cerrar todas las

---

*EE.UU. is one way to abbreviate **Estados Unidos**. E.U. and USA are also used.

tiendas. Así, tomé el metro y volví a la pensión. Aquí estoy, descansando un rato antes de la comida.

Hablando de la comida, eso es otra cosa que encuentro muy diferente aquí. Se almuerza muy fuerte, con tres o cuatro platos más el postre. Y no se almuerza sino hasta la una y media o las dos de la tarde. Todas las tiendas están cerradas durante tres o cuatro horas, porque muchas personas vuelven a casa a almorzar y después a echar (*to take*) una siesta. Ya tengo la costumbre de dormir por lo menos una hora después de comer. Te digo que, con excepción de los restaurantes, es como si el mundo español dejara de existir entre las dos y las cuatro de la tarde. ¿Y sabes otra cosa que me sorprende? La cena es a las diez de la noche.

Pues, eso es todo por el momento. Te vuelvo a escribir la semana que viene.

Tu amigo,

David

A. Conteste en oraciones completas.

1. ¿Dónde se puede comprar champú? ¿jabón?
2. ¿Cuál es la diferencia entre una farmacia de los Estados Unidos y una farmacia de España?
3. ¿Dónde se puede comprar sellos en España? (Mencione dos lugares.)
4. Si se necesitan cigarrillos o fósforos, ¿adónde se va?
5. ¿Qué es un quiosco? ¿Qué cosas se venden allí?
6. ¿Qué venden en una papelería?
7. ¿En qué se diferencian el horario de las comidas en España y el de los Estados Unidos?
8. ¿Cuándo se toma la comida principal en España? ¿Qué hacen muchos españoles después?

B. Pretend that you are a Spanish student studying for the first time in the United States. Write a letter to a friend back home, telling him or her about the culture shock you are experiencing. How will your letter differ from David's?

Ejercicio escrito final

What parts of the Spanish-speaking world are you most interested in visiting? Express your preferences by writing paragraphs to complete the following statements.

1. Si yo estuviera en (Madrid, Buenos Aires, Cuernavaca, ___?___)...
2. Si yo pudiera viajar a cualquier lugar del mundo,...

Verbs

A. Regular Verbs: Simple Tenses

INFINITIVE / PRESENT PARTICIPLE / PAST PARTICIPLE	INDICATIVE					SUBJUNCTIVE		IMPERATIVE
	PRESENT	IMPERFECT	PRETERITE	FUTURE	CONDITIONAL	PRESENT	IMPERFECT	
hablar hablando hablado	hablo hablas habla hablamos habláis hablan	hablaba hablabas hablaba hablábamos hablabais hablaban	hablé hablaste habló hablamos hablasteis hablaron	hablaré hablarás hablará hablaremos hablaréis hablarán	hablaría hablarías hablaría hablaríamos hablaríais hablarían	hable hables hable hablemos habléis hablen	hablara hablaras hablara habláramos hablarais hablaran	habla tú, no hables hable Ud. hablemos hablen
comer comiendo comido	como comes come comemos coméis comen	comía comías comía comíamos comíais comían	comí comiste comió comimos comisteis comieron	comeré comerás comerá comeremos comeréis comerán	comería comerías comería comeríamos comeríais comerían	coma comas coma comamos comáis coman	comiera comieras comiera comiéramos comierais comieran	come tú, no comas coma Ud. comamos coman
vivir viviendo vivido	vivo vives vive vivimos vivís viven	vivía vivías vivía vivíamos vivíais vivían	viví viviste vivió vivimos vivisteis vivieron	viviré vivirás vivirá viviremos viviréis vivirán	viviría vivirías viviría viviríamos viviríais vivirían	viva vivas viva vivamos viváis vivan	viviera vivieras viviera viviéramos vivierais vivieran	vive tú, no vivas viva Ud. vivamos vivan

B. Regular Verbs: Perfect Tenses

INDICATIVE					SUBJUNCTIVE	
PRESENT PERFECT	PAST PERFECT	PRETERITE PERFECT	FUTURE PERFECT	CONDITIONAL PERFECT	PRESENT PERFECT	PAST PERFECT
he has ha hemos habéis han } hablado comido vivido	había habías había habíamos habíais habían } hablado comido vivido	hube hubiste hubo hubimos hubisteis hubieron } hablado comido vivido	habré habrás habrá habremos habréis habrán } hablado comido vivido	habría habrías habría habríamos habríais habrían } hablado comido vivido	haya hayas haya hayamos hayáis hayan } hablado comido vivido	hubiera hubieras hubiera hubiéramos hubierais hubieran } hablado comido vivido

C. Irregular Verbs

INFINITIVE PRESENT PARTICIPLE PAST PARTICIPLE	INDICATIVE					SUBJUNCTIVE		IMPERATIVE
	PRESENT	IMPERFECT	PRETERITE	FUTURE	CONDITIONAL	PRESENT	IMPERFECT	
andar andando andado	ando andas anda andamos andáis andan	andaba andabas andaba andábamos andabais andaban	anduve anduviste anduvo anduvimos anduvisteis anduvieron	andaré andarás andará andaremos andaréis andarán	andaría andarías andaría andaríamos andaríais andarían	ande andes ande andemos andéis anden	anduviera anduvieras anduviera anduviéramos anduvierais anduvieran	anda tú, no andes ande Ud. andemos anden
caer cayendo caído	caigo caes cae caemos caéis caen	caía caías caía caíamos caíais caían	caí caíste cayó caímos caísteis cayeron	caeré caerás caerá caeremos caeréis caerán	caería caerías caería caeríamos caeríais caerían	caiga caigas caiga caigamos caigáis caigan	cayera cayeras cayera cayéramos cayerais cayeran	cae tú, no caigas caiga Ud. caigamos caigan
dar dando dado	doy das da damos dais dan	daba dabas daba dábamos dabais daban	di diste dio dimos disteis dieron	daré darás dará daremos daréis darán	daría darías daría daríamos daríais darían	dé des dé demos deis den	diera dieras diera diéramos dierais dieran	da tú, no des dé Ud. demos den
decir diciendo dicho	digo dices dice decimos decís dicen	decía decías decía decíamos decíais decían	dije dijiste dijo dijimos dijisteis dijeron	diré dirás dirá diremos diréis dirán	diría dirías diría diríamos diríais dirían	diga digas diga digamos digáis digan	dijera dijeras dijera dijéramos dijerais dijeran	di tú, no digas diga Ud. digamos digan
estar estando estado	estoy estás está estamos estáis están	estaba estabas estaba estábamos estabais estaban	estuve estuviste estuvo estuvimos estuvisteis estuvieron	estaré estarás estará estaremos estaréis estarán	estaría estarías estaría estaríamos estaríais estarían	esté estés esté estemos estéis estén	estuviera estuvieras estuviera estuviéramos estuvierais estuvieran	está tú, no estés esté Ud. estemos estén
haber habiendo habido	he has ha hemos habéis han	había habías había habíamos habíais habían	hube hubiste hubo hubimos hubisteis hubieron	habré habrás habrá habremos habréis habrán	habría habrías habría habríamos habríais habrían	haya hayas haya hayamos hayáis hayan	hubiera hubieras hubiera hubiéramos hubierais hubieran	
hacer haciendo hecho	hago haces hace hacemos hacéis hacen	hacía hacías hacía hacíamos hacíais hacían	hice hiciste hizo hicimos hicisteis hicieron	haré harás hará haremos haréis harán	haría harías haría haríamos haríais harían	haga hagas haga hagamos hagáis hagan	hiciera hicieras hiciera hiciéramos hicierais hicieran	haz tú, no hagas haga Ud. hagamos hagan
ir yendo ido	voy vas va vamos vais van	iba ibas iba íbamos ibais iban	fui fuiste fue fuimos fuisteis fueron	iré irás irá iremos iréis irán	iría irías iría iríamos iríais irían	vaya vayas vaya vayamos vayáis vayan	fuera fueras fuera fuéramos fuerais fueran	ve tú, no vayas vaya Ud. vayamos vayan
oír oyendo	oigo oyes	oía oías	oí oíste	oiré oirás	oiría oirías	oiga oigas	oyera oyeras	oye tú, no oigas oiga Ud.

C. Irregular Verbs (continued)

INFINITIVE PRESENT PARTICIPLE PAST PARTICIPLE	INDICATIVE PRESENT	IMPERFECT	PRETERITE	FUTURE	CONDITIONAL	SUBJUNCTIVE PRESENT	IMPERFECT	IMPERATIVE
oído	oye oímos oís oyen	oía oíamos oíais oían	oyó oímos oísteis oyeron	oirá oiremos oiréis oirán	oiría oiríamos oiríais oirían	oiga oigamos oigáis oigan	oyera oyéramos oyerais oyeran	oigamos oigan
poder pudiendo podido	puedo puedes puede podemos podéis pueden	podía podías podía podíamos podíais podían	pude pudiste pudo pudimos pudisteis pudieron	podré podrás podrá podremos podréis podrán	podría podrías podría podríamos podríais podrían	pueda puedas pueda podamos podáis puedan	pudiera pudieras pudiera pudiéramos pudierais pudieran	
poner poniendo puesto	pongo pones pone ponemos ponéis ponen	ponía ponías ponía poníamos poníais ponían	puse pusiste puso pusimos pusisteis pusieron	pondré pondrás pondrá pondremos pondréis pondrán	pondría pondrías pondría pondríamos pondríais pondrían	ponga pongas ponga pongamos pongáis pongan	pusiera pusieras pusiera pusiéramos pusierais pusieran	pon tú, no pongas ponga Ud. pongamos pongan
querer queriendo querido	quiero quieres quiere queremos queréis quieren	quería querías quería queríamos queríais querían	quise quisiste quiso quisimos quisisteis quisieron	querré querrás querrá querremos querréis querrán	querría querrías querría querríamos querríais querrían	quiera quieras quiera queramos queráis quieran	quisiera quisieras quisiera quisiéramos quisierais quisieran	quiere tú, no quieras quiera Ud. queramos quieran
saber sabiendo sabido	sé sabes sabe sabemos sabéis saben	sabía sabías sabía sabíamos sabíais sabían	supe supiste supo supimos supisteis supieron	sabré sabrás sabrá sabremos sabréis sabrán	sabría sabrías sabría sabríamos sabríais sabrían	sepa sepas sepa sepamos sepáis sepan	supiera supieras supiera supiéramos supierais supieran	sabe tú, no sepas sepa Ud. sepamos sepan
salir saliendo salido	salgo sales sale salimos salís salen	salía salías salía salíamos salíais salían	salí saliste salió salimos salisteis salieron	saldré saldrás saldrá saldremos saldréis saldrán	saldría saldrías saldría saldríamos saldríais saldrían	salga salgas salga salgamos salgáis salgan	saliera salieras saliera saliéramos salierais salieran	sal tú, no salgas salga Ud. salgamos salgan
ser siendo sido	soy eres es somos sois son	era eras era éramos erais eran	fui fuiste fue fuimos fuisteis fueron	seré serás será seremos seréis serán	sería serías sería seríamos seríais serían	sea seas sea seamos seáis sean	fuera fueras fuera fuéramos fuerais fueran	sé tú, no seas sea Ud. seamos sean
tener teniendo tenido	tengo tienes tiene tenemos tenéis tienen	tenía tenías tenía teníamos teníais tenían	tuve tuviste tuvo tuvimos tuvisteis tuvieron	tendré tendrás tendrá tendremos tendréis tendrán	tendría tendrías tendría tendríamos tendríais tendrían	tenga tengas tenga tengamos tengáis tengan	tuviera tuvieras tuviera tuviéramos tuvierais tuvieran	ten tú, no tengas tenga Ud. tengamos tengan
traer trayendo traído	traigo traes trae traemos traéis traen	traía traías traía traíamos traíais traían	traje trajiste trajo trajimos trajisteis trajeron	traeré traerás traerá traeremos traeréis traerán	traería traerías traería traeríamos traeríais traerían	traiga traigas traiga traigamos traigáis traigan	trajera trajeras trajera trajéramos trajerais trajeran	trae tú, no traigas traiga Ud. traigamos traigan

C. Irregular Verbs (continued)

INFINITIVE / PRESENT PARTICIPLE / PAST PARTICIPLE	INDICATIVE					SUBJUNCTIVE		IMPERATIVE
	PRESENT	IMPERFECT	PRETERITE	FUTURE	CONDITIONAL	PRESENT	IMPERFECT	
venir viniendo venido	vengo vienes viene venimos venís vienen	venía venías venía veníamos veníais venían	vine viniste vino vinimos vinisteis vinieron	vendré vendrás vendrá vendremos vendréis vendrán	vendría vendrías vendría vendríamos vendríais vendrían	venga vengas venga vengamos vengáis vengan	viniera vinieras viniera viniéramos vinierais vinieran	ven tú, no vengas venga Ud. vengamos vengan
ver viendo visto	veo ves ve vemos veis ven	veía veías veía veíamos veíais veían	vi viste vio vimos visteis vieron	veré verás verá veremos veréis verán	vería verías vería veríamos veríais verían	vea veas vea veamos veáis vean	viera vieras viera viéramos vierais vieran	ve tú, no veas vea Ud. veamos vean

D. Stem-changing and Spelling-change Verbs

INFINITIVE / PRESENT PARTICIPLE / PAST PARTICIPLE	INDICATIVE					SUBJUNCTIVE		IMPERATIVE
	PRESENT	IMPERFECT	PRETERITE	FUTURE	CONDITIONAL	PRESENT	IMPERFECT	
pensar (ie) pensando pensado	pienso piensas piensa pensamos pensáis piensan	pensaba pensabas pensaba pensábamos pensabais pensaban	pensé pensaste pensó pensamos pensasteis pensaron	pensaré pensarás pensará pensaremos pensaréis pensarán	pensaría pensarías pensaría pensaríamos pensaríais pensarían	piense pienses piense pensemos penséis piensen	pensara pensaras pensara pensáramos pensarais pensaran	piensa tú, no pienses piense Ud. pensemos piensen
volver (ue) volviendo vuelto	vuelvo vuelves vuelve volvemos volvéis vuelven	volvía volvías volvía volvíamos volvíais volvían	volví volviste volvió volvimos volvisteis volvieron	volveré volverás volverá volveremos volveréis volverán	volvería volverías volvería volveríamos volveríais volverían	vuelva vuelvas vuelva volvamos volváis vuelvan	volviera volvieras volviera volviéramos volvierais volvieran	vuelve tú, no vuelvas vuelva Ud. volvamos vuelvan
dormir (ue, u) durmiendo dormido	duermo duermes duerme dormimos dormís duermen	dormía dormías dormía dormíamos dormíais dormían	dormí dormiste durmió dormimos dormisteis durmieron	dormiré dormirás dormirá dormiremos dormiréis dormirán	dormiría dormirías dormiría dormiríamos dormiríais dormirían	duerma duermas duerma durmamos durmáis duerman	durmiera durmieras durmiera durmiéramos durmierais durmieran	duerme tú, no duermas duerma Ud. durmamos duerman
sentir (ie, i) sintiendo sentido	siento sientes siente sentimos sentís sienten	sentía sentías sentía sentíamos sentíais sentían	sentí sentiste sintió sentimos sentisteis sintieron	sentiré sentirás sentirá sentiremos sentiréis sentirán	sentiría sentirías sentiría sentiríamos sentiríais sentirían	sienta sientas sienta sintamos sintáis sientan	sintiera sintieras sintiera sintiéramos sintierais sintieran	siente tú, no sientas sienta Ud. sintamos sientan

D. Stem-changing and Spelling-change Verbs (continued)

INFINITIVE PRESENT PARTICIPLE PAST PARTICIPLE	INDICATIVE					SUBJUNCTIVE		IMPERATIVE
	PRESENT	IMPERFECT	PRETERITE	FUTURE	CONDITIONAL	PRESENT	IMPERFECT	
pedir (i, i) pidiendo pedido	pido pides pide pedimos pedís piden	pedía pedías pedía pedíamos pedíais pedían	pedí pediste pidió pedimos pedisteis pidieron	pediré pedirás pedirá pediremos pediréis pedirán	pediría pedirías pediría pediríamos pediríais pedirían	pida pidas pida pidamos pidáis pidan	pidiera pidieras pidiera pidiéramos pidierais pidieran	pide tú, no pidas pida Ud. pidamos pidan
reír (i, i) riendo reído	río ríes ríe reímos reís ríen	reía reías reía reíamos reíais reían	reí reíste rió reímos reísteis rieron	reiré reirás reirá reiremos reiréis reirán	reiría reirías reiría reiríamos reiríais reirían	ría rías ría riamos riáis rían	riera rieras riera riéramos rierais rieran	ríe tú, no rías ría Ud. riamos rían
seguir (i, i) (ga) siguiendo seguido	sigo sigues sigue seguimos seguís siguen	seguía seguías seguía seguíamos seguíais seguían	seguí seguiste siguió seguimos seguisteis siguieron	seguiré seguirás seguirá seguiremos seguiréis seguirán	seguiría seguirías seguiría seguiríamos seguiríais seguirían	siga sigas siga sigamos sigáis sigan	siguiera siguieras siguiera siguiéramos siguierais siguieran	sigue tú, no sigas siga Ud. sigamos sigan
pedir (i, i) pidiendo pedido	pido pides pide pedimos pedís piden	pedía pedías pedía pedíamos pedíais pedían	pedí pediste pidió pedimos pedisteis pidieron	pediré pedirás pedirá pediremos pediréis pedirán	pediría pedirías pediría pediríamos pediríais pedirían	pida pidas pida pidamos pidáis pidan	pidiera pidieras pidiera pidiéramos pidierais pidieran	pide tú, no pidas pida Ud. pidamos pidan
reír (i, i) riendo reído	río ríes ríe reímos reís ríen	reía reías reía reíamos reíais reían	reí reíste rió reímos reísteis rieron	reiré reirás reirá reiremos reiréis reirán	reiría reirías reiría reiríamos reiríais reirían	ría rías ría riamos riáis rían	riera rieras riera riéramos rierais rieran	ríe tú, no rías ría Ud. riamos rían
seguir (i, i) (ga) siguiendo seguido	sigo sigues sigue seguimos seguís siguen	seguía seguías seguía seguíamos seguíais seguían	seguí seguiste siguió seguimos seguisteis siguieron	seguiré seguirás seguirá seguiremos seguiréis seguirán	seguiría seguirías seguiría seguiríamos seguiríais seguirían	siga sigas siga sigamos sigáis sigan	siguiera siguieras siguiera siguiéramos siguierais siguieran	sigue tú, no sigas siga Ud. sigamos sigan
construir (y) construyendo construido	construyo construyes construye construimos construís construyen	construía construías construía construíamos construíais construían	construí construiste construyó construimos construisteis construyeron	construiré construirás construirá construiremos construiréis construirán	construiría construirías construiría construiríamos construiríais construirían	construya construyas construya construyamos construyáis construyan	construyera construyeras construyera construyéramos construyerais construyeran	construye tú, no construyas construya Ud. construyamos construyan
producir (zc) produciendo producido	produzco produces produce producimos producís producen	producía producías producía producíamos producíais producían	produje produjiste produjo produjimos produjisteis produjeron	produciré producirás producirá produciremos produciréis producirán	produciría producirías produciría produciríamos produciríais producirían	produzca produzcas produzca produzcamos produzcáis produzcan	produjera produjeras produjera produjéramos produjerais produjeran	produce tú, no produzcas produzca Ud. produzcamos produzcan

VOCABULARIES

The *Spanish-English Vocabulary* contains all the words that appear in the text, with the following exceptions: (1) most close or identical cognates that do not appear in the chapter vocabulary lists; (2) most conjugated verb forms; (3) diminutives ending in **-ito/a;** (4) absolute superlatives ending in **-ísimo/a;** (5) most adverbs ending in **-mente;** (6) numbers; (7) days and months. Active vocabulary is indicated by the number of the chapter in which it is first listed **(PP = Pasos preliminares);** vocabulary glossed in the text is not considered active vocabulary and is not numbered. Only meanings that are used in this text are given. The *English-Spanish Vocabulary* includes all words and expressions in the chapter vocabulary necessary to do the translation exercises in the text and in the *Workbook.*

The gender of nouns is indicated, except for masculine nouns ending in **-o** and feminine nouns ending in **-a.** Stem changes and spelling changes are indicated for verbs: **dormir (ue, u); llegar (gu).**

In Spanish, words beginning with **ch, ll,** and **ñ** are found under separate headings, following the letters **c, l,** and **n,** respectively. Similarly, **ch, ll,** and **ñ** within words follow **c, l,** and **n,** respectively. For example, **coche** follows **cóctel, calle** follows **calor,** and **añadir** follows **anuncio.**

The following abbreviations are used:

adj.	adjective	*inf.*	infinitive	*poss.*	possessive
adv.	adverb	*inv.*	invariable in form	*prep.*	preposition
coll.	colloquial	*irreg.*	irregular	*pret.*	preterite
conj.	conjunction	*m.*	masculine	*pron.*	pronoun
d.o.	direct object	*Mex.*	Mexico	*refl. pron.*	reflexive pronoun
f.	feminine	*n.*	noun	*s.*	singular
fam.	familiar	*obj. of prep.*	object of a preposition	*Sp.*	Spain
form.	formal	*p.p.*	past participle	*sub. pron.*	subject pronoun
gram.	grammatical term	*pl.*	plural	*v.*	verb
i.o.	indirect object				

Spanish-English Vocabulary

a to (PP); at (*with time*) (PP); **a la(s)** _____ at (*hour*) (PP)
a menos que unless (20)
abierto/a *p.p.* open(ed) (7)
abogado/a lawyer
aborto abortion
abrazar (c) to hug
abrigo coat (6)
abrir (*p.p.* **abierto/a**) to open (3); **abrirse paso** to force one's way
absoluto/a absolute
abuelo/a grandfather/grandmother (3)
abuelos grandparents (3)
abundancia abundance
aburrido/a: estar aburrido/a to be bored (7); **ser aburrido/a** to be boring
aburrir to bore

acá here
acabar to finish (15); to run out of (15); to use up completely (21); **acabar de** + *inf.* to have just (*done something*) (8)
academia academy
acaso: por si acaso just in case (25)
accidente *m.* accident
acción *f.* action
aceite *m.* oil (17)
acelerado: ritmo (acelerado) de la vida (fast) pace of life, living (21)
acelerar to accelerate, speed up
acentuar to stress, accent
aceptación *f.* acceptance
aceptar to accept
acera sidewalk
acerca de *prep.* about, concerning

aclarar to make clear, explain
acomodado/a rich, well-to-do
acomodar to accommodate; **acomodarse a** to conform to
acompañado/a accompanied
acompañar to accompany, go with (19)
acondicionador: (aire) acondicionador *m.* air conditioner (14)
aconsejar to advise
acontecimiento event, happening (24)
acordarse (ue) (de) to remember (15)
acostar (ue) to put to bed (13); **acostarse** to go to bed (13)
acostumbrarse (a) to get used (to) (25)
actitud *f.* attitude
actividad *f.* activity
actriz *f.* (*pl.* **actrices**) actress

actual present (24); up-to-date, current
actualidad *f.* actuality; **en la actualidad** at present, at the present time
actualmente *adv.* at present
acuerdo agreement; **de acuerdo** agreed; **estar de acuerdo (con)** to agree, be in agreement (with) (6); **ponerse de acuerdo** to reach an agreement (23)
adaptarse to adapt oneself to, get used to
adecuado/a adequate; appropriate
adelantado/a in advance, ahead
adelgazar (c) to make thin, slender; **adelgazarse** to become thin
además (de) besides, in addition (to)
adentro *adv.* inside
adiós good-bye (PP)
adivinar to guess
¿adónde? where (to)? (5)
adoptar to adopt
adornado/a ornamented, adorned
aduana customs (26); **derechos** (*pl.*) **de aduana** customs duty (26)
aéreo/a *adj.* air, *of or pertaining to air travel*
aerolínea airline
aeropuerto airport (11)
afectar to affect
afectivo/a affective, emotional
afectuoso/a affectionate
afeitar to shave (13); **afeitarse** to shave oneself (13)
afición *f.* affection, fondness
aficionado/a *n.* fan; *adj.* fond; **ser aficionado/a (a)** to be a fan (of) (19)
afrontar to confront
afuera *adv.* outside (8); **afueras** *n. pl.* outskirts, suburbs (13)
agencia agency; **agencia de empleos** employment agency; **agencia de viajes** travel agency
agente *m., f.* agent; **agente de viajes** travel agent
agitado/a agitated, irritated; stormy
agradable agreeable, pleasant
agradecer (zc) to thank
agradecimiento gratitude
agrícola *inv.* agricultural
agricultor(a) farmer
agua *f.* (but **el agua**) water (10)
aguantar to put up with, endure, tolerate
ahí there
ahora now (3); **ahora bien** now then, well now; **ahora mismo** right now (6)
ahorrar to save (*money*) (22)
ahorros: cuenta de ahorros savings account (22)
aire *m.* air; **aire acondicionado** air conditioning; **aire acondicionador** *m.* air conditioner (14); **al aire libre** outdoors (5)
aislado/a isolated
ajedrez *m.* chess (19)
al (*contraction of* **a** + **el**) to the; **al** + *inf.* upon, while, when + *verb form*; **al (mes, año, etcétera)** per (month, year, etc.)
albóndigas meatballs (10)
alcalde *m.* mayor
alcanzar (c) to get up to; to reach
alcoba bedroom (14)
alegrarse (de) to be happy (about) (18)

alegre happy (7)
alegría happiness, joy
alemán, alemana German (4); **alemán** *m.* German (*language*) (2)
Alemania Germany
alergia allergy
alfombra rug
algo something; anything (5)
algodón: (de) algodón *m.* (made of) cotton (6)
alguien someone; anyone (10)
algún, alguno/a/os/as some; any (10); **alguna vez** once; ever
almacén *m.* department store (5)
almorzar (ue) (c) to have lunch (8)
almuerzo lunch (9)
aló hello (*answering telephone*)
alquilar to rent (13)
alquiler *m.* rent (13)
alrededor de *prep.* around
alrededores *m.* environs, outskirts
altibajos: sufrir altibajos to have ups and downs (25)
altitud *f.* altitude
alto *n.* stop, pause
alto/a tall (4); **en voz alta** aloud, out loud
altura height
allá there
allí there (6)
ama *f.* (*but* **el ama**) **de casa** housekeeper; lady of the house, housewife
amable kind, nice (4)
amante *m., f.* lover, sweetheart
amarillo/a yellow (6)
ambiente *m.* environment, atmosphere; **medio ambiente** environment (21)
americano/a American
amigo/a friend (1)
amistad *f.* friendship (7)
amistoso/a friendly
amor *m.* love (7)
anaranjado/a *adj.* orange (6)
ancho/a broad, wide
anchoas anchovies
andar (*irreg.*) to run, function; **andar en bicicleta** to ride a bicycle
anglosajón, anglosajona Anglo-Saxon
anillo ring (7)
animado/a animated; **dibujos animados** cartoons
animal *m.* animal (21)
animar to animate, excite
anoche last night (13)
Antártida Antarctica
ante before; **ante todo** first of all
anteayer the day before yesterday (13)
anteojos (eye) glasses (13)
antepasado/a ancestor
anterior previous, preceding; (at the) front
antes *adv.* sooner, before; **antes de** *prep.* before (6); **antes (de) que** *conj.* before (20); **antes que nada** first of all, before anything (else)
antibiótico antibiotic (16)
anticipación: con (___ días de) anticipación (___ days) in advance (27)
anticuado/a old-fashioned, outdated
antigüedades *f.* antiques
antiguo/a old

antipático/a unpleasant (4)
antojitos appetizers (10)
antónimo antonym
antropología anthropology
anuncio ad; announcement
añadir to add
año year; **Año Nuevo** New Year (8); **el año que viene** next year; **tener ___ años** to be ___ years old (4)
añorar to long for; to miss (25)
apagar (gu) to turn off (15)
aparato apparatus, appliance (14)
aparecer (zc) to appear
apartamento apartment; **casa de apartamentos** apartment house
apellido surname, last name (3)
apetecerle (zc) a uno to feel like (*eating*)
apodo nickname
apoyo support
apreciar to appreciate, esteem, value
aprender to learn (3)
aprobar (ue) to pass (*an exam*)
apropiado/a appropriate
aprovechamiento advantage
aprovechar to make good use of; **aprovecharse de** to profit by, take advantage of
aproximadamente approximately
aquel, aquella *adj.* that (over there) (6); **aquél, aquélla** *pron.* that one (over there)
aquello that; that thing; that fact
aquellos/as *adj.* those (over there) (6); **aquéllos/as** *pron.* those (over there) (6); **aquéllos eran otros tiempos** it was (things were) different back then (15)
aquí here (2); **aquí mismo** right here; **por aquí** around here
árabe *m.* Arabic (*language*)
árbitro/a arbitrator; referee
árbol *m.* tree (21)
archienemigo archenemy
archivar to file; to store (18)
archivo archives, files
arena sand
argentino/a Argentine, Argentinian
armada fleet, squadron
armario armoire, closet
arquitecto/a architect
arquitectura architecture
arrancar (qu) to start (*with cars*) (17)
arreglar to fix, repair (13); to arrange
arreglo arrangement; repair
arroz *m.* rice (9)
arte *m., f.* art
artesanía handicrafts, folk art
arvejas peas (9)
ascensor *m.* elevator
asequible available
asesinar to assassinate
asesinato murder, assassination (24)
asesino/a assassin, murderer/murderess
así, so, thus; that way (9); **así así** so-so (PP)
asiento seat (11)
asimilarse to assimilate, blend in (25)
asistir (a) to attend, go to (*a class, play, etc.*) (3)
asno donkey
asociar to associate

aspecto aspect
aspiradora sweeper (14); **pasar la aspiradora** to run the sweeper, vacuum (14)
aspirante *m., f.* candidate (*for a job*), applicant (12)
aspirina aspirin (15)
asunto matter
ataque *m.* attack
atención *f.* attention
atender (ie) to be attentive, heed
atento/a attentive, polite
aterrizar (c) to land (26)
atleta *m., f.* athlete
atraer (like **traer**) to attract
atrasado/a late (11); slow, backward; **estar atrasado/a** to be late (11)
atrevido/a daring, bold
auditorio auditorium
aumentar to increase (22)
aumento raise, increase (12)
aun *adv.* even; **aun más** even more
aún *adv.* still, yet
aunque although (19)
autobús *m. s.* bus; **estación** (*f.*) **de autobuses** bus station (11); **parada del autobús** bus stop (28)
automóvil *m.* car, automobile
automovilístico/a of or pertaining to automobiles
autónomo/a autonomous
autopista freeway (21)
autor(a) author, writer
avanzado/a advanced
avenida avenue
aventura adventure
avergonzado/a embarrassed (15)
averiguar (gü) to find out
avión *m.* plane (11)
avisar to advise, warn
aviso announcement; advertisement
¡ay! *interjection* alas!
ayer yesterday (13)
ayuda help
ayudar to help (9)
azafata female flight attendant (11)
azúcar *m.* sugar (8)
azul blue (6)

bachiller *m. title given to one who has completed the bachillerato (studies equivalent to high school, junior college)*
bailar to dance (2)
baile *m.* dance
bajar (de) to get down (from); to get off (of) (11)
bajo *prep.* under
bajo/a short (*in height*) (4); low; **clase** (*f.*) **baja** lower class; **planta baja** ground floor (13)
ballena whale
banana banana (9)
bancario/a banking, financial
banco bank (22)
bañar to bathe (13); **bañarse** to take a bath (13)
bañera bathtub (13)
baño bath; bathroom (14); restroom; **cuarto de baño** bathroom; **traje** (*m.*) **de baño**

swim/bathing suit (6)
barato/a inexpensive, cheap (4)
barbacoa barbecue
barbería barber shop
barco boat, ship
barman *m.* bartender
barra bar, railing
barrio neighborhood (24)
basado/a based
base: a base de based on
básquetbol *m.* basketball (20)
basta enough, that's enough
bastante quite; enough, sufficient; a lot (16)
basura garbage (14); **sacar la basura** to take out the garbage (14)
batalla battle
batería battery (17)
batido milkshake (28)
bautizo baptism
bebé *m.* baby
beber to drink (3)
bebida drink (9)
béisbol *m.* baseball (20)
bello/a beautiful (21)
beneficio benefit
beso kiss
biblioteca library (1)
bicicleta bicycle; **pasear en bicicleta** *n.* cycling; *v.* to go for a bike ride (20)
bien *adv.* well (2); **ahora bien** now then, well now; **bien +** *adj.* very + *adj.;* **está bien** it's okay, fine; **estar bien** to be comfortable (*temperature*) (6); **(muy) bien** (very) well, fine (PP); **pasarlo bien** to have a good time (14); **¡qué bien!** great!
bienes *m. pl.* possessions, property (25)
bienestar *m.* well-being (16)
bienvenido/a *adj.* welcome
bilingüe bilingual (25)
billar *m.* game of billards
billete *m.* ticket; **billete de ida (y vuelta)** one-way (round-trip) ticket (11)
biología biology
bioquímica biochemistry
bistec *m.* streak (9)
blanco/a white (6); **vino blanco** white wine (9)
bluejeans *m.* jeans (6)
blusa blouse (6)
boca mouth (16); entrance (*to a subway*)
bocadillo snack; sandwich
boda wedding (7)
bolchevique *m., f.* Bolshevik
boleto ticket (7); **boleto de ida (y vuelta)** one-way (round-trip) ticket (11)
bolígrafo (ballpoint) pen (1)
bolillo (hard) roll (10)
bolivariano/a *adj. of or relating to Simón Bolívar*
boliviano/a Bolivian
bolsa purse (6); bag
bonito/a pretty (4)
bordado/a embroidered
bordear to be on the edge or border
bosque *m.* forest
bota boot (6)
bote *m.* rowboat
botella bottle

botones *m. s.* bellhop (27)
boxeo boxing
brazo arm (15)
breve brief, short
brillante bright, brilliant
brillar to shine
buen, bueno/a good (4); **buenas noches** good evening, night (PP); **buenas tardes** good afternoon, evening (PP); **buenos días** good morning (PP); **lo bueno** the good thing/part/news (16); **muy buenas** good afternoon, evening; **bueno** *adv.* well
bullicio bustle, noise
busca: en busca de in search of
buscar (qu) to look for (2)
búsqueda search
butaca armchair; seat (*in a theater*) (19)

caballero gentleman
caballo horse (21); **montar a caballo** to ride horseback (21)
cabaña hut; cabin, cottage
caber (quepo) to fit; to be possible
cabeza head (15)
cabo: llevar a cabo to carry out; **al fin y al cabo** after all, in the end
cacería hunt
cada *inv.* each, every (13)
cadena chain
caer (*irreg.*) to fall (12); **caerle bien/mal a alguien** to make a good/bad impression on someone (12); **dejar caer** to drop; **caerse** to fall down (15)
café *m.* coffee (9); café (28)
cafetera coffeepot (14)
cafetería cafeteria, café
caja box, case
cajero/a cashier (22)
calabaza gourd
calcetines *m.* socks (6)
calculador(a) *m., f.* calculator
cálculo calculus
calefacción *f.* heating
calendario calendar
calentar (ie) to heat, warm
calidad *f.* quality
cálido/a warm, hot
caliente hot
calmante *m.* sedative
calmarse to calm down, be calm
calor *m.* heat; **hace calor** it's hot (*weather*) (8); **tener calor** to be (feel) hot, warm (6)
callarse to be silent, quiet
calle *f.* street (5)
cama bed (13); **guardar cama** to stay in bed (16); **hacer la cama** to make the bed (14)
camarero/a waiter/waitress (9); flight attendant (11); *f.* hotel maid
camarones *m.* shrimp (9); **cóctel** (*m.*) **de camarones** shrimp cocktail (10)
cambiar (de) to change (12); **cambiar de lugar** to move (*something*) (15); **los tiempos cambian** times change (15)
cambio change; (rate of) exchange (*currency*); **cambio de ritmo** change of pace (21); **en cambio** on the other hand; **transmisión** (*f.*) **de cambios** manual shift
caminar to walk (16)

camino street, road (17)
camión *m.* truck (24)
camisa shirt (6)
camiseta T-shirt (6)
campeonato championship
campesino/a *n.* peasant, country person (21); *adj.* country
camping; **hacer** *camping* to go camping (19)
campo country(side) (13); field
cana gray hair; white hair
canal *m.* channel (*TV*) (24)
canción *f.* song
cancha (tennis) court (20)
cansado/a tired (7)
cansarse to get tired
cantante *m., f.* singer
cantar to sing (2)
cantidad *f.* quantity, amount
caña (sugar)cane
capítulo chapter
cara face
característica characteristic
cárcel *f.* jail, prison (23)
cargado/a (de) loaded (with)
cargar (gu) to charge (*to an account*) (22)
cariño affection
cariñoso/a affectionate (7)
carne *f.* meat (9)
caro/a expensive (5)
carpintero/a carpenter
carrera course of study; race; career, profession (12)
carretera highway (17)
carro car
carta letter (3); *pl.* (playing) cards (19); **papel** (*m.*) **para cartas** stationery (28)
cartera wallet (6)
casa house (3); **casa de apartamentos** apartment house; **(estar) en casa** (to be) (at) home (3); **regresar a casa** to return home (2)
casado/a married (4)
casarse (con) to marry (22)
casco helmet
casi *inv.* almost (3)
caso case; **en caso de que** in case (20)
castellano Castilian (language)
castigar (gu) to punish (23)
castigo punishment (23)
Castilla Castile (*province of Spain*)
castillo castle
Cataluña Catalonia (*province of Spain*)
catástrofe *f.* catastrophe (24)
catedral *f.* cathedral
causa cause, **a causa de** because of, on account of
causar to cause
cautiverio captivity
cebolla onion
cebra zebra
celebrar to celebrate
cena supper, evening meal (9)
cenar to have, eat supper, dinner (9)
censura censorship
centavo cent
céntrico/a central, focal
centro center; downtown (5)
centroamericano/a Central American

cepillo brush
cerca de *prep.* near, close to (6)
cerdo hog, pig; **chuleta de cerdo** pork chop (9)
ceremonia ceremony
cerrado/a closed (7)
cerrar (ie) to close (8)
cervatillo musk deer
cerveza beer (2)
ciclismo *n.* cycling (20)
ciego/a blind
cielo sky, heaven
ciencias sciences (2); **ciencias naturales** natural sciences (2); **ciencias sociales** social sciences (2)
cierto/a certain; **es cierto** it's certain (12)
cigarrillo cigarette
cine *m.* movie (theater) (7); movies
cinta tape
cinturón *m.* belt (6); **cinturón de seguridad** seat belt
circulación *f.* traffic (17)
círculo circle
circunstancia circumstance; incident
cita date, appointment (7)
citado: estoy citado/a I've got a prior engagement; I'm busy (7)
ciudad *f.* city (4); **ciudad universitaria** campus
ciudadano/a citizen (23)
cívico/a civic (23)
claro/a clear; **¡claro que sí (no)!** of course (not)! (4); **está claro** it's clear, obvious (7)
clase *f.* class (1); **clase turística** tourist class; **primera clase** first class
clásico/a classic
clavado/a nailed
cliente *m., f.* client, customer (1)
clima *m.* climate
cobrar to cash (*a check*) (22); to charge (*someone for an item or service*) (22)
cocina kitchen (14)
cocinar to cook (14)
cóctel *m.* cocktail party; **cóctel (de camarones)** (shrimp) cocktail (10)
coche *m.* car (3)
cochino pig
cola tail; line; **hacer cola** to stand in line
coleccionar to collect
colega *m.* colleague
colegio elementary or secondary school; **colegio mayor** dormitory
colocar (qu) to place
colombiano/a Colombian
Colón: Cristóbal Colón Christopher Columbus
colonia colony
color *m.* color
columna column
comandante *m.* commander, leader
combatir to fight
combinar to combine
comedia play (*theater*) (19)
comedor *m.* dining room (14)
comentar to comment (on)
comentario comment, commentary
comenzar (ie) (c) to commence, begin
comer to eat (3)

comerciante *m., f.* merchant
comerciar to trade
comercio business (2)
comestibles *m. pl.* food
cometer to commit
comí... I ate . . . (9)
cómico/a comic, funny, amusing
comida food (3); midday meal; **preparar la comida** to prepare food (14)
comiste: ¿qué comiste anoche? what did you eat last night? (9)
como as a; like; since; **como si** + *past subjunctive* as if (24)
¿cómo? how? (PP); how's that again? **¿cómo es ____?** what is ____ like? (4); **¿cómo está(s)?** how are you? (PP); **¡cómo no!** of course! (2); **¿cómo que... ?** what do you mean, . . . ?; **¿cómo se dice ____?** how do you say ____?; **¿cómo se llama usted, ¿cómo te llamas?** what is your name? (PP)
cómoda bureau, chest of drawers
comodidad *f.* comfort (27)
cómodo/a comfortable
compañero/a companion; friend; **compañero/a de cuarto** roommate
compañía company
comparación *f.* comparison
comparar to compare
compartir to share (27)
competencia competition
competición *f.* competition
competir (i, i) to compete
complejidad *f.* complexity
complejo *n.* complex
complemento object; **complemento directo** direct object; **complemento indirecto** indirect object
comportamiento behavior
comportarse to behave oneself
compra *n.* purchase; **fue una buena compra** it was a good purchase (5); **¿quieres ir de compras conmigo?** do you want to go shopping with me? (5)
comprar to buy (2)
comprender to understand (3)
computadora computer (*Latin America*) (18)
común common, usual, ordinary
comunicarse (qu) (con) to communicate (with) (23)
comunidad *f.* community
comunitario/a *adj.* community
con with (2); **con frecuencia** frequently (3); **con permiso** pardon me, excuse me (PP); **con tal que** provided that (20)
concepto idea, concept (23)
conciencia conscience
concierto concert
conducir (*like* **producir**) to conduct; to drive (*a vehicle*) (17)
conductor(a) driver (17); conductor
confianza confidence
confirmar to confirm (27)
confundido/a confused (15)
congelador *m.* freezer (14)
congelar to freeze
congestionado/a congested, stuffed-up (16)
conjugar (gu) to conjugate
conjunto totality, whole

conmemorar to commemorate
conmigo with me (6)
conocer (zc) to know, be acquainted with; to meet (9)
conocido/a known, well-known
conocimiento knowledge
conquista conquest
conquistador(a) conqueror
conquistar to conquer
consecuencia consequence
conseguir (i, i) (ga) to get, obtain (12)
consejero/a counselor, advisor (1)
consejo advice; piece of advice (10)
conservador(a) conservative
conservar to conserve, save (21)
considerar to consider, think
consigna baggage check
consigo with him/her/you (*form.*)
consistir (en) to consist (of)
constante firm, perserving, loyal; constant
constipado/a suffering from a cold
constructor(a) builder
construido/a constructed, built
construir (y) to build (21)
consulta consultation, conference
consultar to consult
consultorio (doctor's) office (16)
consumir to consume
consumo consumption
contado: pagar al contado to pay cash (22)
contaminación *f.* pollution (8); **hay contaminación** there is pollution (8)
contaminado/a contaminated, polluted
contaminar to pollute (21)
contar (ue) to count; to tell (about) (15)
contener (*like* **tener**) to contain, hold (17)
contento/a happy (7)
contestar to answer (5)
contigo with you (*fam.*) (6)
continente *m.* continent
continuar to continue
contra against, in opposition to
contraatacar (qu) to counterattack
contraer (*like* **traer**) to contract; **contraer matrimonio** to marry, get married
contrario: al contrario on the contrary
contrato contract
controlar to control (18)
convencer (convenzo) to convince
conversar to converse
convertir (ie, i) to convert, change
copa drink (*alcoholic*) (28)
corazón *m.* heart (16)
corbata tie (6)
cordialidad *f.* cordiality, sincerity
cordillera chain or ridge of mountains
correcto/a correct, right
correo mail; post office (28); **oficina de correos** post office
correr to run (16)
corresponder to correspond
correspondiente corresponding
corriente *f.* current (*electrical*); **cuenta corriente** checking account (22)
cortar to cut (off)
cortés courteous
cortesía courtesy, politeness
corto/a short (*in length*) (4)

cosa thing (1)
costa coast
costar (ue) to cost
costumbre *f.* custom (25)
cotidiano/a daily, everyday
crear to create
crecer (zc) to grow
crédito: tarjeta de crédito credit card (22)
creer (y) (en) to think, believe (in) (3); **creo que sí (no)** I (don't) think so (1)
criado/a servant/maid (13)
cristal *m.* crystal
criticar (qu) to criticize
cruzar (c) to cross (26)
cuaderno notebook (1)
cuadro painting; **de cuadros** plaid (6)
¿cuál? what?, which? (PP) **¿cuál(es)?** which one(s)? (PP)
cualidad *f.* quality
cualquier(a) any
cuando when; **de vez en cuando** from time to time (20)
¿cuándo? when? (PP)
cuanto how much; **en cuanto** *conj.* as soon as (26); **en cuanto a** *prep.* regarding
¿cuánto? how much? (PP)
¿cuántos/as? how many? (PP)
cuartel *m.* quarter; dwelling; home
cuarto room (1); quarter; **cuarto de baño** bathroom; **compañero/a de cuarto** roommate; **(las dos) menos cuarto** a quarter till (two) (PP); **(las dos) y cuarto** (two) fifteen, a quarter after (two) (PP)
cuarto/a fourth (18)
cubano/a Cuban
cubierto/a (de) *p.p.* covered (with)
cubrir (*p.p.* cubierto/a) to cover (20)
cuchara spoon
cuenta check, bill (9); account; **cuenta corriente** checking account (22); **cuenta de ahorros** savings account (22); **darse cuenta (de)** to realize; **tomar en cuenta** to take into account (23)
cuento story
cuerpo body (15)
cuestión *f.* question, matter; **es cuestión de** it's a matter of, it has to do with (23)
cuidado care; **¡cuidado!** careful! be careful!; **con cuidado** carefully; **tener cuidado (de)** to be careful (about)
cuidadoso/a careful
cuidarse to take care of oneself (16)
culpa fault; **tener la culpa** to be responsible for, be to blame for
cultivar to cultivate; to grow
cultivo cultivation, farming
cultura culture (25)
cumpleaños *s.* birthday (8)
cumplir to accomplish, fulfill; **cumplir _____ años** to reach _____ years (*of age*)
cuna crib; cradle (13)
cuota quota
cura *m.* priest
curioso/a curious
curso course
cuyo/a whose, of whom, of which

champán *m.* champagne

champiñón *m.* mushroom
champú *m.* shampoo (28)
chaqueta jacket (6)
charlar to chat
cheque *m.* check (12) **pagar con cheque** to pay by check (22); **cheque de viajero** traverler's check (27)
chicle *m.* chewing gum
chico/a boy/girl; *m.* guy, kid (10)
chileno/a Chilean
chimpancé *m.* chimpanzee
chino/a Chinese; **chino** *m.* Chinese (*language*)
chisme *m.* gossip; misrepresentation
chiste *m.* joke (15)
chocar (qu) (con) to bump into, collide (with) (17); to hit
chocolate *m.* chocolate (5)
choque *m.* collison, crash (24); **choque cultural** culture shock (25)
chorizo type of sausage
chuleta (de cerdo) (pork) chop (9)

dama lady, woman; **dama de honor** bridesmaid
daño harm; **hacerse daño** to hurt oneself (15)
dar (*irreg.*) to give (10); **dar una fiesta** to give a party (14); **dar lugar a** to give rise, cause to **dar un paseo** to take a walk (19); **darse cuenta (de)** to realize; **darse la mano** to shake hands; **¡Qué más da!** What difference does it make! (11)
dato fact
de *prep.* of, from (PP); about; **de la mañana/tarde/noche** in the morning/afternoon/evening (PP); **de nada** you're welcome (PP); **de niño/a (joven)** as a child (young person) (16); **de repente** suddenly (16); **de todo** everything (5)
debajo *adv.* underneath, below; **debajo de** *prep.* under, below (6)
deber to owe; **deber** + *inf.* should, must, ought to (*do something*) (3); **debido a** due to
deber *n. m.* responsibility, obligation (23)
débil weak
decidir to decide
décimo/a *adj.* tenth (18)
decir (*irreg.*) to say, tell (10); **es decir** that is to say
declarar to declare (26); **tener algo que declarar** to have something to declare
decorar to decorate
dedicarse (qu) to dedicate oneself
dedo finger
defensor(a) defender, protector
dejar to leave (behind) (12); to quit (12); to let, allow; **dejar caer** to drop; **dejar de** + *inf.* to stop (*doing something*) (16); **no deje(s) de** + *inf.* don't forget to (*do something*)
del (*contraction of* **de** + **el**) of, from the
delante de *prep.* in front of (6)
delgado/a thin (4)
delicado/a delicate
delicioso/a delicious
delito crime (21)

demás: lo demás the rest, the remaining; **los/las demás** the others (23); **por lo demás** as for the rest; apart from this

demasiado/a *adj.* too much; **demasiado** *adv.* too, too much (5)

democracia democracy

demócrata *m., f.* democrat

demonio demon, devil

demora delay (11)

demorar to delay

demostrar (ue) to demonstrate

denso/a dense (21)

dental: pasta dental toothpaste (28)

dentista *m., f.* dentist

dentro de *prep.* inside

depender (de) to depend (on)

dependiente/a clerk (1)

deporte *m.* sport; **practicar deportes** to participate in sports (16)

deportista *n. m., f.* sportsman/ sportswoman; *adj.* sports-minded (20)

deportivo/a *adj.* sporting, sports

depositar to deposit

derecha: a la derecha de to the right of (*direction*) (6)

derecho *n.* (civil) right; law (23); **derechos** (*pl.*) **de aduana** customs duty (26); **derecho** *adv.* (straight) ahead; **todo derecho** straight ahead (17)

desaparecer (zc) to disappear

desaparición *f.* disappearance

desarrollar to develop (21)

desarrollo development (24)

desastre *m.* disaster (15)

desastroso/a disastrous, miserable

desayunar to eat breakfast (9)

desayuno breakfast (9)

descansado/a rested (14)

descansar to rest (4)

descanso *n.* rest, sleep

descendiente *m., f.* descendant

desconcertante disconcerting, puzzling

desconocido/a unknown

descontento/a unhappy

descortés discourteous

describir (*p.p.* **descrito/a**) to describe

descubierto/a *p.p.* discovered

descubrimiento discovery

descubrir (*p.p.* **descubierto/a**) to discover (20)

descuidado/a careless

desde *prep.* from; **desde que** *conj.* since; **desde luego** of course

desear to want (2)

desempleo unemployment

deseo desire, wish

desesperar to despair, lose hope

desfile *m.* parade

desgracia disgrace; misfortune

desgraciadamente unfortunately

desierto/a deserted

desigualdad *f.* inequality (24)

desinflado/a: llanta desinflada flat tire (17)

desocupado/a unoccupied (27); vacant, free

despacio *adv.* slowly

despedida closing (*of a letter*); leave-taking

despedir (i, i) to fire (someone) (12); **despedirse (de)** to say good-bye (to) (14)

despegar (gu) to take off (*plane*) (11)

despertador *m.* alarm clock (13)

despertar (ie) to wake (*someone up*) (13); **despertarse** to awaken, wake up (13)

desplazarse (c) to move (*to another place*)

después de *prep.* after (6); **después (de) que** *conj.* after (26)

destino destination; destiny

destruido/a destroyed

destruir (y) to destroy (21)

desvalorización *f.* diminishing of value

desventaja disadvantage (18)

detalle *m.* detail

determinado/a determined; specific

detrás de *prep.* behind (6)

devolver (ue) (*p.p.* **devuelto/a**) to return (*something*) (22); to refund, give back

día *m.* day (1); **buenos días** good morning (PP); **Día de Gracias** Thanksgiving Day; **hoy día** nowadays; **todos los días** every day (2)

diálogo dialogue

diario/a daily (13)

dibujo cartoon; sketch; drawing

diccionario dictionary (1)

dictador(a) dictator (24)

dictadura dictatorship (23)

dicho *n.* saying; **dicho/a** *p.p.* said; **mejor dicho** rather

diente *m.* tooth

dieta diet; **a dieta** on a diet

diferencia difference

diferenciar to differentiate

diferente different

difícil difficult, hard (6)

dificultad *f.* difficulty

difunto/a dead, deceased

diga hello (*answering telephone*)

dignidad *f.* dignity

dinámica *n. s.* dynamics

dinero money (1)

Dios *m.* God; **por Dios** for heaven's sake (25)

dirección *f.* address (13); director's office; direction, guidance

directamente directly

director(a) manager, director (12)

dirigir (j) to direct

disco (musical) record (12); **frenos de disco** disc brakes

discoteca disco(theque)

discreto/a discreet

disculpa excuse, apology

disculparse to excuse oneself, apologize

discurso speech

discutir to discuss; to argue, debate

diseñar to draw, design (18)

disfrutar (de) to enjoy

disponible available, on hand (18)

dispuesto/a (a) disposed, willing (to)

distancia distance

distinto/a different

distraído/a distracted, absentminded (15)

diversión *f.* diversion, entertainment, amusement (19)

divertido/a amusing, fun (19); pleasant

divertir (ie, i) to amuse, entertain (13); **divertirse** to have a good time, enjoy

oneself (13); **¡que se diviertan!** enjoy yourselves! (19)

dividir to divide

divorciarse to get divorced

divorcio divorce (7)

doblado/a dubbed (19)

doblar to turn

doble double

dólar *m.* dollar

doler (ue) to hurt, ache (15)

dolor *m.* pain; **tener dolor (de)** to have a pain (in) (16)

doméstico/a domestic (13)

don *title of respect used with a man's first name*

donde where

¿dónde? where? (PP); **¿adónde?** where (to)?; **¿de dónde?** from where?

doña *title of respect used with a woman's first name*

dormir (ue, u) to sleep (8); **dormirse** to fall asleep (13)

dormitorio bedroom (14)

drama *m.* drama, play

ducha shower (27)

duda doubt; **no hay duda** there's no doubt; **sin duda** without a doubt

dudar to doubt (12)

dudoso/a doubtful

dueño/a owner (7); landlord/landlady

dulcería sweetshop, candy store (5)

dulces *m.* sweets, candy (5); **pan** (*m.*) **dulce** sweet rolls (10)

duradero/a durable

durante during (6); for (*a period of time*)

durar to last, endure (24)

duro/a hard

e and (*used instead of* **y** *before words beginning with* **i** *or* **hi**)

economía economy

económico/a economical

economizar (c) to economize (22)

ecuatoriano/a Ecuadorian

echar to throw; **echar la culpa** to blame; **echar raíces** to put down roots; **echar una siesta** to take a nap

edad *f.* age; **Edad Media** Middle Ages; **tener** _____ **años (de edad)** to be _____ years old (4)

edificación *f.* construction, building

edificio *n.* building (1)

editar to edit; **editar textos** to do word processing (18)

educativo/a educational

efecto effect; **en efecto** in effect

egoísmo egotism, selfishness (23)

egoísta *m., f.* egotistical, selfish

¿eh? *tag phrase with approximate English equivalent of* okay?

ejecutivo/a *n.* executive

ejemplo: por ejemplo for example (5)

ejercicio exercise (3); **hacer ejercicio** to exercise, get exercise (16)

ejército army

el the (*m. definite article*)

él *sub. pron.* he; *obj. of prep.* him

electricidad *f.* electricity

electricista *m., f.* electrician

elegir (i, i) (j) to select, choose
eliminar to eliminate
ella *sub. pron.* she; *obj. of prep.* her
ellos/as *sub. pron.* they; *obj. of prep.* them
embarazada pregnant
embargo: sin embargo however
emigrar to emigrate (25)
emocionante *adj.* touching, thrilling
emocionar to arouse emotion in, excite
empezar (ie) (c) to begin (8); **empezar a** + *inf.* to begin to (*do something*) (8)
empleado/a employee (12)
emplear to use
empleo job, employment; **agencia de empleos** employment agency
empresa business, corporation (12)
empujar to push
en in; on; at (PP)
enamorado/a in love; **Día** (*m.*) **de los Enamorados (de San Valentín)** Valentine's Day
enamorarse (de) to fall in love (with)
encantado/a pleased (to meet you) (PP)
encantador(a) charming
encantar (*like gustar*) to enchant (21)
encima *adv.* above, over; overhead; **encima de** *prep.* on top of, above (6)
encontrar (ue) to find (11)
energía energy (21)
enfermarse to get sick (16)
enfermedad *f.* illness
enfermero/a nurse (16)
enfermo/a sick (6)
enfrentamiento conflict
enfrentar (con) to face (up to), confront
enfrente *adv.* in front, opposite; **enfrente de** *prep.* in front of
engordar to fatten, make fat
enojado/a angry
enojarse to get angry (14)
enorme enormous
ensalada salad (9)
enseñanza *n.* teaching
enseñar to teach (2)
entender (ie) to understand
enterarse (de) to find out (about); to learn (about) (24)
entero/a whole, entire (14)
enterrar (ie) to bury
entierro burial
entonces then, in that case; **en aquel entonces** at that time
entrada entrée, main course; (movie, theater) ticket (19); entryway
entrar (en) to enter, go in
entre *prep.* between, among (6)
entregar (gu) to hand in/over (26)
entrenamiento *n.* training
entretener (*like tener*) to entertain
entrevista interview (12)
entrevistador(a) interviewer (12)
entrevistar to interview
época era, time (*period*)
equipado/a *adj.* equipped
equipaje *m.* baggage, luggage (11)
equipo team (*in sporting events*) (20); equipment
equis: rayos equis X-rays

equitativo/a fair
equivocado/a mistaken
equivocarse (qu) to be wrong, make a mistake (15)
escala: hacer escalas to have, make stopovers (11)
escaleras stairs, steps
escándalo scandal
escapar to escape, get away
escasez *f.* (*pl.* **escaseces**) shortage, lack (21); poverty
escaso/a small, limited; little
escena scene
escoger (j) to choose, select
escondido/a hidden
escribir (*p.p.* **escrito/a**) to write (3); **escribir a máquina** to type (12)
escrito/a *p.p.* written
escritor(a) writer
escritorio desk (1)
escuchar to listen (to) (8)
escuela school; **escuela primaria** elementary school; **escuela secundaria** high school
escultor(a) sculptor/sculptress
escultura sculpture, carved work
ese/a *adj.* that (6); **ése/a** *pron.* that one
esforzarse (ue) (c) to make an effort
esfuerzo effort
esmero careful attention; elaborate effort
eso that; that thing; that fact; **eso es** that's right; **por eso** therefore, that's why (4)
esos/as *adj.* those (6); **ésos/as** *pron.* those (ones)
espacio space
espantapájaros *s.* scarecrow
España Spain
español(a) Spanish (4); **español** *m.* Spanish (*language*) (2)
especial special; **en especial** especially
especialidad *f.* specialty; **especialidad de la casa** specialty of the house
especialista *m., f.* specialist
especialización *f.* specialization, "major" (*field of study*)
especializarse (c) to major (*in an academic area*)
específico/a specific
espectáculo spectacle, show
especulativo/a speculative, thoughtful
espejo mirror
espera: sala de espera waiting room (11)
esperanza hope (24)
esperar to wait (for) (9); to expect; to hope
esposo/a husband/wife, spouse (3); **esposas** handcuffs
esquís *m.* skis (20)
esquiar to ski (8)
esquina (street) corner (17)
establecerse (zc) to establish oneself (25)
estación *f.* season (8); station (11); **estación de gasolina** gas station (17); **estación del metro** metro (subway) stop (28)
estacionamiento parking (lot)
estacionar to park (17)
estadio stadium (20)
estado state (4)
Estados Unidos *pl.* United States
estadounidense *m., f.* person from the

United States
estallar to break out (*conflict, war, etc.*)
estancia stay, sojourn; ranch
estanco tobacco stand, shop (28)
estar (*irreg.*) to be (6); **está bien** it's okay, fine; **está claro** it's clear, obvious (7); **está nublado** it's cloudy, overcast (8); **estar aburrido/a** to be bored (7); **estar atrasado/a** to be late (11); **estar bien** to be comfortable (*temperature*) (6); **estar de acuerdo (con)** to be in agreement (with) (6); **estar de moda** to be in style; **estar de vacaciones** to be on vacation (8); **estar listo/a (para)** to be ready (to); **estoy citado/a** I've got a prior engagement (7)
este/a *adj.* this (4); **éste/a** *pron.* this one; **en este momento** at the moment, right now; **esta noche** tonight (3); **este** uh, um
estéreo stereo
estereotipo stereotype
estilo style
esto this; this thing; this matter
estómago stomach (16)
estos/as *adj.* these (4); **éstos/as** *pron.* these (ones)
estructura structure
estudiante *m., f.* student (1)
estudiantil *adj.* of or pertaining to student(s); **residencia (estudiantil)** dormitory
estudiar to study (2)
estudio study (*room*); *pl.* studies, schoolwork
estudioso/a studious
estufa stove (14)
estupendo/a wonderful, marvelous
etapa stage; epoch, period
etiqueta ceremony, etiquette; (price) tag
étnico/a ethnic
europeo/a European
evaluar to evaluate
evitar to avoid
exacto *adv.* exactly
examen *m.* test, exam (3)
examinar to examine
excelente excellent
exceso: en exceso excessively, in excess
excursión *f.* excursion, trip
exigente *adj.* demanding
exiliado/a expatriate, person in exile (25)
exilio exile
existir to exist
éxito success; **tener éxito** to be successful
experimentar to experience; to experiment (25)
experimento experiment
experto/a expert
explicar (qu) to explain
explotación *f.* exploitation
explotar to exploit
exportador(a) exporter
expresar to express
extender (ie) to extend
extendido/a extended
extenso/a extensive
extranjero *n.* abroad (28); **ir al extranjero** to go abroad (28)
extranjero/a *n.* foreigner (1); *adj.* foreign
extrañar to miss (*someone or something*)

extraño/a strange; **es (qué) extraño** it is (how) strange (12)
extraoficial unofficial
extraordinario/a extraordinary
extraterrestre extraterrestrial
extremo/a extreme
extrovertido/a extroverted

fábrica factory (21)
fabricante *m.* manufacturer, maker
fácil easy (6)
facilidad *f.* ease; ability, facility
factor: el primer factor sería... the first factor would be . . . (18)
factura bill, invoice (22)
facturar to check (*luggage*) (11)
facultad *f.* college, school (*of a university*)
falda skirt (6)
falta lack
faltar to be absent, missing, lacking
fallar to fail
familia family (3)
familiar *n. m.* relation, member of the family; *adj. of or pertaining to the family* (3)
famoso/a famous
fantasma *m.* ghost, phantom
farmacia drugstore, pharmacy (5)
fascinante fascinating
fase *f.* phase
fatal fatal; terrible, bad
favor *m.* favor; **favor de** + *inf.* please (*do something*); **por favor** please (PP)
fecha date (8); **¿cuál es la fecha de hoy?** what is today's date (8); **con fecha de hoy** as of today
felicidad *f.* happiness; *pl.* congratulations
felicitaciones *f.* congratulations (14)
feliz (*pl.* **felices**) happy (14); **Felices Pascuas** Merry Christmas; **Feliz Navidad** Merry Christmas
fenomenal phenomenal
fenómeno phenomenon
feo/a ugly (4)
feriado: día feriado holiday
ferrocarril *m.* railway, railroad (24)
festivo: día (*m.*) **festivo** holiday
fiebre *f.* fever; **tener fiebre** to have a fever (16)
fiel honest; faithful, loyal
fiesta party (2); feast; **dar/hacer una fiesta** to give a party (14)
figurita figurine
fijarse to imagine; **fijarse en** to take notice (of), pay attention (to)
fijo/a fixed; **precio fijo** fixed price (5)
filosofía philosophy
filtro filter
fin *m.* end; **fin de semana** weekend (PP); **a fines de** at the end of; **al fin y al cabo** after all, in the end; **en fin** in short; **por fin** finally (25)
final *n. m.* end; **al final de** at the end of; *adj.* final
financiero/a financial
finca farm (21)
firmar to sign
física *s.* physics

físico/a *adj.* physical (16)
flan *m.* custard (9)
flor *f.* flower (10)
florecer (zc) to flower, blossom, bloom
florero flower-pot; (flower) vase
foca seal (*marine mammal*)
fondos *pl.* funds, funding
forma form, manner
formar to form
formulario questionnaire
fósforos matches (28)
foto(grafía) *f.* photo(graph)
francés, francesa French (4); **francés** *m.* French (*language*) (2)
Francia France
frasco flask; bottle
frase *f.* phrase; sentence
frecuencia frequency; **con frecuencia** frequently (3)
frecuentemente frequently
fregadero sink
frenos brakes (17); **frenos de disco** disc brakes
fresco/a fresh; **hace fresco** it's cool (*weather*) (8)
frijol *m.* bean (9)
frío *n.* cold(ness)
frío/a *adj.* cold; **hace (mucho) frío** it's (very) cold (*weather*) (8); **tener (mucho) frío** to be (feel) (very) cold, chilly (6)
frito/a fried; **papa frita** French fried potato (9)
frontera border (26)
fruta fruit; **jugo de fruta** fruit juice (9)
fuera *adv.* outside; **fuera de** *prep.* out of
fuerte strong; severe (23); loud; **plato fuerte** main dish
fuerza force
fumar to smoke (11); **sección** (*f.*) **de (no) fumar** (no-) smoking section (11)
función *f.* function; show, performance (19)
funcionar to function; to run, work (12)
fundar to found, establish
furioso/a furious (7)
fusilar to shoot
fútbol *m.* soccer (20); **fútbol norteamericano** football (20)
futuro *n.* future
futuro/a *adj.* future

galleta cookie (9)
gallina chicken (21)
gallo rooster (21)
gambas shrimp
gana desire, inclination; **tener ganas de** + *inf.* to feel like (*doing something*) (4)
ganar to earn (12); to win (12); to gain (12); **ganarse la vida** to earn a living
ganga bargain (5)
garaje *m.* garage (13)
garantizar (c) to guarantee (23)
garganta throat (16)
gas *m.* gas; heat (13)
gasolina gasoline (17); **estación** (*f.*) **de gasolina** gas station (17)
gasolinera gas station (17)
gastar to use (*gas*) (17); to spend (*money*) (5)

gastos expenses (22)
gato/a cat
gazpacho cold tomato soup
general general; **en general** generally, in general; **por lo general** generally, in general (4); **secretario/a general** registrar
generalmente generally (6)
generoso/a generous
gente *f. s.* people (18)
geografía geography
geólogo/a geologist
gerente *m., f.* manager
gigante *m.* giant
gimnasio gymnasium
gobernador *m.* governor
gobernar (ie) to govern (23)
gobierno government (12)
golf *m.* golf (20)
goloso/a sweet-tooth; **ser goloso/a** to have a sweet tooth
gordo/a fat, plump (4)
gorrión *m.* sparrow
gozar (c) (de) to enjoy
gracias thanks (PP); **Día** (*m.*) **de Gracias** Thanksgiving Day; **muchas gracias** thank you very much, many thanks (PP)
gracioso/a funny
grado degree (*temperature*)
graduado/a graduate
graduarse to graduate (12); **cuando me gradúe...** when I graduate . . . (12); **Ud./él/ella se gradúa** you/he/she graduate(s) (12); **yo me gradúo** I (will) graduate (12)
gran, grande large, big (4); great (4)
grandeza greatness
granjero/a farmer, cattle rancher
gratis *inv.* free, gratis
grave grave, important; serious
gris gray (6)
gritar to shout
grito shout
grupo group
guacamole *m.* avocado dip (10)
guajolote *m.* turkey (10)
guante *m.* glove
guapo/a handsome, good-looking (4)
guardar to keep, hold (*a seat, place*) (11); **guardar cama** to stay in bed (16)
guerra war (23); **guerra civil** civil war; **Segunda Guerra Mundial** Second World War
guerrero/a warlike
guerrillero/a *n.* guerrilla fighter; *adj. of or pertaining to guerrilla warfare*
guía *m., f.* guide; **guía** (*f.*) **telefónica** telephone book
guitarra guitar
gustar to be pleasing (10); **¿le/le gusta... ?** do you like . . . ? (PP); **Sí, me gusta... (no, no me gusta...)** yes, I like . . . (no, I don't like . . .) (PP); **me (te,...) gustaría...** I (you, . . .) would (really) like . . . (10)
gusto *n.* liking, preference; taste; pleasure; **estoy (me siento) a gusto** I am (I feel) at home, comfortable (21); **mucho gusto** pleased (to meet you) (PP); **por gusto** willingly (25)

haber (*irreg.*) infinitive form of **hay** (14); to have (*auxiliary*); **va a haber** there's going to be
hábil skilled
habilidad *f.* ability, skill
habitación *f.* room (27); **una habitación para una persona (dos personas)** a single (double) room
habitante *m., f.* inhabitant
habla *f.* (*but* **el habla**) speech (language); **de habla española** Spanish-speaking
hablar to speak, talk (2)
hace ____ (*period of time*) ago (23); **¿cuánto tiempo hace que (vives aquí)?** how long have you been (living here)? (8); **hace dos años que (vivo aquí)** I've been (living here) for two years (8)
hacer (*irreg.*) to do; to make (8); **hace** ____ **grados** it's ____ degrees (*temperature*); **hace buen/mal tiempo** it's good/bad weather (8); **hace calor (fresco/frío/sol/viento)** it's hot (cool/cold/sunny/windy) (*weather*) (8); **hacer autostop** to hitchhike; **hacer la cama** to make the bed (14); **hacer** *camping* to go camping (19); **hacer cola** to stand in line (11); **hacer ejercicio** to exercise, get exercise (16); **hacer escalas** to have/make stopovers (11); **hacer una fiesta** to give a party (14); **hacer la(s) maleta(s)** to pack one's suitcase(s) (11); **hacer un papel** to play a role; **hacer planes para** + *inf.* to make plans to (*do something*) (19); **hacer una pregunta** to ask a question (8); **hacer un viaje** to take a trip (8); **¿qué tiempo hace?** what's the weather like? (8); **hacerse** to become (15); **hacerse daño** to hurt oneself (15)
hambre *f.* hunger; **tener hambre** to be hungry (9)
hamburguesa hamburger (9)
hasta *prep.* until; **hasta luego** see you later (PP); **hasta mañana** see you tomorrow (PP); **hasta que** *conj.* until (26)
hay there is/are (PP); **hay contaminación** there is pollution (8); **hay que** + *inf.* one must/it's necessary to (*do something*) (17); **no hay** there is/are not (PP); **no hay de qué** you're welcome (17); **no hay más remedio** nothing can be done about it
hecho *n.* event; **de hecho** in fact
hecho/a *p.p.* made, done; **trato hecho** it's a deal
helado ice cream (9)
herencia inheritance, heritage
herida *n.* wound; injury
hermano/a brother/sister (3)
hermoso/a beautiful
hielo ice (8)
hierba grass
higiene *f.* hygiene
hijo/a child (3); son/daughter; **hijos** children (3)
hipopótamo hippopotamus
hispánico/a Hispanic
hispano/a *n.* Hispanic (person); *adj.* Hispanic
Hispanoamérica Spanish America
hispanoamericano/a Spanish American

historia history (2)
histórico/a historical
hockey *m.* hockey (20)
hogar *m.* home, house
hola hello, hi (PP)
hombre *m.* man (1); **¡hombre!** well!, man!; **hombre de negocios** businessman
hondureño/a Honduran
honor *m.* honor; **dama de honor** bridesmaid
honrado/a honest, upright
honrar to honor
hora hour; **¿a qué hora?** (at) what time? (PP); **es hora de** + *inf.* it's time to (*do something*) (20); **por hora** per hour; **¿qué hora es?** what time is it? (PP)
horario schedule, timetable
horno oven
hotel *m.* hotel (27)
hotelero hotel manager, owner
hoy today (PP); **hoy día** nowadays
huelga (labor) strike (23)
huésped(a) guest (27)
huevo egg (9)
humano/a human; **ser** (*m.*) **humano** human being (18)
humilde humble
humo *n.* smoke (10)

ibérico/a Iberian; **Península Ibérica** Iberian Peninsula
ida *n.* departure; **billete** (*m.*) **de ida (y vuelta)** one-way (round-trip) ticket (11)
identificar (qu) to identify
idioma *m.* language (25)
iglesia church (7)
igualdad *f.* equality (24)
igualmente likewise (PP)
ilegal illegal
imagen *f.* image
imaginar(se) to imagine
imitar to imitate
impaciente impatient
imperio empire
impermeable *m.* raincoat (6)
imponer (*like* **poner**) to impose
importancia importance
importar to be important; to matter; **no importa** it doesn't matter
imposible impossible
impresora printer (18)
impuestos taxes (12)
inagotable inexhaustible, never-ending
inaugurar to inaugurate
incaico/a *adj.* Inca, Incan
incierto/a uncertain
incluido/a included
incluir (y) to include
incluso even, including
increíble incredible (12)
independencia independence; **Día** (*m.*) **de la Independencia** Independence Day
independizarse (c) to become independent
indicar (qu) to indicate, point out
indio/a Indian
individuo individual, person (23)
industria industry
inesperadamente unexpectedly

infierno hell
inflamado/a inflamed
influir (y) to influence
información *f.* information (18)
informado/a informed
informalmente informally
informar to inform (24); **informarse** to inquire, find out
informática data processing (18)
informe *m.* report; *pl.* information, news
ingeniería engineering
ingeniero/a engineer
Inglaterra England
inglés, inglesa English (4); **inglés** *m.* English (*language*) (2)
iniciar to initiate
inmediato/a immediate
inmigración: planilla de inmigración immigration form (26)
inmigrante *m., f., adj.* immigrant (25)
inocente *n. m., f.* fool; *adj.* innocent; **Día** (*m.*) **de los Inocentes** Fool's Day (December 28)
inolvidable unforgettable
inquieto/a uneasy
inquietud *f.* concern, worry
inquilino/a renter, tenant (13)
insistir (en + *inf.*) to insist (*on doing something*) (3)
inspector(a) inspector (26)
instalar to install
inteligente intelligent (4)
intensidad *f.* intensity
intensificar (qu) to intensify
interés *m.* interest
interesante interesting; **lo interesante** the interesting thing/part/news (16)
interesar (*like* **gustar**) to interest, be of interest (20)
interno/a internal
interpretar to interpret
intérprete *m., f.* interpreter
interrumpir to interrupt
inventar to invent
invento invention
invierno winter (8)
invitar to invite (9)
inyección: ponerle una inyección to give someone a shot, injection (16)
ir (*irreg.*) to go (5); **ir al extranjero** to go abroad (28); **ir de vacaciones** to go on vacation (11); **¿quieres ir de compras conmigo?** do you want to go shopping with me? (5); **Sí. ¡Vamos al mercado!** Yes. Let's go to the market! (5); **irse** to leave, go away
irlandés, irlandesa Irish
irritado/a irritated; annoyed; **tengo los ojos irritados** my eyes are irritated (16)
isla island
Italia Italy
italiano/a Italian (4); **italiano** Italian (*language*)
izquierda: a la izquierda de to the left of (*directions*) (6)
izquierdo/a left (*direction*) (6); **levantarse con el pie izquierdo** to get up on the wrong side of the bed (15)

jabón *m.* soap (28)
jamás never (10)
jamón *m.* ham (9)
Japón *m.* Japan
japonés, japonesa Japanese; **japonés** *m.* Japanese (*language*)
jarabe *m.* (cough) syrup (16)
jardín *m.* garden
jarro jug, pitcher
jefe/a boss (12)
jirafa giraffe
jornada workday, schedule
joven *n. m., f.* young person (3); *adj.* young (4); **de joven** as a youth (16)
jubilar to retire
juego play (*in a game*) (20); (board, card) game (20); **Juegos Olímpicos** Olympic Games
jugador(a) *n.* player (20)
jugar (ue) (gu) (a) to play (*sports, games*) (8)
jugo (de fruta) (fruit) juice (9)
juguete *m.* toy (13)
junto a alongside of, next to
junto/a *adj.* together
justificar (qu) to justify
justo/a *adj.* precise, exact; **justo** *adv.* exactly
juventud *f.* youth
juzgar (gu) to judge; to form or give an opinion

kilo kilogram (*approx. 2.2 pounds*)
kilómetro kilometer (*approx. .62 miles*)

la the (*f. definite article*)
la *d.o.* you (*form. s.*)/her/it (*f.*)
lado side; **al lado de** beside; **por un lado** on one hand; **por otro lado** on the other hand (5)
ladrón, ladrona thief
lagarto lizard
lago lake
lámpara lamp
lana: de lana (made) of wool (6)
langosta lobster (9)
lanzador (a) pitcher (*sports*)
lápiz *m.* (*pl.* **lápices**) pencil (1)
largo/a long (4); **a lo largo de** along, throughout (the course of)
las you (*form. pl.*)/them (*f.*)
lástima pity; **es lástima** it's a shame (12); **¡qué lástima!** what a shame! (12)
lata (tin) can
latín *m.* Latin (*language*)
latino/a Latin (*person*)
latinoamericano/a Latin American
lavabo washstand; lavatory
lavadora washer, washing machine (14)
lavaplatos *s.* dishwasher (14)
lavar to wash (13); **lavar(se)** to wash oneself, get washed (13)
le *i.o.* to/for you (*form. s.*)/him/her/it
lección *f.* lesson
lectura reading
leche *f.* milk (9)
lechuga lettuce (9)
leer (y) to read (3)
lejos de *prep.* far from (6)
lena spirit, vigor

lengua language (2); tongue (16)
lenguaje *m.* language (*computer*) (18)
lento/a slow
león *m.* lion
les *i.o.* to/for you (*form pl.*)/them
letra letter (*of alphabet*)
levantar to lift, raise (13); to build (*figurative*); **levantarse** to get up, stand up (13); **levantarse con el pie izquierdo** to get up on the wrong side of the bed (15)
ley *f.* law, decree (23)
leyenda legend
libanés, libanesa Lebanese
libertad *f.* liberty, freedom (23)
libre free, unoccupied (7); **al aire libre** outdoors (5); **ratos libres** *pl.* free time (19)
librería bookstore (1)
libro book (1); **libro de texto** textbook (1)
licencia license (17); **licencia de manejar/conducir** driver's license (17)
líder *m.* leader
ligero/a *adj.* light (*in weight*)
límite *m.* limit; border; **límite de velocidad** speed limit
limón *m.* lemon
limonada lemonade
limpiaparabrisas *m., s. and pl.* windshield wiper(s)
limpiar to clean (13)
limpio/a clean (7)
lindo/a pretty
línea line; **línea ecuatorial** equator
linterna lantern
listo/a: estar listo/a (para) to be ready (to); **ser listo/a** to be smart, clever (4)
lo *d.o.* you (*form. s.*)/him/it (*m.*); **lo que** what; that which (18); **lo +** *adj.* the ____ part/thing (16); **lo suficiente** enough
localizar (c) to locate
loco/a crazy
locura madness; insanity
lógico/a logical
los *d.o.* you (*form. pl.*)/them (*m.*)
lotería lottery
lubricar (qu) to lubricate
lucir (zc) to dress to advantage; to show off
lucha fight, fighting
luego then, next (7); later (7); **hasta luego** see you later (PP)
lugar *m.* place (1); **cambiar de lugar** to move (*something*) (15); **en primer lugar** in the first place; **tener lugar** to take place (19)
lujo luxury; **de lujo** deluxe (27)
lujoso/a luxurious (27)
luna moon; **luna de miel** honeymoon (7)
luz *f.* (*pl.* **luces**) light (13); electricity (13)

llamada call
llamar to call (19); **¿cómo se llama usted?, ¿cómo te llamas?** what is your name? (PP); **llamarse** to be named, called (13); **me llamo ____** my name is ____ (PP)
llanta tire (17); **llanta desinflada** flat tire (17)
llave *f.* key (15)
llegada arrival (11)
llegar (gu) to arrive (3); **¿cómo puedo llegar a... ?** how can I get to . . . ? (17); **llegar a ser** to become (15); **llegar a tiempo** to

arrive on time
llenar to fill; to fill out (*a form*) (12)
lleno/a full
llevar to wear (6); to carry (6); to take (*someone or something somewhere*); **llevar a cabo** to carry out; **llevar todos los bienes** to carry (take) all of one's belongings (25); **llevar una vida tranquila (sana)** to lead a calm (healthy) life; **llevarse bien/mal (con)** to get along well/badly (with) (23)
llorar to cry (14)
llover (ue) to rain (8)
lluvia rain
lluvioso/a rainy

madera wood
madre *f.* mother (3)
madrileño/a *of, from, or pertaining to Madrid*
madrugada dawn, early morning
madrugar (gu) to get up early (21)
maestro/a (grade, high) teacher
magnífico/a magnificent, wonderful
mal *n. m.* evil; *adv.* badly (2); ill, not well; **mal, malo/a** *adj.* bad (4); **de mal humor** in a bad mood; **hace mal tiempo** it's bad weather (8); **lo malo** the bad thing/part/news (16)
maleducado/a ill-mannered, rude; poorly brought up
maleta suitcase; **hacer la(s) maleta(s)** to pack one's suitcase(s) (11)
maletero porter (11)
malévolo/a malevolent, mischievous, hateful
mamá mom, mother (3)
mandar to send (10); to order (11)
mandato command
manejar to drive (17); to use, operate (*a machine*) (18); **licencia de manejar** driver's license (17)
manejo operation, use of a machine (18)
manera manner, way
manifestación *f.* public protest, demonstration (23)
mano *f.* hand (13); **darse la mano** to shake hands; **hecho/a a mano** handmade
mantener (*like* **tener**) to maintain, support (*a family, etc.*) (25)
manzana apple (9)
mañana *n.* morning (1); *adv.* tomorrow (PP); **de la mañana** in the morning (PP); **hasta mañana** until tomorrow, see you tomorrow (PP); **pasado mañana** the day after tomorrow (PP); **por la mañana** in the morning (2)
mapa *m.* map
maquillaje *m.* makeup
máquina machine (18); **escribir a máquina** to type (12); **máquina de escribir** typewriter (12)
mar *m., f.* sea
maravilla wonder, marvel
maravilloso/a wonderful, marvelous
marca brand, make
marcado/a marked
marcar (qu) to dial
mareado/a nauseated (16)
mariscos seafood (9)

más more (5); most; **es más** what's more; **más** ___ **que** more ___ than; **¿qué más?** what else?; **¡Qué más da!** What difference does it make! (11)

máscara mask

matar to kill (24)

matemáticas mathematics (2)

materia subject (*in school*) (2)

materno/a *adj.* maternal, motherly, mother

matrícula registration (2)

matrimonio marriage (7); married couple; **contraer matrimonio** to marry, get married

máximo/a maximum; **a lo máximo** at most

mayor older (7)

mayoría majority

me *d.o.* me; *i.o.* to/for me; *refl. pron.* myself

mecánico mechanic

mecedora rocking chair

media: (las tres) y media (three) thirty, half past (three) (PP); **media pensión** *f.* room with breakfast and one other meal (27)

mediano/a moderate; mediocre

medias stockings (6)

medicina medicine; **Facultad** (*f.*) **de Medicina** School, College of Medicine

médico/a *n.* doctor (16); *adj.* medical

medida measurement

medio *n.* means; **medio ambiente** environment (21)

medio/a *adj.* half, middle; intermediate; **clase** (*f.*) **media** middle class

mediodía *m.* midday

mejor better (7); best (4); **a lo mejor** perhaps, maybe; **lo mejor** the best thing/part/news (16); **mejor dicho** rather

mejorar to improve (24)

memoria memory (18)

mencionar to mention

menor younger (7)

menos less; minus; least; **a menos que** unless (20); **menos** ___ **que** less than; **menos cuarto** a quarter till (PP); **ni mucho menos** not at all; **por lo menos** at least (25)

mensual monthly

mentira lie

menudo: a menudo frequently

mercado market (5)

merecer (zc) to deserve (23)

merienda *light snack eaten about 5:00 or 6:00*

mes *m. s.* month (8); **el mes pasado** last month (13)

mesa table (1); **poner la mesa** to set the table (14)

mesita end table

mestizo/a of mixed (Indian and Spanish) blood

meta *m.* goal

metro subway; **estación** (*f.*) **del metro** metro (subway) stop (28)

metrópolis *f. s.* metropolis, large city

mexicano/a Mexican (4)

mexicano-americano/a Mexican-American

México Mexico

mi(s) *poss.* my (3)

mí *obj. of prep.* me

micro- micro (18)

microordenador *m.* microcomputer (*Sp.*)

miedo fear; **tener miedo (de)** to be afraid (of) (4)

miel *f.* honey; **luna de miel** honeymoon (7)

miembro member

mientras while (15); **mientras tanto** meanwhile

milla mile

mimado/a spoiled (*child*)

minidiálogo minidialogue

minoría minority

minuto minute (*time*)

mío/a *poss.* my, (of) mine

mirar to look (at); to watch (3)

mismo/a self; same; **ahora mismo** right now (6); **aquí mismo** right here

misterioso/a mysterious

mitad *f.* half; **a mitad de camino** halfway there

mochila knapsack, backpack (6)

moda fashion; style; **estar de moda** to be in style (6)

modismo idiom

modo: de todos modos anyway

mojado/a wet

mole (*m.*) **poblano** chocolate sauce (*for meat, poultry*) (10)

molestar to bother

molestia *n.* bother

momentito just a minute/second

momento moment; **de momento** right now, for the time being; **en este momento** at the moment, right now

moneda money, currency

monitor *m.* monitor (18)

mono monkey

monótono/a monotonous

montaje: cadena de montaje (*m.*) assembly line

montaña mountain

montar (a caballo) to ride (horseback) (21)

monte *m.* mountain

morado/a purple (6)

moreno/a brunet(te) (4)

morirse (ue, u) (*p.p.* **muerto/a**) to die (14)

moro/a *n.* Moor; *adj.* Moorish

mosca fly

mostrador *m.* counter (*of a ticket window, store, etc.*)

mostrar (ue) to show, exhibit

motor *m.* motor, engine

mozo bellhop (27)

muchacho/a young man/woman; boy/girl

mucho/a *adj.* a lot of, many (4); **mucho** *adv.* much, a lot (1); **muchas gracias** thank you very much, many thanks (PP); **mucho gusto** pleased to meet you (PP); **muchas veces** frequently, a lot

mudarse to move (*change residence*) (21)

muebles *m. pl.* furniture (14); **sacudir los muebles** to dust the furniture (14)

muela molar

muerte *f.* death

muerto/a *p.p.* dead, died; killed

mujer *f.* woman (1); **mujer de negocios** businesswoman

multa fine, ticket, penalty (26); **poner una multa** to give a fine/ticket/penalty

mundial *adj.* world; worldwide (24)

mundo world (17)

muralla wall

museo museum (19)

música music

muy very (2); **(muy) bien** (very) well, fine (PP); **muy buenas** good afternoon/evening

nacer (zc) to be born

nacimiento birth

nacionalidad *f.* nationality (26)

nada nothing, not anything (10); **de nada** you're welcome (PP)

nadar to swim (8)

nadie no one; nobody; not anybody (10)

naranja *n.* orange (*fruit*) (9)

nariz *f.* (*pl.* **narices**) nose (16)

natación *f.* swimming (20)

natal native, of birth; **tierra natal** native land, place of birth (25)

natural: recursos naturales natural resources (21); **ciencias naturales** natural sciences (2)

naturaleza nature (21)

Navidad *f.* Christmas (8); **Feliz Navidad** Merry Christmas

necesario/a necessary

necesidad *f.* necessity, need; **por necesidad** out of necessity, need (25)

necesitar to need (2)

negar (ie) (gu) to deny (12); **negarse a** + *inf.* to refuse to (*do something*)

negocio business deal (12); **hombre/mujer de negocios** businessman/businesswoman

negro/a black (6)

neoyorquino/a native of New York

nervioso/a nervous (7)

nevar (ie) to snow (8)

ni neither; nor; **ni... ni** neither . . . nor; **ni siquiera** not even

nido nest

nieto/a grandson/granddaughter (3)

nietos grandchildren

nieva (*from* **nevar**) it is snowing

nieve *f.* snow (20)

ningún, ninguno/a no; none; not any (10)

niño/a child; little boy/girl (1); **de niño/a** as a child (16)

nivel *m.* level

no no (PP); not (PP); **¿no?** right?, isn't that so? (4)

nocturno/a *adj.* night, nocturnal

noche *f.* night (1); **buenas noches** good evening/night (PP); **de noche** at night, by night; **de la noche** in the evening, at night (PP); **esta noche** tonight (3); **por la noche** in the evening, at night (2); **Noche Vieja** New Year's Eve; **todas las noches** every night (1)

Nochebuena Christmas Eve

nombre *m.* (first) name

normalmente normally

norte *m.* north

Norteamérica North America

norteamericano/a North American; from the United States (4) **fútbol** (*m.*) **norteamericano** football (20)

nos *d.o.* us; *i.o.* to/for us; *refl. pron.* ourselves

nosotros/as *sub. pron.* we; *obj. of prep.* us
nota grade (*in a class*)
noticia notice; piece of news; *pl.* news (24)
noticiario news program
noticiero news broadcast (24)
novedades *f.* news (24)
novela *n.* novel
noveno/a *adj.* ninth (18)
noviazgo courtship; engagement (7)
novio/a boyfriend/girlfriend (7); fiancé(e) (7); groom/bride (7)
nublado/a cloudy, overcast; **está nublado** it's cloudy, overcast (8)
nuestro/a *poss.* our, (of) ours
nuevo/a new (4); **Año Nuevo** New Year; **de nuevo** again
número number (1); issue (*of a magazine*); size (*shoes*)
nunca never (3)

o or (PP)
obedecer (zc) to obey (23)
objeto object
obra work (*of art, literature, etc.*)
obrero/a worker, laborer (24)
observador(a) observant
observar to observe
obtener (*like* **tener**) to get, obtain
occidental *adj.* western
océano ocean
octavo/a *adj.* eighth (18)
ocupado/a busy, occupied (7)
ocupar to occupy
ocurrir to happen, occur; **ocurre: ¿Qué le ocurre?** What do you have? (16)
odiar to hate (10)
oeste *m.* west
oficina office (1)
oficio trade
ofrecer (zc) to offer
oiga(n) hey, listen (*to get someone's attention*)
oír (*irreg.*) to hear (9)
¡ojalá! I wish! (11); **¡ojalá que... !** I hope that . . . ! (11)
ojo eye (16); **¡ojo!** watch out!
ola wave
oleada wave
olvidar to forget (11); **olvidarse (de)** to forget (about) (15); **se me olvidó** (+ *inf.*) I forgot (*to do something*) (14)
oportunidad *f.* opportunity
optar (por) to choose, opt for (25)
oración *f.* sentence
orden *f.* order, command; *m.* order (*sequence*)
ordenador *m.* computer (*Sp.*) (18)
organizado/a organized
organizar (c) to organize
oriente *m.* east
origen *m.* origin
oro gold
orquesta orchestra
os *d.o.* you (*fam. pl. Sp.*); *i.o.* to/for you (*fam. pl. Sp.*); *refl. pron.* yourselves (*fam. pl. Sp.*)
oscuridad *f.* darkness
oscuro/a *adj.* dark
oso bear
otoño fall (*season*) (8)

otro/a other, another (4); **otra vez** again
oye... hey . . . , listen . . . (7)

paciencia patience
paciente *n. m., f.* patient (16); *adj.* patient
padecer (zc) to suffer; to feel deeply
padre *m.* father (3)
padres *m.* parents (3)
paella *Spanish dish made with rice, shellfish, and often chicken, flavored with saffron*
pagar (gu) to pay (for) (2); **¿cuánto pagaste por... ?** how much did you pay for . . . ? (5); **pagar a plazos** to pay in installments (22); **pagar al contado** to pay cash (22); **pagar con cheque** to pay by check (22)
página page
pago payment
país *m.* country, nation (5)
paisaje *m.* countryside, landscape
pájaro/a bird (21)
palabra word (3)
pampas plains of Argentina
pan *m.* bread (9); **pan dulce** sweet rolls (10); **pan tostado** toast (10)
pantalones *m.* pants, trousers (6)
pantalla *n.* screen (18)
pantera panther
papa potato (*Latin America*); **papa frita** french fried potato (9)
papá *m.* dad, father (3)
papel *m.* paper (1); role; **hacer un papel** to play a role; **papel para cartas** stationery (28)
papelería stationery store (5)
paquete *m.* package (28)
par *m.* pair (6)
para *prep.* for (1); in order to (1); **para que** *conj.* so that (20)
parabrisas *m.s.* windshield (17)
parada stop (28); **parada del autobús** bus stop (28)
paraguas *m. s.* umbrella
paraíso paradise
paralizado/a paralyzed
parar to stop (17)
pardo/a brown (6)
parecer (zc) (*like* **gustar**) to seem, appear (19); **me parece que...** I think that . . . (19); **¿qué te parece?** what do you think?, how does that strike you? (6) (10)
pared *f.* wall
pareja couple; partner
pariente *n.m.* relative (2)
parque *m.* park (6)
párrafo paragraph
parte *f.* part; **por mi parte** as for me; **por todas partes** everywhere
particular particular; private
partido game (*in sports*), match (20)
pasado *n.* past; **pasado/a** *adj.* past, last (*in time*); **el (fin de semana, mes, año) pasado** last (weekend, month, year) (13); **pasado mañana** the day after tomorrow (PP)
pasaje *m.* passage, ticket, fare (11)
pasajero/a passenger (11)
pasaporte *m* passport (26)

pasar (por) to pass (through, by) (11); to come by (*for someone*); to happen; to spend (*time*); **pasar la aspiradora** to run the sweeper, vacuum (14); **pasarlo bien/mal** to have a good/bad time (14); **¿qué le pasa?** what do you have? (16); **¡que lo pases/pasen bien!** have a good time! (19)
pasatiempo pastime, diversion (19)
Pascua Passover; **Pascua Florida** Easter **Pascuas** *pl.* Christmas; **Felices Pascuas** Merry Christmas
pasear en bicicleta *n.* cycling (20); *v.* to go for a bike ride
paseo stroll, promenade; **dar un paseo** to take a walk (19)
pasillo hall, corridor
paso step; pace; **cambio de ritmo** change of pace
pasta dental toothpaste (28)
pastel *m.* cake; pie; pastry (9)
pastelería pastry shop (28)
pastelillo small turnover, pastry
pastelito small pastry (28)
pastilla pill (16); **pastilla para dormir** sleeping pill
patata potato (*Sp.*)
patinar to skate (19)
patio patio yard; (14)
patria native land, homeland (25)
paz *f.* (*pl.* **paces**) peace (24)
peatón, peatona pedestrian
pedido *n.* order (*for food, merchandise, etc.*)
pedir (i, i) to ask for, order (8)
pegar (gu) to hit, strike (15)
película movie (7)
peligro danger
peligroso/a dangerous (18)
pelo hair
pelota ball (13)
pena grief (23); **pena de muerte** death penalty (23)
pensar (ie) to think (8); **pensar + inf.** to intend (*to do something*) (8); **pienso que...** I think that . . . (8); **¿qué piensas de... ?** what do you think of . . . ? (8)
pensión *f.* boarding house (27); **media pensión** room with breakfast and one other meal (27); **pensión completa** room and full board (*all meals included*) (27)
peor worse (7); worst
pequeño/a small, little (4)
perder (ie) to lose (8); to miss (*a bus, plane, social function, etc.*) (8)
pérdida waste
perdón pardon me, excuse me (PP)
perdonar to pardon, forgive
perezoso/a lazy (4)
perfecto/a perfect, fine
periódicamente periodically
periódico newspaper (3)
periodista *m., f.* journalist
permiso permission; **con permiso** pardon me, excuse me (PP)
permitir to permit, allow (11)
pero *conj.* but (1)
perro/a dog (3)
persa *m., f.* Persian

persona person (1)
personaje *m.* character (*of a story, play*)
personal *n. m.* personnel; *adj.* personal
personalidad *f.* personality
perspectiva perspective
pertenecer (zc) to relate, belong
peruano/a Peruvian
pesado/a boring (18)
pesar to weigh; **a pesar de** in spite of
pesca catch (*of fish*)
pescado fish (9)
peseta *unit of currency in Spain*
peso *unit of currency in Mexico and several other Latin American countries;* weight
pesquera *adj.* fishing, *of or pertaining to fish*
petróleo petroleum, oil (24)
picante: salsa picante hot sauce (10)
pico top, summit, peak
pie *m.* foot (15); **a pie** on foot, standing; **estar de pie** to be standing (up); **levantarse con el pie izquierdo** to get up on the wrong side of the bed (15); **ponerse de pie** to stand up, get up
pierna leg (15)
pieza piece (*of music*)
pijama *m.s.* pajamas
pinacoteca art gallery
pingüino penguin
pintar to paint
pintor(a) painter
pintura (rupestre) (cave) painting
piscina swimming pool (13)
piso floor (13); **primer piso** second floor (*first floor up*)
pista (race)track (20)
pizarra blackboard (1)
placer *m.* pleasure
plan *m.* plan; **hacer planes para** + *inf.* to make plans to (*do something*) (19)
planear to plan
planeta *m.* planet
planilla (de inmigración) (immigration) form (26)
planta plant; floor (*of a building*); **planta baja** ground floor (13)
plástico plastic
plata silver (*metal*)
plato plate; dish (9); **plato fuerte** main dish
playa beach (8)
plazos: pagar a plazos to pay in installments (22)
pleno/a full
plomero/a plumber
población *f.* population (21)
poblano: mole (*m.*) **poblano** chocolate sauce (*for meat, poultry*) (10)
pobre poor (4)
pobreza poverty
poco/a *adj.* little, few (4); **pocas veces** infrequently, rarely; **poco** *adv.* little, a little (2); **poco a poco** little by little
poder *v.* (*irreg.*) to be able to; can (4); *n. m.* power
poderoso/a powerful
poema *m.* poem
poeta *m., f.* poet
policía *m., f.* police officer; *f.* police (force)
política *n. f. s.* politics; policy (23)

político/a *n.* politician; *adj.* political; **ciencias políticas** *pl.* political science
pollo chicken (9)
poner (*irreg.*) to put, place (8); to turn on (*appliances*) (8); **poner el despertador** to set the alarm clock; **ponerle una inyección** to give someone a shot, injection (16); **poner la mesa** to set the table (14); **poner una multa** to give a fine/ticket; **ponerse** to put on (*clothing*) (13); to become (15); **ponerse de acuerdo** to reach an agreement
poniéndome: estoy poniéndome... I am putting on . . .
por *prep.* in (*the morning, evening, etc.*) (2); for; per; by; through; during; on account of; for the sake of; because of (9); **por ciento** percent; **por Dios** for heaven's sake (25); **por ejemplo** for example (5); **por eso** therefore, that's why (4); **por favor** please (PP); **por fin** finally (25); **por gusto** willingly, out of desire (25); **por hora** per hour; **por lo general** generally, in general (4); **por lo menos** at least (25); **por necesidad** out of necessity, need (25); **por otro lado** on the other hand (5); **por primera/última vez** for the first/last time (25); **por si acaso** just in case (25); **por supuesto** of course
¿por qué? why? (5)
porque because (7)
portarse bien/mal to behave well/badly (15)
portátil portable
portero/a building manager (13); doorman (13)
portugués, portuguesa Portuguese; **portugués** *m.* Portuguese (*language*)
poseer (y) to possess, own
posibilidad *f.* possibility
posible possible
posponer (*like* **poner**) to postpone
postal: (tarjeta) postal *f.* postcard (28)
postre *m.* dessert (9)
postura position (*posture*)
practicar (qu) to practice (2); **practicar deportes** to participate in sports (16)
pradera meadow, prairie
precio price (1); **de todo precio** in all price ranges; **precio fijo** set price (5); **primer precio** first price (5)
preciso: es preciso it's necessary (11)
precolombino/a before Columbus
predecir (*like* **decir**) to predict
preferible: es preferible it's preferable (11)
preferir (ie, i) to prefer (4); **prefiero** + *inf.* I prefer (*to do something*) (2)
pregunta question; **hacer una pregunta** to ask a question (8)
preguntar to ask a question (5)
premio prize
prensa press; news media (24)
preocupado/a worried (7)
preocuparse (por) to worry (about)
preparación *f.* preparation
preparado/a prepared
preparar to prepare (10); **preparar la comida** to prepare food (14)
preparativo/a preparative, qualifying
presentación *f.* introduction, presentation

presentar to introduce; to present
presente *n.* present (*time, tense*)
presión *f.* pressure, tension (15)
préstamo *n.* loan (22)
prestar to lend (10)
prestigio prestige
presupuesto budget (22)
primario/a principal; primary
primavera spring (8)
primer, primero/a *adj.* first (18); **es el primero (dos, ...) de** it's the first (second, . . .) (8); **por primera vez** for the first time (25); **primera clase** first class; **primero** *adv.* first (of all)
primo/a cousin (3)
principiante *m., f.* beginner, apprentice
principio: al principio at the beginning
prisa haste, hurry; **tener prisa** to be in a hurry (4)
privado/a private
probabilidad *f.* probability
probar (ue) to taste, try
problema *m.* problem (1)
producir (*irreg.*) to produce
productor(a) producer
profesor(a) professor (1)
profundo/a profound
programa *m.* program (18)
programador(a) programmer (18)
progresivo/a progressive
prohibido estacionarse no parking
prohibir to prohibit, forbid (11)
prometer to promise
pronombre *m.* pronoun; **pronombre reflexivo** reflexive pronoun
pronóstico prognosis
pronto soon; **tan pronto como** as soon as (26)
pronunciar to pronounce
propiedad *f.* property
propina tip (*given to a waiter, etc.*) (27)
propio/a *adj.* one's own, very
proponer (*like* **poner**) to propose
proporcionar to furnish, grant, supply
propósito purpose; **a propósito** by the way
prosperidad *f.* prosperity
proteger (j) to protect (21)
proteína protein
protestar to protest (23)
provecho advantage
próximo/a next
proyecto project
prueba quiz (12); trial (*for a race*)
psicología psychology
público *n.* public; **público/a** *adj.* public
pueblo town
puente *m.* bridge
puerta door (3)
puerto port
puertorriqueño/a Puerto Rican
pues... well . . . (2)
puesto *n.* position, place in line (11); job (12)
puesto/a *p.p.* put, placed
pulmones *m.* lungs (16)
punto point; dot; **en punto** exactly, on the dot (*time*) (PP); **punto de vista** point of view
puro/a pure (21)

que that, which (3); **lo que** what, that which (12)

¿qué? what? which? (PP); **no hay de qué** you're welcome (17); **¡qué + *noun* + más +** *adj.*! what a + *adj.* + *noun*! **¡qué bien!** great!; **¡qué lástima!** what a shame!; **¿qué más?** what else?; **¡qué más da!** what difference does it make! (11); **¿qué tal?** how are you (*doing*)? (PP); **¡qué va!** good grief!, are you kidding?

quedar to remain, be left (15); **no nos queda(n)** ___ we do not have any ___ left; **quedarse** to stay (*in a place*) (15)

quehacer *m.* task, chore (14)

quejarse (de) to complain (about) (22)

querer (*irreg.*) to want, wish (4); to love (*with persons*); **fue sin querer** it was unintentional, I (he/we, . . .) didn't mean to do it (15); **¿quieres ir de compras conmigo?** do you want to go shopping with me? (5); **quiero (no quiero) +** *inf.* I want (I don't want) to (*do something*) (2); **quisiera +** *inf.* I (he/she/you) would really like to (*do something*) (22); **¿quisiera(s)...** would you like to . . . ? (22)

querido/a dear, beloved (7)

queso cheese (9)

quien who, whom (18)

¿quién(es)? who?, whom? (PP); **¿de quién?** whose?

quiero (no quiero) + *inf.* I (don't) want to . . . (2)

química chemistry

quinto/a *adj.* fifth (18)

quiosco kiosk (*smaller outdoor stand where a variety of items are sold*) (28)

quisiera + *inf.* I (he/she/you) would really like to . . . (22); **¿quisieras... ?** would you like to . . . ? (22)

quitar to remove, take away (6); to take out, withhold (12); **quitarse** to take off (*clothing*) (13); **estoy quitándome...** I am taking off . . . (6)

quizá(s) perhaps (20)

rabino rabbi

radio *f.* radio

raíz *f.* (*pl.* **raíces**) root (25); stem (*gram.*)

ranchero/a rancher (21)

rápido/a *adj.* fast; **rápido** *adv.* fast, rapidly

raqueta racket (20)

raro/a rare, unusual

rascacielos *m. s.* skyscraper (21)

rato short period of time (20); *pl.* spare, free time (19); **ratos libres** free time (19); **un rato** a while

ratón *m.* mouse

raya: de rayas striped (6)

rayo: rayos equis X-rays

raza race (*of people*); **Día** (*m.*) **de la Raza** Columbus Day (October 12)

razón *f.* reason; **la razón por la cual...** the reason why . . . (2); **(no) tener razón** to be (wrong) right (4)

reaccionar to react

real royal; real

realidad *f.* reality; **en realidad** really

realizar (c) to bring about, realize

realmente really

rebelde *n. m., f.* rebel; *adj.* rebellious

recado message

recepción *f.* front desk (27); reception

recepcionista *m., f.* receptionist

receta prescription (16)

recetar to prescribe medicines

recibir to receive (3)

recién + *adj.* recently

reciente recent

recoger (j) to pick up, gather (13)

recomendar (ie) to recommend (11)

reconocer (zc) to recognize

recordar (ue) to remember (14); to bring to mind

recorrer to pass through (21); to cover (*territory, miles, etc.*) (21)

recreo recreation (14)

rector(a) president (*of a university*)

recuerdo memory (4); souvenir (4); *pl.* regards

recursos resources; **recursos naturales** natural resources (21)

red *f.* net (20)

redondo/a round

reducir (*like* **producir**) to reduce, cut down

reemplazar (c) to replace (18)

referente a referring, relating to

referir (ie, i) to refer

refinería refinery

reflejar to reflect

refrán *m.* proverb

refrescante *adj.* refreshing

refresco soft drink (8)

refrigerador *m.* refrigerator (14)

refugiado/a refugee (25)

refugio refuge

regalar to give (*as a gift*) (10)

regalo present, gift (3)

regatear to haggle, bargain (5)

registrar to search, inspect (26)

regla rule

regresar to return (*to a place*) (2); **regresar a casa** to return home (2)

regreso return

reina queen

reírse (i, i) to laugh (14)

relación *f.* relation (7)

religioso/a religious

reloj *m.* watch, clock

remedio: no hay más remedio nothing can be done about it

remunerar to remunerate, reward

renta income

renunciar (a) to resign (from) (12)

repasar to review

repente: de repente suddenly (16)

repetir (i, i) to repeat

reportaje *m.* newspaper report

reportero/a reporter (24)

representar to represent; to present (*a play, etc.*)

república republic (23)

requerir (ie, i) to require

requisito requirement (18)

reservación *f.* reservation

reservar to reserve (27)

resfriado cold (*illness*) (16)

resfriarse to get/catch a cold (16)

residencia residence; dormitory (1)

resolver (ue) (*p.p.* **resuelto/a**) to solve, resolve (20)

respecto: al respecto about the matter; **con respecto a** with respect, regard to; **respecto a** concerning

respetar to respect

respeto respect

respiración *f.* respiration, breathing

respirar to breathe (16)

responder to answer, respond

responsabilidad *f.* responsibility (23)

responsable responsible

respuesta *n.* answer

restaurante *m.* restaurant (9)

resto rest, remainder

resuelto/a *p.p.* solved, resolved

resultado result (24)

resultar to result; to turn out

retirado/a retired

retirarse to retire, withdraw

retraso tardiness; delay

reunión *f.* reunion

reunir to unite; to reunite; **reunirse (con)** to get together (with)

revisar to check, examine, inspect (17)

revista magazine (3)

rey *m.* king; **los Reyes Magos** the Magi, the three Wise Men

rico/a rich (4)

ridículo/a ridiculous

riesgo danger, risk

rigidez *f.* rigidity

rígido/a rigid

río river

riqueza wealth; *pl.* riches

ritmo rhythm; **(necesito) un cambio de ritmo** (I need) a change of pace (21); **ritmo (acelerado) de la vida** (fast) pace of life, living (21)

robot *m.* robot (18)

roca rock

rodear to surround

rojo/a red (6)

romano/a Roman

romper (*p.p.* **roto/a**) to break (15)

ropa clothing (5); **tienda de ropa** clothing store (5)

rosa *n.* rose

rosado/a pink (6)

rota/a *p.p.* broken

rubio/a blond(e) (4)

ruido noise (9)

ruidoso/a noisy

ruso/a Russian (4); **ruso** Russian (*language*) (2)

rutina routine, habit

saber (*irreg.*) to know (9); to know how to (*do something*) (9)

sabor *m.* taste; flavor

saborear to savor; to flavor, season

sabotear to sabotage

sacar (qu) to take (*a photo*); to take out, remove; to get, receive (*with grades*); to stick out (*one's tongue*); **sacar la basura** to take out the garbage (14)

sacerdote *m.* priest, clergyman
sacrificar (qu) to sacrifice
sacudir los muebles to dust the furniture (14)
sal *f.* salt
sala room; living room (14); **sala de clase** classroom; **sala de espera** waiting room (11); **sala de recreo** recreation room, family room (14)
salida departure (11); exit
salir (*irreg.*) **(de)** to leave, go out (8); to appear; **salir a derechas** to turn out right
salsa (picante) (hot) sauce (10)
salud *f.* health (16)
saludar to greet
saludo greeting
sandalia sandal (6)
sándwich *m.* sandwich
sangre *f.* blood
sano/a healthy (16); **llevar una vida sana** to lead a healthy life (16)
santo/a holy, blessed
Satanás Satan
satisfacer (*like* **hacer**) to satisfy
saxofón *m.* saxophone
se (*impersonal*) one; *refl. pron.* yourself (*form.*)/himself/herself/ yourselves (*form.*)/themselves
secadora clothes dryer (14)
sección (*f.*) **de (no) fumar** (no-) smoking section (11)
seco/a dry, barren, arid
secretario/a secretary (1)
secuencia sequence
secundaria secondary; **la (escuela) secundaria** high school
sed *f.* thirst; **tener sed** to be thirsty (9)
seda: de seda (made) of silk (6)
seguida: en seguida immediately (16)
seguir (i, i) (ga) to keep on, continue (17)
según according to
segundo *n.* second; **segundo/a** *adj.* second (18); **Segunda Guerra Mundial** Second World War
seguridad *f.* security, safety
seguro/a sure, certain; **estar seguro/a** to be sure, certain (12); **(no) es seguro que** it is (not) sure, certain that (12); **seguro que** of course
seleccionar to select, choose
selva jungle
sello stamp (28)
semáforo traffic signal (17)
semana week (13); **fin** (*m.*) **de semana** weekend (PP); **fin de semana pasado** last weekend (13); **semana pasada** last week (13); **Semana Santa** Holy Week
senador(a) senator
sencillo/a simple
sensible sensitive
sentado/a seated, sitting
sentar (ie) to seat (13); **¿nos sentamos?** shall we sit down?; **sentarse** to sit down (13)
sentido *n.* sense
sentimiento feeling, emotion, sentiment
sentir (ie, i) to regret (12); to feel sorry; **lo siento** I'm sorry (7); **sentirse** to feel (14); **me siento a gusto** I feel at home (21)

señor (Sr.) *m.* Mr., sir (PP); gentleman
señora (Sra.) Mrs. (PP); lady
señores (Sres.) *m. pl.* Mr. and Mrs.; gentlemen
señorita (Srta.) Miss (PP); young lady
separar to separate
se(p)tiembre *m.* September (8)
ser *v.* (*irreg.*) to be (3); **llegar a ser** to become (15); **ser listo/a** to be smart, clever; **es (son) la(s)** ___ it's ___ (*with time*) (PP); **soy de...** I'm from . . . (3); **ser** (*n. m.*) **humano** human being (18)
serio/a serious
serpiente *f.* snake
servicio service; **servicios públicos** public restrooms (21)
servir (i, i) de to serve (as) (8); **¿en qué puedo servirle?** how can I serve you?, how can I be of service? (11)
sexo sex
sexto/a *adj.* sixth (18)
si if (2)
sí yes (PP); **creo que sí** I think so (1)
siamés, siamesa Siamese
sicología psychology (2)
siempre always (5)
siento: lo siento I'm sorry (7); **me siento a gusto** I feel at home, comfortable (21)
siesta nap; **dormir la siesta** to take a nap
siglo century
significar (qu) to mean
siguiente following, next
silencioso/a silent
silla chair (1)
sillón *m.* armchair
símbolo symbol
simpatía pleasant nature, congeniality
simpático/a nice (4); likeable (4)
sin *prep.* without (5); **sin que** *conj.* without (20); **sin embargo** however, nevertheless
sincero/a sincere
sinfónico/a symphonic
sino but (rather) (25)
síntoma *m.* symptom (16)
siquiatra *m., f.* psychiatrist
siquiera *adv.* at least; **ni siquiera** not even
sísmico/a seismic (*relating to earthquakes*)
sistema *m.* system (18)
sitio place
situado/a located
sobre *n.* envelope (28); *prep.* about, above, on; **sobre todo** above all, especially
sobrino/a nephew/niece (3)
sociales: ciencias sociales social sciences (2)
sociedad *f.* society
sociología sociology
sofá *m.* sofa
sol *m.* sun (8); **hace (mucho) sol** it's (very) sunny (8); **tomar el sol** to sunbathe (19)
solamente *adv.* only
soldado/a soldier
soledad *f.* solitude (21)
solicitar to solicit; to apply for (*a job*) (12)
solicitud *f.* application (*form*) (12)
solo/a *adj.* alone (11); **sólo** *adv.* only (2)
soltero/a single, unmarried (4)
sombra shade
sombrero hat

sonar (ue) to ring (*telephone*) (16); to sound
sonreír (i, i) to smile (14)
sonrisa smile
soñar (ue) (con) to dream (about)
sopa soup (9)
sordo/a deaf
sorprender to surprise, be surprising (12)
sorpresa surprise
sospechoso/a suspicious
sótano basement (14)
soviético/a Soviet
soy I am (PP), **soy de...** I'm from . . . (3)
su *poss.* his/her/its/your (*form. s.* + *pl.*)/their
suave soft; mild, gentle
subir (a) to go up (into, onto) (11); to get on, in (*a plane, car, etc.*) (11); to carry up; to raise
subterráneo/a subterranean, underground
suburbio suburb
sucio/a dirty (7)
Sudamérica South America
sudamericano/a South American
suegro/a father-in-law/ mother-in-law
sueldo salary (12)
suelo floor
sueño sleepiness; dream; **tener sueño** to be sleepy (4)
suerte *f.* luck (15); **¡qué mala suerte!** what bad luck! (15)
suéter *m.* sweater (6)
suficiente sufficient, enough; **lo suficiente** enough (16)
sufijo suffix, affix
sufrir to suffer (15); **sufrir altibajos** to have ups and downs (25); **sufrir muchas presiones** to be under a lot of pressure
sugerencia suggestion (11)
sugerir (ie, i) to suggest
suministro *n.* supply
suponer (*like* **poner**) to suppose
sur *m.* south
suspenso "F," failing grade
sustantivo noun
suyo/a your, of yours (*form. s., pl.*) his, of his; her, (of) hers; its; their, of theirs

tabacalera tobacco shop (28)
tabaco tobacco
tablado stage, platform
taco taco (*tortilla filled with meat, vegetables*)
tal such (a); **con tal (de) que** provided that (20); **¿qué tal?** how are you (doing)? (PP); **tal vez** perhaps, maybe
talla size (*clothing*)
taller *m.* (repair) shop, service station (17)
tamaño size
también too, also (PP)
tambor *m.* drum
tampoco neither, not either (10)
tan as; so; **tan** ___ **como** as ___ as; **tan pronto como** as soon as (26)
tanque *m.* (gas) tank (17)
tanto/a as much; **tanto/a** ___ **como** as much ___ as; **tanto** *adv.* as/so much; **mientras tanto** meanwhile; **no es para tanto** it's not that serious; **por lo tanto** thus
tantos/as as many; **tantos/as** ___ **como** as many ___ as

tapas hors d'oeuvres
taquilla ticket window (19)
tardar: a más tardar at the longest
tarde *f.* afternoon, evening (1); **buenas tardes** good afternoon/evening (PP); **de la tarde** in the afternoon, evening (2); *adv.* late (2); **más tarde** later; **por la tarde** in the afternoon (2)
tarea homework (15)
tarifa price list; rate
tarjeta card (10); **tarjeta de crédito** credit card (22); **tarjeta postal** postcard (28)
tasca tavern
taxista *m., f.* cab driver
taza cup
te *d.o.* you (*fam. s.*); *i.o.* to/for you (*fam. s.*); *refl. pron.* yourself (*fam. s.*)
té *m.* tea (9)
teatro theater (19)
teclado keyboard (18)
teclas keys (*computer*) (18)
técnico/a technician (18)
tecnología technology (18)
tele *f.* television
telefónico/a *adj.* telephone; **guía telefónica** telephone book
teléfono telephone; **(número de) teléfono** telephone number; **por teléfono** on the telephone
telenovela soap opera
televisión *f.* television
televisor *m.* television set (8)
tema *m.* theme, topic
temblar (ie) to shake
temer to fear (12)
temperatura: tomarle la temperatura to take someone's temperature (16)
templado/a warm
temporada season
temprano *adv.* early (2)
tener (*irreg.*) to have (4); **tengo la garganta inflamada** my throat is swollen (16); **tengo los ojos irritados** my eyes are irritated (16); **(no) tengo (nada) algo que** + *inf.* I have (nothing) something to . . . (26); **¿qué tiene?** what do you have? (16); **tener ____ años** to be ____ years old (4); **tener algo que declarar** to have something to declare (*customs*); **tener calor/frío** to be hot, (feel) warm/cold, chilly (6); **tener cuidado (de)** to be careful (about); **tener dolor (de)** to have a pain (in) (16); **tener éxito** to be successful; **tener fiebre** to have a fever (16); **tener ganas de** + *inf.* to feel like (*doing something*) (4); **tener hambre** to be hungry (9); **tener lugar** to take place (19); **tener miedo (de)** to be afraid (of) (4); **tener prisa** to be in a hurry (4); **tener que** + *inf.* to have to (*do something*) (4); **(no) tener razón** to be (wrong) right (4); **tener sed** to be thirsty (9); **tener sueño** to be sleepy (4)
tengo/tienes I have/you have (3)
tenis *m.* tennis (20)
tensión *f.* tension
teórico/a theoretical
tercer, tercero/a *adj.* third (18)
tercio *n.* third
terminación *f.* ending

terminar to finish (3)
término term, expression
terraza terrace
terremoto earthquake
territorio territory
testigo *m., f.* witness (24)
texto text (1); **libro de texto** textbook (1)
ti *obj. of prep.* you (*fam. s.*)
tiempo (*verb*) tense; time (20); weather (8); **a tiempo** on time (11); **aquéllos eran otros tiempos** it was different back then, things were different then (15); **¿cuánto tiempo hace que (vives aquí)?** how long have you been (living here)? (8); **de tiempo parcial** part-time; **hace (muy) buen/mal tiempo** it's (very) good/bad weather (8); **los tiempos cambian** times change (15); **¿qué tiempo hace?** what's the weather like? (8)
tienda shop, store (5); **tienda de ropa** clothing store (5)
tierra land, earth; **tierra natal** native land, place of birth (25)
tino common sense; knack
tinto: vino tinto red wine (9)
tío/a uncle/aunt (3)
típico/a typical
tipo *n.* kind
título title; degree
toalla towel
tobillo ankle
tocar (qu) to play (*an instrument*) (7); **(a mí) me toca...** It's my turn to . . . (14); **¿a quién le toca... ?** whose turn is it to . . . ? (14)
todavía still, yet (7)
todo/a all, every (4); everything (3); **ante todo** first of all; **de todo** everything (5); **de todo precio** in all price ranges; **de todos modos** anyway; **por todas partes** everywhere; **sobre todo** above all, especially; **todas las tardes/noches** every afternoon/night; **todo derecho** straight ahead (17); **todos los días** every day (2)
tomar to take (2); to drink (2); to eat; **tomar el sol** to sunbathe (19); **tomar en cuenta** to take into account (23); **tomarle el pelo (a alguien)** to pull someone's leg, to tease; **tomarle la temperatura** to take someone's temperature (16)
tomate *m.* tomato (9)
tontería foolish thing
tonto/a silly, foolish (4)
tormenta storm, hurricane
torneo tournament, contest
toro bull
torpe clumsy; dim-witted (15)
tortilla omelet (*Sp.*); tortilla
tos *f. s.* cough (16)
toser to cough (16)
tostado: pan (*m.*) **tostado** toast (10)
tostador(a) toaster (14)
total *n. m.* total; *adj.* total; **en total** in all
trabajador(a) *n.* worker; *adj.* hard-working (4)
trabajar to work (2)
trabajo job (12); work (12)
traducción *f.* translation
traducir (*like* **producir**) to translate
traer (*irreg.*) to bring (9)

tráfico traffic (17)
tragedia tragedy
trago drink (*alcoholic*) (28)
traje *m.* suit; costume (6); **traje de baño** swim/bathing suit (6)
trama plot (*of play or novel*) (19)
tranquilidad *f.* peace, tranquility
tranquilizante *m.* tranquilizer
tranquilo/a calm, tranquil (16); **llevar una vida tranquila** to lead a calm life (16)
transbordador *m.* shuttle
transmisión *f.* transmission; **transmisión de cambios** manual shift
transporte *m.* (means of) transportation (21)
tratado treaty
tratamiento treatment
tratar (de) + *inf.* to try to (*do something*) (17); **se trata de** it's a matter of (23)
trato deal, pact; **trato hecho** it's a deal
través: a través (de) through, by means of
travieso/a prankish, mischievous
trébol *m.* clover, shamrock
tren *m.* train; **estación** (*f.*) **de trenes** train station (11)
trigésimo/a thirtieth
triste sad (7)
trompeta trumpet
trofeo trophy
tropezar (ie) (c) to stumble, slip; to strike against; **tropezar con** to bump into (15)
tu *poss.* your (*fam. s.*)
tú *sub. pron.* you (*fam. s.*); **¿y tú?** and you? (PP)
tubería tubing, piping
tumba tomb
turco/a Turkish
turista *m., f.* tourist
turístico/a *adj.* tourist; **clase** (*f.*) **turística** tourist class
tuyo/a *poss.* your, (of) yours (*fam. s.*)

último/a last; latest (24); **por última vez** for the last time (25)
un, uno/a one; a, an (*indefinite article*)
único/a only; unique
unidad *f.* unity
unido/a united; **Estados Unidos** United States
unión *f.* union
unir to unite
universidad *f.* university (1)
universitario/a *n.* university student; *adj.* university, of the university
unos/as some, several, a few
urgencia: sala de urgencia emergency room
urgente: es urgente it's urgent (11)
usado/a used
usanza usage, custom
usar to use; to operate (*a machine*) (18)
uso use
usted (Ud., Vd.) *sub. pron.* you (*form. s.*); *obj. of prep.* you (*form. s.*); **¿y usted?** and you? (PP)
ustedes (Uds., Vds.) *sub. pron.* you (*form. pl.*); *obj. of prep.* you (*form. pl.*)
útil useful
utilitario/a useful
utilizar (c) to utilize, use

vaca cow (21)
vacaciones *f. pl.* vacation (8); **estar de vacaciones** to be on vacation (8); **ir de vacaciones** to go on vacation (11)
valer (valgo) to be worth; **¿cuánto vale?** how much is it (worth)? **¿vale?** okay?
valiente brave, courageous
valor *m.* value
valle *m.* valley
vamos: ¡Vamos al mercado! Let's go to the market! (5)
variar to vary
variedad *f.* variety
varios/as several, some
varón *m.* male child, boy
vaso (drinking) glass (9)
vecino/a neighbor (13)
vegetariano/a vegetarian
velocidad *f.* speed, velocity
vendedor(a) salesperson
vender to sell (5)
venezolano/a Venezuelan
venir (*irreg.*) to come (4)
venta sale
ventaja advantage (18)
ventana window (14)
ver (*irreg.*) to see (9); **a ver** let's see
verano summer (8)
veras: ¿de veras? really?
verbo verb
verdad *f.* truth (10); **de verdad** real; really; **¿verdad?** right?, is that so? (4)
verdadero/a true, real
verde green (6)
verduras vegetables (9)
vestido dress (6)

vestir (i, i) to dress (13); **vestirse** to dress oneself, get dressed (13)
vez *f.* (*pl.* **veces**) time, occasion (8); **a la vez** at the same time; **a veces** at times, sometimes (3); **de vez en cuando** from time to time (20); **dos veces** twice; **en vez de** instead of; **muchas veces** frequently, a lot; **otra vez** again; **por primera (última) vez** for the first (last) time (25); **raras veces** rarely; **tal vez** maybe; **una vez** once
viajar to travel (7); **viajar al extranjero** to travel abroad
viaje *m.* trip, voyage (8); **de viaje** on a trip; **hacer un viaje** to take a trip (8); **viaje por mar** ocean cruise
viajero/a traveler (26); **cheque** (*m.*) **de viajero** traveler's check (27)
vida life (13); **llevar una vida ____** to lead a ____ life (16); **mi vida** dear (*expression of affection*); **ritmo (acelerado) de la vido** (fast) pace of life, living (22)
vieja: Noche (*f.*) **Vieja** New Year's Eve
viejo/a *n.* old man/woman; *adj.* old (4)
viene: el año que viene next year; **la semana que viene** next week
viento wind (8); **hace (mucho) viento** it's (very) windy (8)
viernes *m.* Friday (PP)
vigente *adj.* enforced, prevailing
vinculado/a (a) *adj.* tied (to); based (upon)
vino wine (9); **vino blanco/tinto** white/red wine (9)
virreinato viceroyship, viceroyalty
visita visit; **de vísita** on a visit
visitante *m., f.* visitor
visitar to visit (19)

vista view (13); **punto de vista** point of view
visto/a *p.p.* seen
vivienda *n.* housing (21)
vivir to live (3)
vivo/a *adj.* alive, living; bright (*of colors*)
volador(a) *adj.* flying
volar (ue) to fly (20)
volcán *m.* volcano
vólibol *m.* volleyball (20)
volumen *m.* volume
voluntad *f.* will, purpose
volver (ue) (*p.p.* **vuelto/a**) to return (8); **volver a** + *inf.* to (*do something*) again (8)
vosotros/as *sub. pron.* you (*fam. pl. Sp.*); *obj. of prep.* you (*fam. pl. Sp.*)
votante *m., f.* voter
votar to vote (23)
voz *f.* (*pl.* **voces**) voice; **en voz alta** aloud, out loud; **voz activa** active voice (*gram.*)
vuelo flight (11)
vuelto/a *p.p.* returned; **billete/boleto (de ida) y vuelta** (one-way) round-trip ticket (11)
vuestro/a *poss.* your, (of) yours (*fam. pl. Sp.*)

y and (PP); plus (PP)
ya already, now (1); **ya no** no longer; **ya que** since
yate *m.* yacht
yo *sub. pron.* I
yoga *m.* yoga
yogur(t) *m.* yoghurt

zanahoria carrot (9)
zapatería shoe store (5)
zapato shoe (5)

English–Spanish Vocabulary

a un, una
able: to be able poder (*irreg.*)
above sobre; encima
abroad extranjero; to go abroad ir al extranjero; to travel abroad viajar en el extranjero
absentminded distraído/a
accompany acompañar
account cuenta; checking account cuenta corriente; savings account cuenta de ahorros; to take into account tomar en cuenta
acquainted: to be acquainted with conocer (zc)
addition: in addition (to) además (de)
address *n.* **dirección** *f.*
advance: (____ days) in advance con (____ días de) anticipación
advice consejo
advisor consejero/a
affectionate cariñoso/a
afraid: to be afraid (of) tener miedo (de)
after *prep.* **después de;** *conj.* **después (de) que**

afternoon tarde *f.*; **good afternoon buenas tardes; in the afternoon de/por la tarde**
again otra vez, de nuevo; to (*do something*) again volver a + *inf.*
ago: (two years) ago hace (dos años)
agreement: to be in agreement (with) estar de acuerdo (con); to reach an agreement ponerse de acuerdo
air aire *m.*
air conditioner (aire) acondicionador *m.*
airplane avión *m.*
airport aeropuerto
alarm clock despertador *m.*
all todo/a
allow permitir
almost casi
alone solo/a
already ya
also también
although aunque
always siempre
A.M. de/por la mañana
among entre
amuse divertir (ie, i)

amusement diversión *f.*
amusing divertido/a, cómico/a
and y
angry enojado/a; to get angry enojarse
animal animal *m.*
another otro/a
answer *v.* **contestar;** *n.* **respuesta**
antibiotic *n.* **antibiótico**
any algún, alguno/a; cualquier(a); not any ningún, ninguno/a
anyone alguien; not anyone nadie
anything algo; not anything nada
anyway de todos modos
apartment apartamento
appear aparecer (zc); (*seem*) **parecer (zc)**
appetizer antojito
appliance aparato
applicant aspirante *m., f.*
application (form) solicitud *f.*
apply (for) solicitar
appointment cita
arm brazo
arrival llegada
arrive llegar (gu)

as **como;** as _____ as **tan** _____ **como;** as a child **de niño/a;** as if, as though **como si;** as soon as **en cuanto, tan pronto como**

ask **preguntar;** to ask for **pedir (i, i);** to ask questions **hacer** (*irreg.*) **preguntas**

asleep: to fall asleep **dormirse (ue, u)**

aspirin **aspirina**

assassination **asesinato**

at **en;** (*with time*) **a;** at least **por lo menos;** at the moment **en este momento;** at times **a veces;** at what time? **¿a qué hora?**

attend **asistir (a)**

attendant: flight attendant **camarero/a, azafata** *f.*

aunt **tía**

available **disponible**

avenue **avenida**

avocado dip **guacamole** *m.*

away: to take away **quitar**

backpack **mochila**

bad **malo/a;** it's too bad **es (una) lástima**

badly **mal**

ball **pelota**

ballpoint pen **bolígrafo**

bank **banco**

bargain *v.* **regatear;** *n.* **ganga**

baseball **béisbol** *m.*

basement **sótano**

basketball **básquetbol** *m.*

bath: to take a bath **bañarse**

bathe **bañar(se)**

bathing suit **traje** (*m.*) **de baño**

bathroom **baño**

bathtub **bañera**

battery **batería**

be **ser** (*irreg.*); **estar** (*irreg.*); to be _____ years old **tener** _____ **años;** to be born **nacer (zc);** to be (feel) hot/cold/thirsty/hungry/sleepy/afraid/right/in a hurry **tener calor/frío/sed/hambre/sueño/miedo/razón/prisa;** to be in style **estar de moda;** to be in agreement (with) **estar de acuerdo (con)**

beach **playa**

bean **frijol** *m.*

beautiful **hermoso/a, bello/a**

because **porque;** because of **a causa de, por**

become **hacerse** (*irreg.*) (*p.p.* **hecho/a**); **llegar a ser; ponerse** (*irreg.*) (*p.p.* **puesto/a**) + *adj.*

bed **cama;** to go to bed **acostarse (ue);** to make the bed **hacer la cama;** to put to bed **acostar (ue);** to stay in bed **guardar cama**

bedroom **alcoba, dormitorio**

beer **cerveza**

before *prep.* **antes de;** *conj.* **antes (de) que**

begin **empezar (ie) (c), comenzar (ie) (c)**

behave **portarse**

behind **detrás de;** behind schedule **atrasado/a**

being: human being **ser** (*m.*) **humano**

believe (in) **creer (y) (en)**

bellhop **mozo, botones** *m. s.*

belongings **bienes** *m.*

beloved **querido/a**

below *prep.* **debajo de**

belt **cinturón** *m.*

best **mejor**

better **mejor**

between **entre**

beverage **bebida**

big **gran, grande**

bill (*for services*) **cuenta, factura**

bird **pájaro**

birth: place of birth **tierra natal**

birthday **cumpleaños** *s.*

bit: a little bit **un poco**

black **negro/a**

blackboard **pizarra**

blond(e) **rubio/a**

blouse **blusa**

blue **azul**

board: room and board **pensión** (*f.*) **completa**

body **cuerpo**

book **libro;** textbook **libro de texto**

bookstore **librería**

boot **bota**

border *n.* **frontera**

bored **aburrido/a** (*with* **estar**)

boring **pesado/a; aburrido/a** (*with* **ser**)

born: to be born **nacer (zc)**

boss **jefe/a**

boy **chico; niño**

boyfriend **novio**

brakes **frenos;** disc brakes **frenos de disco**

bread **pan** *m.*

break *v.* **romper** (*p.p.* **roto/a**)

breakfast **desayuno;** to eat breakfast **desayunar**

breathe **respirar**

bride **novia**

bring **traer** (*irreg.*); **llevar**

brother **hermano**

brown **pardo/a**

brunet(te) **moreno/a**

building *n.* **edificio**

bump: to bump into **tropezar (ie) (c) con**

bus **autobús** *m.*

business **negocio, comercio, empresa;** businessman/businesswoman **hombre/mujer de negocios**

busy **ocupado/a**

but **pero;** but (rather) **sino**

buy **comprar**

by **para; por;** by plane **en avión**

café **café** *m.*

cafeteria **cafetería**

cake **pastel** *m.*

call *v.* **llamar;** *n.* **llamada**

called: to be called **llamarse**

calm **tranquilo/a**

camp: to go camping **hacer** (*irreg.*) (*p.p.* **hecho/a**) *camping*

can *v.* **poder** (*irreg.*)

candidate **aspirante** *m., f.;* **candidato/a**

candy **dulces** *m. pl.;* candy store **dulcería**

car **automóvil** *m.*, **coche** *m.*, **carro**

card **tarjeta;** credit card **tarjeta de crédito;** playing card **carta;** post card **(tarjeta) postal** *f.*

care *n.* **cuidado;** to take care of oneself **cuidarse**

career **carrera**

carrot **zanahoria**

carry **llevar;** to carry up **subir**

case: in case **en caso de que;** just in case **por si acaso**

cash: (to pay) cash **(pagar) al contado;** to cash (a check) **cobrar (un cheque)**

cashier **cajero/a**

catastrophe **catástrofe** *f.*

catch: to catch a cold **resfriarse**

certain **cierto/a, seguro/a**

chair **silla**

chalkboard **pizarra**

change *v.* **cambiar;** to change (*something*) **cambiar de;** *n.* **cambio**

channel (*TV*) **canal** *m.*

chapter **capítulo**

charge *v.* (*to an account*) **cargar (gu);** (*someone for an item or service*) **cobrar**

cheap **barato/a**

check *v.* **revisar;** (*luggage*) **facturar (el equipaje);** *n.* **cheque** *m.;* by check **con cheque;** checking account **cuenta corriente;** traveler's check **cheque de viajero;** (*restaurant*) **cuenta**

cheese **queso**

chess **ajedrez** *m.*

chicken **pollo**

child **niño/a, chico/a;** as a child **de niño/a**

children **hijos, niños, chicos**

chilly **frío/a;** to be (feel) chilly **tener** (*irreg.*) **frío**

chocolate **chocolate** *m;* chocolate sauce **mole** *m.* **poblano**

choose: to choose (*to do something*) **optar** (**por** + *inf.*)

chop: (pork) chop **chuleta (de cerdo)**

chore **quehacer** *m.*

Christmas **Navidad** *f.*, **Pascuas** *pl.;* Christmas Eve **Nochebuena**

church **iglesia**

citizen **ciudadano/a**

city **ciudad** *f.*

civic **cívico/a**

class **clase** *f.*, first class **primera clase;** tourist class **clase turística**

clean *v.* **limpiar;** *adj.* **limpio/a**

clear **claro/a;** (*cloudless*) **despejado/a;** it's clear (obvious, understood) **está claro**

clerk **dependiente/a**

clever **listo/a** (*with* **ser**)

climate **clima** *m.*

clock **reloj** *m.;* alarm clock **despertador** *m.*

close *v.* **cerrar (ie);** *adv.* **cerca;** close to *prep.* **cerca de**

closed **cerrado/a**

clothing **ropa;** clothing store **tienda de ropa**

cloudy **nublado/a**

clumsy **torpe**

coat **abrigo**

cocktail **cóctel** *m.;* shrimp cocktail **cóctel de camarones**

coffee **café** *m.;* coffepot **cafetera**

Coke **Coca-Cola**

cold *n.* (*illness*) **resfriado;** *adj.* **frío/a;** it's (very) cold (*weather*) **hace (mucho) frío;** to be (feel) cold **tener** (*irreg.*) **frío;** to catch a cold **resfriarse**

collision **choque** *m.*

color **color** *m.*

come **venir** (*irreg.*); to come by (*for someone*) **pasar por**

comfort *n.* **comodidad** *f.*

comfortable *adj.* **cómodo/a;** *adv.* **a gusto;** to be comfortable *(temperature)* **estar bien**

communicate (with) **comunicarse (qu) (con)**

companion **compañero/a**

complain **quejarse**

computer **computadora** *(Latin America),* **ordenador** *m. (Sp.)*

concept **concepto**

confirm **confirmar**

confused **confundido/a**

congested **congestionado/a**

congratulations **felicidades** *f.,* **felicitaciones** *f.*

conserve **conservar**

contain **contener** *(like* **tener***)*

contaminate **contaminar**

continue **continuar; seguir (i, i) (ga)**

control *v.* **controlar**

cook *v.* **cocinar**

cookie **galleta**

cool: it's cool *(weather)* **hace fresco**

corner *(of a street)* **esquina**

corporation **empresa**

cotton: (made) of cotton **(de) algodón** *m.*

cough *v.* **toser;** *n.* **tos** *f.*

counselor **consejero/a**

country **país** *m.,* **nación** *f.; (countryside)* **campo;** *adj.* **campesino/a**

course **curso;** course of studies **carrera;** of course **cómo no, claro**

court *(tennis)* **cancha**

cousin **primo/a**

cover *v.* **cubrir** (*p.p.* **cubierto/a***); (territory, miles, etc.)* **recorrer;** covered *adj.* **cubierto/a**

cow **vaca**

crash *n.* **choque** *m.*

crazy **loco/a**

crib **cuna**

crime **crimen** *m.,* **delito**

cross *v.* **cruzar (c)**

cry *v.* **llorar**

Cuban **cubano/a**

culture **cultura**

cup **taza**

custard **flan** *m.*

custom **costumbre** *f.*

customer **cliente** *m., f.*

customs **aduana;** customs duty **derechos** *(m.)* **de aduana**

cycling *n.* **ciclismo**

dad **papá** *m.*

daily **diario/a**

dance *v.* **bailar;** *n.* **baile** *m.*

dangerous **peligroso/a**

data processing *n.* **informática**

date *(calendar)* **fecha;** *(appointment)* **cita;** to have a date with **tener una cita con;** what is today's date? **¿cuál es la fecha de hoy?**

daughter **hija**

day **día** *m.;* a/per day **al día;** the day after tomorrow **pasado mañana;** every day **todos los días;** the day before yesterday **anteayer;** New Year's Day **Día** *(m.)* **del Año Nuevo**

dear **querido/a**

death **muerte** *f.;* death penalty **pena de muerte**

declare **declarar**

deeply **profundamente**

delay *v.* **demorar;** *n.* **demora**

deluxe **de lujo**

demonstration *(public protest)* **manifestación** *f.*

dense **denso/a**

dentist **dentista** *m., f.*

deny **negar (ie) (gu)**

department store **almacén** *m.*

departure **ida, salida**

deserve **merecer (zc)**

design *v.* **diseñar**

desire *v.* **desear;** *n.* **deseo;** out of desire **por gusto**

desk **escritorio;** front desk **recepción** *f.*

dessert **postre** *m.*

destroy **destruir (y)**

develop **desarrollar**

development **desarrollo**

dictator **dictador(a)**

dictatorship **dictadura**

dictionary **diccionario**

die **morirse (ue, u)** (*p.p.* **muerto/a***)*

diet: to be on a diet **estar a dieta**

difference: what difference does it make! **¡qué más da!**

different **diferente**

difficult **difícil**

dining room **comedor** *m.*

dinner **cena;** to have/eat dinner/supper **cenar**

director **director(a)**

dirty **sucio/a**

disadvantage **desventaja**

disaster **desastre** *m.*

discover **descubrir** (*p.p.* **descubierto/a***)*

dish **plato;** main dish **plato fuerte**

dishwasher **lavaplatos** *m. s.*

diversion **pasatiempo**

divorce *n.* **divorcio;** *v.* **divorciarse**

do **hacer** *(irreg.)* (*p.p.* **hecho/a***);* to *(do something)* again **volver a** + *inf.*

doctor **médico/a, doctor(a)**

dog **perro/a**

dollar **dólar** *m.*

domestic *adj.* **doméstico/a**

door **puerta**

doorman **portero**

dormitory **residencia (estudiantil)**

dot: on the dot *(with time)* **en punto**

doubt *v.* **dudar**

down **abajo,** to fall down **caerse** *(irreg.);* to get down (from) **bajar (de);** to have ups and downs **sufrir altibajos;** to sit down **sentarse (ie)**

downtown **centro**

dress **vestido**

dressed: to get dressed **vestirse (i, i)**

drink *v.* **beber, tomar;** *n.* **bebida;** *(alcoholic)* drink **copa, trago;** soft drink **refresco**

drive *(a vehicle)* **conducir** *(like* **producir***),* **manejar**

driver **conductor(a)**

drugstore **farmacia**

dryer *(clothing)* **secadora**

dubbed **doblado/a**

during *prep.* **durante**

dust *v.* **sacudir los muebles**

duty: customs duty **derechos** *m. pl.* **(de aduana)**

each **cada** *inv.*

early **temprano;** to get up early **madrugar (gu)**

earn **ganar**

Easter **Pascua (Florida)**

easy **fácil**

eat **comer;** to eat breakfast **desayunar;** to eat lunch **almorzar (ue) (c);** to eat supper/dinner **cenar**

economize **economizar (c)**

egg **huevo**

eighth **octavo/a**

either: not either **tampoco**

electricity **electricidad** *f.,* **luz** *f. (pl.* **luces***)*

embarrassed **avergonzado/a**

emigrate **emigrar**

employee **empleado/a**

enchant **encantar**

end *n.* **fin** *m.;* at the end of **a fines de;** weekend **fin de semana;** *v.* **terminar**

endure **durar**

energy **energía**

engagement *(marriage)* **noviazgo**

engineer **ingeniero/a**

English **inglés** *m.,* **inglesa** *f.; (language)* **inglés** *m.*

enjoy: to enjoy oneself **divertirse (ie, i), disfrutar (de), gozar (c) (de)**

enough **bastante, lo suficiente;** that's enough **basta**

enter **entrar (en)**

entertain **divertir (ie, i)**

entire **entero/a**

envelope **sobre** *m.*

environment **ambiente** *m.,* **medio ambiente**

equality **igualdad** *f.*

especially **sobre todo**

establish (oneself) **establecer(se) (zc)**

even *adv.* **aun;** even more **aun más;** even though **aunque**

evening **tarde** *f.;* **noche** *f.;* in the evening **de/por la noche**

event **acontecimiento, hecho**

every **cada** *inv.;* **todo/a;** everyday *adj.* **cotidiano/a;** every day *adv.* **todos los días**

everything **todo;** de todo

exactly *(with time)* **en punto**

exam **examen** *m.*

example **ejemplo;** for example **por ejemplo**

excellent **excelente**

excuse *v.* **disculpar(se);** excuse me **perdón; con permiso**

exercise *v.* **hacer** *(irreg.)* (*p.p.* **hecho/a***)* **ejercicio;** *n.* **ejercicio**

exile *n.* **exilio;** person in exile **exiliado/a**

expatriate *n.* **exiliado/a**

expenses **gastos**

expensive **caro/a; costoso/a**

experience *v.* **experimentar**

eye **ojo;** (eye)glasses **anteojos**

factory **fábrica**

fall *v.* **caer** *(irreg.);* to fall asleep **dormirse (ue, u);** to fall down **caerse;** *n.* **otoño**

family **familia;** family-related, of the family **familiar;** family room **sala de recreo**

fan *n.* **aficionado/a;** to be a fan (of) **ser aficionado/a (a)**

far *adv.* **lejos;** far from *prep.* **lejos de**
fare **pasaje** *m.*
farm *n.* **finca;** farm worker **campesino/a**
fast *adj.* **rápido/a, acelerado/a;** *adv.* **rápidamente, rápido**
fat *adj.* **gordo/a**
father **padre** *m.*
favorite **favorito**
fear *v.* **temer;** *n.* **miedo**
feel **sentirse (ie, i);** to feel cold/warm, hot **tener frío/calor;** to feel happy/sad **sentirse (ie, i) feliz/triste;** to feel like **tener ganas de** + *inf.;* to feel sorry **sentir**
fever **fiebre** *f.*
few **pocos/as;** a few **algunos/as;**
fewer **menos;** fewer than **menos que**
fiancé(e) **novio/a**
fifth **quinto/a**
fill **llenar;** to fill out (a form) **llenar (una solicitud)**
finally **por fin; al fin y al cabo**
find **encontrar (ue); hallar;** to find out (about) **saber** *(irreg.);* **enterarse de**
fine *n.* **multa;** *adv.* **(muy) bien**
finish **terminar; acabar**
fire *v.* **despedir (ie, i);** *n.* **fuego**
first **primero/a;** first of all **ante todo, antes que nada**
fish *n.* **pescado**
fit: to fit in **adaptarse**
fix **arreglar**
fixed *adj.* **fijo/a**
flat: a flat tire **una llanta desinflada**
flight **vuelo;** flight attendant **camarero/a, azafata** *f.*
floor *(building)* **piso;** ground floor **planta baja**
flower *v.* **florecer (zc);** *n.* **flor** *f.*
fly *v.* **volar (ue)**
fog **niebla**
follow **seguir (i, i) (ga)**
following *adj.* **siguiente**
food **alimento, comida, comestibles** *m. pl.*
foolish **tonto/a;** foolish thing **tontería**
foot **pie** *m.*
football **fútbol americano** *m.*
for **para; por;** for (*a period of time*) **por, durante;** for example **por ejemplo**
forbid **prohibir**
foreigner **extranjero/a**
forget **olvidar;** to forget to (*do something*) **olvidarse de** + *inf.*
form **forma, planilla**
fourth **cuarto/a**
free **libre;** (*unoccupied*) **desocupado/a**
freedom **libertad** *f.*
freeway **autopista**
freezer **congelador** *m.*
French **francés** *m.,* **francesa** *f.;* (*language*) **francés** *m.*
frequently **muchas veces; con frecuencia, frecuentemente, a menudo**
friend **amigo/a, compañero/a**
friendship **amistad** *f.*
from *prep.* **de; desde;** from ___ to ___ **desde ___ hasta ___**
front: in front **enfrente;** in front of **delante de;** front desk **recepción** *f.*
fruit **fruta;** fruit juice **jugo de fruta**

fun *n.* **diversión** *f.;* *adj.* **divertido/a**
function **andar** *(irreg.);* **funcionar**
funny **divertido/a, cómico/a**
furious **furioso/a**
furniture **muebles** *m. pl.*

game **juego;** (*sports*) **partido**
garage **garaje** *m.*
garbage **basura**
gas **gas** *m.;* **gasolina;** gas station **estación** *(f.)* **de gasolina, gasolinera**
gather **recoger (j)**
general: in general **por lo general**
generally **por lo general, generalmente**
gentleman **señor** *m.,* **caballero**
German **alemán** *m.,* **alemana** *f.;* (*language*) **alemán** *m.*
get **conseguir (i, i) (ga); obtener** (*like* **tener**); **ponerse** *(irreg.)* (*p.p.* **puesto/a**) + *adj.;* to get a cold **resfriarse;** to get along well/badly (with) **llevarse bien/mal (con);** to get angry **enojarse;** to get down (from), get off (of) **bajar (de);** to get dressed **vestirse (i, i)** (*p.p.* **hecho/a**) **ejercicio;** to get married **casarse, contraer** (*like* **traer**) **matrimonio;** to get on **subir (a);** to get sick **enfermarse;** to get through (customs) **pasar por (la aduana);** to get tired **cansarse;** to get to, arrive **llegar (gu);** to get together (*on an issue*) **ponerse** *(irreg.)* (*p.p.* **puesto/a**) **de acuerdo;** to get together (meeting) **reunirse;** to get up **levantarse;** to get up early **madrugar (gu);** to get up on the wrong side of the bed **levantarse con el pie izquierdo;** to get used (to) **acostumbrarse (a);** to get washed **lavarse**
gift **regalo**
girl **chica, niña**
girlfriend **novia**
give **dar** *(irreg.);* to give (*as a gift*) **regalar;** to give someone a shot, injection **ponerle una inyección**
glad: to be glad (about) **alegrarse (de)**
glass (*drinking*) **vaso**
glasses (eye) **anteojos**
go **ir** *(irreg.);* to go away **irse;** to go back **volver (ue)** (*p.p.* **vuelto/a**); to go by **pasar por;** to go camping **hacer** *(irreg.)* (*p.p.* **hecho/a**) *camping;* to go down (from) **bajar (de);** to go home **regresar a casa;** to go in **entrar (en, a);** to go on vacation **ir** *(irreg.)* **de vacaciones;** to go out **salir** *(irreg.);* to go shopping **ir** *(irreg.)* **de compras;** to go to (school) **asistir a (la escuela);** to go to bed **acostarse (ue);** to go up **subir (a);** to go with **acompañar**
God **Dios** *m.*
golf **golf** *m.*
good **buen, bueno/a;** good afternoon/ evening **buenas tardes;** good evening/ night **buenas noches;** good heavens! **¡caramba!;** good morning **buenos días**
good-bye **adiós;** to say good-bye (to) **despedirse (i, i) (de)**
good-looking **guapo/a**
govern **gobernar (ie)**
government **gobierno**
grade (*in a class*) **nota**

granddaughter **nieta**
grandfather **abuelo**
grandmother **abuela**
grandparents **abuelos**
grandson **nieto**
gray **gris**
great **gran, grande**
green **verde**
groom **novio**
ground **tierra;** ground floor **planta baja**
guarantee *v.* **garantizar (c)**
guest **invitado/a; huésped(a)**
guy **chico**

haggle **regatear**
hair **pelo**
half **mitad** *f.;* halfway there **a mitad de camino;** it's a half past (two, three . . .) **son las (dos, tres...) y media**
ham **jamón** *m.*
hamburger **hamburguesa**
hand **mano** *f.;* on the other hand **por otro lado;** to hand in, over **entregar (gu)**
handbag **bolsa**
handsome **guapo/a**
happen **pasar, ocurrir**
happy **alegre, contento/a, feliz** (*pl.* **felices**); to be happy (about) **alegrarse (de)**
hard **difícil**
hard-working **trabajador(a)**
haste **prisa**
hat **sombrero**
hate *v.* **odiar**
have **tener** *(irreg.);* (*auxiliary v.*) **haber** *(irreg.);* to have breakfast **desayunar;** to have a fever **tener** *(irreg.)* **fiebre** *f.;* to have fun, have a good time **divertirse (ie, i), pasarlo bien;** to have just (*done something*) **acabar de** + *inf.;* to have lunch **almorzar (ue) (c);** to have a pain (in) **tener** *(irreg.)* **dolor (de);** to have/make stopovers **hacer** *(irreg.)* (*p.p.* **hecho/a**) **escalas;** to have supper **cenar;** to have to (*do something*) **tener** *(irreg.)* **que** (+ *inf.);* to have ups and downs **sufrir altibajos**
he *sub. pron.* **él**
head *v.* **encabezar (c);** *n.* **cabeza**
health **salud** *f.*
healthy **sano/a**
hear **oír** *(irreg.)*
heart **corazón** *m.*
heat *v.* **calentar (ie);** *n.* **calor** *m.;* **calefacción** *f.,* **gas** *m.*
heaven **cielo;** for heaven's sake **¡por Dios!**
help *v.* **ayudar;** *n.* **ayuda**
her *d.o.* **la;** to/for her *i.o.* **le;** *obj. of prep.* **ella;** *poss.* **su**
hers **suyo/a**
here **acá; aquí;** around here **por aquí;** right here **aquí mismo**
hi **hola**
high **alto/a**
highway **carretera**
him *d.o.* **lo;** to/for him *i.o.* **le;** *obj. of prep.* **él**
his *poss.* **su, suyo/a**
history **historia**
hit *v.* **pegar (gu)**
hockey **hockey** *m.*
hold **contener** (*like* **tener**); to hold (*a seat,*

place) **guardar**
home **casa, hogar** *m.;* at home **en casa;** to return home **regresar a casa**
homeland **patria, tierra natal**
homework **tarea**
honeymoon **luna de miel**
hope *v.* **esperar;** *n.* **esperanza;** I hope (that) **ojalá (que)**
hors d'oeuvres **entremeses** *m.*
horse **caballo**
horseback: to ride horseback **montar a caballo**
hot **caliente, cálido/a;** (*spicy*) **picante;** to be (feel) hot (*people*) **tener** (*irreg.*) **calor;** it's hot (*weather*) **hace calor**
hotel **hotel** *m.;* deluxe hotel **hotel de lujo**
hour **hora;** per hour **por hora**
house **casa;** apartment house **casa de apartamentos;** boarding house **pensión** *f.*
housing **vivienda**
how? **¿cómo?;** how are you? **¿cómo está(s)?, ¿qué tal?;** how do you say ____? **¿cómo se dice ____?;** how many? **¿cuántos/as?;** how much? **¿cuánto?**
human being **ser** (*m.*) **humano**
hungry: to be hungry **tener** (*irreg.*) **hambre**
hurry *n.* **prisa;** *v.* to be in a hurry **tener** (*irreg.*) **prisa**
hurt *v.* (*ache*) **doler (ue);** to hurt oneself **hacerse** (*irreg.*) (*p.p.* **hecho/a**) **daño**
husband **esposo, marido**

I *sub. pron.* **yo**
ice **hielo**
ice cream **helado**
if **si;** as if **como si**
illness **enfermedad** *f.*
immediately **en seguida, inmediatamente**
immigrant **inmigrante** *m., f.*
immigration **inmigración** *f.*
impression: to make a good/bad impression on someone **caerle** (*irreg.*) **bien/mal a alguien**
improve **mejorar**
in (the morning, evening, etc.) **de/por (la mañana, la noche, etcétera)**
increase *v.* **aumentar;** *n.* **aumento**
incredible **increíble**
individual *n.* **individuo**
inequality **desigualdad** *f.*
inexpensive **barato/a**
inform **informar**
information **información** *f.*
infrequently **pocas veces**
injection **inyección** *f.;* to give someone an injection **ponerle una inyección**
insist (*on doing something*) **insistir (en** + *inf.*)
inspect **revisar, registrar**
inspector **inspector(a);** customs inspector **inspector(a) de aduanas**
installments: to pay in installments **pagar (gu) a plazos**
intelligent **inteligente**
intend **pensar (ie)** + *inf.*
interest *v.* **interesar**
interview *v.* **entrevistar;** *n.* **entrevista**
into **en**
invite **invitar**
invoice **factura**

irritated **irritado/a**
it *d.o.* **lo, la;** *obj. of prep.* **él, ella**
Italian **italiano/a;** (*language*) **italiano**
Italy **Italia**

jacket **chaqueta**
jail *n.* **cárcel** *f.*
jeans *bluejeans* *m.*
job **trabajo, puesto, empleo**
joke *n.* **chiste** *m.*
journalist **periodista** *m., f.*
juice **jugo;** fruit juice **jugo de fruta**
just: to have just (*done something*) **acabar de** + *inf.;* just in case **por si acaso**

keep **guardar;** to keep in mind **tomar en cuenta;** to keep on **seguir (i, i) (ga)**
key **llave** *f.;* (*computer*) **tecla**
keyboard **teclado**
kids (children) **niños/as, chicos/as**
kill *v.* **matar**
kind *adj.* **amable**
kitchen **cocina**
know (*a fact; how to*) **saber** (*irreg.*); (*someone to be acquainted with*) **conocer (zc)**

laborer **obrero/a**
lack *n.* **falta; escasez** *f.* (*pl.* **escaseces**)
lady **señora, dama**
land *v.* **aterrizar (c),** *n.* **tierra;** native land **patria, tierra natal**
language **lengua, idioma** *m.;* (*computer*) **lenguaje** *m.*
large **gran, grande**
last *v.* **durar;** *adj.* **último/a;** *n.* last name **apellido;** last night **anoche;** last week **la semana pasada;** last year **el año pasado**
late *adv.* **tarde; atrasado/a;** to be late **estar** (*irreg.*) **atrasado/a**
later **más tarde; luego;** see you later **hasta luego**
latest **último/a**
laugh **reírse (i, i)**
law **derecho, ley** *f.*
lawyer **abogado/a**
lazy **perezoso/a**
lead: to lead a ____ life **llevar una vida ____**
learn **aprender;** to learn (about) **enterarse (de)**
least: at least **por lo menos**
leave **salir** (*irreg.*); **irse** (*irreg.*); to leave (behind) **dejar**
left *adj.* **izquierdo/a;** *v.* to be left (remaining) **quedar;** to the left of **a la izquierda de**
leg **pierna**
lend **prestar**
less **menos;** less ____ than **menos ____ que**
let: to let (*someone*) know **avisar**
letter **carta**
lettuce **lechuga**
liberty **libertad** *f.*
library **biblioteca**
license **licencia;** driver's license **licencia de manejar/conducir**
life **vida;** (fast) pace of life **ritmo (acelerado) de la vida**
lift *v.* **levantar**
light *n.* **luz** *f.* (*pl.* **luces**); traffic light **semáforo;** *adj.* **ligero/a** (*in weight*)

like **gustar;** do you like . . . ? **¿te (le) gusta... ?;** no, I don't like . . . **no, no me gusta... ;** yes, I like . . . **sí me gusta... ;** like this/that *adv.* **así**
likeable **simpático/a**
listen (to) **escuchar;** hey, listen (*to get someone's attention*) **oiga(n)**
little **poco/a;** a little (bit) **un poco**
live **vivir**
living room **sala**
loan *n.* **préstamo**
lobster **langosta**
long *adj.* **largo/a;** *v.* to long for **añorar**
look (at) **mirar;** to look for **buscar (qu)**
lose **perder (ie)**
lot: a lot of *adj.* **mucho/a;** a lot *adv.* **mucho**
love *v.* **querer** (*irreg.*); *n.* **amor** *m.;* in love **enamorado/a;** to fall in love (with) **enamorarse (de)**
luck **suerte** *f.*
luggage **equipaje** *m.*
lunch *n.* **almuerzo;** *v.* to eat, have lunch **almorzar (ue) (c)**
lungs **pulmones** *m.*
luxurious **lujoso/a**

machine **máquina;** washing machine **lavadora**
madam **señora**
magazine **revista**
maid **criada**
mail *n.* **correo**
maintain **mantener** (*like* **tener**)
make **hacer** (*irreg.*) (*p.p.* **hecho/a**); to make a good/bad impression on someone **caerle** (*irreg.*) **bien/mal a alguien;** to make a mistake **equivocarse (qu);** to make the bed **hacer la cama;** to make plans **hacer planes;** to make stopovers **hacer escalas**
man **hombre** *m.;* young man **joven** *m.*
manager **director(a); gerente** *m. f.;* building manager **portero/a**
many **muchos/as;** how many? **¿cuántos/as?**
market **mercado**
marriage **matrimonio**
married **casado/a;** to get married (to) **casarse (con), contraer** (*like* **traer**) **matrimonio**
match *n.* (*sports*) **partido**
matches **fósforos** *pl.*
mathematics **matemáticas**
matter **cuestión** *f.;* it doesn't matter **no importa;** it's a matter of **es cuestión de, se trata de**
me *d.o., i.o.* **me;** *obj. of prep.* **mí;** with me **conmigo**
meal **comida**
meat **carne** *f.;* meat market **carnicería**
meatballs **albóndigas**
mechanic **mecánico**
medicine **medicina**
meet **conocer (zc) (a)**
memory **recuerdo; memoria**
menu **menú** *m.*
merchant **comerciante** *m., f.*
Mexican **mexicano/a**
Mexican-American **mexicanoamericano/a**
Mexico **México;** Mexico City **Ciudad** (*f.*) **de México**
middle *adj.* **medio/a;** middle class **clase** (*f.*) **media**

milk **leche** *f.*
milkshake **batido**
mine *poss.* **mío/a**
mineral water **agua** (*f.*) (*but* **el agua**) **mineral**
minus **menos**
miss *n.* **señorita (Srta.);** *v.* to miss (class) **faltar (a clase);** to miss (*someone or something*) **extrañar;** to miss (*a function*) **perder (ie)**
missing: to be missing **faltar**
mistake *n.* **error;** *v.* to make a mistake **equivocarse (qu)**
mom **mamá**
moment: at the moment **en este momento**
money **dinero**
monitor **monitor** *m.*
month **mes** *m.*
more **más;** more than **más que**
morning **mañana;** good morning **buenos días;** in the morning **de/por la mañana**
most: the most difficult thing **lo más difícil**
mother **madre** *f.*
mouth **boca**
move: to move (*change residence*) **mudarse;** to move (*change the location of something*) **cambiar de lugar**
movie **película;** movie theater **cine** *m.*
Mr. **señor (Sr.)** *m.*
Mrs. **señora (Sra.)**
much **mucho/a;** how much? **¿cuánto?**
murder *n.* **asesinato**
museum **museo**
music **música**
must **deber** (+ *inf.*); one must (*do something*) **hay que** + *inf.*
my *poss.* **mi**

name: (first) name **nombre** *m.;* last name **apellido;** my name is _____ **me llamo** _____; what is your name? **¿cómo se llama Ud.?, ¿cómo te llamas?**
named: to be named **llamarse**
nation **país** *m.*
nationality **nacionalidad** *f.*
native *adj.* **natal**
nature **naturaleza**
nauseated **mareado/a**
near *adv.* **cerca;** *prep.* **cerca de**
necessary **necesario/a, preciso/a;** it is necessary **es necesario/ preciso;** it is necessary (*to do something*) **hay que** + *inf.*
necessity **necesidad** *f.;* out of necessity **por necesidad**
necktie **corbata**
need *v.* **necesitar;** *n.* **necesidad** *f.*
neighbor **vecino/a**
neighborhood **barrio**
neither **tampoco**
nephew **sobrino**
nervous **nervioso/a**
net **red** *f.*
never **nunca, jamás**
new **nuevo/a;** New York **Nueva York;** New Year's Day **Día** (*m.*) **del Año Nuevo;** New Year's Eve **Noche** (*f.*) **Vieja**
news **informes** *m.;* **noticias, novedades** *f.;* news broadcast **noticiero**
newspaper **periódico**
next *adj.* **siguiente, próximo/a;** next week **la**

semana que viene; *adv.* **luego**
nice **amable, simpático/a**
niece **sobrina**
night **noche** *f.;* at night **de/por la noche;** every night **todas las noches;** good night **buenas noches;** last night **anoche;** tonight **esta noche**
ninth **noveno/a**
no *adj.* **ningún, ninguno/a;** *adv.* **no;** no one **nadie;** no parking **prohibido estacionarse**
nobody **nadie**
noise **ruido**
none **ningún, ninguno/a**
noon **mediodía** *m.*
North American **norteamericano/a**
nose **nariz** *f.* (*pl.* **narices**)
not **no;** not any **ningún, ninguno/a;** not anybody **nadie;** not anything **nada;** not either **tampoco**
notebook **cuaderno**
nothing **nada;** nothing can be done about it **no hay más remedio**
now **ahora;** now then, well now **ahora bien;** right now **ahora mismo, en este momento**
nurse **enfermero/a**

obey **obedecer (zc)**
obligation **obligación** *f.,* **deber** *m.*
obtain **conseguir (i, i) (ga)**
obvious: it's obvious (*clear*) **está claro**
occasion (*time*) **vez** *f.* (*pl.* **veces**)
occupied **ocupado/a**
o'clock: at (three) o'clock **a las (tres);** it's (three) o'clock **son las (tres)**
of **de**
off: to get off (of) **bajar (de);** to take off (*clothing*) **quitarse;** to take off (*plane*) **despegar (gu);** to turn off (*a light or appliance*) **apagar (gu)**
offer *v.* **ofrecer (zc)**
office **oficina;** director's office **dirección** *f.;* (doctor's) office **consultorio;** post office **correo;** ticket office **taquilla**
oil **aceite** *m.,* **petróleo**
okay: it's okay **está bien;** okay? **¿está bien?**
old **viejo/a; antiguo/a**
older **mayor**
on **en; sobre;** to get on **subir (a)**
once **una vez**
only *adj.* **único/a;** *adv.* **sólo, solamente**
open *v.* **abrir** (*p.p.* **abierto/a**)
open(ed) **abierto/a**
operate (*a machine*) **manejar, usar**
operation (*of a machine*) **manejo**
opt (*to do something*) **optar (por** + *inf.*)
or **o;** either . . . or **o... o**
orange *adj.* **anaranjado/a**
order *v.* **mandar; pedir (i, i);** in order to *prep.* **para;** *conj.* **para que**
other **otro/a**
ought to (*do something*) **deber** (+ *inf.*)
our *poss.* **nuestro/a**
out: out of **por; fuera de;** to fill out (*a form*) **llenar;** to go out **salir** (*irreg.*); to take out **sacar (qu)**
outdoors **al aire libre**
outside *n.* **afuera;** *adv.* **fuera**
outskirts **afueras**
overcast **nublado**

overcoat **abrigo**
own *adj.* **propio/a**
owner **dueño/a**

pace: (fast) pace of life **ritmo (acelerado) de la vida**
pack: to pack one's suitcases **hacer** (*irreg.*) (*p.p.* **hecho/a**) **las maletas**
package *n.* **paquete** *m.*
page **página**
pain **dolor** *m.;* to have a pain in _____ **tener** (*irreg.*) **dolor de** _____
pair **par** *m.*
pants **pantalones** *m.*
paper **papel** *m.*
pardon *v.* **perdonar;** *n.* **perdón** *m.;* con permiso
parents **padres** *m.*
park *v.* **estacionar(se);** *n.* **parque** *m.*
participate: to participate in (*sports*) **practicar (qu)**
party **fiesta**
pass (by) **pasar (por);** pass (*a course, subject, etc.*) **aprobar (ue);** to pass through **recorrer**
passage **pasaje** *m.*
passenger **pasajero/a**
Passover **Pascua**
passport **pasaporte** *m.*
past *adj.* **pasado/a**
pastime **pasatiempo**
pastry **pastel** *m.,* small pastry **pastelito, pastelillo;** pastry shop **pastelería**
patient *n.* **paciente** *m., f.*
patio **patio**
pay (for) **pagar (gu);** to pay attention (to) **fijar (en)**
pea **guisante** *m.,* **arveja**
peace **paz** *f.* (*pl.* **paces**)
peasant **campesino/a**
pen (ballpoint) **bolígrafo**
penalty **multa, pena**
pencil **lápiz** *m.* (*pl.* **lápices**)
people **gente** *f. s.*
performance **función** *f.*
perhaps **quizá(s), tal vez**
permit *v.* **permitir**
person **persona** *f.*
petroleum **petróleo** *m.*
pharmacy **farmacia**
physical **físico/a**
pick: to pick up **recoger (j)**
pie **pastel** *m.*
pill **pastilla;** sleeping pill **pastilla para dormir**
pink **rosado/a**
place *v.* **poner** (*irreg.*) (*p.p.* **puesto/a**); **colocar (qu);** to take place **tener** (*irreg.*) **lugar;** *n.* **lugar** *m.* **sitio;** place (*in line*) **puesto;** place of birth **tierra natal**
plaid **de cuadros**
plan: to make plans to (*do something*) **hacer** (*irreg.*) (*p.p.* **hecho/a**) **planes para** + *inf.;* **pensar (ie)** + *inf.*
plane **avión** *m.;* by plane **en avión**
plate **plato**
play (*instrument*) **tocar (qu);** to play (*sports*) **jugar (ue) (gu) (a);** *n.* **drama** *m.,* **comedia;** play (*in a game*) **juego**
player **jugador(a)**

pleasant **agradable, divertido/a**
please **por favor;** please (*do something*) **favor de** + *inf.*
pleasing: to be pleasing **gustar**
pleasure **gusto**
plumber **plomero/a**
plus **y, más**
P.M. **de la tarde/noche**
politics **política** *s.*
pollute **contaminar**
pollution **contaminación** *f.*
pool: swimming pool **piscina**
poor **pobre**
population **población** *f.*
pork chop **chuleta de cerdo**
porter **maletero**
position *n.* **puesto**
post: post office **correo;** postcard (**tarjeta**) **postal** *f.*
potato **papa, patata;** french fried potato **papa frita**
practice *v.* **practicar (qu)**
prefer **preferir (ie, i)**
preferable **preferible**
prepare **preparar**
prescription **receta**
present *n.* (*gift*) **regalo;** *adj.* (*current*) **actual**
press *n.* **prensa**
pressure **presión** *f.;* to be under a lot of pressure **sufrir muchas presiones**
pretty **bonito/a, lindo/a**
price **precio;** fixed price **precio fijo**
printer **impresora**
prison **cárcel** *f.*
problem **problema** *m.*
processing: data processing *n.* **informática**
professor **profesor(a)**
program **programa** *m.*
programmer **programador(a)**
prohibit **prohibir**
promise **prometer**
protect **proteger (j)**
protest *v.* **protestar;** *n.* **manifestación** *f.*
provided that **con tal (de) que**
psychiatrist **psiquiatra** *m., f.*
psychology **(p)sicología**
public *n.* **público**
Puerto Rican **puertorriqueño/a**
punish **castigar (gu)**
punishment **castigo**
purchase *v.* **comprar;** *n.* **compra**
pure **puro/a**
purple **morado/a**
purse **bolsa**
put **poner** (*irreg.*) (*p.p.* **puesto/a**); to put on (*clothing*) **ponerse;** to put to bed **acostar (ue)**

quarter: it's a quarter after (two, three . . .) **son las (dos, tres...) y cuarto**
question *n.* **pregunta**
quit **dejar (de)**
quiz *n.* **prueba**

racetrack **pista**
racket (*tennis, etc.*) **raqueta**
railroad **ferrocarril** *m.*
rain *v.* **llover (ue);** *n.* **lluvia**
raincoat **impermeable** *m.*

raining: it's raining **está lloviendo**
raise *v.* **levantar;** *n.* **aumento**
ranch **rancho**
rancher **ranchero/a**
rather *adv.* **bastante;** *conj.* **sino**
reach *v.* **alcanzar (c);** to reach an agreement **ponerse** (*irreg.*) (*p.p.* **puesto/a**) **de acuerdo**
read **leer (y)**
ready: to be ready (to) **estar** (*irreg.*) **listo/a (para)**
real **verdadero/a**
realize **darse** (*irreg.*) **cuenta de**
reason *n.* **razón** *f.*
receive **recibir**
reception desk **recepción** *f.*
recommend **recomendar (ie)**
record (*musical*) *n.* **disco**
recorder: tape recorder **grabadora**
recreation room **sala de recreo**
red **rojo/a**
refrigerator **refrigerador** *m.*
refugee **refugiado/a**
registration fees **matrícula** *s.*
regret **sentir (ie, i)**
relative (*family*) **pariente** *m.*
remain **quedar(se)**
remember **recordar (ue), acordarse (ue) (de)**
remove **quitar; sacar (qu)**
rent *v.* **alquilar;** *n.* **alquiler** *m.*
renter **inquilino/a**
repair *v.* **arreglar;** *n.* **arreglo;** repair shop **taller** *m.*
replace **reemplazar (c)**
reporter **reportero/a**
republic **república**
requirement **requisito**
reservation **reservación** *f.*
reserve *v.* **reservar**
resign (from) **renunciar (a)**
resolve *v.* **resolver (ue)** (*p.p.* **resuelto/a**)
resources: natural resources **recursos naturales**
rest *v.* **descansar;** *n.* **descanso**
restaurant **restaurante** *m.*
rested *adj.* **descansado/a**
result *n.* **resultado**
return **volver (ue)** (*p.p.* **vuelto/a**); **regresar** (*with people*); **devolver (ue)** (*p.p.* **devuelto/a**) (*with objects*)
rice **arroz** *m.*
rich **rico/a**
ride: to ride (horseback) **montar (a caballo)**
right *n.* **derecho;** *adj.* **derecho/a;** on/to the right (of) **a la derecha (de);** right? **¿no?, ¿verdad?;** right now/away **ahora mismo, en este momento;** to be right **tener** (*irreg.*) **razón** *f.*
ring *v.* **sonar (ue);** *n.* **anillo**
road **camino**
robot **robot** *m.*
roll *n.* (*hard*) **bolillo;** sweet rolls **pan** (*m.*) **dulce**
room **cuarto, habitación** *f.;* bathroom (**cuarto de**) **baño;** dining room **comedor** *m.;* living room **sala;** recreation room **sala de recreo;** room and board **pensión** (*f.*) **completa;** roommate **compañero/a de cuarto;** waiting room **sala de espera**
rooster **gallo**

root **raíz** *f.* (*pl.* **raíces**)
run **andar** (*irreg.*), **correr;** (*with machines*) **funcionar;** to run out (of) **acabar;** to run (into) **chocar (qu) (con)**
Russian **ruso/a;** (*language*) **ruso**

sad **triste**
sake: for heaven's sake **por Dios**
salad **ensalada**
salary **sueldo**
same **mismo/a**
sandal **sandalia**
sauce **salsa;** chocolate sauce **mole** (*m.*) **poblano;** hot sauce **salsa picante**
save **conservar;** (*money, time*) **ahorrar**
say **decir** (*irreg.*) (*p.p.* **dicho**); how do you say . . . ? **¿cómo se dice... ?;** that is to say **es decir;** to say good-bye (to) **despedirse (i, i) (de)**
school **escuela**
science **ciencia;** political science **ciencias políticas** *pl.;* natural sciences **ciencias naturales;** social sciences **ciencias sociales**
screen *n.* **pantalla**
seafood **mariscos** *pl.*
search *v.* **registrar**
season *n.* **estación** *f.*
seat *v.* **sentar (ie);** *n.* **asiento;** (*in a theater*) **butaca**
second *adj.* **segundo/a**
secretary **secretario/a**
section **sección** *f.;* (no-) smoking section **sección de (no) fumar**
see **ver** (*irreg.*) (*p.p.* **visto/a**)
seem **parecer (zc)**
self *adj.* **mismo/a**
selfishness **egoísmo**
sell **vender**
send **mandar**
sentence **oración** *f.*
serious **serio/a**
servant **criado/a**
serve **servir (i, i)**
service **servicio**
set: to set the table **poner** (*irreg.*) (*p.p.* **puesto/a**) **la mesa**
seventh **séptimo/a**
several **varios/as**
severe *adj.* **fuerte**
shame; it's a shame **es lástima**
shampoo *n.* **champú** *m.*
share *v.* **compartir**
shave (oneself) **afeitar(se)**
she *sub. pron.* **ella**
shirt **camisa;** T-shirt **camiseta**
shock: culture shock **choque** (*m.*) **cultural**
shoe **zapato;** shoe store **zapatería**
shop *n.* **tienda;** confectioner's shop, sweetshop **confitería;** repair shop **taller** *m.;* tobacco shop **tabacalera**
shopkeeper **comerciante** *m., f.*
shopping: to go shopping **ir** (*irreg.*) **de compras**
short (*in height*) **bajo/a;** (*in length*) **corto/a;** (*brief*) **breve**
shortage **escasez** *f.*
shot: to give someone a shot/injection **ponerle una inyección** *f.*
should **deber** (+ *inf.*)

show *v.* **mostrar (ue)**; *n.* **función** *f.*
shower **ducha**
shrimp **camarones** *m.*
sick **enfermo/a**; to get sick **enfermarse**
signal: traffic signal **semáforo**
silk **seda**; (made) of silk **de seda**
silly **tonto/a**
since **como**; *conj.* **desde que, ya que**
sing **cantar**
single (*not married*) **soltero/a**; (*room*) **para una persona**
sir **señor (Sr.)** *m.*
sister **hermana**
sit: to sit down **sentarse (ie)**
sixth **sexto/a**
skate *v.* **patinar**
ski *v.* **esquiar**; *n.* **esquí** *m.*
skirt **falda**
sky **cielo**
skyscraper **rascacielos** *m. s.*
sleep **dormir (ue, u)**
sleepy: to be sleepy **tener (irreg.) sueño`**
slender **delgado/a**
small **pequeño/a**
smart **listo/a**
smile *v.* **sonreír (i, i)**; *n.* **sonrisa**
smog **contaminación** *f.*
smoke *v.* **fumar**; *n.* **humo**
smoking: (no-) smoking section **sección** (*f.*) **de (no) fumar**
snow *v.* **nevar (ie)**; *n.* **nieve** *f.*
snowing: it's snowing **está nevando**
so **así**; so much *adv.* **tanto**; so much *adj.* **tanto/a**; so many **tantos/as**; so-so **así así, regular**; so that **para que**
soap **jabón** *m.*
soccer **fútbol** *m.*
socks **calcetines** *m.*
soft drink **refresco**
solitude **soledad** *f.*
solve **resolver (ue)** (*p.p.* **resuelto/a**)
some **algún, alguno/a**; **unos/as**
someone **alguien**
something **algo**
sometimes **a veces**
son **hijo**
soon **pronto**; as soon as **en cuanto a, tan pronto como**
sorry: to feel/be sorry **sentir (ie, i)**; I'm sorry **lo siento**
soul: All Souls' Day **Día** (*m.*) **de los Muertos**
soup **sopa**
souvenir **recuerdo**
Spain **España**
Spanish **español(a)**; (*language*) **español** *m.*
speak **hablar**
special *adj.* **especial**
spend (*time*) **pasar**; (*money*) **gastar**
sport **deporte** *m.*; sportsman/sportswoman **deportista** *m., f.*; to participate in sports **practicar (qu) deportes**
sports-minded **deportista** *m., f.*
spring **primavera**
stadium **estadio**
stamp **sello**
stand: to stand up **levantarse**; tobacco stand **tabacalera**
start **comenzar (ie) (c), empezar (ie) (c)**; (*with cars*) **arrancar (qu)**

state *n.* **estado**
station **estación** *f.*; gas station **estación de gasolina, gasolinera**
stationery **papel** (*m.*) **para cartas**; stationery store **papelería**
stay *v.* **quedarse**; to stay in bed **guardar cama**; *n.* **estancia**
steak **bistec** *m.*
stewardess **azafata, camarera**
still *adv.* **aún, todavía**
stockings **medias**
stomach **estómago**
stop *v.* **parar**; to stop (*doing something*) **dejar (de + inf.)**; *n.* stoplight **semáforo**
stopovers; to make stopovers **hacer (irreg.)** (*p.p.* **hecho/a**) **escalas**
store *n.* **tienda**; department store **almacén**; *v.* **archivar**
story (*literary*) **cuento**; (*building*) **piso**
stove **estufa**
straight ahead **(todo) derecho**
strange **extraño/a**
street **calle** *f.,* **camino**
strike: to strike (*another*) *v.* **pegar (gu)**, *n.* (*labor*) **huelga**
striped **de rayas**
strong **fuerte**
student **estudiante** *m., f.*
study *v.* **estudiar**; *n.* **estudio**; course of studies **carrera**
stuffed-up **congestionado/a**
style *n.* **moda**; to be in style **estar de moda**
suburbs **afueras**
sudden: all of a sudden **de repente**
suddenly **de repente**
suffer **sufrir**
sugar **azúcar** *m.*
suggestion **sugerencia**
suit **traje** *m.*; swimsuit **traje de baño**
suitcase **maleta**; small suitcase **maletín** *m.*; to pack one's suitcase **hacer (irreg.)** (*p.p.* **hecho/a**) **la maleta**
summer **verano**
sunbathe **tomar el sol**
sunny: it's sunny **hace sol**
supper *n.* **cena**; *v.* to eat/have supper **cenar**
support *v.* **mantener (like tener)** *n.* **apoyo**
sure **seguro/a**
surprise *v.* **sorprender**; *n.* **sorpresa**
surprising: to be surprising **sorprender**
sweater **suéter** *m.*
sweeper **aspiradora**
sweet *adj.* **dulce**; sweets *n.* **dulces** *m. pl.*; sweet rolls **pan** (*m.*) **dulce**
sweetshop **dulcería**
swin **nadar**; swimsuit **traje** (*m.*) **de baño**
swimming *n.* **natación** *f.*
swimming pool **piscina**
swollen **inflamado/a**
symptom **síntoma** *m.*
syrup: cough syrup **jarabe** *m.*
system **sistema** *m.*

table **mesa**; end table **mesita**; to set the table **poner (irreg.)** (*p.p.* **puesto/a**) **la mesa**
take **tomar; traer (irreg.)**; to take away, out **quitar**; to take a bath **bañarse**; to take care of oneself **cuidarse**; to take into account **tomar en cuenta**; to take off (clothing)

quitarse; to take off (*with planes*) **despegar (gu)**; to take out **sacar (qu)**; to take place **tener (irreg.) lugar**; to take someone's temperature **tomarle la temperatura**; to take a trip **hacer (irreg.)** (*p.p.* **hecho/a) un viaje**; to take a walk **dar (irreg.) un paseo**
talk *v.* **hablar**
tall **alto/a**
tank **tanque** *m.*
task **quehacer** *m.*
tax **impuesto**
tea **té** *m.*
teach **enseñar**
teacher **maestro/a**
team (*in sporting events*) **equipo**
technician **técnico/a**
technology **tecnología**
telephone **teléfono**
television **televisión** *f.*; television set **televisor** *m.*
tell **decir (irreg.)** (*p.p.* **dicho/a**); to tell about **contar (ue)**
temperature **temperatura**
tenant **inquilino/a**
tennis **tenis** *m.*
tenth **décimo/a**
test *n.* **examen** *m.*
textbook **libro de texto**
than **que**
thank *v.* **dar (irreg.) las gracias; agradecer (zc)**; thank you **gracias**; thank you very much, many thanks **muchas gracias**
Thanksgiving **Día** (*m.*) **de Gracias**
that *adj.* **ese/a; aquel**; that one *pron.* **ése/a; eso; aquél, aquélla; aquello**; *conj.* **que**; that way *adv.* **así**; that which **lo que**; *adv.* **tan**; that's why **por eso**
the **el/la/los/las**
theater **teatro**; (*movie*) **cine** *m.*
their *poss.* **su**
them *d.o.* **los/las**; *i.o.* **les**
then **luego; entonces**
there **allí/allá; ahí**; there is/are **hay**; there was/were **había**; there will be **habrá**
therefore **por eso**
these *adj.* **estos/as**; *pron.* **éstos/as**
they *sub. pron.* **ellos/as**
thin *adj.* **delgado/a**; to become thin **adelgazar(se) (c)**
thing **cosa**
think **creer (y); pensar (ie)**; to think about **pensar de/en**; what do you think? **¿qué te parece?**; to (not) think so **creer que sí (no)**
third **tercero/a**
thirsty: to be thirsty **tener (irreg.) sed**
this *adj.* **este/a**; this one *pron.* **éste/a; esto**
those *adj.* **esos/as; aquellos/as**; *pron.* **ésos/as; aquéllos/as**
though: as though **como si**; even though **aunque**
throat **garganta**
thus **así**
ticket **boleto, billete** *m.,* **entrada**; (*fine*) **multa**; (*passage*) **pasaje** *m.*; one-way (round-trip) ticket **billete de ida (y vuelta)**; ticket office/window **taquilla**
tie *n.* **corbata**
time **hora; vez** *f.* (*pl.* **veces**); **tiempo; época**; (*short period of*) **un rato**; at times **a veces;**

at what time? **¿a qué hora?;** for the first/last time **por primera/última vez;** free time **ratos libres** *pl.;* from time to time **de vez en cuando;** on time **a tiempo;** timetable **horario;** time to (*do something*) **hora de** (+ *inf.*); to have a good/bad time **pasarlo bien/mal;** to have a good time **divertirse (ie, i);** what time is it? **¿qué hora es?**
tip (*given to a waiter, etc.*) **propina**
tire **llanta;** flat tire **llanta desinflada**
tired **cansado/a;** to get tired **cansarse**
to **a;** (in order) to **para**
toast *n.* **pan** (*m.*) **tostado**
toaster **tostadora**
tobacco: stand, shop **tabacalera**
today **hoy**
together **juntos/as;** to get together (*on an issue*) **ponerse** (*irreg.*) (*p.p.* **puesto/a**) **de acuerdo**
tomato **tomate** *m.*
tomorrow **mañana;** until tomorrow, see you tomorrow **hasta mañana;** the day after tomorrow **pasado mañana**
tongue **lengua**
tonight **esta noche**
too **demasiado;** *adj.* too much **demasiado/a;** too many **demasiados/as;** *adv.* too much **demasiado;** (*also*) **también**
tooth **diente** *m.;* toothpaste **pasta dental**
top: on top of *prep.* **encima de**
toy **juguete** *m.*
track (*race*) **pista**
traffic **tráfico, circulación** *f.;* traffic light **semáforo**
train **tren** *m.*
tranquil **tranquilo/a**
transportation: (means of) transportation **transporte** *m.*
trash *n.* **basura**
travel *v.* **viajar**
traveler **viajero/a**
tree **árbol** *m.*
trip **excursión** *f.;* **viaje** *m.;* round trip **viaje de ida y vuelta;** to take a trip **hacer** (*irreg.*) (*p.p.* **hecho/a**) **un viaje**
trousers **pantalones** *m.*
truck *n.* **camión** *m.*
true **cierto/a, verdadero/a**
truth **verdad** *f.*
try (*to do something*) **tratar** (**de** + *inf.*)
T-shirt **camiseta**
turkey **guajolote** *m.*
turn: to turn on **poner** (*irreg.*) (*p.p.* **puesto/a;** to turn off **apagar (gu);** whose turn is it to . . . ? **¿a quién le toca... ?**
twice **dos veces**
type *v.* **escribir** (*p.p.* **escrito/a**) **a máquina**
typewriter **máquina de escribir**

ugly **feo/a**
uncle **tío**
under *prep.* **debajo de**
understand **comprender, entender (ie)**
unintentional: it was unintentional **fue sin querer**
United States **Estados Unidos**

university **universidad** *f.*
unless **a menos que**
unmarried **soltero/a**
unoccupied **desocupado/a, libre**
unpleasant **antipático/a**
until *prep.* **hasta;** *conj.* **hasta que**
up: to get up **levantarse;** to go up **subir;** to stand up **levantarse;** ups and downs **altibajos**
upon *prep.* **al** + *inf.*
urgent **urgente**
us *d.o., i.o.* **nos;** *obj. of prep.* **nosotros/as**
use *v.* **usar, gastar, manejar;** to use up **acabar;** *n.* **uso;** (*of machine*) **manejo**
used: to get used (to) **acostumbrarse (a); adaptarse (a)**

vacation **vacaciones** *f. pl.;* to be on vacation **estar** (*irreg.*) **de vacaciones;** to go on vacation **ir** (*irreg.*) **de vacaciones**
vacuum *v.* **pasar la aspiradora;** vacuum cleaner *n.* **aspiradora**
vegetable **legumbre** *f.;* *pl.* **verduras**
very **muy**
view *n.* **vista**
visit *v.* **visitar**
volleyball **vólibol** *m.*
vote *v.* **votar**

wait (for) **esperar**
waiter **camarero**
waiting room **sala de espera**
waitress **camarera**
wake: to wake up **despertar(se) (ie)**
walk *v.* **caminar;** to take a walk **dar** (*irreg.*) **un paseo**
wallet **cartera**
want **desear; querer** (*irreg.*)
war **guerra**
warm: to be/feel warm **tener** (*irreg.*) **calor;** it's (very) warm **hace (mucho) calor**
wash (oneself) **lavar(se)**
washer **lavadora**
watch *v.* **mirar;** *n.* **reloj** *m.*
water **agua** *f.* (but: **el agua**)
way: that way **así;** one- (two-) way ticket **billete** *m.* (**boleto**) **de ida (y vuelta)**
we *sub. pron.* **nosotros/as**
wear **llevar**
weather **tiempo;** what's the weather like? **¿qué tiempo hace?**
wedding **boda**
week **semana**
weekend *m.* **fin de semana**
welcome **bienvenido/a;** you're welcome **de nada, no hay de qué**
welfare **bienestar** *m.*
well **bien;** well (now) **pues**
well-being **bienestar** *m.*
what (that which) **lo que;** what? **¿que?, ¿cuál?;** what a shame! **¡qué lástima!;** what do you mean . . . ? **¿cómo que... ?;** what is _____ like? **¿cómo es _____ ?;** what's it about? **¿de qué se trata?;** what is your name? **¿cómo se llama Ud.?, ¿cómo te llamas?;** what time is it? **¿qué hora es?;** at what time? **¿a qué hora?**
when **cuando;** when? **¿cuándo?**

where **donde;** where? **¿dónde?;** (to) where? **¿adónde?;** (from) where? **¿de dónde?**
which **cual;** which? **¿cuál?;** *pl.* **¿cuáles?;** (that) which **lo que**
while **mientras;** a while **un rato**
white **blanco/a**
who **quien;** who? **¿quién?;** *pl.* **¿quiénes?**
whole **entero/a**
whom? **¿quién?;** *pl.* **¿quiénes?**
whose **cuyo/a;** whose? **¿de quiénes?**
why? **¿por qué?;** that's why **por eso;** why not? **¿por qué no?**
wife **esposa**
win **ganar**
window **ventana**
windshield **parabrisas** *m.s.*
windy: it's windy **hace viento**
wine **vino;** red/white wine **vino tinto/blanco**
winter **invierno**
wish *v.* **desear; querer** (*irreg.*); *n.* **deseo;** I wish! **¡ojalá!**
with **con;** with me **conmigo;** with you **contigo** *fam. s.*
withhold **quitar**
without *prep.* **sin;** *conj.* **sin que**
witness *n.* **testigo** *m., f.*
woman **dama, mujer** *f.,* **señora (Sra.);** young woman **señorita (Srta.); joven** *f.*
wool **lana;** (made) of wool **de lana**
word **palabra**
word processing: to do word processing **editar textos**
work *v.* **trabajar;** (*with machines*) **funcionar;** *n.* **trabajo;** (*of art, literature, etc.*) **obra**
worker **obrero/a**
world *n.* **mundo;** *adj.* **mundial**
worldwide *adj.* **mundial**
worried **preocupado/a**
worry *v.* **preocuparse**
worse **peor**
worst **el peor**
write **escribir** (*p.p.* **escrito**)
wrong: to be wrong **equivocarse (qu)**

yard **patio**
year **año;** New Year **Año Nuevo;** New Year's Day **Día** (*m.*) **del Año Nuevo;** New Year's Eve **Noche** (*f.*) **Vieja;** next year **el año que viene;** to be _____ years old **tener** (*irreg.*) _____ **años**
yellow **amarillo/a**
yes **sí**
yesterday **ayer;** the day before yesterday **anteayer**
yet **todavía**
you *sub. pron.* **tú** (*fam. s.*), **usted (Ud., Vd.)** (*form. s.*); **vosotros/as** (*fam. pl., Sp.*); **ustedes (Uds. Vds.)** (*pl.*); *d.o.* **te, os, lo/la, los/las;** to/for you *i.o.* **te, os, le, les;** *obj. of prep.* **ti, vosotros, Ud., Uds.;** with you **contigo** *fam. s.*
young **joven;** young person **joven** *m., f.*
young **menor**
your *poss.* **tu** (*fam. s.*); **vuestro/a** (*fam. pl., Sp.*); **su** (*form.*)
yours *poss.* **tuyo/a** (*fam.*); **suyo/a** (*form.*)
youth **juventud** *f.*

INDEX